LAW IN THE NEW TESTAMENT

J. DUNCAN M. DERRETT

D.C.L. (*Oxon.*)

Professor of Oriental Laws
in the University of London

Wipf & Stock
PUBLISHERS
Eugene, Oregon

Wipf and Stock Publishers
199 W 8th Ave, Suite 3
Eugene, OR 97401

Law in the New Testament
By Derrett, J. Duncan M.

ISBN: 1-59752-231-7
Publication date 6/3/2005
Previously published by Darton, Longman & Todd, 1970

ERRATA

p. 4, n.2: Klein, New Haven 1951), I, XII, 43-65, esp. xviii.

p. 8, n.2: L. Wallach

p. 47 n.1: Legibus III. 159-163 (Loeb edn., vii, 574-576); Plutarch, Lucullus XX.102 (Loeb edn., ii, 532-533).

p. 56 n.4: Ex xxii.25;

p. 71, line 27: with linseed

p. 162, line 3: but the procedure

p. 176, line 7: as a discreet

p. 219, line 24: (Gn xxxiv).

p. 227 n.2: Klemen,

p. 251 n.6: mip_ney

p. 296 n.1, line 1: xxi.34; Mk xi.13.

p. 322 n.1: p. 176 n.3.

p. 340 n.1: above pp. 75-76, 82-83, 316; below pp. 370, 379.

p. 349, line 15: Saul and Jonathan

p. 350 n.3, line 5: MGWJ

p. 353, line 35: Saul would have

p. 373, line 3: may be connived at by

p. 374 n.3; Qid I.1; Ket IV.4;

p. 376 n.1, line 6: sense in which

p. 390, line 16: This way has

p. 409, line 12: (Dt xxvii.25; Ps xv.5).

p. 410 n.2: (Mk xiv.54, 67;

p. 423 n. 1 (CD IX, 1 [

p. 428, line 26: in 223,

p. 441 n.2: on Gn xl.23

p. 473 col.2, line 2: delete 24…219

p. 473 col.2, line 39: 40:23

p. 480 col.2, lines 22-23: delete 14:54…410 n.2

delete 14:67…410 n.2

p. 480 col.2, line 27: 16:19

p. 497 col.1, Mishnah, 'Avot, line 7: IV.22:399 n.7;

p. 500 col.2: For "Samuel,353" read: Samuel, Mar, 315 n.1

p. 500 col.2 After Saul, 346 add 353

p. 500 col.2 Schlatter, A., line 2, read: 462 n.1

p. 501 read Tamar[1], 380 n.1

Tamar [2], 173 n.2

Contents

List of Abbreviations and Abbreviated References

Note. The biblical references are given in the style used in the *Jerusalem Bible* and many other modern works. The only abbreviation likely to puzzle the reader unused to theological literature is Qo (Ecclesiastes). M stands for Maccabees (not Moses), and Ecclesiasticus is indicated by Sir (for Sirach). The references to tractates of the *Mishnāh* or the Talmuds are simple abbreviations (*e.g.* Berakot is shown as Ber.) and the tractates can readily be located by reference to a table of contents or the spines of the volumes. Complete consistency was not possible in this present work since many of its parts were composed separately. On the whole common sense will suffice to expand any abbreviated reference not shown below.

b.	Babylonian Talmud
Bauer-Arndt-Gingrich	W. F. Arndt and F. W. Gingrich, *A Greek-English Lexicon of the New Testament* (1957)
Billerbeck	H. L. Strack and P. Billerbeck, *Kommentar zum Neuen Testament aus Talmud und Midrasch* (1924/1961)
Blackman	P. Blackman, *Mishnayoth* (1951–5)
Blass-Debrunner	F. Blass and A. Debrunner, *A Greek Grammar of the New Testament and other Early Christian Literature* (1961)
BSOAS	Bulletin of the School of Oriental and African Studies, London
BZ	Biblische Zeitschrift
CBQ	Catholic Biblical Quarterly
CD	Zadokite Document, otherwise Damascus Document, or Damascus Rule
Chavel	*The Commandments. Sefer Ha-Mitzvoth of Maimonides*, trans. C. B. Chavel (1967)
C.I.J.	*Corpus Inscriptionum Judaicarum*
Cod.	Justinian's *Codex* in the *Corpus Iuris*
C.P.J.	*Corpus Papyrorum Judaicorum*
CR	Community Rule, or Manual of Discipline

Danby	H. Danby, *The Mishnah* (1933)
Dig.	Justinian's *Digesta* (or Pandects) in the *Corpus Iuris*
DSW	The War Rule, or War Scroll
Dupont-Sommer	A. Dupont-Sommer, *Les Ecrits Esséniens découverts près de la Mer Morte*, 3rd edn (1968)
ET	Expository Times
F. Gr. Hist.	F. Jacoby, *Die Fragmente der Griechischen Historiker* (1958)
Horowitz	G. Horowitz, *The Spirit of the Jewish Law* (1953)
HUCA	Hebrew Union College Annual
ICLQ	International and Comparative Law Quarterly
j.	Jerusalem Talmud
JBL	Journal of Biblical Literature
JE	Jewish Encyclopedia
JJP	Journal of Juristic Papyrology
JJS	Journal of Jewish Studies
Jos.	Josephus
JRL	B. Cohen, *Jewish and Roman Law* (1966)
JQR	Jewish Quarterly Review
JThS	Journal of Theological Studies
Lohse	E. Lohse, *Die Texte aus Qumran* (1964)
LXX	The Septuagint
M.T.	The Masoretic Text
Maim.	Maimonides
Midr. R.	Midrash Rabbah
Moulton-Milligan	J. H. Moulton and G. Milligan, *The Vocabulary of the Greek New Testament* (1914–30)
NEB	New English Bible
NKZ	Neue kirchliche Zeitschrift
NT	Novum Testamentum
NTS	New Testament Studies
PG	Migne, *Patrologia*, Series Graeca
PL	Migne, *Patrologia*, Series Latina
Q	Scroll from Qumran, the preceding numeral referring to the Cave: 1 *QS* = *CR*
RB	Revue Biblique
RE	Pauly's *Real-Encyclopädie der classischen Altertumswissenschaft*
RIDA	Revue Internationale des Droits de l'Antiquité
SBE	Sacred Books of the East
Sonc.	I. Epstein, ed., *The Babylonian Talmud*, English translation (London, The Soncino Press) or the English translation of the *Midrash Rabbah* (various editors) published by the same Press
STh	Studia Theologica
ThWzNT	*Theologisches Wörterbuch zum Neuen Testament*

	(1933/1957–) originally edited by G. Kittel. An English version is appearing in America.
TuU	Texte und Untersuchungen zur Geschichte der altchristlichen Literatur
Vermès	G. Vermès, *The Dead Sea Scrolls in English* (1966)
VT	Vetus Testamentum
ZDMG	Zeitschrift der Deutsche Morgenländische Gesellschaft
ZKT	Zeitschrift für katholische Theologie
ZNW	Zeitschrift für die neutestamentliche Wissenschaft
ZRGG	Zeitschrift für Religions- und Geistesgeschichte
ZSS	Zeutschrift der Savigny-Stiftung für Rechtsgeschichte
ZVR	Zeitschrift für vergleichende Rechtswissenschaft

Preface

THIS PREFACE is devoted chiefly to acknowledgements, but the purposes of the book should be made clear from the outset. This is not a book about 'Christ's law', nor about the conception of law which a Christian ought to have (ought he to have any, rather than a desire for peace, which transcends law?). It is about law in the text of the New Testament. Law obtrudes there somewhat markedly, and it is interesting to know why, and to try to find the significance of the legal allusions with which the gospels and epistles are peppered.

I hope to interest the moderately informed, and to show them a side of Jesus and his contemporaries which they may not already have suspected. This is naturally only one side. But in particular I want to interest lawyers in something theological (which otherwise many lawyers might not undertake), and to interest theologians (particularly biblical theologians) in the everyday law of Jesus's world (a category of information in which very few of them have evinced any real interest until recently). If any lawyers would like to scrutinise the New Testament from a legal standpoint, as their training and temperaments might seem to authorise them to do, they cannot afford to ignore the methods or the results of biblical theologians. These last have made rapid advances in recent years and are about to make several more (as our knowledge of the idiom and mental climate of those times improves). Their approach will sometimes surprise a reader whose experience of Bible study has not progressed beyond the elementary.

As for theologians, I think many will agree that the immense load of scholarship with which every passage is encumbered can lead in desperation to an unconscious selection and over-simplification, which has the further effect of attributing to a particular exegesis of any particular passage the quality of authority from which many theologians in the first half of this century were busily stripping the New Testament text itself. The curious situation therefore operating in theology (which is not found in other non-scientific subjects) in which equally established senior teachers teach concurrently opposite or inconsistent interpretations of identical scriptural passages, and agree privately to differ (indefinitely postponing the task of resolving their differences), has to be understood by the layman who uses the texts for his own historical researches; and he must adjust himself to *not* supposing that a final solution to any purely factual problem can soon be forthcoming, still less an agreed Christian exegesis of any but a few historically innocuous passages.[1] The naïve view that what scripture says can be understood literally and precisely at its face value tends to be rapidly supplanted by the equally naïve fear that no part of the text is of historical value, and that faith must persist entirely divorced from intellectual study of the text. The latter error is indirectly encouraged by our universities which, for quite practical reasons, have to teach students and examine them as if the subject were from first to last historical and objective (*i.e.* a teacher can be equally effective, if not more so, if his own doctrinal position is uncertain), and nowadays no one writes a book of value to theological students for examination purposes upon the footing that his researches should increase or support any particular kind of faith. The position there strongly resembles one which might be imagined if our medical schools put their students through their present arduous training with occasional reminders that 'whatever you have learnt here will have no bearing on your practice as physicians and surgeons which will, as previously, be conducted with the aid of incantations and magic potions'. Thus there is no objection to a man's forming opinions during his theological studies which will clash with traditions surviving in the group which he will serve as minister, and no theological scholar is expected to forbear from proving any hypothesis, however uncomfortable, merely because it would upset faith or conflict with the opinions of others at least as learned and responsible as himself. This is a field in which, in contrast with pre-Reformation times, there is no received opinion, and (with some reservations in the case of Roman Catholics) no academic discovery is heretical.

Nevertheless, theologians have to respond to the times. Unconscious pressures affect them as they affect others. When faith was hindered by obscurantism scholars showed how little we knew of the true meaning of the text, and exposed the gulf between the beliefs of the early Church and those which alone could be attributed to Jesus. The silent implication was that those who professed to be Christians should imitate the latter rather than the former. Now, when indifference to religion has taken a franker tone, and the very survival of Church institutions

[1] An extremely helpful work is Van A. Harvey's *The Historian and the Believer* London, S.C.M. Press 1967).

(which indirectly support the theologians themselves) is in doubt, and reaction from believing Christians of all ages and classes is beginning to be felt, scholars find it possible to detect more of history in the gospels than was previously allowed. The man who went to the New Testament to hear the authentic voice of Jesus was told, not less recently than during my own lifetime, that (with the exception of relatively few sayings) he could only be disappointed. Now the sceptic who relies on academic proofs of the corruption or sophistication of the biblical sources is feeling the draught, and is himself accused of knowing too little about his subject.

But though theologians in common with other scholars tend to supply what their public needs, their difficulties are enormously greater than the average. The historian, for example, is concerned to bridge the gap between his primary source and his immediate public, and the work of his predecessors has only a historical interest for him and for them; yet the theologian who has to act, like other scholars, as a kind of banker for the public, has to produce his clean, new-minted, current coin day by day, while what he takes in is the unrefined ore of the primary sources, the unassayed spoil of heterogeneous minings, the dross of accumulated speculation, the worn and obsolete coinage of previous ages, and the base metal and the counterfeit of the populariser and propagandist: for he cannot neglect any aspect of the Church's research and feeling, nor that of the Church's critics or near neighbours in religious experience, and he must take account of even the most uneducated conjecture unless he is himself to be open to attack for having 'overlooked' something which may turn out to be relevant. In this connection I apologise for causing him to read here yet more matter which, from his point of view, is naïve and undisciplined: in particular I have not interested myself in modern ideas about the Old Testament, since what interests me is its role in the first century.

We must indeed develop a sympathy for the theologian in his situation, and not be offended by him when, in relief at his own prowess in surmounting the immense masses of secondary and tertiary scholarship, not to speak of the minute and far-fetched interpretations which every word in the original sources can call forth, he throws out his chest and gives the world the impression that he alone knows. That is why one welcomes from the best scholars very humble expressions of very relative confidence. Professor Joachim Jeremias, whose books on the parables of Jesus and the eucharistic words of Jesus seem to be the best on those highly intricate subjects, would be the first to react to new information and would never suggest that he has said the last word on those matters. Professor Josef Blinzler, whose book on the trial of

Jesus remains the best on that intensely controversial topic, is employed (in that specific connection) not in teaching what happened so much as in evaluating the multitude of specialised and amateur contributions to a complex of problems which may never be entirely satisfactorily solved. New light on the sources means a reappraisal of the existing mound of learning. Indeed we can copy some of Jeremias's own words, and leave the matter at that: 'Studies . . . not infrequently leave the reader with the uneasy feeling that the author has unconsciously read into the text what he would like to find. Must we not all learn better to listen to the text alone? To do this, research into Jesus's environment provides an indispensable help.'

While the general reader, and the lawyer with him, must seek the aid of the theologian when seeking to understand the meaning of the New Testament text, the question arises whether any, and if any what help will be forthcoming to the theologian if he takes advantage of legal learning. I have no doubt but that if he becomes convinced that it is possible to know what rules of law and custom were in force at that period, and if he can see ground for believing that individual passages are more effective or more intelligible with the aid of the legal information than they were previously in the light of unaided speculation, he will readily acquaint himself with that information and utilise it as he already utilises information of many different kinds. His occasional predisposition to see Jesus as uninterested in law can be put aside sufficiently long to enable him to look into these questions.

Ideally, no doubt, the man to undertake research along the lines of this volume ought to have had the following career: he should be educated in an old-fashioned Jewish home somewhere in the under-developed areas of North Africa or Mesopotamia; he should learn the *Torāh*, *Mishnāh*, Talmud, and *Haggadāh* (terms which are very shortly explained in the Introduction below) as a child and a youth; he should then hold some responsibility as a counsellor or a judge; he should then take to the New Testament (a Hebrew, Arabic, or Syriac copy might come his way by some odd chance); he should come to the West and become acquainted with Christian exegesis (which no doubt would fascinate him intensely): and then at last he would be ready to tell us exhaustively and finally what the more difficult pieces of the synoptic gospels mean, and very many of St Paul's allusions.[1] But I fear that the

[1] If anyone asks, 'Are not the books available to him also available to us, and cannot we also read Hebrew and Aramaic?' the answer is twofold: firstly, that the historical view of Jewish literature and scholarship is itself the product of the western critical mind and therefore out of tune with the tone of the originals; and secondly, that it is not books which made the civilisation, but the civilisation which made the books and continues to make them. The living embodiment of the culture is the best teacher and

'professionals' would insist upon his knowing Greek well, would want him to do a few years' work on the ancient history of the Greco-Roman world, and would want to be sure that he knew all about Jülicher, Schweitzer, Bultmann, and other famous figures, before they would take seriously what he had to say. They would ask him to prove positively that his Jewish learning belonged firmly to the first century, for a theologian thrives on doubt and on the margin of probability, for the more of it he has the more elbow-room there is for him to exercise his gifts. I am afraid it will be many a long day before such a Jewish youth decides to devote his life to Christian exegesis. I already know one who could go a long way towards this if he felt it were really worthwhile. But he has not at present sufficient confidence that Jesus was really so sound a rabbi, and he would not risk the chance that he might be convinced of the contrary if by so doing he would have to run the gauntlet of scholars whose learning would not be entirely confirmed by what he had to teach them. So, in the absence of the ideal, we have to get along as best we can. Perhaps this book will stimulate a Christian to acquire the necessary qualifications?

From what I imagine that I have discovered I am myself tempted to draw certain conclusions. They may be more conveniently offered by way of the 'Conclusion', now postponed until the publication of the companion volume (to be called *Law and Midrash in the New Testament*) which is in contemplation. This book, meanwhile, contains in more or less modified and improved forms the earlier of my studies and three entirely new chapters have been added. These studies, though in places they use somewhat large language, are confined to the particular topics in which I felt there was a legal contribution to be made, and if any general proposition is to emerge from them it need not be explicit.

Chapter 8 (The Lamp which Must not be Hidden) has not previously been published; a somewhat different treatment was privately circulated and the central idea was stated in the form of a question at *Expository Times* 78 (1966), 18. Chapter 6 (The Great Supper) is entirely new, also Chapter 14 ('Render to Caesar . . .'). Chapter 16 (Christ's Teaching on Marriage) originally formed part of a projected study of Jesus's and Paul's uses of 'fundamental law', but the study of the Pauline passage has been postponed, while the treatment of the divorce question seems to fit a volume devoted more particularly to legal teachings.

The remainder of the book has appeared, in one form or another, in various periodicals. I am obliged to the editors and/or proprietors of

the cold, scientific, lexicographical mind has no role in oriental culture—and small hopes of teaching it.

these for their kind permission to reprint so much of already published material as is here reprinted, in so far as such permission was really requisite. This is the sort of reservation which a lawyer can be forgiven for making, and which is (I fancy) too seldom made. Leaving such questions aside I must emphasise that I have revised everything. In particular I have reconsidered most carefully Chapter 17, which deals with the Doctrine of the Redemption and the complex and multi-motivated gospel story of Jesus's so-called trial before the Jewish leaders and his trial before Pilate. My inaugural lecture (October 1965), entitled *An Oriental Lawyer Looks at the Trial of Jesus and the Doctrine of the Redemption* (London, Luzac for the School of Oriental and African Studies, 1966) does not correspond completely, and is still (at the time of writing) available. The present Chapter 17 retains the method of citation found convenient at that time and therefore has its own bibliography appended to it. I did not think this book as a whole needed a bibliography, and the names of scholars whose work has been referred to have been placed in the index.

Chapter 1 started life as 'Law in the New Testament: The Treasure in the Field', in *Zeitschrift für die neutestamentliche Wissenschaft* 54 (1963), 31–42. Chapter 2 appeared originally in the same journal, vol. 56 (1965), 184–95, where its treatment, both of the parable of the Talents and of the two logia which are associated with the same theme, was deliberately abbreviated: it has been possible to make it a little less breathless reading here. Chapter 3, on the Unmerciful Servant, is improved by additional illustrative information; it originally appeared in *Revue internationale des Droits de l'Antiquité* 12 (1965), 3–19. That periodical has earned my especial gratitude for its hospitality and its efficiency, but it was seen by few theologians. Chapter 4, which deals with the parable of the Unjust Steward and the midrashic sub-structure of Lk xvi, has an especial significance for me in that it apprised me of how large a world of Jewish thought, not exclusively legal in character, had totally escaped current New Testament scholarship, in spite of the labours of Lightfoot, Schöttgen, and Billerbeck. If the legal component in Jewish intellectual activity has been underestimated and incorrectly interpreted by western theologians the loss to the common man's understanding of Jesus, his work and his message must be incalculable. It was through the recommendation of Professor C. H. Dodd that that article was published in *New Testament Studies* 7 (1961), 198–219, 364–80, and a special debt is owed to him for his part in that publication, and not less for his patient notes on other parables and *pericopai*, written when he had himself still major undertakings to complete and his strange correspondent's *bona fides* might well have been doubted.

The Indian legal particulars relative to that particular parable were set out more fully at *Zeitschrift für vergleichende Rechtswissenschaft* 65 (1963), 172–82, and the most important of them have been reproduced in their appropriate place below. One might well ask, as some youthful doubters have, 'Why drag in India?' The fact is that the Middle East and the South and South-East of Asia have much in common, and have had throughout history, and more light will be shed on first-century Palestine from Rawalpindi (for example) than will ever be obtained from Rome. This is an uncongenial idea to some theologians and to not a few Jews.[1] The latter in general think of New York as their milieu (or Tel Aviv), and would shudder to think of living in Basra or the Yemen: but it is the Jews of the 'traditional' territories who more closely reproduce the stifling, in-bred atmosphere of the world Jesus belonged to. Hence, notwithstanding the superficial Hellenisation in Luke, for example, it is those who would interpret the synoptic gospels with the aid of Athens or Alexandria who have a case to make, not those who believe that the East can best interpret the East. But this is all by the way. To return to our topic: Chapter 5, on the parable of the Prodigal Son, appeared in *New Testament Studies* 14 (1967), 56–74. Its swift republication is justified by the additional material with which I have been able to enrich it since then. Chapter 7 appeared in the same periodical at vol. 10 (1963), 1–26. Small corroborative illustrations have been added. A short version of it appeared in *Studia Evangelica* II, 170–3. Chapter 9 is my favourite, in that in this parable (The Good Samaritan) the elaborate scholarship and the humanity of Jesus blend so perfectly that a fully intellectual treatise appears as a smooth tale, easily assimilable by an adolescent, or even by a child. The chapter appeared in *New Testament Studies* 11 (1964), 22–37. The argument has been further illuminated with several additions.

Chapter 10 appeared as 'Water into Wine' in *Biblische Zeitschrift* 7

[1] The extraordinarily interesting discovery of Miss Jahnow, published in *ZNW* 24 (1925), 155–8, is still ignored because its implications could not be pursued. In the healing narrative at Mk ii.1ff. and Lk v.17ff. the paralytic, whom Jesus addresses as τέκνον, is let down through the roof, the excuse being that his friends could not have access to the door. Did the friends of the paralytic follow out some eastern superstitious remedy for epilepsy (paralysis is one of the symptoms of epilepsy) which required the patient to be put through a window or to be let down through the roof εἰς τὸ μέσον? How otherwise can we explain the coincidence of their remarkable behaviour with *Hiraṇyakeśi-gṛhya-sūtra* II. 2, 7, 1–2 and *Āpastamba-gṛhya-sūtra* VII. 18, 1 (*SBE* 30 [1892], 219, 286–7)—the cure for an epileptic boy? This has the effect of suggesting enquiry whether other Indian features appear in Jewish practice of the time. For the present it is sufficient to refer to my 'A problem in the Book of Jubilees and an Indian doctrine', *ZRGG* 14 (1962), 247ff.

(1963), 80–97. It was disliked in some quarters because it treated the incident solely as if it actually happened, and neglected the symbolic and transcendental features. This was regarded as dangerous. The occidental mind is quite happy with such stories, provided it is understood that they remain firmly in the realm of symbol. Yet stories in the gospel were preserved as statements of *fact*, of things which were understood to have *happened*. Their value when assessed in mental activity other than the objective appraisal of fact must not be allowed to obscure their primary function. Professor Dr Rudolph Schnackenburg, editor of the *BZ*, was about to publish an earlier draft of my 'Render to Caesar', but kindly released it for this volume.

Chapter 11, 'Peter's Penny', appeared under that title at *Novum Testamentum* 6 (1963), 1–15. Chapter 12 ('The Anointing at Bethany') represents the first of my attempts to participate in the well-patronized congresses organised by the late Dr F. L. Cross at Oxford. It was published amongst the Proceedings in *Studia Evangelica II*, edited by Dr Cross as *Texte und Untersuchungen zur Geschichte der altchristlichen Literatur* 87, p. 174–82. These congresses were altogether enjoyable and their Proceedings are a recognised source of scholarly information. Since my paper was published, however, I have expanded my treatment and added a study of the amusing episode of Zacchaeus. Chapter 13 appeared as 'Fresh Light on the Wicked Vinedressers' in *RIDA* 10 (1963), 11–41. Elaborate as that study was, it has had to be revised in view of a technical error detected by a Jewish colleague, and it has been augmented by several corroborative addenda.

The story of John the Baptist's predicament is important because of its part in Jesus's own story, both as a fact and as an element in Jesus's own self-awareness. Under the slightly bizarre title 'Herod's Oath and the Baptist's Head' I published an article in two parts in the *BZ* 9 (1965), 49–59, 233–46. The material reappears as Chapter 15 in the present book. What started as a study in depth of three words in the gospel text, three words which had never been taken too seriously, turned out to be more adventurous exploration.

The last chapter appeared as 'Fresh Light on Romans vii.1–4?' in the *Journal of Jewish Studies* 15 (1964), 97–108. I had hoped to enjoy again the hospitality of Jewish Chronicle Publications (who have kindly agreed to the republication), but on a matter of policy the authorities concerned determined not to publish under their aegis material which was Christian as opposed to Jewish. The large number of journals devoted to Christian literature may readily excuse this decision; but it remains true that Jesus and Paul, not to speak of the majority of the first Christians, were Jews. Christians can understand their 'founding fathers', and surely their Founder himself, only when in close touch with the semitic orient, if not also at times (as Professor David Daube has shown more than once) with the world of Jewry at large.

I am now brought to the delicate task of acknowledging my personal obligations: delicate because the mention of one scholar or one friend would seem to require the mention of so many as to produce a catena of names, nugatory for each of them. In human as well as scholarly terms I owe a great debt to Dr M. Gertner. My repeated acknowledgements to him in the original publications leave no one in doubt but that this source of inspiration and information has been primary. I surely ought to mention besides especially those few who have helped by giving me the feeling of being useful when they could quite as easily have abstained from doing so. There is no obvious reason why some people entertain unimpressive strangers and some do not. I find that it is some of the busiest who can manage to spare time at a venture. Amongst those whom I wish to record many are very busy people. Professor Dr Joachim Jeremias has several times placed me in his debt. Dr George B. Caird, Fr H. Benedict Green C.R., and Fr C. Spicq O.P., and Professor Dr J. Blinzler have been uniformly positive and encouraging, while Dr Ze'ev W. Falk was kind enough to go through many of my papers and, in commenting upon them, to temper zeal with mercy. Professor David Daube and the late Professor Erich Pritsch have supplied, each in his own way, the lack of an academic leader. My first tutor, Mr J. G. Griffith of Jesus College, Oxford, has often helped me to find the value of a difficult word, and Mr Charles Drage, the Slavonic linguist, has put his knowledge of Greek at my disposal in a comradely spirit. Fr Hasso Jaeger of the Centre National de la Recherche Scientifique never let his own immense labours stand in the way of any help he could give me, and his juridical mind and patristic and biblical bibliographical knowledge have supported me again and again. Preparing this book for the press has been an anxious task and the Principal and Fellows of Jesus College placed me in their debt by giving me house-room while I wrestled with it. It is unfortunate that despite my efforts and the extraordinary diligence of the publisher and printer certain anomalies remain in the style of citation of secondary works. There is no arcane significance in the fact that I cite one edition of a work in one chapter and another in another! The chapters began their lives in different countries, their revised versions are not reproduced here in the order in which they were conceived, and the mode of citation retains some traces of the different experiences they underwent prior to their first being printed. Again, in transliterating Hebrew and Aramaic words I have tried on the whole to aid the reader to pronounce them and to find them in a dictionary: there is no agreed style of representing semitic words in the Roman script, and I must often have made use of more than one method, all, I hope, equally allowable. I trust no one will be misled by any inconsistency which has defied our attempts to eliminate it. A number of my citations are alternatives: I want as many of my readers as possible to look up the sources for themselves.

One of the most intriguing by-products of my adventures into these fields is to discover how vigorously students who are themselves being supervised with rigour will repudiate any inadequacy in the attempts of a newcomer. This discovery (which could hardly have been made otherwise) has enlightened me on the methods I should employ when supervising my own students. One young English graduand told me in effect that if I did not follow European scholars' conceptions of the Law in the History of Israel I ought not to offer anything of mine to the public. There is something in what he says, since until I knew how little people comprehend the Jewish traditional concept of the Law I could not have believed that anyone would find fault with the important (and obvious) word ἀχρεῖοι (unprofitable) in Lk xvii.10. But I am afraid the general truth is that 'O.T.' as studied in our universities has rather less bearing on the law actually obtaining in Jesus's day than Magna Carta has on ours; so, in so far as I am concerned for my own purposes with that law, the European scholar's view of the Old Testament cannot be directly useful to me. If that scholarship was what was required there would have been nothing left for me to do, surely. My young friend added, 'We already have Montefiore (who became, I believe, a Doctor of Divinity) and Strack-and-Billerbeck, and our teachers' commentaries refer to the rabbinical sources wherever these are really relevant and are sufficiently early in date. Even Oesterley said "Billerbeck" was a heap of the barely relevant and the irrelevant. I wonder what you can usefully add to it?' This book (if he reads it) will, I hope, not only provide him with an answer, but also set him off in a similar direction.

Many of my younger colleagues have generously lent me their mental energies. It is not easy to find exactly the right words to express my obligation to them. Whether or not I have deserved well of them, they have deserved well of me—and I trust I may benefit hereafter from the peculiar contribution that youth can make. Especially in the cases of trans-Rhenine scholars-to-be, they have so far seldom allowed comradeship to dilute candour. My gifted young friend Dietrich Fischer's interest in the unexpected treasures of the familiar gospel did not abate upon his defection from theology to the positive sciences. My former student in oriental laws, the Indologist Dr Günther-Dietz Sontheimer, manifested his tolerance towards my apparently irrelevant researches by materially advancing them at Tübingen. Dr Jur. Rolf Knütel after giving me some information on Roman Law paid me the compliment of using some of my studies in some highly successful lectures he gave most creditably in Italy. Willem A. Sinninghe Damsté obtained for me valuable material in Dutch, which Miss H. C. Kamps translated for me. Walter J. Houston made time from his own thesis-writing to point out weaknesses in my detailed approach, accurately and fairly. Researches such as are published here cannot be done (by such a one as I am) in a human vacuum, and it matters a great deal to me in what ambience they are carried on. The negative side of this story would make amusing reading, but would be incongruous here.

My wife deserves more than the conventional acknowledgement. The wife who types her husband's thesis, and sees eye to eye with him in his labours, is not uncommon. The academic profession is blessed with a great many of them. Mine has been sceptical of the value of my normal professional undertakings—as well she may be, given the monumental lack of interest in oriental legal scholarship from which this generation suffers. But of my New Testament doings, which some people have fancied to be a more or less amiable eccentricity, she at any rate has never ceased to approve—though it meant my being away from home when our five children were about the house (none of them yet quite fit to share all the burdens of the home), and my using scarce resources on what might seem to be entirely speculative enterprises. Thus her support has been backed by substantial pledges.

I trust that those who have supported and encouraged me will be repaid indirectly by any results which may flow from my present and my forthcoming book, including any reactions these may provoke from the learned. I should wish such reactions to represent especially a closer factual understanding of what occurred when he whom St Paul called the 'power of God' and the 'wisdom of God' was personally present on earth, and communicated in word and deed with his own generation of ordinary, earthy people.

Introduction

THIS SERIES OF STUDIES is devoted to parables, passages, episodes in the life and teaching of Jesus in which law figures. Not all the passages which contain legal features are dealt with here. They are very many. Interesting legal implications are to be seen in the Annunciation and the Resurrection, to choose for this purpose only extreme points in the biography of Christ. But a fair sample is given of the points of contact between law and the text of the gospel.

My motive is to serve anyone who cares to read the New Testament, Christian and non-Christian. There is a great deal of scholarly information of considerable intellectual and historical value in the New Testament which could be used with profit by many a reader who postpones his own personal judgement on the religious implications of that literature. I, for my part, have tried to see Jesus and his contemporaries as would a historian, a sociologist (of a kind), and as a lawyer. The result is different in some detail and in general from that which is commonly published for Christian readers. It does not follow that the extraordinary problems posed by the gospels and epistles are made easier to solve by such studies as mine. Curiously, it might well be suggested that the closer we get in imagination to the crowd which used to listen to Jesus and to watch his behaviour the harder he is to cope with. The problems are lifted from the plane of mystery and symbolism, out of the depths of unconscious religious yearnings, on to the plane of everyday existence, which can be embarrassing. It certainly *was* embarrassing, intellectually and otherwise, for many worthy and respectable people, who were forced to take Jesus seriously in spite of the indications in his language and behaviour that he was indifferent to many requirements of respectability as these were then commonly understood. However that may be, one should add in fairness to him that he did not disdain, or (perhaps more accurately) he insisted on observing *some* of the traditional taboos which the common people in the eastern world associated with the renunciate and the 'enlightened', rôles which long pre-existed him; and the evidence for this is not confined to suggestions which may or may not have been foisted upon him by pious evangelists or their sources.

This introduction, which contains a few points of substantive detail, is intended to raise a number of generalities which the reader will find it advantageous to consider before he tackles any of the studies independently.

The subject of the law in Old Testament and inter-testamental times and the status of the law as a force in the time of Jesus and shortly thereafter is long and complex, but it is neither its length nor its complexity which is our main problem: what stands in the way of the uncommitted (*i.e.* non-orthodox Jewish) reader is the Jewish attitude to the law, which is at the same time a manifestation of Jewishness and a feature of an antique form of social and intellectual life common at one time to all oriental peoples (with the limited exception of the Chinese) and still very prevalent amongst the unwesternised, *i.e.* the majority, of the world east (and south) of Suez.

The individual laws set out in the five books of Moses[1] have their place in the doctrine of the covenant. Whether this covenant actually happened is neither here nor there for our purposes, since at all material times it was taken for granted that it did happen, and indeed that Jewish history could be understood solely upon such a hypothesis. God chose Israel and Israel acknowledged God, and in an apparently incongruously legal fashion this corporate act on the part of a hypothetical Israel was assumed to have bound all Israelites forever. The laws are the requirements of God. To keep the law is to be obedient. There is punishment for violation but no special reward for fulfilment. A desire for reward manifests itself none the less, and is perhaps the source of the notion that one can claim no reward unless one does *more* than one's mere duty. The law is comprehensive and addressed to all Israel. The authors of the Pentateuch see history preceding the 'giving of the Law' on Mt Sinai as the totally unmerited election of Israel from among the nations. The law is a demonstration of grace by the God who redeemed Israel from Egypt. What God demands is good, but this is to be done not because it is good but because God demands it. This curious notion, which Jews share with Muslims, appeals to a mind which accepts paternal authority without question; and this point must not be lost sight of, since the myth that the Jews were bowed down under a sombre and joyless weight of perhaps as many as six hundred and thirteen commandments enforced by an authoritarian deity has

[1] A very helpful summary of this subject appears in Gutbrod's article νόμος in *ThWzNT*, available in English separately in H. Kleinknecht and W. Gutbrod, *Law* (London 1962) and in the American translation of the *ThWzNT* which is now in the course of publication.

been widely misunderstood in the interests of Christian apologetics. First of all, a great many commandments coincided with timeless taboos and superstitions which no one could have prevented the Israelite from observing (*e.g.* the notion of uncleanness because of the dead); and secondly because the emotional satisfaction of having kept on the right side of the requirements of a super-Father, of having obtained the approval of the chief prestige-holder in an intensely self-absorbed hierarchical society, was a positive and even a beautiful sensation, which the ritualists exploit not as conscious confidence-tricksters but as purveyors of a commodity which was in general demand. Jesus's 'cleansing of the Temple' was by no means so simple an affair as it has seemed to some, and it is no accident that Jesus's whole attitude to the Temple and its elaborate service has long been open to debate.

The Prophets preached what was a new encounter with God. They repeated God's requirements and demanded repentance from those who were (as often in the East, but by no means exclusively there) at one and the same time pious and ungodly. The Prophets made no demands which were new in themselves. Infringement of the written law (Ho viii.12) was apostasy from God. They radicalised law, as when Amos says 'Hate the evil and love the good' (v.15). The cult worship was condemned not absolutely (how could it be?) but in contrast with justice and loving-kindness, which they say God requires.

The author of Deuteronomy, whose work was to appeal so strongly to those ultra-legists,[1] the people of the Dead Sea Scrolls, and who quite evidently served as a prime source for Jesus's detailed teaching, took his stand on the covenant sworn by God to the fathers—the promise, the oath of God. Deuteronomy exhorts the people to follow God's commands for these themselves reveal God's nature. Sincerity is demanded from the individual with an emphasis on ethics rather than ritual. There is no reason to suppose, with some, that ancient peoples were less concerned with ethics: it is a question of what emphasis is at any period sought from the written documents. In Deuteronomy the obligations to the neighbour (*i.e.* brother) are emphasised. Commitment to God will be rewarded with God's blessing. Jeremiah points out that sin can be removed only by a new covenant, but what sort of renewal is left vague.

The exile made it plain that Israel must obey God's law or perish. The historical books of the Hebrew Bible depict periods in which disaster is a righteous punishment for violation of God's will. The cult

[1] A point neatly and significantly made by M. Black in *Studia Evangelica* (*TuU* 73) (Berlin 1959), p. 571.

of the Temple was seen as a fulfilment of the law. The scribes take over the religious leadership of the people (Ezr vii.10).

Torāh originally meant divine direction. Legal, cultic, political and other directions could be described as *Torāh*. Only later did it convey the idea of a legal code.

Law is the basis of all the apocryphal and pseudonymous works of the inter-testamental period. *Torāh* (νόμος) often there means the Pentateuch. The unconditional divine validity of the law is accepted without question: the law is supreme over all other religious functions. The Pharisees were intent on following the law even at the cost of political freedom. Membership of the people was not sufficient if one's attitude to the law was not wholehearted. The separation of the Jews from other peoples was regarded as the main function of the law. The history of the Jews was seen as a matter of rewards for obedience and punishment for disobedience to the law. The law is the hope of the righteous; it is treated as the equivalent of wisdom, and observance of the law as reason. The rabbis were concerned equally with the study of the law and its practice, though they understood that it was more meritorious to learn and to practise than merely to study for study's sake.

Against this background it will be clear that any teacher of first-century Jews must, if he hoped to succeed, appear to uphold the law even if he reinterprets it; he would readily rely upon his audiences' acceptance of the words of the *Torāh* as being essentially and perpetually true.

But that alone does not entirely explain why *we* should concern ourselves with law in the New Testament. We must face up to the special effort required of us. To begin with, what reason have we to think that we know enough about Jewish law of the period; and do we know in what respects the Jewish concept of society differed from that of almost every western society which has tried to understand the gospel from that day to this? We have to go into these questions: we may undertake a task more difficult than that of the apostles themselves (with the very probable exception of St Paul). We have to place ourselves in those streets and beside those waters, and yet at the same time be, as it were, aloft, looking at ourselves and our company as it watches Jesus: we have also to observe ourselves in that situation observing *us*. A naïve attempt to receive the message of Christ as if we were first-century Jews is, by itself, of questionable value. Even if we can imagine that we are first-century Jews (very different from the polished Ashkenazim to be found in college common-rooms and laboratories in Britain or America), which is difficult enough, we have to make the effort of translation, so that we can imagine what effect Jesus's teaching would have had, had he himself directed it occidentally and prospectively—in short if he had consciously taught people far away from him in culture and in time (which of course he did not). The reader will already have grasped that it is *not* recommended that we treat Jesus and his message and the dreadful experience to which his pupils and close friends were submitted as an anthropological and emotional experience of a purely esoteric Jewish kind, relevant only to that place and time.

No doubt for many people that is the right point at which to begin. Let us suppose ourselves working in the relevant kitchen immediately prior to the Last Supper. What 'those people' were about up above would not bother us unduly. We should be quite familiar with holier-than-thou sects, and would not often bother to evaluate their particular programmes or investigate their doctrines. Excited curiosity would be rarer than a customary approval for those who busied themselves with the study of God's word. But everyone would have accepted the simple proposition that Jews are better than Gentiles (however smart the latter might be) and that the latter have something important to learn from the former (did not the emperor himself pay for sacrifices to be performed for him at the Temple?). The religious experiences of the Jews would be, in Jewish eyes, relevant to the whole world: why otherwise did the Jews, racially conscious if any race ever was, offer the Jewish religion and the status of Jew[1] to any proselyte who cared to undergo the necessary discipline and enquiry? No exclusive Hindu racialism this—the religion of the Jews was *true* in a way which no religion claimed to be until the daughter religion, Christianity, and later Islam appeared; and it was a logical sequence of thought which made Jewish religious discoveries significant, in Jewish eyes, for everyone everywhere and always.

Why should Students of the New Testament Interest Themselves in Law?

To the Englishman (perhaps not equally the American) law is a nuisance, and lawyers apparently parasitic. The protective and positive aspects of law are readily (and unfairly) forgotten. Lawyers are always telling each other 'We must charge less for our services, or at least appear to do so!' The legal profession (excluding our judiciary) is regarded by the general public as a clique of 'fixers', whose honesty is less often suspect than their passion for apparently irrelevant minutiae, but their probity too often remains, none the less, a question which

[1] In fairness to facts one must reserve one point here. The proselyte, however righteous, was not entitled, according to the *Torāh*, to be admitted to governmental office, in particular to the throne—a very natural source of embarrassment for the Herodians.

the legal profession itself keeps hidden behind some rather objectionable mystique. Pompous, self-important, and yet oddly remote from responsibility for the way the country is governed, lawyers, and to some extent the law teachers who wish to be associated with them, have attracted to themselves some odium and a lot of indifference. The fact that laymen would do no better than lawyers, or that, if they did, they would have become, of course, lawyers in the process, does not strike the man in the street. Small wonder that in the Anglo-Saxon world one hears emphasis upon the quite mistaken notion that Christ's teaching was anti-law, and that Christ came to free men from law. Away with the letter, and back to the spirit! This is folly. Christ in fact interpreted the *Torāh*, the Jewish corpus of law, in ways which were intellectually possible, by methods intellectually viable—if often with inconvenient implications. The notion that his coming meant the end of law and of legal thinking is false. For *how long* is another matter—we do not know what interval he expected between his own departure and the new age. It is true that Jesus believed, as many then did, that the coming of the Messiah meant the end (or at any rate a modification) of most, if not all, the pre-Messianic regulations and inhibitions with which the *Torāh* was stuffed. Naturally this was a vague concept, as vague as any ideas we might have as to the state of existence after the end of the world, but Jesus could take advantage of this idea and St Paul and many of his Christian contemporaries certainly did so.

To the Anglo-Saxons law is a costly and unpleasing thing, though its power to protect the citizen gives it in America a status which closely approaches respectability. To the world of the civil law, that is to say in countries which draw their jurisprudence historically from Rome, lawyers do not seem so objectionable, and their education and even their manners differ, on the whole, from their Anglo-Saxon counterparts. Jurists are 'knights', fighting for the security of the state in no less ample a measure than the military proper, and study and practice of the law confers social prestige of a substantial character. This distinction between the two major atmospheres in which law is practised is useful to us at present because it helps to prepare the Anglo-Saxon for the unexpected notion that law could be, and was, the *only* substantial intellectual discipline for the Jew, was the mark of an educated man, and carried prestige in a way that no other activity did. To a certain extent this is still true amongst Jews that have not been assimilated into a Gentile environment, nor become infected with Gentile standards.

What we should regard as mean pettifogging and stupid hair-splitting (in fact casuistry in its proper sense) was to them service of the *Torāh*, in fact a *constructive* activity pleasing to God. No one could achieve any superior status in Jewish society unless he were steeped in scripture and in the traditions of the learned. About these traditions something important needs to be said. It is often supposed that the Pharisees, about whom we know a great deal, careless whether they developed hypocrisy at the expense of true piety, foisted upon the public many regulations and taboos of a basically superstitious nature for which the Bible could show no authority. What we must learn is simply this: that piety (and there is no piety like Jewish piety) coexisted in the same head with concern for *observances*. This was a general oriental problem and not confined to the Jews. Our own historical experience of exaltation of observance as opposed to conscientious belief has left a legacy of bitter opposition to observance, and, in the vast majority of people, to 'organised' religion as such. We know perfectly well that religion is an aspect of the healthy, mature personality, and that it does not suffer so much from a lack of organised observance as it does from an overemphasis upon demonstrations of piety. But in the ancient East only one people, namely the Hindu, had really got to grips with the partially conflicting tendencies of the average personality, and theirs has been a running battle ever since.[1] If the Hindus could not solve the problem finally and conclusively no people can; and we need not be surprised that the Jews were at a critical stage in this internal spiritual conflict at the time of Christ. Consequently, while the educated realised that observance had its uses and its value, the mass of the people were inclined to go much further and to suppose that observance was proof of belief; teachers who multiplied observances would tend to be the more beloved, rather than the reverse.

To make the problem more acute, Jewishness, which expressed itself primarily in public and frequent acknowledgement of the sovereignty of God, the God of the patriarchs, was also a political and social reality in a way it has never been since. To be a doubter of the truths of Judaism was to be a traitor to the nation and to the race. In our days this is not a serious problem. Except in primitive societies people are very mobile. Blatant treachery and the abandonment of one's country and even culture pass almost unobserved. The ancient world was very like the primitive societies of today, in that even the democratic societies

[1] In the short, ancient *smṛtis* such as Manu and Yājñavalkya and the *Bhagavad-gītā*, whose date is uncertain but which cannot be much later than the second century A.D. and is usually believed to be much older, is taught a peculiar doctrine: that a mental condition, be it described as knowledge or faith, alone ensures *moksha* ('release') while observances, especially those undertaken for reward (including spiritual reward) lead only to rebirth and continuation in the cycle of existences (which is an evil). Not that observances (*karma*) are evil—indeed they are prescribed, but their role is subordinate to that of true knowledge, and the renunciation of all desires.

(and they were the exception) were fanatically nationalistic and self-centred. Mutual belonging, mutual dependence, common brotherhood, the general absence of objectivity where the apparent interests of the group were at stake—these were almost universal, and the ancient, in-bred, endogamic, hierarchical society of the Jews suffered from these symptoms acutely, as their religious literature reveals constantly and painfully.[1] There was a great deal from which they needed to be liberated ('redeemed' if you like to adopt their emotionally overcharged vocabulary): we should say that they all needed to *grow up*.

The *Torāh* was thus a cult object, actually and figuratively. To interpret the *Torāh*, letter by letter, was a sacred ministry, not an obscure pedantry. The populace did not suspect the lawyer, for all his long gowns and his greetings in the marketplace—it honoured him. Disputes between the learned would have all the disagreeable quality of academic feuding, but it was assumed that in this way 'wisdom was increased'. There was an excellent reason why the *Torāh* should have acquired a second self in the traditions of the scribes, and should be resorted to with pedantic minuteness and imaginative interpretation. Any society which hangs from a single (if imaginary) racial hook, hierarchical in structure, dependent for its norms upon a single and constant *written* source which has stood the complex and constant strain of centuries of battling against fate and foreign nations, must be in a peculiar situation intellectually; it is this situation which we must try to understand when we take up any of Jesus's parables which have (as a high proportion of them have) a legal element. Jesus's debates with the learned of his day are repeated by the Church for numerous reasons, several of which are confidently suspected, and some as good as known. But as actual occurrences (they are all very plausible) they are intelligible only if we know why the *Torāh* was constituted as it was, and why people regarded it as they did. To those who are sincerely interested in the intellectual climate of Jesus's time, the common presuppositions of the learned and the techniques of education the early Christians themselves took absolutely for granted, a recent book is a mine of relevant information. In its way Professor Birger Gerhardsson's *Memory and Manuscript* (1961/1964), followed by his *Tradition and Transmissions in Early Christianity* (1964), opened a new era.[2]

[1] The effect of living in a patriarchal, scripture-revering society, especially at a time when its values are challenged by a freedom-loving individualistic society, is very well brought out in C. Northcote Parkinson's *East and West* (London 1963).

[2] An example of the importance of this work is the demonstration how texts were faithfully transmitted *even though some of the transmitters did not know their significance or implications*—and this 'half-baked' function was an essential feature of education (as in India).

What really interested the Jews? Meticulousness in loyalty and conformity. R. 'Eleazar of Modiim said:[1] 'If a man profanes the Hallowed Things (*i.e.* offerings), and despises the set feasts and puts his fellow to shame publicly and makes void the covenant of Abraham our father (*i.e.* hides the circumcision by plastic surgery or otherwise), and discloses meanings in the *Torāh* which are not according to the *halakāh*, even though a knowledge of the *Torāh* and good works are his, he has no share in the world to come.' Does this not show the scope of their vision, and their order of priorities? What kind of freedom, personal, social, cultural, or intellectual do these words presuppose? Behaviour no doubt deviated from the ideal very often: but the ideal still survives the influence of contact with liberal civilisations, and belongs to the very spirit of Israel.

We ourselves have small respect for statutes or constitutions. Magna Carta, or the Constitution of the United States or of any other country is in our eyes merely an instrument (however useful) to effect purposes, and all can be overturned by the appropriate legislative process. That we should be ruled in thought, word and deed by a statute passed by our ancestors (who were no wiser than we are) would be absurd. Even a law which has been in force, in one way or another, for a very long time commands respect only because no sufficient force has been marshalled to repeal it. If we break a law and are found out we stand a good chance of being punished. This is disagreeable, but that is the long and the short of the matter. If conscience is to be our guide quite different considerations will apply. At a time where parasitism is rampant we still observe some restraints: if we identify with a group (however small or large) we shall not wrong it (as long as we are in health) and shall hope to bask in the approval of the altogether amorphous society to which we belong. Some will help the rich to unload their wealth, and never doubt that this is justice. Robin Hood has many modern counterparts, widely respected. The breach of statute in itself is not a prime consideration in such contexts, especially since statutes are passed which offend the conscience, and the process of government itself involves multiple iniquities. The situation in ancient oriental societies was the reverse of this in ways which concern us intimately for our present purpose.

The situation of the Jews is clarified if we compare the situation of

[1] *Mishnāh*, 'Āvot III.12. It may be argued that liberty of dissent in matters of *halakāh* was formally denied only in the second century A.D. But the authoritarian approach to education and doctrine and the identification of dissent with social malaise goes back to the liberation of the Land of Israel (in the second century B.C.) from the Seleucids, and, in terms of pure psychology, infinitely further.

the Hindus and the Muslims. The last, though they came into existence only in the seventh century of our era, and indirectly owed something to Jewish thinking, in fact take their dependence upon the Qur'an from a social situation unaffected by cultural contacts with the Jews. The first element to be identified is the common, general, inherited sense that laws are essentially permanent and immutable—only *regulations* can change. Legislation is a divine function, and does not appertain to human assemblies. There are many regulations and by-laws of a police character, and they are as lasting as the individuals who issue them in the name of good government—and we are conscientiously obliged to obey them *pro tempore*. But the real law is part and parcel of human existence and derives from the Creator himself. This attitude belongs historically to as far back as the age of the Babylonians and geographically to the areas of settled agriculture with stable climates in the temperate zones of Mesopotamia and the Indus and Ganges valleys. Nature has laws in those regions, as she hardly seems to have in the more northern and western climes. And men were ruled by 'shepherds' and lived what seem to have been very limited, sheeplike lives. An intensely hierarchical social structure made it inevitable that even kings were thought to have their grandsire-like divine masters, and it was never right for anybody to do exactly as he liked.[1] Small wonder that initiative, mobility, and effective individuality belong historically to the west and the north!

We know a great deal about the Hindu and Islamic societies, their politics, philosophy, religion, and law. In both spheres law, though mentioned last here, bulks very large. In Islam law (*fiqh*) is *the* science. In Hinduism its counterpart (*dharmaśāstra*) is the science of righteousness, the only learning binding all castes and groups together and making them partakers of the same civilization. Starting (in the case of Muslims) from the standpoint that the Qur'an cannot err, or (in the case

[1] If one grasps the almost incredibly authoritarian tone of the Jewish Law one understands the frantic zeal to find out what God's requirements were and the excitement about matters we should regard as of no secular interest. A matter of principle in the context of tithe would convulse not only a school but a sizeable section of the public. The tone of Maimonides is typical: 'For the mind is limited; not every mind is capable of attaining knowledge of the truth in its purity. If every man were to follow after the vagaries of his heart, the result would be universal ruin, ensuing from the limitations of the human intellect. How so? Sometimes one will be drawn to idolatry.... Sometimes he will harbour doubts concerning the *Torāh*, as to whether it is of divine origin or not. And such a person, being ignorant of the logical principles which need to be applied in order to attain positive truth, will lapse into heresy. In this regard the *Torāh* exhorts us, "And that ye go not about after your own heart, etc." (Nb xv.39). This means "You shall not allow yourselves to be drawn each one after his own limited intelligence, to imagine that his mind is attaining truth" ' (see Chavel, *The Commandments* II, 46–7).

of Hindus) that the sages who heard truth from the Self-existent himself cannot have misrepresented from age to age what duty was and is, both civilizations have had to develop a science of interpretation. For, of course, in any society which has no legislative machinery, however static it may be, *some* social development is bound to take place, especially as efficient government makes foreign trade contacts profitable and prolonged—and elasticity must be found somewhere. Thus Muslims have the *sunna*, the traditions of the behaviour of the Prophet, interpreted with the aid of the consensus of the learned and regulated analogy; and Hindus have the available pool of custom, the custom of the good (*sad-āchāra*), which is amenable to conformity with the basic principles of the *dharmaśāstra*, and the science of interpretation (*mīmāṃsā*) with the aid of which ancient maxims and propositions of law and good behaviour can be organised to provide a workable norm.

In a similar way the Jews developed first the 'oral law', which, because it was accepted by the majority of the people in theory and to some degree in practice, was attributed (unhistorically) to the time when Moses brought the *Torāh*, the written law, from God to the children of Israel at Mt Sinai. The second stage of development was the identification and study of canons of interpretation, which gave new life or rather lives to the old text. In the application of the written law it was expanded and developed, and occasionally contradicted by this oral law, and, except to some scholars who stuck, as some minority Muslim communities still do, to the literal text of the law without availing themselves of the traditions of men, the combined written and oral material was the standard of public and private conduct and bound every Jew both in conscience and in law. Whether the *Torāh* was *enforced* in any court was a matter of relative indifference. Amongst Hindus the *dharmaśāstra* was exceptionally enforced in petty courts in remote places, rather than as a rule; amongst Muslims the *fiqh* was frequently ignored and the *sharī'a*, the sacred law, was put into effect when it suited the ruler's purposes to be pious and orthodox. But that had no bearing whatever upon the validity of the law! To us no law is law unless it is enforced, and can be enforced predictably. To them its value lay in its being right, irrespective of whether or not it was enforced. What binds ideally and in conscience is much more to the point in a homogeneous, self-contained, fully cohesive society. The activity of judges is a much inferior matter, of limited social significance, and vitiated by temporal, and temporary considerations. The value of a man depends upon so many social factors taken, as always in an old-fashioned society, in the broad, that a well-respected head of a household who treats his neighbours well and gives lavishly in charity will not lose a jot of respect if he bribes a judge to secure his own or his dependant's property: indeed he might seriously lose in prestige if he did not take that easy and almost inevitable step! In this atmosphere bribery is not objectionable *per se:* only if used against the 'innocent'—itself a term implying many more qualifications than mere freedom from criminality (e.g. knowing one's place).

The jurists and their students were a privileged section of the community, an aristocracy of learning. Without them the sacred law would wither away. What judges did, or failed to do, had no bearing upon the structure or development of the law. The teacher was a man who lived righteousness, and his qualities were open to constant supervision from his neighbours and pupils. The latter often lived with him. A good teacher taught only because pupils wanted to learn from him, and believed in him. He had no public appointment, to be won by intrigue or imposture. His learning, namely the sacred texts themselves, and the techniques of interpretation which would make them live in everyday life, was in his head, and although books would certainly be used at various stages in education the most famous teachers would rely entirely on their memory or on the memory of assistants who specialised in memorising traditions. The Asian student to this day despises a teacher who has to refer to books! It is quite certain that Jesus must have known scripture by heart, and the day-to-day teaching he gave his students is not open to any doubt. He will have practised them in the sacred text, putting upon it a gloss of his own which, in spite of its astonishing peculiarity (the teacher himself was the person alluded to constantly in the Prophets and the psalms), must have been technically comparable with that used by the conventional teacher. It was open to any teacher to apply the texts to any situation of his own choice and to adopt an analysis of his own making: but he could get and keep pupils only if what he taught fitted life as they themselves understood it. That he could hoodwink them and blind them with science is extremely unlikely, and altogether inconsistent with what we know of eastern methods of teaching. On the other hand he would be authoritarian in approach, and students who could not stomach his teaching would go elsewhere. There would be no question of a student attempting to change his teacher's point of view. On the other hand the teacher accepted responsibility for his pupils' beliefs and welfare. To be a student was to be a kind of son. A celibate teacher would be rare in the East, though India had long been familiar with them as exceptions. But he would give to his pupils all the love and concern which his sons would have had, and they would expect him to look after them so far as might be. This mental approach, which even the western teacher who has Asian pupils of advanced age knows, overlooks the relationship in point of age. Thus the extremely interesting attitude of Peter, who was almost certainly older than Jesus, to his young master speaks volumes to one acquainted with eastern attitudes on this subject. The teacher is loyal to his student, so long as the latter stays with him and even thereafter, provided they parted amicably; and of course the pupil, no matter what his age, remains loyal to his teacher as he would to his parent, irrespective of personal opinion. It is the relationship which counts. And what relationship meant is naïvely but accurately indicated in the New Testament passages which speak of a man's being converted 'with all his house'.[1]

I think we have reached the point at which the reader can be expected to understand that law was important to the Jews, not merely as a means of adjusting rights and duties and solving disputes, but also as a means of communicating with the divinity and discovering how men should live. In a very special way knowing something about the law made one a Jew. . . . The teacher of religion was therefore a lawyer, and jurists were theologians. There was no clear distinction between the two activities. And this was one of the points of distinction between Jews and Gentiles; one of the many ways in which they felt themselves irreconcilably separate. The western distinction between law and conscience would not astonish the Jew who could come into contact with Gentiles: he would simply say, 'Those benighted people are objectionable in a great many ways. They are idolaters, worshippers of men and of inanimate nature. They go in for homosexuality, and other abominations. And they do not realise that God requires justice in the heart. How could it be otherwise?'

What do we Know about Jewish Law?

The question remains, what do we know about the law to which Jesus and his contemporaries referred? There is a difficulty which cannot be ignored. It had not reached a static or more or less static condition such as the Jewish law of today. It was still fluid because the basic postulates of the Pharisees were either in embryo or in some cases not even so far advanced as that, and there were sections of society, notably the Sadducees, who did not accept that an oral law, or at any rate *their* oral law was needed. Because after the twin disasters of A.D. 70 and 132 the Jewish people were destroyed as a political unit and scattered, no reliable or comprehensive evidence of the legal standpoint of Sadducees

[1] Ac x.2, xviii.8; *cf.* xi.14, xvi.31; *cf.* 1 Tm iii; Tt i.11; Heb iii. And note how the High Priest on the Day of Atonement confesses the sins he committed, 'I and my house' (*bis*): *Mishnāh*, Yoma III.8, IV.2 (based on Lv xvi.11).

survives. Only fragments from, for example, Josephus or Philo (neither of whom was particularly concerned about law in general) remain to instruct us on this subject. The New Testament itself counts as a source-book on the subject of first-century Jewish Law—so that there is a real danger of a non-lawyer moving in a circle. The Pharisees are well represented, for their traditions obtained the form of a miniature code in the *Mishnāh*, which owes much of its material if not its actual form to the period immediately following upon the destruction of Jewish national identity. In that period a great deal was remembered about the law obtaining while the Temple still stood and about the principles of morality and ethics which underlay those highly technical principles. The Talmuds, in essence commentaries upon the *Mishnāh*, contain further material additional to the *Mishnāh* and not inferior to it in antiquity. On the whole one can say that the *Mishnāh* gives a very fair picture of what the Pharisees believed Jewish Law to be in the last years of Jewish self-government, including those when Rome was the political master in fact but before the rebellions had made Jewish social and political life a nightmare. The Talmud naturally contains a great deal more material of various sources. The Babylonian Talmud includes ideas which flowered during a period considerably later than the one in which we are interested. But the highly conservative Jewish communities in Persia and Mesopotamia will have clung, as many still do, to the sacred law with great tenacity, and if the actual rules of the Talmud are not in every case to be read back into the time of Jesus the point of view and outlook can claim a fair continuity with those of his contemporaries.

Most unfortunately the Pharisees, being conscientious people, and much more concerned with righteousness than with law in our sense of that word, were not *invariably* practical. There were places and times in which Pharisees were in the seats of power. Pharisaic rules will have been administered from time to time in Galilee, for example, in the time of Jesus, and we know that before the time of Jesus Pharisees had not seldom been very close to the throne. But by the time of the compilation of the *Mishnāh* wishful thinking coloured some parts of the law as taught. The criminal law especially suffers from this defect and this is the chief reason why Canon Danby was so exceedingly scrupulous about using the *Mishnāh* and Talmuds for the elucidation of the important topic of the trial of Jesus. Now it is a coincidence (or *is* it a coincidence?) that the Jewish law of crime and punishment suffers from impractical scrupulosity more than any other. Attempts to read the puzzling accounts of the trial of Jesus in the light of Mishnaic law are very common, but often futile.

Nevertheless, though caution is necessary in all quarters, far more is gained, especially by the general reader, from acquainting himself with the tone, colour and arrangement of the Jewish Law as now taught than is lost by incurring the danger of being misled upon a question of detail. The 'academic' must have his ifs and buts. He must attempt to assure himself that the rule he finds in the books could have been in force in the time of Jesus, or, what is as good for our purpose, was in the air and was approved by influential people. This is quite often possible. Indeed, the electrifying effect that such tentative conclusions can have, when brought to bear upon the dead text of a particular obscure *pericope*, strongly inclines one to regard the hypothesis as confirmed. But even here, of course, one must be cautious, because the highly plausible is not necessarily true, as we know from our own lives (if the present writer may speak not only for himself), in which the highly implausible and improbable happens.

Our information about Jewish Law is very much better than it was even twenty years ago. The Babylonian Talmud is available in a fine English translation (not to forget a German and less perfect attempts), and the *Mishnāh* in several. Books on Jewish Law, for the general reader and the specialist, are readily available. There is a great deal to be said for these compilations, which take us with the minimum of fuss into the atmosphere of the Jewish struggle to complete and define jurisprudence in all its parts; and their ready availability is an advantage. The works of Maimonides (Moses ben Maimon, *fl.* 1160–80) have a special value. No doubt he was a mediæval scholar, several centuries away from the sources upon which he principally relies. But there are two factors which stand very much in Maimonides' favour. Firstly the continuity of Jewish juridical thought, down to minute details, was still beyond question. The law was added to and developed, but it remained essentially the same, for the Jewish community had been from the time of the last great crisis in the 130's onwards intensely self-absorbed and defensive, and had cherished its *Torāh* as the symbol of its identity and the hope of its redemption. Room for innovation was restricted, and even innovation took the cover of revealing the past through accurate interpretation. Secondly, Maimonides attempted, polymath as he was, to state effectively, completely and permanently what God required of man. His power as a codifier is viewed in many specialist quarters as phenomenal. He was a product of Talmudic technique, and his scholarship was, if not unique, at any rate exemplary. Jewish Law underwent significant changes after his time, but it is possible to overrate the changes it underwent prior to him, and his evidence is good evidence of what Talmudic law was believed to be by the best authorities at a good period in Jewish legal history. Now it happens that we have excellent English translations of his *Mishneh Torāh*, or the greater part of it,[1] and these take the general reader inside the mind of the Jewish jurist rapidly and comfortably. If we find a rule in the *Mishnāh*, the Talmuds, and in Maimonides the burden of proof that the rule did not exist in the first century lies on him who asserts it—and this is a very difficult burden to shift, for great continuity in the recent past argues a still remoter persistence in the further past. Jewish communities, like all Asian communities, have, until the nineteenth century (and sometimes longer) maintained a continuity and identity which mobile, developing societies cannot (and would not wish to) rival. Maimonides' books on the Commandments are also available in a fine translation,[2] and these are not less important than the so-called *Code* alluded to above.

Midrash

We come now to something even more sensitive. If *complete* certainty as to the law in use in the time of Jesus often eludes us, what can be said of that not less important component of Jewish thinking, the Midrash? The same answer applies, for the same reasons.

When law has to be taught to children, and when it has to be interpreted from a written and an apothegmatic substructure into a viable, complete, code of behaviour, numerous techniques must be used which are para-intellectual, and these must be capable of becoming intellectually respectable. I have already shown how a system of law which does not know legislation must have inbuilt flexibilities. So a method of instruction which utilises the sentiments, emotional potentialities and fantasies of the student, and yet keeps close to the letter of the sacred text, will be in vogue—and amongst Jews it always has been. I am not referring here to demonology, astrology, or other para-sciences which were certainly popular. Occasionally good use can be made of the concept of angels. But it is questionable whether good use can be made of all popular superstitions and fancies. Midrash, or the method of expounding scripture to elucidate its hidden spiritual meaning, is

[1] In the present work frequent reference is made to the books published in the Yale Judaica Series, which usually refer the reader to Maimonides' Talmudic sources. The object in citing the older source *and* Maimonides is dual: the busy reader will grasp the point more quickly from the latter, and he will be tempted to wander into more Jewish Law on his own account.

[2] Reference to Maimonides' *Sefer ha-Mitzvot* is beneficial. The whole concept of positive and negative commandments (which seems footling to occidental man) is most fascinating in that it breathes the spirit of the ancient East. In this work frequent reference is made to *The Commandments*, trans. by Rabbi Dr C. B. Chavel, 2 vols. (London/New York 1967).

essential for an intelligent, not to say crafty, people who have inherited a written text, the greater part of which must have a symbolic meaning if it is to have any tolerable meaning at all.[1]

The written text has its covert allusions, say the experts in Midrash, to the great themes of Jewish culture, the great concepts of Jewish religion. The sovereignty of God, the brotherhood of Jews, the obligation of obedience, and of charity: these and other ideas brought out convincingly and interestingly by Max Kadushin in his book, *The Rabbinic Mind*,[2] lie hidden within many scriptural passages which if read according to the Masoretic Text (which is only one of the possible ways of reading the unpointed Hebrew letters) might conceal from the untutored the treasures which it contains. One brings out the beauties of the occasionally bald or even unedifying scriptural passage by bringing similar texts together, by combining ideas from adjacent texts, by reading the letters with alternative vowel combinations and even by altering the reading where the sound would be the same or similar, and by playing various more or less admissible tricks with the grammar. Poetical and ingenious, fecund in allusion to popular myths and commonplace situations, the Midrash serves to make the Bible, and therefore the law it contains, palatable and constantly didactic. 'As a hammer divides fire into many sparks, so one verse of Scripture has many meanings and many explanations', as we read in the Babylonian Talmud.[3] The Midrash is the rabbi's tool for making sermons and for enhancing moral lessons and increasing faith. The capacity of the rabbi to invent new *midrashim* is unlimited, just as the Christian preacher can never run out of material. But the change which came over Protestant styles of sermon-making after it became clear that it was no longer legitimate to apply the biblical historical allusions to the immediate present ('the just', or 'the saints' does not mean Cromwell's soldiers, and so on) has not come to the expert in Midrash. To him the Bible

[1] It cannot be emphasised too vigorously that the Jews saw the written law as a source for their every need. Thus Ex xx.23, 'Ye shall not make with me—gods of silver or gods of gold ye shall not make unto you', is not merely a prohibition of making idols, but of (i) making figures of *human beings* out of metal, stone, wood, etc., even if they are *not* made for purposes of worship; and (ii) appointing judges who would not otherwise be chosen but obtain their position by bribing those in authority. At one and the same time the text carries a plenitude and a multiplicity of meaning, not however exceeding what regulated and disciplined interpreters may attribute to it. In this instance (which serves our purpose well, see p. 330 below) see Chavel, *op. cit.* II, 3–4.

[2] Second edn (New York, etc., Blaisdell 1965). There is also A. G. Wright's 'The literary genre midrash', *CBQ* 28 (1966), 105–154, 417–57 and R. Loewe's 'The "plain" meaning of scripture in early Jewish exegesis' in J. G. Weiss (ed.), *Papers of the Institute of Jewish Studies, London* (Jerusalem 1964), 140–85.

[3] b. San. 34*a* = Soncino translation 214.

speaks always in the present tense, and the flight from Egypt and the Passover is a yearly experience. Indeed, even historically speaking, it seems quite possible that the Bible was written out as we have it in order to produce impressions which combine the intuitive and the historical: the ethical lesson to be learnt from the story of Joseph and his brothers is independent of the historical importance of the way in which the Jews came to Egypt in the first place, but no less important; and at the same time any 'younger brother', any underprivileged person, can see himself in Joseph. The multiple functions of the Bible suggest a multiple and highly subtle policy behind its construction, and the Midrash thus has in general a sound psychological foundation.

One example of rabbinical keenness to yoke interpretation to scripture will serve for our present purposes. It will be noticed how the technique subserves a spiritual purpose. The general rule that a congregation of Jews cannot be less than ten is shown at *Mishnāh*, San. I. 6. But this is too narrow for spiritual purposes. Jesus himself was clear that 'where two or three are gathered together' there was a congregation for prayer (Mt xviii.20). R. Halafta ben Dosa (*c.* A.D. 150 onwards) said:[1] 'If ten men sit together and occupy themselves in the Law, the Divine Presence rests among them, for it is written, "God standeth in the congregation of God" (Ps lxxxii.1). And whence do we know this even of five? Because it is written, "And hath founded his group (*sc.* that which is grasped) upon the earth" (Am ix.6). And whence even of three? Because it is written, "He judgeth among the judges (who must not be less than three)" (Ps lxxxii.1). And whence even of two? Because it is written, "Then they that feared the Lord spake one with another: and the Lord hearkened and heard" (Ml iii.16). And whence even of *one*? Because it is written, "In every place where I record my name I will come unto *thee* and I will bless thee" (Ex xx.24).'

Now it is easy for the modern mind to make a sharp distinction between *halakāh* and *haggadāh*, between law and myth, between the prescriptions of law for purposes of ethics and government on the one hand and stories, fantasies and poetry—hortatory teaching—on the other. To us it would seem that *halakāh* has nothing to learn from *haggadāh*. What, after all, has the jurist to do with the poet? But the first-century population, clever as it was, could not be primarily devoted to studying the *Torāh*. The public at large participated in Bible study and religious education through multiple exploitation of the text. God had revealed, not concealed, his nature by his dealings with the Jews; and every part of those dealings could yield fruit over and over again. The art of the expert in Midrash was therefore ancillary to that of the

[1] *Mishnāh*, 'Āvot III.6.

jurist, but unhampered with the jurist's need to contemplate practical exigencies and at the same time free to depart imaginatively from the literal sequence of the text. The great teachers, like R. 'Aḳiba, were experts in both, and indulged in marvellous combinations of biblical and everyday ideas, pulling (as only the scholar who knows his text by heart can do) allusions and references from here, there, and everywhere.

Our difficulty is to know for certain whether any particular *midrashim* were in vogue in Jesus's time. Two very recent discoveries have opened our eyes to a situation which was previously only occasionally glimpsed, and then only by way of conjecture. The Dead Sea Scrolls have shown conclusively[1] that interpretations of Old Testament texts existed in the first century which gave rise to versions of those texts, with or without variant readings, which agree wholly or in part with versions of the Old Testament found in the gospels and Acts. This shows that genuine Jewish scriptural interpretations lie buried in our Greek sources. Such problems as are raised by Jesus's citing Ps viii.2 in a form nearer to the Greek of the Septuagint than to the Hebrew of our Masoretic Text[2] are now susceptible of a ready solution. We are sure likewise that *halakāh* differing from that adopted by the Pharisees, as also from that propounded by Jesus, existed before the *Mishnāh* and its direct sources.[3] Furthermore, the Palestinian Targum, known from numerous versions and partial or complete variants, including that known as the Targum Pseudo-Jonathan (which will appear frequently in the following pages), has been recovered in its entirety and in a form thought to represent the lost original. The Targum of Onḳelos, the so-called official Targum, seems also to have been available in the time of Christ or not long afterwards, and there is considerable debate as to which was the better known in the synagogues of Jesus's day. These Aramaic translations, or in the case of the Palestinian Targum one might more properly say paraphrases of the Pentateuch, are extremely important, not only because they contain abundant traces of the language spoken by Jesus and his contemporaries, but especially because they give the gloss upon the Old Testament which was most familiar to him and his opponents. Even when this text, properly advertised as a great discovery,[4] is pub-

[1] J. de Waard, *A Comparative Study of the Old Testament Text in the Dead Sea Scrolls and in the New Testament* (Leiden 1965).

[2] There is also the case of the citation of Ps cxviii.22 at Mk xii.10, Mt xxi.42, Lk xx.17. W. O. E. Oesterley, *The Psalms* (London 1953), 94–5. The Messianic interpretation of psalms is now known to have been *one* respectable mode of interpretation in the time of Christ.

[3] M. Black, *cit. sup.* p. xxiii n. 1.

[4] M. McNamara, *The New Testament and the Palestinian Targum to the Pentateuch* (Roma 1966). M. Black, *An Aramaic Approach to the Gospels and Acts*, 3rd edn (Oxford 1967), ch. 3, and see p. 39.

lished and exploited it will give us only a selection of the interpretations of the Old Testament which were available to scholars in Jesus's time: but none the less a new era in New Testament studies will be inaugurated when the expected edition by A. Díez Macho of Barcelona at length appears. True, the Palestinian Targum will only show midrashic interpretations that *were* current, and will incidentally prove that the absence of a *midrash* in our *Midrash Rabbah* and other old sources such as the *Mekilta* does not preclude its existence in highly influential quarters while traditional Jewish learning still flourished unchecked in its ancestral home. True, it will itself not preclude the possibility that yet other readings of the Old Testament text and yet other *midrashim* may have been in vogue. There will ultimately be notions vouched for in the Targumim, in the Dead Sea Scrolls, in the traditional Jewish learning and in the New Testament severally and uniquely, apart from those which will be vouched for in several or even all of them. Whatever the result, one thing is certain, namely that conventional attempts to interpret the more difficult parts of the New Testament from Greek and other pagan sources, and also the once frequent denials that ideas attributed by Jesus to his compatriots were actually acknowledged by the latter must both take to the wall, while sources illuminating the gospel from its homeland are effectively exploited. This will place many of the older generation of New Testament teachers in an embarrassing position, but it will be duly compensated for by the zeal of younger scholars, some of whom already have, as the saying goes, their eye on the ball.

Meanwhile it is exceedingly unwise to attribute to Jesus a technical *midrash*, intended to carry weight in some major context, unless there is evidence that a similar idea existed in his environment. This does not mean that we cannot attribute to him any originality. The fact is that Jews admired marvellous interpretations when they taught what was already well known, when they showed what everybody expected a pious man to show. When it comes to something original and therefore potentially suspect the teacher must rely upon the knowledge which the student already possesses. You cannot communicate in utterly new symbols or figures of speech. Thus, when we see for certain that Jesus used a well-known, or even lesser-known Jewish *midrash*, we are not surprised. He should be using his contemporaries' methods of communication.[1] It would be odd if he were not. He was not an English

[1] Professor J. W. Doeve and Dr M. Gertner have already adventured vigorously into the realm of *Midrash* in the New Testament. Jesus's saying '. . . all who take the sword will perish by the sword' (Mt xxvi.52) has been shown by H. Kosmala to be a quotation from a Targum: *NT* 4 (1960), 3–5. A. Sperber, *Bible in Aramaic* III (1962), 103. J. F. Stenning, *Targum of Isaiah* (Oxford 1953), 170–2.

public-school boy, nor a Lutheran university professor, but a first-century Jew working in an almost entirely Jewish environment. The methods of discussion they respected do not always appeal to us, but one could not communicate with them in any other way—that is to say so far as verbal communication is concerned. Of course Jesus did not stop short at verbal communication, for all that he said was strongly influenced and reinforced by the special life he led, and its even more extraordinary *dénouement*. And it is worthwhile noting in passing that his actions must be read against the background of his contemporaries' fancies, prejudices, taboos, and aspirations—not ours. However, to attribute to Jesus a *midrash* which is not evidenced elsewhere is very risky. One may hit the nail on the head by chance; but to attribute to Jesus an interpretation which is indeed analogically similar to an attested rabbinical one, but which conflicts with Jewish psychology or sociology (as an unfortunate example in recent periodical literature does) is to mislead the reader, and this the present writer has been very careful to avoid. At times this caution may run the opposite risk alluded to above: we may fail to attribute to Jesus some interpretation of scripture which was his own and original, and which survives only in Christian literature. It may be that similar ideas survived once in Tannaïtic (*i.e.* the earliest of rabbinic Jewish) traditional texts, but were expurgated therefrom by zealous anti-Christian rabbis of a later century. But this is a risk which one student at least prefers to take, and he is happy when he finds what is evidently a 'Christian' *midrash* comfortably (and scandalously?)[1] ensconced in Talmudic texts, for example the tractate Sanhedrin which in any case shows abundant signs of the rabbis' reforming tendencies.

More than one reader who already knows something of the contents of one at least of the chapters below may ask, 'So far so good. But how do you account for your own highly original interpretation of the Eucharistic words and actions of Jesus? Have you not attributed to him a *midrash* for which no independent evidence is forthcoming?' I agree. My excuse is simply this, that no satisfactory explanation for the Eucharist has ever been forthcoming, despite every sort of endeavour. The *midrash* I offer, though risky in the extreme, makes sense of the whole affair, and it is consistent with rabbinical techniques in general. Where no rabbi could accept it is precisely the point at which he must make up his mind whether he is willing to risk becoming a Christian. That the *midrash* has not been found elsewhere is therefore not conclusive against the accuracy of the reconstruction. I have taken the risk

[1] This point is made effectively in a different manner by M. Black, *Aramaic Approach*, 237.

deliberately, and time will show whether I am right. Meanwhile I have given the warning such as a scholar in such a situation will owe to his readers, who, he hopes, will give him credit for diligence and for a modicum of self-awareness.

Conclusion

It was an oriental society, in which demons could be met at night round any dark corner. The human personality, cramped under the load of personal obligation to seniors and reciprocating equals, inhibited from unfettered personal enjoyment, deprived of individual responsibility and freedom of association, craved consciously and, even more, unconsciously for contact with God. God meant both the source of all this pressure, and the means of ultimate release from it. God was the explanation for this peculiar, unpopular nation's twin scourges—their inherited aptitudes in financial matters (even in competition with Greeks), in the imaginative arts and in other legacies of long literacy, such as administrative skill, on the one hand (which made them the frequent objects of envy), and their custom of endogamy (which—far more significantly than circumcision—gave them, as it still does, their ambivalent, perpetual identity). God alone could explain and provide the justification for this relatively small nation's refusal to 'integrate' (as the phrase goes) and insistence upon being prominent wherever it went. Teachers who told about God were worth more than all others put together. Since the Jews' *belonging* to their society or to their segment of it was secure (provided individuals were not excommunicated) they had liberty to speculate and to adventure in a search (apart from commerce) which was allowed and prestigious—the search for God himself.

The emotional, the exaggerated, and the poetic were then nearer the surface of the mind. Yet a cool, objective appraisal was not beyond the elders and rulers. An exaggeration does not necessarily imply a flight of fancy. The vast majority of the public, being, in the true sense of the word, in-bred, nurtured notions whose reality was artificially protected from being tested: what could have been falsified readily a few miles away was regarded as a holy truth and removed from critical judgement. The disgraceful behaviour of the effective majority of Palestinian Jews before and during the Roman wars showed that their psychology was closer to that of a primitive tribe of our own day, or the fearful inhabitants of some remote jungle (like the Nāgas of the Indian frontier) to whom ethics are meaningful only within the family, and who would as soon take a stranger's head as buy his bananas. This may seem strong language, but it is needed to counterbalance the tendency still prevalent amongst us to assume that study of foreign and backward cultures exists primarily to educate us theoretically about the nature of man—a tendency which leaves us undisturbed in our prejudice that any peoples from whom we purport to *learn* in a nearer and more personal sense must be peoples we can admire (*i.e.* not very different from ourselves). The developed economy, sophisticated commercial law, and linguistic gifts of the first-century Jews make us suspect that they were a people more or less like the Greeks who, on the whole, hated them (understandably).[1] Their crude family law will correct our vision, and their haphazard attitude to human justice tells us that they thought within a narrow horizon. The fires burning within such people are seldom seen in our world; the nearest approach some of us may have had to such behaviour will have been in Aden (where we were subjected to an Asian variety of blood-feud) and Vietnam. The differences between their world and ours tend to be glossed over by theologians, who, seeking like all teachers to pass from the known to the unknown, take advantage of their hearers' too ready assumption that the ancient Jews were basically men like ourselves. It is high time that some of the dimensions of the differences were pointed out. One utterly unexpected example, which is suitable for our purpose, is fitted for masculine eyes only and has therefore been left to the *Extended Note* at the end of this Introduction. A further example need not be relegated to any such appendix, and can be given at once.

It has often puzzled Christians what Christ could have meant when he said (Mt xix.21), 'If thou wouldst be *perfect* go, sell what thou hast, and give to the poor, and thou shalt have treasure in heaven; and come, follow me!' If well-to-do people were to give lavishly in charity, if they were to give everything away, they would themselves become destitute and swell the numbers of the poor and this could not be to anyone's advantage.[2] The answer falls into two parts. Firstly, in the oriental setting to give lavishly in charity (as the rabbis were always exhorting people to do) did not necessarily impoverish one. Hence the Jerusalem proverb, 'The salt of money is diminution'.[3] In a society having a legal

[1] M. Radin, *The Jews among the Greeks and Romans* (Philadelphia 1915). A. N. Sherwin-White, *Racial Prejudice in Imperial Rome* (London 1967), esp. 86–101. Rome figured as the Jews' protector against the Greeks (96). Anti-semitism was founded on the antipathy of cultures, and of course long anticipated Christianity. L. Cracco Ruggini, 'Pregiudizi razziali . . .', *Athenaeum* 46 (1968) 139 ff at p. 146–7.

[2] Since it is virtuous to give away property Jewish, like Indian, religious teachers insisted that limits should be set to charitable donations. The Indian limit was the reasonable one that the owner should give away only the balance after his dependants' and his own maintenance had been secured. The Jewish solution was probably not less reasonable: you should not give away more than one-fifth of your capital, lest you come to need: b. Ket. 50*a* = Sonc. 286.

[3] b. Ket. 66*b* = Sonc. 405 (*ḥéṣer* sounds like *ḥéṣed*, charity).

system the practical administration of which (in contrast to its academic jurisprudence) was inefficient, capricious and corrupt the only certificate of commercial reliability was a reputation for piety. The more you gave away the more people trusted you with their investments and their business, especially in the big credit transactions which really made money. The history of the fantastically benevolent and very wealthy Parsi and Jaina communities in India evidences this, for the pattern goes back beyond the period when dishonesty could be punished at law. A superstitious regard for 'the poor' such as both Judaism and Islam inculcate with every emphasis is not only consistent with having plenty to give: it is a secret of financial prosperity! Secondly, granted that one gives initially in order to obtain a credit-balance with God, who is the patron of the poor who cannot reciprocate, to go the full length of becoming an ascetic, divesting oneself of all concern for material things was (and still is, as many of our silly lads have discovered in Delhi and Nepal recently), as good as a pension. The public desperately *need* people to whom to be charitable,[1] and it is the poor who confer the favour, by allowing the rich to earn merit through gifts to them! Thus (1) to give lavishly in charity, and even (2) to become a religious pauper were quite practical propositions, and show the oriental spiritual and commercial life in full practical harmony (as any reader of the Talmud will recognise). This will be a surprise to most western readers, who will be scandalised in any case to suppose God acts as a depository for anybody's 'treasure' accumulated in such a fashion!

From what, after all, did Christ aim to redeem these people? Was it from superstitions, or the effects of some of them? Was he diverting their energies into a new direction? Was he utilising for the purposes both of Jews and non-Jews the peculiar prejudices and preconceptions of this nation, hanging on the edge of the Asian world, a thorn in the side of the occident? We should, no doubt, err if we supposed that he viewed his people and his own mission to them as a social anthropologist would be able to do now, or that he was objective in a framework of ideas which was not itself wholly Jewish. Whatever Jesus's intentions, about which there will be a continuing debate, it seems clear that Christianity, for all the problems it has brought to peoples to whom it was offered through the centuries, has had a liberating effect and has put piety and worship upon a much more rational footing: it has brought ethical choices nearer to the front of the conscious mind. It is possible for the choices which men make in religious terms to be

[1] This is why when Jesus says that his hearers will always have the poor with them (see at p. 273 below) he says it not in a tone of pained resignation, but in confident expectation—that road to merit (inferior as it is) will always be available!

visualised as practical matters, exempt (at least in the imagination) from the frantic emotional overheating which previous ages and eastern climes were prepared to take for granted. And there is no ground for asserting that this is an occidentalisation, an imposition upon Jesus of the wishful thinking of his western followers. The old, oriental situation, in which observance is as good as faith, and the observant gains prestige even if he is obviously a rascal and an enemy of God, is now an object of ridicule almost throughout the world. But we, when we go back to the gospel, must remember that that liberation and reformation had not yet begun, and the responsible, respectable and (sometimes) admirable people of the time could not escape intellectual and emotional characteristics which we now despise.

Extended Note

An impressive example of the need for the Christian reader to have some knowledge of eastern ways of thought is provided by Jesus's saying 'If thy right hand offend thee, cut it off' (Mt v.30). The dramatic advice coincides with a similar exaggerated pronouncement by a rabbi quoted in the Talmud, and this has given occasion to so great a scholar as G. F. Moore[1] to suggest that Jesus was warning men and boys against masturbation. On that subject indeed some information of a reliable sort would have been welcome (it lies concealed in the teaching on marriage). But this passage cannot possibly refer to anything of the kind. The Jews, like Indians then and Muslims and many eastern peoples since (excluding the Chinese, who are as indifferent on the subject as we are), made a most careful distinction between the right hand and the left. The left hand is used for lavatory and inauspicious purposes[2] (the left index finger is used in cursing), the right exclusively for blessing, for salutation, for giving (*cf.* Ps xvi.11 and the significant Pr iii.16) and receiving (except in extreme contempt of the recipient or giver), and for showing honour. No doubt the Greeks and Romans too were familiar with the superstitious implications of the difference between right hand and left, from which we inherit the term 'sinister': but the lavatory implications of the left hand dominate in eastern cultures. Those who eat with their hands in fact eat only with one hand, the right hand! Children are most carefully taught never to use the left hand. Consequently anything in the nature of sexual stimulation would be done with the *left* hand, for semen and other natural excretions are believed to be equally defiling (in the superstitious sense). If in fact anyone used the right hand no one would know about it, and no one would ever presume that the right hand could be so used. Therefore Jesus is not referring to anything sexual (in spite of the immediately

[1] *Judaism* (Cambridge, Mass. 1927, 1958) II, 268 n. 4.

[2] Gesticulating with the left hand must be expiated by penance according to the Dead Sea Scroll community: *CR* VII = 1 *QS* VII.15 (Vermès, 84; Dupont-Sommer, 104 n. 6; Lohse, 26). The lavatory: b. Ber. 62*a* (a matter of *Torāh*!).

previous words in the pericope), but to the actions of taking (purloining, stealing, robbing)[1] and giving (bribes, etc.): 'in whose *hands* is mischief, and their *right hand* is full of bribes' (Ps xxvi.10)![2] Indeed it would be difficult to find a neater way of referring in one breath to all the sins that can be committed in respect of ***property***.

[1] b. Ḥul. 91*a* = Sonc. 511 (stretch out the hands to robbery).

[2] *Cf.* Is xxxiii.15. See also *Midrash on Psalms*, 17, § 8 (Braude I, 213).

CHAPTER ONE

The Treasure in the Field

INTRODUCTION: THE DIFFICULTY

Mt xiii.44: Ὁμοία ἐστὶν ἡ βασιλεία τῶν οὐρανῶν θησαυρῷ κεκρυμμένῳ ἐν τῷ ἀγρῷ, ὃν εὑρὼν ἄνθρωπος ἔκρυψεν, καὶ ἀπὸ τῆς χαρᾶς αὐτοῦ ὑπάγει καὶ πωλεῖ ὅσα ἔχει καὶ ἀγοράζει τὸν ἀγρὸν ἐκεῖνον.

The Kingdom of Heaven is like a treasure hidden in the field. A man found it and hid it, and for sheer joy goes off and sells everything he has and purchases that field.

THIS VERY SHORT STORY is a parable, putting across to the hearer a notion he would not so easily acquire, nor so easily retain, if another form of teaching had been used. It is at once obvious that Jesus is utilising people's interest in buried treasure, the very stuff of fairy tale (and not so rare then as now), and is putting his finger on that ubiquitous character of humanity, the desire to gain 'something for nothing' (if possible). But, on reflection, the hearer's pleasure at thinking about buried treasure is overtaken by doubts as the moral quality of the tale seems to be unnecessarily questionable.

The parable perplexes because the finder, in buying the field without revealing the presence of the treasure, has apparently taken a mean, or even dishonest, advantage of the owner of the field. Theologians have tended to ignore this,[1] or to accept too readily a transparently inadequate explanation. In the view of the majority of writers the chance character of the find, the finder's immediate recognition of his luck, his willingness to pay the price, his joyful abandonment of all other possessions and the concentration on the 'find', which concentration itself in a way symbolises the approach we should have to the Kingdom, are the factors which build up the parable's message.[2] We are advised to pay as little

[1] As N. Levison, *The Parables: Their Background and Local Setting* (Edinburgh 1926), 46f. Not so C. H. Dodd, *Parables of the Kingdom* (London 1961), 84 n.: 'He is as unscrupulous in his way as the Unjust Steward himself.'

[2] E. Klostermann, *Handbuch zum N.T. Die Evangelien. Matthäus* (Tübingen 1909), 257–8: 'Ob der glückliche Finder juristisch und moralisch unanfechtbar handelt, darauf kam es dem volkstümlichen Erzähler gar nicht an, wenn nur die Sachlage anschaulich war.' So C. G. Montefiore, *Synoptic Gospels* II (London 1927), 213 (1909

attention as possible to the dishonesty apparent in the story. Others, who realise that if that were to be the outcome Jesus must have been a poor craftsman, or his reporters incompetent, try to show that the finder was strictly justified,[1] but they are too easily satisfied. Neither approach serves the purpose of the parable. Unless we get to the bottom of the problem we are faced with an inescapable dilemma.

The difficulty is emphasised if we invent a parallel (simply for the purpose of clarifying the point). This will show that Jesus was not merely using a drastic metaphor: unless we understand the picture correctly, we are in a hopeless *incongruity*. 'A man left his family and work and all that he had, in order to follow a pretty woman. The Kingdom of Heaven is like such a case.' Is this not absurd? Yet, if previous writers are to be believed, it would be closely similar to our parable. The absurdity, of course, lies in the possibility that a seeker after the Kingdom, one who would recognise it immediately and abandon everything else for it, would do wrong in pursuit of the good: whereas on the contrary the finder in the parable is more likely to have observed the warning of Sir v.8: μὴ ἔπεχε ἐπὶ χρήμασιν ἀδίκοις· οὐδὲν γὰρ ὠφελήσεις ἐν ἡμέρᾳ ἐπαγωγῆς ('Set not thy heart upon unrighteous gains; for thou shalt profit nothing in the day of misery.') Moreover, biblical law is strict about lost property (which must be returned to its owner)[2] and one might suppose that buried treasure would come within at least as great protection in morals if not in law.

Our parable cannot be understood unless we know why the finder behaved as he did. Greeks or Latins could not hope to understand this.[3] To make things worse the Roman law was undecided whether

[1] W. O. E. Oesterley, *Gospel Parables in the Light of their Jewish Background* (London 1936), 80–2. J. Jeremias, *Parables of Jesus*, rev. edn, trans. S. H. Hooke (London 1963), 198–201 (the references to Midr. R., Canticles IV.12 and to B.B. IV.9 are not precisely in point, but the law as set out in this chapter is consistent with them). W. Michaelis, *Die Gleichnisse Jesu*, 3rd edn (Hamburg 1956), 63.

[2] Lv v.21–3 (M.T.) = vi.2–3.

[3] G. F. Hill, *Treasure-trove, the Law and Practice of Antiquity* (London 1934). The

edn, p. 644); W. O. E. Oesterley (cited p. 2 n. 1), 82; G. L. Cary (1900); A. Plummer (1910); A. Maclaren; J. R. Dummelow (1913); B. Orchard and others (1953); G. H. Davies and A. Richardson (1955). The late Erich Pritsch, who was well acquainted with Islamic as well as Assyrian and Babylonian laws, commented (in October 1959) as follows: 'Bei dem Schatzfund handelt es sich sicher um Privatland, denn der Finder will es ja kaufen; ob man sein Verhalten direkt als "unsittlich" bezeichnen kann, ist mir aber zweifelhaft, denn von einem Betrug kann wohl nicht die Rede sein; freilich ist sein Verhalten nicht moralisch hochstehend, weil er sein geheimes Wissen zu seinem Vorteil ausnutzt.' And again (in October 1960), '. . . aber ist das Verhalten eines Arbeiters des Bodeneigentümers, der den Schatz entdeckt hat und das Grundstück erwirbt, um den Schatz für sich heben zu können, so viel moralischer? Unklar sind mir in dem Gleichnis auch die Worte ὃν εὑρὼν ἄνθρωπος ἔκρυψε'.

a finder of treasure was or was not legally entitled to buy the field without revealing his knowledge that the treasure was there. The view which ultimately prevailed was that an owner who did not know of the existence of the treasure did not possess it, though he possessed the land.[1] The finder's conduct would not therefore be an injury to the owner's possession, as he would have none. Independently of the uncertainties of the Roman law on this point, the nuances of the purely Jewish situation would entirely escape them.

When the details emerge from our sources someone may ask, were the original hearers aware of all these points? Jesus's hearers were mostly agriculturalists and others who needed to know the law on these very matters. The topic was, in any case, a favourite one in eastern countries and entered into folk-tales and dreams. The hook upon which the message was hung could not have been chosen better. The rights and duties of landlords and tenants, the prerogatives of landowners, and the general habits of the tillers of the soil could be taken for granted not only in Palestine but also in the more conservative expatriate Jewish communities. Non-Jews, whose laws often differed radically, were not so fortunately placed, and it is strange that, context apart, Matthew gave no clue to help us to see the point of our parable. Perhaps in his day sufficient Jews of conservative origins were to be found in congregations for whom he wrote; or literary artistry relied on a living exegetic tradition.

EUROPEAN JURISTS AND THE PARABLE

Lawyers in non-Jewish communities have been troubled by the parable. Grotius (himself no mean theologian) and others thought that it proved

[1] Paulus, *Dig.* 41.2.3,3: Neratius et Proculus et solo animo non posse nos adquirere possessionem, si non antecedat naturalis possessio. ideoque si thensaurum in fundo meo positum sciam, continuo me possidere simulatque possidendi affectum habuero, quia quod desit naturali possessioni id animus implet. ceterum quod Brutus et Manilius putant eum, qui fundum longa possessione cepit, etiam thensaurum cepisse, quamvis nesciat in fundo esse; non est verum: is enim qui nescit non possidet thensaurum, quamvis fundum possideat. (This reference is owed to Dr Rolf Knütel.)

---

history of the Roman law of ownership of buried treasure is given by Dauvillier (cited below): Hadrian provided that the finder should have *half*—previously all belonged to the owner of the soil. On *thesaurus* in the mediæval Civil law see Baldus, *Baldi Ubaldi . . . in vii . . . Codicis Libros Comm.* (Venetiis 1577), fol. 257*v* (on *Cod.* X, xv, 1 § Nemo). In Islamic Law the finder might keep four-fifths of *rikāz*. At Hindu Law the king owned five-sixths, the finder, normally, one-sixth. Various laws prevailed in Europe generally. That the state owned 'treasure-trove' seems to have been as common as that the owner of the soil owned it. Kerala Act 30 of 1968 gives three-quarters to the finder.

that at Jewish Law the purchase of the field worked a purchase of the treasure, and that therefore the owner of the field must have been the owner of the treasure.[1] If this were so the finder was no better than a thief. He could not hope to acquire the treasure without concealing from the allegedly true owner its presence in the soil: his concealment led, then, to his acquiring something very valuable for a small price. In bargaining for the land he would not only conceal what he knew, but actually cheapen the land as if it were worth less to him than it would in fact be, treasure or no treasure. All the time the object of his efforts belonged (in this view) to another. Morally this amounts to deception of a most reprehensible sort. No system would exculpate him, least of all the Jewish, with its strict law of 'overreaching'.[2]

Naturally other lawyers have had second thoughts. Some have seen that Grotius jumped too hastily to his conclusion.[3] Others suspected that there might be a good case for supposing that the finder was legal owner.[4] But they have not pressed the point, for they could not see how, if that were so (and indeed it is not), it would be necessary for him to buy the land.

For the theologian, particularly the casuist, the parable was particularly interesting since, disregarding Jewish Law, they tended to suppose (for the most part) that it was authority for the proposition that it was

[1] *De Iure Belli ac Pacis* II, viii, 7 (ed. B. J. A. De Kanter-Van Hettinga Tromp, Lug. Batav. 1939, 298–9). The reference to Philostratus VI, xvi is of little value. So also that to Plautus *Trinummus*. S. Pufendorf (otherwise Puffendorf), *De Iure Naturae et Gentium* IV, vi, 13, ed. G. Nascovius (Frankfurt/Leipzig 1744), I, 564; trans. B. Kennett, 4th edn, ed. Carew (London 1729), 396. The same conclusion is wrongly drawn from rabbinical sources by I. K. Madsen, *Die Parabeln der Evangelien und die heutige Psychologie* (Kopenhagen/Leipzig 1936), 148. It remains the current view: Eta Linnemann, *Gleichnisse Jesu: Einführung und Auslegung* (Göttingen 1961), 104, English trans., London 1966, 98–9. At p. 169 n. 4 Miss Linnemann declines to reconsider the notion that only the motives governing the *narrative* (i.e. not the motives of the actors) are significant: but this places in a circle him who, not understanding the story, cannot discover its motive!

[2] It is sufficient to refer to the compendious Maimonides, *Mishneh Torāh* XII (*The Book of Acquisition*, trans. I. Klein, New Haven 1951), I, XII, xviii, 43–65. G. Horowitz, *Spirit of Jewish Law* (New York 1953), 365–6.

[3] J. G. Heineccius thought that our parable showed that the Jews preferred the finder to the owner as claimant of the treasure, and refers to Selden, *A Methodical System of Universal Law* . . ., s. 249, trans. G. Turnbull, I (London 1763), 183. See below, p. 9 n. 1, and next note.

[4] Barbeyrac on Pufendorf V, iii, 3 (English trans., cited above, p. 478) properly says that the parable is not sufficient proof of the Jewish Law in the sense Grotius would have it. He has guessed what is in fact the case, namely that the finder was entirely justified in what he did. Mascovius, in n. 2 and n. 3 to Pufendorf (where cited) follows Barbeyrac, and adds that the treasure was no part of the land—hinc plerique iurisconsulti affirmant recte, adversus emtorem huncce [*i.e.* dominum, venditorem] nec enormis laesionis querelam locum habere.

not sinful to utilise for one's own advantage the knowledge that a treasure lay in another's land, and to buy that land at its market price, so that, in appropriating the treasure on one's *own* soil one displaced the rational and in fact civil law rule that when a man finds a treasure accidentally on the land of another he and the owner would share its value between them. So famous a casuist as the friar Domingo de Soto[1] refers to the parable as being based on this reasoning; so that it is not improper to buy a house (at its market price) *even if appropriation of the treasure was the motive for buying it*! This (one may comment) is hardly loving one's neighbour as oneself. But others were quite satisfied with this notion, as we see from Martinus ab Azpilcueta, the so-called Doctor Navarrus (who does not refer to the parable),[2] and the Fleming Jesuit Leonard Lessius (1554–1623) who relies on these casuists and their predecessor St Thomas Aquinas.[3] Lessius refers deliberately to the parable,[4] and his words are adopted by the German Jesuit Cornelius à Lapide (1566/7–1627),[5] whose work on the Bible is well known as a treasury of linguistic and patristic scholarship. The theory that one may conceal one's knowledge and buy at the market price, thus depriving the owner of the land of the right he would otherwise have in *half* the treasure in case its finding were reported, appealed to the casuists in large part because they thought the parable warranted such an opinion: but it would not otherwise convince anyone commencing with the view congenial to the civil law (which the casuists accepted) that as soon as a treasure is found the owner of the land is no less interested in it than the finder. It is not a sufficent answer to say that Jews were mean and that Jesus and his audience were Jews, because the characteristic Jewish 'meanness', of which we shall note several traces in the parables, is a function of their distinctive and (to many minds) admirable *scrupulosity*. And a scrupulous man would hardly cheat the owner of the land if the latter already had any rights at all.

[1] *De Iustitia et Iure* (Lyons 1582), fo. 151^r, lib. 5, q. 3, a. 3.
[2] *Enchiridion* (Lyons 1592), p. 424, cap. 17, no. 175.
[3] *Summa Theologiae* II^a II^{ae} q. 66, art. 5, *ad secundum*. St Thomas recognizes that the civil law *may* oblige the finder to give a half to the owner of the land, but presumes that otherwise the finder is entitled to the whole since the owner of the land has no possession. The parable illustrates this, he says, quod *emit agrum*, quasi ut haberet ius possidendi totum thesaurum.
[4] In *De Iustitia et Iure* (Paris 1606), II, cap. 5, dub. 15. In the edited version published under the title *De Iure et Iustitia Compendium* from Douai in 1634 the reference to the parable is omitted—but it was in St Thomas.
[5] *Commentarii in IV Evangelia* (*ad loc.*) (Lyons 1681), I, 283. He comments, following Lessius, that the market value is unaffected by the presence of the treasure which lies hidden and unknown. But the whole point is that it is not unknown—the finder knows its presence! And that should have made a difference while the Jewish law on the subject had not been enquired into.

Professor Jean Dauvillier[1] reviewed certain laws bearing on the subject in a contribution of about ten years ago, but he failed to observe the crux of the matter. His information on the Jewish Law was defective.

As we shall see, the upshot of the matter is that the finder was perfectly entitled in morals and in law to do what he did. His behaviour was proper, and indeed inevitable. He would have been an idiot if he had acted otherwise.

THE LAW RELATING TO ACQUISITION

We must see how a treasure could be acquired. But first, was the *Talmudic* law in force in Jesus's time? Seeing that the topic has a permanent fascination alterations in the law are likely to have been notorious. We shall not go far out of our way if we restrict ourselves to the *Mishnāh* and the reports of Tannaïtic teachers' remarks. The subject is rational and commonsensical. It provides little scope for religious, theological, or even moral doctrines. The rabbis are not likely to have interfered with it, and there is no suggestion anywhere that they did so in the first two centuries.

Movables can be acquired only by formal taking of possession (*ḥazāḳāh*). This is lifting (*hāgᵉbāhāh*) in the case of things that can be lifted, and drawing (*mᵉshiykāh*) in the case of animals, etc., that must be drawn.[2] In both cases the act must be precisely as indicated: *i.e.* 'lifting' means grasping and shifting from its position with the intention of acquiring—one must have indicated by this physical act the proprietorial privilege of *moving* the object. Rubbing dirt off a thing is not

[1] 'La parabole du Trésor et les droits orientaux', *RIDA*, 3rd ser., 4 (1957), 107–15. Jewish material is dealt with at p. 111–13. In his view oriental systems ignored treasure as a judicial notion and classified it with the land in which it was buried. This is certainly not the case with Hindu Law (see J. W. Spellman, 'Ownership of treasure trove in ancient Indian polity', *J. Num. Soc. Ind.* 23 [1961], 133–6), and would hardly be correct for Islamic Law. But that the Jewish Law had no special institution called 'Treasure' is correct. Billerbeck, *Kommentar* I, 674, is unhelpful. He cites B.B. IV.8f. inappositely. Buying stones, etc., in a field really means buying stones, etc., *on* a field. See below, p. 8 n. 2. S. Rubin, *Das talmudische Recht. Sachenrecht* (Vienna 1938), § 14 (*Schatzerwerb*) and §§ 21–25, 27–32 (*Erwerb von Immobilien, Mobilien*) are interesting.

[2] b. B.B. 86*a* = Sonc. 350; 156*a* (*Mishnāh*) = Sonc. 679; *ibid.*, 75*b*–76*a* = Sonc. 304–6; 84*b*–87*a* = Sonc. 344–55; B.M. 9*b* = Sonc. 48–9; 99*a* = Sonc. 566; *Mishnāh*, Ḳid. I, 4, 5; 25*b* = Sonc. 123; Ket. 31*b* = Sonc. 173–4; *ibid.*, 76*a* = Sonc. 477. Maim. XII, I (Sales), iii, trans., p. 11ff. Maimonides, *Mishneh Torāh* XI (*The Book of Torts*, trans. H. Klein, New Haven 1954), III (Robbery and Lost Property), xvii, 150f. L. Kirsch, 'Finder of Property', *JE* V, 385; S. Bialoblocki, 'Eigentum', *Encycl. Jud.* VI (1930), col. 344. Note how (as Horowitz notes, *op. cit.*, 349) *mᵉshiykāh* is valid only in a place where the 'drawer' was owner or part-owner, whereas *hāgᵉbāhāh* is valid *anywhere*. I. Herzog, *Main Institutions of Jewish Law* (London 1965) I, 177.

'lifting' it, for example. In cases where neither lifting nor drawing is *feasible* a recognised substitute is required for *m^eshiykāh*.[1] Movables lying on top of the soil[2] pass to a transferee along with the soil, and by means of transfers of soil transfers of movables may take place.[3] But such cases as those are outside the scope of our parable.

A buried treasure can be acquired *only* by being lifted or perhaps dragged. This treasure (*maṭ^emonāh*)[4] was buried out in the open country. It could have been in an underground chamber, loose, but it was almost certainly in an earthenware jar—ἐν ὀστρακίνῳ σκεύει as Paul says at 2 Co iv.7—like most hoards found from those days to our own. It was not buried or found in a dunghill,[5] a street,[6] a courtyard,[7] or a house-wall—all[8] places considered separately in Jewish Law when it is asked what steps should be taken to dispose of lost property found in them. We are intended to assume that the treasure was buried by Amorites.[9] It was what the Arabs call *rikāz*, and not *luḳṭa*.[10] Thus all questions of advertising it or proclaiming the find are avoided, upon which, in cases of recent losses or caches, the rabbis occupy themselves at large.

[1] The whole subject of *kinyan sudār* (a fictional barter) is beyond the scope of this study, but see Horowitz, *op. cit.*, 353f. Herzog, *Main Institutions*, I, 171–2, 181, 183; II, 111.

[2] Stones sold with the field are those 'necessary to it', and those on the surface: B.B. 69*a* = Sonc. 274; *ibid.*, 77*a* = Sonc. 310. Maim. XII, I, iii, 8–9 (trans., p. 13); xxvi, 2 (p. 94).

[3] *Mishnāh*, Kid. I, 5; 27*a–b* = Sonc. 129–31; B.K. 104*b* = Sonc. 605. Maim. XII, I, iii, 8–9. Horowitz, 349, 353.

[4] In the LXX θησαυρός (Bauer, *Wörterb. z. N.T.*, 1958, 2*a*) is a translation of *maṭ^emon* in Gn xliii.23. Jb iii.21; Pr ii.4; Jr xlviii (xli).8: εἰσὶν ἡμῖν θησαυροὶ ἐν ἀγρῷ. Delitzsch, who is usually very reliable, unfortunately translates our θησαυρός by *'otsār*, which emphasises the 'treasury', 'treasure-chamber' aspect, and is not quite the word for 'buried treasure'.

[5] It is presumed not lost, but hidden. B.M. 24*a* = Sonc. 151; 25*b* = Sonc. 158–9 (*Mishnāh*). 'If a man finds a vessel in a dungheap: if covered up, he must not touch it; if uncovered, he must take and proclaim it.' The Jewish law relating to lost property and its finder is perspicuous and rational. For a summary see Maim. XI, III, xi–xviii.

[6] See ch. 2 of B.M., Sonc. 130–76 (the exceptional rules do not concern us). For the 'four cubits' rule see B.M. 10*a* = Sonc. 54–6, Maim. XI, III, xvii, 8–10 (trans., p. 152).

[7] One may acquire through one's courtyard: B.M. 9*b* = Sonc. 48; *ibid.*, 102*a* = Sonc. 581–2; Maim. XI, III, xvii, 8, 10.

[8] *Mishnāh* at b. B.M. 25*b*–26*a* = Sonc. 160f. *Cf.* j. B.M. II.4 = Schwab X, 92–3. The first question is whether it is in the inner or the outer half of the wall. We are not concerned with the detailed rules here. If it were found in an inhabited house other considerations apply. Jesus carefully (or so it would seem) places his treasure in the open country to avoid all such presumptions and considerations.

[9] b. B.M. 25*b* = Sonc. 160f.

[10] *Enzycl. des Islam* III (1936), 38, s.v. *Luḳaṭa*. This is all customary law. C. Hamilton, *Hedàya* (London 1791), II, 264f.; I, 39f. Ibn Abū Zaid (Kayrawānī), *Risala ou Traité Abrégé de Droit Malékite* . . ., ed. E. Fagnan (Paris 1914), 88, 175–6.

The owner of the field could not have acquired the treasure, unknown as it was to his predecessors and thus to himself. An instance of treasure-trove in inherited land is utilised in the Palestinian Talmud to illustrate the question of a woman's limited rights over her acquisitions: but it is not suggested that any problem of ownership arose until, in the course of cultivation, the treasure was found.[1] That he had not found it forms the basis for the parable. It could not be transferred to him by those who never owned it. What they had never possessed they could not transfer by however general a clause in any sale-document.[2] What they could not transfer he could neither buy, nor inherit from them. Nor could he acquire it from them by adverse possession of the field.[3] He had never acquired it at all. And so he did not own it.

[1] j. Ket. IV.6 (Schwab, 1886, viii, 57).

[2] b. B.B. 63*b* = Sonc. 256. If the words 'from the depth of the earth to the height of heaven' are inserted they avail to transfer a well, a cistern, and cavities (cf. Maim. XII, I, xxiv, 15, trans., p. 90)—all of which are naturally known to the seller. See b. B.B. 68*b*–70*b* = Sonc. 273ff. Trees have to be sold separately, since a sale of a field does not sell the trees standing in it: 69*b* = Sonc. 276: Maim. XII, I, xxiv (trans., p. 87–90). A transfer, 'I sell to Reuben my field and all the treasures that may be in it', would be ridiculous: no man may transfer what he does not possess: Maim. XII, I, xxii, 1, 5. It is as a result of *this* that a problem could arise such as suggested the apocryphal tale of Alexander the Great in j. B.M. II.8, 39 = Schwab, X, 94. I. Wallach, *Proc. Am. Acad. Jew. Res.* 11 (1941) at p. 63–71. The problem put to Alexander in the passage in j. B.M. related to a field transferred, not inherited. Thomas (Aland, 109) gives a parable of a treasure in which the original owner did not know of the existence of the treasure, died and left it by inheritance to his son, who took it and then sold it, and the purchaser found the treasure while ploughing. Then he began to lend money at interest to whomever he wished (which seems a gnostic addition such as one will hardly read into the parable of Jesus). R. M. Grant and D. N. Freedman, *The Secret Sayings of Jesus* (London 1960), 183, compare the Aesopic fable no. 42 in Hausrath and no. 98*a*–*b* in Halm. Aesop's debt to India is well known. However, it seems that the characteristically Brahminical tale to be found in an Indian text of perhaps between *c.* A.D. 300 and 900 derives from an Alexander-romance which went to India. Two Brahmins quarrelled about the ownership of a treasure found during cultivation: the one had given the land as a gift to the other, and the question was which of them owned the treasure. The litigants came before the world-conqueror, the righteous king, Yudhishṭhira, each claiming that the *other* must take it! The hero-god Kṛishṇa laughs and says that soon the Kali age will commence during which purer propensities will disappear and people will grab what they can get—*i.e.* time will cure this complaint and the possessor will keep the treasure! *Jaiminīya Aśvamedha* LXV, 29–38 (summarised by Karmarkar, *Mahābhārata, Āśvamedhikaparvan*, Poona 1960, xlii). In view of the numerous Christian (or at any rate gospel) materials reflected in this work (combining Indian, Alexander-romance and gospel themes) we cannot absolutely rule out our parable itself as the true source of this passage in the *Jaim. Aśv.*, though the partial coincidence of themes in both sources may be its occasion there.

[3] J. H. Greenstone, 'Hazakah', *JE* VI, 280. Horowitz, 346f. *Ḥazāḳāh* must be based upon a *prima facie* valid claim. There must be the element of intention. To possess an unknown object is an absurdity in Jewish Law. One's courtyard can acquire objects for one, just as one's agent can acquire objects for one, without one's knowledge, but in either case at the time of acquisition there existed in law an intention on the part of the principal that acquisition of such an object should be made through that means.

What if the finder lifted it? Did he thereby become owner? But the finder did not lift it. It is essential to realise that though he found it and recognised what it was and realised that it was more valuable than the field—and more valuable by a large margin—he did not lift it. He may have rubbed off dirt and examined it *in situ*, though this is not certain. A glance of a few seconds was enough. We must explain why he did not lift it.

THE RELATIONSHIP OF THE FINDER TO THE OWNER OF THE FIELD

There are several possibilities, each of which must be considered. Some are distinctly unlikely. In none of the likely ones would the finder, if he lifted, lift 'for himself'. If he lifted he would be bound to do so for, and so create proprietorship in, someone else. In the less likely possibilities he could indeed have lifted for himself, but he either could not have hoped to dispose of the find for cash (which is what he wanted, of course—the treasure *in specie* would be of no use, since it is unlikely to have consisted of coin still circulating) or would have been exposed to litigation in which he would have been put to discomfort, shame, or, almostly certainly, loss. It is our duty to review each possibility in turn.

(a) *Was he the owner's servant or day-labourer?* The presumption is always that a man is a major and not a minor, a free man and not a slave. The maxim to apply, then, is 'the hand of the workman is the hand of the master'.[1] If he was a day-labourer and his instructions were to do particular work, *i.e.* narrow instructions, he would have been able to lift for himself so long as the lifting was not essential to carry out the prescribed task. This is one of the exceptions alluded to above, and we shall return to it.

The rabbis were aware that workmen might find treasures and they accordingly ruled that where the instructions were broad enough to allow of the workman's finding the treasure in the actual course of the work enjoined upon him he must be presumed to acquire for his employer.[2] The only exception would be where the employer had so engaged the workman that the latter could claim that his orders virtually

[1] b. B.M. 10*a* = Sonc. 52–3. *Cf.* Maim. XII, I, iv, 15, trans., p. 19. It is curious that Heineccius, who was no Jewish lawyer, said, where cited above, that hired workers ought to acquire treasure for themselves even though they had not hired themselves to search for treasure, like digging a pit, etc.

[2] b. B.M. 10*a* = Sonc. 52–3; *ibid.*, 118*a* = Sonc. 670–1.

There is no rule that one's field acquires for one that which happens to have been buried in it. The rule of the courtyard makes this plain.

excluded the lifting of treasures—a somewhat far-fetched proposition, which the rabbis take quite seriously.[1] Since a workman might well see a treasure in the course of his work, and wish to acquire it for himself, he was allowed to drop his work, obtain his discharge from employment, and then, if he could, return and lift the find.[2] It was recognised that no workman could be compelled to work out his day![3] Normally, therefore, lifting by a day-labourer would be lifting for his master so long as he remained in his employment, unless the instructions were so minute as to exclude the possibility of the employer treating the workman as his agent for such purposes—a hypothesis that savours of rabbinical ingenuity.

(b) *Was he the owner's* 'āriyṣ *(servant-tenant)?* The legal status of the *'āriyṣ* was peculiar. In most respects he was more like a mere employee of the landlord than an independent man.[4] He was authorised, and indeed employed, to do the work of cultivation, and since his instructions would be of the widest there could be no doubt but that if he lifted a treasure he would do so for the owner. The treasure is not after all produce of the land, and so the *'āriyṣ* could not even claim a share in it.

(c) *Was he the owner's* soker *(lessee)?* The tenant on a lease was a free man, of a status superior to that of an *'āriyṣ*.[5] His relations with the owner would be very businesslike. The rent would be settled year by year, except where there was a custom to the contrary. The *soker* would do no unusual work if he could avoid it, unless he had a prior agreement with the owner.[6] Our treasure was less likely to have been

[1] B.M. 10*a* = Sonc. 52–3; *ibid.*, 12*b* = Sonc. 69; 118*a* = Sonc. 670–1.
[2] B.M. 10*a* = Sonc. 52–3; *ibid.*, 12*b* (*Mishnāh*) = Sonc. 69–70; 118*a* = Sonc. 670.
[3] b. B.M. 77*a* = Sonc. 445; B.Ḳ. 116*b* = Sonc. 694; *cf. Mishnāh*, 'Āvot II, 15–16. Maimonides, *Mishneh Torāh*, XIII (*The Book of Civil Laws*, trans. J. J. Rabinowitz, New Haven 1949), I, ix. The day-labourer could drop his work when he liked without having to compensate the employer, and without losing his right to proportional payment for what he had done. On this aspect of the subject see Heinemann (cited below) at p. 299, 302, 304, 306. The biblical text is Lv xxv.55.
[4] *'āriyṣ* ('bound', 'engaged') can also mean a field labourer. b. 'Av. Zar. 21*b* = Sonc. 110–11; Ḳid. 52*a* = Sonc. 263–4; B.M. 74*b* = Sonc. 431; *ibid.*, 69*a* = Sonc. 401; B.Ḳ. 113*b* = Sonc. 668; *ibid.*, 119*a* = Sonc. 712; Yev. 93*a* = Sonc. 633; Ket. 80*a* = Sonc. 506. See Midr. R., Lev. I.9 = Sonc. 12: Adam was God's *'āriyṣ* in paradise. J. H. Heinemann, 'The status of the labourer in Jewish law and society in the Tannaïtic period', *HUCA* 25 (1954), 263f., 269.
[5] The *soker* paid a cash rent, whereas a *ḥoker* paid in kind, usually.
[6] '... under the custom recognised by [the Jewish law] the tenant was not expected to make, and seldom did make, any substantial improvements or even repairs, either in house or in farming property' (L. N. Dembitz, *JE* V, 404f.). The reason is made plain by the principles evidently behind the rules at Maim. XIII, I, viii, 2 (trans., p. 27), taken in part from b. B.M. 103*b* = Sonc. 591–2 (*Mishnāh*, IX.1); M. L. Rodkinson's trans. (New York 1901), IV (XII), 274; L. Goldschmidt's trans. (Berlin

found in the course of ordinary ploughing[1] (which would not have been impossible), than in the course of some work which had not been done in that way, or at all, for years, if not centuries. The treasure is to be imagined as found in the foundations of a buried dwelling, in the roots of a tree, in a terrace-wall, or in the wall of a choked well, or side of a ruined water-course. All such works as clearing wells, opening new trenches or restoring old ones, repairing terrace-walls or the like would be done for the owner and upon the understanding that the value of the improvement would be 'set off' against the rent.[2] The whole operation would be agreed beforehand, and the operation by the *soker* would be undertaken as the owner's employee and at his risk, or as his agent. If our finder was a *soker* acting on his own initiative the case would be exceptional and would fall under the special observations alluded to above, to which we shall return. A *soker* in ninety-nine cases out of a hundred would have lifted such a treasure for the landlord.

(d) *Was he an independent contractor?* If he had been engaged for a particular work he was exactly like an agent, and his lifting would be with the owner's authorisation and under his orders, wherefrom it follows that he would lift for the owner.

(e) *Was he an independent contractor's servant?* In that case he would have lifted for the contractor, except in the unlikely case of strict specific instructions to which we referred before.

(f) *Lastly, was he a trespasser?* This is not to be presumed. The normal is to be presumed. A man doing such unusual work as to uncover a treasure could not do it in the daytime without being observed. Unauthorised visitors are watched by children as a matter of course. If one stooped to examine something in the soil the idea 'Treasure!' would occur to the watchers at once, and in a matter of minutes the news would be all over the village. There is no likelihood that he was working at night. His lamp would bring watchers to his elbow. No parable expects us to assume the highly improbable.

Now we may come to the exceptions to the general rule that if our

[1] But Jeremias, *Parables*, 198, refers to j. Hor. 3.48*a* where an ox's sinking into a hole leads to the discovery of a treasure. W. Michaelis, 62. And see above, p. 8, n. 2.
[2] This is deduced from the authorities cited at p. 10 n. 6 above.

1933), 803; A. Sammter, *Talm. Bab. Tractat Baba Mezia* (Berlin 1876) at 103*b* (useful notes). The same principle is to be seen in j. B.M. IX.1, 2 (Schwab X, 145), and more significantly at b. B.M. 109*a*–*b* = Sonc. 623–6, Goldschmidt, 824ff.; and Maim. XI, III, x, 4–10, based on B.M. 101. The principle is evidently that, subject to a contrary agreement, what is essential for demarcating and working the land is provided at the cost of the owner, but nothing more. He is not expected to pay for any unagreed improvement or undertaking by the tenant: hence, no improvements by a tenant without prior authorisation.

finder had lifted he must have lifted for someone other than himself. As a pattern of these exceptions let us take the case where he was authorised, or required, to do particular, specific work, so that, if the treasure was not lifted in the actual course of that work the finder could claim that it was lifted for himself. News of the find reaches the owner, and he at once claims that the find must have been made in the course of work he had authorised or enjoined. Meanwhile the finder has gone to a merchant.

It is essential to observe that most treasures would have to be converted into cash by resort to a merchant. Jesus will hardly compare the Kingdom's finding to the finding of an object which cannot be enjoyed at its full value. This excludes the receiver of stolen goods, the only man who will not follow the Jewish law relating to purchasing objects from suspect sources.[1] We are left with the position that the finder goes to an honest merchant who will pay him as nearly as may be the market value of his find. He will need to be assured that the finder was legally entitled to the object, and his enquiries will be very scrupulous, since the owner of the land could claim the treasure, bring a witness to the circumstances of the alleged engagement, and thus put the merchant to an alternative, either to return the object at the precise amount he paid for it, taking an oath as to this amount (and honest people tried to avoid taking oaths), or to defend the finder's title, that is to say, assert that the finder was entitled to acquire for himself—an assertion that could hardly be within his power.

Further, the owner of the land could claim that the finder was a thief. He could set up a *prima facie* case; and the finder would be put to an oath that the treasure was lawfully his.[2] Either of these thoughts would be in the finder's mind if there was any doubt as to his having been authorised to do the work in question. It would appear that he must so conduct himself as to avoid all chance of litigation: and the straightforward narration in the parable supports this. The same would be the situation if the finder had been, instead of a labourer or *'āriyṣ*, a *soker*. Litigation would operate to a *soker's* disadvantage. For his carelessness in undertaking novel work without an unambiguous bar-

[1] b. B.Ḳ. 118*b* (*Mishnāh*)–119*a* = Sonc. 710–15. Maim. XI, II, vi, 1 (trans., p. 78). Pr xxix.24. Horowitz, 609ff.

[2] The subject of Oaths has a large secondary literature based upon tractate Shevu'ot, *Mishnāh*, ch. VI, and *gemara* thereon. Maim. XIII, IV, i, 3, 7, trans., p. 190–2. Z. Frankel, *Der gerichtliche Beweis nach mosaisch-talmudischem Rechte* (Berlin 1846), 123–7 and notes thereon. J. Rappoport, *JE* IX, 365f. (a reference to B.Ḳ. 46*a* [Sonc. 262]: 'whosoever would oust a possessor must bring evidence to establish his claim'—but where the evidence is deficient the oath may be imposed on the defendant); J. Kohler, *ZVR* 20 (1907) at p. 251–7; also M. Cohn, *Jüd. Lex.* II, 286–8.

gain he would be bound to pay. Thus, even in the exceptional cases the finder would be in danger of deriving no benefit from the treasure if he lifted. But in any case would Jesus's hearers have thought of the exceptional case? Most of them, surely, would have thought first of an *'āriyṣ*, or (as most commentators since)[1] of a day-labourer who comes on the treasure in the course of, and as a normal part of, the undertaking which he was enjoined to complete.

THE BEHAVIOUR OF THE FINDER

No sooner had the finder found the treasure than he covered it up again. The word ἔκρυψεν does not mean that he buried it again.[2] He did not remove it from its position. He took care only that he should not be anticipated by the owner or any other person who might pass that way. He would cover it well, since his behaviour in leaving his work suddenly would arouse suspicion. He would say nothing about the treasure until he had it. Any one who went to the spot could lift it and acquire it, and would owe him nothing.[3] Since the owner of the field had no rights in the treasure there was no reason whatever why he should be told of it: indeed if he were told the whole plan would fail. So the finder manages to buy the field and goes in his own proper person as owner of the field, and not as any man's servant or agent, and lifts it and acquires it for himself.

THE 'TREASURE' AS A 'FIND'

It is convenient to draw attention to the differences now apparent between this parable and the parable of the Pearl.[4] An undue attention

[1] H. Ewald, *Die drei ersten Evangelien . . .*, 2nd edn (Göttingen 1871), I, 292.

[2] As A. Jülicher, *Die Gleichnisse Jesu* II (Tübingen 1910), 581; E. Lohmeyer–W. Schmauch, *Das Evangelium des Matthäus* (Göttingen 1956), 225 (*barg*).

[3] *Mishnāh* at b. B.M. 10*a* = Sonc. 54: 'If one sees an ownerless object and falls upon it, and another person comes and seizes it, he who has seized it is entitled to its possession.' This would apply to our case *a fortiori*. In Qirq Vezīr (see Sheykh-zāda, *Forty Vezirs*, trans. E. J. W. Gibb, London 1886, 380) appears the tale of a Turkoman who covered up a treasure-chamber he chanced upon while ploughing (a parallel noticed by Ewald). But the moral is that great riches in the wrong situation are worse than useless.

[4] The Thomas version is attractive (Coptic text and trans., 1959, logion 76): see C.-H. Hunzinger, 'Unbekannte Gleichnisse Jesu aus dem Thomas-Evangelium', in *Judentum, Urchristentum, Kirche: Festschrift für Joachim Jeremias*, ed. W. Eltester (Berlin 1960), 209ff., 219–20; also H. Montefiore and H. E. W. Turner, *Thomas and the Evangelists* (London 1962), 50, 56, 58–60, 66f. W. Schrage, *Das Verhältnis des Thomas-Evangeliums zur synoptischen Tradition . . .* (Berlin 1964), 155ff. Thomas makes the merchant sell all his merchandise, not all he had. Thomas's parable of the

to the differences, in an attempt to draw a different message out of them, may be undesirable. However, there is reason for believing that Jesus, in giving *both* parables, did not *merely* repeat himself; if this is so the differences between the incidents, so much alike in essential respects, may be significant. Therefore one may place on record the apparent contrasts between the merchant and the finder of the treasure. Our finder was not skilled in finding treasures, nor expecting to find one; his 'find' could not be acquired with the same effort as would be used in the ordinary course of the acquirer's daily life; the treasure could have been found by anyone; yet he could not acquire it without the conjunction of the field, and its owner. Our finder could not enjoy his treasure without altering his way of life and becoming, perhaps quite incongruously, a landowner. His effort was undoubtedly greater. His joy would have been impossible without intelligent and proper exploitation of his opportunity: and evidently that meant more effort for him than the commercial speculation of the merchant.

Not to derive too much significance from these differences, it is perhaps legitimate to claim that they show that Jesus wanted to give information about the Kingdom through pictures of a variety of 'findings' by 'finders' of a variety of qualifications and situations.

Now it happens that Philo, commenting on the phrase 'Noah found grace in the eyes of the Lord' (Gn vi.8), enters upon an interesting discussion of the two kinds of finding, εὕρεσις, which is finding what one had not before, and ἀνεύρεσις, which is recovering what one had lost. Recovering grace after a lapse is illustrated, characteristically, by the law of the Nazirite (Nb vi) to which Philo attributes not only a moral but also a symbolic meaning. Finding of the unknown ('as if the things themselves do of their own accord come to meet them and hasten to offer themselves to view') is illustrated by the popular tale of the husbandman who dug a hole for the purpose of planting a tree and found a treasure, and so encountered a good fortune he never hoped for.[1]

. . . ὥσπερ γεωπόνον φασί τινες ὑπὲρ τοῦ τι τῶν ἡμέρων δένδρων φυτεῦσαι σκάπτοντα χωρίον, θησαυρῷ περιτυχεῖν, ἀνελπίστῳ χρησάμενον εὐτυχίᾳ.

The idea is illustrated by the story of Jacob, who accounted for his unexpected success in finding what his father wanted by saying 'Because

[1] Philo, *Quod Deus sit imm.* XX.91 (F. H. Colson, iii, 57; trans. Yonge I, 361).

treasure (log. 109) has nothing to do with our parable. The trend of opinion is now *against* Thomas's having had access to sources behind our synoptic gospels, though an effort towards 'rehabilitation' has been made by W. H. C. Frend, *JThS* 18 (1967), 13ff. J. Dupont, 'Les paraboles du trésor et de la perle', *NTS* 14 (1968) 408ff. is helpful.

the Lord your God granted me success' (Gn xxvi.20). For, as Philo says, 'When God bestows on anyone the treasures of his own wisdom without any toil or labour then we, not having expected it, suddenly find a treasure of perfect happiness'. Some seek hard and find nothing; others, paradoxically more richly endowed, find without deliberate searching.

Comparing Jesus's parable with Philo's little illustration, one sees how the natural, traditional notion of the farmer and his unexpected find is transformed and developed by the artist. Jesus's work is more elaborate, more subtle. It is quite possible—we may never be certain—that Jesus is alluding to the grace of God and of the soul's instinctive recognition of its spontaneous appearance, in contrast to the equally valid experience of the scholar or the 'man of religion' whose success arises in the course of, and perhaps only because of, his earnest strivings. This is a genuine rabbinical idea. 'Rabbi' said about a certain R. 'Eliezer, 'One wins eternal life after a struggle of years, another *finds* it in one hour'.[1]

THE 'TREASURE' AS GOD'S TREASURE

So far we have concentrated on the treasure in the field, and glanced at the pearl of great price, as if these explained what it should be like when an individual discovers, or tracks down, the kingdom of heaven, and makes it his own. This image is not in any sense untrue, and must not be lost sight of, especially because it is not only to be used straightforwardly, as a hint for the would-be believer and the non-believer, but is also to be used in a topsy-turvy fashion to explain something else, which Matthew quite obviously has in mind. In short, just as a man treasures a chance find or something he is looking for for years, so God will treasure his servants. If an ordinary man will take such pains over a find of bullion or a pearl, how much the more will God gloat, as it were, over those who have served him faithfully. Mt xiii.36–51 is an elaborate little sermon based on Mal iii.16–iv.3. The 'tares in the field', the 'reapers', the 'end of the world', the righteous shining forth 'as the sun', our 'treasure' and the 'pearl of great price', the 'net', and the angels sorting the righteous from the unrighteous, and the householder bringing out 'new' and 'old' from his 'treasure'—all this which we find in Matthew lay unrecognised in the passage of Malachi. It is a wonderful sermon. R. Tanḥuma said, more simply, that the righteous resemble a jewel covered with mowings: only when picked up would their beauty be seen.[2]

The Malachi passage begins, 'Then they that feared the Lord spoke to each other . . . and a book of remembrance was written (with their

[1] b. 'A.Z. 17*a* = Sonc. 88.
[2] *Midr. on Ps.*, Ps i, § 20 (Braude, I, 31).

names?) before him, for those that feared the Lord and thought of his name'. The passage continues, ' "They shall belong to me!", said the Lord of Hosts, "for the Day when I make up (*'oseh*) my own special treasure (*ṣ^e^gullāh*), and I shall deal gently with them, just as a man deals gently with his son who serves him." And then you shall turn and see the difference between the righteous and the wicked, between the one who serves God and the one who does not serve him.'

The point of the difference is brought out in the next verses: the proud will be burnt as stubble, 'neither root nor branch' shall be left. For those that fear the name of the Lord the 'sun of righteousness' shall rise with healing. The wicked shall be trod down. Until that day, needless to remark, the identity of the righteous, as contrasted with the wicked, remains known only to God, with his 'book of remembrance'. The righteous, however, are treasured up and the treasure will become God's very own on that Day, when the choice will be perfect and complete. God will enjoy his treasure and the righteous will be treated with that specially Jewish treatment denoted by the root ḤML, which hovers between 'sparing', 'cherishing', and 'gentle dealing, compassion'.

In our parable Jesus is saying that the word *ṣ^e^gullāh* with its verb *'oseh* explains God's keenness about the righteous, his discernment of them, and his patience towards them. The implication is that they should be keen to be 'found', to be 'treasured', and not be alarmed at their worldly and unappreciated situation. It is *not* a flight of fancy to understand Jesus as saying that God would be prepared to pay a very high price to acquire them, were they not (though in, as it were, foreign possession) already in full measure his. The habit of people to speak of their relatives and friends, especially servants, as 'treasures' silently supports these ingenious parables. The righteous are God's treasures, God's pearls, though they are not yet gathered into his treasure chamber, and he is as keen about them as would be any workman delving in a field or merchant roaming the orient.

The Greek equivalent for *ṣ^e^gullāh* (which sometimes means 'very special possession', and sometimes, in late biblical language, treasure like bullion) is περιποίησις in this very passage of Malachi, and it is a commonplace term in New Testament literature. In the Old Testament the *ṣ^e^gullāh* means Israel, if they obey God: Ex xix.5 is a sufficient example: 'Now therefore, if you obey my voice and keep my covenant you shall be a peculiar treasure (*ṣ^e^gullāh*) for me from among all peoples: for all the earth is mine.' In Ti ii.14, 1 Pe ii.9, and Eph i.14 the same idea appears clearly, and it is associated with redemption. Jesus's parables not only indicate the last days and the judgment but also God's eagerness to acquire his treasure.

CHAPTER TWO

The Parable of the Talents and Two Logia

THE PARABLE OF THE TALENTS (or pounds) (Mt xxv.14–28; Lk xix. 12–27) is not fully intelligible without technical information. References to the legal background have so far been slight.[1] A contribution from Professor Jean Dauvillier[2] has however thrown welcome light. Material necessary for the elucidation of the parable will throw light also on two wandering logia. The problem of the original form of the talents parable requires some reference to the legal knowledge which the hearers of Jesus and their contemporaries can easily have drawn upon when thinking about such a story. If we had legal information directly from the time of Jesus we should be on firm ground. In default of this we note the Babylonian material, the Talmudic material and the (ancient customary) Islamic material: proceeding inwards from both directions we can determine with sufficient sureness what customs will have been familiar to Jesus's contemporaries. The difference between the laws at

[1] J. Jeremias, *Die Gleichnisse Jesu*, 6th edn (Göttingen 1962), deals with the parable at p. 55–60 (in the Eng. trans. [1963] at p. 58–63). Recognition of legal points is seen at p. 57 n. 1 and p. 59 n. 1. Some practical considerations weigh with W. Foerster, 'Das Gleichnis von den anvertrauten Pfunden', in *Verbum Dei Manet in Aeternum* (*Festschrift f. O. Schmitz*, Witten 1953), 37–56. A. Jülicher, *Die Gleichnisreden Jesu* II (Tübingen 1910), 472–93, and L. Fonck, *Die Parabeln des Herrn im Evangelium* (Innsbruck 1902) both show the importance of apparently trifling details. M. Zerwick, 'Die Parabel vom Thronanwärter', *Biblica* 40, 2 (1959), 654–74, counters Jülicher with an excessive allegory indicating that the master is Jesus himself (*cf.* Cornelius à Lapide *ad loc.*, *ubi cit. sup.* I, 450). C. H. Dodd's study of the third servant's behaviour (*Parables of the Kingdom*, London 1961, 108–14) shows how details may lead to a particular application—he sees an attack on the Pharisees. The nature of the over-caution and its cause needs further exploration. Jeremias would see the lesser sums (Luke) and the fewer servants (Matthew) as correct. This writer would incline to favour the Matthaean scheme in both regards. On Billerbeck's contribution see a comment below, p. 19 n. 3. I do not believe this parable has anything to do with Archelaus's trip to Rome, in spite of any element of correspondence there may be.

[2] 'La parabole des mines ou des talents et le § 99 du Code de Hammurabi', *Mélanges Joseph Magnol* (Paris 1948), 153–65. Legrange in part anticipated him. The author was (158–9) somewhat influenced by the alleged allegorical sense of the parable.

both ends, as it were, of this time-scale must be noted, for the sake of accuracy, but the final result is not materially affected by the doubt which remains. The institution of law which is explained in this article is also glanced at in the difficult parable of the Unmerciful Servant, but that topic requires separate attention.

THE PARABLE OF THE TALENTS

INTRODUCTION

This writer accepts the view that both Luke and Matthew preserve versions of an original parable, and that the differences reflect different understandings of the function of that original or its successors.[1] But this chapter is in no way influenced by any such considerations. The residuum obtainable from both surviving versions subserves our discussion adequately. The questions to be asked are these: what is the master–servant relationship alluded to; what does the servant expect to gain; what courses of conduct are open to him and what are their implications? The material within the parable amounts to this: a master is about to be absent; he hands cash to servants with instructions (Luke), or confidence (Matthew), that they should do business with it. The master went away and was out of touch. On his return the two first were found to have made profits, while the third had buried (or hid) the money. The master praises the first two, rebukes the third, making a particular remark about a bank, a peculiarly specific point which has puzzled many.

The servants are *not* slaves. But they are dependants. Psychologically inhibited from free bargaining with their master, they are legally capable of being related to him as *mit'aṣṣaḳiyn*, the correct Jewish name for people who do business with other people's money, partners with capitalists, themselves supplying all the skill and labour. In the East generally servants tend to be maintained at their masters' expense and are bound to him by commensality and loyalty. They do not expect to be treated on a strictly commercial footing.[2] Partnership stems historically from co-heirship and there is nothing incongruous in a servant's being a partner. Jewish stories include a tale of a king who sent out his son to 'do business'. R. Huna tells of one such who was afraid of robbers and pirates; the king gave his son an amulet to give him

[1] Against the view of P. Joüon at *Rech. Sc. Rel.* 29 (1939), 489–94. Lagrange, Oesterley (*Gospel Parables*, 143), Dodd, and W. L. Knox (*Sources*, II, 118) agree that there is one parable behind the two versions.

[2] Note the story of the orphan servant in Midr. R., Deut. III.4 (trans. J. Rabbinowitz, Sonc., 1939, 72).

confidence.[1] *Mit'aṣṣaḳiyn* naturally have rights and liabilities, and these are complicated when the capitalist is also their master.

The servants, as usually in the East, were quasi-relatives, even quasi-sons. The Aramaic word *talya* means characteristically both 'child' and 'servant'.[2] Commensality and loyalty exclude a strictly commercial relationship. They cannot have been slaves. The Israelite slave can indeed act as agent for some purposes. Islamic evidences are in places contradictory. But it is conclusive that the wide powers needed for commercial enterprise and to protect the capital belong to a fully competent agent, which a slave never can be.[3] Economically and psychologically our servants correspond to freedmen under Roman Law.[4]

In the capital-services partnership, a phenomenon not limited to Asia,[5] one partner (P, *primus*) invested capital with one or more trusted

[1] Midr. R., Lev. xxv.1 = Sonc. 313.

[2] M. Black, *Aramaic Approach* (*cit. sup.*), 221.

[3] Dauvillier, 155. δοῦλος as an official: Bauer-Arndt-Gingrich 2, Rengstorf, *ThWzNT* II, 269–70. In Ptolemaic Egypt slaves could not be revenue farmers: *Rev. Laws*, col. 15. C. Préaux, *op. cit.*, p. 26 n. 3 below, at p. 452. The agent is like the principal, and partners are agents. Maliki law agrees: F. H. Ruxton, *Maliki Law* . . . (London 1916), 193–7. Slaves transacting business for their masters are known in Islam, and in pre-British India Gokha women sold at Rs. 50 each because of their commercial ability, but there is no evidence that they engaged in litigation, granted releases, etc., as a Jewish partner would have to do. Billerbeck, *Kommentar* I (1961), 971, *b*, misleads: only a free man can represent another for purposes of litigation. A slave may well lend money as his master's implement (as in Rome)—but our men are engaged in trade (ἐργάζομαι = ἐμπορεύομαι: Pr xxxi.18). Billerbeck also thought that our δοῦλοι earned what they earned for their master. Upon such a view our verses (Mt xxv.24*b*, 26*b*; Lk xix.21, 22*b*) are hardly intelligible. On the meaning of *eved* = δοῦλος see also L. Gulkowitsch, 'Der kleine Talmudtraktat über die Sklaven', ΑΓΓΕΛΟΣ I (1925), 87. The Roman *institor* (factor, agent) might be a slave or free (Ulpian at *Dig.* 14.3.7, 1), but he worked strictly to instructions, as our *mit'aṣṣaḳiyn* did not.

[4] In Midr. R., Exod. XLIII.6 the expression *ben bayit* which usually means 'steward' (literally 'son of (the) house') is applied to an imperial servant engaging in trade. Ziegler supposed him a freedman, but B. Cohen disagrees ('*Peculium*', 226 = *JRL* I, 270).

[5] J.-Ph. Lévy, 'Contractus trinus', in R. Naz, *Dict. de droit canonique* IV (1949), 491–8. B. Beinart (Professor of Roman Law, University of Cape Town), 'Capital in partnership', *Acta Juridica* (1961), 118–55, is essential for the understanding of the parable. Business has features which are perennial. It was commonly assumed that capital was more valuable than labour, thus the capital is *not* presumed (in the absence of agreement) to be common property, *i.e.* it must be returned intact on dissolution. The capitalist alone bears the risk of loss, and the merchant is never debtor in respect of the capital. This corresponds to the *ḳirāḍ* position. Services (Baldus *ad Cod.* IV.37.1, num. 13–15) correspond not to the capital but to its use, *i.e.* interest. Grotius, *De Iur. B. ac P.* II, 12, 24.1, conceives that capital may become joint property (whereupon only a half must be returned—the Jewish view), and Pothier, *Société* I, 4, 16, favours community in capital in the absence of a contrary intention. U. Huber, *Prael. Iur. Civ.*, *ad Inst.* III.26, num. 4 (c), says that equity points the other way. Van der Keessel, *Dictata ad Grotium*, *ad* III.21.5, points out the result—but merchants did in practice

persons, each of whom we may call S (*secundus*), not having capital of his own to adventure in partnership with P. Each treated the other *bona fide*.[1] At the conclusion of the adventure or periodically S rendered an account to P. S has ample discretion, and may choose methods unforeseen by P.[2] Without a breach of faith by S a unilateral termination of the partnership by P would not necessarily be valid,[3] and it might always be immoral. The proportion of profit to be taken by P and S respectively would be fixed by agreement, or by custom. Customs would vary with the region, period, and state and nature of the trade contemplated.

It was good to offer such a partnership to a poor man. R. 'Abba, in the name of the third-century Palestinian Amora R. Simeon b. Laḳish, said: 'He who lends is greater than him who performs charity, and he who "throws into a purse" is greater than all.' It was none the less righteous for its conducing to profit if S were honest and fortunate.[4]

Merchants trading with the king's capital or a temple's[5] were a feature of ancient Babylonia.[6] Ḥammurabi deals with the obligations

[1] See protestations in P. Cair. Maspero 67158, 67159 (J. Maspero, *Cat.* II (1913), 113–17).

[2] Rabbis speak of 'drinking beer', and reject it. R. Tarfon and R. 'Aḳiba illustrate this: Midr. R., Lev. XXXIV.16 (trans., 444). Money intended to be invested in a field was distributed in charity by the 'labouring' partner who, when challenged, cited Ps cxi/cxii.9!

[3] b. B.M. 69*a*–*b* = Sonc. 402; 105*a* = Sonc. 599.

[4] b. Shab. 63*a* = Sonc. 298. Merit increases with risk. *Cf.* Bets. 32*b* = Sonc. 165 (a refusal of an '*iṣḳā*'). For 'purse' meaning a deposit in business see W. F. Leemans, *Foreign Trade in the Babylonian Period* (Leiden 1960), 99. For *Test. Job*, *v. inf.*, p. 25 n. 1.

[5] F. M. Heichelheim, *Ancient Economic History* I (Leiden 1958), 127–8. '... foreign merchants of the ancient orient were almost completely dependent on royal courts and estates, temples and nobles, who alone could lend them sufficient capital ...' See W. F. Leemans, *The Old Babylonian Merchant: His Business and his Social Position* (Leiden 1950), p. 122 n. 308.

[6] E. Szlechter, *Étude Sociologique du Contrat de Société en Babylonie* (Paris 1945), 97ff., 104ff.; *Le Contrat de Société en Babylonie, en Grèce et à Rome* (Paris 1947), 54ff; G. R. Driver and Sir J. C. Miles, *Babylonian Laws*, 2 vols. (Oxford 1955, 1956), I. 186–202; text and trans. of § U (= § 99) and §§ 100–3 are at II, 42–3. The *tamkārum* gives *ana tadmiḳtim* to the *šamallūm* (bagman, agent—not a slave but a paid servant—Leemans [1960], at p. 142, unaccountably calls him an apprentice or helper, which latter he was, but much more, it would seem) and the latter trades with it but is liable for all capital if it is lost otherwise than in trading. The capitalist was entitled to two-thirds of the profits: G. Eisser and J. Léwy, *Die altassyrischen Rechtsurkunden vom Kültepe, Mitt. Vorderas. Ges.* (Leipzig), 33, 35 (3). This partnership is distinguished from *tappūtim* (partnership). *Tamkārum* could mean merchant or money-lender. The *tamkāru* (capitalists) were at some periods royal officials (Driver and

insure capitalists against loss. Beinart leans (140) to the presumption that the capital remains that of the capitalist, but he recognises the possibility of modification. If the merchant were the other's servant (an uncontemplated modification), this would only reinforce the capitalist's right to have his capital intact. See also p. 22 n. 3 below.

of such merchants.[1] In India from perhaps as early as 300 B.C. a similar institution existed.[2] Solomon profited from his merchants.[3] Jews borrowed from kings. At 1 M xiii.15 there is an example. A Jewish parable depicts a king angry with a merchant at his losses.[4] In a *midrash* a king opens his treasures to his minister to find that the latter converts them into tainted assets.[5] The Jewish word '*iṣḳā*'[6] (Heb. '*āṣaḳ*) retains the idea of the relevant Akkadian root, meaning to 'cast lots', 'to divide', 'to allot property' between shares on an equitable basis.[7] Apparently the Hebrew meaning 'business', 'affair' ('*eṣeḳ*) has developed from the sense of 'sharing'.

The importance of '*iṣḳā*' was that, although a profit was obtained by P, no rate of interest on his capital could be stipulated, and therefore usury could be avoided. The Islamic counterpart is called *ḳirāḍ* or *muḍārabah*,[8] very ancient customary law, well documented.

[1] Driver and Miles supersede previous discussions.

[2] See Kauṭilya cited at p. 24 n. 2 below. Also *Gautama-dharma-sūtra* XII.38 (XII.41 in Bühler, *Sacred Books of the East* II, 244). The king must increase his wealth (*Manu-smṛti* III.99, 101) by this method as well as others.

[3] 1 K x.28, also 15 = 2 Ch ix.14 (?).

[4] Midr. R., Gen. VIII.3 (I. Ziegler, *Königsgleichnisse des Midrasch*, Breslau 1903, 253, Anh. lxxxviii).

[5] Midr. R., Exod. XXXI.15 (trans. S. M. Lehrman, 1939, 397). See below, p. 95.

[6] b. Bets. 32*b* = Sonc. 165, B.M. 104*b*–105*a* = Sonc. 598f. Maim. XII, IV (Agents and Partners), vi, 1 (trans., p. 226).

[7] *Assyrian Dictionary* (Chicago, Or. Inst.): *isḳu* 1) lot (as a device to determine a selection), 2) share (of income, assigned by lot), 3) fortune, 4) nature, power. *eseḳu* 2) to apportion lots or shares (see Assyrian Laws B § 1). *isihtu* (by-form of *isḳu*) 1) assignment, assigned working material, share (assigned to officials).

[8] The institution is mentioned by S. M. Stern, *Oriens* (1962), 181. A. L. Udovitch, At the origins of the western *Commenda*: Islam, Israel, Byzantium?', *Speculum* (1962), '198ff. Ben Ali Fekar (Ibn 'Alī Fakār), *La Commande en Droit Musulman* (Lyon 1910). D. Santillana, *Istituzioni di Diritto Musulmano Malichita con Riguardo anche al Sistema Sciafiita* II (Rome 1938), bk. X, ch. iv, 323–34. C. Hamilton (trans.), *The Hedaya or Guide* . . ., 2nd edn. S. G. Grady (London 1870), III, bk. xxvii, 454–71. Freytag, *Lexicon* (1837), 497: *ḳariḍa* = mutuo creditoque dedit, ut lucri ex mercatura redeuntis certam partem cum sorte reciperet. Shafi'ite definition: a contract *sui generis*, mixed of hire and partnership, with a predominance of hire of labour. *Minhaj et-Talibin* (II, 132): 'consigning to someone of a sum of money to be employed in commerce, the profit being on the common account'. In modern Arabic *muḍārabah* means exactly 'speculation', commercially or otherwise. That our parable deals with a *commenda* was observed by G. Eisser at *ZSS* 58 (1938), 395 n. 2.

Miles I, 120, 200, Leemans, 122). E. Szlechter inclines to the view that Ḥam. §§ 99–103 referred to a 'société en commandite' (*i.e.* an '*iṣḳā*') with modifications. An example appears at *id.*, *Tablettes Juridiques de la 1e Dynastie de Babylonie (Genève)*, *Publ. Inst. Dr. Romain, Paris* XVI (Paris 1958), pt. II, 125–7 (the parties engage to return the capital if they lose, which conflicts with Ḥam. §§ 101–2). On the Babylonian *soc. en comm.* see *id.*, 'Revue Critique des Droits Cunéiformes. V', in *Studia et Documenta Historiae et Iuris* 28 (Rome 1962), 470ff., at p. 492–3 (harrānu Vertrag mit einseitiger Kapitalbeteiligung).

'Iṣḳā' was well known *temp. Chr.* See Sirach xlii.3 ὁδοιπόρων and Gospel of Thomas, log. 64/65.[1] The word πραγματεύσασθε should be rendered back into *tit'aṣṣᵉḳu.*[2] In our parable it is actually alluded to twice, once in the investments with the servants and again in the hypothetical deposit with the bank.

THE INVESTMENT

Our P (*cf.* p. 19) chose his S's from amongst his servants. Talmudic law insists that all S's must become, if only *ad hoc*, servants of P.[3] The Pharisees' rule, scrupulously avoiding a suggestion of usury, seems to have agreed with actual custom. For the independent businessman would not often be as attractive as the servant over whom P had ultimate control.

We commence our investigation of the terms of the investment with the Talmudic law, that nearest in time and circumstances to those supposed in the parable. Under that system, which follows the rule of the Nehardeans,[4] there could be a specific agreement as to terms, and the proportions of profit to be taken by each. Naturally profit would not be calculated until the capital had been repaid—this is a universal feature. But if there were no agreement (as would be the case between master and servant) half of the capital was considered a deposit in trust (the risk lying entirely with P), while the other half was a debt, a loan to S.[5] When the *'iṣḳā'* was dissolved, S must restore half the capital if so much or more had been lost in business. S's expenses could not be recovered in such a case, and he would bear them himself.

The reasoning is convincing. Better or worse terms subsisted at other periods. In Babylonian Law the merchant must repay the entire capital in any event (saving *force majeure*)[6]. In Islamic Law none of the capital is treated as a loan to S. P could have no recourse to S's own funds to make good any loss (not due to S's fraud) at the dissolution of the

[1] Guillaumont and others (1959), p. 37, pl. 92. 15–16; R.M. Grant and D. N. Freedman, *Secret Sayings of Jesus* (London 1960), 159–60, which has a better translation.

[2] Billerbeck II, 252, suggests *'āṣaḳ biphragmaṭyā'* for the infinitive. See Jastrow, *Dict.*, 1098–9.

[3] *Mishnāh*, B.M. V.4 (Danby, 356; Blackman IV, 123), b. B.M. 68*a*–69*a* = Sonc. 397–401. Dauvillier, 164. The rule that a *mit'aṣṣᵉḳ* can in any case claim one-sixth of the profit is much later Jewish Law (p. 23 n. 2 below) and does not apply to our period.

[4] Nehardea, a town in Babylonia near the junction of the Euphrates and the Nahr Malka, was the seat of the academy rendered famous by Samuel and other great rabbis.

[5] b. B.M. 104*b* = Sonc. 598. *ha'y 'iṣḳā' palᵉgā' milᵉvāh ū-palᵉgā' piḳādon.* The rule is connected with the ratio of *Mishnāh*, B.M. V.4 (Danby, 356).

[6] Szlechter, *Contrat* 58, relying on Ḥam. § 102.

ḳirāḍ.[1] In between in time the Jewish rule is curiously intermediate in nature. P would not have invested unless he wanted fruit (interest), but without S's labour there would have been no fruit. In the absence of agreement to the contrary the labour of S must be presumed equivalent to the use of the capital of P, and therefore P was entitled (so the Jewish businessmen believed) to the fruit on half, and S to that on the other half. Only half of the capital is treated as a loan, *i.e.* the half on which P was entitled to the 'interest'. His oath as a bailee discharges S from liability for the other half.

What share of the net profit might our S's have expected *if they had not been servants*? Perhaps one-third.[2] But our S's were servants, that is to say their maintenance would be the first charge on the capital or its profits, if any. Their skill was already supposed to be paid for. The proportion would be much less, and it would not be bargained for in advance. A P who in fact profited much from his '*iṣḳā*' would reward the honest S well.[3] S would then obtain absolutely and relatively a larger share than would less successful, or suspect servants.

The greater the risk (as in nautical loans)[4] the larger the percentage of profit is offered by the merchant. Where risks are widely spread demand for capital falls as offers of capital increase, and interest-rates fall. Cato the Elder made money by an ingenious scheme. Greeks, traditionally averse to usury, were shocked and envious. He lent at nautical rates to large mercantile partnerships amongst whom he also figured, through his freedman, as a partner![5] Hopes of participation in profit fluctuate with the anticipated success; with the likelihood that success would encourage further investment and better terms; and the recognition of the investor's actual risk. When many servants played the role of S the competitive and comparative aspects were unavoidable.

[1] Santillana, 330. Hamilton, 454, 464.

[2] So apparently in Babylonia. In the *muḍārabah* (Hamilton, 462), as in Roman Law, half-and-half would be the rule, but variations are contemplated. In the *ḳirāḍ* the texts (Santillana, 326) suggest one-third or one-quarter (at p. 332, the usual proportion seems to have been one-third). Circumstances might at any time justify a partner's agreeing to accept one-third: P. Lond. V, 1705 (p. 110) (sixth century), though half-and-half is almost universal (*e.g.* P. Flor. III, 370, p. 91, A.D. 132). In late Talmudic law the unpaid *mit'aṣṣ^{e}ḳ* is entitled to one-sixth of the profit as remuneration for handling the trust half of the capital, giving him a total of two-thirds of the profit; and he bears only one-third of the loss. This was not generally accepted, but illustrates concern for the unpaid working partner. Maim. XII, IV, vi, 3–4 (trans., p. 227–8).

[3] Under the *ḳirāḍ* the proportion could be altered when the enterprise was over (Santillana, 326). In Old Babylonia the *tamkārum* carrying on trade on behalf of the palace would receive an *ilkum* (land or money in lieu thereof) as his reward (Leemans, *Old Bab. Merch.*, 125).

[4] See p. 25 n. 2 below.

[5] Plutarch, *Marcus Cato*, XXI.6–8 (Loeb edn, ii, 367).

The commencement of the relationship occurred when the cash was committed to them. If we follow the *ḳirāḍ* the partnership would be perfected only by the actual commencement of trading.[1] According to the Matthaean version the master committed amounts varying with the servants' abilities, an entirely plausible scheme. No actual P would do otherwise, for no group of servants will lack differences in skill. Did the third S originally have the smallest amount? Possibly. But it is sufficient if he thought the amount too small for him.

THE OUTCOME AND THE THIRD SERVANT'S BEHAVIOUR

According to Matthew the first two servants multiplied the capital by 100 per cent, which is the minimum profit accepted under the laws of Ḥammurabi.[2] They did what was expected of them. Both versions have two plausible features: the amount received as capital is stated first—there might have been a dispute at that point had it been a real event,[3] and they speak as if their labour had no part in the multiplication—a piece of etiquette as prudent as it must have been usual. Luke shows the first servant reporting 1,000 per cent, a possible and most satisfactory result. The next's 500 per cent was creditable. It is harder to double a small sum than to treble a large one.[4] The original parable might have had a mere skeleton: but the lively force of the details cannot be denied.

Though Luke may have embellished, the features of the third servant's behaviour seem original. The man buried the money and his '*iṣḳā*' never became alive. Luke, saying that he kept the money tied up[5] in a *sudarium*, accuses him of failing to keep the capital itself safe, in itself a breach of the faithfulness required of a servant (who is not a gratuitous bailee),[6] but this prejudicial element is not essential to the parable. But why did he hide the money and not trade with it?

[1] Santillana, 327, 333. Consent alone does not perfect a *ḳirāḍ*.

[2] Dauvillier emphasises this at p. 157, 161. Under § 101 the capitalist is guaranteed a profit of 100 per cent. The merchant is a defaulter if he reports less. For Indian law to a similar effect see Kauṭilya, *Arthaśāstra* III.11, 5–9 (trans. Kangle, 1963, 261–2).

[3] Hanafi Law dilates on who must be believed in a dispute as to the terms: Hamilton, 471.

[4] An observation of general truth but especially true of an underdeveloped economy: T. Fuller, *History of Cambridge* IV (seventeenth-century England). For 'making' profit as an Aramaic linguistic expression see M. Black, *Aramaic Approach* 302.

[5] Mishnaic language. For the *sudarium* see Midr. R., Lev. VI.3 (trans. J. Israelstam and J. J. Slotki, London 1939, 80).

[6] A point observed by Jeremias. Safe keeping is thoroughly investigated at *Mishnāh*, B.M. III.10, 11 (Danby, 352, Blackman IV, 110–11), b. B.M. 42*a*–43*a* = Sonc. 249–56. Samuel said: Money can only be guarded in the earth. Billerbeck I, 971–2. A. Wünsche, *Neue Beiträge* (Göttingen 1878), 317.

He claims fear. 'For I was afraid of you, because you are a hard man: you pick up what you have not put down—you reap what you have not sown (Lk xix.21).' Was it over-caution and cowardice? Rather he suspected he would be left with little of the profit, if any. He believed his master conformed to the (entirely appropriate) saying which pillories a capitalist, or another, who derives (by intimidation or otherwise) an inequitably high proportion from his investments,[1] exploiting the relationship in question. Some capitalists used in the ancient world to try to be 'leonine partners', and there is an inevitable tendency to make the weaker party insure the other against all risks without a premium.[2] Where the merchant insures the capitalist against loss without remuneration it is hardly a partnership at all.

We note in passing the discrepancy between ἴδε ἔχεις τὸ σόν ('Here is your own [money] back!') in Matthew and ἰδοὺ ἡ μνᾶ σου in Luke. The former, typical of wry Jewish humour, is the equivalent of the Mishnaic *harey shelchā l^ephānéychā*. With this expression one disclaims responsibility and defies complaint.[3] The overtones are lost in Luke.

[1] In Luke there is a coincidence with a Greek and a Jewish maxim. Solon (Diog. Laert. I, 57) ἃ μὴ ἔθου, μὴ ἀνέλῃ, quoted by Plato, *De Leg*. XI.913 C as ἃ μὴ κατέθου, μὴ ἀνέλῃ. Josephus, *Con. Ap*. II, 27/28: ὃ μὴ κατέθηκέ τις, οὐκ ἀναιρήσεται. τῶν ἀλλοτρίων οὐδενὸς ἅψεται and again (30/31) ἂν ὑφέληταί τις ἀλλότριον, καὶ ἂν ὃ μὴ κατέθηκεν ἀνέληται, πάντων εἰσὶ κολάσεις, οὐχ οἷαι παρ' ἑτέροις (the Greeks, *e.g.*) ἀλλ' ἐπὶ τὸ μεῖζον. The maxim refers to any unlawful gain including theft. Jb xxxi.8 recalls the maxim (Jn iv.36–8 is a paradox: yet the reaper is employed to do his work so that the sower may rejoice). Philo, *Hypo*. VII, 6 (Colson IX, 427) ἃ μὴ κατέθηκεν, μηδ' ἀναιρεῖσθαι, μηδ' ἐκ πρασιᾶς μηδ' ἐκ ληνοῦ μηδ' ἐξ ἅλωνος comes near to us. The supplementary θερίζεις brings in the peculiar Jewish law that it is forbidden to reap self-sown crops in seventh and jubilee years (the first observed *temp. Chr.*): Lv xxv.5, 11 (implication: 'you will go to any length'). Matthew adjusts, loses the maxim, keeps the θερίζεις point, and adds the double entendre of διεσκόρπισας. This means (i) 'winnowed', (ii) 'scattered' (sown), in charity. Scattering (wasting) leads to wealth (sowing and winnowing): 2 Co ix.6–13 (*cf.* Ga vi.9–10), with citation of Ps cxi/cxii.9 (p. 20 n. 2 above). Matthew indicates, the master acts uncharitably towards dependants, why should he be served *gratis* (oriental dependants are always 'poor')? The righteous capitalist forgives losses incurred by charitable borrowers at *Test. Job* (S. P. Brock, 1967), xi (*cf.* Jb xxxi. 35–7 LXX).

[2] Hamilton, 456. Grotius, *De Iure B. ac P.*, comm. H. L. B. de Cocceii, II (Lausanne 1751), 727. Phaedrus I, 45. *Dig*. 17.2.29, 2. P. Flor. III, 370 (A.D. 132); P.Amh. 94 (A.D. 208). On the ναυτικὸν δάνεισμα see F. Meulenans and M. Verschueren, 'Het nautikon daneisma te Athene', *RIDA* 12 (1965), 157–65. Casson, *Eos* 48 (1957), 89–93.

[3] *Mishnāh*, B.Ḳ. IX.2, X.5. b. B.Ḳ. 66*b* = Sonc. 383; 94*a* = Sonc. 545; 97*a* = Sonc. 566; 98*a* = Sonc. 568; 116*b* = Sonc. 694; 117*b* = Sonc. 703; Shev. 37*b* = Sonc. 223. Illustrations: a stolen coin is dropped in deep but clear water; or usurped land is inundated or occupied by bandits or officials, who have extruded the owner. Also *Mishnāh*, B.M. VI.3 (Danby, 358; Blackman IV, 131); b. B.M. 78*b*, 79*a* = Sonc. 454. The saying is noticed by C. Schöttgen, *Hor. Heb.*, I, *ad Luc.* xix. 8. The example at b. B.Ḳ. 94*a* (above) is particularly interesting because there the one who utters the defiant formula had neglected to treat the property of the unfortunate owner as an honest agent or even friend would have done.

The sauciness of the speech is fascinating.[1] It both upbraids and defies. I really cannot believe, as some do, that he expected commendation—on the contrary this is what he seems to say: 'You gave me too little. Have you so little confidence in me? If there had been any profit, I would have seen little of it. It was within my discretion whether, as well as when, to commence trading. I decided not to start, in the hopes of teaching you a lesson.' The oriental met his dilemma with inaction. If he gained he would obtain a mere trifle out of the profit; if he lost he would be without his expenses[2] or would have to pay (according to the Nehardean rule) half the capital out of his own meagre funds.

Why did the servant omit to deposit the money with the bank?[3] *Some* return would have been certain (ἂν αὐτὸ ἔπραξα). Because, out of the very small rate of interest which banks, engaged in money-changing and highly secure, petty investment, would be able to pay,[4] he, having made no contribution of labour, could expect practically no share. Since the smallest and most secure business would offer him nothing, he declined to do business at all.

The Gospel of the Hebrews version of this parable,[5] the translation of which gives trouble, seems to be a conflation with another, possibly unknown, parable about unsatisfactory servants. This sort of parable was attractive, for a late Jewish text is vaguely parallel.[6]

THE PARABLE AND THE CONCEPT OF TRUST

The Jews thought of God as doing business with men.[7] Commercial

[1] Philo, *Quis Heres* II–VI, 6–22 (Colson IV, 286–95). Note: . . . ταῦτα γὰρ καὶ τὰ τοιαῦτα ἔδεισεν ἄν τις καὶ πρὸς ἕνα τῶν ἐν μέρει βασιλέων εἰπεῖν . . . (§ 20).

[2] Santillana, 330–1.

[3] Such deposits with a *shūlᵉḥāniy* are dealt with at *Mishnāh*, B.M. III.11 (cited above). τόκος (correct) does not mean usury, but increase (out of partnership capital). τὸ ἐμὸν is correct because the capital would remain his. In practice he would, as we have seen, take all the increase for himself, or nearly all of it. A merchant partner had full authority to deposit with a bank: Hamilton, 456. Bankers might handle royal revenues, *cf.* βασιλικαὶ τράπεζαι in Galilee: Jos., *Vita* ix, 38. C. Préaux, *L'Economie Royale des Lagides* (Bruxelles 1939), 280, 291.

[4] Préaux, 282, mentions 24 per cent as high. That was very low for international trade.

[5] Eusebius, *Theoph.*, Migne, *PG* 24, 685–6, reprinted K. Aland, *Synopsis*, 416. Dodd, p. 113 n. 42. Jeremias deals with the Nazaräerevangelium at *op. cit.*, 55. An Indian parable is very similar. S1 gained much, S2 made no profit, S3 lost the capital. The capital = human life; profit = heaven. The parable is apparently borrowed from a gospel. Full references will be found at R. Garbe, *Indien und das Christentum* (Tübingen 1914), 42–3.

[6] Zohar Ḥadash 47*b* quoted by Schöttgen, *Hor. Heb.* I, 217.

[7] *Mishnāh*, 'Āvot I, 3, II, 14, 15, 16, III, 1, 17, IV, 22, VI, 5. *Midrash on Psalms*

metaphors are commonplaces. In the famous multiple allegory of R. 'Aḳiba (*Mishnāh*, 'Āvot III.17) God's 'debtors' are candidates for admission to a feast (*vᵉ-hakol mᵉtūḳān liṣ'ūdāh*), another point of juncture with our parable as given by Matthew. God's 'business' with men is expressed in three contexts as a trust, or deposit for both safe and profitable keeping. These are commonplaces. The soul is a deposit.[1] The *Torāh* is likewise a deposit to be worked with. Lastly the riches of the world are a trust to be employed according to the Master's instructions, with cheerful obedience, if we are to follow Dt xxviii, *cf.* Lv xxvi.[2] The consecration of *property*, possessions, to obedience to God was a practical object with the Dead Sea Scroll community, and on entering the Covenant, that community envisaged (whether they practised it is not certain) a recitation by their Priests of God's blessings and grace, by the Levites of certain curses on the 'men of the lot of Satan', and by both Priests and Levites of a commination, all taken in spirit if not to the letter from Dt xxvii–xxix.[3]

If men are faithful they will prosper. They will lend to others,[4] and this may be construed otherwise than historically. If they disobey they will fail and have no credit.[5] A parable could bring the point home to hearers who knew the scripture and might have assumed that it was to be taken only symbolically. That the treasures of the world are for man to exploit, and do not, in Jewish eyes, begin and end at the rains to which the text is thought to refer,[6] is shown by a *midrash* already alluded to. Moses was God's partner (κοινωνός) in the world's riches.[7] To illustrate the faithfulness with which these treasures should be administered one need only point to the specific obligation to lend (Lv xxv.35–37, Dt xv.7–10, Lk vi.35), which has, however, no direct relation to our parable. It is conceivable that our parable was intended to recall to its

[1] Midr. R., Lev. XVIII.1 (trans., p. 227), *Tanḥuma*, Midrash Shofᵉṭim, § 12 (264*b*). Hermas, *Shepherd* xxviii, Mand. 3.
[2] Dt xxviii is part of the sombre section known as αἱ ἀραί.
[3] 1 *QS* I–II. G. Vermès, *Dead Sea Scrolls in English* (London 1966), 72–4; E. Lohse, *Die Texte aus Qumran* (Munich 1964), 4–8; A. R. C. Leaney, *The Rule of Qumran and its Meaning* (London 1966), 123–4. A. Dupont-Sommer, *Les écrits esséniens découverts près de la Mer Morte*, 3rd edn (Paris 1968), 89–91.
[4] Dt xv.6, xxviii.12.
[5] Dt xxviii.44.
[6] Philo, *Praem.*, 142 (Colson VIII, 401), *Leg. Alleg.* III, 104–6 (Colson I, 371–3). The faithful depend on rain: *Quod Deus*, 156 (Colson III, 89), *Quis Heres*, 76 (Colson IV, 321). God's treasure is only of good: *De Fug.* xv.79 (Colson V, 53). Rain and Israel's merit: Midr. R., Deut. VII.6, 7 (trans., p. 137–8, 139).
[7] Philo, *Vita Mos.* I, 28 (§§ 155–8: Colson VI, 357).

(*Midrash Tehillim*), on Ps lxxix § 5 (trans. Braude, New Haven 1959, II, 46). Midr. R., Exod. XXXI.1 = Sonc. 378.

hearers the famous chapters dealing with blessings and curses, and to reinforce the Deuteronomic recommendation of service with joyfulness of heart.[1]

Luke or his source seems to have rewritten the parable believing that the money was entrusted as a test.[2] A test in loyalty led to the notion of reward, reward in turn to the range of retribution with the addition of *vv.* 14 and 27. The test theme requires *vv.* 17c and 19b, and therefore the implausible equality of investment at *v.* 13 and the equally implausible, trifling sums. That vacant administrative posts remain to be filled fits with the test scheme: yet the men were already his servants—did he not know their capacities? But even a small investment can detect unfaithfulness, and it is not impossible to imagine that detection was suspected to have been behind the scheme from the first. An Indian political writer (Kauṭilya) says you cannot tell whether officials are embezzling the king's money any more than you can tell whether fish are drinking. It is quite plausible to test them in a partnership first, it would seem.

As a reward for faithfulness the first servant receives the money taken from the third. The point is emphasised in Luke. ' "Take the *mina* from him and give it to the man who has the ten *minas.*" And they said to him, "Master, he has *ten minas* (already)" '. Why? P not only resumes the money, but terminates the '*iṣḳā*'—in Matthew he terminates the master–servant relationship also. The partnerships of the others naturally continued. Luke shows administrative and fiscal responsibilities distributed,[3] for which the servants were well fitted, for tax-collectors and dealers in revenue moneys were often the same people and operated in partnership. The interesting and plausible suggestion of Nestle (endorsed by Meyer) that Luke's 'cities' (at xix.17, 19) arose out of misunderstanding[4] *kikᵉrā'* (talent) as *karᵉkā'* (city) would not materially affect the sense, but it would weaken the basic notion (evidenced here and elsewhere) that those who are faithful in a little are entrusted with much: therefore the suggestion is probably unnecessary. The most successful servant was naturally the one whose partnership capital was increased. The others might object, and the master's ultimate share might be reduced. But the apt logion follows. It is the way of the world. Capital chases the lowest risk, even at the cost of interest!

[1] Dt xxviii.47. Sirach xi.22–3. Bounties: 2 Co ix.8. Whole-hearted: Dt xviii.13. Lack of faith in a worker: Midr. R., Lev. XIX.2 (trans., p. 237).

[2] Wünsche, 317, refers to Midr. R., Exod. § 11 (see Sonc. 48–51).

[3] See Sherwin-White, *Roman Society and Roman Law in the New Testament* (Oxford 1963), 133.

[4] M. Black, *op. cit.*, 2–3.

In keeping with the concept of trust, one may suggest an application for the parable. A general application strikes this writer as having a good claim. Moral generalities are worthy of pointed lessons. Those who complain that God has dealt hardly with them, they have a poor heredity, they have not had chances like others, that they are poor, stupid, oppressed, etc., may abandon piety as impractical. They may chide God for expecting of them more than is equitable. But this is not the spirit to adopt, says the parable. You may fail in the search for perfection,[1] but persist, for if success is not met in this world (which need not be excluded), there is the Messianic banquet hereafter. That is what Dt xxviii, for example, promises to those that serve in cheerfulness of heart. To those who survived the destruction of Jerusalem that chapter may have seemed distinctly to anticipate the penalty for failure to serve in the right spirit.

We can compare Jesus's parable with a rabbinical parable in the *Mekilta*.[2] There are striking similarities, but, as usual, Jesus's parable goes further and has subtler overtones. R. Simeon b. 'Eleazar said: 'If they could not manage to keep the seven commandments which were enjoined upon the descendants of Noah how much less could they keep the commandments of the *Torāh*! A king had appointed two governors, one of whom was made superintendent over the treasury of straw and the other over that of Silver and Gold. When accusations were brought against the former he complained that he had not been made superintendent of the treasury of Silver and Gold. The other, who had that post, chided him: "Your administration has been unfaithful in respect of the straw—how much more would this be the case with silver and gold!" One may draw a conclusion *a fortiori*.' On the psychology of the servant who buried his money this parallel throws a good deal of light, but Jesus is concerned to teach a point with which R. Simeon was not immediately concerned, namely the wider implications of 'faithfulness'.

'TO HIM THAT HATH . . .'

This is obviously a saying, appearing appropriately as the culmination of the talents parable.[3] Mt xxv.29 agrees with the version at xiii.12 in the explanatory (but perhaps genuine?) περισσευθήσεται, which tells us that giving increases the capital which the recipient then has. Mk

[1] Note that *mit'aṣṣᵉḳ* means (i) a businessman (as we have seen), and also (ii) a genuine student of the *Torāh* (Jastrow, *ubi cit.*, p. 22 n. 2 *sup.*). Hunter's original notion (*Parables* 79–80) that the third servant represents the selfish, exclusive Pharisee (whose nationalism [?] sterilised his religion [?]) does not attract me.
[2] On Ex xx.2, *Baḥod.* 5 (Winter-Wünsche, 208; Lauterbach II, 236).
[3] Hunter (120) says it tears *vv.* 28 and 30 apart.

iv.25 agrees with Lk viii.18, xix.26, as easily understood as the Matthaean text. It seems paradoxical, which is, after all, its virtue as a saying. How can anything be taken from him who has nothing? It is not (as has been suggested) a question of the rich and powerful receiving presents, nor of lending to the solvent. If a merchant possessing capital shows a profit, people eagerly offer him further capital, while the trader who reports no profit loses the capital entrusted to him. From him that has not (profit to show) is taken (withdrawn) even that (capital) which he still has. This remains true.

παντὶ δὲ ᾧ ἐδόθη πολύ, πολὺ ζητηθήσεται παρ' αὐτοῦ . . .

'Much will be required from every one, to whom much has been given . . .'

Lk xii.48b was understood by the evangelist to throw light on the different treatment awaiting individuals with different degrees of knowledge of God's will, but the saying is cryptic and perhaps always had a double entendre. ἐδόθη and παρέθεντο are in antithesis. The first means 'paid' (wages) and the second 'deposited' in the unexpected sense[1] of entrusted for trade. A movement fom παρατίθεναι to βάλλειν (note βαλεῖν in the next verse) by way of παραβάλλειν is possible. The contrast is, apparently, between those who receive something to be returned in equal measure (as a friendly donation or deposit for safe keeping) and those who receive many and valuable pledges and as a result are constantly applied to for loans. The more and more valuable the pledges they accept, the more readily people beg large sums from them. In the catch-as-catch-can world of business confidence can be induced by restoring deposits of small value in order to attract larger deposits with the hope of misappropriating them. The standard confidence-trick was notorious as far back as the time of Philo[2] and the metaphor of giving and recovering deposits is at one and the same time amusing and instructive. Further (and here the application to servants is valid) money is entrusted to a man, in keeping with his success. The more entrusted to him the larger the profits expected from him. It is easier to multiply a large sum than a small one. The parable showed

[1] Bauer–Arndt–Gingrich 2 b α. C. Spicq, 'Saint Paul et la Loi des Dépots', *Rev. Bibl.* 40 (1931), 481–502, A. Ehrhardt, 'Parakatatheke', *Z. Sav. St., rom.Ab.* 75 (1958), 32–90; 76 (1959), 480–9. D. Simon, 'Quasi-παρακαταθήκη', *ibid.* 82 (1965), 39–66. παρακαταθήκη and παραθήκη (*depositum*) are the same: Phrynichus in Jacoby, *F. Gr. Hist.* 392, 21.

[2] Philo, *Quod Deus sit imm.* XXII.101 (Colson III, 61; trans. Yonge I, 363): καὶ τοὺς τὰς ὀλιγοχρημάτους παρακαταθήκας ἀποδιδόντας ἐπὶ θήρᾳ στερήσεως μειζόνων . . . A fascinating passage deserving further attention from this angle.

that proportionately most could be expected of the servant who received the largest investment.

No equal exchange is desired, or is possible, for the soul, the *Torāh*, or the treasures of the world. But the demands made on the depositary are substantial.

It is true that *profit* in the ordinary sense cannot be made by God out of man, in whom he has made so enormous an investment (Jb xxii.2–3, xxxv.7, cf. Lk. xvii.10). Yet it is not satisfactory to conclude from this that God does not expect a *return*. Jesus's use of the analogy of a deposit for business is as apt as it is suggestive. Quite apart from the fitness of a deposit as a test, it is an excellent way of indicating that man is answerable, responsible, and that too *not* on the basis of strict law unmixed with equity.

CHAPTER THREE

The Parable of the Unmerciful Servant

A DISCUSSION OF THE LEGAL CONTENT and implications of this parable is long overdue. Mt xviii.23–34 contains a number of serious problems. The exegetical problems are already severe, and Jesus's technique in uttering parables may well be misunderstood if, as has often occurred, he is accused of introducing improbable or implausible features.[1] Persons acquainted with the legal thinking of the orient are at once put on their guard by curious features of the parable, which is long and detailed: they are likely to suspend judgement, both on the proper exegesis of the parable and the technique of its author, until the details of usage in Jesus's time have been clarified.

Perhaps the most exhaustive textual examination is that of Fr C. Spicq in his *Dieu et l'homme selon le Nouveau Testament.*[2] There the text is thoroughly checked, word by word. Numerous legal allusions are conjured up. A thorough study, with most avenues of exegesis explored, appeared in Professor Jeremias's *Die Gleichnisse Jesu.*[3] These studies so far outstrip previous examinations[4] that this writer feels reference to previous literature virtually superfluous.

Unlike some parables (for example the kindred parable of Reconcilia-

[1] Jeremias, *cit. inf.*, p. 211, takes the common view that the amounts of money stated are intended for emphatic contrast only. E. Fuchs, 'The parable of the Unmerciful Servant', *Studia Evangelica* I (Berlin 1959), 487ff. at p. 493 insists that the parable is 'intent on the miraculous', an instance of the great influence which reconstructions have on exegesis and, at second hand, on systematic considerations.

[2] *Lectio Divina* 29 (Paris, Le Cerf 1961), 54–61. He turns, however, the request (for such it indeed was) for 'time to pay' into the (theological) prayer for pardon. The temptation to read theologically significant factors into a parable (which must first be read factually and objectively) must at all costs be resisted.

[3] 6th edition (Göttingen 1962), esp. 207–11 (Eng. trans., 1963, 210–14). References to his views below refer to that edition, which (I gather) in fact does not represent entirely his final opinion on the parable. In his then view this was an *Endgerichtsgleichnis.*

[4] Amongst which one may usefully cite W. Michaelis, *Das hochzeitliche Kleid. Eine Einführung in die Gleichnisse Jesu über die rechte Jüngerschaft* (Berlin 1940), 150–68.

tion with the Adversary: Mt v.25) this parable has a folk-tale atmosphere, leaning slightly to the fairy-tale. It is fortunate that we have an analogy in the story of the life of Joseph, son of Tobias (Jos., *Ant.* XII.iv). Josephus' readers will have read this tale with pleasure, and will have yielded up their imaginations to it, without requiring strict proof of verisimilitude. For none of the details is manifestly impossible, and this is how the world believed kings and kingly courts and ministers were. Moreover it is likely that the tale of Joseph and his supersession of the avaricious old High Priest, Onias, was a popular one and still remembered fairly generally in Jesus's day.

But first, to the problems. The story in brief is this: a king is settling accounts with his ministers.[1] The very first one[2] appears in debt to an enormous amount. 'Debtor' means that he owed the money personally, being unable to pay. Unable to offer sureties, one understands, for presumably it was otherwise conceivable that a group of rich men who trusted him might be willing to offer pledges, and so relieve him from his predicament: in fact the debt was there, and he could not pay it. The king ordered[3] him to be sold, his effects, and his family also, with a view to payment of some of the debt.[4] The minister fell down and offered worship, begging for compassion, in fact for time in which he would, he promised, pay all. His master took pity on him, and released him, a term[5] which suggests that he was, as a result of the order, already in the hands of officers. Moreover he released, that is to say forgave, the 'loan'.[6] The story enters its second chapter. Going out[7] the minister found one of his fellow-ministers, who owed him a very small sum. He

[1] δοῦλοι means ministers. Jeremias, 212, cites examples of σύνδουλοι in 4 Ez (2 Esdr) iv–vi. Spicq at p. 54 n. 2 cites a host of authorities to this effect. See also those cited by the present writer when dealing with the Talents (p. 19 *sup.*) In Ptolemaic Egypt slaves could not be revenue farmers: *Rev. Laws*, col. 15 (B. P. Grenfell, *Revenue Laws of Ptolemy Philadelphus*, Oxford 1896). A. Steinwenter, *JJP* 15 (1965), 17–18, thought they *were* slaves as the treatment meted out to the 'hero' could hardly have been applied to a free man. But see below as to revenue contracts and regal rights in such matters.

[2] ἀρξαμένου δὲ αὐτοῦ συναίρειν. The next following word is προσήχθη according to BD, preferred by Aland in his *Synopse*. This is the appropriate expression, and, meaning 'introduced', is abundantly supported in literature. The far better evidenced προσηνέχθη has sacrificial overtones, and is therefore suspect. Jeremias, who accepts this reading, concludes from it that he must have been under arrest. If we accept the *lectio difficilior* with him we are, however, not obliged to assume this; indeed it is impossible since until the accounts are settled so important a minister cannot be under arrest. He is in fact arrested as soon as he confesses inability to pay. But what the word might well mean to imply is that he was previously in hiding or feigning illness and therefore was 'assisted' to be present on the appointed day (see Jewish parallels cited at p. 42 n. 1 below).

[3] ἐκέλευσεν. [4] καὶ ἀποδοθῆναι. [5] ἀπέλυσεν.

[6] τό δάνειον as all the best sources have it. For the implications see below.

[7] ἐξελθὼν δὲ ὁ δοῦλος ἐκεῖνος εὗρεν . . .

seized him, apparently by the throat, the conventional act of the creditor.[1] 'Pay whatever you owe!'[2] The debtor fell down and begged for time, in the same manner as the minister himself had done. But the latter refused, and put him in prison until he should pay what was owing. The other ministers who witnessed this complained to the king.[3] The king summoned the minister and complained to him in these terms: 'I have released all that debt to you, since you begged me (to show mercy towards you). Ought you not also to have had pity on your fellow-ministers, as I had on you?' The king in anger handed him to the gaolers until he paid his debt.[4]

The first problem concerns the enormous debt. Is it not impossibly large? Next, what was the point of ordering him and his effects and his family to be sold? Surely they would not be worth anything like the amount of the debt? Next, would a king release such a huge amount so capriciously? Further, why was the minister so violent with his colleague, or why did the others object? But the most serious problem is the behaviour of the king. He acts in anger, and yet this is supposed to depict the state of affairs as obtaining between man and God.[5] Worse still, he cancels the release which he had solemnly given. For an oriental monarch to rescind a decree was a very serious matter;[6] moreover the

[1] *Mishnāh*, B.B. X.8 (Danby, 382; Blackman IV, 227–8). Jeremias, 209. Billerbeck, *Kommentar* I, 799, had missed this. Incidentally, though not strictly relevant, it has been noted (J. Bonsirven, *Textes Rabbiniques* (Rome 1955), §§ 150, 1559, index 792; Jeremias, 209) that this second minister could not have been sold for the realisation of his debt, and Mekilta on Ex xxii.2 (Winter-Wünsche, 285) has been cited. But the rule applied only to sale for debts arising out of theft.

[2] The Greek idiom seems to be missed by Morton Smith, *Tannaitic Parallels to the Gospels* (Philadelphia 1951), 140. There is nothing *ironical* here.

[3] ἐλυπήθησαν σφόδρα και ἐλθόντες διεσάφησαν. It is desirable to note that this passage occurs not (i) to suggest that the king would act only on complaints; nor (ii) to indicate that without that sympathy the act would have been neutral; but (iii) to show that the king's actions were not capricious or despotic, but conformed to a pattern which the chief minister should have anticipated.

[4] 'Gaolers', or more literally 'torturers' (see *Note* at the end of this chapter).

[5] Mt xviii.23*a*, 35. Grotius and others have felt the behaviour of the king to be despotic. Indeed Dn vi.24 distinctly evokes recollection of the same tyrant at Dn ii.5, 12. On the subject of revocation of divine decrees Jewish tradition evidences contradictory opinions, yet the opinion, that in exceptional cases an unfavourable decree can be revoked (b. M.Ḳ. 16*b* = Sonc. 104. *Cf.* Gn xviii.20ff.; Ex xxxii.7–14; 1 K xxi.19, 29; Jon iii.10), itself betrays the basic conception that divine decrees are irrevocable (as indeed they may well be, given divine omniscience).

[6] οὐ βασιλικόν ἐστι ψεύδεσθαι: Pap. Berol. 13044 = Jacoby, *F. Gr. Hist.* 153 F 9 (cited below, p. 355 n. 3); *cf.* Plutarch, *Alex.* 64 (end) and b. Tamid 31*b*–32*a* = Sonc. 26–9; also the efforts used to avoid breaking the royal word at *Midrash on Psalms*, on Ps vi.2 (Braude I, 97). The point is worthy of emphasis, since, as Jeremias said at p. 210, there might be the recalling of forgiveness of sins, an altogether unpalatable notion, since God cannot be deceived as to the sinner's sincerity and cannot therefore be subsequently enlightened as is the king in our parable.

field being open for imposing on the minister other pains and penalties, it is not clear why the king should, even in anger, reopen, contrary to justice of the most elementary kind, a state of accounts which was already closed. If this is how God is going to behave, many readers must have thought, they would rather be ruled by anyone than by God. In the Old Testament God is depicted as repenting of promises he has made or of arrangements he has provided,[1] but these were always gratuitous. The justice of God is an attribute which has been so central to all religious thought stemming from the Near East that there appears to be something very wrong with this parable. But these problems can be solved if we understand what chapter of law is under discussion, and where the minister went wrong. The cause of his downfall is natural and human, and, seen in the proper light, all too pathetic.

THE LEGAL RELATION BETWEEN KING AND MINISTER

The first question is whether Jewish law is contemplated. If it is, some difficulties arise. But in fact it cannot be Jewish law as such. It will be recollected that Palestine along with many adjacent regions had been for years under non-Jewish rule. In matters of private law the Jewish law obviously prevailed, though some families may have thought it advisable to arrange their affairs in such a way that remedies might be obtained in a court administering any system of justice. In matters of public law the patterns had been set by Ptolemaic, Seleucid and derivative constitutions. Indeed at one period Jerusalem and the rest of Judaea had been under a kind of Ptolemaic–Seleucid condominium[2] with the taxes divided between the two Powers. The kings with whom the public were acquainted, either directly or by way of story and legend, were mostly Hellenistic rulers, and the tone will have been the same whether these were emperors, kings, princelings or other petty rulers who functioned in the time of Jesus or earlier.[3] Fiscal law was evidently not Jewish (for the Jewish state, for so long as it existed, had its own notions of public finance) but what then passed as cosmopolitan. We know a great deal about the Ptolemaic system, and what we know accords perfectly with what is alluded to in the parable. The behaviour

[1] 1 S xv.11, 35; Jr xviii.10. Repenting of evil is another concept, which hardly concerns us here. Because God is capable of an act of grace (as Jesus expects at Mk xiii.20 '. . . for the sake of the elect, whom he chose, he shortened the days') it does not follow that we accept from him an act of unpredictable despotism.

[2] Josephus, *Ant.* XII.iv.1 (154–5; Loeb edn, vii, 81).

[3] A. N. Sherwin-White, *Roman Society and Roman Law in the N.T.* (Oxford 1963), 135, *cf.* 134.

of the ruler, therefore, is not to be paralleled from the Jewish ethic, but from non-Jewish. Appropriately enough, Jewish parables based on the behaviour of kings (and they are many) rely on what actual kings actually were thought capable of doing, and there is nothing specifically Jewish about them: on the contrary their behaviour can be explained only by Gentile habits.[1] The author, wishing to tell of kings, refers to kings people know.

The minister was evidently the chief minister, because he was interviewed first. The size of his debt indicates that he was the greatest debtor to the king.[2] Incapacity to pay so large an amount does not seem so odd as the other's inability to pay the small amount. But both are explicable. The ministers' functions were tax-gathering. In order to gather tax one had to supervise and keep order in the area entrusted to one's rule. Rule and tax-extraction were more or less convertible terms. The idea is given succinctly but accurately at Lk xix.17 (which we have studied already): the servant who had been very successful in relatively straightforward business-operations is told, 'Well done, good servant; because you have been *faithful* in a very *little* context understand that you now have authority over ten cities'—a veritable Decapolis. The test, it seems, was adequate: a business head and, more particularly, faithfulness were required in both contexts. The responsibility was confided to an individual only upon the footing that he was able to perform the task. Normally sureties were taken from the applicant before he was appointed. Two tendencies operated together and were mutually hostile. Bidders bid for the appointment, and the highest bidder, if not disqualified, was appointed subject to his finding sureties.[3] If the sum was too large, and the successful applicant well known,

[1] A Tannaitic parable (a *midrash* on Dt x.17, Nb vi.26: b. R.h.Sh. 17*b* = Sonc. 70) utilizes an entirely non-Jewish institution. A man borrowed money from another swearing to repay by the life of the king. Such oaths made sense in the Hellenistic world. The borrower defaulted. The king forgave him the breach of his oath, but told him he must make this peace (if he could) with the creditor.

[2] But contrary to the general belief the amount is not fantastic. Spicq rightly shows that it is not (p. 54 n. 2). Jeremias's data do not conclude the question. The sum may have been chosen for three reasons: (i) a round figure; (ii) a vast amount; (iii) a sum beyond reach of suretyship (see below). But Joseph son of Tobias contracted for 16,000 talents for Coelesyria, Phoenicia, Judaea and Samaria (Jos., *Ant.* XII. iv, 4; Niese III, 82–3). For a huge sum (1,000 talents) see 1 M xv.31. Ptolemy Philadelphus obtained 14,800 talents from Egypt (Jerome *in Dan.* XI.5); Cicero thought Auletes, father of Cleopatra, took 12,500 talents (Préaux, *cit. inf.*, 424). Vast sums might become irrecoverable through loans to important but unsecured people: for an example see Jos., *Ant.* XVIII.vi, 3 (155–60). Alexander's army's debts amounted to 9,750 tal. (Plut. *Alex.*).

[3] For the whole system of assessment and appointment see Claire Préaux, *L'Économie Royale des Lagides* (Brussels 1939). Jos., *Ant.* XII.iv, 4 (Loeb edn, vii, 93–7) shows the procedure in Joseph's case.

sureties might be waived; for the higher the bid the less likelihood that sureties could be found.[1] It was in the king's interest to take the highest suitable bidder, but the highest bidder might be least well secured. It is certain from the structure of our parable that the first minister was without effective or any surety, and therefore had no defence if he was in default.

The situation in which he stood is easy to understand if one visualises the oriental set-up. The revenue farmer is normally a prestige-holding individual able to command obedience in the area for whose taxes he has bid (ἐπίσημοι, πρῶτοι καὶ ἄρχοντες: Jos., *ubi cit.*, §§ 1, 3). If he is powerful and does not fear the ruler's resentment, and if attachment of property and confiscation will fall on his fellow subjects rather than on him, he will neglect to pay the tribute due from him, as Onias did. If pressure is threatened in earnest what is he to do? He may do as young Joseph advised (rather optimistically?), namely go to the king in person and beg him to forgo (or concede) all the cash payments due, or at any rate part of them.[2]

The word δάνειον in our text (*v.* 27) is somewhat embarrassing (Jeremias understandably said 'Darlehn . . . was hier aber nicht paßt'). We have seen that it means 'loan'. It can hardly be a careless slip since the word is common. But the terminology of revenue practice could give rise to such locution. The minister, when he obtained his appointment, undertook to pay the amount settled at the date of accounting. He undertook to pay no other sum, neither higher nor lower. When the day arrived and the minister could not pay, a crisis occurred which is perfectly well known to the Ptolemaic revenue system. The style and method of the period is all too coarse.[3] There was no other step that could be taken than that which was taken. The minister was personally

[1] Joseph's comical experience points the facts beautifully (*ibid.*): τοῦ δὲ βασιλέως ἡδέως ἀκούσαντος . . . ἐρομένου δὲ καὶ τοῦτο, εἰ τοὺς ἐγγυησομένους αὐτὸν ἔχει δοῦναι . . . αὐτόν, εἶπεν, ὦ βασιλεῦ, σέ τε καὶ τὴν γυναῖκα τὴν σήν, ὑπὲρ ἑκατέρου μέρους ἐγγυησομένους, διδωμί σοί . . .συνεχώρησεν αὐτῷ δίχα τῶν ὁμολογοῦντων, ἔχειν τὰ τέλη.

Jewish *midrashim* point out that there are occasions on which suretyship is useless, either because the sureties themselves would need to be guaranteed, or because no practicable surety is available: see, *e.g.*, *Midrash on Psalms*, on Ps 8, § 4 (Braude I, 124).

[2] συνεβούλευσεν ἀπελθόντα πρὸς τὸν βασιλέα δεηθῆναι αὐτοῦ ἢ πάντων αὐτῷ παραχωρῆσαι τῶν χρημάτων ἢ μέρους. The verb παραχωρεῖν distinctly suggests 'yielding' to one in a position of strength. Our hero, asking for time, is more realistic.

[3] No excuse was accepted. P. Tebt. 703, 852, 853. Goods were sold if there was a deficit. P. Gradenwitz 3. The farmer could be imprisoned and his estate sold for default: P. Tebt. 772 (236); P. Lond. inv. 2308 (Préaux, *op. cit.*, 454–5). Préaux comments on this (446–7, 449): '... cette responsabilité en cascade suscite, entre les fonctionnaires, des relations inquiètes et brutales dont plusieurs lettres nous révèlent le ton (P. Tebt. 704, 751, 758, 759). Et nous verrons qu'elle aura, sur les mœurs administratives, une influence considérable...'

responsible, and he must be sold, likewise anything of his which served as his security. It is quite useless to argue whether Jewish law permitted the sale of wives and children.[1] The atmosphere of this type of business is Hellenistic revenue-practice. 'Pay what you owe or you and your family will be sold as slaves!'

Some scholars have thought our parable fanciful here, evidently forgetting what Diogenes Laertius (who lived about the end of the second century) put into the mouth of Bion of Borysthenes,[2] who lived some three centuries earlier. Bion, obviously with his tongue in his cheek, brings his unlovely autobiography to a climax: ἔπειτα ὁ πατὴρ παρατελωνησάμενός τι πανοίκιος ἐπράθη μεθ' ἡμῶν. His father, who was a *freedman*, fell down upon his obligations under the tax-farming regulations and was sold *with all his house*, *i.e.* 'with us', *viz.* his wife and children including Bion himself. The word παρατελωνησάμενος occurs only here: it is evidently a technical expression, meaning (with the τι) that he did not pay up the amounts for which he was accountable or for which he had engaged, because he had misappropriated, embezzled or defalcated to a certain extent in respect of revenues in his possession. Bion's father, given his freedom from slavery, had acquired some status as a (subordinate) revenue farmer, had failed to keep to the code and suffered the well-known penalty; for otherwise Bion would not have been bought by the orator whose death enabled the enterprising youth to commence his career as a 'philosopher'.

It might be argued that in our case the drastic order for sale was absurd, because the minister would not be worth much as a slave.[3] This is not the point. To extract money from a province or a group of provinces one needed specialised skill. Intimate detailed knowledge of persons and places, of weaknesses and loopholes, of tricks and methods, of conditions and contingencies, of men and their liabilities to pressure; all must have been available to this man, who had been appointed collector for a vast region. His agents, messengers, spies, would have formed a huge regiment. People with such talents and assets are not, in history, especially in the orient, ever discarded. Unless they are blinded or killed they will come up again elsewhere, either in their own

[1] (Jeremias refers to Sọṭāh III.8 (Billerbeck I, 798). Sifre Deut. XXVI (70b) on iii.23 Billerbeck, *ubi cit.*) and P. Fiebig, *Rabb. Gleichn.* (Leipzig 1929), 10 are correct, but do not lead to the conclusion aimed at, namely that the minister was insolvent in the popular sense, *i.e.* that he had no assets at all (which is most implausible). The formal order of sale would not be *executed* (as in that *midrash expressis verbis*) if the cash were forthcoming. Apart from common revenue practice, the references to wives and children may be intended also to draw on ancient Near Eastern folk-memory: Dn vi.24.

[2] Diog. Laert. IV.46 (Loeb edn, i, 425).

[3] Jeremias, 211.

persons or as tools of more ambitious people. Such a man's ill luck would not be a moral fault, and even if it were, moral faults in revenue officials have never counted for much in the East. Rather than that he should be actually sold as a slave someone somewhere would take him up and employ him, and he would reappear as the managing agent of the next appointee to the chief collectorship of the kingdom. But this was very unpalatable to a man who had wielded all but absolute power in provinces. He begged for remission.

It will now be evident why the word δάνειον is used. The stages were these: first he confessed inability to pay the agreed sum (though he might have been able to pay a part of it), and promised that if he were given time he could pay all. What he was proposing was that the debt should be carried on and added to the assessment for the current year. This was practical, for the ill luck, such as famines or rebellions, which had hampered his presenting in cash or bonds the total amount engaged for, might not hamper him in the current year; and secondly, the business transactions in which such ministers certainly engaged, and which had perhaps come to grief on account of dishonest merchants, pirates, or losses at sea, might well succeed, and with a vast capital one could, in those days, make astronomical profits.[1] His suggestion was that the king should loan him the amount due, the ten thousand talents, and he would be able to repay the whole, perhaps with interest (this is only vaguely hinted at). In general ministers kept the interest for themselves, since they were the capitalists who financed merchants out of the revenues of the current year. But if the king would forgo execution on him at that moment he would be able to make the king his partner in whatever profits he made. The proposition is not distinctly uttered, but it lies in the background, and it would be for the king to introduce the notion. Actually, believing the minister to be genuine, and that his inability to pay was due to causes other than dishonesty or inefficiency, or even the 'couldn't care less' attitude which Onias had adopted, and realising that it would be difficult to obtain an assessment of ten thousand talents out of the regions with an inexperienced man in charge of them, the king released him from his plight as a defaulting revenue-official, absolved him from his contractual or constitutional liability to be sold, and forgave him the total which, upon his default, was outstanding as a debt.[2] As soon as he ordered him

[1] On the partnership called '*iṣḳā*' see my study above, pp. 19–21. For high profits in international commerce see W. F. Leemans, *The Old Babylonian Merchant: His Business and his Social Position* (Leiden 1950); F. M. Heichelheim, *Ancient Economic History* I (Leiden 1958). The proportions given in the gospel parable of the Talents are not fanciful.

[2] *Cf.* L. Mitteis, *Reichsrecht u. Volksrecht* (1891), 479.

to be released the debt became, as the minister desired, a loan: immediately afterwards he released or made a free gift of it, and the minister was no longer obliged to pay that ten thousand talents. The miracle which Joseph, optimistically, suggested might happen in Onias's case if he bestirred himself actually happened in this story: kings could act in this way. The steps in our legal ideas are thus faithfully observed by that embarrassing word δάνειον.

The magnificent gesture was not impractical. To exact 20,000 talents might have cost the inhabitants much more than they would bear. Migrations and rebellions might result. The king was wiser than his minister: the minister might have foreseen this, but perhaps it exceeded his expectations, for the king could as easily have entered into any of a variety of compromises.

WHERE DID THE MINISTER DO WRONG?

In immediately imprisoning his own debtor, he enraged his colleagues who were also his debtor's.[1] Why? Was he not legally entitled to seize the debtor? The law, which we can assume without hesitation was not incompatible with the Jewish, certainly allowed this.[2] Then why the

[1] Jeremias refers to Ne v.6. For reasons stated at p. 33 n. 1 above σύνδουλοι should mean not merely any officials but those who were then in attendance for the revenue accounting, *i.e.* revenue-farmers.

[2] A question of importance. Research leans to the view that personal attachment for debt was known in Jewish law at the time: R. Sugranyes De Franch, *Études sur le Droit Palestinien . . . La Contrainte par Corps* (Fribourg 1946); F. C. Fensham at *Nov. Test.* 4 (1960), 1–2; B. Cohen, 'Civil bondage in Jewish and Roman Law', *Louis Ginzberg Jubilee Vol.* (New York, Am. Ac. Jew. Res. 1945, Eng. sec.), 113ff., an article reprinted at *JRL* I, 159ff.; E. Zingg, 'Das Schuld- und Vollstreckungsrecht... nach Moses', *Judaica* 16 (1960), 71–102, 156–71, 207–15; D. Nörr, 'Die Evangelien des N.T. und die sogenannte hellenistische Rechts-koine', *ZSS, r.A.* 78 (1961), 135ff. And this view is fully supported by the attachment of a servant for his master's debt by an innkeeper at Midr. R., Exod. XV.18 (on Ex xii.1) = Sonc. trans., 183 (cited below, p. 218). But Mt v.25, which is carefully written, raises doubts, and one wonders if all De Franch's evidence is valid for all the Near East including Palestine. Should not the debtor be brought to court first (there being no stipulation to dispense with this safeguard)? Spicq for this reason suggests the obligation must have been tortious (or delictual), and he cites *RIDA* (1958), 291–8; Mitteis, *Chrestomathie* (1912) LXXX, 59; Dittenberger, *Or.* II, 669, 15ff.; Taubenschlag, *Op. Min.* II, 135–41, and compares 2 K iv.1. Yet all this is beside the point. Whether a private creditor should take his debtor first before a court, or not, has no bearing on what a revenue official may be able to do. Farmers of revenue had powers overriding all private laws. See what Joseph says at Josephus, *Ant.* XII.iv, 4 on the point. Rights of execution passed with the collectorship or farm as a matter of course and his promise was nothing novel: καὶ τῶν ἁμαρτόντων εἰς τὸν οἶκον αὐτοῦ τὰς οὐσίας ἐκπέμψειν αὐτῷ, καὶ γὰρ καὶ τοῦτο τοῖς τέλεσι συνεπιπράσκετο.

fuss? The parable leaves us to assume that the colleagues, revenue-farmers all, were moral men outraged at a heartless deed. Were these people, the hardest people on earth, such hypocrites? No, it was a question of professional solidarity. This is an aspect of which the king will not have been unaware, but his own point of view is different. He is intent upon detecting signs of dishonesty or unreliability in his servants. He is anxious that his business shall go well at all events.

Many readers of the parable will feel that mercy and compassion are not a minister's normal attributes, and that it was unfair of the king to expect that the minister should imitate him. On the contrary the minister showed zeal and efficiency, indicating that for the future he expected to come up to scratch with his engagements. He meant to show with an auspicious start how he intended to go on. He would be no respecter of persons and would start with the first debtor he found, no matter how highly placed. Or so it would seem at first sight.

The fellow-minister who owed 100 den. was in that situation because the hero of our tale had not exacted it from him. The debt, which presumably had matured, was still owing through the chief minister's forbearance in the past. Why the seizing and imprisoning? Because the debt was unsecured. Why was it unsecured? Because it was so small, and the creditor was so rich and important it would be beneath his dignity to take a security for such a sum. The sums were chosen by the author of our parable in such a fashion as totally to exclude the possibility of a security, and so to indicate solely creditor-debtor relationships: the one debt was too large, the other too small.

The reason why the second minister could not pay at that moment was precisely because he was standing, as it were, in the queue of ministers about to present their accounts. He could have found security, without doubt, but all his available sureties were needed for his business with the king. After the accounting there would be discussion of the current year's assessment, and new engagements would be entered into. The ministers therefore needed their credit free in order to negotiate with the king at this, the most important day of their working lives. The act of the chief minister was due to his being emboldened by his own release. He had come off richer and more powerful than any. His king had shown him unprecedented favour, he was the more free to pursue his own interests, and to make his weight felt. The reaction after his interview with the king is surely part and parcel of the story. Because he had been released he was going to make sure that others did not escape. A rabbinical parable utilises the exact point.[1] Let us

[1] *Midrash on Psalms*, Ps xi.1 (Braude I, 159). See Ps cxviii.6. A king favoured a servant and the latter became puffed up and thought himself unassailable.

notice the king's words, 'Wicked servant, all that debt I have released to you, since you begged me. Ought not you also to have had pity on your fellow-servant, just as I had pity on you?' These words too clearly betray the purpose of the parable, and yet they make sense in the setting.

When the king released the enormous debt it was with the anticipation that the minister would lighten the burdens of the provinces and generally oil all the wheels for the good of the kingdom as well as himself. The king's motives, which should have been known to the minister, were not confined to the immediate beneficiary of his benevolence.[1] The release was for the good of the kingdom. The minister ought to have taken this as an instruction to deal lightly with all inferior debtors, the sub-contractors of the revenue, and others who had had difficulty in supplying their appointed sub-assessments. The purpose of the release was directly frustrated by the seizure of the fellow-minister. The latter was prevented from settling his accounts; and the fellow-subject's attachment of his person precluded the king's dealing with the man (if need be) as he had proposed to deal with the lucky chief minister himself. To attach for a private debt a man who is just about to settle accounts with the sovereign would be insolence in any creditor; it was much worse in one who himself was released in order to facilitate the more effective collection of the royal revenues. Thus the minister's defect was not mere pride or insolence, but failure to recognise that though released from his own debt he was still a servant.

Furthermore, the king had a moral right to call in all the debts owed to his minister when the latter was found unable to pay.[2] When he released the debt it is true that that right disappeared, but the relief of the chief minister should reciprocally have produced relief for the

[1] To issue execution might do more harm than good. Préaux, 515 (the king's long-term interests may be damaged). Kingly generosity to debtors is well evidenced in *midrashim*, and amongst those debtors contractors to produce revenue will have figured. Midr. R., Lev. XXX.7 (trans., p. 389): 'Let bygones be bygones; from now we shall commence a new account.' *Tanḥuma* 56*a* quoted by C. Schöttgen, *Horae Hebraicae* I, 155–6. See Ignaz Ziegler, *Königsgleichnisse der Midrasch* (Breslau 1903), 248 (Anh. lxxxvi, *Yalḳūṭ* I, 318) (a king sends money privily to a servant who is indebted to him and who is afraid to answer the summons to account).

[2] Irrespective, surely, of total insolvency in the popular sense of that word. *Shiy'ᵉbūd* of R. Nathan (Babyl. and Pal., *c.* A.D. 150): b. B.Ḳ. 40*b* = Sonc. 228 (relying on Nb v.7); Ḳid. 15*a*; Pes. 31*a*; Giṭṭ. 37*a*; Ket. 19*a*, 82*a*. Isaac Herzog, *Main Institutions of Jewish Law* II, *Law of Obligations* (London 1967), 209ff. G. Horowitz, *Spirit of Jewish Law*, 476–7. What is contended by the present writer is not that the developed *shiy'ᵉbūd* actually existed *temp. Chr.*, or that, if it did, it was relied upon even incidentally in our parable; but that the rule of equity and common sense which eventually secured a place for the rule in Jewish law as in other systems will have strengthened the picture which the parable paints.

reliever's debtors. The king did a great service for his minister: was the minister in return to squeeze the persons who were indebted to the king? Thus ingratitude as well as unfaithfulness could be laid at the chief minister's door. To take away from him his position, which is what the sentence amounts to, was therefore morally as well as legally just.[1]

It might be argued, as we said before, that it is unjust to rescind a decree. The debt was released, the king must abide by it. But we have already observed that that release was upon a clear understanding that the minister would continue as chief minister and would render accounts for his next assessment at the next accounting. It was specifically with a view to his continuing to serve that he was released. It was assumed he would be *faithful*. The minister accepted his release on those terms. He now shows ungratefulness, dangerous in the extreme in a chief minister, for a minister's ingratitude encourages rival claimants to the throne; and shows disregard for his master's financial welfare, which was the principal concern of all contemporary kingdoms. In what was apparently a very *little* matter he had shown himself unfaithful. He was doubly disqualified to hold his position, and must be degraded. Of course kings had the right to confiscate their ministers' property when they were dissatisfied with their services, or despaired of their loyalty—as Jewish law itself acknowledges.[2]

What then would become of the ten thousand talents? Friends, relations, hopeful subordinates might well rally round and save him; or it might be too late, for once a minister has fallen politically, in a kingdom where the king can nip disloyal tendencies promptly in the bud, no one may care to be associated with him. But the debt became exigible because of the failure to observe the terms in this conditional release.

THE MEANING OF THE PARABLE

'Forgive us our debts just as we forgive our debtors' (*cf.* Mt vi.14–15) fully depicts the attitude signified in the parable. Thus Mt xviii.35

[1] This would be fully comprehensible to the Gentile world governed by Roman law (as it is to their continental descendants). Donations are revocable under that law *propter ingratitudinem donatarii:* Justinian, *Corpus Iuris, Cod.* 8.16.10. We note that the king's generosity was decidedly not *ob causam*, nor *propter obsequia quae donationem merebantur* (which would have altered the position). Casuists would call this *error circa causam principalem* in so far as the king supposed the minister to be a faithful servant: Lessius, *De Iustitia et Iure* II, cap. 18, dub. 10; cap. 40, dub. 2.

[2] b. San. 48*b* = Sonc. 323–4 (Naboth's vineyard, 1 K xxi) as used by Maim. XI, III, v, 13 (trans., p. 109).

('Thus my heavenly Father also will do to you, if each of you does not release unto his brother from your hearts') applies the parable exactly.[1] An unsuccessful businessman trading in the business of life (*cf.* the parable of the Talents) may well throw himself on his employer's mercy, and with good hopes of success. It is in the employer's interests that honest failures should be encouraged. But this mercy must be sought with an open heart, and this means forgoing all claims to compensation from the employer's other servants. Forgive first and then you can be forgiven.[2] This is apparently illogical. Nothing but a simile or parable could be expected to be able to teach it. Paul puts the same point at Rm xiv.4, *cf.* 13. One must not purport to judge 'another's' servant. There is one judge. One can certainly complain to that judge about his servant's behaviour: this is in order. But if one does not rely upon his efficiency and capacity to execute justice one is slandering him. And one cannot slander him and ask for his mercy at the same time, for the points of view are irreconcilable. Those who ask for mercy, and forbearance, cannot at the same time treasure up resentment against their fellows, still less expect to exact vengeance. One particular type of vengeance is especially deprecated: that which sends victims to their account unprepared, hampered, hamstrung. This cannot be forgiven. Pursuit of vengeance may in certain cases (political, sectarian, international, as well as private?) hamper the guilty party in his own relationship with God. *V.* 35, looking back to *v.* 22 (*cf.* Gn iv.24) is appropriate. One might even ponder over the comparison between a sinful Jew and a sinful Gentile: the former being more heavily burdened with commandments (and therefore 'debts') might too readily assume that a Gentile's misdeeds against him came in an altogether different category. And it needed the parable to point out that however we think of God

[1] Jeremias raised with good reason the question whether Matthew confines the rule to Christian brothers, whereas originally it must have applied to everyone. But the notion of a merciless God (*cf.* Mt v.26 '... until you have paid the last penny'), fully brought out at Spicq, p. 61, leads in post-resurrection thought directly to the divine suretyship, whereby the severity of the judgement is indefinitely postponed while faith in the surety (Jesus) survives (see Chapter 17 below). This contrast between pre-resurrection and post-resurrection situations may remove the objection which inspired Jeremias to see in the words attributed to Jesus at the end of the parable merely a symbolic (*i.e.* no theological) significance. Jeremias (Eng. trans., p. 213–14) shows that Jesus teaches in this parable that mercy is in force in the Last Judgement. A. Schlatter's contention (Spicq cites his p. 560 at his own p. 61 n. 3) that the parable teaches the primacy of grace may thus, if only indirectly, turn out to be true.

[2] The reverse is suggested by N. Perrin, *Rediscovering the Teaching of Jesus* (London 1967), 126: '... The experience of God demands a response in terms of imitation of that experience in relationship to one's fellow men.' Though A. M. Hunter, *Interpreting the Parables* (London 1960), 70–1, links the parable with Mt v.7 ('Blessed are the merciful ...'), his explanation of the consequences of refusal to forgive is correct.

our indebtedness (to use the Jewish metaphor) is immeasurably greater to him than can ever be the indebtedness to us of any of our human enemies or wrongers. The parable seems to say that if we ask for mercy and have good reason to suppose, by our preservation, that our prayer has been answered, we should not be emboldened therefore to pursue private rights against other creatures of God who, through unexpiated crimes against us, have still an account to settle with God. We can upbraid them, and call upon them to repent and make restitution, but we must not interfere with their making their peace with God. And perhaps if we adopt towards them the attitude of forgiveness, especially and most relevantly when they ask for it (a rarer thing perhaps in this very secure world than it may have been in the time of Jesus when life itself hung by a thread), they may the more readily and more successfully pursue that task.

It is submitted that this method of exegesis, which utilises every aspect and detail of the parable, is preferable to those methods which select items for emphasis, and which, in any case, have been based upon partial understanding of the legal background to the story.

Parables about creditors forgiving long-standing debts are not, of course, rare in Jewish literature.[1] But it is asserted that no Jewish parallel exists for our parable. This is untrue. So close a parallel exists that it raises the question whether it has been influenced by the gospel. That doubt can however be repelled for the very good reason that the supposed author was notoriously indifferent (not to say hostile) to Christianity, and lived at a period when Christian *midrashim* were viewed with an indifference tending towards horror. R. ʿAḳiba, whose life overlapped with those of contemporaries of the apostles, is an authority on Jewish belief whom no one will question. His life and ideas are thoroughly well known, and this *midrash* accords so well with his undoubted teachings (in particular the celebrated metaphor of the divine business-house: ʾĀvot III.17) that it has every claim to be genuine. But even if it is not genuine the fact that it has been believed traditionally to be genuine tells us what we need to know. Briefly the *midrash* goes as follows:[2] The king is settling his accounts with a number of persons indebted to him who have given him security for their debts. Normally merchants did not do business with the king's

[1] See, for example, *Midr. R.*, Exod. XXXI.1 = Sonc. 378.

[2] Zuta B., p. 19 (Ziegler, 249–50, Anh. lxxxvii). See also *Midrash on Psalms* (Braude II, 46) on Ps 79, § 5. 'When a mortal owes 100 *minas* to his friend, and his friend says, "Give me my money", and he answers, "I have no money", what is there for his friend to do? He must go along! Not so the Holy One, blessed be He. He makes the soul pay . . . Isa. x.18.'

treasury or the king direct, but through the ministers,[1] and from this we guess that the debtors are revenue officials or farmers who have come to pay their assessments, which, as we have seen, are almost always run up, by auction, higher than turns out to be practicable. The *midrash* continues: all the debtors were in danger of losing their pledges, for all had defaulted. The king had it within his discretion whether to take in all the pledges. During the year one of the debtors had been attentive to the king, with acts, we suppose, of obedience, friendliness, etc. These acts, being independent of the contractual relationship, we know from our general acquaintance with the oriental mind and the nature of present-giving and the tensions which it sets up, must operate on the recipient and give rise to a tendency towards reciprocity. The *midrash* continues by saying that that debtor alone was relieved of the necessity to forfeit his pledges. The result, we know, would be to help him enormously in his work during the year then commencing. R. ʿAḳiba now gives the application of his parable. The attentions our king (God) needs, says he (citing Pr xxi.3), are acts of loving kindness and charity during this life. We see the point: by kindness ('mercy') to God's creatures, our 'fellow-servants', we deserve well of God and justify him in releasing to us the debts which legally he could oblige us to pay him. There is an unexpected connection between indebtedness to God and the obligation to show loving-kindness to his creatures which both the parable of the Unmerciful Servant and the parable of R. ʿAḳiba demonstrate, and the parable of R. ʿAḳiba may legitimately be scrutinised to explain the purpose of the parable of Jesus.

A NOTE ON THE 'GAOLERS' (*v.* 34)

The word βασανιστής at Mt xviii.34 has caused a good deal of doubt. The correct meaning 'torturer' (so Schneider in Kittel, *ThWzNT* I, 561) suggests that theological considerations (*cf.* Sap. Sal. XI.9–10) have already contaminated the parable text, with its tendentious 'Thus my heavenly Father also will do to you, unless. . . .' The discovery in *Suppl. Epigr. Gr.* VIII, 246, 8 (2nd cent.), cited by Bauer-Arndt-Gingrich, of βασανίζω ('torture') used in relation to a debtor from whom everything possible is to be exacted, clarifies the position. The idea is of *testing, thoroughly examining*, torture being a method of examination for judicial purposes (*cf.* Sir. iv.17). It is often urged that no amount of 'torturing' would extract the entire 10,000 talents as the text seems to suggest. But in reality, by applying severe methods of

[1] As must have been the case with Herod (Jos., *Ant.* XVI. ix, 1 (279f.), Niese IV, 42; Loeb edn, viii, 321). *Ibid.* XII.iv, 5 (Loeb edn, vii, 95–6: Joseph's business); Préaux, 456.

'examination', all the minister's personal assets would be discovered, and his relations, friends, and dependants would do all in their power to release him (or his blood would be on their heads).[1] The word is therefore entirely apt.

[1] Jeremias, 212 n. 21. Such torture was actually used for this very purpose in the ancient world, as is evidenced most pathetically by Philo, *De Spec. Legibus*, 'On pits', IV (trans. Yonge, iii, 342–3).

CHAPTER FOUR: PART ONE

The Parable of the Unjust Steward

THE NATURE OF THE PROBLEM

DISCUSSIONS OF Lk ch. xvi tend to show the need for background knowledge. Much as commentators disagree as to the meaning of the parable of the Steward,[1] all are agreed as to the embarrassment it has caused.[2] Attempts to connect the parable with earlier and subsequent matter have been few, and scarcely convincing. Because the parable has not been understood, keys to the connection between the

[1] Much of the literature is reviewed by H. Preisker, 'Lukas 16, 1–17', *Theol. Literaturzeitung* 74 (1949), 86–92. L. Fonck *Die Parabeln des Herrn* (Innsbruck 1902), 675–94 at p. 675–6, 690, gives sub-bibliographies including J. C. Schreiter, *Historico-critica explicationum parabolae de improbo oeconomo descriptio* . . . (Leipzig 1803); H. A. W. Meyer, *Kritisch-exeg. Kommentar über d. N.T.* (Göttingen 1898–1902), p. 528 n. 2. Michaelis, *Das hochzeitliche Kleid* (*cit. sup.*), 237–46. Practically no help is forthcoming from W. O. E. Oesterley (1936), H. K. Luce (1936), B. T. D. Smith (1937), J. A. Findlay (1937), P. N. F. Young (1937); F. C. Anderson in *Exp. Tim.* 59 (1948); J. A. Davidson in *Exp. Tim.* 66 (1954); or G. Paul in *Theol.* 61 (1958). While much is gravely misleading there are occasional flashes of light. An instinct to make out that our steward was acting righteously made itself felt in A. Wright, *Interpreter* (1911), 279–87; J. A. Findlay, *Jesus and his Parables* (1950), 82; and F. Davidson and others (eds.), *New Bible Commentary* (1954), 855. Others have since earnt H. Drexler's disapproval by doing the same (*ZNW* 58 [1967] 288 n.). And J. Coutts in *Theol.* 52 (1949), 54–60, correctly observes that there ought to be a progress of ideas from the Lost Sheep to Dives and Lazarus. The suggestion of W. L. Knox, *Sources of the Synoptic Gospels* II (Cambridge 1957), 93 is desperate indeed.

[2] Preisker, *op. cit.*, 'Kaum eine Parabel hat den Exegeten so viel Schwierigkeiten gemacht. . . .' A. Jülicher, *Die Gleichnisreden Jesu* (Tübingen 1910), 495. Th. Zahn (1913) cited by J. Kögel, 'Zum Gleichnis vom unger. Haushalter', *Beitr. zur Förderung christlicher Theologie* 18, vi (1914), 581; A. Rücker, 'Über das Gleichnis vom unger. Verwalter', *Bibl. Studien* 22, v (1912), 1–64. There is a recent treatment in J. Jeremias, *Die Gleichnisse Jesu*, 6th edn (in the Eng. edn, 1963, p. 45–8) which is involved and ingenious (he appears to have disapproved of the present treatment). A novel approach, taking hints from Syriac versions (which are, of course, not independent of our Greek sources), is that of the Abbé E. Larroche, *Bull. de Litt. Ecclés.* 54 (73), 1953, where a keen intelligence grapples with the appalling difficulties which ignorance of the fundamental facts must always produce.

verses which complete the chapter, and indeed between the parable, them, and the first two verses of the *next* chapter, have been overlooked.

As to the parable itself, the chief problems have been these: where does the parable end; who is the κύριος (master) of 8*a*;[1] what and whose is the reason commencing with the word ὅτι in 8*b*;[2] and why, above all, is conduct which appears on the face of it to be reprehensible, held up as instruction, if not example, for the disciples?[3] For the remainder of the chapter various explanations are given, but it is commonly thought that Luke derived parts from different sources, put them together 'with scissors and paste',[4] and perhaps hardly understood what he was using. A case for the reconstruction of the 'teaching' which *could* have inspired the material preserved here and in this order ought to be made out; this was impossible while the theme underlying the passages was unidentified. Naturally, the amount of reconstruction undertaken by Luke is unknown. But the burden of proof lies heavily

[1] Nicoll, Klostermann, Creed, Riggenbach, Schmid, Jeremias, G. Paul, C. K. Williams, and others believe it is Jesus. Ewald, Tillmann, Fonck, Kögel, Hüttermann, Osty, Delitzsch, the A.V. and R.S.V., Leaney and others incline to the steward's principal, the master. T. W. Manson and C. H. Dodd, however, are not firmly decided either way. Schmid and Staab are nearly correct in suggesting that it does not matter who it was that praised the steward; but in fact the master's behaviour is itself part of the parable, as Tillmann, *BZ* 9 (1911), 171ff., shows. If the 'master' is the steward's principal it is easier to account for the stylistic break at ὅτι in 8*b*. Yet it can be argued that this is no indication, since a mixture of direct and indirect speech is normal (Blass-Debrunner-Funk, *Greek Grammar* [1961] §470(2) is cited appositely by I. H. Marshall, *JThS*, N.S. 19 [1968], 617–9); and, properly, 1*b*–9 inclusive are unbroken as the sense plainly shows. Many have said, in effect, 'We like your "solution" but *pace te* we still think the "master" is Jesus!' Let them consider the following explanation of the parable: 'Just as a worldly man will be bound to praise his servant who, in a crisis, acts righteously when it is against his financial interests, so God will praise you if you observe righteousness with your worldly goods (*cf.* Mt vi.25–34, Lk xii.22–31) when no emergency forces you to do so.' Would this not be a neat teaching *a fortiori*?

[2] The main centre of contention here is whether the passage is an explanation of the master's praising, or of the steward's conduct. Every commentator will take this according to his view of the identity of the κύριος, and the nature of the steward's act. For Marshall's comment see last note.

[3] Most commentators think the steward's act was a 'criminal expedient' (Klostermann, *Luk. Ev.*, 1929; J. M. Creed, *Gospel acc. to St Luke*, 1930). Fonck tells some sad results of this view from the time of the Emperor Julian onwards: *op. cit.* 685–6. Tillmann, *op. cit.* 180–1, thought all the characters rascals, and many have seen the debtors as equally tainted with the steward. Preisker thinks the steward was committing himself utterly to *mammon*, but in fact the parable is a continuation of the theme started with the Lost Sheep and the Prodigal Son, and not in antithesis to it. Drexler (see below) makes the most of the steward's *Betrug*.

[4] See the views of Wernle and Harnack at Hüttermann, *Theol. Gl.* 27 (1935), 739ff. Jeremias, *op. cit.* 46, who thought that *mammon* had strictly nothing to do with the parable at all. In his view an existing interpretation has been expanded by a series of further interpretations (xvi.8*b*–13) (p. 108), and this has affected the parable itself. Jülicher, *op. cit.* 513.

upon him who asserts that Luke did not reproduce his material in a form, context, and sequence consistent with tradition still alive, and it is not impossible that that tradition embodied details which were originally more obviously and literally connected than they now seem to be, or than they were when Luke selected them. While an intelligible explanation of the order and content of the verses can be made out, and when reason is shown why the passages should have been remembered as they are reproduced in the chapter, the burden of proof becomes extremely heavy: and if it is not shifted we remain entitled to enjoy the presumption that naturally follows, namely that the material Luke supplies represents actual teaching of Jesus, from which, if properly understood, a connected message can be made out.

The attempt to reconstruct the connections between the passages after the parable of the Steward will be attempted in Part Two of this chapter. It will depend upon the interpretation given to that parable here. It appears that the 'teaching' proceeds from the parables of the Lost Sheep, etc., and the Prodigal Son, right through until after the denunciation of false teachers in xvii.2. The main theme appears to have an embroidery of minor themes, but the whole seems to fit together as a consistent piece of work, the artistry of which now becomes apparent for the first time. Since the treatment of the parable is independent of the conclusions drawn from it as to the construction of the whole chapter, it is given first.

SOURCES OF THE PARABLE

The parable must be seen first as an isolated story, and interpreted as if it had no connection with what precedes or follows. Its strength lies in its being an account of an imaginary, but practical incident. 'This is how people behave.' It is useless to explain the behaviour with reference to any lesson that might be supposed to have been intended to be conveyed by it. The story is partly based on Jewish economic practice, partly upon the Jewish Law, partly upon silent allusion to Pharisaic juridical theory, and partly upon normal public reactions to behaviour which takes those factual data into account.

It is surely useless to look to Roman or Greek law in this connection.[1] Jesus's hearers were hardly acquainted with either. It was many

[1] In the past much learning was expended upon the basis of this assumption, which is in fact unsound. See R. Sugranyes de Franch, *Études sur le Droit Palestinien à l'Époque Évangélique, (i) La Contrainte par Corps* (Freibourg 1946). Professor Jean Dauvillier occasionally verged unhappily near to this position: see his 'La *litterarum obligatio* des pérégrins . . .', *Rev. Hist. de Droit Fr. et Étr.* (1946–7), 136–8; 'La Parabole du trésor et les droits orientaux', *Rev. Int. des Droits de l'Ant.* (3rd ser.) 4 (1957), 107–

years afterwards that comparative legal studies got into their stride in Palestine, and these revealed the utter incompatibility of Greek and Jewish practice in precisely the contexts with which we are concerned here. This must be emphasized, because it explains why non-Jews had to search hard to find an explanation for the parable, why some Christians misunderstood its meaning, and (perhaps) why some sources of the Gospels omitted it entirely, or reproduced it in such fashion as to be unsuitable for general publication in the Greek gospels. Why Luke retained it without providing the key to the meaning is not entirely clear. It may be that he followed his source minutely and was advised that the parable could not be omitted without damaging what followed and was more easily understood. Or it may be that he understood the parable in one of the imaginary interpretations which had influence in earlier centuries. The parable in fact is a jurist's gem: it has a large element of humour in it; it is constructed to reveal the essential weakness of Pharisaic thinking and practice; and must have appealed to both the educated and the simple listener, its humour and its learning clinching the message in an unforgettable manner. The titles of law which were in question were well known to the small businessman and anyone who had occasion to deal with him, let alone more skilled citizens and farmers, and in fact provided fascinating topics for scholastic argument.

The keys to the problem lie in the Jewish law of agency and in that relating to usury. Neither was quite simple, but the second was truly controversial and complex. The notoriously difficult passages of the tractate *Baba Metsia* let us directly into the questions which were still agitated in Jesus's time, and show us as established rules propositions some of which were already well settled then, while others must still have been open to substantial doubt. Jesus was relying upon what was agreed, not upon the views of one particular teacher, of a school or sect. And what was agreed was the law of the Jewish State.

15. And the same may be said of D. Nörr (cited above, p. 40 n. 2, and also in his lecture, 'Civil law in the Gospels', *Irish Jur.*, 1966, 328–40), though he is more cautious. His hypothesis of a 'crypto-law' underlying the formal Jewish and imperial laws is a fruitful notion, deserving further development. In an extraordinary publication Walter Erdmann, who admitted that the Jews retained their native system at least until the time of Vespasian, spent enviable learning upon our parable upon the totally unwarranted assumption that Roman law was applicable: 'Ein römischer *procurator omnium bonorum* in Judäa z. Z. Christi?', *Z. Sav. St., rom. Ab.*, 64 (1944), 370–6. Mitteis, *Reichsrecht und Volksrecht* (Leipzig 1891), 33f. is actually cited to support the view that Jewish law alone was in force. A. T. Robinson, *Luke the Historian . . .* (New York 1920), did well to be cautious. See the interesting legend of the Roman commission to discover what the Jewish law contained in b. B.Ḳ. 38*a* = Sonc. 215, and compare the discussion at B.Ḳ. 113*b* = *ibid.* 667–8.

THE SOLUTION TO THE PROBLEM OF THE PARABLE

We shall patiently look through the law of Agency, so far as it relates to the parable, the law of Usury, the practice which had grown up as a result of the latter, and then the legal positions of the master (or principal), and the steward (or agent), the contracts into which the latter had entered, and the nature and effect of his final acts.

Agency

The three great maxims of the Jewish law of Agency (*sh*^e^*liyḥūt*)[1] are:

1. *sh*^e^*liyḥo shel 'ādām kemoto*: A man's agent is like himself.[2]

2. *'eyn 'ādām shāliyaḥ lid*^e^*var 'averāh*: There is no agency for wrongdoing.[3]

3. *ḥazāḳāh she sheliyaḥ 'oseh sh*^e^*liyḥūto*: It is presumed that an agent executes his commission.[4]

We must assume that the agent has been properly appointed, and that his appointment and authority are not in dispute between him or his master, and third parties. Once appointed, anything done by him within the scope of his agency binds his master or principal.[5] For that reason he must have the legal capacity which his master has.[6] The identification between agent and principal is complete—and this has a theological importance since the word for 'agent' is the original from which the word ἀπόστολος (apostle) was derived. But there is one significant exception. In order that a wrongdoer might not hide behind superior authority, the Jewish Law provides that, if the principal orders his agent to do something which is forbidden by the law, in almost

[1] On Jewish agency see L. M. Simmons, 'The Talmudic law of Agency', *JQR* 8 (1896), 614–31; M. Cohn, 'Die Stellvertretung im jüdischen Recht', *ZVR* 36 (1920), 124–213, 354–460; L. N. Dembitz, *Jew. Encycl.* (1925), art. 'Agency, Law of' (1, 232–3); I. H. Levinthal, *Univ. Jew. Encycl.* (1948), art. 'Agency, legal' (1, 115–17); Maim. XII, IV cited below from I. Klein's trans.; I. Herzog, *Main Institutions of Jewish Law*, 2nd edn, 1967, II, ch. x; G. Horowitz, *Spirit of Jewish Law* (New York 1953), ch. 33.

[2] b. B.M. 96*a* = Sonc. 555; B.Ḳ. 113*b* = Sonc. 667–8; Ḳid. 41*b*–42*a*, 43*a* = Sonc. 216; Nazir 12*b*; Ned. 72*b*. Horowitz, *op. cit.* 538.

[3] b. Ḳid. 43*a* = Sonc. 214–15; B.M. 8*a*, 10*b* = Sonc. 37, 56–7. Shammai (*temp. Chr.*) thought that the principal would be liable by the laws of Heaven and compared 2 S xii.9, but his view was a minority view. Simmons, 623; Horowitz, *op. cit.* 545–6.

[4] b. Erub. 31*b* = Sonc. 219. Simmons, 631; Horowitz, *op. cit.* 556; Cohn, *ubi cit.* 374f.

[5] Horowitz, *op. cit.* 551; Cohn, *ubi cit.* 177f., *cf.* 354f.

[6] A heathen, and a slave, have for various purposes defective capacities to be agents of a Jew. Horowitz, *op. cit.* 539–40.

every case the agent, if he does it, carries the sin on his own shoulders,[1] and in so far as the offence is one of which the civil court takes cognisance the punishment (if any) must be suffered by him and not by his principal. In such cases, we are told, there is strictly no agency at all. If a particular act is wrong by the law, but not recognised as punishable or otherwise cognisable by the court, the agent, if he is careless about his moral welfare and the force of public opinion, may prove a very useful servant for the principal, who can thereby take advantage of his agent's wrongdoing without fear either of sin or of liability to a civil penalty.[2]

The agent may, within the scope of his mandate or commission, fix upon his principal liabilities, just as he may earn for him profits, which were not precisely authorised by the master. So long as his ostensible agency lasts he can bind his master in relation to third parties, and if the two quarrel over loss or profit the law sets out rules for their division.[3] In most cases, an agent with general, or universal, authority could saddle his principal with liabilities and escape personal loss.[4]

The classic example of the agent was not the middleman functioning in the market-place, but the messenger or representative sent to carry a letter of divorce, or to effect a betrothal, on the principal's behalf. The priest is often spoken of as an agent, but[5] he is God's and not man's. The essential quality of an agent is trustworthiness, and wide discretion was inherent in the appointment. No one confused the agent with the paid factor or broker,[6] and no agent was remunerated—he was merely compensated for his expenses.[7] As a result the position was a fiduciary one, and not contractual in the strict sense. Incompetence,

[1] b. B.M. 10*b* = Sonc. 56–7; *cf. ibid.* 71*b* (*ibid.* 413); Ket. 98*b* = Sonc. 626. The numerous distinctions, depending, as some thought, upon the question whether the agent would alone derive pleasure from the act, are irrelevant for our purpose and need not be detailed. For a very special exception, of no relevance here, see Me'il. 20*b* = Sonc. 78–9. Simmons, 624.

[2] A steward could be a means of evading a spiritual penalty, where a husband performs through him duties he has forsworn: b. Ket. 70*b* = Sonc. 436; *Mishnāh, ibid.* VII, 1, where Danby's trans. 'guardian' (p. 254) might mislead.

[3] b. Ket. 85*a* = Sonc. 537; *ibid.* 98*a–b* = Sonc. 625; B.Ḳ. 102*a–b* = Sonc. 593. Maim. XII, IV, i, 5, 209; Horowitz, *op. cit.* 552–3.

[4] Cohn, 144; see also *ibid.* 362f.; Levinthal, 115; correspondingly the principal was not liable for harm sustained by the agent in carrying out his commission: Horowitz, *op. cit.* 549.

[5] The *shāliyaḥ, shāluaḥ* (agent) is literally a messenger, 'one sent'. On the priestly origin of agency, which is an agency for God and not for men (Ḳid. 23*b* = Sonc. 113), see B.M. 71*b* = Sonc. 414, referring to Ḳid. 41*b*.

[6] A broker is *ṣirᵉṣūr*, a paid agent. The difference is brought out in Maim. *ubi cit.* ch. ii.6, trans., p. 213; Ḥoshen Mishpaṭ, paras. 182–4 (see Dembitz, *ubi cit.*). An attorney (for purposes of litigation) was likewise distinct: the *harsha'āh.*

[7] Levinthal, *ubi cit.*; Cohn, *ubi cit.* 142.

misuse of discretion, negligence, and even downright swindling could not raise against the agent an action for debt, nor could the criminal law be brought into play against him. At most he could be compelled to restore what he had taken from his master (if anything) by way of robbery. The law was in any case peculiarly weak in respect of robbery and fraud,[1] for even in Jesus's time and long afterwards it was believed that the *Torāh* omitted to punish robbery because it was desirable that the robber should make restitution out of his own sense of moral responsibility. Thus even a swindling steward could not be punished by any other means than (i) the heaping up of reproaches, and blackening of his character; and (ii) dismissal by unilateral act on the master's part.[2] For this reason care would be used in selecting agents, especially agents with wide or universal authority, such as stewards of their households. Such factotums were usually slaves,[3] but in such a case their authority was limited, for the slave was not 'as the master', and could not do many things which the master might wish done through an agent:[4] hence a free man could be employed as steward, and care would be taken to try to prevent his living by defrauding his master.[5] His 'compensation' consisted in the enjoyment of his master's assets, so that his master's prosperity led directly to his own. The steward was called *ben bayit*, literally, 'child of the house',[6] and he was thus emotionally as well as economically treated as a member of the household. Loyalty and efficiency were normally secured by these means.

It is already apparent that if a steward wanted to release debts owed to his master he could effectively do so while his stewardship subsisted. The debtors could rely on the master to abide by the steward's act, unless he could prove that it was outside the steward's authority.[7] This

[1] H. E. Goldin, *Hebrew Criminal Law and Procedure* (New York 1952), 55–6; Horowitz, *op. cit.* 605f., 615f.

[2] Maim. XII, IV, i, 5, p. 209; Cohn, *ubi cit.* 144; Levinthal, *ubi cit.* 116.

[3] See references gathered by O. Michel in *ThWzNT* V (1954), 151–3, s.v. οἰκονόμος.

[4] See above, p. 52 n. 2.

[5] Note the comment of R. 'Eleazar on 2 K xii.16 in B.B. 9*a* = Sonc. 40: even where there is perfect confidence one must know precisely what one entrusts.

[6] O. Michel, *ubi cit.* It is interesting to see that *ben bayit ne'emān* 'faithful steward' is almost a technical term. Billerbeck gives also the equivalent *gizᵉbār* or *gizᵉbārā'*, but this seems to mean 'manager', 'treasurer' (Jastrow). Delitzsch gives *pāḳiyd*, which suggests 'functionary', 'official'. He was definitely more than an ἐπίτροπος, in spite of P. Fiebig, *Die Gleichnisreden Jesu im Lichte der Rabbinischen Gleichnisse* (Tübingen 1912), 83 and Solazzi's comments on P. Freib. 9 (discussed by Erdmann *ubi cit.*, p. 50 n. 1 above) in *Aegyptus* 5 (1924), 1–19. *Cf.* B.M. 96*a* = Sonc. 556 and the typical steward of Jewish history, Joseph, and also Obadiah.

[7] Roman hearers of the parable would probably know that at Roman law the principal is bound by the acts of his agent whom he has not repudiated publicly or whose authority he has not openly revoked: Ulpianus at *Dig.* 14.3.11, 2–4. This is common sense. Domat, *The Civil Law in its Natural Order* I.16.3, 9 (trans. Strahan [1722] I, 242).

was a difficulty, in view of the presumption which implies not only that the agent does and has done what his original commission expressed, but that what he has done is in fulfilment of his commission. Without such a presumption no one would deal with a man through his steward.[1] This would be extremely inconvenient in matters far beyond commerce. A steward's authority would in any case be notoriously of the widest. His capacity to represent the master's needs and whims would be comprehensive. If the master detected the steward in an act which he believed he might prove (if it were worth his while) to be outside the steward's ostensible authority, it was open to him to ratify it and so remove all possibility of doubt,[2] and all fear on the steward's part that he had forfeited his position.

Our steward was an agent possessing the most comprehensive authority. He had been inefficient and possibly dishonest[3] in his control over the household, whence his title 'unjust', and his master characteristically upbraided him and dismissed him. The dismissal was to operate from the moment when the steward cleared his accounts, that is, gave an account of the state of the property when he last rendered account, of income and disbursements, and the present totals. This account would take time to prepare, and was essential for the purpose of enabling another man to be taken on as steward.[4] Our steward would leave with as little as he first brought with him, save items which might pass his master's scrutiny. His social equals, other stewards, would not welcome him; those who had dealt with him as steward in the past would either scorn him or rejoice at his fall; and re-employment in a similar capacity would be possible only far enough away for news of his dismissal not to have been heard. That would require capital, and good fortune. His situation and predicament are clear. Good will, on a generous scale, he must try to win.

[1] See Horowitz, *op. cit.* 555.

[2] This is an invariable characteristic of laws of Agency. Even where the agent's authority is strictly outlined in his document of appointment (as often in Greco-Egyptian agencies) an excess of his appointment could be remedied, it is believed, by the principal's adopting the act whether specifically or by conduct. For instances of the application of this principle in Jewish law see Horowitz, *op. cit.* 540–1.

[3] Fonck (685) and others (but not Jülicher, 498, nor Kögel, 583) rightly observed that the unrighteousness or untrustworthiness of the Unjust Steward was his characteristic *before* the last dealings with the Debtors. The case is paralleled by that of the Unjust Judge, Lk xviii.6, whose act upon which Jesus places emphasis was in fact as righteous as was our steward's. This partly answers those who stumble at xvi.8: ἐπῄνεσεν ὁ κύριος τὸν οἰκονόμον τῆς ἀδικίας. The interesting and original suggestion of Sophie Antoniadès, *L'Év. de Luc* (Paris 1930), 376f., that ἐπῄνεσεν . . . τ ν οἰκονόμον τῆς ἀδικίας means 'praised the steward *for his dishonesty*' (*cf.* Blass-Debrunner [1954], § 178, p. 115; Robertson, *Grammar of the Greek N.T.* [1934], 511) is shown by the context to be wrong.

[4] E. Klostermann, *Das Lukas Ev.* (Tübingen 1929), 162. The steward was not being given an opportunity to prove his innocence, as Staab suggested.

Usury

Doing his worldly duty by his master, the steward had been lending at interest to fellow Jews. The master was a 'rich man';[1] the choice of description tells us that he did not rely upon simple exchange for the maintenance of a household large enough to demand the employment of a steward—so lending at interest was more or less expected of the latter, if not actually authorised. But this transgressed the steward's moral duty. He could not hide behind his master, as we have seen, for the law of Agency prevented this as effectively in moral as in legal contexts. The hard times, the poverty of the people squeezed by the Romans for taxes, by the Temple for first fruits and other dues, and by the priests for tithes,[2] the consequent rebellion against moral commandments not specifically enforced by the courts, and the general indifference in some well-known producing areas to the sentence of excommunication which the Pharisees' rabbis would otherwise have pronounced against them,[3] all led to men being prepared to postpone a consideration of the moral risks they ran by flouting the law of God. Intending borrowers, after all, press for advances to be made to them, and if they are in need they are notoriously indifferent to usurious terms until the day of repayment awakens their conscience on such matters.

Because of the nature of the law of usury, and the difference between divine and human law, the steward occupied two positions simultaneously, and it is essential for our purposes to observe these independently and again to see the force of each in relation to the man's dealing with the debtors.

The law of God, according to the rabbis of the Pharisees, provided by direct enactment that loans at interest by Jews to Jews were unlawful.[4] The usurer was like a robber, and the two are often spoken of

[1] Jesus distinguishes his characters carefully. He could perfectly well have said 'merchant', 'banker', 'money-lender', 'prince', etc., if he had wanted to do so: there are, after all, ample instances of his doing so in appropriate cases. Jülicher rightly saw (II, 500) that this was not a professional money-lender. Erdmann feels sure he was a Roman *Handelsherr*! Both parts of this description are false. He was most probably supposed to be a well-to-do citizen living in a city at some distance from the estate which may have been his ancestral home, and he was rich in any sort of wealth, and drew his income from any miscellaneous sources of profit that any hearer of the parable would be likely to imagine. That he was primarily and personally engaged in high finance, or that he was a slothful 'oriental' luxury-lover are both probably the sort of exaggerations which Jesus would not expect his hearers' imaginations to harbour.

[2] Baron (who emphasises this aspect of contemporary life in Palestine), *op. cit.* I, 272, 280.

[3] *Ibid.* 278.

[4] Dt xv.7f.; xxiii.20f.; Ex xxii.2; Lv xxv.36f. J. Hejcl, *Das alttestamentliche Zinsverbot im Lichte der ethnologischen Jurisprudenz sowie des altorientalischen Zinswesens* (Freiburg

in like terms.[1] In one striking passage in the Talmud we find the rabbis agreeing that God's commands are expressed in a particular manner because he is able, in those connections, to distinguish between the apparent and the real, and to condemn the robber and the usurer whom the laws of man cannot always reach.[2] The wickedness of usury was so apparent, and so relevant in a society which still preserved characteristics of an ancient agricultural economy and which was suffering notable inequalities of wealth on account of native misgovernment and Roman exactions, that the rabbis applied here their general maxim of erecting 'a barrier round the law',[3] so that the pious Jew might know when he was within the verge of incurring the sin which was unambiguously denounced in the law. Here is the kernel of our question. Was their learning appropriate and adequate? Some of the rabbis' ordinances were almost fantastically apprehensive of 'increase'.[4] Their apprehensions were justified by the fact, which can hardly be doubted in view of the practice of a few well-to-do rabbis themselves,[5] that Jews who were enticed into money-lending or credit-transactions on a large scale used, as they still do and their Muslim cousins have appar-

[1] Tem. 6*a*–*b* = Sonc. 32–4; B.B. 90*b* = Sonc. 372–3 citing Am viii.7; B.Ḳ. 94*b* = Sonc. 548–9; j. B.M. V.13 (Schwab X, 127–8). On the word *gazlan* see Horowitz, *op. cit.* 613.

[2] Lv xxxv.36, 38; Nb xv.38, 41; Lv xix.36 as interpreted by Raba in B.M. 61*b* = Sonc. 366–7. It is important to remember that the *Torāh* prescribes no *punishment* for taking interest as such.

[3] Moore, *op. cit.* I, 33. *Mishnāh*, 'Āvot I, i; Berakot I, i (Danby, 2, 446); b. Ber. 4*b* = Sonc. 13. The doctrine of the fence (*s^eyāg*) is based on Lv xviii.30, but it is not confined to Pharisees: see *CD* X.14–17 (Lohse, 87; Vermès, 112). The doctrine is well discussed in J. Weingreen's 'The case of the woodgatherer (Num xv.32–36)', *VT* 16 (1966), 361–4. See references at p. 58 n. 3 below.

[4] b. B.B. 86*b*–87*a* = Sonc. 353–4. A very full discussion is at B.M. 61*b*–70*a* = Sonc. 368–407; B.Ḳ. 103*a* = Sonc. 598.

[5] See the behaviour and arguments of R. Papa and R. Naḥman, the one a great businessman and the other a somewhat conceited 'notable' (B.M. 66*a* = Sonc. 387), and Raba's comment on the subject: B.M. 65*a*, 68*a* = Sonc. 383, 396. R. Ḥama hired out his coins *in specie per diem* (*ibid.* 69*b* = Sonc. 403). For a general comment on rabbis who made (usurious) mock advance-purchases because they 'wanted a supply of good wine' (!) see B.M. 73*b* = Sonc. 424–5.

i. B. 1907). There is a vast literature on usury. See below, p. 62 n. 1. See references cited in H. L. Strack, 'Wucher bei den Hebräern', *Realencyclopädie f. prot. Theol. und Kirche*, 3rd edn, XXI (1908), 518–21; and Bernfeld, Marcuse, and others cited in S. Eisenstadt, '*En Mishpaṭ* (*Repertorium Bibliographicum* . . .) (Jerusalem 1931), 309–11. L. N. Dembitz, *Jew. Encyc.*, art. 'Usury', XII, 387–90. J. D. Eisenstein, *Ozār Dīnīm u-Minhāgīm* (New York 1917, repr. 1938), art. *Ribbit*, 380–1. E. L. Globus, 'Law of Usury up to the Close of the Talmud' (Heb.), *Ha-Mishpaṭ* II, i–ii (1927), 23–43. E. Neufeld, 'The Prohibition against Loans at Interest in Ancient Hebrew Laws', *HUCA* 26 (1955), 355–412. Maim. XIII, III, iv–x, cited from J. J. Rabinowitz's trans. (1949). S. Stein in *JThS*, N.S. 4 (1953), 161–70.

ently always done,[1] tricks and devices to avoid the applicability of the biblical injunctions.[2]

Even when the Sadducees were powerful in government circles it is possible that only loans with directly stipulated interest could be attacked in a civil court, while those who were concerned with such transactions in any capacity might be subjected to social penalties. By Jesus's time the Pharisees were, though not in political control, vocal everywhere. Their ordinances supplementing and even, on occasion, contradicting the *Torāh*,[3] might, one supposes, have strengthened numerous courts' arm against usurers. Yet such, perhaps characteristically, was not the Pharisees' approach. There was, in their view, and there ought to be, a vast gulf between usury in the courts and usury in conscience.[4] Society and morality unequivocally condemned conduct

[1] The phrase *heyter 'iṣḳā'* (see above, p. 21) is too well known amongst modern Jewish businessmen to require references—it is a fiction of partnership. The general expression *ha'ᵃrāmat ribiyt* (B.M. 62*b*) is referred to as a provision *in fraudem legis* by B. Cohen, *Mordecai M. Kaplan Jub. Vol., Eng. Sect.* (1953), p. 123 n. 92 (reprinted at *JRL* i, p. 45 n. 92). The literature on Islamic fictions and tricks (*Kniffe* in German, *ḥiyal* in Arabic) is very large. See J. Schacht, 'Die arabische ḥijal-Literatur . . .', *Der Islam* 15 (1926), 211–32, where in our present connection reference is made to Juynboll, *Handbuch*, 274ff.; Sachau, *Muhammed. Recht*, 281; al-Ḥaṣṣaf, ed. Schacht, 65, 1ff. There is a reference in Abū Ḥātim Maḥmūd ibn al-Ḥasan al Qazwīnī, *Das Kitāb al-ḥijal fil-fiqh* (*Buch der Rechtskniffe*), ed. and trans. J. Schacht (Hannover 1924), 16–17 (IV, 15). Schacht's article *Ribā* in the *Encycl. of Islam* (III, 1148–50) is invaluable. See also Michaux-Bellaire, 'L'usure', *Arch. Marroc.* 27 (1927), 313–34; Ali Khan, 'The Moh. laws against usury and how they are evaded', *J. Comp. Leg.* 11 (1929), 233–44; Anwar Iqbal Qureshi, *Islam and the Theory of Interest* (Lahore 1946).

[2] On devices see p. 61 n. 1 below and the Christian 'straw man' intermediary described in J. J. Rabinowitz, 'Some remarks on the evasion of the usury laws in the Middle Ages', *Harv.Th.R.* 37 (1944), 49–59. The manner in which Josephus summarises the Law in the first cent. (*Ant.* IV.viii.25) indicates that its reason was racial solidarity and religion—not even food or drink may be lent at usury; one must not derive a profit from the (mis-)fortunes of a ὁμόφυλος; one should lend expecting as reward the borrower's thanks and God's recompense. This excludes, evidently, commerical undertakings from its purview.

[3] b. Yev. 90*b* = Sonc. 614–15; with a reference to 1 K xviii.31f. Moore, *op. cit.* I, 57–65, citing Jos., *Ant.* XIII, x, 5f. On the strictness of interpretation during the procuratorial period see B.M. 30*b* = Sonc. 188–9. It has been suggested that the period of Christ coincided with a tendency to stretch the court-law in the direction of strictness (apart from the Pharisaic tendency always to mitigate punishments), and that therefore there might have been a movement towards tightening up the court-law relative to usurious contracts; but of this in fact no evidence has come to light.

[4] Globus, *ubi cit.* 41 (lines 3–4): 'dust' is forbidden in the Courts of Heaven, though one may be glad that it is not forbidden in the *Torāh*. It is not the duty of the court to force people to obey the spirit of the law. According to Raba the debtor is entitled to delay paying 'dust of usury', for it is not binding upon him in conscience. For a similar contrast between legal freedom and liability to Heaven see Ḳid. 42*b* = Sonc. 212: 'he who sends forth a conflagration by a deaf mute. . .'. The problem regarding usury was of very long standing, and it must be remembered that experience of the practices of the Babylonians and other ancient Near East peoples must have shown

which the courts were powerless to punish. In one view it was ill-advised, as well as blasphemous, to attempt to supplement the provisions concerning punishment. All the Pharisees, so far as we can tell, were agreed that directly stipulated interest (biblical usury), once paid by the debtor by the operation of a lien, or under duress, could be recovered with the aid of the civil court, which could force the lender by flagellation if necessary to pay back what he had wrongfully taken.[1] This was a personal application of pressure to the lender-usurer, and if he died before restitution the interest which he had taken was not tainted so far that his heirs could not obtain it, and they were not themselves bound to make restitution even if they knew that the money was interest.[2] The reason is plain: the usurer, like the robber, must make restitution for fear of Heaven, and the court's power in this case to apply pressure is merely an adjunct to or possibly effectuation of the biblical requirement that the usurer should be enabled to live once again on terms of social approval with his debtor.[3] All this (we have seen) applied only to *directly stipulated* usury, for example a contract expressed in terms of *x* denarii to be repaid after one year at the annual rate of 1¼ den. for every denarius lent, or *x kor* of wheat at the annual rate of 1¼ *kor* for every *kor* lent.

Now we inspect the Pharisees' 'barrier'. Their invention was 'dust of usury', *'āvāḳ ribiyt*. This category of offence is extremely interesting and it cannot be investigated elaborately here. There is no mention of it in our parable, but we must understand it if we are to share the attitude of mind, if not all the information available to, Jesus's hearers. The orthodox definition indicates that the Pharisees regarded any breach of a 'dust' prohibition as nearly as bad as a breach of a major, biblical, prohibition.[4] The purpose of the 'dust' concept was to enable

[1] R. Meir's view that directly stipulated usury was recoverable by the debtor who paid under protest or duress *together with the principal* is not the final view: b. B.B. 94*b* = Sonc. 392–3; *cf.* the view of R. Yanai in j. B.M. V.1 (Schwab X, 115f.); b. B.M. 72*a* = Sonc. 416 and following.

[2] b. B.M. 61*b*–62*a* = Sonc. 368–70; B.Ḳ. 94*b* = Sonc. 548–9, 112*a* = Sonc. 654; j. B.Ḳ. X.1 (Schwab X, 77). The present writer knows pious Muslims who do not touch interest accruing on their bank deposits, but leave it there for their heirs.

[3] Tem. 6*a*–*b* = Sonc. 32–4.

[4] Eisenstein, *ubi cit.* 380, citing Jonathan Eiveshütz. The definition of 'dust' given by

the way to evade the *Torāh* long before the Greeks could have supplied precedents. Pr xxviii.8; Ezk xviii.13; xxii.12; Ps cix.11; cf. Ezk xviii.8, 17; Ps xv.5; xxxvii.26; Hab ii.6; Ezk xviii.22; xxxiii.15; Am ii.8; Jb xxii.6; xxiv.3. Ne v is most interesting, and note the correction from the impossible 'hundredth' to 'debt' in Strack, *REPTK* 21 (1908), 520. On the behaviour of Jews in Egypt some Jewish writers display undue caution, but Stein is obviously right in saying that they did on occasion lend at interest to Jews as well as non-Jews, and loans to be repaid in grain are evidenced: *Corpus Papyrorum Jud.* I (Harvard U.P., Cambridge, Mass. 1957) 165–8.

the pious Jew to avoid even the 'dust', or facet or scintilla, of the biblical wrongdoing. For example, praising a man is 'dust of slander', because, although it is not actually slander, it is a means whereby indirectly slander may be uttered.[1] So 'dust of usury' comprehends a vast range of transactions which enable usurious gains to be made, or might in certain eventualities enable such gains to be made, though not themselves within the biblical prohibition. Contracts and acknowledgements of indebtedness were specially suspect. In a moment we shall look at two acknowledgements, one of them written in Aramaic only a quarter of a century after the death of Jesus—both show plainly the need to evade the overt mention of interest. If, by any chance, 'increase' might accrue to the 'lender' the contract was morally bad. The exceptions are highly interesting.

The theory behind the concept of 'dust of usury' was that the original biblical prohibitions aimed to prevent exploitation. This seems to have been true, and because the spirit of the law, if not its letter, did not comprehend transactions which were intended to bring joint or mutual commercial advantage, there seemed no harm in evading the law by, for example, fictitious partnerships. Naturally, another view of the position was possible. Yet, to pursue the precise point here, in cases where exploitation was totally absent, where more profit would accrue to the community from the exercise of interest-taking under the cover of tricks than harm could arise from people's becoming accustomed to the idea of interest, the concept of 'dust', nominally applicable, would not be applied, and the transaction might safely be entered into even by the most pious Pharisee.[2] Further, if it could be shown that the borrower was under no immediate necessity to borrow the object in question, it seems a loan of such an object in circumstances facilitating

[1] b. B.B. 164*b* = Sonc. 717; for 'dust of usury' see B.M. 61*b*, 67*a* (65*a* in the *Mishnāh* itself); Maimonides, *ubi cit. Hilkot Malveh* = *Mishneh Torāh* XIII, III, vi, 1 (trans. Rabinowitz, p. 97–8). It must be recollected at all times that because a thing is illegal under the developed *halakāh* it need not have been worse than disapproved (by Pharisees, perhaps also Essenes) *temp. Chr.* Horowitz, *op. cit.* 488f. 'Dust of *shevi'it*', Sukāh 40*b*; Ḳid. 20*a* = Sonc. 92–3. 'Dust of idolatry', Tosefta, 'Avodāh Zarāh, 1, 10. 'Dust of robbery', Maimonides, 'Edūt. 10, 4 (= *M.T.* XIV, Judges, trans. Hershman, p. 104). *Talmudic Encycl.* (Heb.), 1, art. *'Āvāḳ*.

[2] Loans of mere temporary convenience (B.M. 63*b* = Sonc. 378); loans between rabbis; loans for the use of the Temple (*heḳdesh*, B.M. 57*b* = Sonc. 341); and loans of the property of minors for their advantage (B.M. 70*a* = Sonc. 405–6).

Rashi (Sukāh 40*b*) is not entirely satisfactory: *miydey dᵉlā' havey 'iykar-hā-'iyṣūr tālūy bo ḳārey 'āvāḳ*. A thing which is not the main prohibited thing but depends on it is called 'dust'. 'Dust of slander' is not real slander but only a 'side', 'facet', of it, *tsad lᵉshon hāra'*. 'Like dust that goes up from a thing that is being ground in a mortar.' But if it were of the same substance it would be the 'main prohibited thing' itself. Rabinowitz translates *'āvāḳ ribiyt* as 'quasi-usury', Klein 'shade of usury'.

the taking of hidden interest was unobjectionable. This at least explains why it was that the strictest Pharisee had accepted by the time of the Talmud, without discussion in our surviving authorities, that a man who 'had a drop of oil' could borrow any amount of oil in circumstances which would otherwise be tainted.[1] It strikes us at once that the same rule would justify morally contracts which were expressed in terms of oil, but in fact were restatements or liquidations of indebtedness which had quite other origins. And it is obvious that every debtor would be likely to have, for example, enough oil to light a lamp, and enough wheat to make a cake: and so oil and wheat were obvious choices for the pious Jew who wanted to enter into a contract which was not biblically usurious, but would have been within rabbinical usury, 'dust of usury', if the commodity had been one which the debtor did not possess. The Pharisees had thus been scrupulous; their scrupulosity had not emended the court-law; and it had been vitiated by an enormous loophole. The reason that loophole was there is stated indirectly by Luke: they were lovers of money, and piety and good business ought not to be incompatible. The excuse for leaving it can hardly claim to be the reason why they left it.

The gains which were tainted by the 'dust of usury' included gains made with the aid of tricks invented to evade the law relating to biblical usury. Such tricks, known to the modern Islamic world and essential to modern commercial expansion, would hardly have remained unknown to the Jews, when they had as their commercial teachers the inhabitants of the Near East, heirs to the Babylonian, Assyrian and other ancient civilizations which had highly developed laws facilitating usury,[2] and the Greeks, who, whatever primitive agricultural tribes may

[1] As a result a man might lawfully borrow wheat, etc., in such circumstances *without fixing a time for repayment* and *even though the market-price is unknown to the parties* (Maim. *op. cit.* XIII, III, x, 2, p. 114). From this two points emerge: (i) even the Pharisees permitted objectionable usurious contracts under colour of a possibly fictitious absence of necessity on the borrower's part; and (ii) a loan of 100 *kor* of wheat *simpliciter* might still be objectionable 'dust of usury' according to the Pharisees if it was a conversion into wheat of a debt of money or some other commodity and the debtor had no wheat at the time of conversion (*Mishnāh*, B.M. V.1 [Danby, 355]; Maim. *ubi cit.* X, 6, p. 115). It is not impossible that Jesus was aiming against the Pharisaic position under (i) above. In any event a contract which concealed usury was against the spirit of the *Torāh*.

[2] *Reallexikon der Assyriologie* II, 123–31 (Darlehen). W. F. Leemans, 'Rate of Interest in Old Babylonian Times', *Rev. Int. des Dr. de l'Ant.* 5 (1950), 7–34. Loans of *naturalien* at interest are evidenced in Kohler and Ungnad, *Assyrische Rechtsurkunden* (Leipzig 1913), no. 309, p. 203, no. 325, p. 210 (where wheat is lent at 50 per cent interest), no. 307, p. 203, and nos. 311–13, p. 204–5 (where barley is lent at the same rate); and compare with these the most important no. 314, p. 205 where 'pure oil' is lent at 100 per cent interest, *i.e.* double the interest payable on grain. Loans of money to be repaid in *naturalien* are evidenced in *Iraq* 16 (1950), 41, ND 2320; p. 45, ND 2335; M.

have thought, were at this period far from hostile to loans at interest.[1]

Our steward, then, lending at interest to Jews, was morally a transgressor, but legally secure, so long as his contracts hid the fact that the loan was usurious.

Agency and Usury Combined

The following propositions can be made with confidence about our steward:

(1) According to God's law, if the contracts with the debtors had originally been usurious in their nature,[2] he was a sinner in entering into them, and in releasing the debtors from the usurious portion of the debts he was acting righteously, and making amends. He was not in fact making restitution for he had not received this very portion as yet;[3] but he was doing something even better, failing to take the usury to which he was legally entitled.

(2) According to God's law, the tainted property did not belong to the master, as he could not authorise the steward to take interest from

[1] That the Greek laws in use in the Levant differed radically from the Jewish is proved (if proof were needed after representative papyri have been studied) by R. S[illegible]'s remarks at B.M. 62*a–b* = Sonc. 371–2. The Romans and Greeks (like any people given to borrowing) disliked interest (*fenus*, τόκος), but while at times its limits were regulated or it was entirely prohibited by law, it was neither immoral by any fundamental code of morality (see, for Cato's practice, above, p. 23) nor, for the most part, illegal unless it were stipulated for above the limit (as in England after the time of Henry VIII). And there must always be a difference between what is prohibited and what is legally unenforcible. See S. Stein in *Hist. Jud.* 17, 7, and Klingmüller in Pauly-Wissowa, *RE* VI, 2187f.; *ibid.* VII, 1207.

[2] That is to say if they had either been usurious when they commenced, or had been restated in a usurious fashion. Note the reservation from the Pharisees' standpoint at p. 61 n. 1.

[3] Thus he was in fact morally in a stronger position, and so, according to the Pharisees, was the debtor who accepted the release. For restitution was not to be accepted lightly, nor in every case, even when it was offered out of regard for Heaven. However, release from a usurious debt was free from objection on every score, for restitution of a specific existing thing was never reprobated (Maim. XIII, III, iv.v, p. 90) even though the restorer ought to be encouraged to be moral.

Schorr, *Altbabylonische Rechtsurkunden* (Leipzig 1913), nos. 49, 50, 52 at p. 82–4; notice also the contract at no. 106, p. 155, where repayment in bricks or money is promised with a penalty for non-payment by a particular month. Driver and Miles, *Babylonian Laws* II, 39. An instance where a 'contract of supply' has a strong speculative character suitable for concealing usury (though in fact in Babylonia, so far as we know, usury did not need to be concealed), and a loan of money had to be repaid in crops at the harvest, so that a much larger amount was promised than could have been bought with the money before the harvest, is discussed exhaustively with references, by Erich Pritsch in 'Zur juristischen Bedeutung der śubanti-Formel', *Alttestamentliche Studien* (*Nötscher-Festschrift*), Bonner Bibl. Beit. 1, p. 172–87 at p. 182–4. This was the model upon which Jewish lenders in Palestine framed that contract which is severely attacked by the Pharisees as 'dust of usury'.

Jews, and therefore the steward's gain was a personal gain whenever he took usury. Any release of rabbinical usury would, therefore, be technically a payment out of the steward's own pocket.

(3) According, however, to the law of man—the court-law—if the contracts contained rabbinical usury, the steward was perfectly entitled to exact the stipulated amount from the debtors and to sell them and perhaps their families also into slavery if necessary[1] in order to recover the amount due. A release of this type of usury would strike at the master.

(4) According to the law of man the contracts, being legally valid, were entered into on the master's behalf, and in releasing the debts or parts of them to the debtors the steward was depriving the master of something to which he was entitled.

(5) According to the law of God as well as the law of man the debtors were entitled to treat the act of the steward in releasing parts of their debts as the act of the master. According to the law of God the steward was doing the righteous thing, and it was presumed that it was his master's wish that he should. According to the law of man it was for the master to prove that he had forbidden the release, or that it was outside the authority of the steward, before the act could be impugned (assuming that he was inclined to impugn it, and that it would otherwise be practicable for him to do so).

The Master's Position

Certain propositions follow from what we already know:

(1) The master might have been ignorant of the usurious character of the original transactions. There is no evidence that he countenanced this conduct, but he may well have assumed that the steward would take all legal steps to increase the wealth of the estate. In any event he could not have authorised him to take biblical usury.

(2) According to the law of God the master was under a duty to release debts to distressed fellow-Jews.[2]

(3) According to the law of man he was entitled even to usurious gains from the debtors, but there was nothing to prevent him from releasing what they legally owed him, and if his steward took such a step without his express authority, he could cure that defect by subse-

[1] LXX, 4 K iv.1; Mt xviii.25 (on which see above, p. 38). R. Sugranyes cited above, p. 50 n. 1.

[2] Luke himself gives us in vii.41–3 an example of forgiveness of debts to distressed fellow-Jews. Jesus constantly urged lending without interest and release of debts, but this was typical Jewish moral teaching. b. 'A.Z. 4*a* (= Sonc. 13–14) cited by Billerbeck II, 163.

quent approval or ratification. And that, we see, is exactly what he did.[1]

What steps the master might take, when he learnt of his steward's proceedings, were severely limited by a factor which we have not hitherto mentioned. The best evidence of a debt was a written acknowledgement attested by witnesses.[2] Since even a witness to a usurious transaction came under a rabbinical condemnation, such contracts were often unattested,[3] but it appears that a holograph document signed by the debtor was good and sufficient.[4] Of course once the original document had been destroyed or cancelled by tearing it was extremely difficult to prove the debt *aliunde*, and the court would certainly not take any steps to coerce an alleged debtor,[5] without either proof of the document in the hands of the creditor or witnesses to an oral agreement.[6] Where the contract was known to have been reduced to writing the calling of witnesses to its terms would be highly unsatisfactory, but no difficulty could exceed that of a plaintiff whose contract was originally so reduced, who had himself, or through his agent, returned the paper in question, and who was in possession of another document which the defendant might swear was given in consideration for the abandonment of the original claim.

[1] The exact force of ἐπῄνεσεν seems to have escaped commentators. It is true that it could have been used to signify merely 'applauded', but the use of the word in general (see Liddell–Scott–Jones, for Arndt–Gingrich are not so clear) supports the implication of adopting, sanctioning, and (to any relevant degree) ratifying, as well as approving and commending.

[2] Horowitz, *op. cit.* 696f.; Maim. XIII, III, xxvii.

[3] b. B.M. 62*a* = Sonc. 371. Hence it was wicked to lend without witnesses (B.M. 75*b* = Sonc. 436)! It must be remembered that at Jewish law, as at Islamic and Hindu law also, witnesses are not merely witnesses to signature or sealing, but are expected to testify to the transaction itself.

[4] Horowitz, 697. The point is illustrated at *Test. Job* (*sup.* p. 25 n. 1), xi.

[5] The Talmud is clear that although (irrespective of liens) the movable property of the debtor could be seized and sold at the court's order (stipulations entitling the creditor to seize the debtor's goods and lands 'as if upon a decree of the court' were usual in Greco-Egyptian usage and seem to have been imitated to some extent in the Land of Israel in transactions between Jews) the plaintiff would not be able to pursue an action unless his documentary evidence was in perfect order. See *Murab.* 18 (Benoit, etc., *cit. inf.* 100ff. A.D. 55/56) cited below. An oral debt did not create a lien over the debtor's immovables: Horowitz, *op. cit.* 717. For examples of the discussion of such evidence and its admissibility see Maim. XIII, III, xxvii, and for the law relating to documentary support of an alleged obligation, L. Auerbach, *Jüdische Obligationenrecht* (Berlin 1870), ch. 2.

[6] Oral agreements were by no means unenforcible, and in remote country districts they must have been frequent, but by the time of Jesus they were distinctly unusual between parties to contracts of any considerable value. Horowitz, *op. cit.* 445f. Maim. XIII, III, xi, 1, p. 116. Our steward exchanges one document for another. Had the entire amount in question been usurious he should (like an Indian lender to this day) have torn the old bond as a sign of its cancellation—B.M. 62*a* = Sonc. 370.

The Nature of the Original Contracts

The relevance of much of what is written above depended upon the nature of the steward's original contracts with the debtors, the contracts embodied in the documents handed back at the interviews which the gospel text so carefully describes. The account of the contracts given in the parable is precisely sufficient to reveal their nature. Here are some specimens of contracts known to the Jews, with rabbinical comments on each:

(1) I will pay Reuben 1 denarius on the 1st day of Nisan and if I do not, then I will pay ¼ denarius annually in addition. *Comment:* Biblical usury, recoverable by the borrower in the courts. *Murab.* 18, dated in the equivalent of A.D. 55/56, is an acknowledgement of a debt: the term of the debt is fixed and if the debtor failed to pay then he must add one-fifth, *even in the sabbatical year* (so much for the law of God!); otherwise he concedes the creditor the right to attach all his goods, present and future. Here usury is hardly concealed.[1]

(2) I will pay Reuben 10 *kor* of wheat on the 1st day of Nisan and if I do not, then I will pay 4 *kor* of wheat annually in addition. *Comment:* Biblical usury, recoverable in the courts.

(3) I owe Reuben 10 shekels of Tyrian silver and will repay it on the 1st day of Nisan, but if I do not I shall pay him any interest which may be ordered.[2] *Comment:* objectionable as contingently usurious.

(4) I will pay Reuben 10 *kor* of wheat at 1 denarius the *kor*. *Comment:* possibly not usurious at all, depending upon what was the value of the loan.

(5) I owe Reuben 10 denarii and will pay him in wheat on the 1st day of Nisan at the price then prevailing. *Comment:* unobjectionable.[3]

(6) I will pay Reuben 10 *kor* of wheat at the harvest. *Comment:* 'dust of usury', not recoverable in the courts.[4] But not 'dust of usury', and unobjectionable, if the promisor had some wheat, however little.

(7) I owe Reuben 10 *kor* of wheat. *Comment:* 'dust of usury', not recover-

[1] E. Koffmahn, *ZSS, r. A.*, 81 (1964), 293.

[2] *Murab.* 114 (A.D. 171): Benoit, Milik, and de Vaux, *Discoveries in the Judaean Desert* II (Oxford 1961), 240ff. The right of attachment is granted as in *Murab.* 18 (above).

[3] b. B.M. 62*b* = Sonc. 372. Maim. XIII, III, xi, 1, p. 114. Because he would be paying *R* not more than 10 den. worth of wheat, and *R* would not be obtaining, either certainly or possibly, any 'increase' on his outlay. Of course all these examples assume that the statement, 'I owe *R* so much', is true. Money-lenders are quite capable of making their clients sign an acknowledgement for double what they receive, but that is another question which we can ignore for the present purpose. Compare with the acknowledgement suggested above the transaction, very similar to that of our steward, detailed and discussed at B.M. 65*a* = Sonc. 382. Maim. XIII, p. 114–15 (ch. x, 2, 4), *cf.* p. 109 (ch. ix, 1): 'no agreement may be made with respect to produce until the market price has been published', and *ibid.* § 5, p. 111.

[4] b. B.M. 75*a* = Sonc. 432. See *ibid.* 72*b* = Sonc. 420–1, which provides an example of the sort of contract in which our steward used to engage on his master's behalf. Maim. XIII, p. 115 (ch. x, 3).

able in the courts.[1] But not 'dust of usury', and unobjectionable, if the promisor had some wheat.

(8) I promise to pay Reuben 10 *bat* of beer to be brewed next year. *Comment:* 'dust of usury', not recoverable in the courts, and objectionable in any case (for the promisor, even if he possesses some of this year's beer, cannot possess beer which is to be brewed next year).

Our steward's contracts were of the seventh variety. Apparently they were perfectly innocent. They might have been forward purchases of comestibles. But in reality they were restatements of the debts[2] owed by the debtors in terms of a common comestible, the time for payment not being stated, the rate and value not being stated, and the whole thing characteristic of an objectionable transaction most probably saved in the eyes of the pious by the loophole in the rabbinical provisions alluded to above.

The amounts were probably worked out in some manner such as the following:

	den.
Original debt	1.00
Interest at 20 per cent	0.20
Insurance against (i) fall in market-price, (ii) low price at easiest time for payment; (iii) adulteration, etc. say, 5 per cent	0.05
Total	1.25

Therefore the amount of wheat fixed in the contract equals, in our example, the amount which 1¼ den. would have bought at the time of the contract—for the time of payment is not stipulated. This was a favourite trick, nominally to help the debtor whose only property is his wheat-field, etc., and who in equity can expect to repay wheat he borrows *to sow* at a considerable rate of interest, but actually to ensure that in any event the creditor is well covered and he obtains his interest on the principal liquidated here as 1 den. The general type of contract was so well known that it had a special name in Hebrew: *ṭarᵉshā'*.[3]

[1] b. B.M. 65*a*–*b* = Sonc. 383–4. Maim. XIII, p. 114 (ch. x, 2). The Jews in mediæval Europe introduced Christians to these well-worn devices, and traces of similar methods of evading citation in the ecclesiastical court for usury are many. Loans, or fictitious loans, of grain or commodities, for sale or otherwise, were commonly resorted to and evidence of these practices is afforded in the statute 37 Henry VIII, c. 9 (1545), F. Bacon's *Draught of an Act against an Usurious Shift of Gain* (*Works* II, 1765, 494), and A. Horne, *Mirrour of Justices* (1642), at p. 165 of the 1646 edn.

[2] For such restatements of principal and interest (common in countries where there were legal bars to the total amount of interest recoverable at one time, as India) see B.M. 72*a* = Sonc. 415, and compare Maim. XIII, p. 115–16 (ch. x, 6).

[3] Literally, 'deaf (usury)', or 'silent (usury)'. b. B.M. 65*a* = Sonc. 383. A specimen is given at b. B.M. 72*b* = Sonc. 420–1.

How do we know that the contracts were usurious? Their very large amounts show that something suspicious was afoot.[1] The debtors were obliged to the master, the causes of obligation being, perhaps, varied.[2] The theory that they were all tenants[3] or all merchants[4] cannot stand. It is impossible that they can have been merchants,[5] and there are excellent reasons for thinking that they cannot have been tenants, sub-tenants, sub-farmers of taxes,[6] or the like.[7] But it does not matter how

[1] The difference between a calculation mentioned by Fonck (p. 682) and that given by Billerbeck is slight. The latter shows that 100 *bat* = 39.456 hectolitres or a little over 868 gallons; 100 *kor* = 393.93 hectolitres or a little less than 1,083⅛ bushels. There is no reason to suppose an exaggeration for effect, and the difference in value between the two amounts, if any, is irrelevant (*cf.* Jeremias, also K. H. Rengstorf, *Das Neue Testament Deutsch* III).

[2] *E.g.* supply of victuals, seed or manure; hire of workmen; advances on crops that failed; loans to pay land-revenue and tithe. Note, as E. Riggenbach, 'Zur Exegese und Textkritik zweier Gleichnisse Jesu', *Aus Schrift und Geschichte . . . (Schlatter-Festschrift)* (Stuttgart 1922), 17–26, that χρεοφειλέτης is after all χρεοφειλέτης. Riggenbach thought that they had had *naturalien* supplied to them, but the amounts are very large, and one may not be right in assuming compound interest, though that is of course not impossible. Jülicher was right (II, 500) and so also W. R. Nicoll (1897) and B. S. Easton (1926), but not Fonck, on the question whether it mattered what was the origin of the debts. Schmid (*cit. inf.* n. 3) at p. 210 shows a proper indifference to the question.

[3] As Fonck (1909) and particularly Kögel (1914), comparing the 'Kolonat' in Africa and adducing the Latin translation *villicus* for 'steward'. The difficulties of 'How much do you owe *my master*?' are not squarely faced. Fonck reasonably wonders how long the 'debtors' ' gratitude would last. Zahn thinks that only the purchase-price of the *naturalien* was owed and compares the tenants' rent in grapes (or wine?) in Lk xx.10. J. Schmid, *Das Ev. nach Lukas* (Regensburg 1951), 209f. and K. Staab (ed.), *Echter Bibel. Das N.T. Das Ev. nach Markus und Lukas* (Würzburg 1956), 97f., think the master was a great landlord. But Jesus would have said so (see above, p. 56 n. 1). Findlay (1937) accepted that they were tenants in arrears.

[4] As Jeremias: 'wholesalers'. Fonck points out some difficulties, but there are others. Staab thinks they were either tenants or dealers. This is a better approach: it does not matter.

[5] Because merchants do not normally respond to an agent's summons in this fashion when the balance happens to be against them; they do not expect to be asked bluntly, 'What do you owe?'; and are not kept standing while being questioned. The last point is conclusive.

[6] A sub-farmer of revenue could be in debt (*a*) to his head-farmer, or (*b*) to a third party who had advanced him money to enable him to acquire the right to subfarm the area in question, or to his surety. In the case of (*a*) the debt would be specifically to the head-farmer in person and not to any 'master'. In case (*b*) there is no distinction from our point of view between such a debt and any other source of indebtedness.

[7] Riggenbach points out that if the documents were really tenancy-agreements the proprietor would not have been bound (the following year?) by the steward's act—certainly the 'debtors' ' position would have been much weaker. He is right in surmising that they cannot have been subtenants, for the loss would have been entirely the steward's own (apart from other objections) and one of the points of the parable would have been lost. The vital point is that under any such agreement the obligee *owes* nothing at all until the time for payment (for example, the harvest) arrives. To this there can be only two objections. First, it may be urged that they may be in arrears.

they became debtors: what matters is what it is they owe. Liquidating debts and restating them in terms of natural products was a characteristic Jewish practice, the reason being precisely this desire to evade the law of biblical usury.

The amount of the releases corresponds to the amount of the interest plus insurance. It is the amount which is oppressive and against the law of God. The last thing a grower wanted to do in prevailing conditions was to mortgage a crop which was not yet in existence: he often wanted to anticipate it by obtaining an advance from a broker.[1] No doubt the debtor of wheat had a wheat-field (if the terms of the contract were not entirely fictitious and the item 'wheat' had not been chosen for the reason stated above, merely for the purpose of choosing a safe medium of indebtedness) and the debtor of oil may well have had olive trees, but it is quite certain that if they could not supply the amount from their own produce they would have been forced to acquire it or an agreed equivalent elsewhere, and the form of the contract covered the creditor in any event.

Twenty-five per cent or thereabouts is the traditional rate of interest on a genuine loan of wheat.[2] That this is exactly what is released to the debtor of wheat is no coincidence. What about the oil? Again a hypothetical sum can be made out:

[1] As contemplated in b. B.M. 73*a* = Sonc. 423.

[2] A range of 33⅓ per cent to 25 per cent is mentioned by Billerbeck, *ubi cit*. Justinian's provisions, if they were ever enforced, assume a state of civil security and easy recoverability of loans with interest which must have been an advance on normal Levantine experience. For India see below, p. 71 n. 2.

Even so, the time for payment of the outstanding debt would be the harvest; and since neither the steward nor the master is depicted as ignorant of economics and indifferent to normal methods of management an explanation would be called for why the alleged tenants had not been evicted and sold up. That they had been allowed to accumulate arrears would be so unusual in those hard times, and would throw so favourable a light upon the worldly pair that express indications of that situation would be expected. Secondly, it may be urged that by coincidence the rents might have been due just then. However, apart from the fact that such a coincidence is not to be expected without express indication (parables are after all not puzzles so far as their basic facts are concerned), the steward had only then been reported for 'waste'. This would occur only when the relative emptiness of the granaries and cellars enabled the informer (and any servant sent by the master to check on the state of affairs) to see at a glance that the master's assets should have been more ample at that time of year and in prevailing conditions. The moment when the harvest was being garnered and rents were about to be paid, when perhaps the assets were beginning to appear, as always at that time of year, at their most abundant, was hardly the appropriate time for such allegations as were made against the steward. But all this is assuming too much. There is no indication that the steward was supervising a predominantly agricultural household. His waste may have been a matter of engaging too many dancers and musicians, paid for out of a chest to which he alone had the key. Assumptions about tenants, rents, and the like are all otiose.

	den.
Original debt	1.0
Interest at 80 per cent	0.8
Insurance (as before) at 20 per cent	0.2
Total	2.0

The clue to the 25 per cent came independently to an Indian peasant several years ago and was reported by a missionary;[1] it and the clue to the 100 per cent came to the present writer from Indian legal sources.

India has and had much in common with Palestine. Objections to usury, once strong, evaporated in the face of commercial expansion.[2] The Indian law tells us that loans of listed articles, all of which are subject to undetectable or inseverable adulteration, for example, oil, wine, soil, base metals, are subject to a very high rate of interest.[3] The

[1] C. B. Firth, 'The Parable of the Unjust Steward ...', *Exp. Tim.* 63 (1951), 93–5. But the interpretation of the discovery was wrong; nor did he grasp the point regarding the oil.

[2] Objections to interest as such vanished before our principal basic texts were compiled, but left clear traces. 'Righteous interest' was fixed at one-eightieth *per mensem* (or 15 per cent *per annum*) on cash loans. The subject is very complex, and we are concerned only with the outlines. See Pāndurang V. Kāne, *History of Dharmaśāstra* III (Poona 1946), 417–18. The *Mānavadharmaśāstra* (G. Bühler, *Laws of Manu*, Oxford 1886, 280) strongly reprobates several types of usury. Manu says at VIII.151: 'Interest on money-loans stipulated at one time shall not exceed the double; in the case of grains, fruits, wool and beasts of burden, it shall not go beyond the quintuple.' An account of the old Hindu law is to be found in R. S. Sharma, 'Usury in early mediæval India (A.D. 400–1200)', *CSSH* 8, no. 1 (1965), 56ff., esp. at p. 64–6 (not all his explanation seems acceptable). One may also consult R. C. Nigam, 'Usury through the ages', *Indian Advocate* 7–8 (1967–8). Loans of some commodities at different rates from loans of cash were recognised as recently as the Cochin Kuries Act, 1932, sec. 45. Paddy as a currency and Manu VIII. 151 are discussed in *Paili* v. *Krishnan* (1944) 36 Cochin 300 (Full Bench).

[3] The reason for the differentiation was not apparent after the original conception behind the scriptural rules had been forgotten, and most late mediæval and modern text-books of *dharmaśāstra* proceed upon the false assumption that the limits applied indefinitely and whatever the rate of interest mutually agreed between the parties *per mensem*. However, the original notion left distinct traces in the commentary of Viśvarūpa on Yājñavalkya II, 40 and Lakṣmīdhara (eleventh century) in his *Kṛtyakalpataru, Vyavahāra-kāṇḍa* (Baroda 1953), 284; and in the denials by the eighteenth-century authority Jagannātha (trans. H. T. Colebrooke, *Digest of Hindu Law* ... I [Madras 1864], 82, 89) of the truth of interpretations which evidently survived even so late as then. Fortunately the same principle which animated the Indian authorities was at work elsewhere also: we have seen the position in the ancient Near East (above, p. 68 n. 2), and Byzantium knew similar rules (*Corpus Iuris, Cod.* 4. 32. 26, 1). The Indian authorities are cited briefly by Kane, *op. cit.* 422–3. Their mutual discrepancies, which are not unusual, can be ignored for our purpose. Kauṭilya (or Kauṭalya) in the possibly pre-Christian *Arthaśāstra* (III, 11 = Trivandrum edn. ii, p. 64; trans. R. Shāma Sāstry, p. 197) strongly suggests that grain repayable at the harvest can carry 50 per cent interest (as St Jerome says was usual in his day) until the harvest, but if the value of the loan has been ascertained and the debt is treated as if it were money there should be no limit. The ancient Indian method of limitation

order of risk, for which the borrower pays, is, from lowest to highest, (i) jewels, gold and silver, fruits (perishables), silk, and wool; (ii) base metals; (iii) oils, wines, clarified butter (even now notoriously subject to adulteration), raw sugar, salt, and soil.

Vasiṣṭha says:[1] 'Where interest runs for a fixed period the maximum on diamonds, pearls, gold and silver is double; on copper, iron, brass, bell-metal, tin and lead it is threefold; on ivory, leather, bone, horn and objects of clay or soil it is limitless, and so with flowers, roots, and fruit.'

Viṣṇu says:[2] 'The maximum increase on gold is double; on clothing triple; quadruple on grain; eightfold on fluids . . . there is no limit on ferment, cotton, thread, armour (or "bark"), weapons (or "implements"), brick, charcoal; on material not otherwise specified the maximum is double.'

Bṛhaspati devotes space to the subject:[3] '. . . on potherbs the interest may make the debt quintuple; on seeds and sugar-cane sextuple; on salt, oil, and spirits, octuple: so on molasses and honey . . .' The same principles are applied by *Nārada*,[4] who is very explicit, and *Kātyāyana*.[5] Oils, liquors, ghee, raw sugar and salt may carry interest up to eightfold; base metals fivefold; soil eightfold. *Vyāsa* has a similar rule.[6] *Bharadvāja* places scented wood in the eightfold category; base metals in the fourfold; ghee eightfold, oils (anomalously) sixfold.[7]

Turning to the rules for debtors repaying their sureties, we find *Yājñavalkya* saying:[8] 'Their progeny is interest in the cases of women and animals (or "female animals"); grain is threefold; clothing has been declared to be fourfold, while a fluid is "remembered" as being eightfold.'

The *Smṛtichandrikā* properly points out (at p. 153/357) that when in the same context *Kātyāyana* speaks of double repayment this can apply only to loans of gold.

[1] Vas. II. 44–7.
[2] Viṣṇu VI, 11–17, trans. Jolly, *SBE* VII, 43–4.
[3] Bṛhaspatismṛti (Reconstructed), ed. K. V. Rangaswami Aiyangar (Baroda 1941), 101–2. L. Renou, *Ét. Véd. et Pāṇ.* XI (1963), 86, 87 (Bṛh. X.17–20, 24). See G. Jhā, *Hindu Law in its Sources* I (Allahabad 1930), 140–1. The earlier part of the text only is cited by Jagannātha (*ubi cit.* I, 82), who gives his own and another interpretation, *ibid.*, 64 and 83.
[4] In two texts of various origins printed in L. S. Joshi, *Dharmakośa*, Vyavahārakāṇḍa, p. 626.
[5] *Kātyāyana-smṛti-sāroddhāra*, ed. P. V. Kane (Bombay 1933), vv. 510–12, p. 217f.
[6] Cited in the *Vy. Mayūkha*, etc.: Jha, *op. cit.* 143.
[7] *Dharmakośa, ubi cit.* p. 635.
[8] II, 57 (Viśvarūpa: II, 59 with slight differences in the text). Kane, *op. cit.* 438. Jagannātha, *ubi cit.* I, 182.

---

was twofold: first it was provided that legal interest should not exceed 15 per cent *per annum* (see above), then that on loans of money the total limit was 100 per cent; on grain, oil, etc., we are not told what was the relevant legal interest, but we are told that the maximum for grain was 200 per cent (a 'triple' return), for fluids 700 per cent (an 'octuple' return)—and of course the multiplication subsumes the corresponding period within which repayment is to be expected.

The Indian system of regulating the amount of interest recoverable was based upon a formal assumption that a certain space of time could be taken by the debtor to pay,[1] and the law attempted to fix what amount could be recovered in all. For the first category the lender could insist upon a maximum of 100 per cent on the basis of the original contract; for the second 400 per cent; and for the third 700 per cent. Repayment of the last would then be 800 per cent, and we find, by comparison with similar provisions elsewhere, that the 800 per cent would be spread over, or could be spread over, 6 years and 8 months, leaving us with an annual increment for oils and wines of something over 100 per cent. Another ancient Indian authority tells us that, over the same period, the maximum recoverable on wheat and other grains is 200 per cent interest, on cloth or clothing 300 per cent. Thus the interest on wheat, for example, would be 30 per cent per annum, which does not differ grossly from the modern rate.[2]

That comestibles carried a higher rate of interest than coin is suggested by the Laws of Eshnunna (§§ 18A, 20) and by Ḥammurabi (§ 50).[3] The ancient Near East shared the situation described by ancient Indian jurists.

Though oil and wheat were valuable crops, staple produce of Palestine, and likely to be found in every home,[4] they were utterly unlike in respect of variability of quality and price at harvest-time. Qualities of oil vary tremendously.[5] Oil-trees bear irregularly, and climate and other factors cause unpredictable vicissitudes in the size and quality of the olive-crop. Whereas adulteration of wheat can be readily sifted out on the creditor's floor, the very easy and attractive adulterations of olive-oil with sesame and other relatively cheap oils[6] cannot be removed and, within certain degrees, are difficult to detect. Thus where a debtor has

[1] See Kāne, 420; Jagannātha, *ubi cit.* 78–90. The above assumption is borne out by the figures, which are corroborated by custom. Wheat must have borne (at least where the orthodox rule was followed) 30 per cent *per annum* (*cf.* the provision of Justinian, which corresponds as to proportion); and oil bore 105 per cent *per annum*. The ancient Indian system is rationalised conformably to what is stated above in the *Vivādārṇava-setu* (1773–5): the very high rates for commodities reflect the possible fluctuations in value at the time the debtor chooses to pay; and assuming that the basic rate of legal interest is 2 per cent *per mensem* the maxima apply when the loan has not been repaid within fifty months (a figure Jagannātha considers) (translator's explanation: N.B. Halhed, *Gentoo Code* [1777], 2, 6–7).

[2] *Yājñavalkya-smṛti* II, 39. The mediæval precedent- and form-book, *Lekhapaddhati*, p. 21, shows 25 per cent as the annual interest on loans of wheat.

[3] Driver and Miles, 173; R. Yaron, *Law of the Aramaic Papyri* (Oxford 1961), 94–5.

[4] Above, p. 61.

[5] On oil-production in Palestine see the invaluable G. Dalman (formerly G. A. Marx), *Arbeit und Sitte in Palästin* IV (1935), 153–281.

[6] See *Encyclopædia Britannica*, art. 'Olive Oil', 14th or current edn. *Enciclopedia Italiana*, art. 'Olivo', xxv, 296f.

nothing left to offer, short of his self and family as slaves, but an amount of natural produce, and where this is a fluid like olive-oil, he must pay dearly for the risks to which he submits his creditor.

The Steward's Acts and their Aftermath

In view of his inevitable dismissal[1] the steward attempts successfully to obtain the support of public opinion until he finds alternative employment. In the last moments of authority[2] he gains that approval by doing what the law of God required of him. The debtors, writing their new acknowledgements[3] and destroying the old ones, were safe. He was safe from his master's resentment; and he suspected that his master, whom in point of morals he was really helping, would adopt his act and, since he had no alternative, take credit for pious conduct which he had not in fact initiated. On dismissal his duty towards his master faded before the practical necessity to recognise his duty towards God. He decided to obey the creator instead of his creature following the rabbinical maxim, 'If teacher and pupil differ in their instructions, who is to be followed?'[4]

The courts for the most part would have enabled the steward (or his successor) to exact every fraction of the debt, concealed usury and all. But it was felt by people in general that a worthy debtor ought, as a favour, to be excused payment of interest as distinct from the capital debt—and we have an actual letter in which *A* asks *B* to intercede with a creditor to extend such a favour to *A's* friend.[5]

The master, who is the κύριος, found that he was in a cleft stick. He did not merely praise the steward, he adopted the latter's acts. He was willing to pose as a pious man, giving us an impression of the pious man who somehow omits to do the right thing until the perfect opportunity is presented to him. That the steward's prudence was beneficial to the steward was evident; that it redounded to his master's reputation with the public was obvious. An ungracious repudiation was out of the question. It is not therefore apposite to ask, with Jeremias, 'how could

[1] Preisker rightly notices that expulsion was irrevocable and discussion was futile. The steward did not beg as in Mt xviii.26.

[2] Riggenbach, *ubi cit.* at p. 18 (*cf. ibid.* p. 24), rightly emphasises that this is the 'point' of the parable, and many others have realised that 'right action while there is time' is a great part of the lesson which it seeks to impart.

[3] As Schmid and Staab see. The wrong notion, namely that the old documents were falsified, is unaccountably found in Billerbeck and elsewhere. Fonck was doubtful: wax tablets were in any case out of the question. Jewish lawyers were alive to the possibilities of forgery. The custody of the document was evidently with the creditor, as appears in the Talmud. The contrary practice of depositing it in safe custody or in the hands of a third party is evidenced from the ancient Near East and from Hellenistic Egypt.

[4] *Div^e^rey rav v^e^-div^e^rey tal^e^miyd, div^e^rey miy ḳod^e^miym?*

[5] *Murab.* 46 (Benoit, etc., *op. cit.* 164ff.).

he have praised his deceitful steward?' The praise may have been tardy, but it was not quixotic. Gathering riches by various expedients, rich men often give lavishly in charity, seeking, especially towards the ends of their lives, a reputation for piety.

It may have struck some legal readers that every steward was liable to be called upon to take an oath of honest dealing at the end of his agency, or indeed at any other time when he came under suspicion.[1] Here the steward had nothing to fear, for of course the oath related to the law of God, not the law of man.

It is to be noticed that the parable contains four dramatis personae: the rich man (the master), the steward, the debtors, and the general public.[2] The need for all these is plain. Without the public's approbation, which is silently assumed, the whole point of the steward's change of loyalties is lost. He, a worldly man, naturally operates in terms of worldly criteria; and that 'honesty is the best policy' is decidedly a worldly criterion. The rich man is needed in order, not only that the steward shall have a reason other than superstition or spontaneous piety for changing his line of conduct, but also that the materialistic world, which he represents, may distinctly approve of the steward's new behaviour. He affords a necessary bridge to Jesus's explanation why the worldly element can behave in such a fashion.

If, as seems certainly to be the case, the steward atoned for his previous life by doing the right thing by his master's debtors and incidentally made an honest man of his master, the question is still unhappily repeated, how could his master praise 'the *unjust* steward'? This question afforded a major reason to Professor Hans Drexler for doubting the reconstruction offered here, which he considered 'unpromising'.[3] No doubt it is more exciting to trace out reasons for why a, or the, master should praise a 'traitor' for his 'treachery'—even if this pushes the whole parable into the background, making it little better than a prologue to later material. Unfortunately for the conservative mind, the words τὸν οἰκονόμον τῆς ἀδικίας do not mean 'the steward

[1] Maim. XII, IV, ix, 1–5, p. 237–9; Horowitz, *op. cit.* 551–2, 679.

[2] This has been missed by all commentators except W. R. Nicholl, *Expositor's N.T* (1897) at p. 584. It has been shrewdly pointed out that the steward, and his imitators, cannot suppose that those whom they have befriended will predecease them! On the construction of the Greek there is no reason whatever to take δέξωνται (*v.* 4) as referring to the debtors, who are not even mentioned until the following verse. Fonck was wrong (p. 687) and Gerda Krüger (*cit. inf.* p. 80 n. 1) in error imagined that the steward wanted his 'present' to produce proportionate gratitude. H. Ewald, *Die drei ersten Evang.* (Göttingen 1871), I, 367–8, took the view that the steward expected, indeed obtained a promise of help from the debtors.

[3] *ZNW* 58 (1967), 286–8. The problem is reduced if one simply imagines quotation marks round the compact semitic phrase.

who remained a rascal/traitor/villain' but simply 'his dishonest steward' who, like most stewards, was tainted with the dishonesty of his previous usurious loans and personal peculations at his master's expense.

An objection might be raised to the foregoing explanation of the parable. Let us admit that the steward is doing the right thing. Let us admit that he is showing charity to the 'poor', namely those oppressed with usury, and doing so at the last moment, and in so doing revealing the human instinct to try to obtain approval when the security upon which we have long relied suddenly collapses. But in this case it was not his money he was donating; he was being charitable with someone else's wealth! Yet have we really grasped, after all, one may object, the real point of the elaborate parable? Is not Jesus really illustrating only cleverness, shrewdness, worldly-wisdom,[1] and indicating thereby how one must approach spiritual questions? Perhaps after all it *was* Jesus who is the 'Master' who 'praised the Unjust Steward', as so many have suspected all along (and continue to suspect)? Yet there is an answer. Charity and righteousness are almost convertible terms, as we have seen near the beginning of this book. Even the vocabulary in Hebrew and Arabic reveal that the righteous is charitable, and the charitable righteous. The parable utilises the public belief that he who voluntarily makes gifts to the poor, when he could well have done otherwise, is entitled to be regarded as righteous. The objection that the Steward is generous with his master's money, and obtains a prospect of hospitality in the debtors' homes on the basis of assets which were never legally[2] his, takes us to the heart of the parable. When we are generous and give to others, whose property do we give away? It *appears* to be ours, at our disposal; just so the Steward could have sued for moneys owed to his master, as he was his master's representative and handled his affairs with complete freedom of discretion. But the true owner of everything is God himself. When we give to God we give him what is his; and when we give to the poor we merely redistribute God's wealth. The Steward is not the less charitable for his manipulating his master's rights, and it is quite proper that his master should commend him.

THE MEANING OF THE PARABLE

The general setting of the parable in the theme of God's law *versus* the law of man will be expounded below. For the present we are concerned with the meaning inherent in the story treated in isolation. We are,

[1] So preachers and popular writers constantly (*e.g. The Times*, 29 July 1961). A. M. Hunter *Interpreting the Parables* (1960), 55: 'resourcefulness in a tight spot'. *Jerusalem Bible*, 'astuteness', 'adroitness'.

[2] *Cf.* above, p. 62 (2): *God's* law.

however, entitled to remember what happened in the parable of the Prodigal Son, and the parallels and divergencies are obvious. One who knows his moral duty, and has been neglecting it for the sake of worldly duty and worldly advantage, is forced by circumstances connected with earlier imprudence and misjudgement to reconsider his position, and seek the goodwill of those whose opinion he had neglected. That goodwill is likened by Jesus to the favour which will enable the Jew to enter the eternal tabernacles.[1] The steward knew by training and instinct that what was righteous was in this instance agreeable to the public. It is worth noting that if the parable had been about a man's abstaining from divorcing his wife, or divorcing his wife whose former husband was alive at the time, it would have been quite unsuitable for the purpose, for there public sentiment and tradition were by no means uniformly in accord with the law of God.

Even those whose approval was unspontaneous (as in the case of the master) assumed without hesitation that the steward was prudent to deal as he did with property which did not belong entirely to his master, and which, if he had taken a shorter view, he could legally (but not morally) have exacted in order to placate his master's anger against him, anger aroused in quite extraneous circumstances. The commodity with which the steward was dealing was 'unrighteous *mammon*'. It is well known to Jewish Law and creates no difficulty.[2] Property earned, even in accordance with the law of man, by means of oppression, usury, robbery, deceit, or otherwise in defiance of the command, 'Love thy neighbour as thyself',[3] is tainted. One does not own it morally even if one is entitled to it legally. God regards the holder of 'unrighteous *mammon*' as a robber. According to the Pharisees such property could

[1] On charity and its power see Billerbeck IV (i), Exk. no. 22, *Die altjüdische Privatwohltätigkeit*, p. 536–58; Fiebig, *op. cit.* 211–12. On 'eternal tabernacles' see the very ingenious R. Pautrel, 'Aeterna Tabernacula', *Rech. de Sc. Rel.* 30 (1940), 307–27. His conclusion at p. 321 seems, however, to be wrong.

[2] G. Kittel (ed.), *ThWzNT* IV (1942), 390–2 (F. Hauck). Augustine (F. Vigouroux in *Dict. de la Bible* IV (1912), 636); Suidas's explanation (ed. Bernhardy III, 679) is wrong (E. Nestle in *Encycl. Biblica* III (1902)). A list of biblical and Talmudic references appears *ibid.* p. 2914, col. 2. Despite Fonck (p. 689), Kögel (p. 588–90) and Riggenbach (p. 21f.) μαμωνᾶς τῆς ἀδικίας which = *māmon dishᵉḳār* is 'wealth which (and which alone) is unrighteous'. R. seems to suspect this at p. 24; *cf.* Hauck, *cit. sup.* para. 2(*a*). A. M. Honeyman, 'The Etymology of Mammon', *Archivum Linguisticum* IV, i, 60ff.; M. Black, *Aramaic Approach to the Gospels and Acts*, 3rd edn, 139–40. *Māmon* meant wealth, and 'unrighteous wealth' was opposed to 'righteous wealth' (*cf.* LXX, Is xxxiii.6). For *māmon* in the sense of 'ill gotten gains', see Hauck, *ubi cit.* para. 2(*b*), (*c*). Unrighteousness is relative to acquisition, not expenditure. So Indian law tells us that wealth could be black, spotted, or white according to its manner of acquisition.

[3] Lv xix.18; Rm xiii.9–10; Ga v.14: the 206th affirmative commandment (Chavel I, 220–1). Moore, *op. cit.* I, 116; II, 85f., 142f., 151.

not be taken in tithe or in offerings to the Temple.[1] The Dead Sea people were concerned not to be partners with those who transgress the word of God.[2] The hymn from the Community Rule says (X.19) 'my soul shall not desire the riches (*hon*) of violence (or 'wrong': *ḥāmāṣ*).'[3] The *Damascus Rule* says: 'They shall separate from the sons of the Pit, and shall keep away from the unclean riches of wickedness (*hon hārishᵉʿāh ha-ṭāme'*) acquired by vow or anathema or from the Temple treasure.'[4] Yet Jesus says that one may gain the favour of 'those'[5] who may welcome us into the eternal tabernacles, by disposing 'faithfully' of 'unrighteous *mammon*'. God expects righteousness to be shown in all our dealings, and will not allow us to sever our means into the clean and unclean, to worship him with the clean, and worship ourselves with the unclean.

'For the children of this world are more prudent (in the context of their own generation) than the children of Light (Lk xvi.8*b*)'—they are more natural and hit a mark which the scrupulous have missed. Is, then, the parable an exemplary parable? It may be sufficient to suggest that it is not precisely exemplary. The message is not exactly, 'Go and do likewise'. After all, the disciples are, if not exactly 'Children of Light', at least candidates for that distinction, and the steward and his master were not. The meaning is that, since worldly people both by training and instinct act, in some crises, upon the assumption that God's standards are the right standards, and deal with worldly property single-mindedly according to their prevailing principles (i.e. *mammon*-directed with all, or God-directed with all) we may learn a lesson from their reactions both as to the validity of God's standards, respect for which is planted even in them by Nature, and as to the applicability of those standards to every department of life and every sphere of activity.

[1] Dt xxiii.18–19; Mt xxvii.6; *Mishnāh*, B.Ḳ. X.1; b. B.M. 7*a* = Sonc. 29–30; Zᵉv. VIII.1; Tem. VI.1f. Likewise, Seventh Year produce was forbidden: *Mishnāh*, Shev. VIII.8; *cf.* Horowitz, *op. cit.* 614, 616. It was a basic rule (as in India) that offerings must be owned. It is of interest that in Islam it has not always been thought objectionable to give ill-gotten gains in charity: J. Sarkar, *Mughal Administration* (Calcutta 1924), 112. But there may be a difference between giving one's own 'unrighteous *mammon*' and giving that which one has inherited from others.

[2] 1 *QS* V, 14 (Vermès, 79; Lohse, 18; Leaney, 173–4).

[3] Vermès, 91; Lohse, 38; Leaney, 249; Dupont-Sommer, 115. Ezk xvi.16.

[4] VI.15–16 (Vermès 103; Lohse, 78). One may compare 1 *QS* V, 16–17. Leaney, 174. An example of sensitiveness to 'unrighteous wealth' is reported from the Islamic Sudan by P. M. Holt, *BSOAS* 30 (1967), 150–1: Ismāʿīl b. Jābir's piety reached such a point that he would not use water which came in the irrigation channels of the Shāyḳiyya, and he said, 'Their oxen (which turn the water-wheels) are taken by force'; and Muḥammad Aḥmad, later the Mahdi, refused to eat food provided by the Turco-Egyptian administration in the Sudan.

[5] God: Billerbeck on xvi. 9*b* (p. 221).

Inappropriate scruples are as much a hindrance to obedience to God as disingenuous or inaccurate juristic subtlety.[1]

[1] A recent translation has 'the children of this world are more astute *in dealing with their own kind* than are the children of light'. This seems to be wrong (my italics here). 'Children of this world' means 'worldly folk'. They are capable, when judged by the standards of their ambience/age/environment, of reaching a higher level . . . Jesus is not suggesting that there could be a contrast between worldly people's dealings with the worldly on the one hand and with the unworldly on the other. Below, p. 79 n. 1.

CHAPTER FOUR: PART TWO

Dives and Lazarus and the Preceding Sayings

INTRODUCTION

IN THE FIRST PART of the chapter the meaning, and the direct implications of the parable of the Unjust Steward were discussed. It remains to attempt to place each part of the chapter in the assumed setting, to which the parable originally belonged, or belonged in the materials from which Luke has taken these passages. It was pointed out that the burden of proof lies upon him who asserts that the passages which appear in sequence are not united by a thread of teaching. As it happens, that thread is not difficult to disentangle, and its reconstruction is the task of this section.

The greatest problem of the chapter, after the parable, remains not so much the sayings, but the story of Dives and Lazarus. That story, which has never been explained *in toto*, contains a plain example of reversal of fates. Lazarus suffered in life, Dives enjoyed luxury: now their experiences are relatively reversed, and heightened into the bargain. But why is the beggar called Lazarus? Another Lazarus rose from the dead, and did both obtain their names from a common traditional source? Do the implications of each occasion upon which the name occurs lie in the meaning, 'God is helper'? The new light shed upon the parable by the material offered in Part One (above) casts a quite unexpected glow upon the story of Dives and Lazarus. Perhaps it is sufficient to prove the connecting thread—for in midrashic discourse, such as Jesus seems often to have used, a connection, even of a much more fanciful kind, serves for the purposes of teaching, without necessarily exhausting the scope of the ideas and texts or other material which are connected. Because the story of Lazarus turns out to have an intimate and surprising connection with the Unjust Steward it does not follow that the story has nothing quite special of its own to contribute to the rich flow of the exposition. But what that connection is must be demonstrated. As the thread passes through the items which are connected, so we must pass from the parable to the story, and develop the ideas as they appear.

The chapter may be analysed into the following parts: (*a*) The parable ending at the end of 8*b*; (*b*) the application of the parable, contained in 9; (*c*) the extension of the parable covering 10–12; (*d*) the summary of the parable and extension (13); (*e*) Jesus's answer to the Pharisees' unspoken objections in 14–18; and (*f*) the summary of the lessons to be learnt from (*a*) to (*e*), with additional matter, in pictorial form in 19–31 (Dives and Lazarus).

THE PARABLE AND PRUDENCE

(*a*) The parable has been examined already. The κύριος who praises the steward and approves his act must be the Rich Man, not Jesus. Jesus gives the reason the Rich Man approves the act, and since Jesus's speech does not end until the end of 13 it is wrong to suppose that we have here an interposition by the evangelist in his own person. The awkwardness of such a break was always evident. The Rich Man's approval is, as we have seen, a crucial part of the parable and the reason he approves is both a part of the parable, and the transition to 9, the 'application'. The reason in 8*b* is most interesting. 'Because the children of this World are more prudent than the children of Light in the context of, or with reference to, their own generation.'[1] It is a fact that in their own generation, which is the 'worldly' phase of human evolution, the sons of this generation know their duty (in the widest sense of the word) better than those who are sons of the generation which has yet to materialise. The worldly people know how to utilise worldly goods to do righteous acts, and to obtain the reward of righteousness, while those who fancy themselves as the 'Children of Light' are either narrowmindedly refusing to 'soil their hands' with tainted

[1] εἰς τὴν γενεὰν τὴν ἑαυτῶν does refer to the steward's dealings with the debtors and the master's reaction (Tillmann 179; Fonck, 688), but does not mean 'in dealings with their like' (as Jülicher, Jeremias), but 'judged by the standard of their generation'. M. R. Vincent, *Word Studies* . . . (1887), 394. A. R. C. Leaney, *Comm. on the Gospel acc. to St Luke* (1958), 220. εἰς is often interchangeable with ἐν and both are used in the sense of sphere or context: Robertson, 589, 591, 594; Blass–Debrunner–Funk, § 206. Bauer–Arndt–Gingrich at p. 229 (5) cite εὔθετος εἰς (fit for), τοῦτο οὐκ εἰς ταύτας τὰς ἡμέρας λέγω (I speak not with reference to these days), λέγειν εἴς τινα (to speak with reference to someone), ἀσθενεῖν εἴς τινα (to be weak in comparison with someone: 2 Co xiii.3), consequently at p. 874 they support the interpretation of our passage given here. *Cf.* '. . . in his generations' (Gn vi.9) with the comment at b. San. 108*a* = Sonc. 741–2.

earnings, or are devising means whereby service to God can be mixed with service to worldly purposes. They are carefully 'watering down' the prescripts of God, so as to enable piety and comfort, fear of God and prestige amongst men, to go hand in hand. Though the *Torāh* forbids the taking of interest, schemes which are barely veiled usury are tolerated under the pretext that if God had wanted to forbid them he should have been more precise! This is not a question of an *a minore ad maius*.[1] The worldly know both when to do the right thing, why to do it, and what means to employ when doing so; we are not to imitate them and outdo them, but are to understand their conduct as proof that our scruples are on the one hand too sensitive and on the other hand not sensitive enough. The facts of life can at times be our teachers, as well as the Law and the prophets.

MAMMON AND FAITHFULNESS

(*b*) Verse 9 is a direct exhortation. 'Unrighteous *mammon*', which the law of man allows you, and will always allow you, to earn, and which in some cases you cannot avoid earning, must be employed in God's service, whether in charity or otherwise. The goodwill of the recipients will be a token by which you can judge whether you have earned entrance to the eternal tabernacles. The steward was driven to it, and hope for Heaven can lead you to it. It does not matter that your motives are, like his, selfish: God is concerned with your state of mind, not with what caused it to change. The Prodigal Son had neither courage nor spontaneous piety, but he obtained his reward because his father was biased in his favour; in the same way the general public appreciate a man who deliberately abstains from interest easily capable of being exacted, because they have sympathy with the poor (which is hardly a high ethical motive). God's 'ideas' of ethics are such that what he requires of us, subject to his penalties, are certain states of mind, which we are free to reach by any path appropriate to the circumstances.

'Unrighteous *mammon*' must not be hoarded, or used for conspicuous consumption; and the same considerations which apply to 'righteous *mammon*' apply equally to 'unrighteous *mammon*'. We notice that Jesus does not recommend that the priestly class should mitigate their objections to such money. Perhaps they were not equally severe—few at this period could afford to be too scrupulous.[2]

[1] As Gerda Krüger, 'Die geistesgeschichtl. Grundlagen des Gleichn. v. ung. Verw.', *BZ* 21 (1933), 170–81, relying on Jerome, *Ep.* 121, 6, 12–13; Augustine, *Quaest. Evang.* 2, 34; Isid. in Migne, *PL* 83, 126; Greg. *ibid.* 76, 207. Kögel (597) and Fiebig (82–3) had anticipated her as to the idea itself.

[2] See above, p. 57.

(*c*) The sentences regarding 'faithfulness' refer to another aspect of the parable, not inconsistent with the first. The promise of the eternal tabernacles would be enjoyed by those who were entitled to it only if they fulfilled the conditions which God had laid down. Using the fanciful rules which placed 'unrighteous *mammon*' *extra charitatem*, the Pharisees had produced a situation whereby disobedience to the spirit of the biblical commands relating to usury, etc., was not only unpunished, but also a source of profit and prestige. One must, if one wishes to possess the promise (the true wealth,[1] 'your own'[2]), be faithful in dealing with (i) unimportant, ill-esteemed, trifling wealth (that is, 'unrighteous *mammon*'),[3] and (ii) property (of both sorts) which is not your own. This includes in general the produce of the earth of which you are stewards and not owners, and in particular other property which according to the law of God belonged to the Temple or the priests or the poor, and not to those who grasped it.

Because the steward in the parable had not been faithful in regard to his master's property of both sorts he had been dismissed. You are in danger of being thought untrustworthy in respect of 'unrighteous *mammon*', whatever be your position with reference to its opposite. The result may be that your title to the genuine wealth, which is yours by right of contract with God, will be jeopardised. For faithfulness, which includes the ability to fulfil contractual and fiduciary obligations to the best of your ability, is a *quality*, and is demonstrated equally effectively in small matters and in great,[4] and because you are not doing what you ought in respect of 'unrighteous *mammon*', which you affect to despise, you cannot claim to be faithful and deserving merely by virtue of your conduct in relation to other property.

[1] A play upon words: *māmon shel 'emet* is the opposite of *m. dishᵉḳār* (Riggenbach, 24). *Cf.* Lk xii.33.

[2] The reading in *v.* 12 which best fits the sense is undoubtedly ὑμέτερον. ἡμέτερον, which could easily be a palaeographical corruption, might be justified on tendentious grounds. It is a pity that Huck–Lietzmann's and also Aland's *Synopse* and the B.F.B.S. edition both print this inferior reading.

[3] Riggenbach, *ubi cit.* 24. See also below, p. 95f.

[4] A somewhat fantastic explanation of 10, reading a pause where hardly any reader would expect to find it, namely 'He who is faithful in the least and the most (or the great) is faithful, and he who is unrighteous in the least and the most (or the great) is unrighteous', is particularly misleading as it might induce one who does not read Greek to suppose that here we had a definition of a 'faithful', and correspondingly an 'unrighteous' person, as one who bore the character respectively in *all* sorts of context and not in *any* sorts only. Hunter, *Parables* (1960), 120 says that Lk xvi.10 does not belong to the parable, since the parable is about resourcefulness, and the saying is about faithfulness in respect of unimportant things. He failed to note the subtle overtones of 'unrighteous *mammon*' (= *e.g.*, usurious gains), and has not observed that the parable is not about resourcefulness but about the instinctive grasp which ordinary people have in contexts where money and morality confront each other.

(*d*) The summary of the parable and of this extension from it is precise. The steward abandoned his master's service when he opted to obey the law of God. To serve *mammon* implies a lack of aversion from accumulating, hoarding, or conspicuously spending 'unrighteous *mammon*'. Riches and 'unrighteous *mammon*' are inseparable in the actual world, which the pious Jew must face as it is, doing his duty in respect of all of it. Just as the steward found the two services incompatible, and (depending upon the point of view) may or may not have been unfaithful towards his master when, whilst still in his service, he obeyed injunctions apparently incompatible with it: so the pious Jew may find he cannot accept employment in certain concerns, but it is equally practicable for him to turn whatever he earns to God's uses, to employ *mammon* for God's ends, and so live obediently even while acting in general under the authority or instructions of a lesser master.

THE LAW OF GOD

(*e*) The Pharisees grimaced. Some may have been attached to acquisitions; more must have felt that it was morally naïve to show that what they had gained legally was not theirs in God's eyes. In their carefully elaborated 'dust of usury' loopholes existed which favoured 'pious' lenders.[1] Was the system self-stultifying? Their prosperity suggested that God favoured them.[2] Jesus's comical parable and the arguments he thought fit to attach to it seemed ridiculous at more than one level. Business and piety could not be incompatible, and the Pharisees' efforts had been directed towards making business standards morally respectable. Was Jesus shaking the bases of 'dust of usury', or was he penetrating deeper into the foundations of Pharisaic theory?

In their view tainted wealth in any case was unsuitable for gifts to God. 'Making friends with' suggests making presents, offerings. If the wages of prostitution, for example, could purchase divine forgiveness, ethical theory was turned upside-down. Was not the *Torāh* itself clear on such points? Falsely earned money is not to be used for pious purposes, as Philo explains with a striking metaphor—tainted wealth is,

[1] See above, p. 61, n. 1.

[2] Preisker, *ubi cit. Cf.* Jb i.10. On Jesus's antagonism to this point of view see Hauck in *ThWzNT* IV, s.v. 'Mammon', para. 3. Perhaps this passage unduly stresses Jesus's objections to wealth as such; the remark satirising charitable donations, etc., aimed at earlier applications of the parable as understood by Fonck and others of that period, appears to be imaginative. It was a matter of fact, as we infer from instances in the Gospel, that a man could hardly be rich in those days without neglecting the command 'Love thy neighbour . . .'. Consequently riches and unrighteous living were virtually synonymous: but circumstances alter cases.

as it were, counterfeit.[1] The rule about the 'hire of a harlot' (Dt xviii.18) is to be extended by analogy to the money of people suffering from passion, vice, or any other soul-sickness.[2] The Community of the Dead Sea Scrolls would have agreed: 'No man shall vow to the altar anything unlawfully acquired (literally tainted with violence)', 'No Priest shall take from Israel (such property)'.[3] The *Torāh*, moreover, was ideally the authority behind the civil law, and judged by legal standards the steward was a thief. A thief purchases goodwill with immoral acquisitions: and this provides an analogy for our entrance into the promise! But were the debts immoral anyway? Unless the whole work on usury were to be done again from the commencement there was a danger of arguing in circles. The existing system was conclusively presumed to rest upon divine foundations,[4] and Jesus's paradox, even if true to life (as might sometimes happen), flouted traditional distinctions. To place the 'spirit' above traditional interpretation was dangerously original, and subversive of the whole system of law which they had constructed and he seemed himself not to reject *in toto*.

Jesus's remarks form a tripartite 'answer' to their unspoken objections. He speaks on (i) justification, (ii) the status of the law of God, and (iii) the special illustration of divorce and adultery. With these three their case is demolished.

(i) The rabbi, says Jesus, is after all only the interpreter of the *Torāh* ('the pupil')[5] and not its author ('the teacher'). The spirit as well as the letter of the commandments must be obeyed: this after all was consistent with the characteristic Pharisee position.[6] The very form of God's commands[7] shows that he is concerned with secret intentions, with the heart, and not merely with actions. In respect of a contract it is the real

[1] Philo, *De Spec. Leg.* I, xix, 104 (Colson VII, 161): ὧν καὶ τὰ χρήματα βέβηλα καὶ παράσημα, εἰ καὶ ταῖς ὕλαις καὶ τοῖς χαρακτῆρσι δόκιμα.

[2] Philo, *ibid.* li, 281–4 (Colson VII, 263–5).

[3] *CD* XVI.13–14 (Vermès, 109; Lohse, 100). See above, p. 76.

[4] Under Dt xxxii.4 it was axiomatic that the Holy One is perfect in the execution of justice.

[5] See above, p. 72, n. 4.

[6] On the aims of the Pharisees see R. Travers Herford in E. I. J. Rosenthal (ed.), *Judaism and Christianity* III, *Law and Religion* (London 1938), 104; Moore, *op. cit.* I, 58, 66. Jesus's comments on the results must be seen against this background only: Moore, *op. cit.* II, 192. On spirit and letter see the stimulating article by Boaz Cohen, 'Letter and spirit in Jewish and Roman Law', *Mordecai M. Kaplan Jubilee Volume. Eng. Sect.* (New York 1953), 109–35 (reprinted at *JRL* i, 31–57, where it is followed by the interesting 'Letter and spirit in the New Testament' (58–64)). As often, the rabbinical scholar takes a jaundiced view of St Paul, but this can be discounted in favour of the learning employed upon the problem in general. Challenging ideas on Jesus's relationship to Pharisees' doctrines are published in H. Merkel, 'Jesus und die Pharisäer', *NTS* 14 (1968), 194–208.

[7] See above, p. 57, n. 2.

intention of the parties, and not the form of words, which interests him. The steward was not *really* cheating his master in releasing part of the debts, and in God's eyes he chose between taking usury (which according to the law of God would have been *de facto* his) and employing it in God's service. In sneering at him the Pharisees have missed the point. Man's law arranges the disposition of wealth to suit worldly standards, and these standards determine prestige on earth: but 'every one who is arrogant is an abomination to the Lord' (Pr xvi.5)[1] and if the Pharisees attribute their current prestige and relative comfort to the accuracy of their doctrines they are deceiving themselves, for *non sequitur*. Elsewhere Jesus pointed out that the Pharisees' attitude was virtually a stumbling-block in their own path.[2]

(ii) Jesus's teaching had elsewhere called in question the traditional (Pharisees') orthodox interpretation of the *Torāh*.[3] Denial of the reliability of the Pharisees' ordinances was obviously fraught with far-reaching consequences. If Jesus verged upon contradiction of the Law his followers were in greater danger than if he interpreted it more strictly, a course open to any puritanical reformer. In the parable of the Unjust Steward he seems to have questioned the distinction between usury and 'dust of usury' as current in the courts. If he allowed that the Pharisees were correct in detecting 'dust of usury', he quarrelled with the scope they allowed it and with their failure to enforce the biblical rules with reference to this class of usury also. God, after all, will judge men by his standard and if the law of man offers no preparation for this test the courts may be failing in their purpose.

Jesus points out (*v.* 17) that the Law and the prophets were eternal and immutable, and would be fulfilled. Divergencies of interpretation are therefore intolerable. It will not do for them to wander after the convenience of the public.

The change brought about by the ministry of John the Baptist altered the basis upon which Jews were entitled to the 'eternal tabernacles'. It is not suggested that the parable of the Steward conclusively disposes of difficulties raised in this saying. Impatient with the Jews, Jesus appears to suggest that others will be admitted to the privilege of which they were unworthy; and to this extent, and not otherwise, the status of the Law and the prophets had altered.[4] There is a sense in which no enlarge-

[1] The significance of this was recognised by Pautrel, *cit. sup.* p. 75, n. 1.

[2] Lv xix.14; Mt xxiii.13; *Mishnāh*, B.M. V.11 (Danby, 357). Preisker, *ubi cit.* emphasises that the chapter is intended to show the Pharisees confronted by the spirit of their own authorities.

[3] The Sermon on the Mount.

[4] This interpretation of the controversial phrase καὶ πᾶς εἰς αὐτὴν βιάζεται (*cf.* Mt xi.12) does not neglect points raised in D. Daube's valuable 'Violence to the

ment in the numbers of the candidature for admission can affect the validity of the original relationship between God and the Jews.

(iii) How deep this assurance penetrates is shown by the near-parallel case of divorce. In usury the rabbis were scrupulous but to no purpose. In the controversial topic which Jesus next raises the rabbis had built up a mass of learning upon a very slender foundation, and had, according to Jesus, missed the fundamental point. Mosaic legislation, intended to meet special needs and therefore (as we shall see) fit to be construed narrowly, ought not to have been so extended as to nullify the propositions relative to marriage and adultery laid down in the Law. Jesus elsewhere explains this, showing that although a man was permitted to divorce his wife (and was obliged to do so where she had committed adultery—the Jews had a horror of actual or potential polyandry) this did not authorise either of them to remarry during the life of the other.[1] The rabbis had assumed that the 'letter of divorce' was an authorisation from the husband to his wife to marry another person, and they had, in fact, thus placed a stumbling-block before the public's feet. The point of *v.* 18 is that even where the rabbis have consistently misled the public the law will be fulfilled, equally with cases (e.g. usury) where they have been, on the whole, on the right track, but have not sought to enforce, or have not insisted upon enforcing, the rules in which they believed. The adulterer and the usurer, it seems, will alike pay the penalty, the standard of adultery and usury being God's and not man's.

SCRIPTURE AS LAW TEACHING

All this is hard. The public may claim that they have not been warned. False teachers worsen the matter. The rules may eventually be applied to those who acted in ignorance and good faith. God tolerates man's law on Earth, which is a travesty of his Law: will mercy be shown to those who are deceived by it?

(*f*) The story of Dives and Lazarus now develops the train of thought. It might well be referred to as the 'parable in reverse' because so many

[1] Dt xxiv.1–2; Mt v.31–2, xix.9; Mk x.11; 1 Co vii.10–11. M. Mielziner, *Jewish Law of Marriage and Divorce* (New York 1901). R. Yaron, 'On Divorce in Old Testament Times', *RIDA* (3rd ser.) 4 (1957), 117f., where references are found to Neufeld, *Ancient Heb. Marriage Laws*, and L. M. Epstein, *Marriage Laws in the Bible and the Talmud*. R. Travers Herford, *Talmud and Apocrypha* (1933), 122; R. H. Charles, *Teaching of N.T. on Divorce* (1921). See below, p. 370. Also Daiches at *JCLIL* 8 (1926), 215ff.

Kingdom', *New Testament and Rabbinic Judaism* (London 1956), 285–300, but it takes a less despairing view of the completeness of the ideas surviving in the chapter.

of its themes refer to the parable, and previous commentators have remained unaware of this aspect of the story.[1] It is, however, much more than the parable in another guise: it summarises pictorially the message of the earlier portions, supplies the answer to questions which they have raised, and adds, with an intriguing touch of irony, the reference to current notions of individual retribution after death.

It has been pointed out that a great deal of popular Jewish mythology underlies the story,[2] and its complete explanation awaits further research. At present I am attempting chiefly to replace it in its context in the chapter.

It is essential to realise who Abraham and Lazarus are. Dodd is certainly right in saying[3] that the presence of the name Lazarus requires to be explained. Abraham, at any rate, is the father of the Jewish people, but is also their patron. He is still alive.[4] He watches the performance of his seed in the land promised to him and to them for ever; *haggadāh* tells that he is interested in them both on earth and in whatever life there is after death.[5] In a sense the Jews on earth are his heirs, or possessors of his inheritance, and he is naturally concerned with the way in which they manage it. In so far as the commandments refer to the Jew's 'brother', they regulate (or attempt to regulate) dealings between descendants of Abraham, and a great part of obedience to God is the fulfilment of duties towards those in whom Abraham has an interest. Charity, for example, is a debt in respect of which not only God, as enjoiner, but also Abraham as the representative of the receivers can figuratively be claimed to be creditors. This type of image is common to all the East, at least in part: acts of charity not merely prepare the way to the everlasting tabernacles, or produce the spiritual effects which correspond to the promise, but also pay one of the human being's debts to his creator, or the power which corresponds to him. Abraham can contact his descendants through his steward, the ruler of all his house. His steward is his representative, 'like' him,[6] and he is competent to be sent to the land to observe how the 'tenants' are dealing with the

[1] Michaelis, *op. cit.* 213–29.
[2] H. Gressman, *Vom reichen Mann und armen Lazarus*, Abh. P.A.W. VII (Berlin 1918). C. H. Dodd, *Historical Tradition in the Fourth Gospel* (Cambridge 1965), 225.
[3] *Ubi cit.* 229. There, at n. 1 he called my identification of Lazarus with 'Eliezer 'more ingenious than convincing', but I am not sure if he realised the midrashic notoriety of 'Eleazar' = Lazarus? See below for the citations from b. San.
[4] b. B.B. 17*a* = Sonc. 86. See *Jew. Encycl.* I, arts. 'Abraham', 'Abraham, Apocalypse of', 'Abraham's Bosom'. Jesus says so at Lk xx.37–8.
[5] See references in previous note. Note how he could be conjured up to rescue the daughter of a digger of wells in B.Ḳ. 50*a* = Sonc. 288 (*c.* A.D. 70). This popular belief throws some light on Jn viii.56–7.
[6] See above, p. 52, n. 2.

property.[1] On this errand Lazarus was sent as a helpless (and therefore sinless) beggar under the noses of a rich and selfish family. For Lazarus, as his name shows, is no other than 'Eliezer, Abraham's steward,[2] who was sent on the very sort of delicate mission which we have seen served as one of the origins of agency in Jewish law.[3] 'Eliezer is a well-known figure of Jewish *haggadāh* and has been the subject of an intriguing short monograph.[4] 'Lazarus' is thus more than a beggar and because the beggar is Lazarus he goes bodily to Abraham's 'bosom' when he 'dies', where he shares the state of those few who went alive to the 'place' where Abraham is. Dives is buried.

The reversal of fates, and 'Lazarus' ' comfort after death were recognised by John Lightfoot more than three centuries ago as pointing to 'Eliezer, the servant of Abraham. Wetstenius, about a century later, did not heartily applaud, but at least he continued (with his modest 'Gn xv.2') knowledge of the clue. But the point of the allusion escaped both of them. The fact is that Jesus, by bringing in Lazarus, and by making the subject-matter of the story a failure of hospitality, and by making the Rich Man refer to his 'five brothers', drew his hearers' attention to the story of Sodom and Gomorrah and the rest of the five cities which were destroyed (Gn xiv.2, xix.24; Dt xxix.23) for their lawlessness. We know that Jesus spoke against the cities in which he had lived and worked, and foretold that in the day of judgement it would go better with Sodom, etc., than with them (Mt xi.24), and that he told his disciples (Mt x.15) that if any city or village was wanting in hospitality towards them it would go worse with them than Sodom, etc. Now in our story of the Rich Man and Lazarus the same theme appears, but

[1] His ability to move about freely is evidenced from the Rich Man's and Abraham's references to him. Naturally we are told that he did not go to the Rich Man's gate on his own feet; in this case he was put down there (by whom, we are not told). See below, p. 95, n. 1.

[2] Lightfoot, *Hor. Hebr. ad* Lk xvi.20. B. S. Easton, *Gospel acc. to St Luke* (Edinburgh 1926), 251; H. K. Luce, *Gospel acc. to St Luke* (Cambridge 1936), 172; *Encycl. Bibl.* III, 2744–5. It is accepted that Lazarus = Lazar = Eleazar. Eleazar and Eliezer are linguistically distinct but parallel forms and in places apparently interchangeable. Several rabbis, for example, are known by both. Josephus, the Letter of Aristeas (*c.* 100 B.C.?) and 2–4 M write Ἐλεάζαρος. But Josephus has our form Λάζαρος at *Bell. Jud.* V, xiii, 7 = V, 567. See Wetstenius. *ad* Lk xvi. 20 for rabbinical instances of the same.

[3] *Jüd. Zeits. f. Wiss. und Leben* 7 (1869), 123–33 (on the biblical text and the *midrash* upon it). That 'Eliezer the Steward of Abraham (Gn xv.2. See also the Genesis Apocryphon xxii [Vermès, 224]) and the servant sent to negotiate for a bride for Isaac (Gn xxiv) were the same is accepted in the Midrash, and no Jewish commentator on Genesis doubts it. *Jew. Encycl.* V, 111. In the treatise *Derech Erez Zuta* (1, 9) 'Eliezer is counted among the nine who entered paradise while still living. 'Eliezer and a miracle: b. San. 95*a* = Sonc. 642.

[4] L. I. Rabinowitz, 'The study of a midrash', *JQR* 58 (1967), 143ff.

highly generalised: those that live as the Rich Man, heedless of warnings, will have the fate of Sodom: for the story of Lot and Sodom is a story for perpetual information, not an old tale to be read and forgotten (*cf.* 2 Pe ii.6; Jude 7). Is i.10–31 commences 'Hear the word of the Lord, ye rulers of Sodom ...' Ezk xvi.46–59 contains the words 'Sodom thy sister hath not done ... as thou hast done ... Behold, this was the iniquity of thy sister Sodom; pride, fulness of bread, and prosperous ease was in her and in her daughter; neither did she strengthen the hand of the poor and needy. And they were haughty ..., therefore I took them away ...'

The lawlessness of the Sodomites lay, according to Jewish tradition, not so much in their sodomy as in their inhospitableness. They were, of course, governed by the law applicable to the descendants of Noah, but their country was a kind of topsy-turvy land in which all right and justice were subverted.[1] The rabbis make merry over the strange rules that obtained there. With Jews, hospitality to strangers and wayfarers (*hach*^{e}*nāṣat 'or*^{e}*ḥiym*) was a cardinal virtue;[2] with the Sodomites it was a vice. 'Eliezer, servant of Abraham, complained of being attacked: 'Give them a fee for bleeding you', said the judge! The beds of Sodom were notorious; they were truly Procrustean, for the rule was that if the visitor was too long they lopped off his feet, and if he was too short they stretched him. The rights of the traveller were completely abrogated. A girl gave bread to a poor man secretly: she was cruelly punished. When a poor man came to a place citizens each gave a single coin, on which the donors wrote their names, but no food: when he died each took back his own coin. It was a rule that whoever invited guests to a banquet should lose his upper garment. 'Eliezer, servant of Abraham, went to test their hospitality. People asked him, 'Who invited you?' He named one after another of those present; they ran away in turn for fear of losing their clothing, till he was left alone—and so could partake of the feast. The Babylonian Talmud solemnly repeats these tales, complete with biblical citations, and a comment by 'Rab' (d.247).[3] The whole is appended to a Mishnaic discussion[4] whether the men of Sodom would (i) partake of the world to come, and (ii) stand at the day

[1] Jos. *Ant.* I.xi. 1 agrees with rabbinical notions in general. Εἶναί τε μισόξενοι καὶ τὰς πρὸς ἀλλήλους ὁμιλίας ἐκτρέπεσθαι. *Cf. Targ. ps. Jon.*, Gn xviii.20.

[2] b. Kid. 39*b*, Shab. 127*a*.

[3] b. San. 109*a–b* = Sonc. 749–52. The passage beings, 'Our rabbis taught: the men of Sodom waxed haughty only on account of the good which the Holy One ... had lavished upon them ...' 'Eliezer, the servant of Abraham, is a useful person. A discussion of his with Shem on conditions in the Ark and Abraham's battle with the kings of the east and the west is reported (b. San. 108*b* = Sonc. 746–7)!

[4] *Mishnāh*, San. X.3 (Danby, 397, Blackman IV, 287–8).

of judgement (for trial). The final opinion (with which Jesus evidently agrees) is that notwithstanding the wickedness of the Sodomites they shall have the benefit of trial on the day of judgment; but it is evident that it was hotly debated. This is the background to our story.

The Jew wishes to enter the eternal tabernacles. The Prodigal Son wished to enter his father's house. The steward wished to enter the houses of the sympathetic public. The Prodigal Son claimed on the basis of his father's pity and affection; the steward in reliance upon the public's regard for the moral law which both knew and respected if they did not normally practice. Lazarus wishes to enter the Rich Man's house in the meanest possible capacity, as a scavenger. The crumbs are not expected to be thrown out of the window, or carried to him by servants. We are correctly told that what he wanted was to be allowed to crawl under the table after the guests had departed and to share the scraps with the dogs. The dogs came out to him after they had enjoyed that in which he wanted (perhaps not entirely silently) to participate. The dogs were apparently the Rich Man's dogs and not merely the ownerless, pariah dogs of the Eastern town. Lazarus's claim rested upon the Law and the prophets: as the Rich Man's brother he was *entitled* to be served at that table. In a sense the Rich Man was his debtor. The Prodigal Son's claim was backed by natural affection; the steward, from being a powerful creditor became a not altogether contemptible applicant for favour. Lazarus typifies those whose 'rights' can never be enforced, whose 'debts' press just so far as the debtor chooses to recognise them, and whose claim is abject and often silent. Lazarus was excluded from the house he was entitled to enter (a symbolic entry would have sufficed), and that was why his unpaid debt directly bears upon the Rich Man's situation, when he in his turn required hospitality thereafter.

The hospitality-theme proceeds even further. We are told that the dogs (who have anticipated Lazarus, and have consumed the spiced fragments of the rich meal) actually licked Lazarus's sores. That licking is connected with the 'drop of water' begged by Dives. Though Jesus's tale expands with that mixture of the dreadful and the comic which some have seen as a feature repeating itself in Jewish humour, not a word is superfluous. The suggestion is not entirely otiose, that the dogs are said to lick Lazarus's sores in order to heighten the horror of his situation, rather than to suggest that the animals took pity upon him while their master did not. But it would appear that, in contrast with Dives's failure to provide any hospitality for Lazarus, Lazarus provided hospitality of a kind for Dives's humblest servants. Watchdogs were certainly then kept in well-to-do houses in Palestine, but it is most unlikely that they would be allowed access to the family's source of drinking-water, or that bowls would be set for them as if they were household pets. This gruesome hyperbole hammers home the fact (meaningful to an oriental) that the natural relationship between rich and poor within Israel had been completely inverted: Lazarus, though a beggar, was, in social terms, the creditor.

In the parable the steward was a man with a bad reputation, and yet he was able to win approval and hospitality from representatives of worldly people; in the story Lazarus, who was without fault and whose claim rested upon permanent injunctions, failed to obtain what he deserved. There are limitations to the perspicacity and sympathy of the worldly and well-to-do. Whereas in the parable the master was painted in neutral colours, and his pressure served to convert the steward in the nick of time; here the Rich Man himself is wicked, dining sumptuously every day with a starving beggar at his door (the very epitome of anti-social behaviour), and though warned against this by the Law and the prophets, in which he was educated,[1] does not heed that relatively less urgent pressure. Here is the answer to our question. Those who are taught the law of God, both the commandments and their exposition and inculcation by the prophets, are, as the lawyer puts it, 'fixed with notice', and cannot escape retribution. Yet up to the last minute those texts could have effected in Dives the conversion which pressure such as is described in the preceding parables is capable of effecting.

Failure to deal righteously with *mammon* leads to 'Hell'. The subtle and nominally God-fearing distinctions of the rabbis have not altered the destination of Dives. He was a flagrant wrongdoer though passive in his wrongdoing. He may not have been a robber or a usurer; he may well have been both, since both methods of being and staying rich were easy in Jesus's time. In any case he neglected his duty towards the poor.

Cannot Lazarus be sent to warn Dives's brothers?[2] Whereas he cannot go to the 'place' where Dives is, there is nothing to stop him returning to the house in question, but in Abraham's opinion the

[1] This is by no means to suggest that all, or even the majority of Jews were literate, but the rich man (even if technically an *'am-ha-'aretz*) was sure to be. In later ages rich Jews found it fashionable to study *Torāh* as a pious act and an intellectual exercise and in order to gain or maintain prestige in their community. We cannot expect that Dives was unacquainted with the text of the Law and the prophets.

[2] It has not been noticed by commentators that whereas Dives has brotherly love for his consanguine brothers, but had no love for his brother Lazarus (equally 'son of Abraham'), he takes it for granted that Lazarus is willing to show concern for his and Lazarus's brothers who are still alive. The fate of all the cities of the plain was decided by the behaviour of Sodom alone (or so it would appear from the biblical text). Naturally, Pharisees would be unwilling to believe that they could have perished without a warning (see below, p. 171).

journey would be useless. 'If they do not hear Moses and the prophets, neither will they be convinced if someone should rise from the Dead.' There is one possible implication of this remark which seems to have been missed by commentators. The Prodigal Son turned to reacquire dependence upon his father as a result of fears for his very life; the steward turned at the last minute as a result of fears for his material future and prestige; in Dives's case no fear enabled him to turn. Whose fault was that? Are Moses and the prophets really upon the same level as worldly stimuli, pressures, fears? It really seems as if Scripture exists (within this limited context) to warn those who are so lucky and independent that no more tangible warning can reach them. Prospects in *this* life impress in a manner quite different from the very uncertain hazards of the next life. Those who are accustomed to grapple prudently and effectively with this life's problems either do not believe that the next has comparable problems, or do not doubt that they will be appropriately equipped to cope with them. News from 'the Dead' falls upon unwilling and uncomprehending ears. Divine commands relating to this life are recognised by the worldly to be valid in strictly worldly contexts. Whatever fear is to be aroused in the individual it must be with respect to what remains of this life. The lesson which could be taught by one who rises from the dead must relate not to the state of things 'there', for that will hardly produce the necessary effect; he will be listened to only if he brings news with reference to the life in which the Prodigal Son, the steward, Dives, and their colleagues believe. When the human being's capacity to be warned has ceased, or in contexts where warning would be inoperative either from its source, its nature, or its lack of force, Scripture must serve as the warning, and since it was intended for just the purpose in question the individual who does not heed it can have no ground for complaint.

Where Scripture fails to instruct, however, everyday experience provides clues, and occasionally gives accurate inspiration. Read in sequence after the parable of the Steward the story of Dives and Lazarus is less depressing. The parable seems to have been intended rather to encourage than to dismay.[1]

[1] The *Jaiminīya Aśvamedha* (? A.D. 300–900) referred to above (p. 8, n. 2) has a grotesquely un-Indian story of a fainting traveller being debarred from all but the sight, scent, and sound of a great feast: the parable of Dives and Lazarus is evidently its basis (chs. VIII–IX). Other gospel traces include an equally un-Indian story at VI.31–54 (the old lady busy with her household affairs says property comes first, religious observances are a 'fraud', and scripture is mere legend: but her stepson has her taken to the divine inauguration-sacrifice *by force*!) which echoes the Martha and Mary episode; and passages at X.57–64, XI.130–7 (about the 'procuress' who recommends 'love' of Kṛishṇa) show what the enterprising Indian author thought was meant by the episode of the forgiven woman (see below, p. 267). As for the Lazarus figure in

The words, 'It were better for him that a millstone were hanged about his neck . . . (than that he should lure or entrap the uninstructed into sin)', complete (xvii.2) the message of our chapter. Nothing is worse than the position of the teacher who expounds Scripture in such a way as to frustrate its capacity to instruct.

All the 'under-senses' of this chapter cannot be dealt with fully here. The word 'steward' at once recalls Pauline doctrines of stewardship; the actual 'stewards' of Jesus's time, the priestly class, are almost certainly aimed at; and also the public in their capacity as assessees to tithe, etc.; not to forget the 'stewards' of the land, the Jewish people as a whole. We have noticed that any steward is an agent, and that the agent is literally the 'messenger' who is like his Master, foreshadowing the apostle. From this chapter it appears that though the Law is binding and effective, and no reference to the law of man can be a substitute for it, actual life, which is the setting for representation of God by those who speak in his name, affords essential clues as to the manner in which they should comport themselves and the uses they should make of practical affairs, both in performing their function and as a medium of instruction. That the Kingdom of Heaven is mixed with this world, inextricably until the end of the age, is after all the message of numerous other parables.

APPENDIX

The exposition of Lk xvi set out above rests upon the supposition that Jesus's 'teaching' can be reconstructed from Luke's material as it lies, a supposition greatly aided by the evident possibility of detecting a rational thread running right through the whole, making it possible to see the relevance of each passage to the chapter and to its neighbouring material. A study of the vocabulary (which reveals that Luke's material came from various quarters) by no means leads to any comparable result—but that is an incongruity for which the scholar must find an appropriate explanation. This present exposition does not depend in any way upon any ingenious guess as to any 'peg' upon which Jesus might actually have hung the 'teaching' itself. If we suppose, as we freely may, that the material derives from notes or recollections of actual sermons and/or discussions, or (though this is a somewhat extreme supposition) of a single sermon, we are by no means obliged to hazard guesses as what text or question might have set the train of thought in motion. We are concerned with the teaching and not with

the *Jaiminīya Aśvamedha* story, his ravenous hunger is relieved at the last, since his divine host was playing a practical joke upon him and thus revealing his power.

its original circumstances, except in so far as these form part of the picture handed down to us. However, there exists a school of thought which has by no means claimed that the time has come for a full-scale demonstration of any general theory, but which steadily accumulates the 'coincidences' between the material preserved in the Gospels and biblical or midrashic counterparts which could possibly have served as texts for and parallels to the material, and in particular the parables, attributed to Jesus.

This school of thought can claim some strange coincidences, all except one of which are beyond the scope of this chapter. Our difficulties in this connection lie chiefly in the absence of definite proof that the surviving *midrashim* bear a close relationship to the *midrashim* current in Jesus's time; that Jesus could cite or rely upon them in front of an audience which may have contained few literate, let alone learned persons; and that if the discourses depended for their comprehension upon midrashic allusions it would have been rational to preserve the gist of the discourses without their connecting and (in that sense) explanatory material. In all fairness it must be added that it has often been suspected that the Sermon on the Mount, for example, would be far more acceptable to Jews and Gentiles alike if the references to the *Torāh* were really meant to be, and understood to have been, references to the *Torāh* with learned and popular commentaries, and not to the bare text as later fixed by the Masoretes.

In connection with Lk xvi an astounding success can be claimed for this type of approach. It is to be remarked that no one suggests that Jesus's teaching is midrashic in anything but method. The public were used to the curious and unexpected links between ideas found in the biblical texts, and to the puns and other types of verbal allusion and purely *ad verbum* exposition of which the teachers commonly took advantage. Passing, as every teacher must, from the known to the unknown, it is extremely likely that Jesus availed himself of didactic methods which relied upon a copious memory for the sacred writings and their fanciful traditional embroideries. The less literate his hearers, the more likely they were to know the tales and utterly unhistorical associations of ideas in which the rabbis then and since have delighted. It is not in the least improbable, therefore, that if midrashic connections exist between apparently unassociated notions, and some corresponding connection exists between verses in the Gospels, Jesus may have been utilising existing habits of association at which none of his hearers would be astonished. But the whole point of this discovery (if it is a discovery) is that Jesus used those associations for new purposes, and hung new teaching upon old pegs.

It was Dr M. Gertner who first drew my attention to *Yalḳûṭ Shim'oni*, sec. 473 (on Is l.10), and to Midrash R., Exod. XXXI. The latter chapter especially is extremely rich in material parallel to, and illustrative of ideas which we have seen to be essential to Lk xvi. Not only the first stages of our parable (see below) appear, but also the verbal connection with divorce, the friends who point out a man's good deeds ('A man's gift maketh room for him': Pr xviii.16, is cited); the duty of the rich man if he wishes to be delivered in the day of evil; the trial to see if the rich man will open his hands to the poor; the wheel idea, whereby the hungry are filled and the rich are sent away empty, and fates are reversed; the faithful servant (in this case Obadiah: 1 K xviii.3—Obadiah who took no usury[1]); the moral weight of abstaining from usury as compared with failure to perform many lesser commandments; and the intimate connection between usury and the exile and other misfortunes of the Jewish people—all these facets of alternative and equally authoritative commentaries on the anti-usury commands of the *mishpaṭiym* section of Exodus strike the reader as marvellously similar to the raw material of our chapter. Space forbids an exhaustive survey, but the English translation will take the reader near the heart of the conceptions, which are characteristically Jewish. That the bearing which this material has upon Lk xvi has never been noticed is to be explained, apparently, by the fact that hitherto no one had realised that the clue to the Unjust Steward and his employer lay in the topic of usury.

The *midrashim* which are available for our consultation supply a further connection (which we have explained above on a rational basis) between the steward, usury, divorce, and 'Eliezer (Lazarus). It is all very clear. We commence the thread of ideas with Is l.1. God puts to the Jews the ironical question in the first verse, 'Where is the bill of your mother's divorcement . . . or which of my creditors is it to whom I have sold you?' God will not 'divorce' or 'sell off' his people, even though he might have a perfect 'right' to do so. The sufferings they endure are not beyond his power to end. In *vv.* 10–11 we have a message of encouragement and warning based upon the song of the Servant. It commences, 'Who is among you that feareth the Lord (*y^{e}rē' yhwh*), that obeyeth the voice of his Servant?' There is a definite connection between 'fearing the Lord' and the redemption of Israel, and 'fearing the Lord' has a technical, narrow, as opposed to the non-technical, wide, meaning.[2] To this we must return. But first we should notice

[1] *Midrash on Psalms*, on Ps xv.5 (trans. Braude, I, 194).

[2] Moore, *op. cit.* II, 147–8, indicates a parallel injunction supported by the words, 'Thou shalt fear the lord thy God', and supplies the reason for the appearance of that formula. He deals with usury succinctly but on the whole accurately, *ibid.* 142–5.

that the commentary on Is l.10 reads, 'Who is among you [that is, really the general body of the Israelites] that feareth the Lord: ... this is 'Eliezer the servant of Abraham. . .'.[1] Naturally the interpretation of the verse differs from that generally accepted now, but the connection between faithful execution of the master's instructions and fitness to trust in the redemption was evident even upon that interpretation.

We return to 'fearing the Lord'. The Midrash R., Exod. XXXI. 6 (on Ex xxii.24)[2] tells us that he who takes usury is not God-fearing; for it is written (Lv xxv.36), 'Take thou no usury of him, or increase; but fear thy God'.[3] The connection between usury and 'fear' is made obvious by the biblical text: *'al-tiḳaḥ ... neshech ... v^{e}yāre'tā me'elo-heychā*. The one who fears the Lord, such as 'Eliezer, therefore takes no usury. The wickedness of usury is expressed in Midrash R., Exod. XXXI.15 (on Ex xxii.24 (25)):

Woe to him who takes usury! This is like a king who opened to one [? of his servants or agents] his treasury, and he [this man] began to oppress the poor with it [*cf.* Ezk xviii.12] ... to strip the people naked ... and to fill the treasury with *lies* [*i.e.* false acquisitions], thus *damaging* the king's treasury.[4] God likewise opens treasure-stores and gives to men of his gold and silver, as it says 'Mine is the silver, and mine the gold (Hg ii.8)'; but man begins to take interest from the poor man. ... God gives him '*mammon* of truth' (*māmon shel 'emet*) and he makes of it untruth (*sheḳer*) [that is, unrighteous *mammon*][5]. ... Therefore you shall pass away from the world ..., and therefore does God warn in the *Torāh*: 'If thou lend money to any of my people thou shalt not be an usurer (Ex xxii.24 (25)).'

[1] This is the second interpretation offered by *Yalḳūṭ*: *d.'a. miy bachem y^{e}re' h. zeh 'eli'ezer shomē'a b^{e}ḳol 'av^{e}do shehiyh 'av^{e}do shel 'av^{e}rāhām 'āveynu* ... Obadiah (1 K xviii.3, 12 *y^{e}rē' 'et-yhwh* San. 39*b* = Sonc. 252–3) would fit the requirements adequately but 'Eliezer's place in Jewish legend is more secure. 'Eliezer, like Abraham, had a sound knowledge of the law and was a stout champion of the right, as well as *the* faithful servant. L. Ginzberg, *Legends of the Jews* (Philadelphia 1947), I, 292. We note the 'Eliezer has the assistance of angels, *ibid.* 294. On Obadiah see *ibid. Index*, sub nom.

[2] Trans. S. M. Lehrman, Soncino Press (London 1939), 384.

[3] Sonc. 397, where Lv xxv.36 is not in fact cited, though Radal inserts the verse (on the authority of Tanḥuma) in the text.

[4] The trans. reads 'fill *himself* with falsehood and generally squander the king's treasures': *v^{e}-gāzal v^{e}-m^{e}mal^{e}'a 'oto sheḳer, v^{e}-miph^{e}ṣiyd 'ots^{e}ro shel melech. pāṣad* or *p^{e}ṣed* is evidently the original of διασκορπίζων. It is curious to note that here the 'robberies' so far from enriching the treasury actually diminished its real value, stuffing it with untrue wealth. That this paradox underlies the Greek term no one would as yet be bold enough to assert, but the point deserves further investigation.

[5] The appearance of these words in the *midrash*, drawn to my attention only after I had completed the reconstruction of the ideas of Lk xvi according to my own theory based primarily on the text itself, struck me as a welcome confirmation of the essential connection between Lk xvi.1–8, 9 and 11: *natan lo māmon shel 'emet v^{e}'oseh 'oto sheḳer*. The *midrash* further cites Ho x. 13: 'Ye have ploughed wickedness ... ye have eaten the fruit of lies (*p^{e}riy-kāḥash*) ...'. See above, p. 75, n. 2.

The usurer is compared by the commentator not merely to one who acquires wrongfully and has 'unrighteous *mammon*' for himself, defying God's commands, but especially with one who uses an opportunity offered by a person of neutral moral position, but ample resources, in order to wrong his fellow men with the result that the character of the resources themselves becomes contaminated. This is a highly characteristic notion. In spite of the late date of this *midrash*, which is supposed to have been based on various old sources,[1] there are no grounds for believing that our parable influenced it, and the contrary supposition is attractive. The parallel between a 'rich man' and a 'king' may be seen again in the two versions of the Wedding Feast parable and of the Talents parable. Our Rich Man approved the steward's act in releasing usurious debts, as we may suppose the king in this rabbinic parable would have gladly rid his treasury of unrighteous *mammon*. The message, that God condemns those who interfere with the divine order of exploitation of the world's produce,[2] is the same in the *midrash* and (as we have seen) in the parable of the Unjust Steward. It is a pity that this remarkably close parallel was not noticed by Billerbeck. Jesus, as we have seen, uses the idea for a much wider purpose, and proceeds from this story to a series of propositions to which the rabbinic *midrash* is not committed.

On the other hand, midrashic confirmation of the connection between usury and divorce is available. It is based upon the point in Isaiah as understood in the *midrash* thereon. God has it in his *power* to divorce, or get rid of, his people who are being punished for their various sins. The people are afraid they have been 'divorced'. A synonym for *divorce* is 'reject'. The root *mā'aṣ* is used in the Bible in the contexts of 'reprobate (counterfeit) silver' and rejection of the people (as at Is liv.6: *timā'eṣ*). Jr vi.30: 'Reprobate silver shall men call them, because the Lord hath rejected them.' Reprobate silver means false money, the money of untruth, and by a metaphorical enlargement of the idea, contemptible or repulsive money (*cf.* ἐλάχιστον), the money which, while it looks 'true' enough and stands physical tests, will not enter the acquirer's ownership because of his having acquired it in a manner contrary to the law of God. We note that *mā'aṣāh shel torāh* means 'rejection or contempt for the Law'. Jr xiv.19: 'Hast thou utterly rejected Judah?' The two phrases *keṣeph nim*^{e}*'āṣ* and *mā'oṣ mā'aṣ*^{e}*tā* establish

[1] H. L. Strack, *Introduction to the Talmud and Midrash*, ch. XVII, 5*c* (New York, Philadelphia 1959), 215.
[2] The notion of ideal equality (into which it is impossible to enter here) is fully set out in Midr. R., Exod. XXXI.5 (*ad fin.*) (trans., p. 383) citing Ps lxi.8 (7), taking the root of *yeshev* to be *shāwāh*!

the connection between usury and rejection, divorce. This is explained in Midrash R., Exod. XXXI.10 (on Ex xxii.24 (25)):[1]

If thou lend money. . . . This is what is written (Jr vi.30), 'Reprobate silver shall men call them'. When Israel was exiled from Jerusalem their enemies . . . used to say: God desires this nation no more, for it is written, 'Reprobate silver, etc.'. God has rejected them. . . . When Jeremiah heard this he went to God and said: 'Lord of the Universe! Is it true that thou hast rejected thy children?' (Jr xiv.19). This is like a king who beat his wife. Her friend said to him, 'How long will you beat her? If you want to *divorce*[2] her, you should beat her until she dies: but if you do not wish to divorce her why do you beat her?' The king said, 'Even if the whole of my palace goes into ruins I shall not divorce my wife'. (Even so) said God to Jeremiah, 'Even if I have to destroy my whole world, I shall not divorce[3] my people . . ., as it is written (Is l.1), "Thus saith the Lord, where is the bill of your (mother's) divorcement . . . ?" I have agreed with Moses about them (Ex xxii.24 (25)): "Thou shalt not be to him as an usurer. . . ." But if you trespass against these commandments I shall pledge you, as it is written (Ex xxii.25 (26)): "If thou shalt take thy neighbour's raiment to pledge. . . ." '[4]

The upshot of this discovery appears to be that the pre-existing connection of ideas was as follows: Usury militates against the redemption of Israel; for their usurious behaviour, their addiction to what is *rejected*, *untrue*, they too will be rejected, put in pawn; 'rejection', however, does not amount to divorce, since it is because God intends to keep the Jews to their contract that he punishes them for breach of its conditions; because divorce is out of the question the rejection is temporary, and at the last minute, as with the pawned garment that must be returned at nightfall (Ex xxii.26), when the people give up their usury, they become 'God-fearing' and the relationship with God becomes perfect. Their redemption from the pawn in question is conditional on their giving up usury.

The present writer does not suggest that Lk xvi.18 is based upon the rabbinic connection of ideas. On the contrary, the teaching is quite distinct. The rabbis say that God will never divorce his people: Jesus says that divorce amongst men as a legal institution has been grievously misunderstood. What is open to suggestion, however, is that Jesus's

[1] Sonc. 388–90.
[2] Or 'drive out'. In the English translation it appears that the notion has been misunderstood, as if the friend were saying, 'if you do not want her to *die*, why beat her?'
[3] Or 'utterly reject', 'banish'. The use of Is l.1 in b. San. 105*a* = Sonc. 714 supports this.
[4] The *midrash* enlarges on the implications of the verse. Moses asked: 'Shall they remain in pledge for ever?' God replied, 'No, only *Until the Sun appears*' (*ibid.*), that is, till the coming of the Messiah; for it is written, 'But unto you that fear my name shall the sun of righteousness arise with healing in its wings' (Ml iv.2).

passage from usury to divorce and thence to antisocial and non-God-fearing conspicuous consumption (the Steward—Mammon—the Law and the Prophets—Divorce—Dives and Lazarus) has arisen from a pre-existing catena of ideas still traceable in midrashic texts.

At this point it may be objected that we have not yet considered whether Lk xvi (part of the Great Central Section) does not derive its structure rather from the sequence of ideas in Dt xxiii–xxiv than from rabbinical *midrashim.*[1] In fact the Hire of the Harlot (xxiii.18), Usury and Brothers (*vv.* 19–20), Vows and their Payment (*vv.* 21–3), Dealing with the Property of Others (*vv.* 24–5), Divorce (xxiv.1–4), Treatment of Fellow-Israelites (*vv.* 6–7), and other topics about the care for the poor follow each other in a sequence agreeing very well with Luke. In fact, once we begin to see the matter in this light it is possible to see Jesus's commands about forgiveness at xvii.3–4 as parallel to the merciful commandment about the 'forty' stripes at Dt xxv.1–3. But what does this mean? There is little likelihood that the text of Deuteronomy was constructed in obedience to canons of rabbinical exegesis. That skilled interpretation was available even at that remote period cannot be denied for one moment, but we cannot go to the length of suggesting that rabbinical notions survived in such perfect continuity in such minute detail. The obvious solution is this: At the time of Christ the connections between the verses of Deuteronomy had been worked out, like other interrelations of scriptural passages, upon a fanciful footing which nevertheless kept close to the fundamental principles of Jewish exegesis. Luke's object was, amongst other things, to provide a Christian 'scripture' which would be read in some more or less close association with the Old Testament. The general arrangement thus provides a peculiar commentary upon Deuteronomy.[2] But this is not to say that the association of ideas was not already firm by another route. Like the tops of submarine mountains which appear on the surface of the ocean as islands, the remnants of Jesus's teaching betray a continental association which a superficial observer would hardly guess. Has Luke arranged the material so as to subserve midrashic patterns (as the linguistic characteristics of the pericopae suggest), or did his informants retain skeleton notes of Jesus's teaching which were explained to him in this way, a procedure which would argue that Jesus followed the midrashic method in any case? Had Jesus the same text of Deuteronomy before him? This might be thought by some to be by far the easiest of the explanations open to us.

Professor Aileen Guilding in her famous *Fourth Gospel*[3] experi-

[1] See below, p. 100, n. 2. [2] *Ibid.*

[3] A. Guilding, *The Fourth Gospel and Jewish Worship* (Oxford 1960), 135f.

mented with Lk xvi to see what would emerge if she supposed that it were intended to be read once a year with the *Torāh* lection appointed in a triennial cycle. She assumed that Lazarus was a point of contact with John's gospel, and to him we must return. Having done so she found that in the first year the chapter would be read with the Joseph story (Gn xlvii), in the second with Lv xxv.14f. (lending free from usury) and in the third year Dt xxiii–xxiv (usury and the treatment of the poor). This is far too much to be put down to coincidence.

It remains to consider Lazarus. Scholar after scholar has evinced an uneasy suspicion that the story of Jesus's raising his friend of that name from the dead has some relation to the Lazarus of the parable. It would seem to be an irrational relation, in any case. Naturally the explicit mention of the personal name attracts attention.[1] A conclusive solution is not to be obtained as a by-product of a study of Lk xvi, for there is evidently much more in the story of the physical reanimation of Lazarus than turns on the name. But our present study makes a contribution to a solution. Jesus had many friends, and their names are forgotten or confused. Names are remembered for some reason, in some cases because of a pun. Some significance was seen in the name, and that gave it weight it would otherwise have lacked. Now 'Eliezer and 'Eleazar are very common names. Jesus named in his parable of the Rich Man (which must have been very popular indeed) the poor man who serves as the touchstone of the rich man's virtue, and called him Lazarus. He did so evidently because he wanted to utilise the common belief to which the author of the Epistle to the Hebrews alludes (xiii.2) that angels can visit men unawares. Lazarus, as we have seen, was one of those people who did not die: some divine power (not clearly visualised) could enable them to revisit the earth and appear as living beings. Lazarus was thus suitable for the purpose. Jesus's actual friend, whose revivification caused such excitement, happened to have the same name —and it was felt to be proof (may we suggest?) that Jesus consorted with a family having this extremely rare (but to the populace well-authenticated) qualification of potential reappearance after death.

[1] Dodd is good on this aspect (*Hist. Trad.* 229) but I reserve an opinion on the whole question of 'solution by formal structure'. That Lazarus-'Eliezer was known to have tested the 'men of Sodom', and the significance of this, naturally escaped him.

CHAPTER FIVE

The Parable of the Prodigal Son

LK xv.11–32, an elaborate, circumstantial, in fact the longest, parable, calls now for the endeavours of a symposium. This chapter cannot do more than open the legal aspects, which have already been handled by Professor David Daube and Professor Jean Dauvillier,[1] and the symbolic aspects, which have been ignored—if we except for the present the work of Professor K. H. Rengstorf, to which references will be made below. A complete investigation of the symbolism is not to be looked for until the midrashic links between the parable and its associated passages in Deuteronomy[2] have been expounded by an expert in

[1] In 'Le partage d'ascendant et la parabole du fils prodigue', *Actes du Congrès de Droit Canonique* (Cinquantenaire 1947: Bibl. de la Fac. de Droit Can. de Paris) (Paris, Letouzey et Ané 1950), 223–8, Professor Dauvillier made a plea for the study of legal materials for the clarification of the text of the New Testament. The notion was then a novelty. D. Daube, 'Inheritance in two Lukan pericopes', *ZSS, rom. Abt.*, 72 (1955), 327ff.

[2] C. F. Evans, 'Central section of St Luke's Gospel', *Studies in the Gospels: Essays in Memory of R. H. Lightfoot* (Oxford 1957), 37–53. R. 'Akiba: 'Every section in scripture is explained by the one that stands next to it' (*Sifre on Numbers*, § 131). It would be highly plausible to see our parable as a sermon on Dt xxxii.6–26 read with Ml i.6*a*, and elaborated with the aid of Dt xxi–xxii. Those chapters contain a series of points: (i) the worst crime can be atoned for (*vv.* 1–9); (ii) those whom God delivers into your hands must receive mercy from you (*vv.* 10–14); (iii) nevertheless justice must be observed in accordance with law, as in the example of the legal right of the firstborn as between two sons (*vv.* 15–17); (iv) yet a stubborn and rebellious son may be denounced (even if he is the elder) and executed (*vv.* 18–21); (v) and he may even hang on a tree (*vv.* 22–3); (vi) therefore one must not hold back from doing good (*e.g.* conversion) out of self-interest (xxii.1–4). That consecutive interpretation of this very chapter was usual in the time of the apostles is shown by Ben 'Azzai, who linked up Dt xxi.10–23 ingeniously, showing how 'transgression draws transgression in its train' (which curiously is illustrated by the younger son's experience in the parable, but that may be a coincidence). See Midr. R., Deut. VI.4 = Sonc. 123. Luke may, as Evans suggests, have used Jesus's words *per contra*, but the position may be even more subtle. The elder brother by alluding to imaginary dissipations on the younger brother's part actually suggests that the spirit of Dt xxi.18–21 applies, and questions whether the younger is not really stubborn, etc., and fit to be executed! The author of Genesis seems to have been aware of these points. Jacob heard his father and mother (thus contrasting with Esau, who qualified in rabbinical thought for Dt xxi.18–21): Philo, in the Loeb edn, *Supplement I*, 548–9, § 244, on Gn xxviii.7.

the technique of delivery of sermons amongst the Jews. Our parable's place in a lectionary cycle has been identified,[1] and the implications of this also must be brought out: in part these will overlap with previous research work, and in part they will reveal the early church's view of the parable's implicit significance.[2] This work, however, will relate to the stage at which the parable became a written document, and to its worth for those who first used it in liturgy. This chapter is concerned with Jesus's own meaning, so far as we can rediscover it from the shape and content of the parable in the light of contemporary attitudes. Though this means covering ground already covered often, and much current exegesis will be confirmed, there is more by way of subtle statement and even more subtle contention in the parable than could have been realised before. Close studies of the vocabulary from Wetstein to J. Jeremias do not help us much at this stage of refinement; but it is interesting to note that in Jeremias's view, well substantiated as to the greater part of the parable, traces of the semitic origin of the document before us are visible throughout.[3]

A preliminary observation is called for. The Jewish public knew the law relating to the family intimately and no more familiar topic could have been chosen. Meanwhile the Jewish public expected sermons to contain references to the leading themes of religious thought, easily evoked, such as that God is father, and the leading themes of Jewish biblical history, including the adventures of the heroes of the nation, will have been utter commonplaces. A comment made privately on my similar treatment of the parable of the Good Samaritan,[4] that Jesus can hardly have expected his hearers to have had *all* those points in their minds, is not entirely answered by pointing out that that parable, unlike this one, is shown addressed to a lawyer: one must insist that

[1] Aileen Guilding, *Fourth Gospel*, ch. 9 (The Feast of the Dedication), esp. p. 132–6, 138. The Genesis passage dealing with Joseph, and the Deuteronomy passages dealing with distribution between sons and the stubborn and rebellious son turn out to be lectionary parallels with our parable. If the parable originally was uttered at a season when these lections would be read many embarrassing problems raised by Professor Guilding's thesis would be totally obviated. The church and the evangelist would then be carrying out the author's intention, not falsifying. See below, p. 120, n. 5.

[2] In the course of a magnificent demonstration of the inadequacies of the post-Jülicher terror of seeing allegory in a parable of Jesus (*cf.* V. Taylor, *Gospel acc. to St Mark*, 210) M. Black conjectures that the father in our parable represents the love of God (*Bull. J. Ryl. Lib.* 42, 2 (1960), 273ff., at p. 283f). A. M. Hunter, whose defiance of Jülicher is admirable (*Interpreting the Parables* [1960], 113–17), sees the father as God, the elder brother as the Scribes and Pharisees, and the prodigal as publicans and sinners (61).

[3] J. Jeremias, 'Zum Gleichnis vom verlorenen Sohn, Luk. xv.11–32', *Theol. Zeit.* 5 (1949), 228–31.

[4] Below, Chapter 9.

the contemporary mind had more leisure to fasten upon what had a multiple emotional appeal such as biblical stories certainly had, and had more zest in holding what it had fastened upon. A parable tailored to suit such a taste must not only elicit sounds of delight, but a determination to reproduce it closely for the benefit of people unable to hear it at first hand.

PARABLE AND PROBLEM

'Don't make difficulties where none exist!' This is how many a friend reacted to my persistent and painful anxieties about the parable. In this view the details, where they seemed to interfere with a commonly accepted exegesis, were, or must have been, insignificant. It did not matter whether the prodigal son was a fool and a liar, whether the father was a dupe as well as weak. The absence of an apparently authoritative application of the parable from Jesus's own lips leaves one free to imagine what the parable could mean, and it must be something simple and straightforward—it is supposed. 'I will arise and go unto my father' is a proposition of such self-evident simplicity that the behaviour of the prodigal son does not require critical scrutiny. If there are faults in the parable these can safely be attributed to Luke or his source. Or perhaps Jesus himself did not mind what misunderstandings might arise? And in view of such uncertainties are close scrutinies called for? Perhaps the situation will seem different when the behaviour of the parties in our story is worked out patiently. There is a close blending of a lifelike tale, such as can easily have happened, with a double (as we shall see) piece of teaching in the course of which the acceptance of one proposition implies, whether the hearer likes it or not, the acceptance of another. The power of insinuation hidden in this parable is on a par with that to be seen in the parable of the Good Samaritan, which is the most artful of the parables treated in this book. To our satisfaction we find, as we do in that case, a point of current social and political thought hidden in the teaching. Most exegetes know (as is shown in *Peake*) that our present parable deals with the attitude of Pharisees towards unorthodox Jews. But with what implications? Is it really an *Antikritik*, as Jülicher would have it? It seems, after all, worth while to point to the problems and do our best with them.

PATENT AND LATENT PROBLEMS

The parable seems to have nothing to do with receiving sinners and eating with them (Lk xv.2).[1] The elder brother (we suppose) ultimately

[1] The hint that Jesus exercises God's prerogative of forgiveness is surely secondary.

dined with one who was reinstated, for the father had received him. The three parables deal with *rejoicing*, and this parable properly makes the bridge between that set and the next, namely, those which concentrate on *warnings*.[1] The prodigal was warned by his stomach, after all, to return. Many wonder how repentance preceded that return. Repentance of *what*? Was he sincere? Was the father as foolish to readmit him as he had been to give him the share initially? Yet when the prodigal decided to return he obviously expected his father to be as harsh as most peasant fathers would have been. The son expected to be paid wages as a servant, with all the humiliation as well as inconvenience which that would have caused. This might well be the fundamental weakness of the parable.

The ne'er-do-well returns to be treated better, as Bornhäuser assured us, than most peasant fathers would have treated him.[2] Does this argue implausibility? Yet undercurrents are hinted at throughout the parable. The sharpness of family conflicts and the tautness of family ties (the latter often producing the former) were taken for granted by eastern peoples, whose descendants still surprise us by their implicit and often irrational obedience to demands made upon them by a father or brother. A slight hint in a parable would be sufficient to show which way the wind blew, especially in a society where an appeal to the fraternal bond between individuals who dislike each other can be guaranteed to produce an immediate and powerful response (*cf.* Ps cxxxiii.1). Though modern exegesis concentrates on the father who 'meets the repentant sinner more than half way' the parable as a whole is concerned with the integrity of a family which the will and intention of the father (with the mother evidently behind him) merely confirms and demonstrates. One who reads the parable as an individualist living amongst individualists, looking perhaps for hints of individual salvation, would be in danger of viewing it from the wrong perspective.

The fatted calf, the robe, the ring are a series reaching from the likely to the unlikely. Had the fond father lost his sense of proportion? If so the parable's function may be jeopardised. How are they to be explained? Implications are already admitted by some scholars, incredulously. One is in danger of forgetting the mental process by which a lifelike factual tale is repeated as a little drama, and the dramatic enhances, without falsifying, the factual element.[3] If the sandals, again,

[1] See p. 91 above.
[2] Hunter, *op. cit.* 63 n. 1, quotes A. T. S. Nygren, *Agape and Eros* (London 1953), 82f: the parable is not self-evident because in real life a father would put the son on probation—and adds that it would be nearer real life if the father had killed, not the calf, but the son himself!
[3] See App. III to Chapter 17 below.

are an embellishment in the parable, what of the singing and dancing? Are there two parables, one about the 'waiting father' and one about the 'evil eye'? Other problems are there, great and small. Does the story, as Professor Rengstorf suggests, belong to a *royal* environment and are the father's characteristics 'positively kinglike'? Was the son, after all, entitled to a share? If not, why was he given one, and what effect would this have? Why so much bitterness on the elder son's part? What, by contrast, about the pigs? Are they rhetorical embellishment, or an integral part of the story as in Mk v.11–16 and parallels? Is the elder son's hypothetical kid declamatory also? Then there is the astounding conclusion: is the father's estate really the elder brother's, when the returning prodigal, who has eaten his cake, shows every sign of proceeding to have it? Theological tendency, to show both sons enjoying the 'inheritance', stumbles here: was the reinstatement *in integrum*, or only apparently so, and would the difference matter? Is there a sly suggestion that the elder son was a hypocrite and was getting his deserts? Hardly, unless we are to take the first hearers as far more tolerant of irony than most orientals are.

THE PRACTICAL SITUATION

No son of a Jewish household was entitled to a share.[1] The son cannot therefore have asked for 'my share'.

Gregory Palama, in his third Homily, comments on the words 'Give me the ἐπιβάλλον portion of the property' in the following way:[2]

> Namely that which belongs to me under the laws, that share which is my just due. But what law is this, and what kind of justice makes fathers debtors to their children? On the contrary. Nature herself proves that children are in debt to their fathers, to whom they owe their very existence. But this little speech fits the adolescent mentality.

Neither at law nor by custom nor according to any sort of reasoning could this son *demand* anything like a share. Nor was he asking for a new legal status.

Jewish Law did not have 'emancipation'; and the father and son were separate in property. But the Jews, like every other eastern agricultural society, treated an ancestral farm as virtually common property in daily

[1] Rightly Tatian, *Diatessaron* xxvi, 13. Indivision amongst sons who are co-heirs is another matter. *Mishnāh*, B.B. VIII.7, IX.3ff. Daube, *ubi cit*. 328. Julius Schniewind, *Die Freude der Busse* (ed. E. Kähler, Göttingen 1956), 56, points out that as the father gives what is asked for so God, whom the father indicates, gives freedom to men.

[2] Migne, *PG* 151.37.

use. Agriculturalists live like co-owners, but when a domestic crisis arises the specialities of the private law reveal themselves. A father might anticipate his death by giving shares to his sons, determining what they would have after him, and obviating disputes.[1] Such arrangements are known from ancient times,[2] and their usefulness is proved by Indian jurists' regarding partition during the lifetime of the ancestor as a prime manifestation of *dāya*, which we should call 'succession'.[3] And Indian conditions resembled Palestinian. Fathers by no means always heeded the advice at Si xxxiii.19, 23 ('. . . give not power over thee while thou livest; and give not thy goods to another, lest thou repent and make supplication for them . . . in the time of thy death distribute thine inheritance'). That reflects experience, sometimes pathetic. The testament developed in our period; the need for careful distribution of assets, avoiding the pentateuchal rule in favour of the eldest son,[4] was already felt, and that occidental institution was embraced so far as the biblical law permitted.[5] In the time of Christ διαθήκη did not mean (in a Jewish context) *testament*, but disposition, and disposition having an ultimate effect similar to a will was well known. It is extremely unfortunate that the legal disquisition of Billerbeck[6] on Lk xv.12–13, upon which Jeremias relies, subtly distorts the

[1] See p. 108 n. 4 below.

[2] Dauvillier speaks of separations initiated by the father, in Sumerian, Assyrian and Babylonian sources. G. R. Driver and J. C. Miles in their *Babylonian Laws* (Oxford 1952–5), as in their *Assyrian Laws* (Oxford 1935), find little trace of our type of partition. An adopted child's share could be recalled for misconduct or failure to maintain (*Bab. Laws* I, 343); a gift could be made to a favourite son to take effect after death (like the Hebrew μετὰ τὴν τελευτήν gift, which Yaron discusses exhaustively). A gift of land normally created nothing more than a life interest: Abraham at Gn xxv.5. The background to the rabbinical legend of the Ishmaelites' complaint to Alexander the Great: Midr. R., Gen. xxv.6 = Sonc. 545–7, *cf.* b. San. 91*a*; Daube, *ubi cit.* 331. The case in Pap. Oxyr. 1, 131 is of ambiguous implications. Judith's partition (Jdt xvi.24) could alone have enabled her beneficiaries to inherit.

[3] H. T. Colebrooke, *Digest of Hindu Law on Contracts and Successions with a Commentary by Jagannát'ha Tercapanchánana* [*sic*] (various editions), book 5, ch. 2. A valid severance may be morally bad.

[4] See the *Mishnāh* cited in the next note.

[5] At *Mishnāh*, Ned. IX.5 (Danby, 276) R. 'Aḳiba dealt with a case where the sons shared equally. The leading discussion is the very thorough study by R. Yaron, *Gifts in Contemplation of Death in Jewish and Roman Law* (Oxford 1960) (extensively and helpfully reviewed by Z. W. Falk at *JJS* 12 [1961], 67ff.). All attempts to reconstruct our parable's legal framework would be futile without this exhaustive background. Yaron himself, with commendable caution, does not classify the transaction between the father and son at Lk xv.12; he contents himself with saying, at p. 44, that it 'conceivably furnishes a case of dismission'. In the present writer's view it is reasonable to call it dismission (*Abschichtung*), though the initiative was the son's: but the results were similar in that the son had no right to participate in his father's estate at his death.

[6] Billerbeck, *op. cit.* III, 550.

evidence and its implications. Yaron's work, fortunately, corrects Billerbeck's learning.

For a son to ask for a share while his father was in good health was a confession that the son could not live in that home. He was not the younger son of an English landed family of the pre-1925 period, to whom the virtue of adventurousness was a necessity. A Jew would see the situation in the opposite light. The younger son should stay at home, labour, and obey. Failing information we must assume that our younger son, aged about 17,[1] who had been a 'son of the commandments' for at least three years, was jealous of his elder brother, intolerant of demands made upon him, thwarted, or under the impression that horizons were wider overseas. The father might have refused the request, but he adopted the policy of treating the nearly grown-up son with kindness.[2]

The younger son asks for τὸ ἐπιβάλλον μέρος. What was it? The definite article shows that no unexpected or uncertain item is wanted. 'Επιβάλλον could mean 'falling (to me)' (*cf.* Tb vi.12), not in any case 'what would fall (to me)'. It *could* mean 'proper', 'suitable'.[3] But does the father's discretion enter into it? No doubt he had discretion whether to give a share and, if so, what its size should be; yet what he is asked for is evidently something known to customary law and usage. Deplorable, but not unthinkable. A liberty is allowed which should preferably not have been asked for: but people had successfully asked for it before. The boy's motive is not then mentioned in so many words. He does not intend to set up a separate household, but to emigrate. Either occasion would have justified his demand and his father's acquiescence. It is not necessary to suppose that he was a spoiled child, son of a favourite wife. This would be *our* embellishment. But we are justified in noting that the father met impatience with patience. All peoples are familiar with

[1] So K. Bornhäuser in his very full study at *Studien zum Sondergut des Lukas* (Gütersloh 1934), 103–37, at p. 105. This would be very young for emancipation, but Jewish law did not know emancipation as a means of terminating the father's moral (and later also, in emergencies, legal) right in the son's acquests. The lad's age is indicated by the extreme improbability of his being married. Had he been married he would have been settled. If he were married his sinfulness in leaving and behaving as he did would be multiplied out of all proportion and the parable would become lop-sided. Jeremias, *op. cit.* at p. 129 (Eng. trans. 1963, p. 129), agrees that he was unmarried.

[2] Maimonides, *Mishneh Torāh* XIV (Book of Judges), III, vi, 9 (trans. Hershman, p. 156) (Lv xix.14. b. M.Ḳ. 17*a* = Sonc. 107). The word μέρος excludes *ṣᵉgūllāh* (*peculium*), on the implications of which see B. Cohen at *Proc. Am. Ac. J. R.* 20 (1951), 135–234, which is reprinted at *JRL* I, 179–278.

[3] This aspect is somewhat obscured in Bauer–Arndt–Gingrich, but is plainly seen in the references provided in Stephanus and in Liddell–Scott–Jones at II.7. The force of the ἐπί must not be lost sight of. It is the share which (hypothetically) is bound to come to him. Jülicher, *cit. inf.* II, 338, correctly summarizes the position, but his supposition of the third must be wrong.

a situation where the share which must fall to a child at the parent's death is anticipated at, for example, a marriage. There is nothing derogatory in asking for this kind of help at such a time. Usually the one who asks is so keen to have it that he forgoes the possibility of sharing in profits made after his share is separated. Other parties do not mind, either because the taker forgoes future participation, or the law has grown sufficiently sophisticated to ensure that these 'advancements' are brought into hotchpot at a distribution after the parent's death. That was certainly not envisaged at our present partition. But that does not mean that the father in this case was obliged to accede to the request. The law did *not* oblige the father to furnish a young son with capital—on the contrary it did not at that time even oblige him to maintain the boy.[1] But it was obviously better to give him his chance than to compel him either to remain in the family against his will, or to decamp without a penny. Thus he could well give a share, but, emphatically, he did *not* give it with permission to alienate it or dispose of it absolutely (a point which the Jerusalem Talmud[2] notes as relevant). The point of this we shall observe presently.

It has been suggested that the share was a third.[3] But this can hardly be. In many such calculations the special rights of the eldest would be observed, but in a distribution in the ancestor's lifetime the elder could not count on obtaining his precise double share. First let deductions be made from the capital for the maintenance of dependants of the family including unmarried females, deduct again something to secure the maintenance of the father and his wife, and the balance is available for this disposition. The younger might not be awarded above a half of what the elder might hypothetically be supposed to have—for, who knows?, the elder himself might wish to decamp, and should the father then be left with all the responsibilities and no capital? One may suggest a share of two-ninths as more like what the boy would be given. If he was not satisfied he could wait until the charges on the estate were fewer, and the father's own claims were otherwise secured. The Jews were well aware of the old man who, out of fondness for his issue, splits his assets amongst them, and later, Lear-like, calls in vain to heaven and earth to relieve him. The Babylonian Talmud tries to explain the phrase 'he who acquires a master for himself' (*ha-ḳoneh 'ādon le'atsmo*) in a maxim about the three who 'cry out in vain'. It may

[1] A father could be compelled to maintain children *under puberty* only from the second century: b. Ket. 65*b* = Sonc. 397. Those above puberty could never insist upon being maintained.

[2] On *Mishnāh*, Ket. IV.8: Schwab VIII, 60.

[3] So Dauvillier, for example, at p. 225. Bornhäuser thought the capital could, and should, remain intact (p. 107). Jeremias obtained an opposite impression.

well mean 'he who transfers in writing his property to his children during his lifetime' (*ha-kotev n^e^kāṣeyv livnāyv b^e^ḥayyeyv*).[1] This pathetic figure would never be far from any middle-aged man's mind. Our father will by no means have prejudiced his own position, as the parable clearly hints. The way the servants run around him tells its own tale, and we shall explain the elder son's behaviour in a moment. Nevertheless, the younger son, having taken his share, could not later have any claim on his father's estate: so that he would be entitled, once his father agreed to his plan, to see that his share was a reasonable one *rebus sic stantibus*. All legal critics of the parable are agreed that no further participation could have been contemplated by the parties. The boy himself would have been content to be a hired servant, and a typical Jewish father might actually have contemplated such an arrangement, at least until the prodigal's reformation had been confirmed in the ripeness of time.

The owner of a big farm would not carry out this division orally or haphazard. Since this is a parable no unusual or far-fetched method can be contemplated. He would write the younger son a document giving him the share outright,[2] whatever it was. Shall we stop there? The father need not have affected the elder son. But διεῖλεν αὐτοῖς τὸν βίον fairly suggests a formal division in which the elder also would play a rôle. Moreover, the elder brother's reaction and the father's answer reveal that something was done for the elder upon which the latter ought to have relied.[3] There is an excellent reason why that indeed should have happened, not merely because when a father *kātav livnāyv* he will have followed custom in writing documents for all of them. The younger might conceivably have returned after the father's and the elder brother's deaths and demanded a share *as heir* from the latter's children. These would have been embarrassed to prove that their uncle had been given his share of his own choice, if he denied this. To protect the elder and his issue it was absolutely necessary that the father should use the well-worn expedient, that kept the image of the silly old man at a good distance, and provided for all contingencies. He will have written the elder son a document giving him the remainder of the estate 'from today and after my death' (*mē hayom ū-l^e^'aḥar mītāh*).[4] By means of this formula he gave the latter no right to possession as he gave the

[1] b. B.M. 75*b* = Sonc. 436.

[2] T. W. Manson, *Sayings of Jesus* (London 1949, 1957), 286–7, thought that the father wanted to give him a share as from the moment of his death, and this the young man must have rejected. This would be a gratuitous denigration of the young man's character.

[3] Jülicher II, 337, surmised correctly.

[4] b. B.M. 19*a* = Sonc. 119. E. Bammel (*NTS* 6, 1960, p. 315 n. 6) suggested a *matt^e^nat bāriy* (a gift in health).

younger—who could proceed to demand partition and arrange an auction if necessary (συναγαγὼν πάντα)—but a right to succeed at the father's death and to question meanwhile all alienations including gifts which were outside the father-donor's legal powers.[1] This explains the elder son's saucy behaviour, and his attempt at argument. The full effect of the answer we shall explore in due course.

Once again the English reader must be asked to consider himself ill equipped to study this story. A French reader, for example, would be protected by his own country's legal history. A son who is given a share is not thereby relieved of all responsibility to the family. No one acquainted with customary laws in general or oriental laws in particular[2] would mistake the moral, if not also legal, situation of our prodigal. *We* would think of that two-ninths, or whatever it was, as his absolute property. Hardly any other nation or culture would suppose it was. An old man cried in vain to Heaven or the courts, because Sadducee rabbis had no legal procedure whereby they could compel the issue to maintain the fond parent, just as they could not compel the parent to maintain the child. But this legal weakness rather reflected than denied the moral bond, and Pharisees were not behindhand in supplying the law's deficiencies. We must remember, too, the Jewish interest in money and what one does with it. To be casual with money is utterly un-Jewish and, as we see from many parables of Jesus and his near contemporaries, was so in his times. The biblical command to honour the parents was not a merely ethical rule.[3] Just as God must be honoured with one's finances[4] so must the parents. The honour a son owes his parents was considered (not unreasonably) as a heavy duty,[5] fully comparable with

[1] The law is stated plainly at *Mishnāh*, B.B. VIII.7 (Danby's *Mishnāh*, 377; Blackman, *Mishnayoth-Nezikin* IV, 212): 'If a man assigned his property in writing to his son (for) after his death, the father cannot sell it since it is assigned (or written) to the son, and the son cannot sell it because it is within the *rāshūt* (dominion, absolute control) of the father. If the father sold it, it is sold until he dies; if the son sold it the purchaser has no claim until the father dies.' J. Bonsirven, *Textes Rabbiniques* (Rome 1955), § 1831. Yaron, *op. cit.* 49. This fits the situation described in our parable. The elder son has what is called in English law a vested interest. This metaphor is quite suitable for theological purposes.

[2] Plato, *Laws* IV, 717; Arrian's *Epictetus* II, x.7; Seneca, *De Benef.* VII, 6; Domat, *The Civil Law in its Natural Order* (various editions of the text and Eng. trans.), II, ii, tit. 2, sect. 2 and § x. At Roman law children could be given *beneficium bonorum quaerendorum*, but they were still liable to maintain the parent: *Dig.* 25.3.5, 1. See Max Kaser, *Das römische Privatrecht* II (Munich 1959), § 226, iii, p. 145–6. For Hindu law see G. D. Sontheimer, 'The joint Hindu family . . .', Thesis (unpubl.), Ph.D. (London 1965), 180, 207, where the texts of Haradatta on Āpastamba II, vi, 14, 1 (*vibhāgāt ūrdhvam*) and *Tesavalamai* I, 8 (South India and Ceylon) are noticed.

[3] Ex xx.12; Lv xix.3; Dt vi.13; Pr iii.9. Maim. *ubi cit.* § 3.

[4] References at p. 224 n. 4 below.

[5] Midr. R., Deut., trans. J. Rabbinowitz (London 1939), 122. O. Eissfeldt, 'Sohnespflichten im alten Orient', *Syria* 43 (1966), 39–47 is useful here.

the honour owed to God himself.[1] The obligation, incidentally, is applicable, by analogy, towards the teacher and the elder brother. Obedience and maintenance were included within the word 'honour'. One who honours his father does not covet (we are told); one who covets will dishonour his father: why else, said R. Ḥananiah (a first-century Tanna), were the commandments written opposite to each other?[2] The share taken by our younger son was therefore impressed with a tacit but certain, if contingent, reservation in favour of his father. Had the father told him to go, suggested that he need not return, or otherwise exonerated him, it would be another matter. As our text shows, he divided the property—and so left the fundamental obligation in full vigour. True, a Sadducee court might not flog the son for failing to maintain the father if he were, by chance, left destitute; but that does not mean that in Galilee or elsewhere Pharisees would not insist upon children's maintaining their indigent parents, especially out of assets obtained from the latter, and would not flog them and ultimately excommunicate them if they refused. Such refusals are known. After the fall of the Temple it was established that sons must maintain their parents, and such maintenance was enforced out of funds obtained from those parents. It might be argued that this was an innovation. But the rabbis who are known to have insisted upon this, which is unquestionably Talmudic law, did so in following out a principle of practical as well as religious importance. For unless this tacit hypothec over the aided child's share were recognized parents would never part with their assets till their last gasp.

The principle is still alive: an instance is recorded of a decree for maintenance being passed against the sons of a 100-year-old resident of Baqa al-Gharbiya in 1965/6. He had shared his estate between them and they had forced him to sue them for his very livelihood.[3]

It is established that amongst the Jews the duty to honour, and so to maintain, the father was not diminished by any discourtesy, unfairness or favouritism on the part of the parent.[4] No one will doubt but that

[1] Mekilta, *Baḥodesh* viii (Lauterbach II, 257–8; Winter–Wünsche, 1909, 217–18).

[2] *Ibid.* (Lauterbach 264–5; Winter–Wünsche 220–1); Philo, *De Dec.* XXII–XXIII (!).

[3] *Muslim Bulletin* (Jerusalem) 10, pts. 1–2 (1966), p. 3.

[4] Maimonides, in the chapter cited, reproduces the Talmudic position. The children's duty to their father who has partitioned his property between them is referred to at length in j. Ket. IV, 28*d* bot. (see Schwab, 1886, VIII 59–60): Jastrow, *Dict.* s.v. *shammashā'* (p. 1602). Food, drink, clothing and attendance are obligatory: b. Ḳid. 31*b*–32*a*, even if the father greatly provokes the son, *ibid.* 32*a* = Sonc. 153–7. R. Elai said in the name of Resh Laḳish (a celebrated Amora of the second generation) that it was enacted at Usha that if a man assigned all his estate to his sons in writing he and his wife might nevertheless be maintained out of it (b. Ket. 49*b* = Sonc. 285). R. Jonathan (an Amora of the first generation) compelled sons to maintain their

Jesus himself taught that property was subject to moral responsibilities, and that membership of his community could not be obtained until this was recognized in practice, a point which we need not pursue further here (see Mk vii.11–13—the Korban [*ḳārᵉbān*] point).

This is where the prodigal sinned. Not in his dissipation, though waste of assets is a sinful act,[1] for this may be attributed to youth and inexperience; but in his forgetting that his father had a moral claim on his property, that his father, so long as he lived, had a right to call, in case of necessity, upon the son's labour and his savings. The Englishman may pooh-pooh the idea: but hardly anyone of another nationality will: such is the effect of legal history. The young man realised what he had done only when the money was gone, and when his capacity to earn (upon which he had obviously relied as axiomatic) dramatically ceased. He had sinned against Heaven[2] (hence his wretched predicament, which the pigs will have reinforced for him), and in the sight of his father, for, appropriately, he had disobeyed the fifth commandment and at one and the same time injured both God and his father. No wonder he felt signs of not enjoying any long days in the land which the Lord his God had given him! One who really repents of a wrong done must at the same time make his peace with the one he has wronged and offer penitence to God.[3] Hurrying home with a prepared speech of contrition was the obvious remedy. In fact the formula 'I have sinned against God and (this man)' would find a place in the ritual of the Eve of the Day of Atonement and the words would require no excogitation.[4] To be reck-

[1] Dt xx.19 (b. Ḳid. 32*a* = Sonc. 156). See below, p. 213 n. 2. The error, that the sin adverted to in the parable was dissipation (St Thomas Aquinas, IIᵃ IIᵃᵉ q. 119, a. 1, arg. 3), was very natural.

[2] Philo, *De Dec.* XXIII (beg.). I incline to reject the suggestion of Billerbeck (*Kommentar* II, 217) that he meant that his sin was so great it reached up to Heaven (citing Ezr ix.6, 1 Esdras viii.74, Resh Laḳish at 'Arak. 15*b* = Sonc. 87). There is after all a big difference between 'gegen' and 'bis an'. Jülicher II, 348. Jülicher's view of the nature of the lad's sin seems correct.

[3] *Targ. ps. Jonathan*, Lv vi.5–6 (Etheridge ii, 160–1). So Jesus himself at Mt v.23–4 ('leave there thy gift before the altar . . .').

[4] *Service of the Synagogue, Day of Atonement*, pt. I (London 1904), p. 49. The *basic* elements of the service will go back to the first century or earlier. b. Yoma 87*b* = Sonc. 437. Moore, *op. cit.* II, 59–60. For transgressions between a man and his fellow the Day of Atonement effects atonement only if he has appeased his fellow. It has crossed my mind that Jesus may have wished his audience to imagine that the prodigal returned on the Day of Atonement, to which the penitence, followed by a 'sacrifice', a dressing in fine garments and general merrymaking, would provide some sort of counterpart. It is impossible to be sure, but this might have formed part of a sermon for *Yom ha-kippūriym.*

---

fathers in such circumstances, and we can assume that the principle long antedated the 'enactment' at Usha (the Academy's second remove after the destruction of Jerusalem). b. Ket. 49*b*–50*a* = Sonc. 286, cf. j. Ket. (Schwab, *cit. sup.*). See also j. Peah i. 15*d*.

less whether or not you can perform your moral obligation is as sinful as failing to perform that obligation; in this case the youth did not know, while he was away, how his father was faring with that elder brother, who, as we know, was capable of arriving from the field and asking 'what these things might be'. Or had that brother been obliged to go to the wars, leaving the father to the servants? Because he did not know he should have cared more. This writer, like others, repudiates the idea that the prodigal's sin lay in his 'having a good time': we know nothing about that. If, as is quite probable, he, an unmarried lad, spent time with 'harlots', as his elder brother's imagination suggests, there is ample doubt whether a contemporary Jew would regard this as remotely comparable with the sin against the father and the sin thereby involved by breach of the commandment. The elder brother's point is that his father's 'livelihood' (σου τὸ βίον, *i.e.* the money out of which the father had a moral right to be maintained in case of need) had been eaten up, no matter how. An unsuccessful investment would have been another matter: the point is that the money was squandered. Correspondingly the prodigal's merit was that he did not see any excuse in his youth and inexperience, and when he 'came to himself' he had grown up. Working as a *hired* servant (sleeping off the premises) he could see to it that eventually with his wages, if not in other ways, he could give his father what, so long as the father lived, was only his due.

THE FATHER'S FORGIVENESS

The father must have been notified of his son's approach by small boys running from the next village, if not sooner. He has had ample time to wonder what mischief his son had been embroiled in. What has the son been doing? He lived with Gentiles, as so many non-observant Jews did,[1] and like them became attached to one of the godless (*cf.* Dt x.20). Pharisees would find this very touching, they who spared no pains to make converts even in the diaspora. Our lad was occupied in the most degraded occupation known to the Jews.[2] At the approach of the Messiah pigs, the natural abode of devils, must hide themselves and pig-

[1] It is not correct to observe, as Bornhäuser did, that the lad abandoned the Jewish faith. The Jews of the diaspora and on the fringes of the Gentile world adopted many compromises which would not amount to this. It was *observance* which was in point.
[2] *Mishnāh*, B.Ḳ. VII.7 (Danby, 342; Blackman, 62; Bonsirven, § 1636): 'And no one (*lect. var.* no Israelite) may raise swine in any place, *b*ᵉ*kol māḳom.*' b. B.Ḳ. 82*b*. Even the shepherd was despised socially on account of his flocks' eating private property, whatever prestige the occupation of shepherd might have in the eyes of allegorists. *Midrash on Psalms*, Ps 23, § 2 (Braude I, 327).

keepers must fear for their safety.[1] Pigs and Gentiles seem to have been held in about equivalent esteem. One can imagine parents whose boy goes to find his fortune in the diaspora wondering, will he be forced even to keep pigs? Our lad, keeping pigs, makes one think of the Jews before the Covenant, in the 'house of bondage'. Some have suggested that the lad's master did not give him his food, but this is so incredible that we cannot force it into the parable. What the text seems to mean is that he was so hungry, especially seeing the pigs consuming the carob-pods, that he fancied he could eat them (as indeed he could have done). Rather than share the pigs' diet he wanted charity, but no one gave him any. The suggestion that he stole his diet[2] is superfluous, but is evidence that theologians have wondered what after all the boy's sin was. Charity however must have helped him on his way home, a point by no means to be neglected in our reading of the story.

The father does not ask about the past. He hears the words of repentance and submission, which are more than enough. The fact that the lad has come back shows that all pride has gone, a point which will not have failed to strike home while other aspects of the parable have been forgotten. A special robe is placed on him, and the ring is put on his finger, an act which symbolises that whatever the son might have missed at home before is now given him. He is to consider himself his father's deputy, for it is no mere ornamental ring, as the symbolism confirms, but a signet-ring.[3] The ex-prodigal was willing to be a servant, as the elder brother was content to be thought (*v.* 29),[4] but the father insists upon his being a son with the privileges that entails. The servants put

[1] Mk v.11–16 par. has not previously been interpreted in this way. There is a well-known legend about a pig, and the attempt to hoist it up the walls of Jerusalem before the time of Christ which caused widespread earthquakes. This evidences a folk-belief that the pig itself was a forbidden object, of whose presence the Messiah was naturally bound to take notice (so the census-coin and the coins of the moneychangers in the Temple, which must either be thrown away as valueless or trampled underfoot). The topic of Jesus and forbidden objects has still to be worked out.

[2] A further blemish in the thorough and extremely helpful study of the parable by J. Jeremias, *Die Gleichnisse Jesu*, 6th edn (Göttingen 1962), 129. The point is seen at p. 130 of the Eng. trans. (1963).

[3] See the discussion at *Dig.* 31.1.77, 21. Wetstein, *ad loc.*, cites 1 M vi.15; Gn xli.42; Est iii.10, viii.2. The very elaborate, illustrated, research of K. H. Rengstorf (cited below, p. 115 n. 3), serving to prove that the ring signifies might and jurisdiction (of divine origin), is extraordinarily interesting (p. 30ff.) but the rings depicted from the sculptures of the ancient Near East are quite evidently not finger-rings. Would the father refer to such a ring as δακτύλιον, and if he did would not this symbolism escape the hearer?

[4] *Diatessaron* xxvi.30. Theologians will compare Ga iv.6–7; 2 Co vi.18. Bornhäuser, *ubi cit.* 116. Rabbis said that God accepts as servant one who calls himself a servant: *Midrash on Psalms*, Ps 18, § 4 (Braude I, 231) citing Gn xviii.3, xxvi.24, xxxii.2; Is xliv.2, etc.

his sandals on as a sign that they accept him as their master—indeed no order could have expressed this more conclusively.[1] The elder son is about to be compelled to celebrate what is in effect his own discomfiture. His insolence to his father soon justifies his being treated as lower than his brother.[2] The order to kill the fatted calf is the height of hospitality, though the lad is not a guest.[3] The elder brother complains, as he has a right to dispute expenditure of the estate which had been written over to him on the terms explained above. He forgets, in his hurry, that ever since the gift 'from today and after my death' was executed he has been living on the farm and enjoying its profits. As his father reminds him (*v.* 31), if in the past he has been obliged to eat nothing better than was provided for the father's own table (whether or not this exceeded the value of his labour on the farm), the full value of this frugality, if frugality it was, is stored up for him till the day when his interest, as lawyers say, vests in possession. The complaint was legally competent, but, on the facts, invalid.

The younger brother and his dependants will now be able to live at the expense of the farm during the father's lifetime. The elder, who had not given overt cause for complaint until now, must take second place so long as the father lives. No doubt the younger would with time have made peace with the elder (as Jacob did with Esau: Gn xxxii, xxxiii), but the process has been swept aside by the father. How different this is from the story of the prodigal son as retold by Buddhist scholars a century or more afterwards! There the prodigal is carefully tested to know whether he is fit to enjoy the wealth he can claim.[4]

T. W. Manson described the father's behaviour as reckless unselfishness. This may not be quite accurate. He was entirely within his rights, and his behaviour was prudent and wise. One must not put a stumbling-block before the feet of the blind, and the door of repentance must be kept open. His elder son disputes his action as unreasonable and too soft. The father's rebuke is remarkably measured. To understand it we must grasp that over the remainder of the estate which had been assigned 'from today and after my death' the father's rights persisted.

[1] Mk i.7; Lk iii.16; Jn i.27 ('the latchet of whose shoes . . .').

[2] Philo, *Supp. I*, p. 522, § 224, comments on Esau's claim to be a son (Gn xxvii.31*b*) whereas, as a wicked man, he was not fit to be numbered among the attendant servants.

[3] 1 K i.9; Pr xv.17; Mt xxii.4 ('my oxen and my fatlings are killed').

[4] *Saddharmapuṇḍarīka*, IV, at p. 99–108, H. Kern's trans., *Sacred Books of the East* XXI (Oxford 1884). The work was compiled in stages (the oldest Chinese trans. belongs to A.D. 265–316) and this chapter is of later growth (p. xxi). W. T. de Bary, ed., *Sources of Indian Tradition* (Columbia University Press 1958), 165ff. G. A. van den Bergh van Eysinga, *Indische Einflüsse auf evang. Erzählung* (Göttingen 1904), 57ff. (a second edn appeared in 1909). The relationship between Buddhist texts and the gospels is discussed by me at *ZRGG* 19 (1967), 33ff.

These were confined to taking the profits (*e.g.* a fatted calf) and using them for the comfort of anyone of his choice. Not only the father's personal maintenance and that of his personal dependants, but also that of his casual guests is comprehended. As the *Mishnāh* puts it with characteristic terseness:[1]

hā-'āv tolēsh ū-ma'^{a}chiyl l^{e}kol miy sheyyir^{e}tseh. 'The father (-donor) may pluck up and feed (the produce) to whomsoever he pleases.'

True enough, all his estate did belong to the elder son, so that the assignment stood unimpaired. The younger brother having, as it were,[2] come to life again, the father's right to maintain him came again into existence, and the circumstance should be a cause of rejoicing. The very right which the elder son relied upon as the foundation of his complaint was itself derived from his sonship of that father, and did not, when examined, support his complaint at all. This solution, as it takes into account all parts of the parable literally, instead of resorting to figurative interpretation, is superior to previous reconstructions. The elder son is therefore shown in the wrong, disobeying the fifth commandment in his turn.

Professor K. H. Rengstorf recently published a study of our parable[3] in which he utilises the archaic Jewish institution of *ḳ^{e}tsātsāh.*[4] Whether it was actually in use in the time of Jesus is not certain, but if it is relevant it would not be fit to be overlooked merely because it was antique. The ceremony was used in order to 'cut off' or separate a man who had broken one at least of the fundamental rules of the tribe, in particular by disposing of property in a manner disapproved of by the public. After the ceremony he was treated as a kind of outcast, and by a ceremony of a similar kind he could be reintegrated.[5] Professor Rengstorf suggests that 'my son was dead and has become alive again' fits the notions of a community in which an individual could be ceremonially 'cut off', and then, if his behaviour was fully approved thereafter, could be solemnly reinstated in his old position with his old right to communal or tribal facilities.

[1] B.B. VIII.7 (Danby, 377). The point is not dwelt on by Yaron, *op. cit.* 49.

[2] For the concept of being 'dead' through impiety see references gathered at Schöttgen, *Hor. Heb.* I, *ad* 1 Tm v.6; Billerbeck *ad* Mt viii.22 (I, 489). Rm xi.15.

[3] *Die Re-Investitur des Verlorenen Sohnes in der Gleichniserzählung Jesu Luk.* 15, 11–32 (Köln/Opladen 1967).

[4] Or *ḳ^{e}tsiytsāh. Encycl. Judaica* ix, s.v. *Kezaza.* j. Ḳid. I, 60^{c} = j. Ket. II, 26^{d} (Schwab VIII, 34); b. Ket. 28*b* = Sonc. 157–8; Midr. R., Ruth VII.11 = Sonc. 87.

[5] Midr. R., Ruth, *ubi cit.* The similarity of the broken cask of nuts, etc., with the water-jar which figures in Hindu 'excommunications' (Manu XI.184, 187) is interesting, especially as it throws light on Falk's comments on *ḳ^{e}tsātsāh* at *Ivra* 17 (1966), 173. The *ḳ^{e}tsātsāh* was considered briefly already by Daube (*ZSS* 72 [1955], 332–4) in connection with this parable.

Unfortunately for this original and interesting suggestion, what we know of the *ḳᵉtsātsāh* does not apply to the prodigal son's situation. It does, however, serve to emphasise the great social importance attached by the Jews to property-transactions and to the proper recognition of property-rights. The ceremony used to take place if family property, an heirloom, were sold to an outsider, or if a man married beneath his social rank. He would be doing what the law allowed him to do, only subject to this social penalty, resembling excommunication. A man might legally sell his paternal estate, but he *ought* to retain it for his own descendants. Now our prodigal, so far as the parable goes, was not penalised, nor ostracised by his family. He was assuredly not cut off. He asked for what his father might well give him, and the latter gave it to him. A reprehensible thing to ask, perhaps, but, as we have seen, by no means unknown.

The *ḳᵉtsātsāh* illustrates how bitterly relatives could be disappointed if their expectations with regard to property were frustrated, and to that extent this institution (if it still existed in full vigour) parallels the bitterness of the elder son when his brother is unexpectedly reinstated. But it is important to see from the parable that no formal reinstatement, no placating of relatives, no proof of 'coming to heel' was necessary before the father welcomed the lad home.

Meanwhile there is a rabbinical parable similar to ours in tone, purpose and content—though inferior to it in conception and artistry (as we shall see). A father, who was a physician, was angry with his son, who was disloyal to him; the son at length fell ill and was glad to have the ministrations and remedies his father hastened to supply to him. Thus God forgave Israel in spite, we are told, of his serving false gods.[1]

THE THEME OF THE YOUNGER BROTHER

To have *two* brothers calls in the theme of the 'younger brother'. The patriarchs after Abraham were younger brothers.[2] Even Moses has no posterity, while Aaron emphatically has. The Bible emphasises in this way a theme easily overlooked. Though Aaron is the elder brother he shows great respect for Moses, who was meek, and this is what God commanded.[3] Younger means inferior and weaker, the object of patronage. Both *ḳāṭon* and *tsā'iyr* have the further sense of 'unimportant'. The inferiority of the younger is pointedly emphasised at Jb xxx.1

[1] Midr. R., Exod. XLVI.4 = Sonc. 530–2.
[2] There is a marked change after Abraham. Not only is he an eldest son himself, but the youngest at Gn ix.24 receives a curse.
[3] Nb xii.3, 7–9, 11 ('Oh my lord . . .), on which we have a rabbinical comment at Mekilta, '*Amaleḳ* 1 (Lauterbach II, p. 140).

('they that are younger than me have me in derision . . .'). Younger brothers achieve fame because (and only because?) they are *chosen.* Aaron was chosen (Ps cv.26). The Jews, who long viewed themselves with self-pity,[1] were a chosen people.[2] God's law (often honoured in the breach) respects the elder, chooses in practice the younger.[3] Levi obtained seniority over Reuben.

When we think over the stories of the younger brothers of the Old Testament we notice how many of them *went out, migrated, left home, journeyed* actually or figuratively, and for how many a final homecoming is shown or posited. The theme of the wanderer's return is indeed the theme of the children of Israel themselves.

Younger brothers are traditionally rebels.[4] The elder is worldly, niggardly,[5] orthodox, hypocritical. The younger is idealistic, rebellious, but fit for repentance.[6] Pharisees may praise him who sits and commits no transgression.[7] But this is a counsel of perfection. Philo, who has much to say on this theme, says those are elders who are in fact faithful and wise (irrespective of age), and the younger are those who actually rebel against God.[8] Abel, the righteous, is virtually the elder because he undertook pastoral work, which prepares one for kingship, while Cain occupied himself with the earthy and inanimate.[9] Philo says the

[1] See the expressions in the apocryphal psalm (Ps. 151A) at J. A. Sanders, *Discoveries in the Judaean Desert* IV. *Psalms Scroll of Qumrân Cave* 11 (Oxford 1965), 55–6.

[2] Dt vii.7; Is xliv.2; Ml i. 2–5. K. Galling, *Die Erwählungstraditionen Israels* (Giessen 1928).

[3] A king loved his younger son, the dirty one, better than the elder, who was clean: *Midrash on Psalms*, Ps 9, § 1 (Braude I, 131). The choice of the Jews is depicted as favouritism in the matter of dividing a paternal inheritance (*ibid.* Ps 16, § 6 [Braude I, 199]). Dt xxxii.8–9 is called up. The nations had their shares, but Jacob, the Lord's people, are the Lord's share. A parable of a king: he loved his youngest child most. When he was to apportion their inheritances there was one lot of great beauty which each child coveted, so the king said, 'Let this parcel of land remain as my own portion' (see Dt xxxii.8–9). He gave his own portion finally to his youngest child. This is about the land of Israel (*Midrash on Psalms*, Ps 5, § 1 [Braude I, 82]), but it could be given a spiritual application. So at *ibid.* Ps 27, § 1 (Braude I, 365), citing Ps xcvii.11. Billerbeck, *op. cit.* 212 cites Gen. R. § 98 (61*d*) against Lk xv.12, to the same effect as the above (Midr. R., Gen. XCVIII.6 = Sonc. trans. II, 954).

[4] As the Greek vocabulary testifies. Psychologists would guess that it is the link between the father and the elder son (of whom he expects far too much) which really excites the younger son's resentment.

[5] Cain, a lover of self, sacrificed and took home all but the blood . . . (Gn iv.4–5): Philo, on Cain and Abel, *Suppl. I, Questions and Answers on Genesis* (Loeb edn 1953), p. 38.

[6] He who sins and is ashamed is kin to him who does not sin at all, as the younger brother to the elder: Philo, *ibid.* p. 40 (on Gn iv.7).

[7] Mishnāh, *Makkot* III, 15 (Danby, 408; Blackman, 329).

[8] *De Abrahamo, ad fin.* XLVI, § 274 (Colson VI, 133; Yonge ii, 452). This is why Abel is mentioned first at Gn iv.4–5 (*Suppl. I,* 37). On the righteousness of Abel see Hb xi.4 and Mt xxiii.35 (*contra* Kilpatrick, *NT* 5 [1962], 114).

[9] Philo, *Suppl. I*, p. 36, on Gn iv.2.

younger is good, the ruler of the natural elder (Gn xxv.23).[1] The good alone is ruler, and the foolish is poor and his servant.[2] The toiler, even though younger, who makes progress in the virtues will obtain from the Father not only the birthright of the elder but the whole inheritance, just as did Jacob, who took refuge in God's mercy (Gn xxxiii.11)![3]

In the case of Jacob no aspect of the relationship between the brothers or between them and their father is overlooked.[4] The two stories of Esau's rejection and Jacob's installation as his heir both tend to the same end. The father's authority is emphasised. The rebellious behaviour of Joseph's brothers (whose unkindness to him conferred so strange a benefit upon him) led the children of Israel into Egypt, the proximate cause being the coat of many colours.[5] The younger brother was not only their saviour but the model of the practical man, the prototype of the politician.[6] He has his robe and ring.[7] His own sons are given preference over his elder brothers, while Jacob expatiates on the merit of the younger (Ephraim).[8] Moreover, Esau and Edom did not 'go down to Egypt'. God appointed Judah above his senior, Simeon.[9] God's choice of the prestigeless Saul could hardly be more emphatic,[10] and those who doubt Saul's power are 'worthless fellows'.[11]

Two redeemers of Israel, Gideon[12] and David, were both younger brothers. Both had opposition, the latter markedly from Eliab,[13] 'My god is Father'. If he had had his way Israel would have perished. David's heir, in a situation contrasting with the Esau–Jacob struggle,[14] was another younger brother. Solomon paid his father's debt by building the Temple. Supernatural elements occurred in the choice of David and Solomon.[15] Parental approval is present in both, as also in the story

[1] Philo, *Suppl. I*, p. 441–2.
[2] *Ibid.* p. 542, § 230 (Gn xxvii.37).
[3] *On the Sacrifices of Abel and Cain*, 42, 124–5. *Cf.* καί ἔστι μοι πάντα at Gn xxxiii.11 with Lk xv.31.
[4] Jacob and Esau dwelt together (Gn xiii.1ff., xxxvi.6ff.). *Midrash on Psalms*, Ps 25, § 14 (Braude I, 356).
[5] Gn xxxvii.
[6] The theme of Philo's *Treatise of the Life of a Man occupied with Affairs of State*, or *On Joseph* (Colson, Loeb edn, vol. VI).
[7] Gn xli.42.
[8] Gn xlviii.8–22.
[9] Jg i.1–3, iii.9.
[10] 1 S ix.2, 21–4, x.22–4.
[11] 1 S x.27.
[12] Jg vii–viii.
[13] b. Pes. 66*b* = Sonc. 338. Whoever becomes angry, even if greatness has been decreed for him by Heaven, is cast down. Eliab is the example. 1 S xvii.28; *ibid.* xvii.6ff. God favoured Eliab until he was angry. The rabbis say that like a first-born who is entitled to two portions of an inheritance, David inherited a double portion of kingship, one portion in this world, and the other in the world to come: *Midrash on Psalms*, Ps 5, § 4 (Braude I, 84).
[14] 1 K i–ii.
[15] 1 S xvi.12–13; 1 K ii.15.

of Gideon.[1] When Adonijah, after bowing to the divine will, schemes against the settlement, he is destroyed. Neither Eliab nor Adonijah are models for anyone.

No redeemer, however, was more popular than Judas Maccabaeus, a younger brother.[2] His services were acknowledged by heavenly fire, as were those of Solomon and Gideon before him.[3] Obedience is required of all these younger brothers, and without it their services for the nation would have been impossible. The Church saw the younger brothers of Jewish biblical history as 'types' of Jesus.

SYMBOLIC CONNECTIONS

In a real sense the 'dead' brother came to life and this is celebrated with feasting and merrymaking. What has this to do with the younger-brother theme? And what connects this younger son with the younger brothers of Jewish history? Esau and Jacob must be the starting-point. Both seek to please their father. What actually pleases him is the kid,[4] which is both his meal and the means of deception. Consuming a kid is less extravagant than killing and eating beef. The elder brother is aggrieved by the fatted calf, to which he pathetically and indignantly refers. This implies his own abstemiousness in comparison with the younger generally.[5] Esau's garment, which was believed to have been the garment of Adam, is worn by Jacob as a means of acquiring the blessing.[6] The elder brother's garment is a symbol of the younger overcoming the elder. The garment of Joseph we have already referred

[1] 1 S xvi.20, xvii.20; 1 K ii.1–9; Jg vi.31.

[2] 1 M ii.4.

[3] H. E. Del Medico, 'Le cadre historique des fêtes de Hanukkah et de Purîm', *VT* 15 (1965), 238–70; Jg vi.21; 2 Ch vii.1. Note that David too was 'answered by fire': 1 Ch xxi.26.

[4] Gn xxvii.9, 16. *Cf. Targ. ps. Jon.* Gn xxxvii.31 (a kid in the Joseph story).

[5] According to rabbinical law the stubborn and rebellious son gorges himself on beef. *Mishnāh*, San. VIII.2 (Danby, 394), b. San. 68–70. Maim., *ubi cit.* III (Rebels), vii, 3.

[6] Gn xxvii.15. That the robe of Esau was that of Adam, and thus the 'first' robe, is to be seen from *Targ. ps. Jon.* on this passage. For the importance of the Targum ps. Jonathan as evidence of the *midrashim* that had accumulated round the Bible before Jesus's time see P. Kahle, *Cairo Geniza*, 2nd edn (Oxford 1959), 202–3, 208. Jülicher, *Gleichnisreden* II, 351, is, as usual, scornful of the identification of the robe in our parable with that which Adam lost—an identification made from at least as early as Origen (according to Jülicher) and beloved of the Council of Trent 'nach unzähligen Vorgängern'. This is yet another example of the early Church taking over and developing for its own purposes a *midrash* which was well established in the synagogue. The details of the legend of Adam's celestial garments are given very fully in L. Ginzberg, *Legends of the Jews* V, 103–4, 276–7. The sequel is handled by M. Harl, 'La prise de conscience de la "nudité" d'Adam', *Studia Patr.* 8 (*TuU* 93) (1966), 486–95.

to. The Esau theme is pointed to openly by describing the elder brother as coming from 'the field' (where Cain killed Abel):[1] Esau is *agroikos*, unpolished, crude, a slave. Our elder brother is as jealous as Esau.[2] Esau is traditionally wicked.[3] A tiller of the soil is one who satisfies bodily wants above everything. The father in the parable seems to abstain from quoting Isaac, 'with corn and wine have I sustained him; and what then shall I do for thee, my son?' (Gn xxvii.37) because our elder brother is somewhat better placed than was Esau. Meanwhile the connections with the Joseph story go further. He was virtually exchanged for sandals, so the mention of sandals is appropriate.[4] The rejoicing of the father resembles that of Joseph himself and of his own father.[5] We have alluded to the ring. A connection with Gideon emerges in the first of a series of 'fatted calves'. It is convenient to review them together. The calf is mentioned three times in the parable. It occurs in the Saul story as a symbol of refreshment.[6] In the Elijah story and the Gideon story it symbolises the perfect burnt sacrifice.[7] It has a definite connection with the repulse of idolaters and foreigners. The connection with David is obvious, though we have not sufficiently emphasised as yet the function of David as a herdsman of small beasts. At Ps lxxviii.70–2 we read 'He chose David his servant and took him from the sheepfolds ... to be the shepherd of Jacob his people, of Israel his inheritance. With upright heart he tended them. . .'. We have referred to Eliab,[8] who accused David of leaving his pastoral occupation for the sake of amusement.[9] David apparently defends himself by quoting his father's orders.[10] Adonijah slew 'fatlings', and, as an elder son, misunderstood

[1] It appears that a Hebrew text of Gn iv.8 circulated (unlike the M.T.) in which the word 'field' (*sādeh*) occurred *twice* (Kittel *ad loc*).

[2] Philo, *Suppl I*, p. 524–5, § 227 (Gn xxvii.34).

[3] D. Daube, 'How Esau sold his birthright', *Cambridge Law Journal* 8 (1942), 70–5. Ob *v.* 10 is conclusive. Gn xxv.27 should be taken allegorically, says Philo, *Suppl. I*, p. 450, 451–2, 489, §§ 165, 166, 199. Esau was a savage (*Midrash on Psalms*, Ps 9, § 7, Braude, I, p. 139). Hated by God (Ps 9, § 13, *ibid.* 146, citing Ml i.3). A plotter of murder (Ps 13, § 2, 3, *ibid.* 182–3, referring to Jr xlix.7ff.; Ezk xxxv. 15). b. B.B. 16*b* = Sonc. 84 (he committed five sins, of which spurning his birthright is the last—he had also denied the resurrection). *Midrash on Psalms*, Ps 9, § 7 (Braude I, 137). He pursues bodily lusts: Philo, nine citations in the index to the Loeb edn. He represents the worse part of the soul and ignorance: see *e.g. Leg. All.* III, 2. He is both ἄγριος and ἄγροικος. He is of an unbending character. He is a criminal: Midr. R., Gen. LXIII. 12 = Sonc. 567.

[4] *Targ. ps. Jon.* Gn xxxvii.28.

[5] As noticed by Guilding, *op. cit..* 135.

[6] 1 S xxviii.24 (LXX: δάμαλις νομάς). At Dt xxi.4, 6 the same animal is a satisfaction. The coincidence is to be noticed, as Dt xxi was parallel to our chapter in the lectionary.

[7] Jg vi.25, 28 (LXX). 1 K xviii.25, 26 (note the fire from heaven at *v.* 38).

[8] Above, p. 118 n. 13.

[9] 1 S xvii.28.

[10] *Ibid.* 29, if it refers back to *vv.* 17–18. A disingenuous response? But the meaning is not plain.

his situation and got into trouble with his 'feast', Adonijah who had never displeased his father or earned a rebuke.[1] David's and Solomon's activities led to singing and dancing.[2] This connects our parable at second hand with the dedication of the Temple, a feast conducted in Jesus's time as a domestic ceremony with socio-political overtones.[3] Beef was sacrificed and rejoicing followed at the start of the David story.[4] The word εὐφρανθῆναι at Lk xv. 32 strongly suggests praise of God. The word θύω which means both 'sacrifice' and 'kill' has been retained to suggest sacrifices, dedications and other occasions for rejoicing. The Judith story, a biblical precedent for the Judas Maccabaeus story, has no equal as a 'younger sibling' theme, and was read in the home during the festival of the dedication. There cannot be any doubt but that our younger brother, who has undergone a rebirth, is regarded in the parable as rededicated to a better life. Judith tells of feasting and rejoicing.[5] Mourning was forbidden during this period, and likewise in our parable the elder brother is ordered to rejoice. The themes of the turning of the year coincide with the themes of the parable. Biblical redemption stories, post-biblical history, myth and moral theology join in one pattern. The lectionary cycle claims this part of Luke for the Hanukkah period.[6]

THE TEACHING RECONSTRUCTED

The allusions go beyond the lections as at present understood, so that there can be no question of this parable having been tailored to fit the lections as such, but there is no reason why the vocabulary and tone should not from the first have reflected Jesus's knowledge that at that period the hearers would be hearing determined passages of scripture, and if this is so we know which passages these were. But leaving this aside for our hypothetical symposium, let us see what the parable as it stands tells us.

First a *ḳal vā-ḥómer*: if a human father could act like this, a father whose foresight, means and patience are limited, how much more will

[1] 1 K i.6, 9, 33, 38–41, especially 41, seems strikingly like our parable, if for *Joab* we read *Adonijah*, Solomon's elder brother.
[2] 1 S xviii 6; 2 S vi; 1 K iv.20, viii.65.
[3] See p. 195 n. 1 below, also *Megillat Ta'anit*, § 23. Theodor Schärf, *Das Gottesdienstliche Jahr der Juden* (Leipzig 1902), 92–6. Maimonides *op. cit.* III, x, 3, trans. S. Gandz and H. Klein, *Book of Seasons*, 463ff. Jos., *Ant.* XII, 316–25 = vii.6–7; *Contra Ap.* II, 118 = ii.9. Philo, *De Congr. Erud. gratia* XXI, § 114 (Colson IV, 514–17).
[4] 1 S xvi.2, 5.
[5] Jdt xvi.20.
[6] Ezk xxxiii, xxxiv, xxxvii are most apt. For Hanukkah see below, Chapter 8.

God, whose foresight, etc., are unlimited, receive those who 'come to themselves' and repent of their disobedience and unfaithfulness? The road to repentance is not so hard as it seems, and if such a father exacts no terms from his prodigal, how much less will God exact terms, for example, punishment, from the truly contrite! Manson was worried because Christ was not in this parable, a conclusion which Jülicher had accepted. Some on the contrary will see him, not as the father,[1] which seems to be an error, but as the divine spirit which induces a father to come so wholeheartedly towards his son in such circumstances. The parable shows Ps li.17 in action. Both son and father do what is right; the third must be taught that love does not admit of strict sharing. God does not 'despise' a contrite heart: how can others presume to do so?

The elder son is taught in the parable, and teaching must be contained in this for the audience. Not necessarily a single or simple teaching. The direct lesson is surely that no one, whatever his self-righteousness, can ever claim to determine the rights of others to whatever status they occupy. A hard lesson, which only such a parable could teach, perhaps. This can be applied to the Pharisees who had difficulty in seeing how sinners could be admitted to ordinary Jewish society without trial and perhaps also penance (no one claimed that they were entitled to be *ḥaveriym*, for that idea implies some kind of club). They are here given a reason why they should rethink their position.[2] Their argument seems to have been that only strict obedience to the Jewish Law could enable Jews to profit from the expected redemption. Many Jews, including sinners, were evidently of the same mind—hence their joy that Jesus was prepared to recognise them as sons of Abraham without any costly, humiliating, or compromising preliminaries (Jn viii.39, x.26–30).

The parable contains at least one powerfully symbolic feature which we have not yet explored: and it is full of teaching. We have seen that when the servants put sandals on the returned prodigal's feet they acknowledge him as their master. But to what end? The biblical allusions of the requirement to be shod are threefold and highly suggestive. Firstly, do not be in awe![3] Secondly, mourning is over, rejoice![4]

[1] Jeremias's interpretation sees (p. 131) the behaviour of the father as an indication of the nature of God, which must be correct. A view which anticipated that expressed here appeared in R. Schippers, *Gelijkenissen van Jezus* (Kampen 1962), 162ff. Bornhäuser saw the father as Jesus.

[2] Lv xxv.50 (equality of Jews) is pointed to by τῶν μισθίων σου.

[3] Ex iii.4–6 ('. . . put off thy shoes from off thy feet . . .'); Jos v.15 (the same in the mouth of 'the captain of the Lord's host'). That Gabriel does not insist on Mary's removing her sandals (Lk i.28) might be very significant, if it were not obvious that she (in an inner room) was not wearing any.

[4] Ezk xxiv.17 ('put thy shoes upon thy feet'), 23. It is well known that according to

Thirdly, be ready to go somewhere, do something.[1] What the prodigal is to do is itself the subject (indirectly) of another parable, that of the Great Supper. The reinstatement of the prodigal is the preliminary to his being a leader, a leader in a very important enterprise; that is a rôle from which unfortunately his elder brother, the prestige-bearing member of the group until now, is excluded at least for the while, if not permanently.

Underneath lies, apparently, yet another lesson. The Pharisees', like the Dead Sea Scroll community's, notions were based upon a concept, natural in itself, that a section of Jews could triumph in a national sense, achieving national independence and the spiritual rewards hereafter, by faithfulness to the *Torāh*, and by separating themselves from fellow-Jews as a means of furthering this. The Pharisees are quite right, Jesus seems to say, in their insistence that moral law must be worked out in practice, but they do not go far enough (*cf.* the parable of the Unjust Steward).

You have agreed that the prodigal was wicked and that his repentance was justified. You have agreed that the father was entitled to reinstate him as a member of the family. And you are satisfied that this can be done without loss to those to whom by contract the inheritance belongs. Have you not, thereby, admitted that the elder son's argument is wrong (as it obviously was), and therefore that the non-religious, the last-minute-pious, are as much entitled as you are to the Father's favour? If you still cherish doubts about this, to whom are you to be likened? To Cain, Adonijah, Eliab, elder brothers of Joseph? To the Midianites, and still worse the Edomites?

Can the elder brother resemble Edom? What a suggestion! Edom is none other than Rome.[2] True, we cannot be sure that Jesus used the common rabbinical pseudonym, but the hated foreigner, whose lackeys the Hellenisers seemed to be, was later referred to most appropriately as the descendant of Esau. Jealousy of the younger brother is the mark of characters scorned by Bible and myth alike, and unconsciously makes the elder brother an ally of the very power the Pharisees aimed by their piety to expel.

[1] Ex xii.11; Mk vi.9; Ac xii.8; Ep vi.15.

[2] b. Gitt. 56*b*, 57*b* = Sonc. 260, 266. *Midrash on Psalms*, Ps 10, § 6 (Braude I, 155), Ps 14, § 2, 3 (*ibid.* 183–4); Ps 17, § 12 (*ibid.* 217). *Cf.* Ps 21, § 3 (*ibid.* 295). Midr. R., Num. IV.8 = Sonc. 103. Midr. R., Gen. LXIII. 9, 10 = Sonc. 565, 566. The Messiah will trample Edom down, *Midr. on Psalms*, on Ps lx.10 (Braude I, 516). *Jer. Targ.* Gn xv.16; b. Ber. 62*b* = Sonc. 392.

Jewish custom mourners must not wear boots, though the prohibition of wearing boots nowadays applies only to those made of leather (G. Friedlander, *Laws and Customs of Israel*, London 1921, p. 226, § 3).

The family festival about Christmas time, when each male lights his little lamp in honour of the miracles of liberation effected in his fathers' days, is a good time at which to show that common sonship of the common father binds the Hellenisers, the unorthodox, the separatist and the Pharisee. We do not know whether this parable was part of a Christmas sermon, but it could well have been.

We should not leave the parable without noting a possible misunderstanding and seeing what its justification might be. The early church could have seen the parable as explaining how it was that the robe of the priesthood and the ring of authority passed, while the Temple still stood, from the sons of Aaron back to the sons of Abraham at large. The synagogue must give way to the Church.[1] The Church certainly saw the robe as apostolic wisdom and the ring as proof of the true faith.[2] For the Temple at Jerusalem another temple was dedicated. Was this a plausible understanding of the text? Treated already as scripture, yes. Did Jesus expect his words to be treated as scripture? A problem too big for this occasion: it certainly cannot be ruled out. Paul has no difficulty in setting out the younger-brother theme in a most difficult context, proving that (just as the Jews were chosen, though inferior) the Church is the younger brother and the recipient of Christ's favour and authority. To be born earlier conveys rights which are not disputed. Paul at Ga iv.21–v.1 allegorises,[3] and concludes that Christians, being the seed of Abraham by way of Isaac (*cf.* Ga iii.29), would have been inferior, being descended from the younger brother, but were senior by the election[4] of God. The argument is that the promise was made to the seed, and although on the surface of the story both Sarah and Hagar were *wives* of Abraham (Gn xvi.3), Hagar was really a female slave, so that her son did not qualify, much to Abraham's own surprise, for favour. It is curious, and gratifying, to note that the connection of Abraham with Hagar was the outcome of a pact (*cf.* Gn xvi.2–6) between Sarah and Abraham: Hagar did not take the initiative. The child was connected in some way with Arabia and Egypt, and was the child of a

1 *Targ. ps. Jon.* at Gn xxvii.27 clearly identifies Esau's garment, as worn by Jacob, as a priestly robe to be worn in the Temple. Allegories listed by St Jerome may well reveal traces of midrashic activity in the early church, *e.g.* . . . *duos filios, Judaeos et gentes, quia Judaeis prius data est lex.* See Migne, *PL* 30, coll. 574–5; Ambrose *ad loc.*, *PL*, 15, col. 1761. Like Philo, Jerome sees *in agro* as signifying *immundo desiderio.* Very similar to the Latin allegories are those of ps. Chrysostom, *PG* 59, coll. 515–22. A. Jülicher, *Die Gleichnisreden Jesu*, 2nd edn, 1 (Tübingen 1910), ch. 6.

2 See references in previous note.

3 For a discussion of the *midrash* see J. W. Doeve, *Jewish Hermeneutics in the Synoptic Gospels and Acts* (The Hague 1953), 109. See also *Letter of Barnabas* XIII, 2. H. J. Schoeps, *Aus frühchristlicher Zeit* (Tübingen 1950), 154.

4 1 Co i.20–9: Christians are prestigeless but chosen.

covenant. The Ishmaelites were treated equitably by God, but not allowed the rights of a firstborn, obviously because of the antecedents of the marriage (Dt xxi.16). The birth of Isaac, however, was not the result of a contract (*cf.* Ga iii.16–18), but was a blessing freely bestowed. The children of Abraham by way of Isaac are believed entitled to rely upon the promise, whereas the status of the Ishmaelites symbolises the status of the descendants of Hagar as inferior, just as the Pharisees and others who placed their entire trust in the *Torāh* are enslaved to a covenant which was none of their making. The Church is the younger brother, chosen by God, heir to the promise, and mocked by the elder brother as Isaac was by Ishmael (Gn xxi.9; Ga iv.29). Thus the Church may have followed the younger-brother pattern, and seen the elder brother of the parable as the synagogue. This left the Pharisees and other adherents of the *Torāh* still in possession of their rights under the covenant, for what that was worth, since God's covenant could not be broken: but they would live under rebuke, not enjoying the forgiveness which the father of the parable lavished on the younger brother. Thus the early Church's view of itself can consist with the Pauline allegory. This view of a possible application of the parable would be considerably enhanced if in fact Pharisees had *mocked* the first Church for its inclusion of harlots and those who had recently consorted with such: and there is no reason to doubt that that is what happened. The reply that the Pharisees in such a situation were Ishmaelites, Midianites, Edomites and the like, would, if it happened, have produced a balance of mutual abuse that would have suited the atmosphere of the period.

CHAPTER SIX

The Parable of the Great Supper

THE NOTORIOUS DIFFICULTIES in the two parables[1] of the Great Supper and the Wedding Feast could, it seems, be solved if it is accepted as a hypothesis that Jesus's tale is an artistic *midrash* on Zp i.1–16, concentrating on *vv.* 7–8, in the context of the Holy War. Dt xx, and occasional verses from Dt xxiv, xxv, and xxviii, along with Ex xvii and other references to 'Amalek', not forgetting Is lxv, supply the complex of, as it were, underground streams which feed that source, which is the ostensible intellectual starting-point of the parable. The divergencies between Lk xiv.15–24 (*cf.* Thomas § 64) and Mt xxii.1–14 could be explained on this footing as intentionally differing versions of a single story which could have been told once, or even more than once. The allegedly separate little parable of the man who came without a wedding garment turns out to be an actual, or at the least an inherent, or potential part of the main parable (a part which Luke did not need, as we shall see), and the maxim 'Many are summoned but few are

[1] G. Bornkamm, *Jesus of Nazareth*, 2nd edn (London 1966), 18–19: the parable's versions illustrate the unhistorical, timeless nature of Jesus's word. E. Linnemann, *Parables of Jesus*, 3rd edn (London 1966), 88–97; J. Jeremias, *Parables of Jesus*, rev. edn (London 1963), 63–5, 176–8, 187–8, 230; R. Bultmann, *History of the Synoptic Tradition* (Oxford 1963); W. Trilling, 'Zur Überlieferungsgeschichte des Gleichnisses vom Hochzeitsmahl', *BZ* 4 (1960), 251–65; V. Hasler, 'Die königliche Hochzeit', *Theol. Z.* 18 (1962), 25–35; E. Linnemann, 'Überlegungen zur Parabel vom großen Abendmahl', *ZNW*, 51 (1960), 246–55; R. Swaeles, 'L'Orientation ecclésiastique de la parabole du festin nuptial . . .', *Ephem. theol. lov.* 36 (1960), 655–84; K. H. Rengstorf, 'Die Stadt der Mörder', 106–29 in W. Eltester, ed., *Jüdentum . . .* (*Fests. J. Jeremias*), 1960 (*BZNTW* 26); S. Pedersen, 'Zum Problem der vaticinia ex eventu . . .', *STh*, 19 (1965), 167–88; G. Eichholz, *Einführung in die Gleichnisse* (Neukirchen–Vluyn, 1963), 54–77; W. Michaelis, *Das hochzeitliche Kleid* (*cit. sup.*), 1–72; J. van Goudoever, *NT* 8 (1966), 110ff. at p. 115, 118–19 (a study of Israel in St Luke). In O. Glombitza, 'Das große Abendmahl', *NT* 5 (1962), 10–16, an attempt is made to show that the Lucan text is not a parable at all but a piece of instruction developed from the pious ejaculation at xiv.15, and depending from the admonition at xiv.12–14. That a connection between the two pericopes was evident to Luke can hardly be doubted, but what is explained below shows that it was not the literal connection Glombitza conjectured, but an important step forward.

chosen'[1] belongs to this parable. Indeed, if we exclude the doubtful reading in the parable of the Workers in the Vineyard, it could fit hardly anywhere as well as here.

The parable is a tale which, contrary to popular opinion, has no implausible elements, and which, as in the case of other parables we have studied, utilises features and words at the story level to call up biblical passages by way of *midrashim* which themselves reillustrate and document the parable, as it were by invisible footnotes. As soon as these 'footnotes' are restored the intellectual effort of the author is revealed, the efforts of the evangelists are disclosed for what they are, and the meaning is clarified. Regrettably, little of current theological reliance upon the parable seems substantiated by this process, and most of the critical work on the parable turns out to have been to small purpose. There is no evidence, for example, that the Gentiles are referred to: nor is urgency or crisis to the fore. What seems remarkable is that Jesus's method of teaching, by plain tales to the simple and by scholarly poetry to the learned at one and the same time, has remained unknown for a preposterous period of time.

An essential prerequisite to the whole is a retranslation of Zp i.7–8. The two versions we need for our purposes are the Masoretic Text and the *Targum ps. Jonathan.* It is a great pity Fr R. Swaeles[2] did not consult the latter, for if he had it is almost certain that he would have found the source of the parable. Since Kahle we know the extreme importance of *Targum ps. Jonathan* for rediscovering the understanding which first-century Jews in Palestine had of the *Torāh* and the prophets. It must be emphasised that Jesus and his contemporaries knew the text in Hebrew with the Aramaic gloss, each of which would instantly call up the other, an allusion to one being automatically an allusion to the other; and doubtful words, especially in the Prophets, would tend to be taken rather in the Targum than in the Septuagintal sense, especially in a non-Greek-speaking area.

Zp i.7–9 M.T.: 'Be silent before the Lord God, for the day of the Lord is at hand; the Lord has prepared a sacrifice/feast and sanctified/consecrated[3] the guests/persons-who-have-been-summoned. And on the day of the Lord's sacrifice—I shall visit/punish the officers and the

[1] 'Eine crux interpretum . . . was allen anderen Stellen zuwiderläuft, zumal da vollends Apk 17, 14 κλητοί, ἐκλεκτοί, πιστοί gleichmäßig nebeneinander genannt werden. Dieser Widerspruch kann und soll nicht vertuscht werden.' Schmidt, *ThWzNT* III (1935), 496, and refs.

[2] See p. 126 n. 1 above, *Eph. theol. lov.* 36 at p. 680–1.

[3] Compare the formula *ḳiḍesh milᵉḥāmāh* (see also Jl iv(iii).9, Mi iii.5), and Is xiii.3. For a consecration leading to an eating of meat see Nb xi.18.

sons of the king and all who are clothed in strange clothing.' The Palestinian Targum (*Targ. ps. Jonathan*) has the following variants: instead of 'has sanctified the persons who have been summoned' it reads 'has summoned his fellow-diners/guests'; for 'sacrifice' it reads 'the slaughtering that is to come'; for 'visit/punish' it has the slightly less menacing 'visit/inspect' (reducing the force of the '*al*). In the context of the holy war, God is shown inspecting his troops before a banquet to which they are invited guests. The relevance of the double *midrash* on the verses will appear presently when we turn to our parable. Further instead of 'all who are clothed in strange clothing' we have a gloss, 'all who busy themselves to worship idols'. This fits both what we know of the practices of Baal-worshippers,[1] and the immediate as well as general context of Zephaniah. Now it is evident that if we accept the Targum's as the correct reading of the Hebrew passage we must envisage a holy war (with which the words 'Be silent' are fully consistent)[2] which will be won with troops who have to be scrutinised to exclude individuals suspected of corruption, etc., and persons actually tainted by irreligion, or at least a lack of that faith in God which is the actual weapon used against the enemy. God inspects the troops to see that they are faithful. Then the war will take place, which will be won by the troops purged of disloyal elements, and immediately afterwards the banquet will celebrate the victory. It is to be observed, meanwhile, that people rejected at such a review or muster are looked to in the words in *v.* 13, 'Though they build houses they shall not inhabit them; though they plant vineyards they shall not drink wine from them'. The point of this will appear presently.

Not to delay with specimens of Jesus's use of this source, we may at once observe that the 'servants' to whom the king speaks in the so-called little parable of the wedding-garment (Mt xxii.13) whose denomination in Greek differs from that of the servants who have figured in the parable at *v.* 10 (which commentators have viewed as a suspicious circumstance) are none other than the 'children of the king' in Zp i.8, and, in the picture which Jesus paints, these are different (warrant-officers, as it were) from the servants who have been seeing to the preparations for the banquet! Readers will be prepared for the method by which we are to look into the parable, identifying Jesus's material and seeing how it is called up by his vocabulary which is masquerading

[1] 2 K x.22. See how Cyr. Alex. takes this (*In Soph.* 585A, Pusey): ἐνδεδυμένους... τουτέστιν εἰς τοῦτο λοιπὸν ἀφιλοθεέας ἰγμένους, καὶ τῶν πάλαι διὰ Μωυσέως τεθεσπισμένων καταφρονεῖν ᾑρημένους, ὡς μηδὲ... τὸ σχῆμα τηρεῖν... See also Is xxiv.21–3.

[2] G. von Rad, *Studies in Deuteronomy* (London 1953), ch. 4: 'Deuteronomy and the Holy War'. At p. 48 he points to the phrase 'Hold your peace': Ex xiv.14, etc. For the holy war see R. de Vaux, *Ancient Israel*, 2nd edn (London 1965), ch. 5, p. 258ff.

as simple story-telling. Even the word ἑταῖρε (*ḥaver*), with which the king addresses the unfortunate whose uniform is dirty, exactly fits the situation: the invitee is a table-companion of his host and also his comrade in war. In fact he was an impostor, but this was not known until no excuse could be elicited from him to explain his improper dress. One may continue, pointing out that θεάσασθαι, an action which has surprised some readers (did hosts go round inspecting their guests?), renders the Hebrew *ū-pāḳadᵉtiy* like the Aramaic *vᵉ-'aṣᵉ'ar* ('inspect') as well as could be attempted, and applies equally appropriately to a review or a muster of troops[1] and a formal greeting of the assembled guests by their host, who has not previously had the opportunity of meeting them. It is in this spirit that we too must 'visit' our text; but first the intellectual background must be set out so that we are as well placed as Jesus's original hearers.

A further prolegomenon: it is discussed below whether the parable belongs to the season of Purim (the great feasting season amongst the Jews). It is *not* asserted here that the parable was part of a sermon for Purim: but the question is raised, if it is not a sermon for Purim how is one to account for the heightened appropriateness of the details of the story once one applies the law relating to Purim to our parable? There is every reason to understand why the early Church should suppress any allusion to Purim which might have existed in the tradition: but that is not to say, of course, that such conclusive allusion ever existed.

DT XX.1–9 AND JEWISH MIDRASHIM THEREON

It has already been observed that Lk xiv and surrounding passages keep closely to the order and themes of Dt xx and adjacent material.[2] The purpose of this may be lectionary, or it may be to show how that extremely popular book of the *Torāh* was reflected or even improved upon by Jesus's teaching, the teaching which supplemented, fulfilled or corrected that of Moses. Without prejudice to whatever may have been Luke's motive, it is evident that hearers of our parable in Luke's gospel will have been reminded deliberately of Dt xx, 'When you go forth to war against your enemies . . . you shall not be afraid. . . . Then

[1] Xen., *Cyr.* V.5, 1. The verb is equally suitable in either context.

[2] C. F. Evans, 'Central section of St Luke's gospel' (cited above p. 100 n. 2) at p. 37ff., esp. p. 47–8.

the officers shall speak to the people saying, "What man is there that has built a new house. . . . Let him go back . . .".' They will have been reminded by two distinct motifs: first Luke gives a parable in which a *choice* occurs which is itself met by *excuses* (a feature of Dt xx.1–9), and then Luke gives us a pericope on worthiness, counting the cost, which looks directly to the topic of wholeheartedness (the need that adherents shall leave utterly behind them all attachments to 'home'), the central idea of Dt xx.5–8, followed by the small parables in which Jesus speaks of going to war (which is not directly spoken of in *vv.* 15–24) and military strategy which is the subject of Dt xx.10–19.[1] Now what connection is there between Dt xx and our parable, the excuses apart? A linguistic connection, as we shall see, justified by Zp i, exists between going to war and feasting, but consistently with our scheme we must proceed with the thematic connections, the fundamental points to which the linguistic curiosity, after all, only alludes.

Reverting to Dt xx.1–9, we find that the war spoken of is an aggressive war, in which Jews 'go forth'. The cause is not openly stated, but God will certainly give the victory, in which everyone must have faith (*vv.* 3–4). That this Deuteronomic rule was still regarded as good law in Jesus's time seems to be indicated by 1 M iii.56. The 'enemies' are midrashically understood to be in reality a single enemy.[2] Who is he? This depends on the context. If the war is an actual war he may be any foreign power, in which case this chapter supplies rules which are still part of the Talmudic law on the subject.[3] In an actual war it is politic not to place in the front line troops whose minds are continually drawn to their homes. As Philo puts it, in a passage worthy of our attention, οὐχ ἅπασαν τὴν νεότητα καλεῖν οἴεται δεῖν, ἀλλ' ἔστιν οὓς παραιτεῖται προστιθεὶς αἰτίας εὐλόγους τῆς ἀστρατείας . . .[4] They should be excused, whereupon they are occupied with the war-effort in the rear, *e.g.* working on the roads.[5] They are by no means useless. It is of extraordinary interest that the rabbis believed that even those who ***have***

[1] We should not overlook the fact that Luke may have misunderstood xiv.31–3, which looks very much like a parable about *God's* preparedness: see von Rad, *op. cit.* at p. 47.

[2] So the M.T. and *Targ. ps. Jon.* (J. W. Etheridge, *Targums of Onkelos*, etc., London 1865, II, 617). *Cf.* Ex xv.1*b*. Mekilta, p. 119 (when Israel do God's will).

[3] Maimonides, *Mishneh Torāh*, XIV, V (Kings and Wars), vii (trans. Hershman, p. 224ff.); *Book of Divine Commandments* (trans. Chavel, 1967), I 205–6: positive commandment no. 191.

[4] *Virt.* 23 (Colson VIII, 176; Yonge iii, 417). 'He does not think it expedient to summon forth all the youth, but some he excuses, stating reasonable causes for their exemption from military service.'

[5] 'They return home and provide water and food and repair the roads': *Mishnāh*, Soṭāh, VIII.2 (Danby, 302). b. Soṭ. 44*a* = Sonc. 222.

begun to enjoy new assets may be exempted from a secular war for one year, deriving the principle from Dt xxiv.5 ('When a man is newly married he shall not go out with the army . . .'), which was interpreted so that those who have actually engaged in any of the new enterprises mentioned in Dt xx are temporarily free both from military service at the front and from works of supply and communications.[1] Dt xxiv.5 is no doubt capable of this *midrash* with Dt xx, but it is doubtful whether even the newly married could properly claim his exemption from 'any business' (*cf.* xxiv.7 LXX) in other than military contexts.

Dt xxviii.30 says that the disobedient (*v.* 15) shall 'betroth a wife and another man shall lie with her'; shall build a house and shall not dwell in it (*cf.* Zp *sup.*); shall plant a vineyard, and not have the fruit of it. These are therefore commonplaces for frustration as the penalty for disobedience. Avoidance of these, which form parts of the sombre chapter of 'curses', will weigh heavily in a righteous war. Those entitled to the excuse should avail themselves of it lest they die and the 'curse' develop.

Meanwhile a distinction is to be observed. If the war is not for a religious purpose (as some of the wars of David were not) those excuses were available; but if the war is required by religion (*e.g.* against Amalek) even the bride out of her bridechamber should go to war.[2] The disqualifications from front-line service do *not* apply if the war is for a religious purpose. Nevertheless one rabbi reasonably opines that even in such a war those whose hearts are still at home and certainly those who are still 'fearful' in spite of God's promises ought to be exempted from the front line,[3] lest (*scilicet*) the curses seem to operate. The Dead Sea Sect certainly wanted the faint-hearted to be exempted from the field, and also the '*halt, the blind and the lame*' and those ritually defiled, for it was the holy war about which they were meditating.[4] A very recently publicised scroll belonging to that sect deals in

[1] *Mishnāh*, Soṭāh VIII.4 (Danby, 303). For a discussion of Philo's two accounts of Dt xx.1–9 with the allegorical meaning (*Virt.* 27–33, *cf. De Agr.* 148–56) see Colson VIII, 441–2.

[2] *Mishnāh*, Soṭāh VIII.7. b. Soṭ. 44*b* = Sonc. 223. Note the reliance upon Jl ii.15, *cf.* i.14.

[3] b. Soṭ. 44*b* = Sonc. 224. This was insisted upon by Gideon (Jg vii.3): the rabbinical doctrine thus has good support.

[4] Yadin (*inf.* p. 134 n. 5), 65–71. Y. Yadin, *The Message of the Scrolls* (London 1957), 139. *DSW* VII and X, 5–7, p. 290, 304. G. Vermès, *Dead Sea Scrolls in English* (London 1966), 132–3, 136 (*cf.* the badly damaged passage at *CD* XV.15f., Vermès, 109). E. Lohse, *Die Texte aus Qumran* (Munich 1964), p. 196, *ll.* 4–5: *piṣeaḥ 'o 'iwer 'o ḥiger* . . . The coincidence with Lk xiv.21 (*cf.* 13) is remarkable. It seems possible that a connection between 2 S v, Lv xxi.18 and the holy war existed prior to both the Dead Sea Sect's *haggadāh* and that of Jesus, but the evidence for this has yet to appear.

detail with this war, with the division of the nation for the prosecution of it, and with the rules of ritual cleanness which must be observed in the context.[1]

Now Jewish scholars linked Dt xx, xxviii, and Is lxv.21–2 ('They shall build houses and inhabit them; they shall plant vineyards and eat their fruit... and my chosen shall long enjoy the work of their hands...'). It is evident that the 'chosen' (Is lxv.15) are people who need fear no curse, because they obey God. Therefore those who take advantage of the excuses set out in Dt xx.5–7 do so because of consciousness of sin.[2] They will die in battle (though God will give the Jews the victory) because of their sins. Likewise those who are fearful (*v.* 8) are said by R. Jose the Galilean to be fearful because of the sins 'in their hands'.[3] God has promised to his chosen the right to expect the fruit of their enterprises, and this in Is lxv: the same chapter at *v.* 13 shows the same people feasting at a feast from which the men who did not listen to him are excluded, and endure pain and anguish instead. Our first substantial connection between fighting and feasting is plain: those who are chosen are sinless, do not die, are not frustrated, and sit in comfort at the banquet from which the others are consciously excluded, like Dives in the parable.

All these general principles have several points of coincidence with the myth of Amalek, to which we must now turn.

AMALEK

If the war in Dt xx is symbolic it may be taken as against Amalek. It is true that Amalek is not mentioned in Dt xx.17, but the correspondence between the tales of Amalek in scripture and *haggadāh* on the one hand and the scheme of Dt xx on the other justifies a midrashic connection between them.

From the chapter we see that it is a religious obligation utterly to exterminate the enemies of Israel and of God. Now the first enemy of Israel and the last is Amalek (Nb xxiv.20). The psalmist is thinking of Amalek when he sings 'Thou hast rebuked the nations (*goyim*); thou hast destroyed the wicked'.[4] Amalek symbolises God's chastising Israel

[1] A communication by Professor Y. Yadin at the conference of the Palestine Exploration Society (Jerusalem 1967) reported in *The Times* for October 23, 1967.

[2] So *Targ. ps. Jon.* on Dt xx.8ff. (Etheridge II, 617–18). For the text see Ginsburger (1903), 334–5 (where *ḥwv'* is constantly repeated).

[3] *Mishnāh*, Soṭāh VIII.5 (Danby, 303), b. Soṭ. 44*a*–*b* = Sonc. 222f. M. Kadushin, *Rabbinical Mind*, 2nd edn (N.Y., etc. 1965), 100. *Yalḳūṭ* on Dt xx.8.

[4] Ps ix.6 (5) as explained at *Midrash on Psalms*, *ad* Ps ix, § 7 (Braude I, 137).

when they doubt him.[1] Amalek exploited[2] (and exploits) weakness. Amalek is an answer to unbelief, and victory over him is the reward of faith. This enemy, of all the peoples, must be remembered. The double commandment, to remember and not to forget,[3] gives Amalek a curious privilege. In Joshua's fight against Amalek chosen men took part, and the remnant in the rear, the fearful and sinful, were it seems alone destroyed.[4] This shows how, even before the commandments were given at Sinai, the principles of Dt xx applied.

The notion that God is the leader in war, and that if the people have faith in him and listen to his word (however improbable) the fight will be won for them without suffering on their part, is fully documented at 2 Ch xx.14–29 ('. . . the battle is not yours, but God's').

Amalek is no ordinary enemy; his is no ordinary enmity: so that rabbis identify him with Esau's stock,[5] the embodiment of the evil inclination unchecked, Edom, which we know meant Rome.[6] Haman was an Amalekite,[7] and Esther's and Mordecai's victory over him was a re-enacting of the first victory. Purim celebrates God's vengeance and the continuing defeat of Amalek by the Jews,[8] provided the latter (as

[1] Midr. R., Exod. XXVI.3 = Sonc. 320; *Yalkūṭ ad loc.*; Midr. R., Num. XVI.18 = Sonc. 685. Amalek came before the serpent was raised aloft: *Targ. ps. Jon.* Nb xxi.9. *Refidim* is explained at Pes. d. R. Kahana *ad* Ex xvii.8–16. The men *chosen* to fight Amalek were those, said R. 'Eliezer ha-Moda'y, who fear sin.

[2] U. Cassuto, *Commentary on the Book of Exodus* (Jerusalem 1967), 206. When Israel had sown, the Midianites came up and the Amalekites . . . and they encamped against them, and destroyed the increase of the earth . . . (Jg vi.3–4, 33, vii.12). The non-destruction of the Amalekites by Saul was the cause of his rejection (1 S xxviii.18). It can be no wonder that these 'historical' details were construed symbolically.

[3] Dt xxv.17–19. Maimonides' 189th positive commandment. Chavel, *op. cit.* I, 202–4 should be consulted.

[4] Josephus, *Ant.* III, ii (39–62). This contains some *haggadāh*, as for example that after the victory Moses instituted a feast (like Purim). Note at 50: βραχὺ δέ τι περὶ τὸ ὕδωρ ἔταξε τῶν ὁπλιτῶν . . . *Targ. ps. Jon.* on Dt xxv.17–19: the Amalekite slew those who were thinking to go aside from my word and men of the house of Dan in whose hands were idols. *Cf. ibid.* on Ex xvii.8 (Etheridge I, 502).

[5] Midr. R., Num. XVI.18 = Sonc. 685. Jos., *Ant.* II, 2 (5). Midr. R., Deut. II.20 = Sonc. 47. b. Sanh. 99*b* = Sonc. 674. Amalek is wicked: Midr. R., Gen. LIII.5 = Sonc. 465; *cf.* Philo, *Leg. All.* III.186f. (Yonge i, 157; Colson I, 426), also *Ebr.* 24, *Mig.* 143f. To be destroyed by 'Joseph' (quoting Ex xvii.13): Midr. R., Gen. LXXV. 12 = Sonc. ii, 698–9. *Yalkūṭ ad* Ex xvii.8–16. The biblical authority is, of course, Gn xxxvi.12,16.

[6] Amalek = Edom: 1 K xi.16. b. B.B. 21*a*–*b* = Sonc. 107–8. Midr. R., Num. IV.8 = Sonc. 103. For Rome see *Midrash on Psalms*, Ps 10, § 6 (Braude I, 155); Ps 14, § 2, 3 (*ibid.* 183–4); Ps 17, § 12 (*ibid.* 217). *Cf.* Ps 21, § 3 (*ibid.* 295). The Messiah will trample Edom down: *ibid.* on Ps lx.10 (Braude I, 516). *Targ. Jer.* Gn xv.16. H. Loewe, '*Render unto Caesar*' . . . (Cambridge 1940), 28.

[7] 1 S xv.2. *Yalkūṭ* on Ex xvii.8–16 (ref. Dt xxv.19).

[8] Ex xvii.8–16 is a Purim lection. For Dt xxv.17–19 see *Mishnāh*, Meg. at b. Meg. 29*a*–30*a* = Sonc. 178ff. Esther's victory is remembered (!) in Ex xvii: Mekilta at '*Amaleḳ* II, on Ex xvii.14 (Wünsche, 173); b. Meg. 7*a* = Sonc. 35. *Yalkūṭ ad loc.*

scholars tardily realised ought to be stated plainly)[1] have faith in God and rely upon prayer to him.

Amalek's memory is to be kept, and yet it is to be blotted out. How? God will destroy Amalek in the last days, by means of the King Messiah.[2] Remembrance of Amalek is therefore remembrance that he will be destroyed, along with other enemies of Israel, in the Messiah's war.[3]

A passage in Paul (1 Co x.10) neatly alludes to Amalek (whom he refers to as 'the destroyer': ὀλοθρευτής = Satan?) in an elaborate Christian *midrash* on the Exodus story. The children of Israel perished because they *murmured* against God (Ex xvi.2, 7–12, xvii.2–7; Nb xiv. 27–35, 43, 45), therefore Christians must equip themselves to receive, and withstand, such temptation as God sends them.

THE MESSIAH'S BANQUET AND AMALEK

We have seen how in Is lxv the chosen will feast with God; Is xxv.6, indeed, explains ταῦροί μου καὶ τὰ σιτιστὰ τεθυμένα, the delicacies. The picture of the Messianic banquet is a familiar one to which Jesus himself refers.[4] That there would be a final war, in which the chosen would triumph and the enemies of the Messiah would become his foot-stool, and after which the Messiah would preside at a banquet seems to have been a common Jewish[5] as it subsequently became a Christian belief. It is important to realise that the day of vengeance (Is lxi.2–3) is also a day of joy.

The Matthaean parable begins 'The kingdom of heaven is like a king who made a marriage feast for his son . . .', and it ends '. . . there shall be weeping and gnashing of teeth. For many are summoned but few are chosen.' There exists a parallel to this amongst Jewish *midrashim*, coming, as do so many of our parallels, from the *Midrash Rabbāh*, which

[1] The notorious discrepancies between the LXX versions of Esther and the M.T., and the debates between the rabbis as to the book's sanctity. For the LXX now see the Göttingen Septuaginta, VIII, 3, *Esther* (1966).

[2] *Cf.* Ex xvii.16 LXX. The discussion of the three commandments given to Israel, of which the first was to appoint a king, and the second to cut off the seed of Amalek, deserves mention, but not analysis here: b. Sanh. 20*b* = Sonc. 108–9.

[3] 'But of the days of king Meshiḥa you shall not be unmindful': *Targ. ps. Jon.* on Dt xxv.19. *Cf. ibid.* on Nb xxiv.20.

[4] Mk xiv.25 par., Mt xxi.31, Mt viii.11f. = Lk xiii.28f. On Lk xxii.30 see p. 148 below.

[5] 1 En. lx.7, 24; 2 Ba xxix.4; 4 Ezr vi.49, 51–2; *Targ. ps. Jon.* Gn i.21. Ps l.10. Pirḳe d[e] R. 'Eliezer, trans. Friedlander (1916), 70, 72, 222. Those who partake are not necessarily the 'remnant'. Y. Yadin, *The Scroll of the War of the Sons of Light* . . . (Oxford 1962). Dead Sea Scrolls, *Messianic Rule* (Vermès, *op. cit.* 121, *cf.* 49). J. Klausner, *Die messianischen Vorstellungen des jüdischen Volkes* . . . (Krakau 1903, also Berlin 1904), 86–103. J. Jeremias, *Jesus' Promise to the Nations* (London 1958), 55–6. Rv xix.9, 17–18.

contains old, tannaitic material. The passage to be explained is Ex xii.19 ('for whoever eats that which is leavened, that soul shall be cut off . . . whether he be a sojourner, or one that is born in the land'), which raises the problem how foreigners could partake of the essentially Jewish Passover ritual meal. The parable goes as follows: 'God was like a king who made festivities (*simᵉḥāh*, a joyous occasion, such as a wedding feast) in honour of his son and slew his enemies. The king then announced: "He who rejoices with me may come to the festivities of my son, but he who hates me shall be slain with my enemies.' So God made a day of rejoicing for Israel when he redeemed them, and he proclaimed: "All who love my sons may come and rejoice with them." The virtuous Egyptians came, celebrated the Passover with Israel and went up with them . . .'[1] Now there is no question here of the 'son' being the Messiah —he is simply a symbol of the children of Israel, God's favourites. But the same type of idea could as easily be used by a teacher intending to show how a banquet, and the extermination of God's enemies can go together; and, unlike the Jewish parable reproduced above, his parable could show how those who, out of negligence as well as enmity, decline to come to the banquet in fact automatically incur association with the enemy. Accept our invitation, whoever you are, be with us and not against us! If you refuse the invitation you choose the camp of the enemy and are doomed. Jesus's parable is more complex and subtle than the *midrash* from *Midrash Rabbāh*, but it is evidently based on one and the same image, and the comparison is enlightening.

JESUS'S MIDRASH ON DT XX

What war is alluded to in Dt xx.1? Is it not the war alluded to in Dt xx.12–18? A war backed by God's intention (*v.* 1). The invitation to go forth to war involves the fighting in the front line by chosen men, *i.e.* those who are not disqualified. In a religious war, such as that envisaged here, no one is exempted and no one is disqualified unless he disqualifies himself. This could happen. When you go out to war an individual can absent himself or disqualify himself, with the natural result that he will not partake of the banquet after the victory. But do not read *milᵉḥāmāh* simply as war: read it as 'eating of bread', *i.e.* a feast.[2] In Pr xxiii.1 also we have the same double meaning.[3] To knead

[1] Midr. R., Exod. XVIII. 10 = Sonc. 226.

[2] See Gesenius and Koehler–Baumgartner, *lāḥam* II, to make a meal. Pr iv.17, ix.5, xxiii.1, 6; Ps cxli.4; Dt xxxii.24.

[3] The passage is interpreted (i) as a warning against the foe, the evil inclination, (ii) as a warning against speaking out of turn.

and to struggle, to fight and to feast—the linguistic connection is there.[1] One may disqualify himself from fighting, and so disqualify himself from feasting—what then of the feast that is prepared? Obviously it will be enjoyed by those who are undisqualified. Who are these? It is as if a man were preparing a feast in this world and invited guests. They can disqualify themselves by refusal. Others will take their places, provided they have no disqualification of their own. Thus if midrashically we read 'when you go forth to an eating of bread' (following Zp i), the text tells us that certain excuses are available even when God is the master and leader: when individuals have taken advantage of such excuses 'commanders shall be appointed at the head of the people (*v.* 9)', *i.e.* the fight (and therefore the feast) will start without them, and a system of discipline commences for the remainder.[2] If we are interested in a war against God's and Israel's enemies Dt xx tells us about disqualifications which exempt the individual from the battle and from the banquet. The parable is needed to probe more closely into the nature of self-disqualification and its consequences, and in it Jesus employs a varied technique. It is of interest that he almost certainly avails himself of the interpretation of Dt xx.10–12 given in the *Targum ps. Jonathan*, according to which *agents* (*pūliyn*) are sent to the city to *invite* (*lᵉmiḳᵉry*) it to peace, and *all* the people that are *found* are to pay, if they accept the invitation, *tribute* to their 'inviter'. If so, this proves that he accepted the midrashic linking of the later with the earlier parts of the chapter. Since the occasion is not merely an ordinary war but a holy war the word 'commanders', which we might pass over without thought, acquires a new significance, and to this we shall return presently.

THE PARABLE IN DETAIL

The excuses. Were the guests deriding their intended host? Apparently not. They agree less with the Deuteronomic pattern than with something more to Jesus's purpose if Luke's sequel is to be noticed. Luke's excuses are specific, whereas Matthew speaks of 'disregarding', they 'go away, one to his own field and one to his trading'. But Luke's field, yokes of oxen, and wife follow the Jewish teaching that a young man

[1] For the sake of completeness it is desirable to add that the *Torāh* itself is referred to as bread (*inter alia*) at Midr. R., Gen. XLIII.6 = Sonc. 356; Exod. XLVII.7 = Sonc. 542; XXV.7 = Sonc. 307, *ibid.* 8 = 312. Study of the *Torāh* is also battle; b. Meg. 15*b* = Sonc. 90 (*cf. milᵉḥāmāh* at Is xxviii.6*c*); San. 42*a* = Sonc. 272 (Pr xxiv.6); *cf.* b. Ḥul. 6*a* = Sonc. 22–3. At b. Ḥag. 14*a* = Sonc. 84–5 the *Torāh* is both bread and battle. *Cf.* the symbolism of 'Bethlehem', and also the language of Tt iii.9 (?).

[2] Dt xx.9; *Mishnāh*, Soṭāh VIII.6 (Danby 303). In particular the appointment of officers to prevent flight or rout.

should first acquire a source of income, then a means to live on it, and then only marry a wife and begin a family.[1] Thus all the excuses, so far as they go, are legitimate. They are not 'fatuous' as Bornkamm would have it. The man who bought the field may already have seen it, or he may have bought it through an agent. The phrase he uses, ἔχω ἀνάγκην ἐξελθὼν ἰδεῖν αὐτόν, 'I am obliged[2] to go out (of town) to view it', is consistent with the period immediately after the agreement to buy. Should the field be depreciating in value he may want to retract from the sale.[3] Or, if this was an area in which land could not be acquired without a written conveyance,[4] or even otherwise, he has a good reason to go and do an act on the land such as will manifest his acquisition, so that neighbours and his vendor know that he has 'made *ḥazāḳāh*', asserted his title, taken possession.[5] Moreover, even from the standpoint of religion he must surely see it to know what is needed for cultivation and to avoid the inconveniences that would arise from breach of commandments relative to agriculture. This is no doubt the spring. The rich man who has bought so many oxen (not necessarily on approval) is thinking of ploughing, he has many fields to plough and as all farmers know there is a right moment for ploughing—otherwise the number of acres to the plough would not be a known entity.[6] One who has just married a wife has a social and religious reason for attending to his own festivities. All three excuses are plausible, and they are expressed politely[7] in our Lucan version. The Thomas version (reproduced in most recent studies)[8] is interestingly devoid of the supposed

[1] Pr xxiv.27. b. Soṭ. 44*a* = Sonc. 221: a man should build a house, plant a vineyard, and then marry a wife. *Cf.* Tos., Sot. VII.20. This teaching is based directly on Dt xx.6,5,7(!), and failure to observe it leads to the imprecations directed to the fool at Dt xxviii.30(!): Maimonides, *op cit.* I (Book of Knowledge), II,v,11 (text and trans., M. Hyamson [Jerusalem 1965], 54*a*). That Luke understood the parable to be connected with Dt xx and xxviii is thus confirmed.

[2] The expression implies that it is not customary to do otherwise. So ἀνάγκην δὲ εἶχεν at Lk xxiii.17 is most appropriately explained by M. Black, *Aramaic Approach* (*cit. sup.*). 228: and ἔχει δ'ἀνάγκην at Euripides, *Hipp.* 634 (interpolated) (one cannot help getting married!). Moulton-Milligan cite P.Oxyr. VII.1061 and P.Flor. II.278.

[3] *Mishnāh*, B.M. VI.2; b. B.M. 77*b* = Sonc. 447. The subject of retraction is not free from difficulty, due to the contradiction of traditions (Herzog, *Main Institutions* I [1965], 147ff.).

[4] b. Ḳid. 26*a* = Sonc. 125.

[5] Herzog, *Main Institutions* I, 154ff.

[6] Jeremias, *Parables* (*op. cit.*), 177, cites Dalman, *Arbeit und Sitte* II, 47f.

[7] ἔχε με παρῃτημένον cannot be ironical. The absence of the apology at *v.* 20 is due to delicacy (what answer could be returned?) rather than reliance upon any commandment of the *Torāh*.

[8] See W. Schrage, *Das Verhältnis des Thomas–Evangelium zur Synoptischen Tradition* . . . (Berlin 1964), 133ff. The alternative reference to Thomas is 92.10–35. The passage is handled from numerous points of view (see their index) by H. Montefiore and H. E. W. Turner, *Thomas and the Evangelists* (London 1962). Montefiore, at p. 62, finds Thomas superior to Luke.

allegorising details which are said to obtrude in Matthew's version, yet it shows some signs of development. It is ingenious in elaborating the excuses: the guests had legitimate business to do, but it is assumed that businessmen *ipso facto* fall short of perfection. True, each of the excuses shows an abiding interest in the world, oblivious that it will end soon, but why not? The parable is not to be read as if the guests knew whom their host represented. A simple invitation to a feast, even if urgent, cannot take priority over a provident concern for the future—unless, that is to say, the social prestige of the host introduces another factor.

There is no suggestion that in making these excuses the guests acted illegally. That is one reason why the third invitees take offensive action, so that Dt xx.10–19 obtains its scope. Those, says this *midrash*, who despise the invitation with excuses may go about their business at their own risk, but the war commences not merely against the Hittites, etc., but also against those who, not content with refusing to fight *with* you, actually side against you.

The reaction to the excuses. Both versions (but not Thomas) state that the intending host was 'angry'. Matthew implies that his anger was aroused by the ill-usage meted out to his servants. Justifiably. The oriental setting must be understood. Hospitality is a function of social cohesion. In turn those who are able to entertain do so, and their equals are expected to accept as a matter of duty, and to reciprocate.[1] Oriental and primitive societies indulge in present-giving and in exchanges far more than we do, as constant pledges of mutual belonging. The distinction between charity and hospitality is clear and definite, as Jesus's words at Lk xiv.14 explain ('. . . and you will be blessed, because they cannot repay you'). When the feast was prepared, the lavishness of which is emphasised dramatically at Mt xxii.4, the host contemplated that his equals in giving and taking (with whom he stood upon terms of parity) would, if politely invited, come and rejoice with him, not because his food would be better but because such reciprocity as obtained meant that in all public respects these men could be relied upon. The general invitation had been accepted in principle and so he was expecting a good proportion of them actually to come.[2] When they refuse, even upon adequate excuses, he is bound to suspect that they

[1] On reciprocity see below pp. 232–5. The parable attributed to R. Gamaliel (b. B.Ḳ. 79*b* = Sonc. 452 = Bonsirven, *Textes Rabbin.* § 1635) shows that to banquets (including wedding feasts) social superiors should be invited, but to neglect social equals was not less reprehensible.

[2] Invitations were circulated so that people would hold themselves in readiness, and later a notice was sent round when the meal was ready—the unpredictability of oriental arrangements rendering this method necessary, especially in view of the etiquette that guests should not be kept waiting.

despise him or have indirect motives: after all it is to avoid such implications that even *we* go some distance to attend a function in which we are not interested if it is given by a person with whom we do not want a 'misunderstanding'.

The guests took this risk. They mistook their man. They were under the impression that if he misunderstood them the loss would not be significant to them. They apologised assuming that he was bound to accept their apology. And no doubt he would have done so had they not all, by an unfortunate coincidence, refused 'upon one impulse'.[1] This altered the situation. Individually they *could* be misusing him; collectively they *did* misuse him.

What, then, were the motives he could suspect? In the Lucan examples it is plain enough: they weighed the possibility of immediate inconvenience and the cost of having to contemplate reciprocity, and found that together these outweighed the chances of the intending host's displeasure. Matthew, by insisting on the *midrash* on Zp i, and making the host the king, implies something further. Refusing a king's invitation is very rare: but in the petty kingdoms of the Syrian orient acceptance had overtones.[2] First, since reciprocity was impossible a present would have to be brought; and since this was a son's wedding it would be as large a present as the unfortunate invitees could manage to bring. Next, attendance at the banquet implied approval of the matrimonial alliance, and allegiance to the king.[3] His position was obviously doubtful at that very moment, just as local politics must often have jeopardised the standing of many a small monarch throughout the first century. Thus for him positively to insist on their coming was nothing less than an enforcement of authority which one-third of the invitees (as we have seen) thought it prudent to dispute in the characteristically downright Jewish fashion.[4] The invitations thus carried implications, and the refusals likewise. The host's chagrin, 'anger', was therefore quite reasonable.

[1] In spite of the Hebrew and Aramaic learning indicated by M. Black, *An Aramaic Approach*, 3rd edn (1954), 113 approved by Jeremias, *Par.* 176, it appears that the idiom ἤρξαντο ἀπὸ μιᾶς [ἀρχῆς] is paralleled in Greek. The meaning is that though their *motives* may have differed their *impulse* was one and the same.

[2] A. N. Sherwin-White, *Roman Society and Roman Law in the New Testament* (Oxford 1963), esp. at p. 134. The biblical parallel (and one should always be welcomed in a parable of Jesus) is Saul's being despised by the sons of Belial: 1 S x.27, *cf.* 1 S xxx.22, 2 S xx.1.

[3] One may compare the extreme fuss attending Sir Thomas More's failure to attend the coronation (1534) of 'Queen' Anne Boleyn.

[4] See below, pp. 298–9. It is not true, as is said from time to time, that the Wicked Vinedressers had a right to beat up the owner's messengers while our men were acting completely without excuse—the cases are in fact parallel, in that both sets of villains were resisting a demand the implications of which were unacceptable to them.

It is fair to say that no invitation is without strings.[1] To put it coarsely, you cannot get something for nothing. The story of Esther's double invitation to the king and Haman[2] emphasises what, after all, everybody knows. The alternative is not modern casual 'dropping in', but charity, in which a prestige-less class of the population receive, and thus confer spiritual merit on their benefactors. It is more blessed to give . . .

The host is disappointed by the implications and the coincidence that all invitees, all the chosen, have turned the invitation down (which in the case of the king-host raises political questions). They have collectively proved that they are socially incompatible with the host, they are not 'worthy'. They must be punished. How? For a social offence a social penalty. They must be insulted. To summon all who can be found in the streets to sit (or rather lie) down with the host in his hall is the most deliberate insult that could possibly be offered to the invitees and their families. The Lucan account stresses first that the poor, the blind and the lame are called, and then whoever happens to be in the streets and walls of the village or city. This makes a midrashic allusion to the Deuteronomic passage concerning excuses, for those who are properly, or compulsorily, disqualified from front-line service are to be employed on the roads and, one may add reasonably, the fortifications.[3] True enough at first reading one thinks of beggars or vagabonds hiding under hedges, or, more realistically, of people who have no house to be in at dinner-time; but the rabbinical allusion is there none the less.

Two points must be noted here. The Jewish host was supposed to think of the poor. But this does not mean that the poor and the handicapped are normally fed along with the polite company.[4] Jesus suggests at Lk xiv.12–13 that the man who is well enough placed to hold an entertainment should imitate divine bounty and invite the underprivileged. They alone, unable to reciprocate, should be invited. They indeed will have no scruples about accepting. When the poor are fed

[1] Abraham's guests suspected he wanted to establish a spurious claim by inviting them: b. B.M. 87*a* = Sonc. 502. And note the relationship between a banquet and a request at Midr. R., Cant. on i.4 = Sonc. 48–9.

[2] Est v.6, vii.2.

[3] The *Mishnāh* and *gemara* do not say specifically that the 'rejects' are to be employed so, but it is obvious from the sense that they engage in non-combatant but essential tasks. φράγμα is a means of defence; φραγμός is a fence or fortification: Liddell–Scott–Jones, also Stephanus, esp. *Geop*. V.55. Not observed by W. Michaelis at *ThWzNT* V, 68–9. The Jebusite blind and lame were, according to one version, placed on the walls of Jerusalem.

[4] The interesting case of Mephibosheth: 2 S ix.3, 7, 10–11, 13; *cf*. xvi.3–4, xix.24–30, xxi.7. It is obviously unique and casts light on David's character. The hyperbole is evident in Jeremiah's making the blind and the lame the guests of the Most High (after building and vineyards) at xxxi.8.

at a time that polite company are entertained, the 'broken meats' are handed out to them, as it were, by the back door. The distinguishing even between classes of guests is reasonable, as an unnoticed Jewish parable shows. A king of flesh and blood prepared a banquet for his servants (*i.e.* the ministers, etc.), but to his personal friends he sent (*m^{e}shager*) portions from the plates set before himself. This means, in fact,[1] that those who *earn* will get their reward, but those to whom the host's free grace goes out, who are faithful *whether or not they are hired*, have not necessarily distinctly better entertainment, but a more intimate, and, one remarks, at the same time a separate one.

Portions of a meal are sent, as we see, to friends (especially out of the house at Purim), and our habit of sending portions of a celebration cake to the unavoidably absent may be a vestige of such a sentiment. Portions are also sent out to the poor.[2] Having this usage in mind we understand Lk *v.* 24: 'none of those people whom I invited shall (so much as) taste of my dinner', *i.e.* I shall not send him even a token of recognition and continuing reciprocity.

It is an ill wind that blows no one any good. Our host has his moral satisfaction. Like the master of the Unjust Steward, he is righteous by accident, which is gratifying.[3] The dinner was meant to be eaten, and eaten it is, in spite of the preoccupation and indifference towards it on the part of the invitees. His situation is actually used in a little-known rabbinical parable intended to explain God's concern for men: he is grateful for man's acceptance of his bounty.[4]

But one gets nothing for nothing. The host would have obtained from his guests reciprocity, or, in the case of the king, loyalty, acknowledgements of sovereignty. In the case of the lame and blind, etc., the host would have obtained merit. This universal semitic and further eastern notion is based upon God's justice and men's stewardship of the world's goods. The underprivileged, the humble, the depressed and

[1] b. Mid. 70*b* = Sonc. 491. R. Ḥiyya's comment on Pr ii.6. The point is that faith obtains the same reward as study, but spiced, as it were, with the host's favour. The word *shiyger* is used of 'sending', *e.g.* from the dining hall no further than the females' apartments: b. Ber. 51*a–b* = Sonc. 310.

[2] See Ne viii.11, 12.

[3] It is a remarkable thing for a king to do, to build a palace, prepare a banquet, and then assemble wayfarers (to enjoy it): b. San. 38*a* = Sonc. 240–1 (noted by Schöttgen, *Hor. Heb.* I, *ad* Lk xiv.16, 21).

[4] The parable of R. Jose bar Ḥanina at *Midrash on Psalms*, Ps xxv, § 9 (Braude I, 352). The banquet was announced early but the guests did not arrive until evening. The king said, 'Had you not come, I should have had to throw the whole banquet to my dogs'. So the Holy one, blessed be He, says to the righteous, 'I created my world because of you . . . (Ps xxxi.20) . . . otherwise to whom could I give it?' Jesus's parable, obviously better than this one, adequately illustrates by what a margin he excels the teachers who shared his cultural background.

handicapped are in a sense God's creditors, and others may pay his debts for him. Then God will reward them at the 'resurrection of the just'. 'Justice' in man is only another word for charity. The overtones are beyond the scope of this study, but it suffices if we notice that the rights of the poor spilt over, long before the time of Christ, into moral channels: the 'poor in spirit', the righteous, even if financially comfortable, are 'poor', 'humble'.[1] Religion assumes that those who feed the poor, the blind and the lame, losing prestige or profit thereby in social terms for want of reciprocity, gain spiritually—they store up treasure for themselves in heaven. To pursue our point: when services have been performed for him the king can reward his servants by entertaining them, especially at a victory-banquet; the ordinary host expects his guests to do something for him hereafter. If he is already successful, and to support him would be advantageous, people will readily accept his invitations, disregarding any inconvenience involved, for people like to participate in an upward movement.[2] A man may test his popularity and his progress by arranging a festivity, and nothing offends people more than premature festivities, as the well-known and (for us) highly relevant story of Adonijah shows (1 K i.9–10, 19–20). However, entertainment of the underprivileged is always practicable since in an effort to attain spiritual merit one can engage in conspicuous consumption without arousing any individual's personal jealousy.

The wedding (or rather 'festal') garment. It has already been pointed out that this could have meant nothing other than clean, preferably white clothes.[3] If it was for some reason impracticable to wear such, naturally less than clean clothes would have been condoned. Clean white clothing signifies in the Near East and South Asia gladness, rejoicing, what is auspicious. Dirty clothes fit a dirty deed.[4] Dirty clothing signifies mourning.[5] At a time of mourning clean clothes are forbidden. At a feast mourning garments are forbidden. To turn up at your host's home in dirty clothes implies that the occasion is an inauspicious one. The king saw it as a deliberate insult. Now the other intended guests had shown contempt for the occasion—a Jewish

[1] See the exhaustive articles πτωχός by Hauck and Bammel in *ThWzNT* VI, 885–915. God chooses the poor: Jm ii.5, etc. I am obliged to Dr M. Gertner for explaining the extremely important semantic and linguistic contacts between *'āniy*, *'ānāw*; *'innūy* = affliction, *ta'aniyt* = fast. In Arabic *fakir* means both 'poor' and 'an ascetic'. We may note in particular Is xli.17, xlix.17, liii.4, 7, liv.11; *DSW* xi, xiv.7.

[2] The amusing instance at Jb xlii.11. Note how they bring presents.

[3] Not a standard garment. Jeremias, *Par.* 187ff. Zc iii.3–5. *Mishnāh*, Ta'an. IV.7–8.

[4] b. M.Ḳ. 17*a* = Sonc. 107. b. Ḳid. 40*a* (when a man's evil inclination masters him, let him don black . . .).

[5] Or asceticism, *i.e.* a refusal to feast or rejoice. P. V. Kane, *Hist. of Dharmaśāstra* V, 1386 (top).

parable completely clarifies this point[1]—but he showed no ability to apologise. He was 'fearful' within the meaning of Dt xx.8, *i.e.* sinful, and kept silent. When the king rejoices his guests must rejoice (*cf.* the provision at Est iv.2), and if they neglect this the implication is that the king should not rejoice. A king reviewing guests who are also his troops may inflict disciplinary measures, for the guest who was not *with* his host was understood to be against him. The allusion to Is lxv.14 (*cf.* Ps cxii.10) has already been explained. It has already been explained that Matthew's treatment of the king's anger at xxii.7 reflects a *midrash* of the entire Dt xx. At Is xxiv.21–2 God himself *visits*, and imprisons.

'MANY ARE SUMMONED BUT FEW ARE CHOSEN'

This saying, which is obviously a maxim, occurs only in Matthew. The expression 'chosen' has obtained a theological life which the New Testament passage or passages do not entirely warrant. In the prime passages from the Old Testament cited above, and in the portion of Ex xvii which deals with Amalek, the word occurs in different senses leaving a certain vagueness which justifies various hypotheses. But our maxim has an express meaning which we are now able fully to appreciate. The trumpets are sounded, and all able-bodied men fall in. The maxim refers to a muster. Volunteers are needed for a particular mission. Those who are over age for the task or suffer from impediments or handicaps relative to the work are rejected. The others are 'chosen'. It is the chosen who, having faith in God, defeated Amalek though he was much more numerous and the children of Israel were faint and weak. After the Covenant *all* the 'chosen' mustered and *ate* (Ex xxiv.11 LXX).

But what of those that are not 'chosen'? It does not follow that they[2] are useless. Quite the contrary. The lame and the blind are quite able

[1] j. Sanh. 6, 9, f. 23*c* (line 31) (Krotoshin edn 1866) = j. Ḥagh. 2, 2, f. 77*d* (line 43) (Schwab VI, 1883, 278) reproduced at G. Dalman, *Aramäische Dialektproben*, 2nd edn (Leipzig 1927), 33–4. This is the story of Bar Ma'yan, heavily relied upon by W. Salm, *Beiträge zur Gleichnisforschung*, Diss., Göttingen 1953. Salm is cited appreciatively by Jeremias and Linnemann, and also W. Grundmann, *Das Evangelium nach Lukas* (Berlin 1964), 299. But unfortunately this story (reproduced again by Loewe, '*Render unto Caesar*' . . ., 57–8) is misleading, and the conclusions of Salm are quite unacceptable. There is no reason whatever for supposing that the host in our parable was a tax-gatherer or any other sinner. Because Ma'yan's invitations were refused (because of the social implications) he gave his feast to the poor, so that it should not be wasted. This parable illustrates that ignoring an invitation is a form of contempt and social ostracism, and that the poor could conceivably benefit from this: but beyond that we cannot go. That Jesus's words should be ironical, etc., is extremely improbable.

[2] See E. E. Sutcliffe, *Ir.Th.Q.* 28 (1961), 126–31.

to defend Jerusalem,[1] indeed only a strategem enabled David to defeat them and he would not have treated them as he did had they not been Jebusite lame and blind.[2] The weak, the lame and the blind will divide the spoil.[3] In other words, the prayers of the underprivileged and handicapped are as effectual for the victory in which God is interested as the valour of the man in the front line.

Now if we look again at Matthew we see that the sending is not detailed or repeated, hence impostors could be mustered—as fits Zp i.8; Luke avoided this by carefully enlisting first the poor, etc., and then the people with genuine excuses, *i.e.* those who, with the best will in the world, cannot fight in the front line, and so are entitled to man the home front (whether in the strict rabbinical or the Dead Sea Sect's opinion). Impostors are thus excluded by the host's explicit instructions, though one has to know the *midrash* to observe the point.

The parable of the Workers in the Vineyard, to which our maxim is appended in some manuscripts, is clear enough in general, though details still need much explanation. The workers are 'mustered' at the break of day in the marketplace, but the choice depends on special circumstances and does not take place once for all. The services of some are required only for an hour, and yet they are as essential to the harvest as those of the men who worked all day. Those who had to wait all day were physically less appealing to the hirer at earlier stages; but at the eleventh hour even they were required, and their reward was the same, though a peculiar order of payment was employed (*cf.* the publicans and sinners at Mt xxi.31). In the same way the Messianic banquet will be enjoyed by the front-line troops and those who served behind the lines, including those who could contribute nothing but silent prayers.

PURIM AND THE PARABLE

The law relating to Purim existed in embryo in the time of Christ.[4]

[1] 2 S v.6–8. Jos., *Ant.* VII, viii, 1 (61ff. Loeb edn, v, 391ff.). Oesterley and Robinson, *History of Israel* I, p. 215, n. 2. I am obliged to Professor D. Winton Thomas for an exposition to me of the state of this enigmatic text and its probable meaning. The suggestion by E. E. Bishop at *ET* 61 (1949), 355 is of no help to us. The biblical passage was exhaustively discussed in the *Z. des Deutsche Palästinavereins* 73 (1957), 73–99, an article utilised in the careful (but perhaps not final) treatment by H. W. Hertzberg, *I and II Samuel* (London 1964), 266, 268–9. The Jebusite city, and the rock-cut water channel, shaft and tunnel, are studied and illustrated in Dame Kathleen M. Kenyon's *Jerusalem* (London 1967), 21–2, figs. 3, 4.

[2] In view of the command to exterminate that people amongst others at, *e.g.* Dt xx itself.

[3] Is xxxiii.13–24 M.T. with *Targ.* and LXX. *Cf.* Jg v.30; Ps lxviii.12. In the holy war all spoil is *ḥerem*, so that the metaphor is not to be pressed too far.

[4] Jos., *Ant.* XI.vi.13 (284ff.) (agreeing with Est xix, LXX). It is not possible to accept

Purim, like Hanukkah, was an overtly anti-Gentile festival,[1] and therefore is not directly alluded to in the New Testament. At Purim, which is a spring festival, work may be done, provided it is of a conservative and not initiating description. Marriage at Purim would however be appropriate. Buying fields, ploughing, and marriage all strike one as appropriate spring occupations. Mourning is forbidden. Feasting is obligatory and it starts *early* in the day so that people can get drunk comfortably—the one day in the year when drunkenness is obligatory. Since each household will normally have its own celebrations those who have not previously arranged for their feast would not be particularly pleased to be invited elsewhere. Since Purim is celebrated in certain walled towns one day later than in other towns and villages,[2] the reading of the scroll of Esther, which is compulsory, is done on different days in different places and each individual has to make his own arrangements to read or to hear it read. The blind are naturally privileged in this respect.[3] Invitations will take account of all this and it would be exceptional to invite to one of the walled towns for Purim a man whose home celebration will hardly have worn off. But exceptional circumstances might justify such a step. If he were already within range of his own Purim a repeated invitation would then be required. The poor as always must be thought of, but at Purim there is an especial obligation. Purim requires (1) that the miracles of God should be remembered, (2) that Haman (Amalek), Esther and Mordecai should be remembered and the *haggadāh* associated with their names, (3) that all Jews should rejoice, and that therefore all should have the means wherewith to feast, and (4) that all Jews should congratulate one another on God's fighting for them. Thus all the poor are entitled to the Purim collections without any discrimination: good and bad alike are to participate.[4] Portions of food may be given to them as well as money, and if they are stationed at road junctions they will do well from many households, so that an invitation to dine at one house would

[1] *Jüdisches Lexikon*, IV/1, 1182ff. ('Purim'); *Jewish Encyclopaedia*, X, same title. T. Schärf, *Das Gottesdienstliche Jahr der Jüden* (Leipzig 1902). G. F. Moore, *Judaism* I, 245f., II, 51f. For the lections and psalms see any Prayer Book and I. Elbogen, *Der jüdische Gottesdienst* . . . 4th edn (Hildesheim 1962), 130, 132, 156, 184ff. R. de Vaux, *Ancient Israel*, 2nd edn (London 1965), 514–17 ('It was a popular feast, of suspect origin . . .'). Later, anti-Gentile elements were softened: see D. N. Mackenzie at *J. R. As. S.* 1968, 68–75.

[2] *Mishnāh*, Meg. I, 1–2 (Danby, 201). Maimonides, *op. cit.* III, x, 1, § 10 for detail.

[3] *Mishnāh*, Meg. IV.6 (Danby, 207).

[4] b. B.M. 78*b* = Sonc. 452.

W. Robertson Smith's contention at *The Old Testament in the Jewish Church*, 2nd edn (London 1908), 183–7, since the fast may have been superseded without the feast's having been interfered with.

have to be pressing, for on that day they would rather be more easily accessible. Then portions of food must be sent to friends' houses, since the friends are presumed to be having their own Purim feast. Each will 'taste' of his friends' celebrations. Amongst work allowed on that day would be counted all the items found in the gospel parables, including the king's chastisement of his enemies. The appropriateness of the details is rather striking. So also is the complacent remark of the fellow-diner at Lk xiv.15, 'Blessed is he who eats bread in the kingdom of God'. The kingdom of God will not take place until Amalek is conquered; and Amalek and the Messiah's war and banquet are in people's minds at Purim. Luke's setting is appropriate to the parable, for rabbinic thought relies on Is lvii.15 here—the poor should be fed rather than friends because the poor and contrite are the especial objects of God's concern.[1]

Jesus is teaching about the individual's fitness to be present at that last banquet over which he intends to preside. His warnings would be authoritative. Matthew keeps the king of Zephaniah and emphasises the conflict between him and his foes, near and far; Luke emphasises the *midrash* on Dt xx.5–8 (three excuses only) and brings out the sequel, the actual composition of the partakers of the feast. Purim would be the best time, in fact, for such a feast.

THE SUGGESTED MEANING OF THE PARABLE: THE 'OPEN' HAGGADĀH

Many parables have penumbrae of meanings, and a choice from amongst them is bound to be made by commentators ancient as well as modern. But the meanings of this parable seem to have been both more vague and more narrow than the meanings attributed to it by our commentators. Jesus does not look at non-Pharisees, or at Gentiles, as such. He seems to look, by implication, at Rome, and perhaps at the zealots who want his leadership in war if he is indeed their Messiah. But what emerges is briefly this. For an earthly banquet guests utilising legitimate excuses risk their host's ire, and a consequent fall in prestige: how much the more will God exclude those who excuse themselves hypocritically, illegitimately, or inadvertently from his combined invitation to fight, to conquer, and to 'rest' afterwards?

Those who wish to participate in the Messiah's banquet must have one of the following qualifications: (1) if they have been chosen to fight in the war they must not have disqualified themselves by such an

[1] Maim. *op. cit.*, III, x, 2, § 17; *cf.* iv, 6, § 18 (trans., p. 303).

attachment to alternatives as would imperil their efficiency, *i.e.* their obedience to God (and so would bring them within the curse of Dt xxviii), in other words they must accept wholeheartedly the appointment in God's service. Or (2) they are 'poor', that is to say underprivileged or handicapped, and so not chosen, provided they have forwarded the war by their prayer or by other services which, in view of their handicaps, God accepts in lieu of active participation. And they must not have disqualified themselves by sin. The fighters will be at the banquet, and those who help in the war-effort in the senses indicated. If any believe they are *entitled* to be present by reason of their status or other merits and irrespective of their services, they are to expect a rude shock—no such consideration will be shown them, rather the reverse.

And the enemy is not the Amalekite, the Edomite, or Rome, but the evil inclination. Those who conquer themselves are God's victors: thus allusions to Isaiah and Zephaniah enable the actual moral amelioration of the ancient laws of war carried out by the author of Deuteronomy to flower in a lively tale. The Church took up the idea and expanded it in the conception of God's rest, from which the disobedient (who tempted him in the wilderness—and thus incurred Amalek—*cf.* Ps xcv) are excluded (Heb iii.7–iv.12).

THE HIDDEN HAGGADĀH

To grasp an inner meaning it is necessary to read on into Lk xiv. The question is raised there, cannot all the youth to whom the previous idealistic appeal is made join up, as it were, under Jesus's leadership? (We note that the Church later saw Jesus as depicted by Joshua in the Amalek story.)[1] They too must be prepared to sacrifice in order to warrant their being chosen for the front line. God has worked it all out; so must they. Jesus shows that the banquet is not in this life, and so both leader and troops must be prepared to give their lives to attend it. On this footing the victory can be won.

In this holy war Dt xx is, as we have seen, relevant. Dt xx.9 speaks of the *captains of the hosts* (*sārēy tsᵉvā'ot*, *i.e.* the commanders of the army now constituted free from unsatisfactory elements. Joshua, who defeated Amalek, prostrated himself (Jos v.14) before some divine being who described himself as 'captain of the host (*sar-tsᵉvā*') of the Lord'. Twice, therefore, Joshua won important victories in obedience to supernatural guidance, and the captain of the host (which Joshua himself seemed to be) was in fact some other force, supernatural aid.

[1] Fathers at Nicephoros, Σειρά (*Catena Patrum*, Leipzig 1772), coll. 745–50.

A closer look at 'Amalek' is required. The strange story in Ex xvii deserves a commentary such as considerations of space now preclude. It provides the beginning of a beautiful, ancient, and still popular hymn[1] in which the Jews acknowledge that as they look up, following the direction of Moses's hands, they prevail. As in the case of the serpent in the wilderness, the Jew's mind and spirit are sent upwards, and by faith in God he overcomes. Now Moses's hands held up, fixed, lest they drop from exhaustion, until the going down of the sun, appeared as if in prayer, but the rod or staff of God was in them. How? Our imagination will have to serve as its like served the generation of Jesus. Moses's rod which dried the Red Sea, found water in the desert, and held up the life-giving serpent, was the material instrument whereby God ministered to wavering faith. This rod could have been held by the two hands, and it was while the hands were held up that Joshua triumphed. Now this rod was a part of a tree. Here evidently we have the symbolism which Jesus himself saw behind the σταυρός which, for all its incongruous origins, could be turned to haggadic account, as the Church insisted later.[2] Those who enlist in God's active service must be prepared to carry such a stake[3] in imitation of their leader, their only weapon, like faith, the only weapon of the warrior in the holy war.

It is of great interest to discover, in a region of Luke which is not normally considered a single pericope, a series of concepts which, read in the light of the foregoing, form an intellectual continuum. First we have the cross (Lk xxii.26–7 should be compared with Mk x.45), then temptations (Amalek symbolises the response God makes to those who lack faith in him; Amalek comes only because of sin:[4] *cf.* πειράζειν at Ex xvii.7) (Lk xxii.28), then the coming kingdom (xxii.29), then the Messianic banquet (xxii.30), which will take place provided Satan is repulsed upon Jesus's prayer for the faith of Peter. Peter must turn *to* [the fight] and not turn away (*cf.* Dt xx.5–7), and then 'make firm'

[1] b. R.H 29*a* = Sonc. 133–4: *v*[e]*kiy yādāyv shel Mosheh 'osot mil*[e]*ḥāmāh.* Note that a reference to the fiery serpent of Nb. xxi.8 follows this hymn. Mekilta, '*Amaleḳ* 1 (Lauterbach II, 143–5). *Cf.* Philo, *Mos.* i, 215ff.

[2] Jn iii.14. *Targ. Onḳ.*: the serpent was put on an ensign. Theodoret ('the greatest Greek interpreter of Scripture in Christian antiquity': Altaner), *Quest. in Exod.* XIX.34 (*MPG* 80, 260–1): τοῦ σταυρωθέντος ὑπὲρ ἡμῶν ἐπλήρου τὸν τύπον . . . Amalek is the διαβόλος. This is without prejudice to the symbolism of the tree at Ex xv.25 (*cf. Targ. ps. Jon.*). Justin Martyr, *Dialogue* §§ 49, 90, 97, 111–2.

[3] For a totally different view of Lk xiv.27 see E. Dinkler, *Signum Crucis* (Tübingen 1967), 77–98. The parallel, Mk viii.34 (ἀράτω τὸν σταυρὸν—Luke at ix.23 understandably adds καθ' ἡμέραν [for it refers to the war against sin]) is suggested by Brandon (*Trial*, 1968, 34 n. 59) to have been 'a well-known Zealot saying'. But Zealots were not (even theoretically), primarily missionaries against sin.

[4] Mekilta, '*Amaleḳ* 1 (Lauterbach II, 135, 139).

(στήρισον, *cf.* Ex xvii.12, *bis*) his 'brethren'. Biblical motifs can be used over and over again, and here Jesus sees himself as Moses encouraging Peter, either as Joshua or as an imitator of Jesus or as both, to lead his troops to victory, so that they may partake of the great banquet in the 'kingdom' which is not hypothetical, but actually 'appointed' (more correctly 'disposed': διατίθεμαι, διέθετο) for the faithful companions of the leader.

Let us look at the Amalek story again, and once again with the commentary upon it of the *Mekilta*, which preserves so many old *midrashim*. The rabbis fastened upon Moses's words 'Choose *us* out men . . .' (Ex xvii.9). Why 'us'? To show that Moses in this context regarded Joshua as his equal—the relationship is a very special one, and the subordination of the 'pupil' is modified: from this we learn that the teacher must hold the pupil as dear to him as himself.[1] Why 'men'? 'Men', say two of the rabbis (exemplifying two ways of reaching the same interpretation), means ultimately 'men who fear sin'[2]—the criterion of choice is that the select shall be righteous. It is obvious that though the 'soldiers' are to fear sin and to abhor temptation, *i.e.* they are exactly those whom Amalek would hope to overcome, they are in fact the élite from amongst whom exclusively the front-line troops are picked. Moreover Moses suffers discomfort in two ways because of his position. His hands are heavy because of the inevitable sins of the children of Israel in their hour of trial, and he is supported by a stone, which signifies a want of comfort or refreshment so long as the battle lasts.[3] To the student of ancient religion the stone is a magical factor, signifying stability, strengthening: Moses is trying to impart strength to his troops by supporting himself on a stone. But to the student of rabbinics (whose point of view is much more conducive to our purpose) the stone indicates that while his troops suffered at the foot of the hill, Moses himself suffered with them. We may now turn to Jesus's exchange of 'identifications' with Peter in Matthew (xvi.15ff.) where two other allusions to the Amalek episode appear. Simon acquired the name Cephas (Aram. *kēyphā'*, a rock or stone) (Jn i.42) which is the same as πέτρος, πέτρα (a word having its own allusive character, calling up the earlier part of the Moses story in Ex xvii and elsewhere), and could equally be translated λίθος. Jesus now identifies Peter as a stone *upon which* (not 'onto which') Jesus will build (*i.e.* create, form) his ἐκκλησία, usually translated 'church'. We are immediately told that the 'gates of Death' shall not prevail against it.[4] The passage has enjoyed many very

[1] *Ibid.* 140. [2] *Ibid.* 141.
[3] The Mekilta does not give this *midrash* in full. See b. Ta'an. 11*a* = Sonc. 48.
[4] O. Cullmann examines the passage, with references, at *ThWzNT* VI (1959), 99–109.

careful examinations,[1] but for our purposes it is needful to remember that the word 'prevail' is exactly that used in Ex xvii about the combatants, while the stone reminds us of the stone placed under Moses. 'Εκκλησία is literally an assembly mustered upon some principle of selection, however wide. The 'church' founded with Peter as its first member is the same as the 'chosen' who will fight (with him as captain?) against evil to final victory. The chosen are to 'put on' as clothing (Col iii.12–14) virtue, and as armour (Rm xiii.12; Ep vi.11, 13–17) qualities including similar virtues and faith and the gospel, in order to withstand, in military fashion, the 'wiles of the devil'. If we are inclined, as is legitimate, to search the psalms for hints about the Messiah, his sufferings and victory, we note Ps xxvii as relevant to our present theme. Leaving aside critical and historical questions (which will not have interested contemporaries of Jesus) we notice the sequence of ideas: a host encamps against him, yet he still trusts in Yahweh, whose temple is his protection; his head is lifted up, he is set on a rock and his foes are now beneath him; he will sing and praise Yahweh. No doubt the rock (LXX: ἐν πέτρᾳ) was originally that of Ps xl.2, a symbol of security in an insecure world. But midrashically linked with Moses's stone it does more than symbolise security—it implies the founding of a victorious establishment against which the host of foes (temptations to sin) will be powerless.

The image of the soldier of Christ is sufficiently established. The author of the Second Epistle to Timothy couples in his injunctions to Timothy the lessons of the faithful soldier (*cf.* the metaphor of the muster) and of the agricultural worker who is entitled to his reward:[2]

> Take your share of suffering as a good soldier of Christ Jesus. No serving soldier involves himself in the business ventures of ordinary life, since his intention is to satisfy the one who enlisted him. And if one engages in a fight he is not crowned unless he has fought fairly. It is the labouring cultivator who ought to take the first share of the crops.[3] Think over what I say, for the Lord will give you understanding in everything.

It is worth adding that the double meaning in 'fight' and 'crowned' would be apparent to a contemporary reader. 'Fighting', whether serious or mock, implies both struggle, especially wrestling (*cf.* Jacob)

[1] J. Ringger, *Fests. O. Karrer* (Stuttgart, 1959), 271–347. [2] 2 Tm ii.3–7.

[3] The word 'labouring' does not refer to the amount of labour but to its sincerity, nor does 'first' necessarily signify priority as between the labourers, *i.e.* so that those who work longer should be paid first. On the contrary the meaning seems to be that the labourer shares before the non-labourer, such as the landowner. Mt xx. 1–16 can be read with 1 Co iii.5–9 ('according to his labour' does not mean 'proportionately to the *amount* of his labour', as one might otherwise suspect).

and contest; 'crowned' refers not only to the crowns given to individual victors in public games, but to the crowns habitually worn at banquets, Jewish or Greek. The allusion to the banquet for the victorious warriors, who fought in the war in which Christ was both enlisting officer and commander was not too recondite. The author of the passage is no doubt self-consciously sewing together elements from 1 Co ix, etc.,[1] but there is no reason to suppose that he was unaware of the significance of the parables which lie behind his teaching, and he seems impelled (as do many self-consciously clever people) to point to his own smartness: a biblical *midrash* is (somewhat remotely) at the back of the sequence of ideas, and reference to Jesus's teaching will clarify the points. Meanwhile the terms 'fellow soldier' and 'fellow worker' became commonplaces (Ph ii.25).

AN OBJECTION

If this is the meaning, it may be objected, a serious difficulty arises. The parable, in either of its transmissions, should make sense literally, and the symbolic and allusive elements should be harmonious with the everyday story. Yet what was to happen to the banquet if the intended guests had all accepted? Would the poor have got nothing? Would no lame and blind have been invited? It is this consideration which has urged commentators to suppose that the reference, possibly by the evangelist, is plainly allegorical, and that by the *guests* are meant the chosen people, Israel, who rejected Jesus (or so we are told), and by the *lame* and the *blind* are meant the Gentiles—and this understanding seems persuasive, even though it is quite evident that the Gentiles have not been called immediately before the banquet, and there is no reason for supposing that the 'day' was thought by Jesus to be hard on his heels, or that, if this was so, he or anyone else had by that time actually called any Gentiles.

The problem so far as Matthew is concerned soon melts. Weddings are occasions when all and sundry come, and those who turned down the individual invitations would have been a small fraction of the guests expected. The lame and the blind and the poor would have been at the back door, as it were, in numbers. The Lucan position is not so simple. There was no question of calling the poor nor the lame and the blind until the invitees had turned down the invitations. What otherwise would have happened to those handicapped people? Notwithstanding their merits and loyalty, are they conceived as due to lose the banquet

[1] 'Who goes to war at any time at his own expense? Who plants a vineyard without eating its fruit later?' That is to say no undertaking is without hope of reward.

unless those who are not handicapped choose to decline? Had the Jews or their leaders accepted Jesus would the Gentiles never have been called? We know that in prophetic terms, and to keep the balance between the life of Jesus and the haggadic role of the Messiah, rejection by the leaders has to take place. But did this parable require that the invitees must fall down on their social obligation in order that others who were not fit to be invited along with them should have a chance of entering the hall?

The answer is not long in coming. We must remember that Jesus's audience thought first of corporate and later of individual salvation—the salvation of the people was their concern. Jesus speaks in this idiom. The people is of course led by its prestige-worthy elements, the householders, the middle-aged people. These are the ones commonly involved in worldly affairs. The rest of the population are either handicapped physically or mentally, underprivileged financially or otherwise, or young. It is the 'poor' who have the virtue of humility, contrition; the young who have the quality of idealism. When the middle-aged and prestige-worthy, the 'rich', turn down the summons, supposing that they are perfectly entitled to do so on prudential grounds, will the banquet be lost, thrown to the dogs, or will the 'rest' God has promised fail to take place? The banquet is a banquet to celebrate a victory, and the rest is rest after honourable fighting. Consequently the victory and the honourable fighting must take place. Theoretically the middle-aged and prestige-worthy are exactly the people to conduct the war: the responsibility is upon them. But if they excuse themselves, surely the others must set to and take the responsibility which has devolved upon them? And they will win, and the banquet will be theirs, and the host will make merry with them. As we shall see below, Jesus was keen to create an equality of status between his followers (Lk xxii.26). And, as both prophets and the rabbinical writers saw such a situation, the people who really had no faith in the invitation (they knew too much), would like to withdraw their refusals—would like to participate though it is too late. Their status, they hope, will secure them a place. They are forced to stay outside where there is weeping and gnashing of teeth: a somewhat unchristian way of punishing them, but true to the spirit and the letter of the prophetic passages. Thus there is no question of the poor, etc., representing the Gentiles or indeed any Jewish group specifically. Those who are naturally bearers of responsibility may assume that their status will give them rights on the 'day', but it is actual service that counts, and when the front line (the 'great') back down (whether their excuses seem adequate or not) the other forces (the 'inferiors') must go forward and win, and it is assumed that since the power to conquer lies somewhere it must lie there. This is logical, fits our knowledge of life, and enables even the Lucan version to be true at once to the purpose of the parable, and to the biblical imagery which lies behind both.

Both Luke and Matthew preserve a story bound up with *midrashim* on Old Testament texts. It may be that we have two rewritings of one story, or a faithful version and one not unfaithfully rewritten, and indeed there are other possibilities. But the kernel of the idea and the concept of the banquet as the joy of the actual victors, whoever these are, may safely be attributed to Jesus as a typical specimen of his teaching. That the Church has fastened upon some aspects as suited to its situation may well be true, but we now have a plausible explanation for all the elements of the tale, and it is no longer necessary to attribute as much to the Church's rewriting of the parable as was formerly supposed desirable.

APPENDIX

SUGGESTED SOLUTIONS FOR DIFFICULTIES

(A) *Practical Difficulties in the Story*

Mt xxii.5. The invitees all make light of the king's invitation. This seems implausible,[1] but political implications account for it. They are basically disaffected.

Mt xxii.6. The same is to be said for those who illtreat the king's servants,[2] and there is no need to assume an imitation of the parable of the Wicked Vinedressers.

Mt xxii.7. The king's anger and destruction of the city are not implausible because he lacked time, for the city need not be far off, it is unlikely to have been his own city,[3] it could have been quite small, and prompt action is seemly in kings.

[1] K. H. Rengstorf, *Das Evangelium nach Lukas* (Göttingen 1962), 178–80, finds the whole parable frankly unrealistic. G. V. Jones, *The Art and Truth of the Parables* (London 1964), 97–8, is a recent victim to these ideas. Eta Linnemann's suggestion (p. 89, 161) that the refusals were absolute in Matthew but only postponements or apologies for coming late in Luke (except in the case of the newly married, whose presence in the series she thus unwarrantably suspects) is rightly rejected by Jeremias. Such were the difficulties of the supposedly lucid parable.

[2] W. O. E. Oesterley, *The Gospel Parables in the Light of their Jewish Background* (London 1936), 126.

[3] Oesterley, *Gosp. Par.* 123. C. G. Montefiore, *Synoptic Gospels* II (1927), 288. R. V. G. Tasker, *The Gospel according to St Matthew* (London 1961), 207.

Mt xxii.8. The king calls the defaulters 'unworthy'. This is not too feeble,[1] because he means that he intends to insult all of them.

Mt xxii.12. The man had no wedding-garment. This is not implausible on the ground that he had no time to get one or that the king was unfair to demand one in the circumstances,[2] because all the others had the correct dress, and even beggars can manage to wash a garment or, failing that, to explain why that was impossible. The rabbinical parallel[3] shows that great haste in arrival was not normally expected.

Mt xxii.13. Binding hand and foot is dramatic but not implausible,[4] as the insult must be avenged according to contemporary notions.

Mt xxii.14. 'Many are summoned...' is not inappropriate on the ground that in fact the hall was filled,[5] because the meaning is *ad hominem*: 'True you were mustered with the others, but subject to my right to reject you if you are unfit for service.'

Lk xiv.18. It is not implausible that all the invitees should reject at the last moment an invitation which they had accepted in principle, because they were not in collusion, it was a coincidence, and to a great feast each invited guest would not consider himself personally bound by acknowledging a general invitation, any more than we are bound to turn up to a wedding to which we have been invited.

Lk xiv.18–20. All three excuses are plausible, though they involve the risk that their non-acceptance will result in social retaliation. See above on plausibility.

Lk xiv.21. It is not implausible[6] that the house should be filled from people near and far who were not themselves already dining, for

[1] A. H. McNeile, *Gospel according to St Matthew* (London 1915, 1952), 315. B. T. D. Smith, corrected by Tasker, *cit. inf.* at p. 208.

[2] Linnemann, 94, 165–6; Oesterley, *ubi cit. sup.* Montefiore, *op. cit.* II, 289. McNeile, *op. cit.* 316. As this is no allegorisation so it is not polemical in the sense suggested by Trilling.

[3] Wetstenius *ad* Mt xxii.11, Billerbeck, *Kommentar* I, 878 and Montefiore, *Rabbinical Literature and Gospel Teaching* (London 1930), 310–11 cite b. Shab. 153*a* = Sonc. 781–2 (attributed to Joḥanan b. Zakkai) and Midr. Ḳoh. on IX.8 (42*a*) = Sonc. 235–6. Clean clothes must be kept as soon as the preliminary invitation is received. Both the versions cite Is lxv.13f., which is significant, as Oesterley notices at p. 130. Jeremias, *Par.*, 188.

[4] The reading of D ignores the military overtones and is therefore to be rejected (otherwise Linnemann, p. 167, n. 21).

[5] P. Gaechter, *Das Matthäus-Evangelium* (Innsbruck, etc. 1963), 690–7. McNeile, 317. Linnemann, 97, B. T. D. Smith, *The Parables of the Synoptic Gospels* (Cambridge 1937), 206. Sarcastic remarks appear at Montefiore, *ubi cit.* 289–90. Hunter's notion that no real host insists on filling his hall has no foundation, since Asian hosts are very proud of entertaining crowds—the more the merrier, and since the very word for hospitality (*hachᵉnāṣat 'orᵉḥiym*) is literally kindred to *kᵉnéṣet*, an Assembly!

[6] Jeremias, *Par.*, 178.

the host gains merit and his social equals will be the better affronted.

Lk xiv.24. The final words are addressed not by Jesus,[1] but by the host not to the servant(s)[2] but to the company he then had, to the effect that not even tokens of comity would pass from his kitchens to the host's friends (he was wild with them).

(B) *Critical Difficulties in the Story, as Reviewed in the Light of the Above Clarification*

Mt xxii.6–8 are not insertions from elsewhere,[3] for they illustrate that the king-host will utterly destroy those who are his open enemies [*cf.* 2 S x.4, xi.1, xii.30–1], in contrast with those that neglect his summons with or without valid excuses (this is reading Dt xx.10–18 with 1–4). The rabbinical parallel explains this.

Mt xxii.11–14 is not an additional parable added to make an additional point,[4] but a continuation of the theme. The surreptitious enemy is disclosed by 'visitation', 'review'. He is the man whose lack of faith is not disclosed until a late stage. In terms of the Zephaniah passage with which we commenced this paper, the 'officers' (or 'great ones', 'magnates') are visited by having their city destroyed. Those in strange clothing, *i.e.* worshippers of other gods, are detected at the end. Is xxiv.21–3 implies exactly this.[5]

Mt xxii.14: 'Many are summoned . . .' summarises the whole theme, since the banquet is for the victorious army; and since not all the men who answer the call are fit for service, and none but those who are 'present and correct', as it were, can expect a place at the tables.

[1] Oesterley, *Gosp. Par.*, *ubi cit.*

[2] ὑμῖν in *v.* 24: Linnemann, 90; Jeremias, 177; Smith, 205.

[3] Oesterley, *ubi cit.* R. Bultmann, *op. cit.* 175, 197, 413, citing Kümmel, Jeremias and W. L. Knox (*Sources*, II, 112f.). The assertion that *v.*7 is a prediction of the destruction of Jerusalem is frequent (R. Bultmann in F. C. Grant, ed, *Form Criticism* (New York 1962), 49) but without any foundation.

[4] Linnemann, 95. Jeremias, 65, 187ff. Oesterley, *ubi cit.* Bultmann, *op. cit.* 175; Tasker, 207; G. D. Kilpatrick, *The Origins of the Gospel according to St Matthew* (Oxford 1946), 30, 82 (followed by A. R. C. Leaney, *St Luke*, 2nd edn, London 1966, 214). Hunter, *op. cit.* 56 n. 1 ('Matthew thought the parable made salvation too easy').

[5] Following the M.T. and the Targum. The word *mārom* is ambiguous, implying both (host of) heaven and the (army of) Sion. The 'kings of the earth' fit the rebels of the parable. As in Zp, *yiphᵉḳod* implies 'he shall visit/punish'.

CHAPTER SEVEN

The Woman Taken in Adultery

THE NATURE OF THE PERICOPE[1]

IT IS ADMITTED that the celebrated Pericope de Adultera (Jn vii.53–viii.11) is a piece of authentic tradition going back to the beginnings of the Church, though it is extra-canonical[2] and its text evidently suffered from its independent wanderings before it found its way into the canonical gospels.[3] It was readily used to show that, as our

[1] U. Becker, *Jesus und die Ehebrecherin. Untersuchungen zur Text- und Überlieferungs-geschichte von Joh.* 7.53–8.11 (*Beih.zZNW* 28) (Berlin 1963). A draft of the present chapter was discussed with Professor Dr Joachim Jeremias in 1961 to whom it owes some of its tone and certain references. It was complete before the works of Van Vliet and Becker came to hand. Dozent Dr Becker courteously sent me the typescript of his dissertation (1959). I have found it difficult to see eye to eye with him, despite the vast, model learning of his work (which, however, pays more attention to theology than to law). A summary of this article was delivered at 'New Testament Today' (Oxford 13 September 1961) and appears in *Texte und Untersuchungen* 87, p. 170–3. Acknowledgement is due to Dr J. Rosenwasser (of the British Museum) for bibliographical help, for a helpful discussion of *soṭāh*, and for the warning that Danby's translation of Soṭāh I, 5 (Danby's *Mishnah*, 293) is wrong (*shoveret* means 'quittance', cf. commentary of Obadiah di Bertinoro and the correct translation at b. Soṭ. 7*a* in Sonc. 30).

[2] The commentaries on John by Zahn (1921), Schlatter (1928), Strachan (1943), Hoskyns, ed. Davey (1947) treat the pericope seriously, especially the last in a useful appendix (563–72). It is ignored by Bultmann (1956), Barrett (1956), Bouyer (1958), and Lightfoot (1957). The New English Bible (and the Greek text edited by R. V. G. Tasker) relegate it to an appendix to the fourth gospel.

[3] H. Frhr. v. Soden, *Die Schriften des neuen Testaments in ihrer ältesten erreichbaren Textgestalt*, I (Berlin 1902), 486–524. Becker, *ubi cit.* 9ff. The reason why the pericope appears frequently at the head of Jn viii is differently explained by Schilling (cited below), who suggests silent references in John to Daniel, and by Becker (p. 79) who sees the explanation in vii.24 and viii.15. I incline to take a third view. Note vii.51, which refers to evidence. Note the rest of viii which is preoccupied with the important question of the *admissibility* and *compelling* quality of Jesus's claims—a question leading in typically Jewish fashion to the question of the *sufficiency* of his evidence. The link between evidence in our pericope and Jesus's own awareness of difficulties regarding his testimony would strike Jewish editors. There is a discussion of viii.17 by J.-P. Charlier, 'L'exégese Johannique d'un précepte légal', *Rev. Bibl.* 67 (1960), 503–15. Aileen Guilding, *Fourth Gospel and Jewish Worship* (Oxford 1960), p. 110–12, 214 n. 1, accounts for the situation of our pericope in both John and Luke upon her theory of lections: her claim that the passage did not *stray* where it now appears seems to be convincing.

Lord was supposed to have shown mercy, if not actually unasked forgiveness, to an adulteress, so the Church ought to deal leniently with offenders.[1] Other doubtful interpretations have been and are placed on the passage;[2] and the story, as it lies baldly on the paper, might well give offence. Perhaps this helps to explain why it was not used by the compilers of our gospels. In any case it has its obscurities, and it is the purpose of this chapter to attempt to clear them up. From the material submitted here it may be possible, by the use of strict reasoning, to recreate what actually took place.

If this can be achieved we are placed in a favourable position. Very few passages of scripture have been immune from dissection and 'criticism'. Whether any of the varying 'interpretations' of other passages is correct is beside our present question; but a passage which can be shown to have been preserved intact, sealed by its own opaqueness against corruption, dilution, or 'secondary' accretion, has the distinction of taking us directly to the scene of Jesus's activity. What we make of this experience is another matter, but the advantage obtained from being in that position, if only for a moment, cannot be denied.

It may be urged that a passage which first appears on the scene at a relatively late date, and the text of which is more than commonly debatable, can hardly be alleged to be free from suspicion of corruption. The latest researcher, Dr Ulrich Becker,[3] finds several of the verses[4] to

[1] H. Riesenfeld, 'Die Perikope von der Ehebrecherin in der frühkirchlichen Tradition', *Svensk Exegetisk Arsbok* (Uppsala), summarised in *Int. Zeits. Bibelw. u. Grenzgeb.* II (1953/4), no. 500. *Apostolic Constitutions*, II, 24. Schilling, cited below, p. 168 n. 5, says (96), 'J. shows God's willingness to forgive even without an audible prayer for mercy'. Since not condemning is very different from forgiving, this may not be accepted. St Augustine objected to the passage on the ground that it might imply 'easy forgiveness'. The authenticity of the story is doubted (Jesus seems to forgive the unrepentant) on inadequate grounds by, *e.g.* F. C. Grant, *Translating the Bible* (Edinburgh, Nelson 1961), 118.

[2] Hoskyns (above); K. Bornhäuser, *NKZ* 37 (1926), 353–63; T. W. Manson, *ZNW* 44 (1952/3), 255f.; T. A. Burkill, *Vig. Chr.* 10 (1956), 80–96; B. Weiss, *Z. wiss. Theol.* 46 (1903), 141–58. W. Beilner, *Christus und die Pharisäer* (Vienna 1959), 123–7 is good. Bultmann says (*Geschichte der synoptischen Tradition*, 3rd edn, 1957, 67): '. . . aber schon Jesu anfängliches Schweigen ist singulär und darf als novellistisches Motiv bezeichnet werden; vor allem aber ist dann der ausführliche Schluss, der das Gespräch mit der Frau bringt, ganz novellistisch und sekundär.' J. Blinzler's investigation, 'Das Synhedrium von Jerusalem und die Strafprozessordnung der Mischna', *ZNW* 52 (1961), 54–65, esp. 56, is of great value for our historical reconstruction, especially the canons propounded at p. 59: but in fact each rule has to be seen independently—see p. 174, n. 1 below. Wensinck's excellent point is referred to below. C. G. Montefiore valued the passage (*Synoptic Gospels* I, 1909, 242): '. . . we seem to find Jesus, not condoning or belittling sin, but yet nobly unwilling that the woman should be singled out for scorn and punishment.' In fact Jesus's *silence* obeys Ps xxxix.1!

[3] *Jesus und die Ehebrecherin* (cited above) at pp. 74–91.

[4] A bare skeleton is left. Verses 3*a* (οἱ γρ. καὶ οἱ φαρ.); 6*a* (τοῦτο . . . αὐτοῦ); 6*b* (κάτω κύψας . . .); 8 (πάλιν . . .); 11, and indeed the greater part of the ending are swept

be 'secondary'. He favours us with a new text (73–4) but even this does not give us an entirely historical account, in his view. However, it will be noted from his work, first, that those passages are found to be secondary which are hard to account for without recourse to speculation, and secondly, that, while his grounds[1] admit of their being secondary, they by no means prove that they must be secondary. One will in any case approach with suspicion a tendency to strip to a mere skeleton a text, parts of which cannot be understood as they stand. This, it is submitted, is a case where it will pay to be patient.

The claim made here is that, if the assumptions are correct, we are taken to the position which Jesus's questioners occupied on that day; that is to say we are in a better position than his audience, who heard but did not see all that went on. If any of them asked him what had transpired it is by no means certain that he would have told them. But it is equally possible that they understood well enough what he said, and that he was never asked, for example, what he had written on the ground, or what was in his mind when he wrote. The satisfaction of having grasped what an intelligent man has done in a crisis often outweighs curiosity to confirm how he did it. In fact a reader of the pericope as it stands today would have little difficulty in understanding what it was all about, provided that he had a general knowledge of Jewish law, and a common acquaintance with the Pentateuch and with contemporary notions on the subjects which were necessarily in question. What is quite extraordinary is that these facts have not been assembled before.

THE SITUATION

A question that has interested many is whether Jesus was being approached as a prophet or as a rabbi. The fact that he is actually addressed by the term appropriate to the latter[2] does not really settle the question. One puts questions to rabbis, and addresses them as 'rabbi', 'teacher', 'Master': prophets are not met with commonly and the formula of address would not come readily to the tongue, especially if the question were exactly one that would be put to a rabbi, a *iuris-*

[1] Chiefly comparison with rabbinical and N.T. arguments, upon the assumption that any rare or unique feature here must be false; accompanied by the assumption that some words are unnecessary and appeal to popular imagination, filling out an otherwise crisp and sharp-climaxed tale.

[2] Verse 4: διδάσκαλε. For instances see Bauer–Arndt–Gingrich, *s.v.* C. H. Dodd, 'Jesus as Teacher and Prophet', *Myst. Chr.* 30, 53–66.

away. Becker says (91) '. . . so können wir jetzt antworten: die Perikope . . . stellt eine stark überarbeitete bzw. erweiterte Form eines synoptischen Streitgespräches dar.'

prudens. The fact that there is no proof that Jesus was regularly ordained to the rabbinate[1] is not so conclusive as might be supposed. The strict rules of the period of the Talmud, which envisage ordination before the *ius respondendi*, and which inhibited a pupil from uttering pronouncements within a certain radius of his teacher, were not necessarily in vogue, even in embryo, at our period. On the other hand the right to be approached for answers to problems of ritual or civil law cannot have lain promiscuously with anyone who had studied the Law. Particularly in a period noted for its sectarian and even messianic teachers, one would expect care to be exercised in the choice of referee, and of the questions that might be put to him. Questions of criminal law, in particular, would not be referred to unqualified (still less actually disqualified) persons, when authoritative tribunals were still sitting, and a regular body of precedent was to hand. Still more care would be exercised at a period when criminal jurisdiction was itself a matter of controversy. In some respects it is more natural to see Jesus being approached here as a prophet. Difficult questions are reserved for the solution of a future prophet.[2] There would, indeed, as we shall see, be ample justification for approaching him in this capacity at that juncture; but the approach itself is much more important than the reason why it was made. Jesus was being asked a question of practical law, not a matter of academic interest,[3] and the celebrated teacher of the law was being asked to settle a matter of life and death. He refused, we know, to accept judicial responsibility in a civil matter:[4] now he was asked to settle doubts in a matter of crime carrying a death-penalty. The rabbis have always distinguished *diyney māmonot* from *diyney n^ephāshot*, and the weight of responsibility attached to judges in the latter cases is invariably regarded as heavier, and the rules of the law are to be more strictly applied.[5] There is no reason to suppose that non-Pharisees at this period took any other view of the distinction than that which permeates the Talmud. In whichever guise Jesus was approached he acted (if we take the episode as a whole) as a rabbi, but it is a matter of

[1] A. Wünsche, *Neue Beiträge zur Erläuterung der Evangelien aus Talmud und Midrasch* (Göttingen 1878), cites b. 'Erub 63*a*; Soṭāh 22*a*; *Mishnāh* Sanh. XI, 2.

[2] 1 M iv.46.

[3] As, for example, in Mk x.2–10; x.17; xii.18, 28.

[4] Lk xii.13–21. Note how the refusal to *judge* is immediately followed by moral exhortation directed to the would-be litigant and the matter at issue.

[5] *Mishnāh* Sanh. IV, 1. In all references to *Mishnāh*, *Tractate Sanhedrin*, the reader may find it helpful to use *Mishnayoth*, IV, *Order Nezikin* (pointed Hebrew text . . . translation, etc.), ed. Philip Blackman (London 1954); H. Danby, *Tractate Sanhedrin, Mishnah and Tosefta* (London 1919) (superseded as to translation to a limited extent by his *Mishnah*, Oxford 1933); and H. E. Goldin, *Hebrew Criminal Law and Procedure* (*Mishnāh*: Sanhedrin, Makkot) (New York 1952).

little importance for the understanding of his answer in what precise character he purported to act. Christians, however, will see him in a guise of more than a *iurisprudens*: for them he acted not merely as a referee, but also as a legislator. Hence we must scrutinise the episode with minute care.

A woman had been caught in the very act of adultery. There is no reason to doubt but that she was a married woman, though the word μοιχεία will admit of other possibilities.[1] She had been caught in the very act, and since her stoning was in question there can be no doubt but that two or more persons had seen her in the act.[2] Since a husband cannot be a witness against his wife[3] these two, or more, must have been in addition to, or exclusive of, the husband. They must have been male adults, Jewish, and free.[4] What they did is not immediately apparent to the modern reader, but a perusal of Jewish law, in the light of the common semitic customs which served also as a foundation for the Islamic rules on the subject, makes it clear that these two or three saw this woman and man actually *in coitu*.[5] There is absolutely no question of their having seen them merely in a 'compromising situation', for example, coming from a room in which they were alone, or even lying together on the same bed.[6] The actual physical movements of the

[1] See pp. 371–2 below. The parallel study of πορνεία by J. Bonsirven, *Le Divorce dans le Nouveau Testament* (Tournai 1948) is relevant.

[2] Dt xix.15, exhaustively and convincingly shown to have been taken for granted in N.T. times and earlier by H. van Vliet, *No Single Testimony: A Study on the Adoption of the Law of Deut. XIX, 15 par. into the New Testament* (Utrecht 1958). One notes his statement that the requirement of *two* witnesses is unique for the oriental legal world (47). Quite apart from Islamic law, which almost certainly did not borrow from Jewish law here, the requirement of two witnesses is notoriously a Hindu rule, of great antiquity, as ought to have been known to Van Vliet, since Frankel (whom he cites) conscientiously considers Manu in his *Gerichtliche Beweis* at pp. 249, 250, 255, 260.

[3] A fine digest of the Jewish law of evidence, compiled in a spirit of comparative research, is Z. Frankel's, *Der gerichtliche Beweis nach mosaisch-talmudischem Recht. Ein Beitrag zur Kenntniss des mosaisch-talmudischen Criminal- und Civil-rechts* (Berlin 1846), see p. 121, 285.

[4] *Ibid.* 118.

[5] *Ibid.* 116. R. Samuel at B.M. 91*a* = Sonc. 524. With our κατείληπται ἐπ' αὐτοφώρῳ compare the opposite at Nb v.13*c v*[e]*'ed 'eyn bāh v*[e]*hiw' lo' nit*[e]*pāsāh* where *'ed* does not, of course, mean 'witness', but 'evidence'. (For the rabbinical interpretation of *nit*[e]*pāsāh* = 'violated' see b. Soṭ. 2*b* = Sonc. 3.) Evidence as to intercourse need not include evidence of both penetration and emission (below p. 164 n. 4, Horowitz, *Spirit*, 203), but there is excellent reason for supposing that the witness of copulation (as opposed to 'seclusion') could have prevented it (see below, p. 164). Doubt is, in any case, enough. Jesus's own reaction is explained if we assume that he was alive to this doubt.

[6] If she is found after the departure of, for example, a tradesman, with dishevelled clothing, she obtains a bad name and goes out with *k*[e]*tūbāh* and without any requirement that she should have been warned: Maimonides, *M.T. Hilkot Ishūt* XXIV, 15. This is the position emphatically if there is *not* clear evidence of her unchastity.

couple must have been capable of no other explanation, and the witnesses must have seen exactly the same acts at exactly the same time, in the presence of each other, so that their depositions would be identical in every respect.[1] The evidence upon which a life could be taken was 'solid', that is, the evidence of the second witness could not be severed from that of the first, for it was only upon the evidence of two or three witnesses that a life could be taken, and such evidence could not be made up of fragments admitting of discrepancies.[2] Since a regular judge, in the Sanhedrin, would as a matter of moral obligation and common contemporary usage ask the colour of the cloth covering the couple, or the colour of the material upon which the woman was lying,[3] the witnesses would have taken in the whole scene, to eliminate all possibility of discrepancy. If the culprits had been caught in a ruined building the witnesses would have memorised the state of the structure overshadowing them. Failure to agree in all details would be fatal to the criminal case they themselves would promote (for the witnesses were the accusers), and might bring penalties upon their own heads, as we shall see.

How were two or three persons in such a position? Hardly by chance, one would suppose. People in love are notoriously careless, though in a crowded city filled with people who believed that adultery deserved death one would expect precautions against discovery. The situation at once raises a doubt whether the whole thing was not planned beforehand. It seems that the husband had suspected his wife, had had his suspicions confirmed, and had called some 'respectable' citizens to hide and to watch. The woman was caught, it seems almost certain, in a trap. People are hardly ever caught in adultery, but to require that they shall be seen *in coitu* by two or three people is to make convictions for adultery rare indeed.[4] It was for this very reason that the Jewish Law and custom provided an elaborate ordeal (*soṭāh*) to which a husband, *suspicious*, yet not on well-authenticated grounds, could subject his

[1] b. San. 30*a* = Sonc. 185. Mekilta on Ex xxiii (Lauterbach, III, 169–70). Maimonides, *M.T.* XIV (Judges), trans. Hershman, II, iv, 89. The principle remains even if we abstract the element of Pharisaical finickiness, as the experience of Islamic countries confirms.

[2] San. 30*a* = Sonc. 187. O. Bähr, *Das Gesetz über falsche Zeugen nach Bibel und Talmud* (Berlin 1882), 7–8 (the book is preoccupied with the *zomemiym*, who do not concern us, being a rabbinical development from Dt xix.15–19). Maimonides, *ubi cit.* II, iv, trans. 91.

[3] *Mishnāh*, San. V. 2 (Danby, *Mishnah*, 388). Maimonides, *ubi cit.* II, ii, 1f., 84f.

[4] As evidence that in Tannaïtic times compelling evidence of adultery was possible, traces survive of hypothetical cases from that period: Tosef. San. vi, 4*b*; Maimonides, *ubi cit.* II, xxi, 10, p. 133–4. Observing intercourse is discussed as a practical possibility at b. Giṭṭ. 73*b* = Sonc. 349; 81*a–b* = Sonc. 389.

wife.[1] Despite the disgrace for both parties, the procedure alone was sufficient to act as a deterrent. 'Drinking the bitter waters' was certainly in use in Jesus's time, and the procedure became obsolete when, about the time of the Fall of Jerusalem, adultery and general sexual licence became so constant that the institution lost its meaning.[2] Why had the husband not adopted that course? Probably because he had the best possible proof, and had obtained such proof in order to put himself beyond the point at which he had the alternative whether to divorce her or to promote the ordeal. A woman who had obtained a 'bad name' by being discovered in a compromising situation could lawfully be divorced by her husband, who would be amply justified in depriving her of her *keṭūbāh* (ketubbah), the sum secured to her by her marriage-settlement.[3] If the husband chose not to divorce her, he was prevented from having intercourse with her (she was 'forbidden to him' by a cause greater than mere suspicion—'jealousy' as the text puts it—that would lead to *soṭāh* and lesser than the legal proof leading to a criminal penalty) and could not marry again without being a polygamist. The only reasons for this man's preferring to promote her rapid execution would be (1) willingness to listen to 'pious' exhortations not to compound the offence; or (2) a mean refusal to divorce her, with the prospect of her running to or even marrying her paramour;[4] or (3) a mean desire to succeed to her property as her heir, a benefit he would lose if she were divorced! It was doubtful whether, after hearing of her 'bad name', or becoming 'jealous', he had not hired the witnesses[5] and so proceeded to this point under the influence of pseudo-religious or mean motives, or both. Mean husbands, and their responsibility for their reputations, are characterised in an old *midrash*. What does a man do

[1] Nb v.11–31. Tractate *Soṭāh*. Danby, *Mishnah* 293f.

[2] J. Z. Lauterbach, 'The Pharisees and their Teachings', *HUCA* 6 (1929), 124f.

[3] See p. 160 n. 6 above. D. W. Amram, 'Adultery', *Jewish Encycl.* I (1901); D. W. Amram, *Jewish Law of Divorce according to Bible and Talmud* (London 1897), 122–3; Marcus Cohn, 'Ehebruch' in art. Eherecht, *Jüdisches Lexikon* II, 267f.; S. Bialoblocki, 'Ehebruch', *Encycl. Jud.* VI (1930). On the *keṭūbāh* itself see any Jewish encyclopaedia under Ketubbah; also Z. Frankel, *Grundlinien des mosaisch-talmudischen Eherechts* (Leipzig 1860); M. Duschak, *Das mosaisch-talmudische Eherecht* (Wien 1864); M. Mielziner, *Jewish Law of Marriage and Divorce in Ancient and Modern Times . . .* (Cincinnati 1884), 85–9. Examples of pre-C.E. *keṭūbot* are examined by R. Yaron, *J. Sem. Stud.* 3 (1958), 1f.; 5 (1960), 66f.

[4] Talmudic Judaism does not recognise the marriage of a woman with her former paramour, but this was an age when adultery was a capital offence: moreover the rule may only have been developing in Jesus's time.

[5] Hiring of witnesses in this connection is mentioned in b. Ket. 46*a* = Sonc. 262. The comfortable rule is laid down precisely in b. Ket. 46*a* = Sonc. 263: if there are witnesses to adultery after the marriage the woman is put to death and no *keṭūbāh* has to be paid. The husband's heirs also have a direct interest in her being put to death: Soṭ. 25*a*–*b* = Sonc. 126.

when a (dead) fly drops in his wine? The sort of man who would continue to let his wife behave in an unseemly way, possibly committing adultery, and gloat over his 'rights' is one who would take the fly, suck it and then drain the cup to the bottom. Here we have a genuine Jewish comment on our husband.[1]

Jesus's own prescription would have been different. Van Vliet has persuaded us that Mt xviii.15–17 are not 'spurious'.[2] On the whole *vv.* 15–16*a* have been little attacked, and they would show that Jesus, relying upon Lv xix.17 and Dt xix.15 and the rules regarding warning to which we shall return, believed that in loving kindness a brother (or 'sister', *e.g.* wife) should be warned, privately, then (if necessary) solemnly, and only then subjected to excommunication and/or civil penalty if the condoned offence were repeated. The Community of the Dead Sea Scrolls are shown from the *Zadokite Document* or 'Damascus Rule' which they valued to have had a very similar outlook. Like contemporary sects,[3] Jesus believed that reclamation should be tried before the offender was condemned on the evidence of two witnesses, whom, in fact, a court would be bound to believe if their credit was not undermined.[4]

But where was the adulterer? It is just possible that he had already been stoned: but the other possibility is more attractive. The woman had no free property of her own[5] with which she might redeem herself from her husband's wrath. Her paramour was in a better position: at the least he had his labour to pledge. *He* could arrange matters. The

[1] Midr. R., Num. IX. 12 on Nm. v.14 = Sonc. 261–2; A. Wünsche, *Midr. Bemidbar Rabba* (1880), 153. A similar simile occurs at b. Giṭṭ. 90*a*–*b* = Sonc. 438.

[2] *Op. cit.* 94–6.

[3] 1 *QS* V. 25–VI. 1 (Vermès, 80; Lohse, 20; Leaney, 178–80; Dupont-Sommer, 100); Zadokite Fragments or Damascus Rule, IX. 2–8, 17–23, both cited *in extenso* by Van Vliet at pp. 57–8. For more modern citations see below, pp. 172 n. 1, 184. W. D. Davies, *Christian Origins and Judaism* (London 1962), 103. Lv xix.17 is recalled in Lk xvii.3; Ga vi.1; Jm v.19. Note also Si xix.13–17.

[4] The distinction between the then doctrine of compelling testimony, 'legal proof', and the modern system of judicial enquiry (in which the court weighs evidence and is less concerned with admissibility than with credibility) is well brought out by Van Vliet, 2, 7–10.

[5] The husband had the usufruct of all the wife's property acquired before or after the marriage, and owned all her earnings and chance acquisitions made after the mairrage. All her property was under his control, and she could not alienate it without his consent, and even so such a sale affected only the corpus and not the usufruct. If she predeceased her husband he inherited her property. Horowitz, *Spirit of Jewish Law* 295–307, 387. *Mishnāh*, Ket. IV. 4; VI. 1; VIII. 1f.; IX. 1f. It might be argued that this woman might own *melog* ('plucking' property as distinct from 'iron flock'), which she could transfer to her husband (Horowitz, 296, 300; Danby, *Mishnah*, 795): true, but he would be little advantaged thereby (for he had all the profits of it already), and she *alive* could give him no more than he would gain from her at her *death*. It would be difficult to find a clearer case of doubtful motives.

witnesses, as 'respectable' and righteous men, would surely not allow this? The law requires that both the culprits be put to death.[1] But the witnesses can be 'squared', especially if, as we suspect, they have been planted by previous arrangement and are a little doubtful of their fairness in spying on a fellow male.[2] He can buy his life by suitable agreements with each of them—immorally, but, if we may judge from Proverbs,[3] by no means inconsistently with actual usage.

Thus the situation spells doubt; doubt whether the husband has not deliberately engineered a situation, which implies failure to prevent the crime from being committed; doubt whether the husband and/or the witnesses have not corruptly allowed the adulterer to escape; and lastly the virtual certainty that the witnesses 'stood by' and allowed the crime to be commenced, and proceeded with. *Res ipsa loquitur*. Moreover the Jews were frankly conscious of the length of time required for intercourse as distinct from coition, and a witness to a woman's 'seclusion' was a different witness from him who witnessed her intercourse—the latter must have been an eyewitness for a longer period![4] As a result no one could have doubted but that a sound from one of them would have disturbed the couple, and made it impossible for the evidence of copulation to be deposed before a court. The whole affair reeks of doubt, but the witnesses' sin in not attempting to prevent what might easily have been prevented admits of little doubt. Jesus will have grasped the last point immediately, and what seems doubtful about the remainder to us will have seemed doubtful to him. We must repeat: the law of adultery and its means of proof was *not* that of modern states.

Thus the woman is brought in and placed between Jesus and his audience (Jn viii.3: ἐν μέσῳ), her escort being 'the Scribes and the

[1] Lv xx.10; Dt xxii.22. Not necessarily *together*: Blinzler, cited p. 168 n. 3 below, at p. 38.

[2] E. Stauffer, *Die Botschaft Jesu* (Bern/Münich 1959), 81. Hauck, *ThWzNT* IV, 737. Traces of inequitable deviation to the disadvantage of women lie in Book of Jubilees (*c.* 110 B.C.), xxx.8, 9: a man must be stoned for adultery, but the woman burned alive (cf. *Mishnāh*, San. IX. 3). Some consciousness of unfairness is evidenced in Ho iv.14 (see below, p. 187 n. 3). That the adulterer may have 'done a deal' is supposed by I. Abrahams, *Studies in Pharisaism and the Gospels* I (Cambridge 1917), 73–4.

[3] vi.32–5 says of the (respectable) husband, 'he will accept no compensation, nor be appeased though you multiply gifts'.

[4] The beginning and end of intercourse are referred to in b. Ḳid. 10*a* = Sonc. 38 (*A* betroths *B* while *B* is at the first stage of coition with *C*!); that time is required is noticed in Yev. 11*a* = Sonc. 53–4; Ket. 11*b* = Sonc. 61. The time needed for 'seclusion', that is sexual contact as opposed to full intercourse, is the time needed to walk round a date-palm: a discussion of this ancient estimate appears at Soṭ. 3*b*–4*a* = Sonc. 13. That for some purposes penetration is as good as full coitus is shown by Yev. VI.1, and the view of some to this effect is evidenced at Soṭ. 26*b* = Sonc. 132. But that coitus in general means the distinctive movements and not mere penetration is asserted in Shev. 14*b* = Sonc. 68; 18*a* = 91; 18*b* = 92–3.

Pharisees' (*ibid.*). It is supposed that 'Scribes and Pharisees' is some sort of formula, and stands merely for Jesus's opponents. We are told (*v.* 6) that their motive was to trap him and to obtain material for an accusation against him. But it is never impossible to take the phrase literally. We may here understand that a small group which included representatives of Scribes who were not Pharisees and Pharisees who might or might not have been Scribes, and whose points of view on the subject in question may have differed radically, joined in approaching Jesus in the hope that he would resolve a doubt in favour of one point of view, or produce a third and more generally acceptable answer. If he resolved their doubts, well and good: he might even provide means whereby he himself could be removed from the scene. The nature of the question, if we rightly explain it below, was admirably suited to such mixed motives. We may assume that some, if not all, were anxious to trap Jesus, and they appear to have been as interested in this as in the punishment of the guilty woman. The way they hang over him and press him for an answer indicates an intense interest in the answer itself, and in the mode in which it will be given. Whatever else the situation imported, it was certainly a test for Jesus.

Some bystanders we can expect, yet amongst the small crowd standing around Jesus and partly blocking his audience's view we can surely predicate certain other elements. *Res ipsa loquitur*. The witnesses will have been there, and since they cannot have been related to each other[1] they cannot have been twins, from which it results that one of them was older than the other: that they were unrelated but of the same age would be a coincidence for which few would make allowance, and if a doubt remains it can safely be neglected. The point of relative age will appear shortly. Apart from the witnesses there will have been one or two elderly 'respectable' citizens whose presence would lend authority to the proceedings and give an air of responsibility to the decision which had to be taken. The witnesses cannot be judges,[2] for it is before others that their testimony has to be uttered, and someone of prestige has to hear their testimony and satisfy himself that it is reliable. Since age teaches the wisdom of sharing such responsibility at least two elders are almost certain to have been there. Perhaps they were Scribes or Pharisees: indeed all the persons identifiable as belonging to one of the classes or both may have been elders willing to take personal responsibility for the woman's death. Besides these there must have been a few who would act as the 'people', to finish the stoning as soon as the

[1] Frankel, *op. cit.* 122, 287.
[2] In a normal criminal trial, that is: b. B.Ḳ. 90*b* = Sonc. 522.

witnesses had let their stones fly.[1] The more 'respectable' the witnesses the less chance that their aim would be good or their cast forceful, and the mob were necessary. The ages of these persons are a matter of indifference, but a few young zealots, keen to purify the people of sinners, can certainly be expected. Their aim would be improved by zeal, and their ability to gather ammunition would more than compensate for any lack of practice.

THE WOMAN'S PREDICAMENT

She was not being taken for a regular trial,[2] for the only court which had jurisdiction to try her by Jewish Law seems to have been deprived of jurisdiction in capital cases not long before.[3] If she were on her way to a trial in any case the approach to Jesus could only mean that his questioners intended to obtain arguments or authority from him which would aid their advocacy in the Sanhedrin. But apart from the inherent improbability of this we are told that their motive was not to rely upon him but the reverse. Even if the statement of their motive embodies the redactor's guess the state of our knowledge renders it as nearly as

[1] Dt xiii.9; xvii.6–7. On the procedure, see p. 182 n. 2 below.

[2] As thought by Bornhäuser and now Becker who, at p. 166f. shows that he was influenced by P. Winter's book (cited below).

[3] San. 41*a* = Sonc. 267 (closed *c.* A.D. 30); for this and other authorities see Goldin, 26 (he points out that Maimonides, *Hilkot San.* XIV. 13, *i.e. Mishneh Torāh, Book of Judges*, transl. A. M. Hershman [1949], 41, was of that opinion, but adds the references, *e.g.* Sanh. 37*b*, for the opinion of the school of Hezekiah that the right to inflict the death penalty was taken away only in A.D. 70); Dt xvii.10; *Megillat Ta'anīt* (A.D. 68) records a feast on the 22nd Elul to commemorate the reimposition of capital punishment for offences against the law (Dalman, *Aramäische Dialektproben* [Leipzig 1927], 43). J. Jeremias, 'Zur Geschichtlichkeit des Verhörs Jesu vor dem hohen Rat', *ZNW* 43 (1950–1), 145–50. E. Stauffer, *Jesus, Gestalt und Geschichte* (Bern 1957), 16f. T. A. Burkill, *ubi cit.* p. 2 n. 1 *sup.* Hoenig, cited p. 174 n. 1 below, goes, at p. 209, beyond his authorities. Amram, cited p. 162 n. 3 above, at p. 217 seems a little too positive as to the husband's alternatives at this period. Paul Winter (*On the Trial of Jesus* [Berlin 1961], 15, 67f., 75f.) defies Maimonides in the choice between Jewish traditions. His arguments that the Sanhedrin still possessed the right to put culprits to death are forceful, but ignore *Megillat Ta'anīt* (above), rely too much on Burkill, on an over-elaborate method of subverting the evidential value of Jn xviii.31*b*, and on happenings in following decades which can be explained partly by lynchings, and partly by a genuine restoration to the Jews of greater measures of autonomy before the final catastrophe. His further defence of his treatment of the passage in John at *N.T.S.* 10 (1963/4), 494ff., is yet another step in his attempt (an attempt shared by many Jewish writers, including S. Zeitlin) to prove, come what may, that the Jews had little to do with the death of Jesus or at any rate much less than Pilate. But see below, p. 433. Mantel (*Studies*, 315–16) thinks that Jn xviii.31, if genuine, deals only with political offences.

possible certain that there was no question of the woman receiving a *formal* trial. Nor was she being conducted to execution after a trial.[1] Since there was no court there can have been no trial, but for those who reserve doubt as to whether there was a court sitting Jesus's words οὐδείς σε κατέκρινεν; (*v.* 10*c*) are conclusive.[2] He asks the woman finally whether this group, or any of it, has passed sentence upon her, informal as that sentence would have been, though effective enough from her point of view. To suppose that he meant to ask whether she had been condemned to be *executed* (as contrasted with any other sentence) is to wander into fantasy. He was interrupted in the course of a lecture, had given his mind to her case, had disposed of the problem, and found her remaining between him and his audience when he resumed his discourse. Further, to suppose that after a regular sentence had been passed upon her the Scribes and Pharisees would put to him a pure point of law, as if by way of appeal from the highest tribunal in the land, is to suppose something unreasonable in itself. Pharisees hostile to the woman's being stoned might have tried this as a final attempt to save her, but in that case the question would have been differently put: he is asked to comment on the effect or applicability of the law of Moses (*v.* 5*b*),[3] not to suspend or delay the course of regular justice.

But all this is otiose. They wanted to lynch the woman,[4] because that was the only way in which she could be punished. Whether in fact she would have been stoned, or, as the *Mishnāh* says, strangled, might have been open to debate—but the basic question was whether she should be lynched. Because the Sanhedrin was not allowed to hear cases involving the death-penalty, at any rate in Jerusalem itself, the constitutional

[1] As thought by Blinzler, Jeremias (*ZNW* 43, 148–9), Grundmann (1959) and Stauffer (*Botschaft* 80f.).

[2] In Theod. Sus. 41 it means 'condemn'. So Moulton–Milligan. Bauer (*WzNT*) is clear, Arndt–Gingrich adequate, Liddell–Scott–Jones definite. All N.T. examples go the same way, with the possible exception of 2 P ii.6. In the LXX κατακρίνω = *gāzar* (condemn). Epict. III, xviii, 9 (κατακρινεῖν) instances 'pass adverse judgement'; *ibid.* I, i, 30 (κατακέκρισαι) beautifully instances 'condemn to (exile, etc.)'. κατάκρισις is naturally 'condemnation'. On the other hand κατάκριμα implies 'punishment following upon sentence'; in papyri it means 'judgement', or even 'penal servitude' (see Moulton–Milligan). Grundmann (*op. cit.* 246), seems embarrassed: 'keiner hat ... an ihn die Verurteilung vollzogen?' But this is unnecessary.

[3] ἐν δὲ τῷ νόμῳ ἡμῖν Μωϋσῆς ἐνετείλατο τὰς τοιαύτας λιθάζειν· σὺ οὖν τί λέγεις; Some manuscripts read σὺ ... λέγεις περὶ αὐτῆς. The difference is not considerable. οὖν here continues the narrative. Liddell–Scott; Blass–Debrunner (10th edn, 1959), § 451, p. 283–4 (trans. R. W. Funk, Cambridge/Chicago 1961, p. 235, col. i); J. D. Denniston, *Greek Particles*, 1st edn (Oxford 1934), 416, 425–6.

[4] Bornhäuser rejected this for insufficient reasons: *NKZ* 37 (1926), 353–4, but see E. Stauffer, 'Neue Wege der Jesus-forschung', *Wiss. Z. d. U. Halle-W.* 7 (1958), 451f. at p. 456, 466.

method of seeking a penalty against her would have been to approach the Roman governor. The law prescribed how and by what means an adulteress should be punished; but its application was hindered so far as regular administration was concerned, and the Romans provided no attractive alternative. No Roman judge would condemn to death a woman taken in adultery,[1] and that was what the crowd (and the husband) wanted, it would seem, to happen to her. A smaller legal punishment, or even a penalty at the judge's discretion, would by no means satisfy their zeal.

It was once thought that she must have been a betrothed girl.[2] We know now that the traditional punishment for adultery by a married woman was stoning.[3] The Pharisees developed the theory that she should be strangled,[4] but all evidence relevant to our period points to stoning. The story of Susanna, which in point of date and subject-matter is relevant to our pericope,[5] shows, in one version,[6] that casting down a precipitous place (cf. Lk iv.29) and death by mangling on or by rocks (*i.e.* in effect stoning) was a penalty for adultery not so very long

[1] The law applicable was the celebrated *lex Iulia de adulteriis coercendis* (Mart. VI, 7, 22; Justinian, *Dig.* 4. 4. 37, 1; 48. 5; *Cod.* 9. 9. 3, 17; *Inst.* 4. 18, 4—but beware of imperial revision of the provisions of the *lex*!). Adultery became a capital offence in the third century (*Cod.* 2. 4, 18; 9. 9, 9). The position is explained concisely in Th. Mommsen, *Römisches Strafrecht* (Leipzig 1899), 698–9.

[2] References at Blinzler (next note), 34, 40.

[3] Ezk xvi.38–40; xxiii.45–8. J. Blinzler, 'Die Strafe für Ehebruch in Bibel und Halacha zur Auslegung von Joh. viii. 5', *NTS* 4 (1957–8), 32–47.

[4] Blinzler, *ubi cit. sup.*, last note, at p. 40.

[5] Date: *c.* 80 B.C. For the texts (LXX and Theodotion) see A. Rahlfs, *Septuaginta*, II, 864f.; H. B. Swete, *Old Testament in Greek* (1912), III, 576f.; R. H. Charles, *Apocrypha and Pseudepigrapha of the Old Testament* (1913), I, 647f. For discussion, W. O. E. Oesterley, *Introd. to the Books of the Apocrypha* (London 1953), 281–6; E. J. Goodspeed, *Story of the Apocrypha* (Chicago 1939, 1956), 65f.; C. C. Torrey, *Apocryphal Literature* (New Haven, London 1945, 1953), 107–11; F. Zimmermann, *JQR* 48 (1957–8), 236–41; M. Waxman, *Hist. of Jewish Literature* (New York, London 1960), I, 15; Van Vliet, *op. cit.* 51–2. For relevance note the collocation of the pericope with Susanna in the Missal (Sat. after 3rd Sunday in Lent); also Goodspeed, *cit. sup.* 69–70, 124. D. Daube, *N.T. and Rab. Jud.* 91, says Daniel here 'advocates a Pharisaic innovation' and the book demonstrates (230) 'the superiority of the rational modern method' (*cf.* his article in *Rev. Int. des Dr. de l'Ant.* 2 (1949), 200f.)—*sed quaere?* F. A. Schilling, 'Story of Jesus and the Adultress', *Ang. Theol. Rev.* 37 (1955), 91–106 at 98f.; Becker, 151f. There is no real ground for supposing (as Schmidtke, cited by Becker) that our pericope is a conscious fabrication antithetical to Lv xx.10 and a counterpart to Susanna; nor that the pericope is intended to show Jesus as an anti-Daniel, compassionate rather than severe (as Schilling, 98–9).

[6] LXX Sus. 60–2: καὶ ὡς ὁ νόμος διαγορεύει ἐποίησαν αὐτοῖς καθὼς ἐπονηρεύσαντο κατὰ τῆς ἀδελφῆς καὶ ἐφίμωσαν αὐτοὺς καὶ ἐξαγαγόντες ἔρριψαν εἰς φάραγγα. (Becker takes this as evidence of Pharisaic development of the law, *sed quaere?* For his explanation of the whole passage as a controversy between Jesus and the upholders of the Sanhedrin, its competence and its law, see 165–74.) Theodot. merely refers to Dt xix.19: . . . καὶ ἀπέκτειναν αὐτούς.

before our incident.[1] Jesus himself narrowly escaped lynch-justice,[2] the followers of Jesus including Paul himself, actually experienced it.[3] Notwithstanding the procedural developments in Jewish law until the coming of the Romans, the positive obligation to stone, for example for blasphemy, was taken for granted. Stoning was the traditional penalty from remote antiquity, to be resorted to wherever the law said 'he shall certainly die' or words to that effect without prescribing a different penalty. The provisions of the Talmud on this subject might mislead us, for they embody the speculations of Pharisees who believed that the mildest penalty possible should always be chosen, and who wanted not to disrupt the skeleton, and who, from the Fall of Jerusalem, had few opportunities to test their theories in practice.[4]

The questioners were therefore not in doubt but that if she was to die at all, stoning by the witnesses and the mob was the method to be adopted. This implied a rapid execution, as near as might be on the spur of the moment, by persons inspired by zeal. It should allow the least possible interval between detection and execution. For this reason the Pharisees later established doctrines encouraging delay.[5] But Jesus's questioners wanted a quick answer, to deal with the woman out of hand. They had, after all, a splendid biblical precedent upon which to rely. The story of Phinehas,[6] which later gave the Pharisees so much heart-searching,[7] was of great persuasive force.[8] Phinehas was no ordinary person: he won the rare privilege of living for ever because of his (to the Jewish mind) noble act—and this piece of *haggadāh* added strength to the case of those who sought the opinion of Jesus (see the *Note* at the

[1] Because the elders were given the punishment which would have been inflicted upon Susanna: D. Daube, *N.T. and Rabbinic Judaism* (London 1956), 307 n. 1.
[2] Dt xiii.9–10; Lk iv.29; Jn x.31f.
[3] Ac v.26 (narrow escape); xiv.5, 19 (non-Jewish jurisdictions); 2 Co xi.25. The case of Stephen (Ac vii.58–9) was almost certainly a lynching. *Cf.* Lk xx.6.
[4] Frankel, *op. cit.* 104 is frank. Danby, *Tr. Sanh.*, introd., likewise. *Mishnāh*, Sanh. IX. 3. Blinzler, 'Die Strafe ...', at p. 38–9 refers to A. Büchler, 'Die Todesstrafen der Bibel und der jüdischnachbiblischen Zeit', *Mon. Gesch. Wiss. des Judenthums*, 50 (1906), 539–62; 664–706, esp. 683–6. Daube, *op. cit.* 304ff. Winter's chapter 'Jewish Death Penalties' is not his most successful. He casts doubt on the Pharisees' theory (see p. 71, refs. at p. 189) but his substitute is not entirely convincing.
[5] But not excessive delay. Cases were not to be heard at night, adverse sentences were to be postponed (*Mishnāh*, Sanh. IV. 1; V. 5), and opportunities were offered for holding up proceedings.
[6] Nb xxv.5–15. Phinehas's act was ratified *ex post facto*, which evidences discomfort even amongst Jews who were proud of him. Zimri seems to have defied a proclamation, however (*v.* 6). Boaz Cohen, *cit. inf.* p. 170 n. 2, at pp. 116–17.
[7] b. San. 82*a*–*b* = Sonc. 545–8.
[8] On Phinehas as a model in pre-Christian centuries see 1 M ii.19–21, 26–7, 54; 4 M xviii.12. See the very relevant remarks of W. R. Farmer, 'The Patriarch Phinehas: a Note on "it was reckoned to him as righteousness" ', *Ang. Theol. Rev.* 34 (1952), 26–30, particularly at p. 28.

end of this chapter). While the constitution was suspended and the Sanhedrin could not be convened in capital cases what better course could be followed than to imitate Phinehas? Zeal to purify Israel there led to the death of a sexual offender. Other instances of mob-execution,[1] severe instances of 'self-help', survivals from the pre-juridical age,[2] were not wanting but Phinehas was the case in point. The Jews have always set much store by precedent.

THE QUESTIONERS' MOTIVES

We have seen that some if not all were keen to obtain material wherewith Jesus himself might be accused. Accused of what? In Talmudic times it was axiomatic that majority decisions enabled certain doctrines, ritualistic and juridical alike, to be established as authoritative. The 'rebellious teacher, or elder' who interpreted the law differently from the received opinion was a sad feature of the Jewish Law far older than the time of the Talmud.[3] It was possible for him to be put to death even in a time of violent controversy and extreme difficulty in deciding what was the received opinion. To make matters worse, the possibility of invoking the relevant biblical rules remained even if the difference related to innovations effectuated or proposed to be effectuated by the Romans, upon which, in the very nature of things, serious doubts must have been widely held. But Jesus was safe provided he did not give a *decision* in a practical matter.[4] Moreover, if he gave an answer which denied the applicability of the law of Moses, or denied the validity of the Roman constitutional settlement he would be in

[1] b. San. 81*b* = Sonc. 542; *Mishnāh*, Sanh. IX. 6. Those who take in the act may punish: if they do not they cannot charge the guilty person before the *Bet-dīn*.

[2] Boaz Cohen, 'Self-help in Jewish and Roman Law', *Rev. Int. Dr. Ant.* 3rd ser. 2 (1955), 107–33, at p. 112f. (the article is reprinted at *JRL* II, 624–50, and Phinehas appears at p. 633f.). He cites Palestinian rabbinical modifications: the offence must be in public: j. Sanh. IX. 7 (Schwab, XI, 38). There is a very short discussion of self-help at b. B.Ḳ. 27*b* = Sonc. 144. H. E. Goldin, *Heb. Crim. Law* (p. 159 n. 5 above), 30off.

[3] Dt xvii.12–13; *Mishnāh*, Sanh. XI. 2; San. 86*b*–89*a* = Sonc. 572–89. *Cf.* San. 99*a* = Sonc. 672: 'one who gives an interpretation of the *Torāh* not according to the *halakāh* has no portion in the world to come.' Maimonides, *ubi cit.* XIV, III, iii, iv (trans. Hershman, p. 143ff.). Wünsche, *Neue Beiträge, cit. sup.* 529. Winter attempts (129–30) to show that the concept 'orthodoxy' was non-Jewish, and that Jesus's *teaching* did not lead to his death. There is much in the latter point (though he dismisses evidence of Jesus's being watched and tempted as inventions of the Church), but he ignores the force of biblical law.

[4] If the law then was according to *Mishnāh*, Sanh. XI. 2 (Danby, 399–400). Since it is common sense, the rule could have been argued for long before Mishnaic times.

danger from one side or the other, and many commentators have already observed this dilemma.[1]

But a genuine doubt existed. If the trial had been before a regular court the witnesses might have had to establish that the woman had been warned. In Talmudic law it is settled that they must depose that they *themselves* had warned the woman and received her acknowledgement of the warning.[2] This was justifiable on semantic grounds, for 'eye-witness' and 'warning' both use the root 'WD.[3] From the rule that they must prove that she acknowledged the warning and persisted in the crime notwithstanding the warning we can be sure that the rabbis intended to make death-sentences for adultery impossible. Such was certainly the intention of Muḥammad when he introduced comparable legislation.[4] But there is evidence that women could be executed for adultery,[5] and even if we assume (which seems inevitable) that the maxim *'eyn 'on^eshiyn 'ellā' 'im kēn maz^ehiyriyn*, 'No penalty without a warning', was far more ancient than the Talmud, we are not driven to assume that in Jesus's time[6] the witnesses had to prove anything more

[1] So Hitzig (1843), Jeremias, Grundmann, Westcott, and Lightfoot, but apparently not the editors of the *Catholic Commentary on Holy Scripture* (1953), 997. On the attitude of the Roman government to Jewish messianic sects, and political implications, Winter, *op. cit. passim*, is excellent.

[2] b. San. 40*b*–41*a* = Sonc. 262–7; 80*b* = Sonc. 535–6. Blinzler, *op. cit.* utilises this rule at p. 41. Jeremias, 'Untersuchungen zum Quellenproblem der Apostelgeschichte', *ZNW* 36 (1937), 209–11, gives many references.

[3] See the lexicons under *he'iyd* (cf. *Mishnāh*, B.Ḳ. ii. 4) and *ha'^adā'āh* (cf. Ex xxi.29). See p. 172 n. 3 below.

[4] Because it is 'laudable to conceal and cover infirmity' four witnesses must see the couple in the very act: C. Hamilton, *Hedaya* (London 1791), II, 3f. It is rational that two *pairs* of witnesses should depose to an act which (as *zinnā'* alone) cannot take place without the simultaneous criminality of two people acting mutually. But reason is not referred to. The authorities are Qur'ān iv. 19 (early) and xxiv. 4 (late Medinan). The 'revelation' dealt with a scandal attaching to Ayesha, Muhammad's favourite wife (on which see p. 300 n., of Palmer's trans., World's Classics Ser. or Sale's note to his trans. of Q. xxiv. 11–20). Subject to repealing legislation, the rule persists in many Islamic countries and renders adultery virtually impossible to punish, except upon confession.

[5] The indirect references contained in hypothetical cases in rabbinical literature: p. 161 n. 4 above. The case of Mariamne, wife of Herod, is perhaps no precedent (she was put to death on suspicion and partly on political grounds), and indeed the acts of Herod are hardly to be taken as cases in Jewish law. Josephus is curiously silent (*Ant.* IV, viii) about the penalty for adultery by a married woman: this may imply rather that he avoided his readers' unfavourable comment than that he regarded the rule as impractical.

[6] For the Dead Sea Scrolls Community's rules, which are slightly less strict than the rabbinical see, *CD* IX, 20–23 (Vermès, 111; Lohse, 84–6). Rabbinical rules developed after Jesus's time. A good instance is the provision regarding the 'stubborn and rebellious son'. The rabbis so developed this (b. Sanh. 68*b*–72*a* = Sonc. 465–89; J. Kohler, *ZVR* 20 [1907], 237) that execution was impossible. Yet instances were actually alleged to have occurred: *ibid.* 71*a*. And Herod refers to the institution as

than that the woman had received warning of some sort, whether from her husband or elsewhere in front of witnesses, and had misconducted herself in the face of an existing effective warning.

The fact that warning was *in theory* essential before a wrongdoer could be capitally punished, or even excommunicated from a sect to which he had adhered, is established by numerous contemporary and near-contemporary texts.[1] The rule, as understood by the Pharisees, goes back at least as early as Tannaitic times.[2] After all, God himself *warned*, sometimes repeatedly.[3] The alleged exception of the Ḳaraites, who are said not to have believed in the necessity of warning,[4] asks for further investigation, but it is possible that Scribes of Sadducean tendencies objected to proof of warning, still more to proof of warning by the witnesses themselves, as an essential prerequisite to conviction of the crime alleged. The principle, that God will 'require the blood', *viz.* of any who die for their crimes without having been warned by the 'watchman unto the house of Israel', at the hands of the 'watchman' who failed to warn them; but that, on the contrary, the one who warns the wicked shall deliver his soul even if the wicked disregards the warning, is biblical, being stated plainly at Ezk iii.18–19. But it is, of course, a moral principle.

Women gave rise to controversy. Non-Pharisaic Scribes may well have argued that a married woman needs no warning: however young she might be she would know that adultery was a crime. Moreover the actual biblical texts regarding adultery and establishing the penalty do not in fact say anything about warning, and the *Pharisees* drew out their rules about warning from biblical hints which could have been clearer.[5]

[1] Zadokite Document X. 16 (Charles, *Apo. and Pseud.* II, 825). *CD* IX, 3 (Vermès, 110; Lohse, 82–4 Dupont-Sommer, 164f): no one may accuse his comrade without rebuking him before witnesses (an interpretation of Lv xix.17–18). If only one witness sees, the matter is to be reported and the offender rebuked. An act repeated before two different witnesses will be a completed punishable offence (*CD* IX, 16–20). 2 Co xiii.2.

[2] Van Vliet, 38, 53. The rabbis knew that the Romans and other heathens did not require proof of previous warning: San. 57*b*; Midr. R. Gen., trans. Freedman (1951), p. 279.

[3] Gn iv.6; Ex xix.21–2; Dt xxx.19–20; xxxi.19, 21. The law is God's 'witness' (xxxi. 26), 'warning' (see above, p. 91). Van Vliet, 72, draws attention to this, and to *'edūt* (Admonition, Testimony) in 2 K xvii.13 (*wayyā'ad*) and Ne ix.29 (*wattā'ad*). See also Soph. Sal. xii. 2, 10, 20, 25–6, and an interpretation of the commandments referred to by Jeremias, *ZNW* 36, 210–11.

[4] B. Revel, *Ḳaraite Halakāh* (Philadelphia 1913), 51, cited by Van Vliet, 141 (n. 537).

[5] Lv xx.17: 'see'; Dt xxii.24: 'word'; Ex xxi.14: 'presumptuously'; Nb xv.33: 'gathering'. b. San. 40*b* = Sonc. 263. Horowitz, 167–9, calls *hat^{e}rā'āh* (warning) a 'merciful impracticality'.

operative (Jos. *Ant.* XVI, xi, 2, Niese, IV, 54–5, Loeb edn, viii, 355) and Josephus himself gives a good full account of it as current and effective (Jos. *Ant.* IV, viii, 24, Niese, I, 213–14, Loeb edn, iv, 601).

If warning by two witnesses or in front of two witnesses were essential in all cases what sense was one to make of Dt xxii.25–6? All surviving Pharisaic discussions of 'warning' are suspiciously silent about the case of the man who rapes a betrothed girl who 'cried, and there was none to save her'. Admittedly the girl herself could be one witness, but by definition another witness was not present to save her, or to warn him![1] Moreover, this is precisely a topic where an exception (if this is one) ought not to be made.[2] True, later the Pharisees made exceptions to their own rule. These exceptions could easily have been recognised earlier, and they betray acknowledgement of a principle which would support our assumed scribal outlook. The scholar never required a warning,[3] nor did the heretical teacher[4] (for the law was their warning),[5] nor did *zomemiym*,[6] nor did the enemy, nor 'pursuer',[7] for there the biblical texts introduced the germ of an exception. That a woman,[8] who was presumed to be illiterate, needed a warning, if only of the nature of the penalty she was incurring, was taken for granted in *Mishnāh* and *gemara*.

It is true that in the story of Susanna (to which we return shortly) the witnesses who nearly succeeded in destroying her were not required to

[1] The presumption is that she 'cried out', *i.e.* the court must believe that she was forced, so that she herself avoids the death-penalty (Dt xxii.24, 26). That she can be a witness against him is clear from the principle in the sodomy case: b. Yev. 25*a* = Sonc. 154.

[2] All systems of law are alive to the tendency of girls who regret illicit, but consensual, intercourse to claim that 'someone', or a particular person, committed rape. As a result 'corroboration' is invariably insisted upon. Thus justification for the *Torāh's* abandoning the alleged principle of 'warning' before two witnesses in this one instance will be hard to find. 'Warning' as such (irrespective of witnesses) is there, of course. She herself has warned him! See the case of Tamar (2 S xiii.11–14).

[3] b. San. 8*b*, 41*a* = Sonc. 37, 265; 72*b* = Sonc. 494. Makk. 6*b* = Sonc. 34; 9*b* = Sonc. 58. Maimonides, *ubi cit.* I, xii, 2 (trans., 34), says that even a scholar must be warned; this is a late development. Warning is needed to elicit the distinction between ignorance and presumption.

[4] Sonc. San., index, *Mesith*; *Prophet, false*; *Rebellious elder*. A *mēṣiyt* was a layman seducing Israelites to idolatry; the Pharisees later gave him an opportunity to retract.

[5] The reasoning is too complicated for discussion here: see San. 88*b* = Sonc. 587.

[6] The rabbinical 'false witnesses', *i.e.* those refuted because, being elsewhere, they could not have seen what they say they saw: San. 40*b* = Sonc. 259; 86*b* = Sonc. 570. See p. 161 n. 2 above.

[7] b. San. 72*b* = Sonc. 494–5. The enemy is virtually warned: Makk. 9*b* = Sonc. 56–8.

[8] *Cf.* b. San. 8*b* = Sonc. 36–7 (R. Papa speaks of a scholarly woman!). San. 41*a* = Sonc. 264; Soṭ. 25*a* = Sonc. 122–3. *Cf.* also the anomalous dictum, 'A man is always regarded as forewarned . . .' (on thieves breaking jugs), in San. 72*a* = Sonc. 490. Maimonides, *ubi cit.* II, xxi, 5 (following Talmudic sources as always) gives examples of testimony of a woman's secluding herself with a paramour, and testimony of adultery: due warning is essential for *her* liability, and for *their* refutation (evidence that cannot be refuted is inadmissible). See also warning followed by adultery followed by divorce in the *Mishnāh*, Soṭāh vi. 1.

show that they had warned her. But the story of Susanna, apart from its archaic origins, stands as a tale of warning and not as an indirect precedent in *this* respect. The old men, like Herod, were decidedly not patterns to be followed. On the contrary the *practice* of warning people before putting them on trial for a repetition of their offence was certainly in use in Jesus's time. The apostles were warned as well as 'threatened'.[1] Jesus and his disciples were themselves warned, and not always only by Pharisees.[2] A sensible principle, which virtually 'allows the dog his first bite', was part of the customary legal background of the time. One might wonder how, with the rule that two eyewitnesses were required, and the rule that proof must be tendered of warning having been given, convictions could be obtained in the case of persons whose guilt was notorious, for example him who struck down a sleeping man in the presence of a witness too far off to be able to intervene. This was taken care of. The biblical penalties could not be imposed, but there were others, not necessarily less deterring, the details of which do not concern us here.[3] Where God was silent, there were many possibilities: we are concerned with a situation where it was alleged that he had prescribed exactly.

But would proof of warning before witnesses apply in all its force to lynchings, where meticulous taking of evidence could not be expected? Did Phinehas, after all, warn his victims? Just as blasphemy is self-condemnatory, so adultery is a definite act, admitting of no ifs and buts,[4] and if the Pentateuch provides a death-penalty for adultery proved by two witnesses who are we to insist upon requirements which it does not state in so many words? Room for dispute certainly existed here between Scribes or non-Pharisees and Pharisees.

The question put to Jesus was not, then, whether or not the woman was liable to be stoned as contrasted with some other penalty,[5] but whether, in view of Moses's provision, she could lawfully in the circumstances be stoned. The questioners expected an interpretation of the relevant passages of the Law, a *midrash*. The bare text admitted of doubts, and here was a perfect test-case.

[1] Ac iv.17; ix.1. Jeremias, *ZNW* 36, 211–13, following Bornhäuser, *NKZ* 33 (1922), 332–3. It is of interest to notice another rule favoured by the Pharisees (that of the 39 strokes) which was in force *temp. Chr.*: 2 Co xi.24; Jos. *Ant.* IV, vii, 23; XIII, x, 6 cited by S. B. Hoenig, *Great Sanhedrin* (Philadelphia 1953), 209 (his conclusions, however, seem to go too far: each rule must be seen separately).

[2] Mk ii.24–8 (Jeremias, last note, also Stauffer, 'Neue Wege', 457); iii.2, 6; Jn v.10. In 3 M ii.24; v.18, 30, 33, 37; 4 M iv.8, 24; vii.2; viii.19; ix.32; xiii.6; xiv.9 ἀπειλή seems to be *hat^{e}rā'āh* 'warning', but it shades into 'threat', as in 1 P ii.23.

[3] b. San. 81*b* = Sonc. 541; *Mishnāh*, Sanh. IX. 5.

[4] b. San. 33*b* = Sonc. 211.

[5] Becker, 165ff.

JESUS'S REPLY

(1) *The First Writing*

It was open to Jesus to refuse the question. Then the elders would have given the woman a summary trial, a mockery of the regular procedure, and rushed her off to execution. They might consult someone else, but that would mean further delay, and impartiality and freedom from party or sectarian allegiance were perhaps not easily found, nor a rabbi who would willingly incur all the risks involved. The intrusion was an embarrassment, though not unthinkable. Many suggestions have been made why he should have written on the ground.[1] All except the traditional one, that he wrote the sins of his questioners,[2] shirk the necessity to link the writing with the oral answer. Is it 'profitless to enquire what he wrote'? The question put to him was a question of pure law, and a life was immediately at stake. The oral answer was a prescription of pure law. The final conduct of the questioners related to a legal sentence (*i.e.* they abandoned their accusation [*vv.* 9*a* and 10*b* as read in EF and numerous other manuscripts] and so the programme they had anticipated). Everything points to Jesus's concern for the woman's position, though not to any particular sympathy for her. It points in any case to serious reflection.[3] He was concerned, to judge from the oral reply, that

[1] For A. J. Wensinck see below, n. 3. Orchard and others (he doodled); Strachan (meaningless marks); Westcott (unwilling to speak); Macgregor, Dummelow, Hoskyns and others (he refuses to give judgement); Temple (hides his confusion); Manson (ironically pretends to draft a judgement). R. Eisler, 'Jesus und die ungetreue Braut', *ZNW* 32 (1923), 305–7, at p. 306 suggested that he indicated the vanity of the questioners and their questions, citing Jr xvii.13. A far-fetched suggestion in an otherwise helpful discussion. Becker, who cites previous explanations (86–7), would excise the passage and eliminate the problem. A suggestion by Dr Gertner ought to be recorded: the husband's 'jealousy' (Nb v.14) leads to a taking of the dust of the floor of the tabernacle and a writing of curses (*ibid. v.* 17, 21–3) or at any rate an allusion to the *soṭāh* ritual. But the husband is not present, Jesus was not a priest, confession was otiose (and in the ritual she must refuse to confess), and allusion to curses is hardly appropriate. In any case we must remember that Nb v was an improvement upon the situation obtaining before, evidenced in Judah's conduct at Gn xxxviii.24. Jesus can hardly appeal by allusion to *soṭāh* in a situation incompatible with *soṭāh*. Philo (*De Spec. Leg.* III, x, 52–9: Colson, VII, 509–11) indicates that the dust and water of the ritual symbolise innocence. Guilding, *op. cit.* 112 suggests Jesus wrote the decalogue, since Dt ix.10 is related as a lectionary reading to Jn vii–viii. See p. 176 n. 2 *infra*.

[2] *E.g.* a few manuscripts' reading of *v.* 8 and the Armenian 'Papias-text' (Becker, 106). Perhaps encouraged by the interesting form κατέγραφεν (v.l. ἔγραφεν). The former is more commonly used for 'entering up', 'setting down', 'consigning', and even 'conveying' (Moulton–Milligan, p. 325). It *does* imply serious and bold writing, as if of more permanent value than the circumstances permitted. A suggestion which, oddly, has not been proposed is that Jesus continued (like a teacher at a blackboard) to write texts he was expounding to his audience (in view of the ritual significance of writing scriptural texts, mentioned below).

[3] A. J. Wensinck, 'John viii.6, 8', *Amicitiae Corolla* (Fests. *J. R. Harris*) (London 1933), 300–2, uses an Islamic tradition of the Prophet's writing with a stick on the

whatever was to be done should be done in righteousness. The two acts of writing therefore ought to have formed a piece with the oral reply, and can most easily and naturally be explained as acts directed towards the establishment of a proposition of law. If this is so the possibilities are very few, and our choice is greatly facilitated.

Could he have written some general proposition, say from a Psalm?[1] (R. 'Eleazar just scored a line[2] and wrote Ps xxxix.1 as discreet *caveas!*) Hardly. The effect of his writing, and pausing after writing, was to produce from those in a position to watch him an insistence upon his giving his sentence (*v.* 7*a*). What he wrote was not unintelligible, but it did not satisfy them. This need not mean that it was irrelevant, but that it was provoking, teasing, or partial. It made them more anxious than ever to hear what he would say. What is more likely than that he reminded them (and, as it were, himself) of the principal source upon which he would rely if he were to give judgement in the case? Better still, he could have written the first words of a chain of texts (if one can be found) which supply all a man needs to know if he is to take responsibility in such a nasty business.

But why should he write? If it was a text which was bound to apply in such a case, why should he not proclaim it aloud? There are excellent and manifest reasons why he should do nothing of the sort. First, a real judge never cited his authorities.[3] The position in our day is somewhat different, though the matter has not escaped critical discussion.[4] The very nature of things requires that a judge in a practical case (particularly a single judge from whom there may be an appeal) shall say 'Guilty', or 'Not guilty', or 'You must make delivery', and so on. The reasons are a professional secret, and if the matter went to a fuller court the whole thing would be heard all over again. Secondly, to utter the

[1] *E.g.* Ps i. 1–2; Sap. Sal. i. 5f.; Si xi.9; xiii.1. [2] b.Giṭṭ. 7*a* = Sonc.22 (*sharᵉṭēṭ*).

[3] b. B.M. 69*a–b* = Sonc. 402–3. When a Samaritan litigant accused R. Papa of partiality he condescended to cite his authority—obviously a phenomenon. The Talmud is filled with examples of sentences of the great rabbis, the reasons of which were a matter of speculation even amongst their pupils and academic descendants. See Maimonides, *Mishneh Torāh* XIV, xxi, 10 (trans. Hershman, p. 65), where he cites Ex xxiii.7*a*. Odd as it may seem now, reasons were not given in English judgements within historical times: Coke, 3 Rep. preface, v. And the typical judgment in Canon law through the centuries did not cite its authority or authorities.

[4] K. H. Nadelmann, 'The Judicial Dissent. Publication vs. Secrecy', *Amer. J. Comp. Law* 8 (1959), 415–32. The Jewish law relating to the 'rebellious elder' took cognisance only of cases where the rabbi's *reasoning* failed to agree with that of the supreme court.

---

ground when pondering over a question: 'this is the gesture of one who is reflecting upon a serious question', and not of one attempting to evade it. He does not consider whether the tradition is not copied from Jn viii.6, 8! But the point is valid, and he cites other examples from Islamic contexts.

principal text or texts would be to deprive them of much of their meaning. Jesus was not asked to give a lecture interpreting a text. To speak a text[1] was to show at once the 'punctuating' upon which the speaker *primarily* relied. That did not preclude his later giving other pointings, etc., but the virtue of simultaneously suggesting two or more interpretations would be lost. All possible senses must be obtained from the characters, unpointed. A Scribe needed only a few characters to be written before a whole web of readings and interpretations would be presented to his mind. A short group of words would at once conjure up a connected passage as currently interpreted by various teachers. Thirdly, writing instead of speaking impressed upon those who saw it the referee's attention to the basic source of the law. That source provided all the necessary information, if one looked in the right place. The letter of the law had been appealed to; to the letter the referee applies his mind. If our choice of his text is correct we see at once that this, the perfect method of allusion without assertion, shows the letter carrying a heavy burden of the spirit of the legal system it codified. Writing *with the finger* was symbolic of divine 'legislation' (*cf.* Ex xxxi.18; Dt ix.10), a fact upon which the Church will later have fastened. Fourthly and lastly the words of the *Torāh* should ideally not be uttered except as an act of reading—reading the well-known words was itself a ritual act, for the culture made a fetish of the written word (*cf.* Jos i.8). R. Judah b. Naḥmani the public orator of R. Simeon b. Laḳish (*c.* A.D. 200–250) discoursed as follows: 'It is written, "Write thou these words" (Ex xxxiv.27) and "For according to the mouth of these words" (*ibid.*) . . . It means that the words which are written thou art not at liberty to say by heart, and the words transmitted orally thou art not at liberty to recite from writing.'[2]

He was sitting (*v.* 2*c*), probably on a low stool a little distance from the ground (whatever his height above his audience), and bent down to write and to study what he had written (*vv.* 6*b*, 8), and he wrote with his finger (*v.* 6*c*) and not with any instrument. Dust is dust and sand is sand and no one of average or above-average height can write more than sixteen Hebrew characters in a row from such a position and in such an attitude. We need not dwell on the possibility that he wrote and erased and wrote again, or that he wrote in a manner that was illegible to him and to those who would be reading upside-down or from the side. What he wrote he paused and appeared to ponder over.

[1] For Jesus's oral citation of *Torāh* to Scribes and Pharisees see Mk vii.10; but that is a spontaneous, independent reference to texts to which his questioners were not alluding.

[2] b. Giṭṭ. 60*b* = Sonc. 284. B. Gerhardsson, *Memory and Manuscript*, 159.

Those that stood in front of him could read what he had written as easily as he could. What did he write? We need a text of sixteen characters or less, a text of law bearing on accusation and execution of offenders including adulteresses, a text applicable to all executions inclusive of lynchings. Since his oral answer relates to the sinlessness of those who commence the stoning, that is the witnesses themselves,[1] the text is likely to relate to the function of the witnesses predominantly. They, after all, are accusers, provers of the case, and executioners.[2] The law properly spends many words on them. If we examine all the possibilities we find that all except one are unsuitable for one or more reasons.[3] In every other case the implications are too narrow, the relevance is not clear, or the vital words refuse to be fitted into our limited space, and that too by a clear margin. The one text that fits our requirements would be a splendid choice and deserves close discussion. It is Ex xxiii.1*b*:

'al-tāshet yād^e^chā 'im-rāshā^c^ [lih^e^yot 'ed ḥāmāṣ
Place not thy hand with the wicked (to be a false witness).

This text, up to the bracket, was used by the rabbis to prove that in all situations, not merely in those of giving evidence in a trial,[4] one should take care with whom one associates oneself, and to whose project one lends one's countenance and authority. It is a sin to join with, or help, or intervene in, an affair with an evil man. The word *rāshā^c^* is to be taken in a broad sense, including 'unjust', 'wicked', 'godless', 'guilty'. Including the words beyond the bracket, the text warns us that in

[1] Dt xvii.7. [2] Horowitz, *op. cit.* 640. Above p. 166 n. 1.

[3] Vague references to false witnesses, *e.g.* Pr vi.19, are wide of the mark since they do not touch the members of the crowd who were not witnesses, nor was the 'falsity' certain. The rule that *two* or three witnesses are required (Dt xvii.6; xix.15) does not touch an issue. Lv v.1 is not in point as no one suggests that vital evidence is being withheld. The commands not to bear false witness (Ex xx.16; Dt v.20) suffer from defects mentioned above. Lv xix.16–17 are not irrelevant but vague, and not exactly to the point: moreover a phrase of satisfactory length is not forthcoming—the only exception, the famous commandment *lo' ta'^a^mod 'al-dam re'échā*, has in fact a totally different connotation, namely, the Jew's duty to save his brother from physical as opposed to moral (*v.* 17) danger. The elaborate exposition of the penalties for 'false witness' in Dt xix would be cumbersome, not to the point, and difficult to allude to in the space available. Serious thought must be given to Dt xvii.7. This text directly affects the situation, and is linked with Jesus's words. Moreover, we have the key word *bāri'shonāh* to which Jesus might actually allude, and its correlative *bā'aḥaronāh.* But it is mechanical, no one doubted its meaning, everyone present was relying upon it anyhow, and no suitable group of words comes within sixteen characters. Texts dealing with adultery as a crime and even the not irrelevant Hosea are out of the question, for no one disputed that adultery was a crime, or what its ingredients were, and the passages are not related to the procedure to which Jesus certainly applied his mind, as we see from the answer.

[4] Midr. R., Lam. iv. 2, 3–4 = Sonc. 218 (do not attend a dinner . . ., do not sign a deed . . .).

giving evidence which is to be vitiated by wickedness, falsehood, violence, or fraud, it is a sin to join with a wicked person, even if one's evidence is factually true.[1] *'ed ḥāmāṣ* and *'ed sheḳer* mean not merely lies, and the liar, but the evidence of one who is disqualified and the disqualified man himself. The opposite of *'ed sheḳer* is *'ed ne'emān.*[2] All the rabbis' elaborate and somewhat over-systematised rules on the important subject of disqualification of witnesses hang upon this text.[3] Their highly interesting but under-generalised propositions may not already have been developed as they stand by Jesus's time, but the principle that evidence, however true, is not to be heard from an incompetent (*unfähig, unzuständig*) witness, is far older than our period, is reflected in the texts relating to 'false witness', and is firmly rooted in the semitic as in other branches of the human race.[4] It reappears in

[1] b. Yev. 25*a* = Sonc. 154. See n. 4 below. Also Horowitz, *op. cit.* 685. Mekilta on Ex xxii.1*b* (Lauterbach, III, 160–1).

[2] The implications in the former are of corruption and malice, and in the latter reliability and faithfulness. See Is viii.2; Jr xlii.5. On *'ed* see Van Vliet, 49, 67, and refs.

[3] *Mishnāh,* San. III. b. San. 25*a–b* = Sonc. 146–60; B.Ḳ. 72*b* = Sonc. 415; Yev. 25*a* = Sonc. 154 (*cit. sup.*). Maimonides, *ubi cit.* II, ix, 100f.; x, 102; I, xviii, 50f.; xix, 53f. (a vast number of disqualified persons). Z. Frankel, *Gerichtliche Beweis,* 118–21, 246–80. J. Kohler, *ZVR* 20 (1907), 257f. Note the law relating to *zomemiym,* 'plotting witnesses', evidencing the Pharisaic tendency to limit the application of severe punishment, is post-C.E. in so far as it unreasonably limits the definition of one liable to the penalties set out in Dt xix.18–19; but the general principle is of course far older.

[4] Jos. *Vita,* § 49 (Loeb edn, i. 97) (cited by Van Vliet, 27–8); *Ant.* IV, viii, 15 (Niese, 1, 206) is sound. The requirement of 'competence' is bound up with Ex xx.16; xxiii.1; Dt v.20; xix.15–19. Jewish law, like Islamic and Hindu law, was concerned with competence of witnesses where today we are concerned with the credibility of evidence tendered. A consciousness of the Jewish meanings of 'false' witness is present in tit. IX of the very interesting *Mosaicarum et Romanarum Legum Collatio,* ed. Th. Mommsen, *Collectio Librorum Iuris Anteiustiniani* (ed. Krüger *et al.*), III (Berlin 1890), 167f. There, discussing *de familiaris testimonio non admittendo,* Ulpian's rules on the *lex Iulia de ui publica et priuata* (see *Dig.* 22. 5. 3, 5) are compared with Ex xx.16 (*falsum testimonium non dabis*). In Islamic Law great attention is paid to the requirement that a witness must be *'ādal*: the similarities with Jewish law are striking but both draw on a common customary source. C. Hamilton, *Hedaya* II (1791), 671–92. Professor Dr O. Spies summarises the position (in a letter): 'Adal ist einer, der keine große Sünde begangen hat noch sich gewohnheitsmäßig Verstösse gegen das Gesetz zuschulden kommen läßt.' A comparison of Koranic and rabbinical provisions on evidence was made by R. Roberts, *Social Laws of the Qorân . . .* (London 1925), 34–5. A peculiarity of Islamic law is that the court is obliged independently to inquire into the competence of witnesses. For Hindu law (*dharmaśāstra*) we have noted, p. 160,n.2, references to Manu (VIII, 61–71) by Frankel. There is also Manu, V, 106; and other sources are authoritatively represented in A. Thakur, *Hindu Law of Evidence or a Comparative Study . . . according to the Smṛtis* (Calcutta 1933), 84–96, 108f.; P. V. Kane, *History of Dharmaśāstra* (Poona 1946), III, 334–41; L. Rocher, 'Theory of proof in ancient Hindu law', *Recueils de la Société Jean Bodin* 18 (*La Preuve*), at p. 342ff.

other forms even in modern systems of criminal procedure. In Jesus's time the opinion at least of the Dead Sea Scrolls Community is known. In cases both of life and property witnesses must be 'trustworthy' (*ne'ᵉmān*); in a case where the death penalty is appropriate the witness must also be, not merely God-fearing, but also free from unexpiated transgressions of any commandment; he must also be twenty years of age or above. One who was not with these categories could not be considered 'trustworthy' (*'al ye'āmen*).

The text of Exodus was, of course, *not* pointed. By stopping at RSHᶜ emphasis would have been laid upon *association* rather than corrupt motive (another interpretation, equally sound, placed ᶜM–RSHᶜ with the words that followed it,[1] making no less acceptable sense). Now if one reads *reshaᶜ* instead of *rāshāᶜ* (an instance of an *'al tiḳᵉrey*)[2] the result is impressive. Jesus is then considering a joining with Evil in the abstract, associating in an evil matter. Some of his questioners will resent the implied attack on them, or some of them, as wicked people. But others are at liberty to suppose that he means (i) that no respectable man will associate in this nasty affair, and (ii) that he himself is unwilling to take any part in a business which is, or almost certainly will turn out to be,

[1] The technique of interpretation is described (under the term *sᵉmūkiyn*) by M. Mielziner, *Introduction to the Talmud* (Cincinnati, 1894), 178–9. On the great importance of the Targum Onḳelos as a source on the language and beliefs of the time of Christ see P. Kahle, 'Das palästinische Pentateuchtargum und das zur Zeit Jesu gesprochene Aramäisch', *ZNW* 49 (1958), 100–16. Onk. has *l' tshwy ydch 'm ḥyyv' lmhwy lyh ṣhyd shḳr* (ed. Sperber, 1959, 127). Etheridge translates, I (1862) 396: 'Nor set thine hand with the wicked to be a false witness *for him*'. Vulg.: *ut pro impio dicas falsum testimonium*.

[2] M. Gertner, 'Midrashim in the New Testament', *J. Sem. Stud.* 7 (1962), 267f., at p. 270, 272, 280, 283, 292; also *idem*, 'The Masorah and the Levites', *VT* 10 (1960), 241f., at p. 262, 274–5. He refers to b. San. 34*a*, and to an example at Ber. 64*a* (end). At Mekilta, *'Amaleḳ* 1 (Winter–Wünsche, 168–9; Lauterbach, II, 138) there is an astonishing *'al tiḳᵉrey* of 2 Ch xxiv.24: SHPṬYM is read not as *shᵉphāṭiym* ('judgements' ?) but as *shᵉphūṭiym* or *shippūṭiym* ('childish folly', 'sodomy')—also Midr. R., Exod. VIII. Note the ease with which the vowel *vāv* is inserted. See also in the New Testament at Mt ii.6 where in Mi v.1(2) *bᵉ'alufey* (princes) is read for *bᵉ'alᵉfey* (thousands). A flamboyant illustration occurs at Midr. R., Lev. XVIII. 1 (on Lv xv.1f.) = Sonc. 223. There BR'CH is read (i) *bore'echā* (thy creator); (ii) *be'erchā* (thy well); and (iii) *borechā* (thy pit). That our very verse (Ex xxiii.1) was subject to an *'al tiḳᵉrey* is shown in Pes. 118*a* = Sonc. 607–8 (also Makk. 23*a* = Sonc. 161), where, instead of *tisā'* an alternative reading *tāshiy'* is used to connect *slander* with *being cast to dogs* (by the technique of interpretation by proximity to other verses—in this case Ex xxiii.1*a* is read harmoniously with the immediately preceding Ex xxii.30 (31*c*)). That different pointings of ḤMṢ (Ex xxiii.1*c*) were in use is suggested by Mekilta *ad loc.* (Lauterbach, III, 160–1). For the technique of *'al tiḳᵉrey* see A. Rosenzweig, *Die Al-tikre Deutungen, ein Beitrag zur talmudischen Schriftdeutung* (Breslau 1911); Zvi Zinger, *Textus* 5 (1966) 119; S. Talmon, *Textus* 4 (1964), 132; for examples in addition to those given above b. Bek. 44*b* = Sonc. 302; Ta'an. 7*b* = Sonc. 29; b. 'Erub. 54*b* (B. Gerhardsson, *Memory*, 151); Kadushin, *Rabbinic Mind*, 118 n. 30; Bonsirven, *Exégèse Rabbinique et exégèse Paulinienne* (Paris 1939), 120–2, 127.

contaminated by immorality. If he had spoken the words great parts of the implications would have been lost, and direct attack on some of the questioners could hardly have been avoided. As it is, his refusal to be a party to what may be an unrighteous decision merges imperceptibly with a warning to the questioners that their own activities must be justifiable, and that it is not sufficient that they or some of them saw her in the act of adultery.

Moreover the passage in the code to which this text will have introduced them contains several propositions which are highly relevant to the situation. Let us see them with their contemporary or later glosses:

Ex xxiii.2: *lo'-tih*^{e}*yeh 'aḥ*^{a}*rēy-rabbiym l*^{e}*rā'ot . . .*

Though decision by majority is not excluded, one must not follow the majority to do evil, and in convicting a person one must not give one's sentence merely because others are of that opinion.[1]

Ex xxiii.3: *v*^{e}*dāl lo' teh*^{e}*ddar b*^{e}*riyvo.*

Justice is to be given impartially, without regard to the claims accused persons have upon one's sympathy, or the reverse.[2]

Ex xxiii.4: *kiy tiph*^{e}*gga*^{c} *shor 'yiv*^{e}*chā 'o ḥ*^{a}*moro . . .*

An enemy, one whom you know personally to be a sinner, shall be aided as an act of reconciliation. If his ox or ass strays you must take the initiative to preserve it; how much more must you preserve him if he strays. Thus you must admonish, and reason with one who wrongs you.[3]

Ex xxiii.5: *kiy-tir*^{e}*'eh ḥ*^{a}*mor shona*^{a}*chā rovēts . . .*

This, like the preceding, teaches that activity in a spirit of revenge is wrong. The ass lying under the burden, like the body lying under a load of temptation, must be raised, and a brother must help his brother to avoid sin.[4]

Ex xxiii.6: *lo' tāṭṭeh mish*^{e}*paṭ 'ev*^{e}*yon*^{e}*chā b*^{e}*riyvo.*

[1] *Targ. Onk.* (Etheridge, 396). The rabbinical rule is that one must follow the majority (of proofs or instances, of opinions), e.g. Midr. R. S.S. vii. 5, 2 = Sonc. 286. That Ex xxiii.2 meant that a majority should always be followed was a hermeneutical distortion, on which Dr Gertner's treatment of Decision by Majority in Jewish Law is awaited.

[2] b. Ḥul. 134*a* = Sonc. 762.

[3] With both Ex xxiii.4, 5 *cf.* the tone of Dt xxii.1–4. *Targ. ps. Jon.* (Etheridge, I 522, II 622). Philo, *Supp. II, Questions and Answers on Exodus*, trans. R. Marcus (Cambridge, Mass. 1953), 45–6 (on Ex ii.*11, 12). Midr. R., Gen. XXXVIII. 3 = Sonc. 303 (ref. Ex xxiii.5): evil must not be rewarded with evil. Midr. R., Lev. IX. 9 = Sonc. 115; xxiii.4 and 5 are maxims making for peace.

[4] See Philo, Midr. R. Gen. cited above. In b. Pes. 113*b* = Sonc. 583 this is used to show that accusation by a single person is a possibility: however, one may *hate* someone only when his fault is observed by two witnesses. Maimonides (*op. cit.* XI, *Book of Torts*, V,xiii, 14, p. 236) takes the view that one may hate the Israelite wrongdoer whom one alone has seen committing the offence: but one is bound to help him.

Unfair advantage must not be taken of underprivileged or helpless people: human justice must be strictly impartial and technicalities should be employed for acquittal rather than conviction. Moreover 'poor' means also 'wicked': one must not pervert judgement in favour of the wicked.[1]

The implications are plain: the husband should have helped his wife to avoid adultery in a spirit of loving kindness, and not conspired (as would seem to be the case) to effect her destruction; and her 'brothers' should consider whether their conduct in conniving at his scheme does not make them such as 'place their hand with the wicked' (Ex xxiii.1*b*).

(2) *The Oral Reply*

He is pressed for an answer. Those who see a covert attack upon themselves in the written text feel that their guilt is not in question, but rather hers. 'Let him among you who is without sin cast first upon her a stone'[2] does not deny that she may be stoned, but insists upon the innocency and therefore the competence of whoever stands forth against her as accuser and witness.[3] Even in a lynching matter the biblical requirements must be met. Now we know what is the principal meaning of our Ex xxiii.1*b* in this context. Are the witnesses really competent? The facts of the case raise doubts.[4] Even if one witness were untainted, the other would incur guilt by standing forth with him. Both watched a crime they could have interrupted, and then pounced. Both, it seems, had very recently been through the experience of watching human beings in sexual intercourse, which oriental peoples regard as an in-

[1] It is understood as a helping-verse with xxiii.2: a judgement for conviction requires a majority of two and not a bare majority (San. 36*b* = Sonc. 228). Mekilta, *Kaspa* iii, Lauterbach, III, 168.

[2] ἀναμάρτητος = 'without sin' (*cf.* 2 M viii.4). So, correctly, Wünsche (*Neue Beiträge* 530) as far back as 1878, and Grundmann, *Ev. nach Markus*, 2nd edn (1959), 245–7—not, as Schlatter, 'Wer unter euch nicht gesündigt hat. . . .' Rengstorf (*ThWzNT* I, 338) agrees that the word implies freedom from *all* sin, but his reasoning is not apt (Becker). We have seen, p. 169 n. 4, that many Pharisaic rules of the post-C.E. rabbinical texts were not in force *temp. Chr.* The elaborate rules regarding stoning (*Mishnāh*, San. VI, 4; b. San. 44*b*–45*b* = Sonc. 293–9; Maimonides, *ubi cit.* I, xv, 1, p. 42) according to which the *second*, *i.e.* the younger, witness casts the first (heavy) stone, fit excellently with our situation, but are *not* presupposed by Jesus's reply, and it is unlikely that in practice the younger threw first.

[3] This exact point appears in the anonymous Syrian Chronicle of the World which here stems from the chronicle of Zacharias Rhetor, in which our pericope appeared as an episode. The entire version shows that the explanation given in this article was understood in eastern Mediterranean circles in the late fifth century. Ahrens-Krüger, *Die sogen. Kirchengeschichte des Zacharias Rhetor* (Leipzig 1899), 164f., cited by Becker.

[4] Suborned witnesses were certainly disqualified: b. Makk. 6*a* = Sonc. 31. The general point was seen by Wünsche, *Neue Beiträge* 530.

evitable prelude to jealous, lustful, sinful, and possibly harmful thoughts: 'Whoever witnesses a suspected woman in her disgrace should withhold himself from wine' is a typical comment.[1] Had the witnesses rid themselves of this private taint? Even the elders who were not witnesses are implicated if they lend their approval to a stoning when there are doubts as to the competence of the witnesses. No one, however factually guilty, can be lawfully convicted and executed on the evidence of incompetent witnesses. They would be 'joining with the wicked' if they allowed her, for all her adultery, to be a victim of injustice. The witnesses, and the elders, are put on their guard.

(3) *The Second Writing*

If we are right in our choice of Ex xxiii.1*b* for the first writing, because of its eminent fitness and its subsequent undoubted authority for propositions entirely relevant to our situation, and if we are right in seeing in Ex xxiii.2–6 rules which a citation of 1*b* would automatically bring to a Scribe's mind, there can be no doubt what it was Jesus wrote to round off his 'opinion'. Ex xxiii.7*a* says: *midd^{e}var-sheḳer tir^{e}ḥāḳ [v^{e}nāḳiy v^{e}tsadiyḳ 'al-tāh^{a}rog kiy lo' 'ats^{e}diyḳ rāshā^c*. 'From a false matter keep far [and the innocent and righteous slay not; for I shall not acquit the guilty]'. The ambiguities of the last passages are helpful:[2] God is the source of retribution, therefore human justice need not strain his laws in order to award penalties in a hard case; moreover, those who slay the 'innocent and righteous', who include, according to interpretation, those who have escaped, on technical or other grounds, a penalty they would otherwise have had to pay, or have narrowly escaped a penalty which they did not deserve,[3] are the peculiar objects of God's promised retribution. Verse 7*a* is the very text upon which the rabbis later hung the rules that one must not associate with a sinner as co-judge or co-witness, nor enter upon judgment merely on the basis of evidence without ascertaining the truth—both of which points are relevant to our present problem.[4] At the time of Christ the same text was used by the Dead Sea Scroll Community (along, curiously, with Is ii.22) as authority for the much wider proposition that no kind of consorting is

[1] b. Sot. 2*a* = Sonc. 2.

[2] The LXX had a different reading, possibly because of a need felt at some time for a contrast rather than a threat. This proves that the text was open to various interpretations at the period in question. *'ats^{e}diyḳ* means that God will not 'justify', declare righteous, the *rāshā^c*, lit. 'wicked', as at *v.*1*b*.

[3] *Targ. ps. Jonathan* (Etheridge I, 522).

[4] b. Shev. 30*b* = Sonc. 170–1. *Targ. Onḳ.* translates *-d^{e}var-* by *pit^{e}gāmā'* which, like DVR itself, has the connotation 'decree', 'affair', 'rule', or even, as in Is viii.10, 'communication consistent with conspiracy or enmity'. Maimonides, *op. cit.* XIV, I, xxiii, 10, p. 68 (citation of Ex xxiii.7), so also xxiv, 3, p. 72–3.

to be allowed with the 'men of falsehood who walk in the way of wickedness' who are not reckoned in God's (*i.e.* the Community's) Covenant. These vain people must not be joined socially, in their work (*'ᵃvodāh*) or their property (*hon*), lest they contaminate the members of the community.[1] The *Manual of Discipline* or *Community Rule* goes on with words which have been variously translated but which clearly tend to separate the Community from such people 'in all matters of *Torāh* and judgement' (which would certainly cover Jesus's situation).[2]

As a moral rule the text's force is wide and undeniable.[3] On moral grounds you should scrutinise the probity of those who are requiring your aid in some scheme they are promoting. The second witness is invariably the younger man.[4] Upon the younger man then falls the responsibility of guaranteeing the probity of the elder.[5] If the disqualification of the elder witness can be proved by a bystander, the younger labours under the sin of association with the 'wicked', and the entire testimony falls to the ground.[6] When the older men reflect upon this position the implications are uncomfortable. Their zealous juniors are entitled to inquire into every type of sin, not merely the stereotyped list of the Talmud, long though it is, but others which come within the principle. What of the sin of standing by and not preventing the sin of one's brother? There is a positive obligation to rebuke and to prevent a brother's sin;[7] and from many sins (some of which had a sexual character) a Jew might lawfully be saved *even at the cost of his life.*[8]

[1] 1 *QS* V, 14–20 (Vermès, 79–80; Lohse, 18). The text is read as *mikol dᵉvar sheḳer tirᵉḥāḳ*, 'From *every* false matter keep far'. Dupont-Sommer, 99.
[2] 1 *QS* V. 15–16: *va-'ᵃsher lo' yāshiyv 'iysh mē'anᵉshēy ha-yaḥad 'al piyhem lᵉchol torāh ū-mishᵉpāṭ*. Leaney, 174–5 ('No member of the community shall respond to their authority on any teaching or decision'). Gaster, *Scriptures of the Dead Sea Sect* (1957), 57, translates, 'No member . . . is to abide by the decision of such men in any matter of doctrine or law'. Vermès (79) has, 'No member . . . shall follow them in matters of doctrine and justice', while Lohse (19) prefers *Und keiner . . . darf Antwort geben, wenn er von ihnen gefragt wird, betreffs irgendeines Gesetzes oder Gebotes*. Likewise Dupont-Sommer (*ubi cit. sup.*) 'et qu'aucun . . . ne réponde à leurs questions concernant toute loi ou ordonnance'. The English versions given above seem preferable.
[3] *Cf.* Ps. ci. 3, 7.
[4] The nature of things makes this inevitable, but it is attested in *Mishnāh*, Sanh. III. 6; Sanh. 29*a* = Sonc. 175; Maimonides *ubi cit.* XIV, I, xii, 3, p. 35.
[5] Since he takes upon himself the sin of 'joining with another . . .' if he adds his testimony to that of a person whom he believes to be 'wicked'. Naturally, he does not guarantee the freedom of the elder man from sins of which he has no knowledge and of which in the ordinary course of events he ought not to have had knowledge. It was just *possible* that the younger man was not told by the husband or his elder colleague the purpose of their visit to the place, and that he did what he did more or less innocently. He need not have been over 14 years of age, after all (according to the Pharisees' *halakāh*).
[6] See p. 161 n. 1 above, also San. 8*b* = Sonc. 37–8.
[7] See p. 163 above.
[8] b. San. 73*a*–75*a* = Sonc. 495–506; *Mishnāh*, Sanh. VIII. 7. Goldin, *op. cit.* 177–8.

By far the most valuable aspect of this text is its recalling of the Susanna story. Like that of Potiphar's wife, this must have come from the mists of antiquity.[1] It had fairly recently been revived and retold under the influence of a definite historical movement to amend the law of evidence.[2] It is nearly certain that a leading Jewish elder had had reason to reform the manner in which evidence was relied upon in capital cases under the impact of a personal tragedy.[3] Ever since the public had been awakened to the need for thorough investigation of evidence, the Susanna story had been connected not merely with adultery but also with the peril of accusers whose accusation is vitiated by malice or fraud. If Susanna was a popular story, the populace were concerned with public executions by stoning. Every stoning, especially a lynching, must depend on public approval. In Susanna a young man called Daniel, who was popularly identified[4] later with the most popular of the prophets,[5] saved the unjustly accused woman by searching questions addressed to the 'elders',[6] the 'respectable' witnesses. He flung at them[7] the very words that appear in Ex xxiii.7*b*, words that a Targum shows were indicative of the right of any person to escape if, at any time, his sentence could be revoked, or an acquittal could be obtained.[8] When their falsity was proved out of their own mouths it was this text that was believed to have sent them to their deaths, the mode of death being that which they had envisaged for their intended

[1] The description of the court-scene is obviously Hellenistic and betrays the foreign origin of the surviving versions; what concerns us is the framework of the story as we know it existed contemporaneously with our episode. On its history see W. Baumgartner, 'Susanna. Die Geschichte einer Legende', *Archiv. f. Religionswiss.* 24 (1926–7), 259–80, particularly at p. 277f., 279f. Also the same, 'Der weise Knabe und die des Ehebruchs beschuldigte Frau', *A.f.Rel.w.* 27 (1929), 187–8. M. Wurmbrand, 'A Falasha Variant of the Story of Susanna', *Biblica*, 44 (1963), 29–35.

[2] Oesterley, *Aprocr.* (cited above), 283–6. Was there an allusion to Susanna in Ps. Sal. (LXX), iv. 4?

[3] Previous note. Simeon b. Shetaḥ's advice is preserved in part in *Mishnāh*, 'Āvot I. 9. See succinct note at Sonc. trans. Makkot, p. 27 n. 7. Van Vliet, 52–3. Baumgartner, 261f.

[4] Susanna was at one stage included in the book of Daniel. In b. San. 93*a* = Sonc. 624–5 the villainy of Ahab and Zedekiah towards Nebuchadnezzar's daughter is related and Jr xxix.21–3 is connected with the Susanna story. Schilling, cited above, p. 168 n. 5, at p. 99–100.

[5] Jos. *Ant.* X, xi, 7 (Niese, I, 317).

[6] πρεσβυτέροι, πρεσβῦται. Both versions of Sus. 41 (Theod. 41*b*) emphasise that it was because they were πρεσβυτέροι (the very word in Jn viii.9*a*) they were believed by the court. The *Didascalia* (cited by Zahn, *Ev. des Johannes*, 1921, 726–7) says, *num condemnaverunt te presbyteri, filia mea.* Daniel's questions appear at Sus. 51–9.

[7] Sus. 53*c*: ἀθῷον καὶ δίκαιον οὐκ ἀποκτενεῖς.

[8] *Targ. ps. Jon.* (Etheridge, I, 522). Ex xxiii.7*b* was also used by the rabbis to show that no conviction might be arrived at upon *circumstantial* evidence: Maimonides, *op. cit.* XIV, I, xx, 1, p. 60.

victim.[1] These two horrible old men were the subject of many scandalous stories,[2] and their fate was obviously the subject of general satisfaction. If an elder ignored the warnings published so graphically in the current texts of Susanna it would be to these disgusting types that he would liken himself. 'From a false matter keep far . . .' was a warning addressed particularly to the elders, the leaders of this group. It is not surprising that the group began to melt away, 'starting from the elders (or the oldest)' (*v.* 9*a*). As the leaders departed the responsibility for maintaining the affair would remain with those who stayed behind, and the speed of withdrawal must have increased.

In case it might be feared that, notwithstanding the citation of Ex xxiii.7 in Susanna, the midrashic interpretation of the chapter was post-Christian, we may refer to a passage in Philo which brings allusions to Ex xxiii.1, 2 and 7 together.[3] Assenting to evil, he says, is morally equivalent to the crime of breaking the prohibition against 'false witness': διὸ πολλαχοῦ παραινεῖ τῆς νομοθεσίας ἀδίκῳ μηδενὶ συναινεῖν, μήτε ἀνθρώπῳ μήτε πράγματι. There is even a reference to Daniel and Susanna within the passage cited, and we find Philo occupied with the effect of majority rule—a topic obviously relevant to lynch-trials.

CONCLUSION

'Woman, where are they?', or, as other manuscripts have it, 'Woman, where are those who were thy accusers?', was the question of one who had been studying the last matter he had written, and looked up, in anticipation of the accusers' next step. Whether the question is sarcastic, or humorous, is not clear, or it may be that it was a way of saying, 'So they have abandoned it?' Without the accusers there could be no evidence, no judgement, no execution. An interval had occurred, reflection had taken place, zeal had lost its edge, the precedent of Phinehas seemed less clearly applicable. No one wanted her to be stoned under the conditions pointed out by Jesus. Jesus was himself in no position to condemn her (*v.* 11*b*). She waited for something to be done or said. Previously rooted to the spot, she was sent away with the warning to which she had been entitled (*v.* 11*c*), but had not had. This time the warning was given before a group, some of whom would certainly be competent witnesses. If she was caught again in adultery nothing could save her.

Here we have a story which, somewhat like Mk xii.13–15,[4] illustrates Jesus's ability to emerge from a critical situation. Here, however, a life

[1] Above, p. 168 n. 6.
[2] Above, p. 185 n. 4. Goodspeed, *op. cit.* 65f.
[3] *De Spec. Leg.* IV, viii, 41–7 (Colson, VIII, 34–5).
[4] See below, Chapter 14.

was at stake. Here, as there, he avoids a direct interpretation of the Law; he merely reminds his questioners of its requirements. He does not directly abuse or accuse anyone for his part in the affair. By implication we know that had she been warned and had the accusers been sinless her stoning could have taken place with his approval.

If one is entitled at this stage to draw an inference from the story it is that Jesus required the whole Law to be applied even in contexts where the usual formalities would be relaxed. Criminal justice ought to lie in clean hands. Brotherly love admitted the possibility of chastisement, but only in the last resort. A wicked man, one who 'hated his brother in his heart', or one whose motives were devious, could neither accuse, nor testify, nor condemn.

It is not difficult to believe that his audience understood this as his meaning. The belief that only competent, sinless people should accuse or should condemn is deeply rooted in many nations.[1] The Pharisees certainly shared Jesus's approach. While the ordeal of the 'bitter waters' was still in vogue it was established, according to their doctrines (based on Nb v.31), that it could only be employed if the husband, promoter of the ordeal, even though acting upon information from witnesses,[2] were himself without fault.[3] If the husband were himself vitiated (not necessarily in sexual relations only) the ordeal would not work; in other words the provisions of the *Torāh* in that connection were valid only on condition that the accuser was himself pure.

There are no grounds for assuming that Jesus had any additional intention in behaving as he is recorded to have behaved. The motives of the early Church in preserving and transmitting the pericope in its present shape, even if they were fully known to us, would not assist us in any further interpretation.

[1] See Rm ii.1. If it is not in the *dharmaśāstra* it is because there the litigant cannot be a witness in his own cause, and the rules relating to competence of witnesses (p. 179 n. 4 above) need not be extended to cover the complainant himself: Vācaspati Miśra, *Vyavahāracintāmaṇi*, ed. Rocher (Ghent 1956), 189ff. The point is taken in Shakespeare's *Measure for Measure*, Act II, sc. 1. The civil-law position on witnesses is set out at length in Bartolus and Nellus respectively in their *Tractatus Testimoniorum* (in Bartolus *Super Authenticis* and other editions). Its hostility to tainted accusers is shown in G. Durandus, *Speculum Judiciale*, and, for example, in *Baldi Ubaldi Perusini in* [*Nonum*] *Codicis Librum Comm.* (Venetiis 1577), fo. 190*v*, col. ii (tit. *de iis qui accusare non possunt*): 'repelluntur [ab accusando] propter infamiam vitae, periculum participationis, ut excommunicati . . ., rationem poenalitatis, ut banniti. . . .'

[2] *Mishnāh*, Soṭāh I. 1; VI. 3.

[3] *m*e*nūḳeh mē'āon*. Soṭāh 28*a* = Sonc. 137–8; 47*b* = Sonc. 251–2. Becker, 60, aptly cites Tar. Onḳ. *meḥoviyn* for M.T. *mē'āon* at Nb v.31. The connection between the text of Hosea (iv.14) which is cited most relevantly in the b. (see Soṭ. 47*b*, *cit. sup.*), the history of Soṭāh, and our pericope was noticed and understood as long ago as the beginning of this century: see D. W. Amram (cited above), *JE* I, art. 'Adultery'. Stauffer utilises the point differently at 'Neue Wege' (cited above), 469.

A NOTE ON PHINEHAS

Origen [? 185–253] relates (*in Joan.*, *tom. vi*: Migne, *P.G.* XIV, 225), in connection with Jn i.21 ('They asked him, What then? Art thou Elijah?'), that the Jews traditionally accounted Phinehas to be Elijah. This, he says, was surprisingly achieved, οὐκ οἶδα πόθεν κινούμενοι, evidently by a *midrash* of the words 'my covenant [a covenant] of peace' in Nb xxv.12, which were supposed to convey immortality upon Phinehas. Origen adverts to Herod's misconception, and to a confusion Elijah–Phinehas–John–Jesus at least as a possibility. If the *midrash* in question existed at the time of our pericope (which is nearly certain) we should be entitled to suppose (i) that Phinehas's action was of prophetic value as a precedent, and (ii) that Jesus might be expected to be, if not an enthusiastic, at any rate an authoritative commentator upon it. Origen's report is supported by *midrash* and *targum*,[1] and the whole subject of Phinehas's reward and fame has been expounded in a learned article by A. Spiro, who shows[2] that the ascension of Phinehas was necessitated by certain Jewish–Samaritan polemics, and fully disposes of Origen's puzzlement.

[1] SHLWM has a defective *vāv*. Ps. Philo, *Bibl. Ant.* XLVIII (trans. M. R. James, 1917, p. 210–11). See Mid. R., Num. XXI. 3 (Sonc., 829, n. 7); Sifre Num. § 131 (Kuhn, 527; Levertoff, 143); *Targ. ps. Jon.* (Etheridge II, 436); Pirḳe d^{e} R. El. § 47, trans. G. Friedlander (London 1916), 213, 371.
[2] 'The ascension of Phinehas', *Proc. Am. Ac. Jew. Res.* 22 (1953), 91–114.

CHAPTER EIGHT

The Lamp Which Must Not Be Hidden (Mk iv.21)

JESUS'S SAYING ABOUT LIGHTING and placing a lamp is very famous, having given rise to the popular comment about a man that he hides, or does not hide, as the case may be, his light under a bushel. But there is no certainty as to the original form of the saying, and none whatever about its original meaning.[1] It is plainly a wandering saying, which had lost a definite identity well before the synoptic gospels were compiled and, since Luke uses it twice in two different contexts and forms, we have reason for thinking that even his highly skilled advisers had lost contact with a distinct tradition as to its real meaning. We recollect that distinctness, opposition, 'not this, but that', is an occidental and not an oriental intellectual virtue—the oriental being far more inclined towards 'both this and that', more tolerant of the overlapping and the incongruous—but that is no consolation to us, as we grope for traces of an original occasion when the saying could first have been uttered. There is room for imagination here, and it has (as usual) not been wanting.

To make matters worse, the second of the Lucan versions immediately precedes a very difficult passage about the 'lamp of the body', and it has naturally been a matter of doubt whether originally the two

[1] The synoptic material and its earlier interpretations were fully considered by A. Jülicher, *Die Gleichnisreden Jesu* II (Tübingen 1910), 79–88. Also R. Bultmann, *Die Geschichte der Synopt. Trad.* (1931 edn), 96f., who shows that Lk xi.36 is meaningless except to prove that *vv.* 35–6 are attempts to explain a dark saying. J. Jeremias supposed that the alternative to placing on the stand was extinguishing the light—a careful note at *Parables of Jesus*, 6th edn, rev. trans. S. H. Hooke (London 1963), p. 120–1. See also W. D. Davies, *The Setting of the Sermon on the Mount* (Cambridge 1964), 249, 457. Bultmann, in *Form Criticism* (*cit. sup.*), 54 compares Mk iv.21 with the saying 'You don't beat a drum under a rug', and then suggests (55) that 'the primitive community placed in his mouth many a beautiful saying that was really derived from the treasure of Jewish proverbial lore'. Wisdom-sayings are not, says Bultmann, really significant, and are probably unauthentic. K. Kundsin's idea (*ibid.* 108) was that our saying was owed to the early Church as it determined that the message must be released and made public.

sayings about lamps had any contact with each other. Since the difficult passage is nearly unintelligible without some clue which has eluded us, there is an advantage in assuming before we start that an intellectual, midrashic, link was there prior to Luke's incorporating the passage, and that the saying about the lighting of a lamp was retained for the second time because it had an integral intellectual connection with the puzzling passage in question. This is a guess, though a reasonable one: we shall find below that it works out very well. Meanwhile no one will undertake research into the sayings about the lamp without first consulting Dr Conny Edlund's *Das Auge der Einfalt*,[1] which appears to have an exhaustive bibliography. His conclusions embrace the subjects of *simplicity* and *generosity*, utilising a full investigation of the language of the sayings in Greek and Hebrew counterparts. But he has not stumbled on the clues which will be given below: it would have been interesting to see how different his conclusions would have been if he had.

We must first tackle the saying about lighting a lamp. On the surface it is a very silly saying. No one lights a lamp *in order* to hide it. The saying is reported by the evangelists in a form which is recognisably halakic. Jesus is evidently making a legal pronouncement, as we shall see below. And this gives a clue. The words 'in order to' can refer to an *intention*, and intention is frequently a factor of great juridical importance. It is a commonplace of Jewish thought that when a man complies with a commandment he must act in obedience to it, with the intention of fulfilling it. This is one reason why the blessings which form so large a part of the observant Jew's ritual day refer explicitly to the commandments and rehearse the fact that the action which is being sanctified is one which is commanded, whether by the biblical or the rabbinical law. Therefore Jesus's saying, if correctly reported, must have had something to do with a lamp the lighting of which is a religious–legal obligation, and which must be lit with a particular intention in mind. The

[1] *Acta Seminar. Neotest. Upsal.* 19 (Kopenhagen/Lund 1952). He points out, citing M. Dibelius, *Die Botschaft von Jesus Christus* (1935), 135, that the saying is completely dark. A great merit of Dr Edlund's work is the demonstration that Lk xi.34*b–c* is the kernel of the passage to which the rest is appendage. The whole concept of 'simplicity' is studied, and general approval is given to C. Spicq's article, 'La vertu de simplicité dans l'Ancient et le Nouveau Testament', *Rev. Sc. Phil. Theol.* 22 (1933), 5–26 (our passage is dealt with at p. 15–18: the lamp is the doctrine of Christ; the single eye is that which enables one to see straight). The fact that ἁπλότης is a leading notion in the Testaments of the Twelve Patriarchs is of great interest (Edlund, 62ff.), and these works may quite possibly be pre-Christian. In Dr Edlund's view the best exegesis of the logion is Mk x.15. Neither Dr Edlund nor Fr Spicq have much use for the study by W. Brandt, who dealt with 'Der Spruch vom lumen internum' at *ZNW* 14 (1913), 97–116, 177–201.

actions he refers to (if he did refer to them) must be such as relate to that intention. As one might well guess, it turns out that there is no proposition in Jewish law that a man must light a lamp with the intention of hiding it! Is this a truism then?

Apparently it is not a truism. The saying was so good that, far from being cryptic to the point of being unusable, it has been used, it would seem, too often! Many different meanings were read into it, as the evangelists witness. This places the scholar in very grave difficulties. Is this a case where the Jewish pious mind has put Jesus's saying to uses for which he himself would never have allowed room? A common difficulty. All we can do is to cast out our net, and see what we catch. What we shall not reject should be either (1) what Jesus meant, or (2) what he could reasonably have been thought to mean by those in a good position to form an impression on the subject. Since so able a person as Our Lord must have taken account of the possible difference between (1) and (2)—he was after all communicating with people, not making pronouncements in the air—there is some justification for rejecting, at our stage in the research, only what cannot reasonably be included within either of those categories.

In order to arrive at the original *form* of the saying we need to know whether Jesus could have referred specifically to the places where the lamp might be hidden. Up to now it has been supposed that Jews would never want to hide a lamp under a 'bushel' or a bed. But since it is a fact that they would wish to do so, and that too in a rather interesting connection, and since 'bed' is really the 'punch' word of the saying, there is good reason for assuming that Jesus actually referred to the bed—better still to the actual means of hiding mentioned in Mk iv.21 in so many words—and going on to see what situation he could have had in mind. Jews did act somewhat high-handedly with lamps.

LIGHTING A LAMP AND HIDING IT

Let us grasp these facts first, and then state our problem and offer the solution.

The inverting of a vessel over a lamp, or placing a partition between it (the lamp) and people is a perfectly well-known act in Jewish law. It would tend to happen on numerous days within the Jewish year, and on none so obviously as the Hanukkah days. The topic shows Jewish fussiness at its best, and is quite fun to follow through. The problem arises because certain lights must not be extinguished. Various tricks were tried to induce lamps to go out, but the rabbis resolutely forbade any extinguishing of a lamp at any time when extinguishing fire was 'work' and so forbidden. It is known to everyone that kindling a fire or extinguishing a fire (including lamps, of course) was forbidden on the Sabbath and on the festival days (the beginning and end of Passover, Pentecost, New Year, and first and eighth day of Tabernacles). Lamps would therefore burn until they went out naturally. One would see to it that as little oil was put in as necessary and the shallow little lamps that most people had were not built for all-night illumination. Now it is (or ought to be) not less well known that sexual intercourse was forbidden (or at any rate taboo) in the immediate presence of a lighted lamp. Yet intercourse (though it could conceivably be classed as work) was commended by Pharisees, though not actually commanded, on the evening or night of the Sabbath;[1] and it certainly was not forbidden on the festive and joyous occasions, which must often coincide with the prohibition of extinguishing the lamp. This created a problem which everyone knew about. The obvious answer was to take one or other of the three following courses (note them carefully!): (1) to cover the lamp by placing a vessel on top of it, as by inverting the vessel (*k^e^liy*); (2) placing a partition between the light and the people concerned (whether that partition consisted of a vessel which could not be inverted or some other suitable substance or division); or (3) carrying the light into some other room, building or structure.[2] In order of ease, perhaps No. 2 would come first. Before conjugal intercourse it would often happen that the wife tested herself to make sure that no breach occurred of the very severe taboo against contact with a menstruant, and the need for the lamp was plain. So to shove the little lamp under the bed was the easiest and most obvious thing to do with it. Or one could turn a pot over on top of it (and one can think of a pot suitable for the purpose).[3]

On the days when work was forbidden, and when people were bound to eat as well as ever they could and to rejoice, the likelihood that conjugal intercourse would take place was particularly strong. Therefore the problem of what to do with the lamp was one with which

[1] Maimonides, *Mishneh Torāh* III (Seasons), I, xxx, 14 (trans. Gandz and Klein, New Haven, 1961, p. 197) relies upon b. Ket. 61*b*, 62*b* = Sonc. 369, 376 (referring to Ex xxi.10). Older sects, perhaps including the Essenes, disapproved of intercourse on the Sabbath (Jub l.8). On the last passage see R. H. Charles's note at *Apocrypha and Pseudepigrapha* II, 81–2 (but the rule need not belong to the 'fanatical period' to which he alludes). That the Samaritans disapproved is most interesting.

[2] Maimonides, *Mishneh Torāh* III, IV, iv, 4 (trans. p. 286) relies upon *Mishnāh* Bets. IV.4 (Danby, 196) and b. Bets. 22*a* = Sonc. 113, 32*a–b* = Sonc. 165. Jeremias, *ubi cit. sup.*, referred to Bets. 22*a* but failed to catch the point.

[3] It is important to realise that the nature of locally-produced vessels and the level of the domestic floor would seldom produce an air-tight seal, so that to invert the vessel would not necessarily extinguish the light (as Jeremias suggests)—therefore one could invert without intending to extinguish the lamp (which was a forbidden intention).

everybody will have been quite familiar. But the days of Hanukkah created a special problem, which rendered the action of the couple with regard to their lights the subject of greater attention than usual. We have seen the third alternative above. On the festival nights one could take the lamp and put it in an underground room, or cupboard, or any more or less 'hidden' place. The lamp, after all, had no significance in itself once it had been lit. But the Hanukkah lamp was different. It was lit as a lamp not to give light but to advertise something abstract (as we shall see in detail below), so that it must not be extinguished, for a different reason from that which obtained with the Sabbath and other festival lights. These last could not be put out because extinguishing would be work. On the eight nights of Hanukkah work as such was not in itself forbidden. Extinguishing a lamp was not forbidden then, so obviously people who did not care much for Hanukkah (if there were any such—and one could be scrupulous if wastage of oil was at stake!) would simply extinguish the lamp. The Pharisee rabbis would object very strongly to this, and so would ardent patriots, as we shall see. Now assuming that the household took Hanukkah seriously, and regarded their Hanukkah lamp as an object to be reverenced, what would they do with it at bed-time? Eight days (or rather nights) is a long time, and the problem experienced on festival nights would arise in an acute form. Naturally people would want to extinguish the lamp, or if they scrupled to do this they would, just as naturally, adopt the normal course with the Sabbath and festival lamps. But there was a difficulty about the third alternative. A Hanukkah lamp, being on the way to becoming a cult object in itself (that is to say irrespective of its superstitious survival, if it did so survive, from pre-Jewish cults), could not be moved about. It must be lit and placed where it is to shine, and must not be carried around. It is, after all, as we shall see, not intended for illumination as such. So, strictly speaking, it should not be carried out of the room and placed in a cellar, still less in a draughty place where it might blow out. Thus people who cared, as a great many must have done, for the Hanukkah lamp, would be quite used to putting it under the bed, under utensils, or inverting utensils over it. Now our present study is about the implications of this—the implications which one could legitimately draw from this common domestic habit, at first hand, and also at second hand.

But we have not done with the simple act of inverting a vessel over something. We have seen that the lamp might be hidden to enable the master of the house and his wife to pursue their normal conjugal life without transgressing a taboo. The action of inverting the vessel recalls yet another situation, and that a most inauspicious one: when someone was dying in the house anything which ought to be protected from death-uncleaness must either be removed or placed in a container or underground chamber and covered. *e.g.* with an inverted basket.[1] The inverted vessel is thus a symbol of the presence of death, the greatest source of ritual pollution.

Now let us look carefully at our texts. They have to be scrutinised synoptically, individually, and in context, against the background of this new information.

THE TEXTS AND OUR PROBLEM

In Mt v.15 we read: 'Nor do men burn a lamp and place it under the bushel (or "measure": μόδιος), but on the lampstand, and it shines for all in the house.' The language of Mark is more idiomatic, argumentative (iv.21): '... surely the lamp "comes" not in order to be placed under the bushel or under the bed? Is it not in order to be placed on the lampstand?' Literally the Marcan version could be taken to refer to an *unlit* lamp (so Austin Farrer takes it),[2] but the other four versions show that the lamp is lit: and in any case an unlit lamp hardly 'comes'. The two Lucan versions (viii.16 and xi.33) insist upon the lamp's being 'lit'. The first speaks of under a 'utensil' (σκεῦος is exactly *k^eliy*) and the bed as unsuitable places for the lamp, the second speaks of a 'cellar' and the 'bushel' (or 'measuring vessel'). Both agree that the action disapproved of in the saying is a hiding. Both agree, as against Matthew and Mark, that the motive for the correct procedure is that 'those who come in' shall 'look upon' or 'see' the light. In Luke's case we doubt whether the two versions came from a single original, or from two originals, themselves derived from, perhaps, a single ultimate source. The fifth piece of evidence is in 'Thomas' (§ 33 in Aland's *Synopsis*, App. I).[3] The undesirable alternatives are there in the reversed order, while the motive offered for the correct placing is that the light may be seen by those who go in *and come out*. The variations between Matthew and Luke have until now been understood as reflecting the different milieux of the evangelists. It is often said that Luke envisages a Hellenistic, Matthew a Jewish home. Here we offer another suggestion. The

[1] *Mishnāh*, *'Oholot* (prop. *'Āh^alot*) V.6, XI. 8–9 (Danby, 656, 666; Blackman VI, 221–2, 257–8). On the insusceptibility of wooden receptacles to uncleanness—and thus their fitness to serve as a protection (for the lamp itself) against pollution—the intricate rules of Kel. XV, 1 (Danby, 625; Blackman, VI, 103) are of interest.

[2] *A Study in St Mark* (London 1951), 244. Farrer is misled by the prevailing motif of the context, hiding, concealing until the moment of revelation: and of course a lit lamp could not be 'stowed away'. But the Jewish facts disperse this notion.

[3] Log. 34 (87.10–18) in earlier publications.

Hanukkah lamp, which has a long history and an involved cultural significance, could serve to explain the divergencies between the versions, and perhaps explain what was the original saying itself, and how it came to have the applications which we find attached to it. It is far from certain that the saying, with its elaborations, could have applied to any ordinary lamp; we have seen that the problem of extinguishing a Sabbath or festival light was less serious than that of extinguishing the Hanukkah lamp.

HANUKKAH—ENCAENIA[1]

Though the festival known as Hanukkah was popular in Jesus's time, the synoptic gospels do not refer to it directly. It was the festival of lights referred to by Josephus,[2] alluded to vaguely by Philo.[3] It was distinctively Palestinian, and required (as we see from 2 M, the prefatory letters of which appear to belong to the second century before Christ) explanation to expatriate communities. Hanukkah corresponds roughly to Christmastide,[4] which to this day it strikingly resembles in outward manifestations. Every adult male Jew must, as a religious obligation, rejoice and advertise his rejoicing by kindling a lamp on each of the eight nights of the festival. The origins of the festival were really pre-Jewish. The 'historical' documents of the Maccabaean period fostered a myth to explain the custom, and Talmudic learning shows the myth in full flower.[5] The two great themes of Hanukkah were the coming of

[1] Properly *ḥanukkāh*. See Ps xxx (the festival psalm). Kaufmann Kohler, 'Ḥanukkah' (*Jewish Encyclopaedia* vi [1925], 223–6). Theodor Schärf, *Das Gottesdienstliche Jahr der Juden* (Schr. des Inst. Jud., Berlin, no. 30) (Leipzig 1902), 92–6 is most important, but contains post-Talmudic material. The blessings are found there and at Maimonides, *Mishneh Torāh* III, x (Hilkot Megillāh ve Ḥanukkāh), 3 (trans. p. 454–5), and in the Prayer Books, where the Megillat Ḥanukkāh (*Megillat Ta'anit*, § 23) is reprinted, *e.g.* at p. 546–7 of A. Hyman Charlap's *Sidur Tifereth Jehudah* (New York 1912, etc.). For further references see E. Schürer, *Geschichte des Jüdischen Volkes im Zeitalter Jesu Christi*, 2nd edn, i (Leipzig 1890), p. 161–2 n. 58 (in the trans. of J. Macpherson (Edinburgh 1890), i, 217–18); also G. F. Moore, *Judaism* II (Cambridge, Mass. 1927, 1958), 49–50. O. S. Rankin, *The Origins of the Festival of Hanukkah* (Edinburgh 1930). F.-M. Abel, 'La fête de la Hanoucca', *RB* 53 (1946), 538–46. R de Vaux, *Ancient Israel*, 2nd edn (London 1965), 510–14.

[2] *Ant.* XII.316–25 = XII.6–7; *Contra Ap.* II.118 = II.9.

[3] *De Congres. Erud. gr.* XXI.114 (Colson IV, 514–17).

[4] Commencing on the 25th Chislev (see the Megillat Ta'anit, *ubi cit. sup.*) Moses dedicated *his* altar, so says *haggadāh*, on that day (the proper day for the rededication of anything): Midrash R., Exod. LII.

[5] Nehemiah's sacrifice (2 M i.22, 32) is read with the Maccabaean rededication (1 M iv.36–50, 56, 59; 2 M x.1–8); b. Shab. 21*b* = Sonc. 92; Meg. Ta'an., *cit. sup.* M. Gaster, 'The scroll of the Hasmonaeans' in Gaster, *Studies and Texts* I (London 1925–8) 165ff. at p. 183. W. O. E. Oesterley, *Books of the Apocrypha* (London 1914),

light as a gift associated with God, and the coming forth of the hidden (*e.g.* the returning sun) from the depths (*i.e.* the solstitial darkness). The allusions associated with the festival are important for us. 'Kindling the lamp' could be a parable for morally significant behaviour.

At Hanukkah the Jews remembered the miraculous fires which played important rôles in biblical history.[1] God 'answered prayer by fire' (1 K xviii.24). One called to mind occasions when divine fire was associated with the redemption motif and kindred crises of the Jewish nation:[1] Moses, Lv ix.24; Gideon, Jg vi.21; Manoah, Jg xiii.19, 20; Elijah, 1 K xviii.38; David, 1 Ch xxi.26; and Solomon, 2 Ch vii.1. Gideon, approved with heavenly fire, did his redemptive work with the aid of lights emerging from darkness,[2] in a story which obviously blends symbolism with an otherwise exciting narrative. Judas Maccabaeus's rededication of the Temple drew all the themes together. This was the proximate example, in Jesus's time, of God's manifesting his concern for Israel by some heavenly fire. This was also the last non-biblical miracle,[3] and therefore to some extent a parallel or test for the miracles of Jesus. Hanukkah itself was supposed to have been founded by Judas Maccabaeus to commemorate his triumph, and the Jews commemorated this and the miraculous lights of the occasion together by lighting the Hanukkah lamp. Pharisees debated—and the debate can be traced to the schools contemporary with Jesus—how many lights should be lit on each of the eight nights, but this discussion is not important, except in so far as it shows that some scholars were anxious to inculcate Jewish, and minimise pagan, motives in the lamp-kindling—for the method whereby the number of wicks was increased from one to eight fitted pagan sympathetic magical practices too neatly.[4]

[1] Notice how explicitly Moses, Solomon, Nehemiah and Judas Maccabaeus are connected at 2 M ii.8*b*–14. Solomon kept the eight days: 2 M ii.13 (*cf.* 1 K viii.65–6). J. Morgenstern, *The Fire upon the Altar* (Leiden 1963) is of general interest in this connection.

[2] Jg vii.20. Gideon was the Moses of his day; b. R.H. 25*b* = Sonc. 111. The redemption theme is manifested during Hanukkah by the daily recital of the Hallel (Ps cxiii–cxviii). Gideon showed how lights must come *out* of pots and *shine*!

[3] b. Yom. 29*a* = Sonc. 136; *Midrash on Psalms*, Ps. xxi, § 10 (Braude I, 306).

[4] C. Colpe, 'Lichtsymbolik im alten Iran und antiken Judentum', *Studium Generale* 18, no. 2 (1965) (an issue devoted to light and darkness), 116–33.

490–2. H. E. Del Medico, in 'Le cadre historique des fêtes de Hanukkah et de Purîm', *VT* 15 (1965), 238–70 gives additional information on the current justification of the feast of Hanukkah. The *Yosippon* has been scrutinised and provides new material. At p. 242–6 we are shown the account of miraculous discovery of fire, and again at p. 247–50 we are told of Judas Maccabaeus's purification, in which fire came from the stones on the altar. The work, therefore, combines all the legends which are elsewhere separate. See also S. Zeitlin, ed., *II Macc.*, trans. S. Tedesche (New York 1954), 43–6, 101–15. J. Morgenstern at *HUCA* 20 (1947), 1–136; 21 (1948), 365–496.

Together with the series of heavenly fires, and the victory over the Gentile desecrators of the Temple, those who celebrated Hanukkah were celebrating the coming forth of something hidden (not in fact the 'hidden' sun, but hidden fire or the hidden flask of pure oil supposed to have been discovered), the revelation in due time of that which was deliberately hidden, hidden only in order to be revealed. This is evident as we read the various ancient accounts of Judas's dedication of the Temple.[1]

Talmudic teaching tells what was done with the Hanukkah lamp in the third century. The information is in principle relevant for earlier times, since there is no reason why the customs should have changed significantly. Every Jewish home must rejoice with this lamp, and must spend the necessary amount of oil (at least half-an-hour's worth). The lamp was blessed by a blessing special to it. In effect, when lit, the lamp manifested socio-political solidarity.[2] The defeat of the Gentiles of 165 B.C. was celebrated. But religion required the lighter of the lamp to bless God, recalling 'the miracles Thou has done *in days of old* for our fathers *at this season*'. The words in italics are taken from a more modern form of the blessing,[3] but one notices that the constant factor is the recalling of *miracles*, not merely the 'miracle' of the returning light after the solstice, nor the miracles of the heavenly fire nor the light in Judas Maccabaeus's candlestick, but the miracles done by God for his people. Now it is essential to notice that, because of the advertisement-principle, not only he who lights a Hanukkah lamp but also he who *sees* one must say a blessing.[4] Whether this rule was known in Jesus's time is not clear: but the Talmudic rule derives directly from the fundamental function of the Hanukkah lamp, and fits exactly with what Luke and 'Thomas' say about the lamp of which Jesus speaks—indeed it is the only lamp whose function is to cheer 'those who come in', as we shall see.

A household with a window on to the street placed the lamp where the light could be seen outside; in Talmudic Law the lamp must be placed in the window.[5] A house which opened on to a courtyard would naturally display the lamp where the light was visible both to the occupants and passers-by. One recollects that the Maccabaean miracle was supposed to have occurred with relation to the candlestick in the

[1] See p. 195 n. 1 above.

[2] Note the tone of the 2 M account (*cit. sup.*). In time of danger the lamp may be placed on a table (and not in the window): b. Shab 21*b* = Sonc. 92.

[3] Maimonides gives the blessing as follows: 'Blessed art Thou, Lord . . . to light the lamp of Hanukkah, and hast done miracles for our fathers . . . '.

[4] b. Shab. 23*a* = Sonc. 99.

[5] b. Shab. 21*b* = Sonc. 91.

Temple. This would justify an attempt to keep the lamp in the appropriate place in the living-room of the family (perhaps their only room), provided that the light could be seen from outside. When dwellings opened regularly on to the street the usage developed of having the lamps at the left of the entrance, whether or not they could be seen from within. But most homes had more than one adult male, so that a Hanukkah lamp within the living-room and one or more at the entrance would be possible. The lamp is expected to be stationary. A lamp placed on a lampstand in the entrance of the living-room from the courtyard would serve both purposes, domestic celebration and advertisement of the miracle. When placed outside, the Jewish Law will not allow the lamp to be too high or too low. It would be in a sconce or bracket (not exactly a lampstand). It could actually endanger passers-by.[1] But if we imagine the living-room entered from a central courtyard, where the Hanukkah lamp was in its most important place, the focus of the family, a certain complication and an embarrassment arose even earlier than bedtime and the problems we have indicated above.

THE RELIGIOUS CHARACTER OF THE HANUKKAH LAMP

The lamp undoubtedly had political implications, but to light it was a religious obligation.[2] The home must imitate the Temple where the miracle of the candlestick was believed to have occurred. The family must rejoice in the light, but not *profit* from it. This is normal with things which the *Torāh* says one must have as a religious obligation—one has not fulfilled the obligation if the thing is used for a secular purpose. One of the modern blessings said over the lamp actually mentions the 'commandment' not to use the light of the lamp. One must not count coins by that light,[3] and *a fortiori* one must not do any work of a secular character. According to normal Pharisaical reasoning it would be wrong to spare one's oil, to light only the Hanukkah lamp, and so to kill two birds with one stone. As there was an obligation to feast,[4] work of some kind would often follow the lighting. If the family could afford a candlestick (*m*ᵉ*norāh*) the secular lights were placed on top, and the Hanukkah light lower down (as in the modern Hanukkah lamp the 'servitor' lamp is to be seen higher than the eight Hanukkah

[1] *Mishnāh*, B.Ḳ. VI.6 (Danby, 340); b. Shab. 21*b* = Sonc. 93.

[2] Rabbis seeking for scriptural support for it at length chose Dt xvii.11 or xxxii.7 (b. Sukk. 46*a* = Sonc. 213–14). But it is equally a commandment, whether based on written or oral tradition.

[3] b. Shab. 22*a* = Sonc. 94.

[4] It was sinful to fast: b. Shab. 21*b*; 'Er. 41*a* = Sonc. 283; R.H. 18*b* = Sonc. 76; Ta'an. 15*b* = Sonc. 72.

wicks). If the Hanukkah light was on the floor it could not be proved what or how much work was illuminated by rays of light from the festive lamp. If the house had no *m^e^norāh*, and there were few or no other lamps, the Hanukkah light had somehow to be hidden, not so that its rays would not be seen, still less so that it might be extinguished, but so that no rays illuminated work. The alternative was to enjoy the light, but to be idle. The Talmud mentions hiding the lamp in times of intolerance;[1] so that to light the lamp and then hide it was not unthinkable—but there had to be a good excuse.

If one covered or hid the lamp one could work. If one did not, out of respect for the lamp and what it symbolised, one played party games or told stories of Judith or other tales of suitably edifying anti-pagan prowess. If one was going to hide the lamp, where would be the best place? Somewhere where, without setting fire to anything or extinguishing the lamp, the rays would be visible and yet not able to illuminate work. The measuring vessel, with its four legs,[2] a vessel which could be inverted, or the bed, kept off the ground (except in time of mourning) for fear of insects, etc., would be ideal places. We have already seen that when bed-time came people had an additional reason for hiding the light by such methods.

THE FORM OF THE SAYING

Because of the variations between the versions there is some fear that Jesus himself might not have referred to the 'bushel' or the bed. The lighting and the lampstand are no doubt fixed and certain points in the saying.

That the pronouncement is halakic, normative, is obvious.[3] The

[1] b. Shab. 45*a* = Sonc. 204.

[2] K. Galling, 'Die Beleuchtungsgeräte im israelitisch–jüdischen Kulturgebiet', *Z.d. Deut. Palästinavereins* 46 (1923), 1–50; A. Dupont-Sommer, 'Note archéologique sur le proverbe évangélique: Mettre la lampe sous le boisseau', *Mélanges Syriens ... René Dussaud* II (Paris 1939), 789–94.

[3] D. Daube, *The New Testament and Rabbinic Judaism* (London 1956), 90–102, draws attention to the distinction between the biblical positive and negative commandments and the rabbinical form. The form 'No one does ...' may be found in fact where the prohibition is against an act which is only barely conceivable, *e.g.* 'No addition may be made to the City or to the Temple Courts except by the (decision of the) king ...' (*Mishnāh*, Shev. II.2: *'eyn mosiyphiyn 'al hā-'iyr v^e^-'al hā-'^a^zārot, 'ellā' b^e^-melek ...*). At Ga iii.15 Paul uses the form in regard to the all-too-tempting. So at 2 Tm ii.4. But one must admit that the 'No one does ...' form hovers at times between the 'One must not ...' and the 'One need not'. An example appears in connection with giving alms (other than trifles) to door-to-door beggars (b. B.B. 9*a*): '... they do not attend to him (*'eyn niz^e^ḳaḳiyn lo*) means both 'they are justified in not attending to him' and 'it is not the custom to attend to him'. In our instance 'No one lights ...' should mean 'It is not the (correct) practice to light ...'. And so we should have a parallel with *Mishnāh*, 'Er. VIII.6, *'eyn m^e^mal^e^'iyn*, 'no one draws (water on the Sabbath)'.

scribes phrase their ordinances in the form 'They do . . .', or 'They do not', the last implying 'No one does . . .', and therefore 'Don't . . .'. As we have seen, the idea 'in order to' refers to intention. When lighting the lamp the intention must not be to hide it for the family to pursue secular tasks or personal pleasures, but to celebrate miracles. The implication is that it is sinful to light the lamp with such incongruous motives. From this we get the idea that you light the lamp with the correct intention, fully realising that you do so at the cost of any inconvenience that may be caused thereby to yourself.

That Jesus particularised the 'bushel' and the 'bed' is very likely, because they at once call to mind the motives which ordinary people had for paying lip-service to the obligation whilst pursuing their normal affairs. The bushel symbolises the cooking and other domestic tasks before bed-time, the bed indicates what it most obviously would.

Mark's version already tells us that an oral explanation was available. The word 'the' prefixed to 'lamp' indicated that a special lamp was in view;[1] the definite article appears again at Lk xi.36. 'The' lamp would, if it is original, mean only such a lamp as would give rise to the action immediately spoken of, and in Jewish Law in all its strictness it is the Hanukkah lamp which meets the requirements. 'The' candlestick would refer to the lampstand of the home, perhaps not without an allusion to the candlestick of the Temple: the same word meant either.[2]

The Church supposed that Jesus associated physical and spiritual illumination with the season of Hanukkah, for it was at that season that the man born blind was given his sight.[3]

THE USES OF THE SAYING IN THE GOSPELS

Does the saying refer to Jesus himself, to his disciples, or to the truly pious? Was the lamp actual, metaphorical or both?

Matthew already has a spiritual interpretation incorporated in the

[1] The other view, that the definite article is purely generic, is frequently held (for example, C. H. Dodd, *Historical Tradition in the Fourth Gospel* [Cambridge 1965], 380).

[2] λυχνία in the LXX invariably renders *m^enorāh*, so also in the apocryphal literature. One may compare the implications of the word in Revelation. There is no ground for arguing that *m^enorāh* could not have meant the household lampstand, but if Jesus's saying had included *bim^eḳomo* ('in its place') without the reference to the lampstand which is a fixed point in all our versions of the saying, that objection would be removed. But the argument is unnecessary. λυχνία, though it means *m^enorāh* in all the LXX contexts, has the general meaning of 'lampstand', the place for holding a lamp or lamps, and that is, after all, all that is required.

[3] Jn x.22.

saying, irrespective of its context: οὐδὲ καίουσιν λύχνον καὶ τιθέασιν αὐτὸν ὑπὸ τὸν μόδιον, ἀλλ' ἐπὶ τὴν λυχνίαν, καὶ λάμπει πᾶσιν τοῖς ἐν τῇ οἰκίᾳ. Since Matthew mentions only 'measure' it has been suspected that his version is nearer to the original than Mark's.[1] But we may well wonder, knowing what we now do. 'Measure' seems to have been used as a catch-word at an early stage,[2] but that may be quite irrelevant. Matthew insists that the light burns for all in the house (including those who are not inconvenienced by it?). But placing the lamp on the stand would hardly have that effect, unless the family were intent on celebrating the miracle. Matthew wants the lamp and what it symbolises to be central to the family's thoughts. The Children of Israel ('in the house') must rejoice in divine miracles, amongst which, of course, those of Jesus are to be counted. It is just possible that in 'house' we have a covert allusion to the Temple, which is referred to as 'the house'.

The Marcan formulation seems to point to a miracle, and to Jesus himself. He is to be placed on some kind of 'lampstand'. . . . μήτι ἔρχεται ὁ λύχνος ἵνα ὑπὸ τὸν μόδιον τεθῇ ἢ ὑπὸ τὴν κλίνην; οὐχ ἵνα ἐπὶ τὴν λυχνίαν τεθῇ; The hidden is to be revealed. If this is correct it is only a step to Jn viii.12*b* ('I am the Light of the World'), and indeed to Jn i.9: Jesus shines upon all men, whether or not they accept it. The variant reading ὑπὸ τὴν λυχνίαν, which occurs in respectable manuscript tradition, must not be ignored. A careless scribe could well have written ὑπό for ἐπί: but the wide retention of the error (if it is one) could be permitted only on conscious reflection. A scholarly Jewish reader will have known that the lamp, if not hidden, must be placed perceptibly lower than the secular lights, and so the very odd expression 'under the lampstand' looks rabbinically correct. Jesus no doubt wants the lamp to have the chief place, provided that is also the proper place.

Though Mark does not say so, we are justified by the terms of the Lucan and Matthaean versions in believing that Mark too understood Jesus to have anticipated that the light of the lamp would be *enjoyed.* This is important, because otherwise we might have suspected from the references to 'measure', 'bed' (which could be a board on which a dying person was lying), and 'cellar' that the lamp he had in mind was that customarily lit for the dying. Indeed logically no one lights this lamp in order to protect the lampstand from ritual pollution (the point is irrefutable), but that was not the point, because Jesus unquestionably

[1] J. Jeremias at *ZNW* 39 (1940), 237–40.
[2] Vincent Taylor, *ad loc.* (263), citing Bultmann and R. H. Lightfoot. J. Jeremias, *Parables* (*cit. sup.*), 71. D. E. Nineham, *St. Mark* (London 1963), 141.

had in mind an auspicious lamp, to give pleasure, which (on that very account) is not to be treated lightly.

The Lucan textual story is naturally very involved. The idea of the hidden appears in both. At xi.33 the emphasis in the context is hardly on hiding; the unexpected words εἰς κρύπτην (literally 'into a cellar' or a similarly dark spot in the building) make sense when one realises that that is what could be done with a lamp on festival nights *other than* a Hanukkah night—but the literary effect of a literal climax, from cellar to floor-level and thence to the lampstand would have attracted some minds.

Lk viii.16	Lk xi.33
οὐδεὶς δὲ λύχνον ἅψας καλύπτει αὐτὸν σκεύει ἢ ὑποκάτω κλίνης τίθησιν, ἀλλ' ἐπὶ λυχνίας τίθησιν, ἵνα οἱ εἰσπορευόμενοι βλέπωσιν τὸ φῶς.	οὐδεὶς λύχνον ἅψας εἰς κρύπτην τίθησιν οὐδὲ ὑπὸ τὸν μόδιον, ἀλλ' ἐπὶ τὴν λυχνίαν, ἵνα οἱ εἰσπορευόμενοι τὸ φέγγος βλέπωσιν.

In both versions the proper motive for lighting the lamp is not, as in Matthew, so that the family may rejoice, nor, as in Mark, so that the lampstand shall perform its function, but in order that strangers or homecomers shall 'look upon' the light. φέγγος, *splendor*, already has heavenly implications. This agrees perfectly with the Hanukkah light, which is no ordinary light, and which could well be placed (and in Talmudic law must be placed) near an opening or the entrance. It advertises a household loyal to Judaism.

'Thomas' does not share Luke's interest in the conversion of those who are not 'sons of the house'. He wants the light of the enlightened ones to serve for the admiration of the rest of the world, the non-adepts, '... for no one lights a lamp (and) puts it under a bushel, nor does he put it in a hidden place, but he puts it upon the lampstand, so that all who go in and come out may see its light'. Both Luke and 'Thomas' think that oil is to be spent on the stranger and not on the family, and both attribute to the lamp a function which is, in Jewish law, distinctively that of the Hanukkah lamp.

THE SAYING AND ITS SEQUEL IN LUKE

To Matthew the world has a perpetual light in the illuminated ones.[1] It must be seen by strangers. One works at Hanukkah while the lamp

[1] The title *nēr 'olām* for a distinguished rabbi (*Fathers acc. R. Nathan*, § 24, cited by Schöttgen *ad loc.*) is here probably turned by punning into an admonition.

burns: correspondingly the illuminated ones ('you') acquire honour for 'your' Father, who is honoured by the lighting of that lamp, by 'your' deeds. It is a rabbinical commonplace that good deeds, especially in dealings with the non-Jewish world, sanctify the Holy Name (*ḳ*^e^*dūshat ha-Shem*) whereas bad deeds profane it (*ḥiylūl ha-Shem*), thereby discrediting Israel and God.[1] Matthew is concerned with the attraction of converts, no doubt within Israel.

To Mark the saying proved that Jesus was interested in the coming forth of the hidden. The hidden fire and the flask of oil emphasised the pagan theme (see 2 M ii.5–7). Some saw Jesus's sign as that of Jonah. No sooner has Mark emphasised his point than he himself proceeds to deal with Jesus's own miracles (iv.35ff.), true both to the theme of Hanukkah and to the theme of the hidden shining forth.

It has been argued that there is no thematic connection between the saying of the light and the parable of the Sower with its appended matter.[2] Dr M. Gertner has pointed out[3] that the variant reading *nēr* (LXX) for the Masoretic text's *niyr* at Ho x.12, connected with *niyru*, *niyr* ('plough', 'ground') at Jr iv.3, would enable us to recover a comment of Jesus upon Jeremiah as follows: 'Plough the ground, kindle the fire (of thorns), light the lamp (of knowledge).' But it seems that this *midrash* was hidden from Matthew and Luke. In support of Dr Gertner's suggestion one finds in Jr iv.4 the divine fire, playing a role dramatically opposed to the fires celebrated at Hanukkah, a fire which Jeremiah threatens will burn if the command in the immediately previous verse is not obeyed. The parable of the Sower itself may as easily have stemmed from a sermon on Jr xii.13 (where the ambiguous NYR does not appear) as from one on Jr iv.3. We are left, then, with the impression that to Mark the saying meant that kindling must precede far-shining, with the inference that the miracles of God and the custom of the Hanukkah lamp 'prove' Jesus's character and mission, misunderstood, obscure, unrecognised, but finally emerging triumphant and crowning all miracles and all celebrations.

Luke's two passages provide evidence that the saying was interpreted by Christians in two different ways, one of them very ingenious. In ch. viii we have a reproduction of the theme and application closely

[1] Ex xxvi.20. See *e.g.* b. 'A.Z. 28*a* = Sonc. 139; Mekilta on Ex xv.2, Lauterbach II, 25–6; Winter–Wünsche, 124; Moore, *Judaism* II, 104–5. I Pe ii.12.

[2] For the sower-parable (irrespective of its subsequent matter) as a development of the 'seed growing secretly' theme, see K. D. White at *JThS* 15 (1964), 306–7. Also B. Gerhardsson at *NTS* 14 (1968), 165–193.

[3] 'Midrashim in the New Testament' (*Journal of Semitic Studies* 7 (1962), no. 2, p. 267–92, at p. 271–3). For further light on the techniques see the same, 'The Masorah and the Levites' (*VT* 10 (1960), no. 3, p. 241–84, at p. 261–6).

similar to that in Mark. In ch. xi a more impressive movement is undertaken.

We move from the sign of Jonah, which recalls the theme of the hidden and remote, into a passage which is usually slighted as platitudinous or nonsensical (*vv.* 34–6). The technique requires to be explained. At the head of each explanation of Jesus's saying as Luke found it the saying would have had to be repeated as is normal in surviving Tannaitic *midrashim*, where several interpretations are given in turn and the biblical text is recited at the commencement of each. In Mt xxiii.27 and Lk xi.44 we have two different midrashic interpretations of Jesus's saying about Pharisees: Matthew and Luke there preserved independent but supplementary interpretations of Jesus's allusion to Ps v.9.[1] This may well be a parallel case.

Luke's second passage must be compared with its Matthaean counterpart, which has a relatively feeble air and may have been the result of simplification.

Mt vi.22–3	Lk xi.34–6
ὁ λύχνος τοῦ σώματός ἐστιν ὁ ὀφθαλμός. ἐὰν οὖν ᾖ ὁ ὀφθαλμός σου ἁπλοῦς, ὅλον τὸ σῶμά σου φωτεινὸν ἔσται· ἐὰν δὲ ὁ ὀφθαλμός σου πονηρὸς ᾖ, ὅλον τὸ σῶμά σου σκοτεινὸν ἔσται. εἰ οὖν τὸ φῶς τὸ ἐν σοὶ σκότος ἐστίν, τὸ σκότος πόσον.	ὁ λύχνος τοῦ σώματός ἐστιν ὁ ὀφθαλμός σου. ὅταν ὁ ὀφθαλμός σου ἁπλοῦς ᾖ, καὶ ὅλον τὸ σῶμά σου φωτεινόν ἐστιν. ἐπὰν δέ πονηρὸς ᾖ, καὶ τὸ σῶμά σου σκοτεινόν. σκόπει οὖν μὴ τὸ φῶς τὸ ἐν σοὶ σκότος ἐστίν. εἰ οὖν τὸ σῶμά σοι ὅλον φωτεινόν, μὴ ἔχον μέρος τι σκοτεινόν, ἔσται φωτεινὸν ὅλον ὡς ὅταν ὁ λύχνος τῇ ἀστραπῇ φωτίζῃ σε.

One must be patient with Luke's pun. The passage is in two parts. (1) 'The lamp of the body' is of course contrasted with some other lamp, which is presumably that previously spoken of, which we would identify with the Hanukkah lamp. That lamp advertises the beliefs of the family, so the lamp of the body discloses the state within. The method of disclosure has been misunderstood by modern critics. The lamp does not illuminate what is within, but by its quality (the light in the pupil) shows whether the 'wick' is 'trimmed' and the 'oil' good and sufficient. The curious word ἁπλοῦς is appropriate for the loosely twisted ancient wick. The lamp might smoke, resulting in both the

[1] A study of the passages is forthcoming.

absence of light and the addition of 'darkness'. An untrimmed lamp is a good metaphor for an untended soul (cf. Mt xxv.7; Lk xii.35). The eye, which reveals the state of affairs within, is an indicator. In other words something (which we shall suppose is biblical or if non-biblical then in any case authoritative) is midrashically interpreted so as to 'mean' the eye. Here we have a piece of interpretation actually reported. After we have learnt about an actual lamp we learn from it about a metaphorical lamp. Just as the lamp shows, so the eye shows. Commandments or rules relative to the lamp can be transferred by analogy to the maintaining of the eye.

The lamp is the eye, and so the lampholder is the body, or better still, the body is the lamp itself and the eye is the wick. The lamp will be in the dark if the wick is smoking. 'Your light must not be darkness' means simply, 'Tend your soul, your eye will be bright, with all the consequences for yourself and others which that implies.' Certainly ἁπλότης implies integrity.

This metaphor is not yet coupled with the Hanukkah themes; the author proceeds to couple it, so it seems, by an agile application of the figure. (2) The quality of illumination you can cast for others may correspond to the illumination you yourself receive. Every lamp has to be lit. You cannot give light until you have received it. An actual lamp may give more or less than the lamp from which it is lit. If your lamp is, after being lit, entirely light-filled (because your wick is perfect, *i.e.* your eye is bright, *i.e.* your soul is perfect), you yourself are an effectively illuminated person, just as (spiritually) you are when illumination is provided for you by the flash of the light of 'the' lamp. The Hanukkah lamp will cause joy to the beholder. But why a 'flash' (ἀστραπῇ)? Flashing is not expected of any oil lamp. A miracle is referred to. 'Flash' recalls at once lightning (*nogāh, cf.* Hab iii.11). It takes up the φέγγος at *v.* 33 (= *nogāh, cf.* Is lxii.1) which was deliberately chosen instead of φῶς (*cf.* Hab iii.3 LXX) to indicate heavenly illumination. Instantly the secular but sanctified light kindles the Hanukkah lamp; instantly the heart is illuminated; just as the heavenly fire came to the altars throughout biblical history and at Judas Maccabaeus's rededication. Does not the Hanukkah fire ignite you as well as illuminate you? Your eye is (and therefore you are) illuminated by the flash of heavenly light, being ignited by it, and you go on shining afterwards with the perfect brilliance that only heavenly ignition can give. If the eye, as a wick, catches spiritual fire, the body, as the lampstand, lives in the light (without impurity). 'You cannot illuminate others unless you yourselves are entirely irradiated, having taken fire from heavenly splendour'. The populace would understand this. The eye is a commonplace metaphor for the soul, its defects are the defects of the heart and the conscience.[1] For the spirit of man is the lamp of the Lord (Pr xx.27) which allows no dark corners in the 'body'.

THE APPLICATION OF THE SAYING

Jesus may have alluded to this lamp at the most appropriate time, namely Hanukkah, weaving a picture of the coming redemption of Israel round the synagogue lections for that period. Those lections deal with the themes we have mentioned.[2] The burden of the sermon or sermons could have been that what people were celebrating at Hanukkah was a process about to reach fulfilment. The points of such a sermon could have included the following:

1. The redemption of the people has utilised the hidden and the unexpected, and is doing so again.

2. Celebration of the miracles requires not only symbolic lamp-lighting but also revitalised lives.

3. Attention to the festive lamp is praiseworthy. It symbolises the attention we must give to the 'lamp of the body'. Our wicks must be kept 'single'. The illumination and festivity is truly complete when we cause God to be praised and glorified by the godly works which we do.

4. But this end cannot be achieved unless we are ourselves enlightened, and for this we must undergo heavenly illumination. The Redeemer is the immediate source of illumination.

CHRIST IN THE SAYING

The contrast between the domestic disregard for the little lamp and its heavenly significance is striking, not to say harsh. Surely there is yet another lesson in it.

Jewish law teaches, if nothing else, the need to be constantly alert. There may be a deep significance in a trifling act. One must watch one's motive at all times. As St Paul points out in a passage which Christian

[1] Mt vii.3–5; xx.15; Mk vii.22.

[2] Nb vii–viii; Zc iv; 1 K vii.40–50; Lv xxiv. So b. Meg. 30*b* = Sonc. 186–7, 31*a* = Sonc. 190. See on this subject Guilding, *The Fourth Gospel and Jewish Worship*, ch. 9, where great attention is paid to Hanukkah and to Luke. As she shows in her skeleton scheme of lections, Gn xlvi–xlvii and Dt xvii–xviii were set for Hanukkah-time. Have these as much relevance as the others? Genesis deals with family rejoicing and family feasting, while Deuteronomy deals at length with two themes very much to the point, the first false worship, in particular sun-worship and the like, and the second the prophecy of the coming of the prophet (*v.* 16 refers to 'this great fire', a phrase offering midrashic possibilities).

commentators must take to heart,[1] many a biblical commandment has a symbolic meaning far more potent than its literal meaning: the 'wages' of the ox which treads out the corn prefigure not merely the salaries of the clergy but much more besides. The Sabbath lamp is not lit to be extinguished. The Hanukkah lamp is lit for purposes extending beyond the lighting itself which is an obligation. Neither light may be extinguished, but for different reasons. A man who lit the Hanukkah lamp with the intention of afterwards covering or hiding it did not do his duty by lighting that lamp, and the mere fact of having lit it would not avail him. It is a hypocrite who lights a light with seeming joy but with the secret intention of hiding it when an impulsive urge, a human but lower appetite, overcomes him. Indeed all one's acts should be for God's sake: *kol-ma'ᵃseychā yihᵉyū lᵉshēm shāmāyim* (*Mishnāh*, 'Āvot II.12). Those who can be compared to a lamp must be allowed to perform their function, and must not allow themselves to be hindered in performing it. That which is to be a source of joy must not give place to the banal, still less should it be associated with the unclean.

Jesus was welcomed, patronised, praised, and advised. Those who found him useful and edifying could not face the prospect of his being lost to them. He on the contrary was going to give a demonstration of courage such as has not been surpassed, and to set an example which many have emulated, but without it perhaps would have lacked adequate strength. Those who argued with him and told him he was deceived as to the path he should tread[2] are neatly answered by this saying. Just as the little light kindled at Hanukkah is intended to burn itself out in praise of God and his miracles, though people did not scruple to push it under the bed, so it is sinful to disregard heavenly illumination or in any way to impair its capacity to illuminate.

[1] 1 Co ix.9–11.
[2] Mt xvi.22–3.

CHAPTER NINE

The Parable of the Good Samaritan

Lk x.25–37 is variously interpreted and is usually attacked as clumsy and inharmonious. Luke's contrived contexts are so many that one suspects that the parable must be independent of its context.[1] Yet about both much remains to be said. The formerly debated status of the Samaritan *vis-à-vis* Jews was clarified by Professor Joachim Jeremias in his *Jerusalem zur Zeit Jesu*,[2] and other problems still demand attention.

The various interpretations given to the parable through the ages have been studied exhaustively by Werner Monselewski,[3] but the ingenuity and faith exhibited over the centuries have not bridged the gap between Jesus and his predominantly non-Jewish followers. Critical scholarship, not perceiving the true function of the parable, has tended to proceed on the assumption that the author of the pericope lacked intelligence or skill or even both. The point of the parable (and it *is* a parable as well as an illustrative tale or 'wonder story') would escape anyone unacquainted with rabbinical techniques of interpretation, and the same must be said about the parable's relation to its context. A dilemma in everyday life typically tests the Jewish Law, the manifold *Torāh*, and its techniques. Can we place ourselves in the position of the original hearers of the parable? The very specific particulars make the parable seem like a lecture; the story is condensed, and one wonders whether all the details are of substantive value. There is room for an investigation which assumes that they were. What impressions would these details create on an ordinary Jewish audience, and what lessons

[1] M. Black, 'The Parables as allegory', *Bull. J. Ryl. Lib.* 42, 2 (1960) at p. 285 says that the context does not fit and asks whether the parable was addressed to self-righteous *Sadducees*.

[2] 3rd edn (Göttingen 1962), 387–94. See also Kittel–Friedrich, *ThWzNT* VII (1960), 88–93.

[3] *Der barmherzige Samariter* (*Beit. z. Gesch. d. bibl. Exegese* 5) (Tübingen 1967). See also J. Daniélou, 'Le bon Samaritain', *Mélanges André Robert* (Paris 1957).

could be learnt from them? Is the parable a direct indication of how people should behave, or is it directed to answering an intermediate, and much more specific question?

(I) THE TALE ANALYSED

'A man', whom the audience would see as a Jew like themselves, was going down the road from Jerusalem to Jericho, known for its robberies.[1] The priest certainly,[2] the levite probably, and the Samaritan possibly were going in the same direction. One might travel to Samaria *via* Jericho; the reverse journey is depicted in 2 Ch xxviii.15. The priest and levite were making (one may suppose) for Jericho, inhabited by numbers of both classes,[3] rich and abounding in tithes. Highwaymen, perhaps zealots, ambushed our 'man'. The deep *wadis* on the pre-Roman road[4] would make the word περιέπεσε quite appropriate.[5] Stripped and unconscious as he was,[6] the Jew's race and community were not ascertainable at a glance. The priest and levite, according to the better text, acted alike, or more accurately were alike in deciding not to act. The Samaritan, a merchant, with two or more asses,[7] came near, and curiosity was overtaken by compassion.

The Samaritan's acts of kindness can be categorised. He employed personal care and expended energy; he expended his goods; he made available facilities, finally placing himself at risk personally and by pledging his credit with the innkeeper. His conduct perfectly exemplifies charity (*g^e^miylūt ḥasādiym*) at its widest, which is greatly superior to mere alms-giving.[8] The inn is unknown: it could be at Jericho or even Jerusalem. It need not have been a Samaritan inn.[9] Pharisees will have had their inns, or put up stoically with others. The innkeeper must be

[1] K. Dannenbauer in *Der Bote aus Zion* 70 (1955), 15–21, cited by J. Jeremias, *Die Gleichnisse Jesu*, 6th edn (Göttingen 1962), 201, corresponding to p. 203 of the Eng. trans. (1963).

[2] E. Stauffer corrects J. Jeremias's *JZJ* (above), 1958 edn, at *NTS* 7, no. 3 (1961), 273–4.

[3] Billerbeck, *Kommentar* II (Munich 1961), 180–1.

[4] R. Beauvery, 'La route romaine de Jérusalem à Jéricho', *Rev. Bibl.* 64 (1957), 72–101. Josephus, *Bell. Jud.* IV, viii, 3 (474, Loeb edn iii, 141).

[5] Wetstenius *ad loc.* shows that the phrase is in any event a cliché.

[6] So Arabic *Diatessaron*. Wis. xviii.18; *cf.* 4 M iv.11. B. Weiss cites Galen, *de morb. diff.* 5: the word (ἡμιθανῆ) does not exclude a power of movement.

[7] See Bauer–Arndt–Gingrich *s.v.* κτῆνος; *Diatessaron*, 34, 22–45.

[8] b. Suk. 49*b* = Sonc. 233. An interesting debate on the parable and its contents took place between Professor E. Stauffer and Professor W. G. Kümmel which is reported by O. Merk, 'Ein Beitrag Jesus-Frage: das Gleichnis vom barmherzigen Samariter', *Marburger Blätter*, 70 (1961), 11–12. The difficulties generally experienced with the parable have led to imaginative conclusions as to its origins and implications.

[9] As supposed by K. Bornhäuser at *Z. f. syst. Theol.* 9 (1932), 558.

visualised as a Jew. Innkeepers were often lax people, in touch with thieves.[1] A man who trusted an innkeeper knew what he was about. The Jew's arrival will at once have raised the question of payment for his keep. If the priest or levite had reported what they saw it by no means follows that aid would have been sent—quite the contrary, for the innkeeper might well have been too busy or indifferent to such calls. The end of the tale anticipates the Jew's recovery. The Samaritan weighed things up; did what he believed was his duty; and went.[2] Everyone in the tale had behaved rationally.

(2) THE RAW MATERIAL

Little of the tale is original. Jewish biblical history supplied most of it. Ho vi is most important. Its textual history leaves a reliable residuum of words.[3] The treasured[4] story of the young prophet from Jerusalem and the old prophet of Samaria (1 K xiii.11–32) is also relevant; also that of the conscience-stricken 'Samaritans' in 2 Ch xxviii.8–15 (expounded at *Mishnāh*, Soṭāh VIII, 1 and referred to by Josephus at *Ant.* IX, xii, 2). Sense and wording agree in relevance. Since 1914 it has been realised that the parable was connected with the Chronicles passage.[5] Rashi in his commentary on Dt xx.1, 3 ('against your enemies') draws on 2 Ch xxviii.15 for the pattern of brotherliness such as will exclude enmity, so that the connection goes back very far.

The injured man is present in the Kings passage, in Chronicles, and, by anticipation, in Hosea (where 'man' at any rate appears); Jerusalem is present in Hosea, Kings, Chronicles; Jericho is present in Chronicles and (by a stretch of imagination) in Hosea, where the way, road or

[1] b. Ta'an. 21*a* = Sonc. 104–5; b. San. 109*a* = Sonc. 747.

[2] Attending to the facts we find the Samaritan's generosity was not boundless, though extensive.

[3] E. Nielsen, *Shechem* (Copenhagen 1955), deals with vi.9 at 19n., 26, 283n., 290f. and 323n. He translates: 'As robbers lie in wait, / a gang of priests / along the road they murder unto Shechem, / yea, wicked plans they carry out.' Adam is ed-Damije. For the dialect, H. H. Hirschberg, *VT* 11 (1961), 382ff., 382–5. To the Qumran people *v.* 9 proved that God will requite the Seekers-after-smooth-things at Jerusalem, and they inserted it between the commentary on Is xxx.18 and 19: Vermès, 228; J. M. Allegro, *J. Bib. Lit.* 77 (1958), 215–21, 219. Studying the LXX, Syr., Symm. and the Qumran reading, the Vulg., Theod. and the Quinta we have the following words at our disposal: (1) lying in wait; (2) a man; (3) robbers; (4) company, association; (5) priests; (6) road; (7) they murder; (8) towards Shechem.

[4] Midr. R., S.S. II, 5, 3 = Sonc. 107; b. San. 89*b* = Sonc. 594, *ibid.* 104*a* = 706 (cf. 2 Ch ix.29); Jos. *Ant.* VIII, ix (236–45); *Constit. Apostolorum*, IV, vi, 6. L. Ginzberg, *Legends of the Jews*, VI (Phila., 1959), p. 211, n. 133.

[5] F. Orth, *Protest. Monatschr.* 18 (1914), 406–11, 410; K. Kastner, *BZ* 12 (1914), 29–30. Noted by Bultmann, *Gesch. d. syn. Tr.*, 4th edn (Göttingen 1958), 221–2; Hauck, *Lukas* (Leipzig 1934), 146f.; M. Black, *Bull. J. Ryl. Lib.* 42, 2 (1960), at p. 285; *Peake's Commentary on the Bible*, ed. M. Black, H. H. Rowley (London 1962), 318*e*.

direction towards Shechem is present; robbers are present in Hosea, an injury on the road in Kings, wounds in war, taking captive and spoil in Chronicles; people passing by on the road in Kings, priests and a killing on a road in Hosea, people indifferent to suffering in Chronicles (xxviii.14); Samaria appears in all three sources, most closely in Hosea because of the reference to Shechem; binding-up is done (we suppose) for the dead body in Kings, is mentioned in Hosea (vi.1), and is present in Chronicles (xxviii.15) by implication; oil appears in Chronicles (*ibid.*), but not in the other sources; the ass appears over-prominently in Kings, and is present in Chronicles. The inn is lacking, but the young prophet is brought 'home' in Kings, with emphasis on brotherhood, and the theme appears in Chronicles, where the injured are taken to Jericho, to be looked after. One notices that the levite and the wine are missing.

(3) THE BEHAVIOUR OF THE PRIEST AND LEVITE

Why is the levite here? The threefold encounter has the advantage of the threefold act, fitting the folk-tale and the legal presumption equally well. Would not Priest, Israelite, Samaritan have been possible? Hardly, because the priests and levites were the bearers of prestige, the teachers and examples.[1] An Israelite, lacking their instructed outlook, might well have done what the Samaritan did. The suggestion that instead of the Samaritan an Israelite originally appeared[2] is superfluous. Priest and levite are in antithesis, for the purposes of the parable, not to an Israelite, but to a Samaritan who rejects the worship at Jerusalem and does not accept Jewish priests as his spiritual guides. Samaritans in any case knew that the temple worship at Jerusalem was wrongheaded.[3] It may not be out of our way to recognise that priests and levites would share suspicion of being callous through association with the ritual slaughter of animals. It is not possible to prove that no one applied to levites the restrictions scripturally applied to priests; but it is possible to argue that a levite might, had he wished, have allowed himself more latitude than would a priest, a member of the group qualified by the twenty-four qualifications and endowed with the twenty-four endowments.[4]

[1] Philo, *De Spec. Leg.* IV, xxxvi; Jn i.19; Dt xvii.9ff.; xxi.5; Ezr viii.24–30; 1 Ch xxiii.4, cf. xxvi.29; Sir xlv.17. Jeremias, *Jerusalem*, p. 234 and n. 2, 304–5.

[2] J. Halévy, *Rev. Étud. Juives* 4 (1882), 249–55. C. Montefiore, *Synoptic Gospels* II (London 1927), 466–7 (corresponding to 935–6 in the 1909 edn). G. V. Jones, *The Art and Truth of the Parables* (1964), 116: 'Jesus may have introduced the priest and the levite as an example of what scrupulous observance of the Law could do to people, rather than as a condemnation of a class.'

[3] b. 'Av. Zar. 22*a* = Sonc. 111. Jos. *Ant.* XVIII, ii, 2 (29f.); Jeremias, *Jerusalem*, 389.

[4] *Mishnāh*, 'Āvot VI, 6; b. B.Ḳ. 110*b* = Sonc. 646–7.

Bornhäuser suggested (and he was followed by Oesterley) that the man's injuries might have seemed a divine punishment, with which the 'clerics' feared to interfere[1]. Bornhäuser's inference turns out to be false,[2] and the notion does not fit with the ethics the author of the parable presupposes in his audience. Lk xiii.1–5 and Jn ix.2–3 ('Who sinned, this man or his parents . . .?') testify, in fact, to a popular belief that misfortune springs from sin, but not to indifference to suffering.

The priest did not hesitate long; but he obviously made a decision. To us his predicament may seem worse than it did to the original audience; they will have seen any predicament in terms of conflicting commandments, and a balancing of commandments would be the normal mental response to such a situation.[3] Self-consciousness and awareness how far the final balance would reflect ulterior motives might not have been so well developed as it is after centuries of Christian sensitiveness to hypocrisy.

Was any obligation incumbent on the priest? If the man were still alive the priest must not stand idly by the blood of his 'neighbour' (Lv xix.16*b*). If the priest could be sure he was a neighbour he must make an effort to save his life.[4] Before long a maxim emerged that no Jew need trouble himself to save a Samaritan's life,[5] so we know that the definition of 'neighbour' was crucial. Then the man might die in his proximity, whereupon he would in any case be defiled, which was forbidden (Lv xxi.1);[6] and he would be obliged to procure his

[1] *St. z. Sondergut d. Lukas* (Gütersloh 1934), 69ff. He observed Muslim behaviour, but failed to understand it.

[2] Prof. N. J. Coulson denies that such an outlook has any place in Islamic teachings; Mr E. Cotran, a Palestinian Arab and a lawyer, describes the idea as 'nonsense'.

[3] A story of a Jew actually cogitating whether to rescue a disabled man at the risk of breaking the sabbath laws appears at Midr. R., Eccl. 91*b*, of which a version appears in C. Schöttgen, *Horae Hebraicae et Talmudicae* (1733) I, 279. It is significant that the benefactor 'mastered his evil inclination' (see below), and was rewarded by a miracle. We note, moreover, that he was afraid of his and his family's missing their meal, as well as a breach of a ritual law.

[4] b. San. 73*a* = Sonc. 495–6 (if a man sees his fellow [*ḥavero*] drowning, mauled by beasts, *or attacked by robbers*, he is bound [*ḥayyāyv*] to save him); Sifra, *par. Ḳᵉdoshim* (trans. J. Winter, Breslau 1938, p. 506). *Fathers acc. R. Nathan*, ch. XVI (trans. J. Goldin, *Yale Jud. Ser.* X, New Haven 1955, p. 86). Billerbeck, I, 359. Paul broke this: Ac xxii.20. It is the point of Ps xxxviii.12*a* (M.T.).

[5] b. San. 57*a* = Sonc. 389. Maimonides, *Mishneh Torāh*, XI (*Torts*) V, iv, 11 (trans. H. Klein, p. 208) (heathen and Israelite raisers of small cattle are not 'thy neighbour' within Lv xix.16!). Lightfoot, *Hor. Hebr.*, *ad* x. 29.

[6] Sifre on Num., § 130 (on Nb xix.22), trans. K. G. Kuhn (Stuttgart 1959), 500f. b. 'Av. Zar. 37*b* = Sonc. 182–3. Billerbeck, *ubi cit.* 183, is imperceptive. H. J. Schonfield, *Authentic New Testament* (London 1962), 120n. J. Jeremias, *Gleichnisse*, in earlier edns gave weight to this aspect (see *Parables of Jesus*, trans. S. H. Hooke, London 1954/8, p. 140–2), but in his latest edn, p. 202 (Eng. trans., 1963, p. 203–4), he voices doubts. Stauffer shared them. These are answered here. Hunter, *op. cit.* 73 n. 1, rightly suspects that ritual defilement was the point.

burial[1] (provided he were a Jew, which he might well be!); and he would be obliged to rend his garment, which conflicted with an obligation not to destroy valuable things.[2]

If the man were dead, on the other hand, the first two inconveniences would ensue, provided the man were a Jew, unless the priest confined himself to arranging for the burial and kept his distance. But he would not do this unless he knew the man to be a Jew. The duty either to assist or to bury was certainly incumbent under Lv xix.18 ('. . . and thou shalt love thy neighbour as thyself'), but in either case provided the man were a 'neighbour'. A gloss on this verse found amongst the Dead Sea scriptures leaves us in no doubt but that 'neighbour' means 'brother'.[3] In order to resolve the doubt whether the man was alive or dead the priest must come within four cubits.[4] If he were dead the man would thus be defiled. A priest must not 'overshadow' a corpse. If he bends over a dead body, even in ignorance of its existence, he may escape guilt, but not, of course, defilement.[5] Poking with a stick would not avoid this.[6] An overhanging rock would, if the priest came within its shadow, extend the radius of defilement even beyond the four cubits.[7] Yet the *Torāh* obliges us to avoid transgression and defilement: '. . . be ye holy, for I am holy' (Lv xi.44; xix.2, etc.).

The true positive commandment, Lv xix.18, and the virtual positive commandment ('not to stand . . .') at Lv xix.16, were both conditional, and could not overcome the unconditional commandment not to defile.[8]

[1] Tb i.17–19, ii.1–9; Philo, *Hypoth.* vii, 7 (Colson, IX, 1941, 427–8); Jos., *Cont. Ap.* II. 29; b. Meg. 3*b* = Sonc. 13–14; Sifre on Num., § 23, trans. Kuhn, p. 76; Mid. R., Levit. XXVI, 8 = Sonc. 338. For priests and the *met-mitsvāh* see b. Ber. 19*b* = Sonc. 119; *Mishnāh*, Naz. VII, 1. J. Mann at *JQR*, n.s. 6 (1915–16), 415–22 seems on the wrong track. There is no reason to suppose the lawyer was a Sadducee.

[2] b. Ḥul. 7*b* = Sonc. 30. b. Ned. 87*a* = Sonc. 268. b. M.K. 22*b*, 25*a*; Maim. *op. cit.* XIV, IV, ix, 11, trans. Hershman, p. 189. Note the delightful story at b. B.Ḳ. 91*b* = Sonc. 529 (a rabbi raised his skirts while walking amongst thorns; challenged to explain this behaviour, he replied that skin would grow again, the cloth would not); b. Ḳid. 32*a* = Sonc. 156; also *cf.* b. Ta'an. 23*a*. On priests and such rending see b. Hor. 12*b* = Sonc. 90, 94. Dt xx.19; Maim., *ubi cit.* xiv, 24 (trans., p. 203); XIV, V, vi, 10 (trans., p. 223)—the rabbis may administer a disciplinary beating to one who destroys wantonly.

[3] *CD* (DR) VI, 20–21 (Lohse, 79; Vermès, 103; Dupont-Sommer, 147).

[4] b. Sot. 43*b*–44*a* = Sonc. 218–19. He would incur a disciplinary flogging: Maim., *op. cit.* XIV, IV, iii, 13.

[5] There is a relevant discussion at b. Nid. 15*b* = Sonc. 104.

[6] *Mishnāh*, 'Oholot XVI, 1 (Danby, 672; Blackman VI, 278).

[7] See Blackman on *'Oholot*. Danby, *op. cit.* index, 842. b. Pes. 90*b*–91*a* = Sonc. 485–6. Maim., *op. cit.* X, I, i, 13 (reference to a Gentile may be post-Mishnaic, but in any case there was a doubt—and in doubts regarding death uncleanness the inference is positive, see *Mishnāh*, Taharot IV, 11 (Danby, 722, Blackman, *ubi cit.* 498)).

[8] b. Yev. 20*b*. Mekilta, *Kaspa* 2 (Lauterbach III, 166–7). A commandment which is both positive and negative cannot be overruled by a positive commandment: b. B.M. 30*a* = Sonc. 186 (a priest and a lost animal in a cemetery).

But the strength of the opposing commandments would be a matter for tradition, and to some extent for personal preference, as we shall see. In a situation of doubt, however, which was the priest's situation, preference must be given to that which is certain. A story exemplifies this.[1] A rabbi hoping to redeem captives wanted to cross a river. The river (citing Qo i.7) declined to divide and allow a passage saying, 'We are both doing the will of our Maker but I am certain of fulfilling my task, whereas it is not certain that you will achieve yours.' The *Torāh* required sin-offerings to be offered for those who doubted whether they had transgressed a negative commandment breach of which involved extirpation, not those who doubted whether they had broken a positive commandment.[2] This indicates the outlook. The priest was thus entitled to pass on. There is no anti-clerical sarcasm here.

Defilement, of course, was inconvenient and costly. The ashes of the red heifer could hardly be had for nothing (Nb xix),[3] and the 'water of sprinkling' which had to be used on the third and the seventh day would hardly be 'sprinkled' *gratis*. Priests lived on tithes. There might be competition for tithes.[4] A defiled priest could not eat tithe, which had to be eaten in 'holiness'.[5] He could not collect or distribute it. *Terumāh* was highly susceptible to defilement. Even third-grade uncleanness could render it *pāṣūl*, which must be burnt.[6] Defilement of the head of the family would in practice prevent the whole family, including the servants, from eating tithe.[7] Transport of tithe to Jerusalem was a priestly task.[8] Scrupulous agents would have been expensive to employ.[9] An agent could not be appointed by an 'unclean' priest.[10] The right (conditional on ritual cleanness) to eat tithe was a valuable asset, which could be pledged to the Israelite who tithed to the pledgor.[11]

[1] b. Ḥul. 7*a* = Sonc. 28–9. *Cf.* the problem of circumcising on the Sabbath a child not sure to live: *Mishnāh*, Shab. XIX, 3 (Danby, 117); b. Shab. 134*b* = Sonc. 678–87. b. B.B. 158*b*–159*b*. Maim. *op. cit.* XIII, V, v (trans. Rabinowitz, p. 273ff.): a man died leaving a son and hermaphrodyte issue; a house fell on a man and his father, etc.

[2] Lv iv.27–8, v.17–18. Maim. *op. cit.* IX, IV, trans. H. Danby (New Haven 1950), 93ff.

[3] Midr. R., Deut. I, 15, Sonc. 16. b. Soṭ. 44*b* = Sonc. 225ff. See *Mishnāh*, Parāh III,

[4] Jos. *Ant.* XX, viii, 8 (Niese IV, p. 258); also *ibid.* IX, 2 (Jeremias, *Jerusalem* (1962) II. 121–2).

[5] b. San. 82*b* = Sonc. 550 (death at hands of Heaven).

[6] Maim. *op. cit.* X, V, i, vii, viii, trans., p. 5ff., 278ff. Danby, *Mishnah*, p. 714 n. 3.

[7] Uncleanness is communicated to most utensils and garments. Maim. *op. cit.* X, I, v, trans. Danby (1954), 23ff. Philo, *De Spec. Leg.* I, xxiv–xxv (Colson VII, 167–73).

[8] b. Ta'an. 27*a* = Sonc. 143 (on *Mishnāh*, Ta'an. IV, 2).

[9] Read with caution Midr. R., Levit. VIII, 1 (trans. J. Israelstam and J. J. Slotki, London 1939), 227.

[10] An agent is as oneself. For an analogous rule see b. B.Ḳ. 110*a* = Sonc. 640 (an aged priest).

[11] *Mishnāh*, Giṭṭ. III, 7 (Danby, 310), b. Giṭṭ. 30*a*. It was possible to become rich on tithes (Josephus, *Vita* 12), therefore they could be secularised and converted in terms of money.

Priests at Jericho would have known the implications of defilement and would have striven habitually to avoid it.

Justification for a priest's defiling himself, however, should he wish to do so, was not wanting. To save life he might so do,[1] that is, he must have the intention of saving the life of a living person. Some might take the view that he could take the risk. The Babylonian Talmud in the gemara to *Mishnāh* Pes. VIII. 6 (rescuing one who may turn out to be dead, or to have been dead when one commenced rescue work)[2] and to Yoma VIII. 6–7 touches on the ritual commandments and the duty to save life.[3] Doubt there operates in favour of life. '. . . Even if it is doubtful whether he is an Israelite or a heathen [which will include a Samaritan for our purposes] one must, for his sake, remove the débris (even on the Day of Atonement).' The mere possibility of being rendered unclean by working above a man whom he is attempting to rescue, but is in fact dead, will prevent a priest from eating tithe until the facts are known.[4] Priests were thus justified in working in such cases of doubt, but strictly at the risk of losing their right to eat tithe. It would seem therefore that though in the eyes of Pharisees the priest was entitled to pass by, he would have been justified in stopping and doing what he could. Unless a duty authorised a priest to incur defilement he actually risked becoming temporarily disqualified even from his temple service (with all its secular advantages), and this could be embarrassing. The *Mishnāh* at Bekh. VII. 7 says, 'He that suffers uncleanness because of the dead is unqualified until he pledges himself to suffer uncleanness no more because of the dead'.[5]

Much depends upon the inclination with which one approaches such a dilemma. A priest may not defile himself. What if his parents, whom he must obey, order him to do so? He must not defile himself, so says the rabbinical law.[6] What if in order to restore a wandering ass[7] a priest must enter a graveyard? Indeed he must not enter the graveyard for so speculative a purpose.[8] But if he fails to show honour to respectable people by observing the rule against defilement he may incur censure. R. 'Eleazar b. Zadok, a priest during whose youth the Temple still stood, said, 'We used to leap over (and thus 'overshadow') coffins containing bodies to see the Israelite kings'. There would be no dis-

[1] b. Yoma 82*a* = Sonc. 404: 'There is nothing that can stand before the duty of saving life'.
[2] Danby, 147.
[3] b. Yoma 84*b*–85*b* = Sonc. 416–21. The Palestinian Talmud is more emphatic: Schwab V, 254 ('celui qui s'informe [au lieu d'accourir] équivaut à un assassin').
[4] *Mishnāh*, 'Oholot XVI, 4 (Blackman, 281).
[5] Danby, 539.
[6] Mekilta, *Kaspa* 2, *cit. sup.* For the principle see also b. Ḳid. 32*a*.
[7] Ex xxiii.4, 5; Dt xxii.1–4.
[8] b. B.M. 30*a* = Sonc. 186. b. Ber. 19*b* = Sonc. 118–19.

crimination against Gentile kings. Were the coffins so spacious[1] that they might serve as a (protecting) 'tent'? No, R. 'Eleazar and his colleagues did not ascertain the fact before leaping over them! The need to show respect overcame the negative commandment to avoid defilement. In a Tannaitic *midrash* a priest who owned an orchard in which human remains were interred sent for two figs from it.[2] When his servant was insulted he declared he would visit the defiling ground himself to punish the disrespect shown to his servant. 'Great is human dignity, since it overrides a negative precept of the *Torāh*.'[3] Our priest, in 'turning aside', took a course which was not unjustifiable; had he decided otherwise his conduct would have been allowable. The ethics of the time gave no decisive guidance. It was certainly not a case of pure cowardice, as Stauffer has supposed.

That contemporaries of the apostles believed in the claims of the distressed is proved by the story of Naḥum of Gimzo.[4] His animals had once been laden with good things. A beggar stopped him. He asked him only to wait, but in the interval the beggar died. He tried in vain to revive him, and gradually brought upon himself the miseries his neglect had consummated.[5] An Israelite might not have taken the view the priest and levite took. Unlike him both classes were entitled, biblically, to live on tithes. The situations of the priest and the levite had an essential difference, which adds to the piquancy of the story. Fear of possible defilement was reinforced by fear of being deprived temporarily of tithes. In the view (reflected in the *Mishnāh*) of some Pharisees, the biblical rule (Nb xviii.21–32), whereby the Israelite tithed to the levite and the latter again to the priest, was still ideally valid, and doubtless levites would have agreed whether they were Pharisees or not.[6] Philo apparently did not regard the levites' right as obsolete. But John Hyrcanus (134–104 B.C.), abrogating the public avowal of payment of this tithe (*Mishnāh*, Ma. Sheni V, 15, *cf. ibid.* 10), recognised that levites had ceased *de facto* to receive their biblical tithe.[7] Consequently

[1] b. Ber. 19*b* = Sonc. 117–18. j. Naz. VII § 1, fol. 56ᵃ, *l.* 43. *Yalḳūṭ* on Is xxvi.2, § 429. H. Loewe, *Render unto Caesar* (Cambridge 1940), 23–4, 30.

[2] Midr. R., Exod. XV, 19 (on xii.1) = Sonc. 183–4. For priests' avoidance of graves see Midr. R., Lev. (Ḳᵉd.) XXIV, 7 = Sonc. 309; XXVI, 5 = Sonc. 329–30.

[3] b. Ber. 19*b* = Sonc. 118; b. Meg. 3*b* = Sonc. 13–14; b. Shab. 81*b* = Sonc. 387.

[4] Or Gamzu. Abrahams, *Studies* II, 39. Bacher, *Agada d. Tannaiten* 1 (Strasbourg 1903), 57ff. J. Mann, *JQR* n.s. 6 (1915/16), 421, refers to j.Pea 21*b*. C. G. Montefiore and H. Loewe, *A Rabbinic Anthology* (New York/Philadelphia 1963), 421. Gimzo was a pupil of Joḥanan b. Zakkai and teacher of R. 'Aḳiba (b. Shevu. 26*a* = Sonc. 138).

[5] b. Ta'anit 21*a* = Sonc. 104–5.

[6] M. Sheni V, 9; Ter. IV, 2. For forestalling by Levites see b. 'Er. 31*b*=Sonc. 216–17. A levite shows how to rinse before eating tithe at b. Ḥul. 106*b* = Sonc. 591.

[7] b. Yev. 86*b* = Sonc. 584; Soṭ. 47*b* = 253; Ḥul. 131*b* = 743. J. Jeremias, *Jerusalem*, 121–3.

a taboo which, a century after Hyrcanus, remained meaningful only in terms of hereditary prestige was a taboo of a different description from that which the priests observed. It had not even a practical justification. Prestige, money, domestic comfort, corporate feeling, all created an inclination such as would operate against the injured Jew's welfare. The behaviour could be satirised, but wives, servants and colleagues might well applaud it. Intelligence, intellectual equipment and training were used to financial advantage. But the intellectual position would have been quite different if everyone had known what 'neighbour' truly meant in Lv xix.18.

(4) THE BEHAVIOUR OF THE SAMARITAN

This has no less complex features, not obvious to a non-Palestinian Jew. However, we readily see that a Samaritan will not have respected the behaviour of the priest and levite, one of whom he will have been bound to see or pass in whichever direction he was travelling, in view of the nature of the man's injuries and the contours of the road, which make a long lapse of time and prolonged absence from view unlikely. Indeed Samaritans, who were also sons of the commandments,[1] feared defilement from the dead.[2] But the Samaritan was moved by compassion, and this obviated fears about his own or his animal's or wares' contamination. He persisted with his charitable work even after he discovered (when the man regained consciousness) that he was not a Samaritan, but in fact, in the view of some (cf. ἀλλογενής at Lk xvii.18), an 'enemy'. Proceeding to the inn on foot he rendered himself a better possible target for robbers.

At the inn he entered, on the following day,[3] into a piece of business carefully detailed for us. 'Take care of him, and whatever you lay out in addition (to the two denar.) I, at my return hither, shall repay to you', is equivalent to a formula long discussed by rabbis, 'Give him ... and I shall repay you'. This is *ḳabb*^{e}*lānūt* (principal indebtedness), and not '^{a}*rēvūt* (suretyship).[4] The two are conversing apparently alone. The

[1] J. Jeremias, *Gleichnisse*, 202 ('der das Liebesgebot erfüllt') (the Eng. trans., p. 204, 'duty of love' is less striking). A. Schlatter, *Lukas* (Stuttgart 1931), p. 286.

[2] b. Nid. 56*b* = Sonc. 395–6; *Masseket Kuṭim* I, 16.

[3] On ἐπί Blass–Debrunner, 9th/10th edn, § 233 (3), trans. (1961), 122, have doubts; but Bauer–Arndt–Gingrich III, 2, *a* (289) are content. So Klostermann, *Das Lukasevangelium*, 2nd edn (Tübingen 1929), 121. Recovery should be within three days to fit the symbolism: Midr. R., Gen. (Miḳḳets) XCI, 7 = Sonc. 842–4; *ibid.* (Vayera) LVI, 1 = Sonc. 491 (both cite Ho vi.2). Yet, M. Black, *Aramaic Approach*, 3rd edn (Oxford 1967), 205–6, suggests only a temporal sequence.

[4] b. B.B. 174*a* = Sonc. 765–6. Maim. *op. cit.* XIII (Civil Laws) III, xxv, 5 (trans. Rabinowitz, p. 174). For the distinction and relevant details see I. Herzog, *Main Institutions* II (1967), ch. 14.

Samaritan is pledging his credit. He asks the innkeeper to make a gift to the Jew of the excess (above 2 denar.) of his cure, his keep and shelter, and conveyance if necessary. Otherwise the Jew would not have left the inn at all. Personal arrest for debt was in use. A release from an innkeeper is described in a *midrash*,[1] and there is other evidence.[2] The Samaritan enabled him to 'get out of town'. The Samaritan it was that (surprisingly) did a deed of 'supererogation'.

It would be charming to think that he never contemplated recompense, though he more or less invited the innkeeper to incur expenses, even lavishly,[3] and undertook to pay them. Must we assume this? He was a merchant, and the age was scrupulous about rights. Thieves do not rob people who have no valuables. Those who voluntarily help others in distress have a moral, and normally also a legal, right to recompense.[4] But the situation was peculiar. The Samaritan appointed the innkeeper his agent to make necessary disbursements. By receiving the two coins the innkeeper bound himself to carry out the commission.[5] The legal link from Samaritan to injured man seemed complete. Had the benefactor been a Jew he could have forced the Jew to repay, when he was fit and well, all that had been spent on necessaries. The innkeeper's sole testimony could have been supported by the plaintiff's oath. But the legal situation was iniquitous. The innkeeper could sue the Samaritan on the agency which the Samaritan could constitute, but since a Jew cannot constitute a Samaritan his agent[6] the Samaritan could not pursue any legal rights by virtue of the implied agency of necessity. Agency being a fiduciary relationship the agent was liable to an oath; but the oath of a Samaritan was not accepted.[7] The scroll he

[1] Midr. R., Exod. XV, 18 (on xii.1) = Sonc. 183.

[2] R. Sugranyes De Franch, *Études sur le Droit Palestinien à l'Époque Évangélique. La Contrainte par Corps* (Fribourg 1946). A. Deißmann, *Light from the Ancient East* (trans. Strachan, London 1910), 267, 334 (1927), 369–70. E. Zingg, *Judaica* 16 (1960), 72–102, 156–71, 207–15. B. Cohen's 'Civil bondage in Jewish and Roman law', *Louis Ginzberg Jubilee Volume, Eng. Sec.* (1945), 113ff., has been reprinted at *JRL* i, 159–78. See above, p. 40 n. 1.

[3] This is the implication of δαπανᾶν in προσδαπανήσῃς (spend).

[4] Romans hearing our parable would at once assume that the law of *negotiorum gestio* (or some hypothetical Jewish equivalent) must apply, and would apply if the Samaritan could get the Jew whom he had benefited before a non-Jewish official with judicial powers.

[5] M. Black, *op. cit.* 136. For the contemporary law we must look behind the fictitious considerations, the *kinyan sudar*, *q.v.* in any textbook and encyclopaedia of Jewish Law. See also below, p. 408.

[6] Cohn, *ZVR* 36 (1920) at p. 148–50. *Cf. ibid.* 422–42, ref. b. B.B. 138*a*, b. B.M. 9*b*. Here no mandate could have been given.

[7] J. Blumenstein, *Die versch. Eidesarten* . . . (Frankfurt 1883), 15. *Mishnāh*, Giṭṭin I, 5 (Danby, 307). Montgomery, *Samaritans* (Philadelphia 1907), 185. Eta Linnemann, *Gleichnisse Jesu* (Göttingen 1961), 60 (trans., 1966, 54).

would hold would not be sacred in his eyes, for the Samaritan Pentateuch differed. No alternative was possible in a Jewish court. At one time Samaritans could not get justice in a Jewish court.[1]

Our Samaritan had no hope of enforcing reimbursement. His generosity was exercised while he must have been indifferent to the outcome, whether the Jew would be grateful, would recompense him, or not. The coincidence with what Jesus requires of the initiated Christian at vi.35 is striking: '[Even sinners lend to sinners in the hope of obtaining thereby reciprocity][2] but love your "enemies" and do good (to them) and lend (Lv xxv.35; Dt xv.7–8), abstaining totally from despair,[3] and your reward shall be great. . . .' The commandment is to lend to those (including 'enemies') from whom neither repayment nor reciprocity can be counted upon.

(5) SYMBOLIC FEATURES IN THE STORY

The raw material provides a web of allusions. It is not possible to set bounds dogmatically to the midrashic potentialities of any of those passages, but we can confine ourselves to the obvious and the plausible. Brotherly love as inculcated in the story of Joseph and his Brethren is alluded to in the context.[4] So in the 1 K xiii passage: Jeroboam had built Shechem (xii.25) in his programme against Jerusalem; the young prophet cried by the word of the Lord against the high places of Samaria, and Joseph and Shechem were associated.[5] Ho vi.9 points directly to the story of Simeon and Levi and the slaughter at Shechem (Gn xxiv).[6] Shechem is the birthplace of the Joseph story, and the scene of the Samaritan–Jewish conflict. Jericho recalls Rahab (Jos ii, vi), Rahab who became a Jewish heroine of loving-kindness.[7] The road is

[1] b. San. 57*a* = Sonc. 388. *Masseket Kuṭim* II, 28: 'When they renounce Mt. Gerizim . . . he that robs a Samaritan shall be as he who robs an Israelite.' Montgomery, *op. cit.* 203. *Cf.* b. B.Ḳ. 113*a* = Sonc. 664; *Mishnāh* at b. B.Ḳ. 37*b* = Sonc. 211. 'Rab' (d. 247) said that Dt xxix.20 applied to one who returned a lost object to a Samaritan: b. San. 76*b* = Sonc. 517.

[2] τὰ ἴσα does not mean the capital, for sinners do not lend to sinners (or anyone else) in hopes of obtaining only the *capital* back (they want interest too). H. Montefiore's 'if they are to be repaid in full' (*NT* 5 [1962] 160) is thus wrong.

[3] ἀπελπίζοντες cannot mean 'expecting therefrom' or 'expecting in return', not merely because it is unexampled, but because such a transaction would emphatically not be a *loan*, but a *gift*.

[4] 'Do this and live' (*v.* 28*b*) recalls Gn xlii.18.

[5] Midr. R., Deut. VIII, 4 = Sonc. 152.

[6] Midr. R., Gen. (*Vayyishlaḥ*) LXXX, 2–3 = Sonc. ii, 736–7. J. Theodor and Ch. Albeck, *Bereschit Rabba*, par. XLVIII–LXXVI (Berlin 1927), 953. *Yalḳūṭ Shim'onī*, § 523 (Jerusalem edn II, 850). Levi paid (Ex xxxii.26)—see *Yalḳūṭ*, § 955 (I. Ziegler, *Königsgleichnisse*, Breslau 1903, p. 249). On b. Soṭ. 22*b* = Sonc. 112 see M. Gertner, *BSOAS* 26 (1963), 260, 262. Shechem was destined for evil: b. San. 102*a* = Sonc. 292.

[7] Heb xi.31; Jm ii.25.

significant. On the *way* the traveller must talk of the commandments (*e.g.* Dt vi.4–5) and meditate on them (*ibid.* 7).[1] The apparently unnecessary ὁδεύων of our *v.* 33 suggests *holēch* (3 K vi.12: ἐὰν ὁδεύῃς τοῖς προστάγμασί μου)—it was the Samaritan who was the traveller on the way of life.

The oil and wine are more than conventional first aid for wounds. They correspond to the sacrificial elements in the temple worship (see Apoc. vi.6), especially the daily burnt offerings,[2] of which Hosea speaks. 'I desired mercy and not sacrifices; knowledge of God more than burnt offerings.'[3] See 1 S xv.22. Amos at v.21–4 demands a flow of righteousness, not burnt offerings, spiritual sacrifices (1 P ii.1–5). Sirach says (vii.30): 'Love him that made thee with all thy might, and forsake not his ministers'. Who are these, those that sacrifice or those that do his will? To show what is the *ḥęṣed* which God demands one cannot be more apt than to show oil and wine employed to heal an injured man. The oil and wine of the Temple, specially obtained, stored in a special place, were handled only by priests.[4] Josephus states that to divert them from the sacrifices was such sacrilege that it merited the destruction of Jerusalem.[5] Micah (at vi.6–8) contrasts the rivers of oil which represent the offerings with love of *ḥęṣed* and *walking* humbly with God. Origen, alive to the allusion, sees the oil in our parable as a reference to Is i.6—the work of God is to bind up the wounds of Israel and mollify them with oil.[6]

The reference to oil and wine (which the reader will note is not essential to the story as such) could also be humorous. Oil and wine are forbidden objects if they emanate from a Samaritan,[7] when they are also *demai* (they will not have been tithed). Unless the wounded man were one of the 'accursed' *'amme ha-'ārets* 'that know not the Law', he would certainly have refused to benefit from either, upon religious

[1] b. Ber. 11*a* = Sonc. 60–3. Max Kadushin, *Rabbinic Mind*, 125. The *Sh^ema'* in the view of some need not be said on the way if one was afraid of *robbers*!

[2] F. X. Kortleitner, *Arch. Bibl. Summ.* (Oenip., 1906), 119–21. R. de Vaux, *Ancient Israel* (*cit. sup.*), ch. 10. Maim. *op. cit.* VIII, V, ii, 12 (trans. Lewittes, Yale 1957, p. 170). Philo, *De Spec. Leg.* I, clxxix (Colson VII, 201). Any wood might be burnt on the altar *except* olive and vine: Mid. R., Levit. VII, 1 = Sonc. 90.

[3] Loisy saw the relevance, but Lagrange denied it.

[4] b. Yoma 24*b* = Sonc. 113 (*cf. Mishnāh* at b. Yoma 25*a* = Sonc. 116). *Mishnāh*, Menaḥot IX at b. Men. 86*b* = Sonc. 522; *ibid.* XII (end) and Sonc. 641–2, 658. Cell (or Chamber) of the House of Oils (see any plan of the Temple). *Letter of Aristeas*, § 92.

[5] *Bell. Jud.* V, xiii, 6 (Niese V, 565, vol. 6, p. 511, but the text of S. A. Naber [Teubner 1895] is better). G. A. Williamson, in his translation (London 1959, p. 302), oddly drops the word 'wine' and replaces it with 'corn', for which there appears to be no manuscript authority. A *hīn* is a liquid measure. *Cf.* Jdt xi.13.

[6] B. Gerhardsson, *Good Samaritan* (Copenhagen 1958), p. 15.

[7] A. Cohen, introd. to Sonc. trans. b. 'Avodāh Zarāh (London 1935), xiii.

as well as financial grounds. He was in no position to redeem the proportion which should have been tithe.[1] To absorb oil through the skin, whether broken or whole, was equivalent to consuming it through the mouth,[2] and it was wicked to rub *demai* oil on oneself without providing for tithe. The wine, and to much the same extent the oil also,[3] of a Samaritan was so objectionable to the Pharisaic mind (aware of dietary notions dating from well before the time of Jesus)[4] that willingness to consume the wine of a Samaritan was proof of incapacity to control the inclinations. That these rules could be ridiculous perhaps needed to be pointed out. Or perhaps the point was that priorities could be confused.

The sort of religious exclusiveness which Jesus incidentally alludes to in his parable, showing what its logical conclusion is, continued to have some scope in Jewish society afterwards. The famous story of Ben Dama illustrates the kind of religiosity which real life (apart from fantasy) abhors. The rabbi was bitten by a snake. A disciple of Jesus used to cure such sufferers with a remedy (of a magical character) known only to Christians. The rabbi sent for him. His uncle remonstrated. The nephew died before the Christian could attempt the cure. The uncle rejoiced: 'Blessed art thou, Ben Dama, that thou hast gone in peace . . ., and hast not broken down the fence of the wise!'[5] Similarly Pharisees would have blessed our victim if he had said, 'Begone, Cuthean, I will have none of your oil or your wine!', and the parable of Jesus shows how idiotic such notions were (and are—for they are not yet dead).

(6) THE TEACHING

The tale perhaps seeks to present more than one idea.

(1) *Ḥéṣed* may be shown, as the result of natural sympathy, even by

[1] b. Yoma 55*b* = Sonc. 263, b. B.Ḳ. 69*b* = Sonc. 399 (Cuthean wine!). Mixed substances might not be titheable. b. Ḥull. 6*a* = Sonc. 24. Were the two poured simultaneously, as insisted by Ps.-Chrysostom, *In parab. eius q. incid. in latr.*, Migne, *PG* 62, vol. 755, 757—ἀναμίξας? *Cf.* b. Shab. 134*a* = Sonc. 673.

[2] *Mishnāh*, Demai, I, 4 (Danby, 21); Shab. IX, 4 (*ibid.* 108). M. Schwab, *Talm. de Jérus.* III (1902), 210–11 (Masser Schéni II, 1). From Dt xii.17 it is deduced that anointing amounts to consumption.

[3] Wine: Dt xxxii.38 ('Av. Zar. 31*a* = Sonc. 147); *Mishnāh*, 'Av. Zar. II, 3 (Danby, 438), b. 'Av. Zar. 31*a* = Sonc. 155–6; b. Nid. 56*b* = Sonc. 397, 57*a* = 400. Oil: *Mishn.* 'Av. Zar. II, 6 (Danby, 439), Sonc. p. 171, n. 8. *Cf.* Jos., *Vita* 13. R. Judah II permitted the oil: 'Av. Zar. 35*b*–36*a* = Sonc. 173–6. Some points of importance, suggesting that oil was originally a test substance, arise in J. M. Baumgarten, 'The Essene avoidance of oil and the laws of purity', *Revue de Qumran* 6 (1967), 183–92.

[4] Jdt x.5; xii.1–4, 19; Dn i.8; b. Shab. 13*b*, 17*b*.

[5] Baraita at Tos., Ḥul. II. 22–3; b. 'Av. Zar. 27*b* = Sonc. 137. J. Klausner, *Jesus of Nazareth*, trans. H. Danby (New York 1959), 40.

a sectary or heretic, and that too in a situation where God's formal agents may omit to show it. This agrees with experience.

(2) One who does *ḥéṣed* identifies himself with the object of it, according to his own power and the other's needs. Results show whether *ḥéṣed* has been at work. This draws upon common knowledge.

(3) A ritualistic approach to duty will manifest itself even in dilemmas of daily life, but it can lead to dramatic failures to show *ḥéṣed*. This too fits experience.

(4) Methods of reasoning which balance commandments like commodities having weights can, through self-deception, permit the very breaches of commandments which they were designed to prevent. Teaching about behaviour which needs such methods may be defective.

(5) The Samaritan–Jewish problem must be reviewed. Biblical-historical authorities show that the hatred between the peoples was not natural, ancient, continuous, or proper.[1] This hatred is here condemned or ignored. A contemporary might be startled by this reinterpretation of history, especially in the light of more recent events, but the point was at least arguable.

(6) If real life can find such defects in the Pharisees' ordinances it is high time that their fundamental structure was re-examined. Opponents of Pharisaism would enjoy the point, which is put as delicately as it is inescapable.

The Context

In a sense the message transcends its context, but can it be grasped in its fullness without it? If the present context is not inappropriate[2] the burden of proving that it is not original lies upon those who assert it, and, as we shall see, their chief argument is found to have no substance, since it has escaped notice what the relationship between the parable and its context really is. The position as between other passages in Luke and their respective contexts is beside the point.

Jesus is depicted as a legislator.[3] He plays a role similar to that of

[1] Does O. Cullmann go too far, in *Early Church* (London 1956), 186 (race-prejudice)?

[2] Jeremias points out (Eng. trans., p. 205) that any inconsistency between the scribe's question and Jesus's question to him at the close of the parable is to be resolved from the nature of the subject-matter. The scribe's approach is theoretical, Jesus's practical, and the word *rea'* reciprocal in any case.

[3] 'Do this and live' recalls Dt v.30; vi.24; Lv xviii.5. 'Go' recalls Ex iii.16, iv.12, 19; xxxii.7. *Cf.* Mt ii.20; Ac ix.15; Lk xvii.19. The word is attributed to Jesus in this conclusive sense: Lk v.24; vii.50; viii.48; Jn iv.50; viii.11. But 'hither' at Lk xviii.22*d* (sequel to the deuteronomic section) is, as it were, an improvement. It appears to be gratuitous to suggest that Jesus wanted the lawyer to put himself in the wounded man's place, as J. J. Vincent, *Studia Evang., T. u. U.* 73 (1959), 90, after Gordon, Scheitlin, Pirot. T. W. Manson said (*Teaching of Jesus*, Cambridge 1955, p. 301) that Jesus refused to legislate, but this is using the word 'legislate' in another sense.

Moses. This point is not necessitated by the parable, but is not incompatible with it. The parable is in fact concerned with the interpretation of the *Torāh*, the ethical and practical 'law' (which is the business of a νομικός), and in particular with Lv xix.18, with special reference to one word in it, 'thy-neighbour'. The priest and levite acted as they did because 'thy neighbour' could be taken to mean only a Jew. Had that word meant 'Jew or non-Jew' the dilemma could not have existed in that, or indeed in any conscientious form.

The parable is about *ḥéṣed*, which is, *inter alia*, a variant of *'ahavāh*, the subject of both Dt vi.4 (5) and of Lv xix.18—indeed it is *va-'āhavᵉtā* in each which brings them together.[1] The word 'neighbour' does not occur in the parable. But its lesson, as we have seen, is that *ḥéṣed* has nothing to do with community or sect, but is a spontaneous, natural thing. Thus the original context must have had to do with the nature of *ḥéṣed*. This should call in Dt vi.4 (5) and Lv xix.18, which have that paradox in common, the command to love. The two great divisions of the *Torāh*, duties to God and duties to man, were summarised in those two.

Texts from various quarters (since there is no temporality in the *Torāh*) may be read together for mutual illumination.[2] The much discussed dictum of R. Simeon b. 'Azzai, a contemporary of the apostles, seized upon Gn v.1ff. ('This is the book of the generations of Adam. In the day that God created man, in the likeness of God made he him . . .') as a text superior to Lv xix.18, itself manifestly a portmanteau commandment.[3] R. 'Aḳiba would have chosen the latter as the greatest commandment,[4] though without asserting that 'neighbour' includes non-Jew.[5] B. 'Azzai hinted that if one recognises God's creation of man (not necessarily all men) one loves man and therefore loves God. Because men are made in God's image one cannot love him without loving his creatures.[6] That is one lesson from placing Deuteronomy before Leviticus, as here and in Mk xii.28–34.[7] In both passages Jesus

[1] There was an Aramaic Targum that read RḤM in place of the original's 'HV (*Midrash on Psalms* 18 § 7, Braude I, 235). On that basis the commandment suggests the idea of God's mercy and the need to *show* compassion.

[2] Sifre on Num. 131. Mk xiv.62 appears to contain an example (below, p. 424).

[3] Rm xiii.8–10; Ga v.14; Jm ii.8–12. Sifre, 782. Midr. R., Levit. (Ḳᵉd.) XXIV, 5 = Sonc. 307–8.

[4] Sifra, *para. Ḳᵉdoshim* (trans. Winter, p. 507). Bacher, *Agada* I, 417–18; Moore, *Judaism* III (Cambridge, Mass. 1927/58), 85; I. Abrahams, *Studies* I (Cambridge 1917), 18–29; W. Foerster, *Neutest. Zeitgesch.* 3rd edn (Hamburg 1959), 199; Billerbeck, *op. cit.* I, 357–8. J. Schmid, *Das Evang. nach Lukas*, 3rd edn (Regensburg 1955), 190 denied that the texts were linked in rabbinical literature.

[5] So Kosmala, referring to Weiss and Bacher, at *Judaica* 4 (1948), 248ff.

[6] 1 Jn iii.17; iv.20. *Fathers acc. to R. Nathan*, cited above. *Didache*, I, 2. Jm iii.9–10.

[7] W. E. Bundy, *Jesus and the First Three Gospels* (Cambridge, Mass. 1955), 339–40.

and his interlocutor agree that this *midrash* is correct, obtaining the full meaning from Deuteronomy and Leviticus. 'How readest thou?' means, 'May I hear your authorities with exposition?'[1] But if Leviticus is explained by Deuteronomy it follows that the word 'neighbour' merely acts as an object for the verb. The *ratio* of B. 'Azzai (unknown to him?) produced this very interpretation, for God also created the non-Jew. R. 'Aḳiba certainly thought that Lev. allowed one to insist upon equality (*cf.* Mt v.43–8).[2] It is *from our parable alone* that we know that Jesus accepted the *ratio* behind the famous dictum, and that to him 'neighbour' for this purpose means 'man'. Mark's and Matthew's version of the *midrash* leaves it open whether 'neighbour' means any Jew, for the implications of πλησίον, the LXX rendering of *re'a*, are not conclusive.

A parable which shows that *ḥéṣed* is a natural emotion and that it is to that that God referred in demanding *ḥéṣed*, might seem to be the perfect commentary on the two verses, and to fit our context as a hand fits its glove. Jesus and the scribe agree somewhat emphatically in Mark that the difficult word *m*^{e}*'od*^{e}*chā* must be glossed, as the rabbis themselves gloss it.[3] They choose the intellectual faculty. Whether we say διανοίᾳ or συνέσει (Mk xii.33) God needs to be loved not merely with financial and other resources (*m*^{e}*'od*^{e}*chā*),[4] but also with the intelligence (*maddā'achā*).[5]

Context and Parable

The Samaritan–Jew paradox of the parable fits the old-prophet–young-prophet paradox of 1 K xiii. At 2 K xxiii.17–18 there is a reference to

[1] 'Av. Zar. II, 5 (Danby, 439). J. Jeremias's suggestion (after Lightfoot) at *ZNW* 26 (1926), 129, though plausible linguistically, is not now adhered to. Lightfoot, *Hor. Heb.* (*Works*, London 1823, xii, 99) draws attention to a similar amoraitic usage.

[2] *Fathers acc. to R. Nathan*, trans., p. 112. Mekilta, *Kaspa* 2, cited above. Billerbeck, *op. cit.* I, 358.

[3] *Mishnāh*, Ber. IX, 5 (Danby, 10), b. Ber. 54*a* = Sonc. 328: *middāh, modeh, me'od. Midrash Tannaim . . . Devarim* (Hoffmann), 25, 26. Rashi, *ad loc.* Wünsche, *Neue Beiträge*, 437.

[4] *Mishnāh*, Ber. IX, 5; b. Ber. 61*b* = Sonc. 385; b. San. 74*a* = Sonc. 502; Shab. 56*b* = Sonc. 264; Yoma 82*a* = Sonc. 404; Pes. 25*a* = Sonc. 114–15; *Targ. Onḳelos*, Dt vi.4*b* (5). The LXX trans. *me'od* as ἰσχύς only at II Kings xxiii.25, and as δύναμις only at Dt vi.5 (!).

[5] So Delitzsch. 'Alef and 'Ayin are interchangeable and may be removed or added according to the *'al-tiḳ*^{e}*rey* technique. b. Ber. 32*a* = Sonc. 195. D it Mcion, omitting καὶ ἐν ὅλῃ τῇ διανοίᾳ σου may be betraying an intention to follow Dt vi.5 in ignorance of the *midrash*. διανοίᾳ is not an additional rendering of *levāv*. Thus one answers S. E. Johnson's doubt at *Harv. Theol. Rev.* 36 (1943), 146–7.

W. L. Knox, *Sources of the Syn. Gos.* II (Cambridge 1957), 57–8. Tatian fits Lk x.28*b*–37 on to Mk xii.32–34*a*. Matthew comments on Mk xii; 29*b* is excised and the misleading xxii.38–39*a* added. Mt xxii.40 seems to be an explanation of Mk xii.31*c* for the unlearned. M. Rade, 'Der Nächste', *Festgabe f. A. Jülicher* (Tübingen 1927), p. 71, held Mark and Matthew to be a doublet preferable to Luke.

the two prophets. Josiah, whose righteousness was axiomatic,[1] says, 'Let him alone; let no man move his bones'. Josiah recognises the sanctity of the old prophet because his bones were mixed with those of the young prophet. According to 2 K xxiii.25, there was no king before or after (!) Josiah that 'turned to the Lord with all his heart . . . according to all the law of Moses'. The words are an evident quotation from Deuteronomy.[2] Josiah must have obeyed Lv xix.18, and yet he was a persecutor of the cults of Samaria. The patriot, the national hero, was paralleled by the righteous king, David, who glories in Ps cxxxix in his perfect hatred of those who are opposed to God.[3] This seems to prove, as is obvious to the modern scholar, that 'neighbour' in Lv xix.18, as in so many other places,[4] has a limiting force, and does not mean 'man'. The question 'Who is my neighbour?' is merely an assertion that there can be a non-neighbour.[5] This is in order to obtain the true meaning of the *midrash*. If *v*. 29*a* was introduced by the evangelist it was not without good reason. The question can have been put *bona fide*.

[1] Jr xxii.15–16; Sir xlix.1–4. b. Shab. 56*b* = Sonc. 264.

[2] B. S. Easton, *Gospel acc. to St Luke* (New York 1926), 168. 2 K xxiii.3 takes up Dt iv.19; x.12; xi.13; xiii.3; xxvi.16; xxx.2, 6, 10.

[3] *Fathers acc. to R. Nathan*, XVI (trans. Goldin, p. 86): '. . . as thyself: I am the Lord. And why is that? *Because I have created him* (Is xlv.8). Indeed, if he acts as thy people do, thou shalt love him; but if not, thou shalt not love him.'

[4] Billerbeck, *ubi cit.* J. Fichtner in Kittel–Friedrich, *ThWzNT* VI (1959), 210–14. Only in Ex xi.2 can the word *re'a* mean 'non-Jew' exclusively—and the context is peculiar. Ex xx.16, 17; Lv xix.13; xx.10; Dt iv.42; xix.4, 5, 14 are doubtful, but rabbinical exegesis confines the second Leviticus citation to Jews: b. San. 52*b* = Sonc. 356. The following are certain examples of *re'a* meaning Jews: Ex xxi.14; xxii.7, 8, 9, 10, 11, 26 (cf. 25); Lv xix.17 (= brother); and Dt xv.2. Lv xix.34 is evidence, but why was it necessary to add it? The *ger toshav* was therefore not a 'neighbour' in the sense of *v*. 18. Dt x.18–19 proves that what was meant was charity. The choice of *v*. 18 to go with Dt vi.4 (5), ignoring *v*. 34, calls for emphatic comment. Lv xxiv.17–22 is not to the point. Dt xxiv.7 was never taken in the inclusive sense.

[5] H. Montefiore, *NT* 5 (1962), 157–70. The Testaments of the Twelve Patriarchs may well have been in existence *temp. Chr.* The contrary view elaborated by M. De Jonge in several works from 1953 onwards (see more recently *NT* 5 [1962], 311ff.) is unfortunately weakened by the actual discovery, amongst the Dead Sea Scrolls, of fragments of the Testament of Levi and of the Testament of Naphtali (A. Dupont-Sommer, *Les Écrits Esséniens* . . . 3rd edn [1968], 313–18), in versions corresponding or analogous to the known Greek text. From this it follows that the presence in Test. Issachar V.2, Test. Dan V.3 of instances of the citation of the two great commandments together may well be evidence that such a combination was a commonplace in some quarters in Jesus's time—*i.e.* those 'testaments' in those versions may well turn up among the Scrolls. *But this does not mean that re'a was understood to include the gentile* (H. Montefiore, 158). So violent a change in oriental cultural and social thinking must be accounted for. Even many centuries afterwards rabbis were prepared to presume that any girl over three years and a day, or any *animal*, left with a Gentile would be 'covered' by the latter! Inter-racial or inter-communal charity deserves a firmer foundation than this. And Maimonides (master of law and religion) says that *re'a* in Lv xix.18 means the Israelite and the proselyte: *op. cit.* I, II, vi.3–4 (trans. Hyamson [1965], 55*a*).

The parable answers[1] this assertion about the non-neighbour perfectly. Look to 2 K xxiii.17–18, where Josiah approves of the old prophet, and then see what the old prophet did (1 K xiii). See 2 Ch xxviii.15, and the Joseph story and Rahab. And then there is Dinah with whom it all began. Hosea gives the foundation, with which Mi vi agrees. Hosea explains (at *v.* 14) the lion in the Kings passage. Binding up the wounds caused by the robbers (who are a chastisement sent by God himself)[2] is part of God's work, his saving grace.[3] There is no fixed and formal method whereby salvation comes: one cannot, for example, rely on the hierarchy and rule out even the most improbable channel. God's arrangements may (perhaps often will) disregard even the sacrosanct caste system. In order to explain Lv xix.18 one needs only to concentrate on the word *'āhavᵉtā. 'Ahavāh* existed before the commandments.[4] Our parable therefore is an explanation of 'neighbour' in Lv xix.18, taking its scriptural support principally out of Ho vi, and utilising biblical-historical texts as justificatory precedents. Some might think this is an ideal parable.

That Dt vi.4 (5) and Samaritans were in fact linked in rabbinical thought, and that too (curiously) by way of wine, is proved by a Tannaitic *midrash*. We must love God with both our inclinations, the good and the evil. One must master the evil inclination. The story tells how Samaritan wine (very good wine) was sold to a rabbi on the understanding that he could control his inclinations, that is, resist the temptation to drink it.[5]

That Luke thought the parable was a commentary on Dt vi.4 (5) is indicated by the passage's position in the great central section, where it is found opposite to Dt vi–vii, and parallels in the wording abound.[6]

CONCLUSION

The parable thus answers the lawyer's question. The method of the lawyer's admission, given quite frankly, underlines this. The semitic tone is obvious. By saying *hā'oseh 'immo ḥéṣed* (*cf.* Gn xxiv.12) or the like he proves that he has grasped how *'ahavāh*, *ḥéṣed*, and Deuteronomy

[1] ὑπολαβών in *v.* 30 indicates lively debate, therefore the parable is a retort (so Lagrange). The word appears 22 times in Job.

[2] Jr xviii.22; Jb v.18. 'Lions and thieves are "by the hand of Heaven" ': b. Ket. 30*b* = Sonc. 167.

[3] Jr xxx.17. Midr. R., Levit. XVIII, 5 = Sonc. 233. Midr. R., Deut. III, 3 = Sonc. 70, 71. Midr. R., Num. (*Shᵉlach Lᵉcha*) XVII, 1 = Sonc. 698.

[4] Ex xx.6. Gn xxix.20; xxii.2, xxiv.67; xxv.28, xxxvii. 3, 4, xliv.20.

[5] Midr. R., Deut. II, 33 = Sonc. 61–2.

[6] C. F. Evans, 'Central Section of St Luke's Gospel' (cited above), 37–53 at p. 43. The paradox is that the foreigner (*cf.* Dt vii.2) has mercy on us.

and Leviticus are bound up together. From an artistic point of view the answer is conclusive.

The parable is shown as a kind of *midrash* on Ho vi.6 and adjacent verses, or at least a sermon hung on that passage by allusion; we have seen that there are other parables which are *midrashim* of a very similar kind, a complicated and highly organised teaching hooked, as it were, upon scriptural authorities. But the special feature of this parable is that it enjoins action. Cut the knots of 'if' and 'but', let the noble instinct do its work, and the commandments of God are fulfilled. We shall see a case[1] where the human instinct worked the opposite way, so that there is no danger of supposing that our present parable sanctifies instincts as such.

One might wonder, how far could general ethical teaching be derived from this highly technical parable? The principal teaching comes more directly from the *midrash* placing Deuteronomy and Leviticus together. The parable subserves that *midrash*. It is a highly scientific piece of instruction clothed in a deceptively popular style. The specific dilemma of persons belonging to specific castes does not by itself afford any rule of life for the ordinary man. But in explaining the true meaning of Lv xix.18, which is linked firmly to Dt vi.4 (5), it tells us that unless we show love to all humanity with the enumerated powers and attributes we cannot claim properly to have loved God, and so to have obtained entrance to the Messianic age.[2]

[1] Chapter 13 below.

[2] I derived some profit from discussion with K. G. Klemm, at that time (1964) a pupil of Professor E. Stauffer and about to complete a thesis on this parable.

CHAPTER TEN

Water into Wine

THE FIRST MIRACLE OF JESUS (Jn ii.1–11) may be studied from two purely objective standpoints: what happened, and why was it recorded as it appears in John? Many apparently fanciful interpretations have been placed upon the passage, and it forms the object of open and veiled scepticism, while the actual circumstances which must have obtained if our text is to be relied upon have not been explained.[1]

A considerable amount of research has gone into both pre-Christian[2] and post-Christian[3] use of wine-symbolism in religious contexts, not without stories of miracles: but, though these throw valuable light both on the mentality of St John's contemporaries and on the potentialities

[1] R. Schnackenburg, *Das erste Wunder Jesu* (Freiburg i. Br. 1951) not only reviews the deeper meanings of the episode, allegorical, sacramental, messianic, the 'history of religions' aspect, and the christological meaning, but notices (as commentators do not), at p. 6, that presents were usual and that wine was often brought as such. Many writers say it is vain to 'speculate about the historical conditions of a fact which does not belong to strict history' (A. Loisy, G. H. C. Macgregor, R. H. Strachan). W. F. Howard, *Fourth Gospel*, 4th edn (London 1955), 190 says all that happened was that Jesus ordered the wine to be diluted! H. van der Loos, *The Miracles of Jesus* (Leiden 1965), 590–618 gives a good survey of previous ideas and the background. Amongst other recent studies the following are to be noted: R. J. Dillon, 'Wisdom tradition and sacramental retrospect in the Cana account', *CBQ* 24 (1962), 268–96 and M. Rissi, 'Die Hochzeit in Kana' in F. Christ, ed., *Oikonomia* (Hamburg 1967), 76–92, which is highly allegorical. C. H. Dodd, *Historical Tradition in the Fourth Gospel* 223–8, starts (as in his *Interpretation of the Fourth Gospel*, 1953, 297–300) with the proposition that the story is a highly theological demonstration of a sign; Christ the giver of the knowledge of God which is eternal life (as distinct from mere purification) comes at the moment he chooses—'the hour comes and now is': but the story, though intended to be understood symbolically, is a pure miracle story. However, as he shows, much of the symbolism picks up synoptic ideas (*e.g.* 'new wine', which is not readily accepted), and he guesses that the traditional nucleus may have been a wedding parable. This is attractive; but it totally ignores what we find the *pericope* actually shows Jesus *doing*, and that particular kind of reciprocity can be done only by a miracle-worker, and hence cannot form part of a parable of which Jesus (or the rabbis) would be author.

[2] H. Noetzel, *see below*, p. 245, n. 3. Dodd, *ubi cit.*, 224–5. Folk-tales, he says, forget their origins: but could this notorious Dionysos-myth have been forgotten?

[3] E. S. Drower, *Water into Wine: a study of ritual idiom in the Middle East* (London 1956), usefully reviewed at *JJS* (1957), 250–1.

of such ideas later, they do nothing to clarify our biblical story as it stands.

No one can say *how* Jesus changed water into wine. But *why* he did so, and what he meant by that curious response to his mother are not beyond recovery. For the first, Jewish Law retains sufficient information to enable us to see Jesus's moral situation at that wedding-feast, and also to enable us to see the significance of the gift of wine. As for the other problem, it has not been noticed that, if Jesus actually used those words, they expressly allude to a not altogether dissimilar miracle connected with that well-known provider of food and drink, the prophet Elisha. Apart from this, a careful and comparative study of *shosh^{e}viynūt* reveals its idiomatic character and shows what was in Jesus's mind when his mother approached him. Why she approached him, and what she expected him to do also appear from this reconstruction.

WEDDING-GUESTS

We are concerned with the habits of Jews in Galilee in the first century. We have very little information bearing directly upon contemporary practice with regard to invitations to wedding-feasts—but what we have is significant.[1] It has already been made evident that the parents of the bridegroom, or the bridegroom himself, were responsible for the entertainment of the guests, and indeed took the initiative with regard to the betrothal, the solemnisation of matrimony (the homebringing of the bride), and the invitation of the guests.[2] We know that, since it was not usual for marriages to be arranged by the parties in person, the prospective bridegroom's parents employed a man to act as their agent in effecting the betrothal of their son. The interests of the bridegroom were represented by this independent 'go-between', and the selected bride's family saw to it that they too were represented by what may not improperly be described as an agent.[3] When it came to the actual ceremony of marriage the bridegroom's representative saw his work come to fruition and assisted at the critical moment.[4] Since the financial situation of the bride would be affected if it emerged that she was not a virgin, the Jews, like many oriental peoples to this day, provided that evidence of her virginity should be forthcoming, and should remain in

[1] P. Billerbeck, *Kommentar* I, 500ff. Non-tannaïtic material has only an indirect bearing on our problem.
[2] G. F. Moore, *Judaism* II, 119–22. *Jew. Enc.* III (1925) 126f.
[3] *Tanḥuma*, Korah 8; Tosefta and the Talmuds cited by Jastrow *op. cit.*, 1543 (*shosh^{e}viyn*).
[4] Whence Jn iii.29 ('The friend of the bridegroom, who stands and hears him, rejoices greatly at the bridegroom's voice. . . .').

the custody of the bride's representative. The witnesses, and the agents, had what may be called an economic as well as ceremonial and social role to play.[1] Their 'business' was not concluded with the betrothal or the declarations under the canopy. At least one night must pass during which the couple would come together.

The Talmud evidences an indelicate, but probably ancient, custom whereby the bridegroom would signify a successful attempt at intercourse by pronouncing the *Sh^{e}m'a* ('Hear, O Israel . . .!'), a duty from which he was exempted from the evening of the wedding until that time had been reached—to pronounce it earlier was misleading, even in one of established piety! Oriental peoples who favour marriage at or about puberty between people who have hardly met, let alone fallen in love, are aware of the young spouses' difficulties, and the two families prefer to be together for much longer than a day and a night.

Difficulties of travelling, the rareness of opportunities for relations and friends to meet, and the psychological factors referred to above, all joined to make it convenient for the wedding to be an affair of three days or more, and in the case of the marriage of a virgin, a full week. Naturally the time is spent in festivities, and naturally the males get intoxicated.

Some of these details are learnt, in respect of the Jews, from relatively late sources: but habits with regard to weddings die hard. The law relating to the relationship between the bridegroom's friend and the bridegroom will hardly have been open to change, since there is nothing about it to attract the reforming eye of the Pharisee, and we actually come upon it buried, unobtrusively, in the law relating to intestate succession, one of the most static chapters of ancient law. Mishnaic information will certainly be available for our purposes, especially when it accords with common sense. An Indian parallel, very much alive to this day, is far from unhelpful to us, as we shall see shortly.

At the wedding feast those who have stood by the bridegroom and especially those who have negotiated the marriage, will be in high honour. The degree of intimacy extended to the 'best man', in Hebrew *shosh^{e}viyn*,[2] might be no greater than that subsisting between the bridegroom and his parents and other relations and friends, and therefore the inner group of friends feasting with the bridegroom will be *shosh^{e}viyniym*, and will be somewhat distinct from other people who are invited to the feast out of courtesy, or charity, or a desire to obtain prestige.[3]

[1] One may consult b. Ket. 12*a* = Sonc. 63 for an account of Judaean and Galilean customs.

[2] *Jew. Enc.* III, 127f.

[3] For the distinction note phrasing at b. Sukk. 25*b* = Sonc. 111. *Shosh^{e}viyniym* included others besides those who accompanied the bridegroom on his procession to

There were, therefore, two categories of wedding-guests. There were the personal friends of the bridegroom or his parents, including cousins and other relatives, of whom the most significant would be his age-mates, males, comrades, whether or not fellow-villagers. From amongst these would be chosen the best man, or best men, who would act in the negotiations for the betrothal.[1] Secondly, there would be the remoter relatives, females, fellow-villagers, business connections, and tenants. These would be expected at a wedding, though their presence would not be essential. Again there would be guests whose presence lent dignity or prestige, such as the local representative of the ruler, other notables (if they could be induced to appear) and the aristocracy of the nation which would include rabbis.[2] At a suitable distance from them there should be some poor neighbours.[3] The reason for placing these categories apart lies in the vital question of wedding-presents. The Jews, as is evident throughout the Talmud, thought a great deal of rights and duties, and found it in them to count the financial implications of almost every relationship in cash to the nearest *p^erūṭāh*.[4] Everyone would be aware of his obligations, and those of his neighbours, and a wedding-guest who fell short of what was expected of him had to face not merely scorn but a civil suit into the bargain. This sounds strange to modern European ears, but there is no doubt about the facts.

It is not desirable to think of the Jews as isolated in these respects from developing and ancient societies in general. Reciprocity and the social and psychological functions of exchange (*i.e.* it is nonsense to think of *gift* as by nature isolated from reward of some kind) have been studied in the classic work[5] of Marcel Mauss, who was at one and the same time a social-anthropologist, a classical scholar and an orientalist; and against the background of his study the episode of Christ's turning water into wine comes to life in a fashion unpredictable from mystical–mythical–allegorical studies of the pericope by modern theologians.

[1] *Shosh^eviynūtā'* means both connection by 'groomsmanship' and blood relationship and intimacy (Jastrow). *Shosh^eviyn* = 'friend', 'guardian of the interests of the bride': Midr. R., Exod. XLIV. 4 = Sonc. 509–10. God (naturally!) was *shosh^eviyn* to Adam: b. Ber. 61*a*.

[2] Midr. R., Eccl. III.2, 3 = Sonc. 78; b. Ber. 9*a* = Sonc. 45.

[3] Waiters might not attend to all guests equally: b. B.B. 145*b* = Sonc. 625.

[4] A marvellously vulgar passage appears at b. B.B. 145*b* (*cit. sup.*).

[5] To be read in M. Mauss, *The Gift. Forms and Functions of Exchange in Archaic Societies*, trans. I. Cunnison, with an introd. by E. E. Evans-Pritchard (London 1954). The French original appeared in 1925.

fetch the bride. The *b^eney ḥophāh*, *b^eney g^enānā'* *i.e.* the υἱοὶ τοῦ νυμφῶνος of Mk ii.19; Mt ix.15; Lk v.34 include *shosh^eviyniym*. They are wedding-guests collectively. They must feast, and not fast, for they are attending an observance of a religious character of a joyous nature.

The poor neighbours invited out of charity would not be expected to provide wedding-presents. The aristocracy and notables would be invited in the spirit of compliment, and though they would not be expected to provide anything they certainly would make some contribution (which could hardly be calculated beforehand) for otherwise they would be under obligation to their inferiors, which is not tolerable in the East, if anywhere. This fact is to be noted in passing, since it explains why in Mt xxii the king's invitation was declined and why the king reacted as he did: private citizens stood to lose if they had to waste their time in feasting, and had not a marriage of their own or of their sons in contemplation.[1] Remote relatives, tenants, business connections and others who were more or less equals with the bridegroom's family would make some contribution to the festivities. The principle was that the guests rejoiced *with* the bridegroom and not at his expense.[2] It is exemplified very clearly when we come to the first category, the bridegroom's friends, that is to say his personal friends and equals.

In the case of the *shosh*^{e}*viyniym* the duty of sending a wedding-present is wrapped up with the status of *shosh*^{e}*viynūt*. Indeed exactly the same word means both the status of a *shosh*^{e}*viyn*, bridegroom's friend or groomsman, as he is somewhat inelegantly called, and the present he is obliged to send. The procedure is as follows.[3] The bridegroom, whom we shall call *A*, asks his classmate *B*, who is unmarried, to his wedding. *B* sends 10 denar. a few days prior to the feast. Of those 10 denar. part is spent on preparations for the feast and part on household utensils for the use of the bridal couple. *B* then comes to the feast and eats and drinks and is satisfied. *B* in turn gets married, and *A* is at once under an obligation to reciprocate. Reciprocity is inherent in *shosh*^{e}*viynūt*.

The rabbis lay down that *A* must return exactly the same sum, *i.e.* 10 denar., unless the marriage of *B* differs in some material respect from that of *A*.[4] We are left to suppose that originally any difference in

[1] See above, p. 139.

[2] The passage from B.B. cited above (Sonc. 625–6) shows that all guests brought presents (except the poor, presumably) and that one could estimate from rank the value of the present ('guests usually consume up to a *zuz* . . .').

[3] The authorities for what follows are to be found in *Mishnāh*, B.B. IX, 4 (Danby, 378f.; Blackman's *Mishnayoth* IV, 216, where the notes indicate a somewhat different interpretation; Windfuhr, 82–3, where 'at the time of the wedding' is omitted); b. B.B. 145*a*–*b* = Sonc. 624–6; Maimonides, *Mishneh Torāh*, XII (Acquisition), II (original acquisition and gifts) vii (trans. Klein, p. 133ff.). The last words of *Mishnāh*, B.B. IX, 4 may be taken as referring to the guest sending (or delivering) a present to his friend, the bridegroom. This is natural, Maimonides so takes it, and we may follow him despite Blackman and Danby's teacher. One who disputes with Maimonides must be very sure of his ground, and the text of the *Mishnāh* is strongly in M.'s favour.

[4] b. B.B. 145*b* = Sonc. 626. The principle is old, and based upon common sense.

the expense undergone by *B* for setting up house or entertaining friends at the feast (as for example where *B* is actually a widower and is marrying a non-virgin) would be reflected in the amount. In such cases *A* would not expect to eat and drink and to be satisfied in the same way as *B* did at *A*'s wedding, and therefore he would be entitled to deduct something, and, say, 5 denar. might suffice. But let us assume that *B*'s wedding did not differ from *A*'s. *A* must send 10 denar. before the feast, and of course he is entitled to turn up to the feast without specific invitation.[1] If *A* is unable to attend he is not entitled to omit to send the present: he can deduct from the 10 denar. the amount *B* must have eaten and drunk at his own wedding. In case of a dispute between *A* and *B* as to the amount *B* drank no doubt the matter could go to arbitration and witnesses would be questioned as to *B*'s degree of intoxication at the nuptials of *A*. Farcical as all this seems, this is the spirit of our authorities.[2] Reciprocity is the condition of many so-called gifts in the semitic family of nations.[3] Indeed one can extend the principle further. Generosity, without expectation of reciprocation, is rare everywhere; and prestige is wrapped up with giving and receiving in civilisations from America to Polynesia.

If *A* failed to send the wedding-present in the circumstances mentioned above *B* could commence a suit against him in court, for the obligation counted for this purpose as a debt.[4] This particular feature of the Jewish Law may not be unparalleled, but the present writer has not come across a counterpart. There is a *faint* possibility that in Jesus's time the obligation did not amount strictly to a debt, and that *B* would not be entitled to seize the property of *A* as security for its payment. But if the *Mishnāh* makes out that *shoshᵉviynūt* is equal to a debt we can be sure that in Jesus's time the duty of reciprocation was taken very seriously indeed.

In India there is an obligation to invite (*nimantraṇa*, *nyota*) families to one's weddings (and similarly auspicious functions) which have the relationship, often hereditary, of reciprocal invitation and present-giving. The guest may be even of higher or lower caste: he is a particular

[1] b. B.B. 145*b*.

[2] Maimonides, *ubi cit.*, vii, § 6.

[3] J. Kohler, 'Darstellung des talmudischen Rechtes', *ZVR* 20 (1907) 179f. All presents must be given publicly, publicity being of the essence of transactions between persons (as contrasted with merely charitable and pious donations). For a semitic practice closely similar to *shoshᵉviynūt cf.* the *mesnit* of the Bogos: J. A. W. Munzinger, *Über die Sitten und das Recht der Bogos* (Winterthur 1859), 47, 72; G. Mazzarella, 'L'Esogamia presso i popoli semitici', *Riv. ital. di Sociologia* 5 (1901), at p. 11 of the offprint.

[4] Not an ordinary debt, for it had exceptional features, but these do not interest us here, Maim. *ubi cit.* vii, 2, 13. The *Mishnāh* says plainly (B.B. IX, 4) *ha-shoshᵉviynūt nigᵉbeyt bᵉ-veyt diyn.*

type of friend (called, *e.g.*, *nyotaharī*, *nautaharā*); his presents are valued and recorded, and strict reciprocity is a matter of honour. Even the poor will face indigence rather than fail to produce the expected *nyota* present when the friend's marriage takes place. The institution is of immemorial antiquity with agriculturalists, as with the Jews.[1]

Naturally, guests who were themselves married, and who were therefore not likely to anticipate reciprocal treatment, or those to whose weddings our bridegroom had not come, so that they were under no duty to reciprocate, would have some method of contributing to the festivities which would be outside the scope of the *shoshᵉviynūt*, properly so called. This is not to suggest that a married man could not be a *shoshᵉviyn*. On the contrary the most eligible person to perform the delicate functions of 'best man' would be older than the bridegroom and most probably married. In fact the custom was, so far as practicable, to call upon a person of somewhat higher status socially, a person of rather higher prestige, than the bridegroom's family, even if this meant going to the edge of those who could be described as intimate: one went down for one's bride, but up for one's *shoshᵉviyn*.[2] Thus we can be sure that even men who were not age-mates would be within the scope of reciprocal presents. But there must have been many guests who for one reason or another would not count technically as *shoshᵉviyniym*, and we have reviewed many such. The custom accordingly provided that a gift of wine or other comestibles at the actual time of the wedding counted as a gift of affection, and was non-reciprocating. Our sources tell us so in so many words, and we find wine mentioned first of all, for obvious reasons.[3]

In the case of a young *shoshᵉviyn* who lived in the Jewish joint family, with little or no earnings of his own, it would often be difficult for him to provide his own *shoshᵉviynūt*. Consequently the custom was for the father to send the sum. He had a choice, whether to attach to it the

[1] An interesting extreme example of reciprocity are the mutual entertainments in Malabar called *Changngātikkuṛi Kalyāṇam*, explained by Graeme in his *Glossary of Words and Phrases* reprinted in W. Logan, *Malabar* II (1887), clxxiii–clxxiv.

[2] b. Yev. 63*a* = Sonc. 421; b. Ber. 61*a* = Sonc. 383.

[3] *'avāl ha-sholeaḥ la-ḥavero kadey yayin vᵉ-kadey shemen, 'eyn nigᵉviyn bᵉ-veyt diyn, miphᵉney she-hen gᵉmiylūt ḥaṣādiym. ḥaver* means 'fellow', 'comrade', 'pal', and therefore is an odd word for 'brother', which is what Blackman and Danby's teacher apparently thought (p. 232 n. 3 *sup.*). What is intended is the friend's 'friend', *i.e.* the bridegroom. *sholeaḥ* does not imply that one cannot make the gift in the presence of the bridegroom and at the time of the wedding. Maimonides says explicitly *bᵉ'et hanisu'iyn* 'at the time of the wedding'. *gᵉmiylūt ḥaṣādiym* (see p. 209 above) is a general term for an act of loving kindness for which the reward (if any) is in Heaven. Carrying a bier, or condoling with mourners, would be examples. 'Charitable deed' gives too restricted an impression. Maimonides adds that the law relating to groomsmen's gifts (*diyney shoshᵉviynūt*) applies only to gifts of money.

name of a particular son, or to leave it as a family present. In the first case this was virtually a present to the son indicated, since at that son's wedding the bridegroom would have to reciprocate. In the second the first son to marry would have the right to call for reciprocation. The head of the family paid the present, and its repayment counted as a hereditary asset, divisible between the brothers after the father's death if he died in the interval.[1]

THE SITUATION AT CANA[2]

We are told that the mother of Jesus 'was there'. She was evidently on terms of intimacy with the bridegroom's parents and was 'behind the scenes' enjoying the festivities in the more dignified, though not less convivial, atmosphere of the inner apartments. She, together with the other women, would be much nearer to the domestic quarters, and would become aware sooner than the male guests in their dining-room of the situation with regard to the supply of food and drink. She may even have been helping the bridegroom's mother with the preparation of dishes,[3] but this is a guess, and not necessary to the reconstruction, though it is difficult to see how she can have given the instructions to the servants if she had no such concern at the time.

Jesus and his disciples 'were invited'. The question has been raised whether they were invited at the commencement of the feast. One does not wish to exclude absolutely the possibility of their appearing later than the commencement, but the custom of sending invitations personally as soon as preparations were ready, or of otherwise notifying the commencement by ringing a bell, and the custom of a solemn gathering for the blessings tend to make it improbable that Jesus came later than the commencement. The picture that has been painted by some, of guests coming and going during the week, is not quite accurate: strangers, the poor, and people employed in government and other service might well 'drop in' for a while. Friends of the family, the family themselves, and honoured guests would expect to stay for as long as possible. If Jesus had stayed for two or three days out of the seven, that would have been entirely fitting from every point of view—but he may well have stayed longer.

The invitation was extended to him because of a childhood associa-

[1] b. B.B. 144*b* = Sonc. 620. See citation from Kohler above.

[2] The real Cana was at the ruined place called Khirbet Ḳāna (8½ m. N. of Nazareth), not the popular 'holy place' Kafr Kenna, in spite of falsifications connived at by modern Israelis (C. Kopp, *The Holy Places of the Gospels* [Freiburg/Edinburgh 1963], 144–54).

[3] So Schnackenburg, 5. Zahn (1921) thought the obedience of the servants also to be a miracle!

tion, which might have been intimate, or because he was one of the very distinguished people in the neighbourhood, or for both reasons. If we doubt whether Jesus could have accepted merely to add to the prestige of the family, his mother's presence confirms the doubt. He must have wanted to rejoice with the bridegroom in the customary manner. But the invitation was not to him alone. He was invited together with the disciples. Naturally. They were his 'family'. As head of the family he accepted the invitation, and had it been a normal family he would have been obliged to contribute to the feast. In so far as his company consisted of marriageable young Galileans the status of *shosh^{e}viynūt* would arise. Some would marry. They were mostly poor, living as mendicants, wandering from place to place,[1] but that would not last indefinitely. Many would settle down and found families. Others, following their master, would eschew family-life. Mary knew well that Jesus would not marry. However, on behalf of some at least of his disciples Jesus ought to have provided a reciprocating wedding-present, whilst on behalf of others he ought to have provided some non-reciprocating contribution to the feast. The only way to avoid this would be to accept in the guise of beggars, as objects of charity. This the text does not suggest. It is highly unlikely that beggars would be invited to stay till a point when the good wine would normally be replaced by inferior wine. In respect of some of the disciples, possibly a large proportion of them, acceptance implies a moral obligation to make a substantial contribution.

Had Jesus the means? Had any of the disciples? Some, no doubt, still had access to family funds. The contribution of others to the common stock must long since have been exhausted. Widows and other patrons of the band could hardly be looked to in an emergency such as this. Jesus was no longer at the carpenter's bench; he was about his Father's business, which meant complete absence of visible means of support. Could he ask patrons to finance his and his disciples' feasting at a wedding-feast? True, such feasts were supposed to be religious occasions, but common sense precludes any such application as that suggested.

The evidence that Jesus was well acquainted with the law and usages of his people is overwhelming.[2] He can hardly have accepted the invitation in a fit of abstraction or indifference. The hardy wanderers, many of them youthful, probably had excellent appetites. They will have eaten and drunk freely. The company were already past knowing

[1] See Mk vi.8; ii.23; viii.14; x.28; Lk viii.3; ix.58.

[2] The episodes of the Unjust Steward; the Woman taken in Adultery; the Anointing at Bethany and the Temple-tax question leave us in no doubt.

how good the wine was. The *architriclinos*—whom the present writer, in spite of the learning of lexicographers, sees as the master of ceremonies[1]—was clearer-headed than anyone present except the servants.[2] The invitation was a 'block invitation'. Even so early in Jesus's ministry his 'family' amounted to a dozen, or even more. Our information is neither precise nor exhaustive. There could have been many more. A group of a score of guests could hardly be more abstemious than the remainder. Small wonder the wine ran out, or was in imminent danger of running out! The bridegroom or his parents had underestimated the capacity of their guests, and a substantial section of them had made no contribution, or no contribution worth the name, to the good cheer.

The position was serious for the bridegroom. He could, as we have seen, expect a wedding-present from all but the beggars (if any). It is possible that, apart from Jesus and his disciples, the guests had not been as numerous as expected, or had sent inadequate presents, or some accident had prevented the laying-in of sufficient refreshment. We are not concerned, except to notice that if the wine ran out, as we are told it did, the disappointment of the company and their host would vent itself in the comment that a group of guests had been refreshing themselves virtually at the expense of the others. The loss of prestige of the bridegroom, who was the nominal host,[3] would be considerable if guests departed unexpectedly early, unsatisfied. But that would not be the end of the matter. When unmarried guests eventually married they would expect their *shosh^{e}viynūyot* to be reciprocated with an additional payment: we can be sure that the principles of this reciprocity (which

[1] Cremer-Kögel and Bauer are clear, and they are followed by most commentators. Hoskyns (1954), 188; Wikenhauser (1957), 75. J. E. Belser (1905), 76, actually thought the *Tafelmeister* was complaining! A head waiter would be in better contact with the servants, and would not dare to summon, or shout to, the host, especially in such vulgar and evidently 'merry' terms. The word must have, perhaps at different periods and in different contexts, represented more than one sort of functionary. In no oriental feast would a servant have made the comment as alleged, whereas a professional or semiprofessional master of ceremonies might well do so. We may rely on Sirach xxxii (xxxv). 1 (see notes at R. H. Charles, *Apocrypha and Pseudepigrapha*, I (1913), 424). The whole fundamental attitude and method of H. Windisch, 'Die johanneische Weinregel', *ZNW* 14 (1913) 248–57 deserves minute appraisal: many of his suppositions are wrong, and his conclusions questionable or superfluous. What, for example, is there to show us that the guests were 'great drinkers'? Whether there was a rule or not, what is important was that the man believed that there was—a rule not of custom, of course, but of usage.

[2] Many (if not most) were already 'merry' (ii.10). To get 'merry'—and even to dance—was an ancient custom and quite respectable: b. Ber. 30*b*–31*d* = Sonc. 188. A professional master of ceremonies would have a good head, naturally.

[3] b. Ber. 47*a* = Sonc. 284. *Jew. Enc.* VIII, 340–7. Jn ii.9*c* shows that the bridegroom was host in form if not in fact. φωνεῖ may mean 'shouted over to'. But was he with the bride, or asleep? If so the light φωνεῖ throws on etiquette and the taste of the wine is remarkable.

we have discussed) required, in such alarming circumstances, nothing less than compensation to the guests.

A had invited *B* to his wedding-feast; *B* has sent 10 denar.; but had left the feast prematurely having consumed less than the 5 denar. worth he had expected to consume, less, shall we say, by 2 denar. Then when *B* marries, *A* will be expected to send not less than 12 denar. At this rate, assuming that a dozen marriageable lads went away disappointed, our bridegroom stood to lose financially—say, up to about half the value of the presents Jesus and his party ought to have brought—as well as in point of reputation.

Mary would be alive to the implications of the failure in the supply of wine. It is possible that she overheard comments from the bridegroom's family. Her son's presence had complicated, if not actually caused, the calamity. Her son's wisdom and independence, and his authority over his followers, were known to her; and she evidently assumed that he should be told what the situation was. So, ignoring the breach of etiquette involved in disturbing the male guests, she entered and told him of the bridegroom's plight.

'WHAT HAVE I TO DO WITH THEE?'

This striking reply, which Mary interpreted as an acknowledgement of his willingness, if not actual obligation, to take some action, has been very diversely interpreted.[1] The appellation 'woman' causes no difficulty: it is universally recognised that it implies no hostility or rudeness, though the correct explanation, namely that a religious devotee or ascetic will speak to a woman, if unavoidable, only in the most formal terms, seems not to have attracted attention. The rhetorical question itself seems rude. It suggests distance. It has been seen as a divine repudiation of the claims of the earthly mother.[2] On the other hand rabbinical sources have been scrutinised, and biblical parallels examined, with the suggested result that the phrase means, 'What reason can there be (or, is there?) for your saying this to me?'[3] An older scholar, looking at classical and Hellenistic material, found the denial of common interest to be implied, and this interpretation is the one followed in the

[1] It is superfluous to give all the attempts. The best study is P. Gächter, 'Maria in Kana', *ZKT* 55 (1931) 351–402, especially at p. 364–73. H. van der Loos (*cit. sup.*) sees it definitely as a refusal. The instances he cites do not necessarily support this interpretation. The *Jerusalem Bible* has 'Woman, why turn to me?'–which suggests an impatient refusal (obviously a slip of the tongue in the circumstances), which is hardly rational.

[2] Chr. Wordsworth, *NT* 1, 277.

[3] Billerbeck, II, 401. Much that is cited is not relevant, while 2 K iii.13 (the vital citation) is omitted.

New English Bible recently.[1] An impressive study of the phrase was undertaken by Gächter,[2] but from his results I am obliged to differ.

The words are evidently a quotation from the Old Testament. Of the many possible passages to which allusion might be made that concerning Elisha and the three kings is the one which at once makes an appeal. Was Jesus deliberately making an allusion to that passage? We can assume that he was, and interpret the phrase in that light; or we can assume that it was a coincidence, and that Jesus independently meant by that phrase what any man steeped in the Old Testament could mean by it. It might be that only afterwards were the compilers of the gospels in a position to see the significance of the choice of words. If we assume that John includes something that the synoptics thought it better to omit, we may believe that the story was controversial and even embarrassing at a very early period. Whichever course we adopt we are bound to find out what τί ἐμοὶ καὶ σοί; essentially means. There is no better way than to examine all the passages, and to extract the common element. This means going, very briefly, over ground covered by Gächter, but the difference in result will be apparent. It is at once evident that the expression is idiomatic, verging upon the colloquial. The verbal meaning does not indicate the true meaning. Linguistically parallel, but semantically distinct expressions cannot help us.[3]

1. Shimei curses David, and Abishai, son of Zeruiah, remonstrates and asks for permission to kill Shimei (2 S xvi.5, 9). David rebukes Abishai, saying (*v.* 10) ***māh-liy vᵉlāchem*** (LXX: τί ἐμοὶ καὶ ὑμῖν;—similarly elsewhere), on

[1] Which adopts the 'we are not concerned about the same thing' interpretation. It is possible that Alexandrian and other Greek-speaking Jews used τί ἐμοὶ καί σοί in a narrower sense than Greeks. Josephus's paraphrases however are valuable information. See J. J. Wetstenius (Wetstein) Η ΚΑΙΝΗ ΔΙΑΘΗΚΗ, I (Amsterdam 1751), at p. 355 (on Mt viii.29). Note that Epictetus, I, i, 16 uses τί ἡμῖν καὶ . . . in just the sense of *māh liy vᵉ-lᵉchā*, except that it is addressed otherwise than to the person remonstrated with: 'What have we to do with the north wind? It ought to cease troubling us.' Similarly II, xix, 16, 19. The instance at II, xx, 11 is of the wider variety, implying no community of interest or concern.

[2] Cited *sup.*, p. 238 n. 1. He understands the phrase as a refusal, whereas Mary manifestly understands it as an *agreement*. So Wikenhauser (73) interprets the phrase in a purely negative sense. Schnackenburg (31) sees a limited 'Trennungstrich'. Dodd, *ubi cit.*, 226 asks if this is not a reference to traditions of tension within the family: *cf.* Mk iii.32–5, Lk ii.48–50, Jn vii.3–5. Mary's ὅ τι ἂν λέγῃ ὑμῖν, ποιήσατε ('Do whatever he tells you') is well known to be a reminiscence of Gn xli.55 LXX. What is not so well known is that the implications of this are (i) that if Mary was applied to by the distressed family she had perfect confidence in her son, as Pharaoh had in Joseph, and (ii) Jesus's relief of the 'famine' was on the basis of reciprocity (Joseph *sold* to the Egyptians).

[3] H. van der Loos (*op. cit.*), 594 does not make the distinction adequately. I would exclude Ho xiv.8–9; 2 K ix.18; Ezr iv.3; Jr ii.18; Is iii.15, xxii. 1; Jos xxii.24. On the other hand the expression *'eyn lāyy* (?) at 2 S xxi.4 seems semantically parallel.

the ground that Shimei was perfectly entitled to curse him. Evidently the phrase means here, 'Do not tell me what to do, I am not obliged to respond to your suggestion'. David thought himself justified in listening to Shimei's curses; and Abishai unjustified in indirectly questioning David's patience.

2. Shimei apologises to David, and Abishai recommends that Shimei be put to death (2 S xix.16–21). David complains, using the same phrase as before. He claims that Abishai is acting in a manner hostile to himself, tempting him to do something inauspicious. The meaning is, 'Do not tell me what to do. You have no right to make so improper a suggestion'. Light is thrown on his attitude towards Shimei by 1 K ii.8–9, *cf.* 44. Josephus's paraphrase implies that David was impatient with Abishai's persistence.[1]

3. Necho king of Egypt advanced against Charchemish by the Euphrates, and Josiah king of Judah attempted to interfere. Necho complained in our phrase, explaining that he had no grievance against Josiah, and furthermore God had ordered him to do what he was doing. Josiah ignored the latter warning and was wounded and died (2 Ch xxxv.20–3). Necho's use of the phrase implies, 'Do not interfere. I have no quarrel with you, and in any case right is on my side'.

4. Jephthah, a man with a grievance, is called in as a leader. He complained to the aggressors, using our phrase, and enquiring their reason for invading. They reply, giving a *prima facie* ground for their conduct (Jg xi.1–13). The phrase seems to mean, 'What claim have you against me?', implying that they have none—not, as we should say, a leg to stand on.

5. The woman befriended by Elijah has a grievance against him. Though he could (she supposed) have prevented it, her son has fallen sick. Without preamble she accosts him with our phrase. Had he come to recall her sins to her, and to slay her son? His reaction is to restore the son to health. The phrase can only mean, 'What have you against me (that you should attack me, or let me down, in this way)?', implying that her misfortune was in large measure (in her opinion) undeserved, and Elijah's negligence uncharitable and unworthy of him. When he responds to her complaint—for as such Josephus sees her behaviour[2]—she recognises his true character (1 K xvii. 17–24).

6. We come at length to the most significant example. Jehoram initiates an expedition against the king of Moab. He is joined in turn by Jehoshaphat and the king of Edom. All three become short of water. Jehoshaphat suggests enquiring of the Lord by a prophet. Elisha is suggested as he is in the vicinity. As soon as Elisha saw Jehoram he used our phrase (2 K iii.13). He recommends him to consult his usual, or ancestral prophets. Jehoram explains that the three armies will be defeated due to the lack of water. Elisha refuses to be prompted by him, but professes to be moved by the presence of Jehoshaphat; he calls for a minstrel, and prophesies. The result of his instructions is that a flood appears, filling the ditches they had dug. This flood serves not

[1] *Ant.* VII, 265 (xi. 2); cf. VII, 208–9 (ix. 4).
[2] *Ant.* VIII, 325 (xiii. 3); cf. V, 261 (vii. 9).

merely as drink for the hosts and their cattle, but, because of its blood-red appearance, deceives the enemy in such a fashion that they are induced to make a tactical error which leads to their defeat. At first sight Elisha's greeting to Jehoram is rude in the extreme. But when we recollect that Elisha had foreknowledge of events,[1] and saw what was happening at a distance, we realise that he knew the needs of the armies before the three kings' visit. He did not care for Jehoram's prompting. There is no evidence that he hesitated to do his duty. On the contrary the elaborate snub to Jehoram shows that he did not want any implication to be placed upon his act which would embarrass him in future. The phrase means, 'You have no claim upon me. I shall not act at *your* bidding'. Josephus paraphrases the expression, τοῦ δὲ μὴ διοχλεῖν αὐτῷ φράσαντος, ἀλλὰ . . . implying, 'Do not trouble me',[2] but though this shows what Josephus thought the phrase meant it cannot be a final interpretation of it.

7, 8, 9. Three further episodes (Mk v.7; Mt viii.29; Lk viii.28; Mk i.24; Lk iv.33–4) have a common feature. Unclean spirits shout out our phrase as soon as they see Jesus. In the first example the cry seems to be of fear; in the second of indignation; in the third of despair. In all the cases they know that there is a strong likelihood that they will be dislodged. They are trying in a pathetically human fashion to fend off this disaster by appealing to their antagonist's sense of fairness. They seem to be saying, 'We have done you no harm. Though you have the power, do not harm us, for you have no claim against us'.

It is permissible to construe the occurrence in Jn ii.4 by reference to the other nine examples. Each one of them is a remonstrance. Indignant, pathetic, impatient, rational (as in Elisha's case), or irrational (as in the widow's)—whatever the tone, the meaning is a remonstrance. In every case the speaker asserts that the person addressed has no right, claim, or justification for taking this course with him. Personal affront is suggested. 'Why do you take this course with *me*?' 'What have *I* done to deserve this?' 'There is no need for you to take this course.' Gächter reports from Mittermaier at second hand[3] a saying in east Syrian 'chaldaean' a phrase from modern Kurdistan corresponding word for word with τί ἐμοὶ καὶ σοί. It is *man bain anta un ana*. Its meaning is a 'Beteuerung der innigsten Sinnesgemeinschaft' *i.e.* protestation of a deep unity of ideas or motives. It is noteworthy that this turn of phrase should survive, corroborating our reconstruction of τί ἐμοὶ καὶ σοί; as a protestation that there is not, or should not be, a difference of viewpoint, still less a dispute, between the two personalities. 'Between *us*', the speaker insists, 'there can be no quarrel; and if you have sup-

[1] 2 K iv.16, vi.26. In iv.27 Elisha explains an exception.
[2] *Ant.* IX, 34 (iii, 1 *ad fin.*).
[3] From 'Die Mutter Jesu auf der Hochzeit zu Kana', *Passauer Theol.-Prakt. Monatsschr.* 3 (1893) 713–16.

posed a basis for one existed, you are wrong.' This does not by any means exclude a meaning, according to context, 'Why do you interfere?', 'Why behave like this?', or even 'Let me alone'. But it depends on the context, and the underlying meaning must be as set out above. No one suggests that in order to use the phrase one must be the wiser, or the party who really has right on his side.

Since we know that Jesus must have been aware, from the commencement, of the difficulty which his acceptance of the invitation might involve, he needed no prompting. His mother's report was met by the response, 'You (and your friends) have no reason to blame me and my family here. The problem is taken care of'. He intends to remedy the deficiency. She does not know how, but probably expects him to send out for some wine.[1] She knew that he had resources which might be relied upon in case of need.[2]

Why did Jesus say, '. . . my hour is not yet come?' This did not mean that he was not yet ready to depart, as someone has rather ingeniously suggested; nor has ὥρα, as elsewhere, a mystical or eschatological significance. The most natural meaning should be the right one. He will have already considered the most convenient and least disruptive method of fulfilling his moral obligation. If the wine had run out earlier, while guests were sober enough to grasp what was going on, one at least might have learnt, or accidentally seen,[3] the drawing of the wine from the jars. Such a sight would have brought the festivities to an end. The feast would have broken up in confusion.[4] The last thing a convivial party wants is a miracle; and the man who brings such a party to its senses risks a reputation for folly.[5] The appropriate time would have been when the supply ran out, when a new supply would have been looked for, and when no one would care where it came from. The awed waiters carried out their task, but that was hardly arduous. Their astonishment would not upset the party. Jesus did not intend to attract notoriety, or to increase his following. The phrase, 'my hour has not yet come', seems to mean no more than, 'I shall choose the appropriate moment, and if the wine has already run out it is not due to my indifference. On the contrary . . .'. The moment is his moment, since it

[1] Scholars are divided as to whether Mary expected a miracle. Gächter is against her expecting a miracle, and this seems the better view. Bultmann (cited below) disagrees.

[2] Apart from the widows, we have recently heard of Nathaniel (i. 48–50).

[3] It is absurd to suppose that the jars were in the dining-room itself. They must have been in a passage communicating with the courtyard where the well would be: for a gulley or drain must have led from the space where they were kept directly into the courtyard.

[4] A point missed by Windisch, 256f.

[5] Compare the man who broke some crockery when the rabbis were 'merry': b. Ber. 30*b* = Sonc. 188.

is his present on behalf of his family. The word ὥρα can very well bear this sense.[1]

WHAT DID JESUS DO?

Jesus and his disciples had received an unlimited invitation. He provided an almost unlimited supply of wine at the feast. This was perfect, perfectly timed, giving. The bridegroom was spared embarrassment; he and his family escaped obligation of reciprocity to the disciples, for this was a non-reciprocating present. Mary's prompting was not operative. When Jesus had accepted the invitation he undertook tacitly to care for the bridegroom whom he had agreed to honour with his and his disciples' company. We do not know whether Jesus was the most prestige-worthy person present. The guests might not have recognised him as a natural leader. But it is conceivable that he was asked to pronounce the bridegroom's blessing, and if he did this he occupied a place of honour in the feast.[2] A young man was technically the host. Jesus did not displace him, on the contrary he intended to preserve his prestige. Yet the guest who was not likely to contribute any money, whose fellow-guests were likely to be expensive to entertain, gave the most valuable present of all: valuable for its quality, its quantity, its timeliness, and its non-reciprocating character. Like the episode of payment of temple-tax, this miracle recognised moral obligations without Jesus's swerving from his self-imposed duty of poverty and non-concern for finance. The bridegroom or his parents invited Jesus without reckoning what it might cost them; and Jesus in accepting knew that their faith was not misplaced.

THE EARLY CHURCH AND THE STORY

We may consider briefly what the story may have meant to the evangelists. Did John, or his source, fabricate the story? We have seen that the explanation of the act of Jesus lies in Jewish law and custom. A largely Greek, or assimilated Jewish, community would have been unable to understand it. The story, without trace of explanation, and with economy of words, stems from an un-selfconscious Jewish source. To deprecate this miracle it is freely alleged that Mk ii.18–22; Lk v.33–9; and Mt ix.14–17 are synoptic archetypes for Jn ii.1–11. Other explanations are offered for the appearance in John of a story whose central

[1] Lk xxii.53; Jn xvii.1; and possibly xvi.21. Scholars, including Jeremias, lean against ὥρα having an eschatological significance; so held Weiss and Zahn. Barrett (cited below) takes the opposite view.

[2] Midr. R., S.S. II, 2, § 4 = Sonc. 96f.

event had notorious pagan counterparts. Unfortunately those counterparts do not fit very closely, and the deviation (if there was a deviation) is not accounted for; and the halakic *responsum* in the passages referred to above ('Can the children of the bridechamber fast, while the bridegroom is with them? While they have the bridegroom with them they cannot.') does not fit our story in the least. We have seen that Jesus does *not* usurp the function of the host, does not act as bridegroom; on the contrary he appears in a beautiful combination of the divine and the friend—an image as far from the *responsum* as from the pagan wine-deities. No Jew could see in the bridegroom analogy used in the *responsum* any similarity with the function which Jesus served at Cana.

We may proceed by noting that the synoptics had a choice between miracles, and made a selection from their material. Could this story have been available to them? If it was, why did they reject it? Here is no difficulty at all. The wonder is that John admitted it—but after all his standards evidently differed from theirs. The authority to resist the increase in the number of miracles recorded would have been very strong as soon as the meaning and importance of the accredited and canonised miracles was established. If one seeks to edify the congregation far more can be said against our pericope than for it.

The feeding of the five thousand, for example, is better accredited: the observers were sober, they were free men, competent to act as witnesses. Cana is suspect: Mary, a woman, is offered as the only witness of the exact words spoken to her, which provide the crucial allusion to Elisha. The drawing of the wine is done by servants, who (for all we, and the Church, know) may have been slaves and so incompetent witnesses. The miracle of the loaves and fishes conforms to Elisha's miracle with the cruse of oil. An existing element is multiplied, which (to the literal mind) is very different from turning one substance into another. This dubiously authenticated miracle is hardly necessary? Would Jesus himself care to have his presence celebrated in connection with a vulgar wedding-feast? No one knows who the bridegroom was. We are not told that he 'had faith': this is a sad deficiency. The vast quantity of wine, taken from jars of humble purpose, differs in many respects from Elisha and the widow's cruse. The latter ceased to pour when all the vessels were filled, and all the oil was used for the purpose intended. At the feeding of the five thousand, for example, all the remnants were collected in baskets.[1] Here Jesus supplies more than enough wine for people who were already too tipsy to recognise his bounty, and no one cares what happens to the residue. In the nature of

[1] 2 K iv.44 leaves us in doubt whether the leavings of Elisha's miraculous meal were actually preserved.

things some wine will have been left at the bottom. It would be diluted with fresh purification-water, or (more probably) swilled out into the gutter. This is as unedifying as the very vulgar remarks of the master of ceremonies—and both are much too vivid to be inventions. This was a miracle which need not become canonical.

The tendencies at work when John was written are well known. Aileen Guilding[1] demonstrates how our story would appear in this position, and the intricate web of allusion and association upon which the actual words might rest. The symbolic meaning of the wine to one who intends to show the superseding of water-baptism by Spirit-baptism, the abundance of the life of the Spirit given by Jesus, is evident. The putting aside of the Jewish ceremonies for the new power of the Spirit is observed by all commentators and must have been evident to the early Church. The gift of wine also serves a eucharistic purpose in John. Guilding shows that lections for what she regards as the appropriate part of the year provide a vocabulary as well as ideas that knit our text into a pattern of association with various passages, assuming a variety of lectionary cycles. The ingenuity postulated of the evangelist is not impossibly great. Correspondences are striking, and even the size alleged for the vessels is accounted for by reference to 2 Ch iv.2ff. and 1 K vii.26.[2]

All these symbolic considerations would serve to qualify the miracle for admission to a gospel: moreover the comment of the evangelist himself, which proves that readers strove to explain the miracle in an edifying and consistent manner, tells us that, in increasing the faith of his disciples Jesus deliberately utilised the Cana situation, and consecrated it. Our own suspicion that the disciples learnt of the event afterwards, and that it was not essentially for that purpose, has nothing to do with the early Church's problems, and does not remove the significance of John's revelation of his evaluation of the story in that situation in his gospel. No doubt the gift of wine to people (note: the gift was not to believers as such) qualified Jesus in the eyes of pagans as a deity, for they were used to such theophanies.[3] But would this

[1] Cited above. Ch. 12, particularly p. 180–6, is relevant.

[2] Guilding, 185.

[3] The alleged parallels are made much of by R. Bultmann, *Das Evangelium des Johannes* (Göttingen 1950), 83; C. K. Barrett, *Gospel according to St John* (London 1955), 157. The benefit of this learning is passed on without reserve to the parish clergy by E. Dinkler, Das Kana-Wunder, *Fragen der wissenschaftlichen Erforschung der Heiligen Schrift* (Sonderdruck aus dem Protokoll der Landessynode der Evangelischen Kirche im Rheinland, January 1962), 47–61, particularly at p. 53–5. A comprehensive study of the parallels appeared in H. Noetzel, *Christus und Dionysos. Bemerkungen zum religionsgesch. Hintergrund von Joh. ii, 1–11* (*Arb. z. Theol.* 1) (Stuttgart 1960).

consideration have carried weight with the Jews who, at such an early stage, put the story into its verbal form? It might well be meaningful after missionary-activity had progressed far. Thus perhaps it is true to say that while we see why the synoptics could have rejected the story, we are satisfied that John for characteristic reasons adopted it. This, it is submitted, leaves the door open for the miracle's being genuine.

If the reader has come with me so far perhaps he will be willing to accompany me further? A recent, admirable commentary on John ignores the human scene and dwells upon the symbolism and mystery:

> The wedding feast lacked wine, not water; yet it is precisely to the water, concerned with the admission to the feast by purification, that Jesus turns to supply the deficiency of wine . . . That which had, as water, never been able, and never would be able, in any quantity, large or small, to prepare men by an adequate purification to enter worthily even into an earthly marriage or union of persons, was to turn, in the presence of the true bridegroom, and by his grace and power, into the very substance of the joy of the divine marriage between God and his people . . . And to believe in him is quite evidently not to believe that he can turn water into wine, but rather that he is the real bridegroom who will replace the inadequate rites of purification established among the Jews with the reality of a communion (marriage) with God achieved through his own sacrificial death for all . . . Jewish water is anticipation; Christian wine is for all time the reality. The one is but a promise, the other fulfilment . . .[1]

Such, no doubt, were the reflections of the Church for whom John actually wrote. But what do I see in the Wedding at Cana? I see a young man, who knew that he would not experience some of what are considered life's chief joys, giving pleasure to a young friend by attending his nuptials. And at those nuptials he demonstrated, in material form, his solidarity with that friend, that ordinary youth—and in that solidarity he willed that his friend should not come to shame. He willed, and so it was.

[1] John Marsh, *Saint John* (London 1968), 146–8.

CHAPTER ELEVEN

Peter's Penny

THIS STORY (at Mt xvii.24–7)[1], especially because we are not told in so many words that Peter found the *stater*, is often dismissed as a distorted report[2] or a playful argument.[3] H. Montefiore, influenced by fashionable 'critical' techniques, sees the last verse of the pericope as 'a compressed version of a Jewish Christian *haggadāh*, taken from Jewish fable and adapted to this context in order to give special sanction to the payment of the temple-tax by Christians before A.D. 70'. An interesting view favoured by Dodd will be dealt with below. In a typical comment, following an ingenious criticism to a banal conclusion, a scholar of an older generation called it 'an example of half-baked legend-formation which has halted half way in the course of its literary development'. That it is a sober record of an event in Jesus's life is seldom accepted. H. van der Loos[4] says 'Jesus regards the payment of the tribute as a financial matter, an obligation which, if necessary, can be fulfilled by catching a fish'. On the other hand great importance was placed on it by G. D. Kilpatrick, who used it to date Matthew.[5] Recently much information has come to hand which places it in a very different light. The attempted dating fails, though we are left with a still useful indication of the age of the passage as it stands. Moreover

[1] Almost contemporaneously with the article on which this chapter is based there appeared in *NTS* 11 (1964), at p. 60–71, a well-rounded article by H. Montefiore on the same subject. Except for the legal implications (which he misunderstands) the information he gives is recommended to the present reader.

[2] So A. H. McNeile, *Gospel according to St. Matthew* (London 1957), 257, 259. His statement about the didrachm seems questionable. A similar approach, borrowing something from Kilpatrick, appears in *Peake's Commentary* (1962), 687 O: 'The miraculous element serves this dialectic by letting the Father supply the coin. The tendency of the story seems to be that Jesus's action could not be made a basis for making Christians continue to pay the Temple tax.'

[3] So T. H. Robinson, *Gospel of Matthew* (London 1951), 150. A comment on the approach of Professor C. H. Dodd appears below (Appendix to the chapter). The notion that 'Peter's Penny' is a parable unaccompanied by a narrative of fact is bequeathed to the general public by B. W. Bacon at Hastings, *Dictionary of Christ and the Gospels* I (1906), 594.

[4] *The Miracles of Jesus* (*cit. sup.*) 680ff. at p. 687.

[5] *Origins of the Gospel According to St. Matthew* (Oxford 1946), 41–2, 129.

we are able to understand what happened, gaining much insight into the moral doctrine intended to be conveyed.

Before we commence the study we should notice that there is a certain connection between the Jew's liability to the temple-tax under the indigenous, self-supporting, Jewish Law and his liability to pay taxes *de facto* and, it would seem, *de jure* also to the actual ruler, whoever he might be. But the connection is not a close one, and it would be altogether wrong to assume any kind of equivalence or other balance between the two obligations.[1] In Chapter 14 below we shall deal with the highly interesting question of a Jew's religious obligation to recognise the rights of the ruler, whoever he may be.

THE 'HALF-SHEKEL'

By the beginning of the month of Nisan, in which Passover falls, every free male Jew over 20 was liable to pay a 'half-shekel' of silver (*i.e.* half a '*temple*-shekel') as his personal contribution to the cost of public worship in the Temple.[2] The payment ought to be made at Jerusalem, but the State provided collectors, armed with powers to collect, to transmit collections from remoter districts to that city. The tax had all the appearance, superficially, of a poll-tax (*Kopfsteuer*) such as the Romans levied in many parts of their empire. But the δίδραχμον was not a Roman tax as a numismatic historian incautiously suggests.[3] But it was a sin to avoid its payment, and the collectors were probably not professional tax-gatherers and had no opportunities to cheat either the Temple or their fellow-Jews. The Jews were proud to pay the tax, and no doubt it was an honour to be appointed a collector in the country districts or overseas.

The amount due was 2 *zuz* of coined silver. To consider first the *imperial* coinage, the Antioch didrachms, being approximately 2 *zuz*, might have been suitable in point of weight, but they, as well as the tetradrachms (approx. 4 *zuz*) from the same mint, were of less fine silver than the Tyrian coinage, which was reputed to be the nearest to temple-shekel money that one could reach in practice.[4] Both Tyrian

[1] H. Loewe, '*Render unto Caesar*', 66ff.

[2] Ex xxx.13, xxxviii.26. J. M. Powis Smith, *Origin and History of Hebrew Law* (Chicago/Toronto 1960—first publ. 1931), 158–9 (a shrewd but sarcastic comment). A *third* of a shekel is engaged for in Ne x.32 (33) (2 Esd xx.33): discrepancy noticed but hardly explained by Smith, *op. cit.* 119. The *Mishnāh* says collections began outside Jerusalem a fortnight before the end of the old accounting-year. See also Maimonides, *Mishneh Torāh*, III (Seasons), VII (Shekel dues), 1 ff (trans. Gandz and Klein, 1961, p. 411). The 171st positive commandment (Chavel, I, 180–1).

[3] M. N. Tod, *Num. Chr.* 1960, p. 10–12.

[4] b. Bek. 50*b* = Sonc. 346, 348; B.Ḳ. 36*b* = Sonc. 204. A. Reifenberg, *Ancient Jewish Coins*, 2nd edn (Jerusalem 1947), 30–2.

and Antioch coinage had a didrachm, approximately equivalent to 2 *zuz*, and a tetradrachm, known as a *stater*. Surviving specimens of the Tyrian stater, which for practical purposes was the 'temple-shekel' (*i.e.* the shekel referred to in scripture), weigh between 13.98 grammes and 14.14 grammes, but the standard (which refers to perfect mint specimens) was apparently 14.5 grammes.[1] The Antioch tetradrachms range more widely in weight. I was shown specimens of 14.86 and 15.32 grammes.

The currency of the Temple was the temple-shekel, while the due for each male was a half-shekel. The didrachms had to be changed into temple-shekels, and in view of the losses contemplated in the changing, and in compensating for the lack of weight in the didrachms when weighed in bulk, a premium was charged in practice, called the 'agio'.[2] Naturally, if a perfect didrachm were presented at the treasury in Jerusalem no agio would be demanded. When *two* people paid in Jerusalem in the form of a good Tyrian *stater* for both of them, it appears no agio would have to be paid by either; whereas payment for two people by a *stater* outside Jerusalem would require payment of an agio for *one* of them.[3] Out of Jerusalem and still more out of the land of Israel there was a financial advantage in offering a *stater* on behalf of two males.

In the Jewish climate of thought one who paid on behalf of another would do so as agent, as a loan, or as a matter of charity.[4] In a case of loan, would he loan the agio as well? Or would the two have been deemed to divide it between them, so that he loaned half the agio? Such questions would arise, and are reflected in the texts, but we need not pursue them. Where, however, one man paid on behalf of a beggar or ascetic he was *totally* relieved of the agio.[5] His *stater* sufficed in practice for both of them. Prior to the Jewish wars such cases must have been exceptional, but no doubt they were well known to the collectors. We can be sure that men tried as far as possible to work in

[1] F. W. Madden, *Jewish Numismatics* (London 1874–6), 260–1, 267–70; F. v. Schrötter, *Wört. d. Münzkunde* (1930), *s.v.* Stater. G. F. Hill, *British Mus. Cat. of Greek Coins* (1910), *s.v.* Phoenicia, Tyre, p. 233. Mr R. A. G. Carson of the Department of Coins and Medals, British Museum, most kindly showed the present writer the coinage circulating in Palestine at our period and explained it.

[2] *Mishnāh*, Sheḳ. I. 6, 7. Maimonides seems to have thought the agio was needed to pay for re-changing into half-shekels, but actual knowledge of the procedure must have been lost a thousand years before Maimonides (his discussion is at *Mishneh Torāh* III [Seasons], VII, iii, 417ff. of the translation).

[3] *Mishnāh*, at § 6 (Danby, 153).

[4] Discussion at *ibid.* § 7.

[5] *Ibid.* He would also be relieved if he paid on behalf of a 'comrade'. It is to be noted that when the Romans took over the collection they continued to demand a surcharge, in connection with which, perhaps, the notorious abuses developed.

pairs in paying the half-shekel, so that collectors expected pairs of men to offer a Tyrian shekel (if available) between them.

Naturally Tyrian shekels were to be had at a premium in the month in question. Many could not pay as members of pairs. The great hoard of 3,400 Tyrian shekels, 1,000 half-shekels, and 160 Roman denarii found at Isfiya on Mt Carmel[1] shows that at least 1,000 people in one community could not manage to join with a fellow each to pay in shekels.

Now we approach the vital question of liability to the tax. A man who was poor, and for whom no one would pay the tax, could be squeezed by all the processes known to the law in order to realise the sum. The collectors could take pledges,[2] and in default of securities they might confine him, or sell his labour until he had worked off the debt. Yet there were at least two communities which denied liability to the tax, one which denied liability totally—a freedom from liability which the Pharisees, and doubtless other schools of interpretation, accepted (as we shall see)—and another, a sect whose views have been preserved amongst the Dead Sea documents,[3] which denied liability beyond the first payment in each lifetime in order formally to comply with the *Torāh*. The first case can conveniently be examined first, since it depends upon a common-sensical interpretation of the law. It seemed illogical that the *priests*, whose maintenance was provided for by the law, should out of that provision provide for the common offerings in the Temple. God would be taxing himself, if his servants, whose entire maintenance had been provided for by him, had to contribute to the cost of Temple worship. Many of the animals slaughtered, for example, provided the priests' meals. So, although the scriptural texts did not exempt priests, they held themselves to be exempted by interpretation. Moreover, in the hands of a rabbinical scholar the text in Ezr vii, whereby Artaxerxes provides that the priests and all other servants of the Temple shall be free from all sorts of taxation, signified that by divine providence all servants of the Temple were immune from taxation by the Jewish State. Upon the basis of this text *rabbis* later on

[1] Leo Kadman, 'Temple dues and currency in ancient Palestine in the light of recent discovered coin-hoards' (A paper read to the International Numismatic Congress, Rome, Sept. 1961), *Israel Numismatic Bulletin*, 1 (1962). His argument that the hoard was a consignment of temple-dues is convincing. We note that the 160 denarii represented 8 per cent on 1,000 didrachms (half-shekels), 8 per cent being the *agio* (approximately) stated by R. Meir in the *Mishnāh*.

[2] *Mishnāh*, Sheḳ. I. 3.

[3] J. M. Allegro, 'An unpublished fragment of Essene halakhah (4Q ordinances)', *J. Sem. S.* 6 (1961), 71–3. Vermès, 249. The document is closely discussed in connection with our pericope by David Flusser, 'Mt. xvii 24–7 and the Dead Sea Sect' *Tarbiẓ*, 31, 2 (1961), 150–6 (summary at p. iii).

(and even at our period?) claimed complete exemption from tax, toll and forced labour.[1] At the time of Jesus scholars accepted that priests ought not to be forced to pay the half-shekel.

R. Judah said: Ben Bukri testified at Jabneh that if a priest paid the shekel he committed no sin. Rabban Johanan b. Zakkai answered: Not so! but, rather, if a priest did not pay the shekel he committed sin; but the priests (continues the *Mishnāh*) used to expound this scripture to their advantage: 'And every meal offering of the priest shall be wholly burnt: it shall not be eaten'—since the *Omer*[2] and the *Two Loaves*[3] and the Shewbread[4] are ours, how can they be eaten?[5]

At the time of this debate the Temple no longer stood. Johanan was incensed at the priests' artful interpretation of Lv vi.23. The reason why the half-shekel was not exacted from them was that the collectors respected their conscientious objection (so long as the law could not be clarified authoritatively) *out of regard for the ways of peace.*[6] It is a fundamental rule of the Jewish law that lacunae in the rules could be filled, and doubts could be resolved, by recourse to the fundamental command to seek peace.[7] 'Great is Peace . . .'.[8] The *Mishnāh* gives a most instructive paradigm of situations in which, though the right does not exist at scriptural law, the sages allow it under our maxim. It would be beyond the scope of this paper to analyse the examples,[9] but one may summarise their purport in this way: a rule may be enforced, even if not specifically laid down in the *Torāh*, if (1) the spiritual welfare of the nation require it; (2) the higher needs of the community as a whole require it; or (3) in particular, litigious or quarrelsome tendencies are inhibited or frustrated. Many a good rule has, therefore, become established because, though not directly enjoined, it is wise to follow it *out of regard for the ways of peace.* Avoiding unnecessary disputes would be a motive within this principle. The priests could, therefore, plead

[1] b. B.B. 8*a* = Sonc. 33. Michael Avi-Yonah, *Geschichte der Juden im Zeitalter des Talmud in den Tagen von Rom und Byzanz* (*Studia Judaica: Forschungen zur Wissenschaft des Judentums*, ed. E. L. Ehrlich, II), Berlin 1962, p. 98–102.

[2] 'Sheaf': Lv xxiii.10. All these are paid for out of the Temple's public shekel fund. If the priests contributed they would eat (and not burn) their 'own'.

[3] Of Pentecost: Lv xxiii.17.

[4] Ex xxv.30; Lv xxiv.5–9.

[5] *Mishnāh*, Sheḳ. I. 4 (Danby, 152).

[6] *miphney dar^{e}chey shālom.* This appears in so many words in *Mishnāh*, Sheḳ. I. 3, as read in the Babylonian text; the Jerusalem text seems to mean, 'because of the respect due to them', but this may well be a gloss, explaining what the maxim means in the context. There is no *gemara* in the Babyl. Talm. on this tractate.

[7] Ps xxiv.14; Pr iii.17; Ezk vii.25; Zc viii.16; Ml ii. 6. b. Yev. 109*a* = Sonc. 761 Midr. R., Num. XXI 1 = Sonc. 827.

[8] Maimonides, *op. cit.*, III (Seasons), X, iv, 14 (trans., p. 471).

[9] These are of considerable juridical interest. See *Mishnāh*, Giṭṭ. V. 8, 9; b. Giṭṭ. 59*a*–61*a* = Sonc. 277–87.

their immunity, and the collectors did not enforce the collection of the half-shekel from them: and the basis of the immunity in practice was the doubt as to the correct interpretation of the *Torāh*.

The sect known from the Dead Sea documents had the peculiar notion that its members, once they had complied with the commandment, and had paid once, were under no obligation to pay again. The history of this notion is not yet established, and we do not know if it is really old.[1] Since the document goes back to the Roman occupation, and the text may be still earlier, it seems quite possible that objections to paying the tax on conscientious grounds existed while the Temple itself stood. Samaritans naturally refused, notwithstanding their belief in the *Torāh*, to contribute to the offerings at Jerusalem. Sects which had lost faith in the value of the daily sacrifices, or even sacrifices in general, and which would sympathise with Jesus's teaching on that subject, evidently could honestly contend that the scriptural text did not mean exactly what it said. Thus we have two very different grounds for asserting that the scriptural text was contemporaneously 'interpreted' to mean something very much less general and comprehensive than it appears to mean from the bare words. Yet we know that the collectors were authorised to exempt only priests who claimed their caste privilege.

THE COLLECTORS AND PETER

Jesus with his disciples was passing through Galilee, on his way to Jerusalem for the Passover, for his trial and crucifixion (xvii.22–3). At Capernaum[2] Peter was met by collectors. The question and answer admit of more than one interpretation: 'Does the teacher of your group not pay the half-shekel? He says, Yes.' Collectors do not speak as if they expect refusal. But Jesus had been called a Samaritan (Jn viii.48), and he might have been a teacher of a sect like our Dead Sea sect. It was only because the group had come down into the town that they had met them. They would however have been well aware that they would be asked for their half-shekels. They would have faced a demand before as many may have been over twenty years old. The question almost certainly means, 'We propose to collect the half-shekel from your teacher. Does he object?'

Jesus and his disciples were living entirely on charity.[3] It is very

[1] Allegro (cited above) at p. 73 suggests that the interpretation of Ex xxx.11ff. was legitimate, and it may have been old.

[2] G. Dalman, *Orte und Wege Jesu*, 3rd edn (Gütersloh 1924), ch. 8. Our incident is mentioned at p. 144, and the fish at p. 143. J. Finegan, *Light from the Ancient Past* (London 1955), p. 303–6. Billerbeck, *Kommentar* I, 159ff.

[3] Mk ii.23, viii.14, x.28; Lk viii.3, ix.58.

likely that their treasurer[1] hoped to use the rich city of Capernaum to collect supplies for the final stage of the last journey. Collectors would not put beggars under an obligation to supply pledges; but they knew that wealthy patrons were at hand. If Jesus were confined, the half-shekel no doubt could be found from some such source. But the collectors were not tactless. It has been suggested that the picture of Jesus (resting?) in a dwelling and Peter outside is merely a literary device to enable Jesus and Peter to have a juridical discussion behind the collectors' backs. But the collectors would certainly avoid putting the question to Jesus directly. Irate rabbis were people to be avoided, and Jesus's reaction to a direct demand was unknown. Peter, as the leader of the disciples, was obviously the person to approach. If Jesus ultimately admitted liability, the disciples would have to pay theirs (if possible) *a fortiori*. Peter's answer by no means signifies that Jesus *had* paid previously; though it may well have been paid on his behalf in the past. To temple-tax collectors the obvious answer was 'Yes . . . I shall look into the matter', not to bluster and deny liability out of hand. Peter did *not* mean that Jesus had proposed to pay, that he had ordered payment to be made, or that he was contemplating a method of obtaining the money.

JESUS AND PETER

It was not tactful for pupils to initiate discussions except upon invitation. Peter would not say, 'The collectors are outside', or 'Had you not better give instructions . . .?' Naturally the discussion is opened by Jesus, who knew of the demand and must have anticipated that it would have to be faced. To Jesus the question was one of *halakāh*, fit to be discussed with his juridically minded pupil. 'From whom do the kings of this world, the kings of flesh and blood, take customs or poll-tax (κῆνσος)?' The temple-tax, as we have seen, is virtually a capitation-tax, with which the Jews were perfectly familiar.[2] 'Do they collect them from their children or from strangers?' Peter answers, 'From strangers', and Jesus concludes, 'Consequently[3] the children are free'.[4]

[1] Jn xii.6; xiii.29.

[2] See Chapter 14 below. Note the wording of Ex xxx.13 (*cf.* Nb iii.47). For Roman taxation see Adolph Büchler, *Economic Conditions of Judaea after the Destruction of the Second Temple* (London 1912), 63ff. Avi-Yonah, *op. cit.* 49. For a Talmudic reference, b. Yev. 46*a* = Sonc. 301.

[3] For the force of ἄρα γε see Bauer–Arndt–Gingrich 4, Blass–Debrunner–Funk §§ 440 (2), 451 (2).

[4] *ḥāpheshiym* as in 1 S xvii.25. H. Montefiore suggests (*ubi cit.*, 70) that Jesus may have taught that only *free-will* offerings should be given. At any rate he denies legal liability.

Most translators have missed the point.[1] Jesus was not referring to the Roman–Jewish problem, but the normal situation in Near Eastern kingdoms. It is perfectly true (and this has misled many) that the Romans imposed κῆνσος on *non-citizens* and not on citizens, but it is not certain that in Matthew's words τέλη ἢ κῆνσον at xvii.25*b* there is any intention of referring directly (*i.e.* overtly) to the Roman practice. Mr Sherwin-White was puzzled by this, and others have been misled.[2] Jesus is speaking of the 'kings of (this) world' in contrast to the heavenly king for whose sake the temple-tax is collected and his reference is purely general. But even if this were *not* the case, the words τῶν υἱῶν αὐτῶν ('their own folk' = *bᵉneyhem*) do not distinguish citizens from non-citizens, but merely subjects from non-subjects. Whatever the Romans may have done in respect of non-citizen subjects, everyone knows that citizens also paid taxes. Jesus plainly also had in mind for example excise, the internal revenue imposed, in particular, on imports, whether the importers be citizens or foreigners. Land-tax in fact was paid in Roman provinces by citizens (unless they had received an immunity) and non-citizens too. This is conclusive. Oriental and other rulers derived the greater part of their revenue out of their own subjects, as anyone who reads Josephus's account of revenue-settlements of Ptolemaic Palestine[3] can see for himself. Land-revenue, poll-tax, excise duties, and so on, would be paid by those whom the ruler could squeeze. The suggestion that aliens are more notably liable to taxation than citizens is absurd, and one wonders how it can have weighed with the majority of our translators. If there were any doubt about it Billerbeck, thirty years ago, drew attention to the very relevant story told by R. Simeon b. Yoḥai and repeated by R. Joḥanan.[4] God owns everything, so how can he be cheated? Yet he wants honesty in payment of tithes, and so on. Apparently superfluous preoccupation with *terumāh*[5] and the like breeds careful dealings with one's neighbour. To set a good example even a human king will have his own goods taxed. Why? To tax his own goods is to tax himself and is stupid: *but* if the king himself

[1] Taking υἱῶν to be 'subjects' or 'citizens'. H. Montefiore gets this wrong (*ubi cit.* 65) and his reconstruction is vitiated thereby. So McNeile. C. C. Torrey (1947) keeps 'sons'. J. B. Phillips's translation hits the nail exactly. Delitzsch naturally renders it by *bᵉneyhem*, from which one cannot go astray. Cornelius à Lapide, *ad loc.*, had the answer already in the seventeenth century, and from Chrysostom: *an ab alienis?* id est, ab aliis subditis, qui non sunt filii: alienos enim opponit filiis . . . regum filii cum sua familia iure communi [!] immunes sunt a tributo per regem indicto. . . . The argument which follows, namely concerning liability to *civil* taxation is, however, irrelevant.

[2] A. N. Sherwin-White, *Roman Society and Roman Law in the New Testament* (Oxford 1963), 126. C. G. Montefiore, *Synoptic Gospels* II (London 1909), 673, is astray here.

[3] See above pp. 33–7.

[4] Billerbeck, *op. cit.* I, 771, citing b. Sukk. 30*a* = Sonc. 133.

[5] 'Heave-offering': Danby, *Mishnāh*, 797

follows the regulations his subjects will acquire and keep the habit of obeying them cheerfully. So it was a commonplace that citizens, subjects, paid excise-duties.

Who then were exempt? The 'children', *i.e.* their households. All their dependants, and employees, all those maintained at the charge of the rulers, were automatically exempt from taxation, and general statutes demanding tax were subject to this common-sense exception. Jesus thus interprets the *Torāh* subject to principles of fundamental common sense. As long as the 'family' of God are entirely dependent on him and not earning their living otherwise they are logically free from obligation to contribute to his worship in the Temple. They have no superfluity to be taxed! In Jesus's own words he was 'about his Father's business', and his disciples were evidently in the same position so long as they accompanied him. Jesus indicates that he and they could claim exemption if they wanted to do so. They were legally not liable to pay the temple-tax, he said, because the *Torāh*, properly interpreted, exempted them.

That this is the way to interpret his reasoning is indicated not merely by common sense but also by some documentary evidence from an unexpected quarter. The *Milindapañha*[1] contains a simile or parable about four chief ministers whom their king orders to impose a tax on the people. The question is whether these ministers are inspired with fear of being taxed themselves. No. 'Why not?' 'They have been appointed by the king to high office. Taxation does not affect them, they are beyond taxation. It was to the rest that the king referred when he gave the order to tax.' The *Milindapañha* is a Buddhist work of about A.D. 150 and retains ample traces of its author's acquaintance with the gospels.[2]

'SO AS NOT TO OFFEND THEM'

Nevertheless Jesus says that the tax, to which they are not liable, must be paid in this instance. The reason offered is remarkable. Here again we have a fatal mistranslation. The verb σκανδαλίζειν is very seldom found in the sense 'to offend', 'to give offence', the senses in which translators take it. The New Testament examples are debatable.[3] One

[1] IV, 2, 3 (trans. I. Horner I, 205; quoted by J. W. Spellman, *Political Theory of Ancient India* [Oxford 1964], 188).

[2] Derrett at *ZRGG* 19 (1967), 33ff., at p. 57–9. One should add to the Indian counterpart to Lk iii.2–5 the following reference: Mahābhārata III, 73, 9.

[3] The debate is evident from Bauer–Arndt–Gingrich *ib.* In their 2 instances as late as Athanasius and Palladius are quite inconclusive. The meaning of Jn vi.61*b* is arguable. So Mt xv.12, where also it may mean 'to be led into unbelief, to be thrown

(2 Co xi.29) has been assigned by some to the other meaning, and the rest may with equal plausibility be so assigned. Other examples are late, in most cases very late. By the time of Jesus this special derivation from the general meaning may not have emerged. The meaning of σκάνδαλον and its derivatives is beyond doubt.[1] In xvi.23 and xviii *passim*, on both sides of our pericope, we find the words in their usual sense. Other examples are numerous and compelling.[2] σκάνδαλον (*mik*ᵉ*shol*) is the 'stumbling-block', the temptation, fear, or suspicion which causes the unwary to trip, to hesitate, to fall. The smooth, even path of faith and obedience is obstructed with obstacles over which one trips if not warned. σκάνδαλον may be evil, its effects are evil, and one who places it is partly responsible for any sin that is committed. There is a command, put to all sorts of applications, which prohibits the placing of a stumbling-block.[3] False teachers are 'scandalisers'. A bad example is 'scandalous'.

Who are the people whom Jesus says must not be scandalised? The collectors themselves.[4] Jesus was not afraid of *offending* them.[5] But his refusal might lead them into sin, indeed would inevitably do so, and in this rather interesting way. If Peter reported, 'We claim exemption from Ex xxx.13 on the basis that we are fully employed in God's service', the collectors would have no choice but to refer the question to Jerusalem for a ruling. Jesus was under observation.[6] Any claim that he was a member of God's family would be no surprise at Jerusalem. His *respon-*

[1] I find myself in closer agreement with A. Humbert, 'Essai d'une théologie du scandale...', *Biblica* 35 (1954), 1–28 at 26ff. than with G. Stählin, *Skandalon* (Gütersloh 1930), at p. 247ff.

[2] Ign. *ad Eph.* xviii.1 and Ga v.11 may well be examples of what is argued for in p. 255 n. 3 above: the cross not only arouses opposition amongst enemies (as it may) but serves to turn away weaker members amongst the faithful, being a 'stumbling-block' to them. Bauer–Arndt–Gingrich 2.

[3] Lv xix.14; Rm xiv.13.

[4] αὐτούς (27*a*) = αὐτοῖς (27*d*).

[5] As H. Montefiore supposed he was (*ubi cit.*), and likewise S. Zeitlin, *Rise and Fall of the Judaean State* II (Philadelphia 1967), 161.

[6] This aspect of Jesus's experience is brought out well by E. Stauffer, 'Neue Wege der Jesusforschung', *Wiss. Z. der Martin-Luther-Universität Halle-Wittenberg* (Ges.-Sprachw. vii/2, March 1958), 451–76, at p. 455 etc. Stauffer points out repeatedly how Jesus's teaching could well be described as 'scandalising', and that reservation of (and presumably diminution of) one of the rights of God would be characteristic of a heretical teacher.

---

into error (from the point of view of the speaker)'. In both instances a saying had turned otherwise loyal or sympathetic hearers off the true path, their loyalty, their faith, had been jeopardised, and they had been caused to sin (or so it appeared). Mt xiii.21 may well be another example, but it is arguable. All the rest are clear cases in favour of the present submission: Mt v.29f., xviii.6, 8f., xxiv.10; Mk iv.17, ix.42f., 45, 47; Lk xvii.2; Jn xvi.1, and especially Mk xiv.27, 29. Sir xxii.8 and xxxii.15 (particularly the latter) are corroborative.

sum, going back to fundamentals, would not surprise them either, for they knew his doctrine on divorce. But refusal to pay the tax might be a refusal to obey a ruling on law from the supreme tribunal, and that would bring him within the power of authorities hostile to him.

The collectors are no rabbis. They would be given notice of Jesus's objection, and its grounds. Yet they would be bound, for practical purposes, by the reply from Jerusalem. If the orders were unlawful, as, for example, to exact the money by any normal means, the collectors would be unlawfully exacting money from a man not liable to the tax after warning by him. Accordingly they would be sinning, according to Jesus's understanding of the situation. They could not hide behind their instructions, and would have to bring a sin-offering. Jewish jurisprudence did not allow an inferior to escape liability for the unlawful instructions of his superior.[1] Thus, although Jesus was not liable to the tax he was obliged by the *Torāh* to save the collectors from the sin of compelling him to supply the half-shekel. *Therefore* it would be a sin to refuse to pay the said half-shekel! This extraordinary conclusion, of so much importance, has been missed by commentators and for that reason translators have misunderstood the vital verb.

Why then did Jesus not order the treasurer to pay the money? The scrupulous Jewish mind is again at work.[2] Jesus knows that the half-shekel *as such* is not due to the collectors. He is concerned only for their moral welfare. Could not the treasurer put his hand into the common purse and find the needful coin? This assumes that they had money, collected from their patrons recently, which is quite likely. Moreover, here was a genuine need. They had important business in Jerusalem and did not want to be detained at Capernaum. But this was not the method to be followed. The money in hand had been collected from patrons for pious purposes, namely for the group's maintenance. Jesus scrupled to use that money for unauthorised purposes. The patrons gave implicitly believing that the expenditure would be lawful; otherwise there would be a breach of trust. And here Jesus conscientiously believed that the half-shekel was not due to the Temple! His discussion with Peter shows (1) that the question of payment was relevant, but (2) there was no question of payment out of any available funds. It would be an ideal method of getting out of the dilemma to ask patrons whether they would contribute in order to save the collectors

[1] 'He that can depend on himself is culpable, but he that *must* depend on the court is not culpable.' *Mishnāh*, Horayot I, 1. The collectors were not servants of the Temple, still less of the court. See also b. Ḳid. 42*b* = Sonc. 212; 43*a* = Sonc. 214–15 (the limitation on the liability of a servant or agent).

[2] Amongst many instances of scrupulosity with charity collections one may note b. B.M. 106*b* = Sonc. 611 (Purim collections).

from sin: but this might have stretched some patrons' credulity beyond its strength. What was wanted was a combination of satisfying the collectors, without admitting that Jesus or his disciples were contributors to the Temple service. A perfect method of dealing with this difficulty presented itself in the shape of a lost stater in a fish in the harbour.[1]

PETER'S PENNY

A Tyrian shekel, sufficient for a poor man's payment for himself and a friend, was in the fish. This was an unowned coin, and the first taker would be its owner. Coins are not identifiable when found singly, and the owner must long since have given up hopes of recovering it. The last is a test at Jewish law whether the property is 'lost' or not.[2] Lost property would be ideal for the purpose. Jesus constituted Peter his agent to acquire the coin for him, and instructed him to offer it to the collectors on their joint behalf. The collectors were doubtless as well satisfied with this coin as they would have been by a coin obtained from a patron: but charity money had not been used, and the important admission had not been made. The earthly king would provide that his servants were not liable to customs duty; but the heavenly king in this case, caring for the souls of the collectors, would provide for the payment of the half-shekel. God enabled the need to be met, but he did *not* admit the liability to the due as such.

Did Peter take the coin? Why are we not told? The obvious answer is probably correct. Jesus himself tells us, near our very passage itself, that matters are substantiated by two or three. Did Peter gather some friends before he went? Or did he rush as fast as he could lest the fish get away? Jesus said the coin was for himself and Peter: no one else was entitled to be present. There were no witnesses, and Peter would not stand as authority for the story were it not literally true to the best of the early Church's knowledge. What interested the latter was not Jesus's amazing knowledge, but the juridical and moral point.

There is no doubt whatever but that the Tyrian shekel could be in the fish. There is only one possibility as to the fish. This is the cat-fish, known as *Clarias lazera* to us and, it seems, to the Greeks as κορακῖνος.[3]

[1] I am anticipated in this explanation by A. Jones in a brief comment at B. Orchard and others, *Catholic Commentary on Holy Scripture* (London 1953), 883.

[2] b. B.Ḳ. X, 2. See Maimonides, *Mishneh Torāh* XI (Torts) III, vi, 1 (trans. H. Klein, p. 110). On *yā'ash, ye'ush* see below, pp. 303–4.

[3] *Bell. Jud.* III, x, 8 (519–20). Kopp, *Holy Places* (1963), 174–6. The fish is referred to in E. W. Gurney Masterman, *Studies in Galilee* (Chicago 1909), 45–6; Aharoni, app. to Max Blanckerhorn, *Naturwissenschaftliche Studien am Toten Meer und im Jordantal* (Berlin 1912), 435; E. F. F. Bishop, *Jesus of Palestine* (London 1955), 83.

It is an omnivorous predator. Its commonest food is smaller fishes. It likes shallow water, and scavenges around the landing-places where edible matter spills from containers. Almost blind, it feels by taste and touch, sensitive to lateral movements in the water. It can grow to four feet or more. A bright disk, which would not drop like a stone, would attract it. In East Africa it is often caught with a hook baited with tinfoil. It is scaleless, prohibited by Mosaic Law. No one would dream of fishing for catfish, and their lives would be long.

If Peter did what was very unusual, and fished with a hook,[1] the first thing to bite would be a catfish, whether or not he used bait. He would have to be told to take up the *first* fish (τὸν ἀναβάντα πρῶτον), for otherwise he would not think of taking out the catfish. Though this fish can cough or spit out objectionable matter, a disk about an inch in diameter and 14 grammes in weight could easily be caught in the framework of the hinder part of the mouth if it initially escaped being drawn into the stomach. There it might well remain, if it did not irritate too much, as long as several days. Jesus says the mouth is to be opened: *i.e.* the fish is not to be shaken, as would be natural—the implication is that the coin was jammed well down at the back of the mouth. We know the coin, we know the fish: are we in a position to refute the suggestion that here we have once again the folk-tale or fairy story about riches found in fishes?[2] Are we obliged, as previous writers, to discard all the factual detail which the story calls for simply because a myth is more credible? One notes that here we have a slightly more probable story; the vision of the fisherman Peter rushing to fetch up a *Clarias* with a hook is so incongruous that its genuineness seems certified. Again, the coin in the fish is an appendage to an intricate

[1] b. B.Ḳ. 81*a* = Sonc. 461.

[2] Midr. R., Gen. XI, 4 end (8*b*) (not in the Sonc. trans. at p. 83); Shab. 119*a* = Sonc. 586; L. Ginzberg, *Legends of the Jews* IV (1947), 171; notes, VI, 300, a citation from *Bet ha-Midrash*, ed. Jellinek, II, 86–7. The story in Herodotus III, 42, has a counterpart in the famous Indian drama of Kālidāsa, the *Abhijñāna-Śākuntalam*. C. H. Dodd adds sceptically (*Historical Tradition in the Fourth Gospel*, 1965, p. 225 n. 7) a report from Cyprus in 1961 of 'a whole series of similar tales'. Repetition blunts the critical faculty, and I must point out that the constant allusion by scholars to this recurrent folk-tale (which relies on the fact that some fish swallow and retain bright objects) does *not* reveal an essential similarity between Jesus's prediction and the tale. There is no question of Peter finding an unusually valuable object he himself had lost.

It is curious that the head of this, the *barbuṭ*, used to be sold to tourists, . . . auf dessen unterer Seite verschiedene Heiligenbilder und Szenen aus dem hl. Lande aufgetragen waren (Aharoni). I am grateful to Dr P. H. Greenwood of the Department of Zoology, British Museum (Natural History), for explaining the fish of the Sea of Galilee and showing me a skeleton of this *Clarias*. The fish is illustrated in G. A. Boulenger, *Catalogue of Fresh-water Fish of Africa* . . ., II (London 1911), p. 236, fig. 197. Canon Tristram obtained a specimen from Galilee, to be seen in the British Museum.

juridical and moral discussion, and is not the highlight of the tale. The value of lost property in solving Jesus's practical problem is quite beyond exaggeration; and no property is so indubitably lost as a coin in a fish.

THE IMPLICATIONS OF THE STORY

One objection to the genuineness of the story might be that we are told only about payment on behalf of Jesus and Peter. What of the other disciples? This is no problem, since where God had apparently showed the way Jesus's patrons in Capernaum would have little difficulty in following the example. But perhaps we need not go so far. Once the collectors had received payment on behalf of two of the group they might be satisfied that no point of principle remained in dispute, and might be only too glad to have escaped so lightly from an embarrassing situation.

It is worth considering whether Jesus knew the coin was in the fish by any ordinary means of knowledge. A boy on the jetty may well have seen the coin drop from the purse (*cf.* Lk xii.33; b. B.K. 98*a* = Sonc. 569), or whatever had held it, and seen the big fish swallow it. But no one could predict that the coin would stick in the mouth instead of entering the stomach, that it would be retained, or that the same fish would rise to the hook. There would be many catfish about at the time. Jesus's sixth sense, or supranatural perception, seems once again to be demonstrated: but that can hardly be the reason for the episode's admission into the canon.

It has been observed that when, after the destruction of the Temple, the Romans diverted the half-shekel to the uses of Jupiter Capitolinus—the *fiscus Iudaicus*—Jews by race would be assessed to it as well as Jews by religion. We knew a great deal about that *fiscus*.[1] The tax was called Ἰουδαϊκὸν τέλεσμα, formerly τιμὴ δηναρίων δύο Ἰουδαίων = *denarii duo Judaeorum*. Jews made great efforts to escape being taxed. Christians afterwards noted that Jews were liable while they were not, so that at some period the Church could be recognised as non-Jewish, or at least

[1] S. Krauss, *Jew. Enc.* V, 402–3; M. S. Ginsburg, 'Fiscus Judaicus', *JQR* n.s. 21 (1930/1), 281–91. On the persistence of the tax see references at p. 290. Rostowzew in Pauly-Wissowa, *RE* VI, 2403. Of importance for us are (1) the citation from Suetonius, *Domitianus* XII: praeter caeteros Iudaicus fiscus acerbissime actus est: ad quem deferebantur, qui vel improfesso Iudaicam viverent vitam, vel dissimulata origine imposita genti tributa non pependissent; (2) the references regarding Nerva's reform; (3) the official of the time of the Flavians bearing the title procurator ad capitularia Iudaeorum. V. A. Tcherikover and A. Fuks, *Corpus Papyrorum Jud* I (Harvard U.P., Cambridge, Mass. 1957), 80–2; also sec. ix in vol. 2 of that series, p. 112ff. Avi-Yonah, *op. cit.* 49.

non-Jewish Christians could go free. The Church would be anxious not to have to pay the didrachm on behalf of clergy; and it would be argued on behalf of the community that priests under the old religion were free and since the same conditions applied after as before those who were free before should be free now, and their counterparts. To this the obvious answer on behalf of the Roman administration was that Jesus himself had paid the tax, though he did not believe in the Temple-service as then organised, and the apostles likewise. But our pericope proves that Jesus only paid the tax with the *ad hoc* motive of saving the Jewish collectors from sin, whereas this motive could not possibly apply to a collection by Roman collectors for the benefit of Jupiter Capitolinus. One has sought to go further,[1] and Kilpatrick suggests that as the *fiscus Iudaicus* was abolished, as he believed, by the emperor Nerva, the date of Matthew can be determined with some accuracy: for no one would retain this passage, which other gospels do not know, after its principal usefulness had expired. Most unfortunately the *fiscus* was not abolished at that time. It went on well into the third century,[2] when it disappeared because inflation will have made it too expensive to collect. Nerva had merely reformed the administration as his inscription on a coin, *fisci Iudaici calumnia sublata*,[3] indicates. However, though we are deprived of a firm date, it remains a fact that an early Judaeo-Christian community alone would be interested in the precise reason why Jesus and the apostles *appeared* to have acquiesced in the organisation for the Temple-service. The episode is most relevant to a period of stress between rabbinical Judaism and the Church, when it was taught by the latter that Jesus superseded the Temple made with hands, its worship, and the vast catena of taboos connected with it and subservient to it.

Yet far more important than these considerations is the light cast on Jesus's concept of duty. The commandment not to place the stumbling-block was so important that action ought, if possible, to be taken, even though it might precipitate a misunderstanding upon a matter of intellectual doubt. The Church knows from this that it must deal kindly with the orthodox Jewish world, and have patience with it. Jesus cared

[1] McNeile, *op. cit.* 258 speaks of anti-Jewish feeling throwing doubt on the genuineness of the story.

[2] As Montefiore correctly notes. In 145/6 or 167/8 it was 9 dr. 2 ob. for one male at Karanis, Arsinoite *nome*: P. Ryl. 594, col. 1 = *Corp. Pap. Jud.* III (1964), 460, line 7. Origen *ep. ad Afric. de hist. Sus.* 14, Migne, *PG* XI, c. 81.

[3] The coin is illustrated by A. Reifenberg, *Israel's History in Coins* (London 1953), p. 34, fig. 32 (where the erroneous legend occurs: 'Abolition of the Jewish tax'.). What did Nerva do? The suggestion that he freed Jews resident in Italy from the tax is made in the richly elaborated article of I. A. F. Bruce, 'Nerva and the Fiscus Iudaicus', *Pal. Expl. Q.* 96 (1964), 34–45.

for the souls even of those who would be predisposed, or forced, to take an attitude hostile to what he knew to be right. Out of a regard for the ways of peace one is justified in making what might appear to be admissions against what one knows intellectually to be true.[1] The avoidance of sin is more important than the obstinate pursuing of an academic argument, however justified the latter might be. If we are right in believing that the stater was in the fish, and that Peter caught it and took the coin, there was every reason for the Church to believe that the position Jesus adopted had his Father's approval.

APPENDIX

Is this a pronouncement story on the way to becoming a miracle story?

In his inestimable *Historical Tradition in the Fourth Gospel* Professor C. H. Dodd, who, in common with the most celebrated theologians active nowadays in New Testamental research, accepts the concept that the traditional material out of which the gospels were formed can, and perhaps ought to, be classified in formal categories for their readier identification and evaluation, propounds a far-reaching idea about the story of Peter's Penny.[2] This *pericope*, he says, is not a miracle story (no miracle is certified as having happened), nor a story of action of any kind; it is a pronouncement story. We have seen in what has been set out above that it most certainly *is* a story which was important for its pronouncement, rather than as proof of Jesus's miraculous knowledge about the first fish to be caught. Dodd goes on to suggest that here we have a parabolic saying almost in the act of making the transition from a supposed parabolic origin into a miracle story. The idea is that Jesus was telling a parable in which, perhaps, a man was pressed to pay a tax and paradoxically relied upon God to meet his needs. This parable was then associated with Jesus's personal history, the reasoning became a dialogue, and the direction to apply to a miraculous source of money took the place of an appeal to chance gains such as everyone knows occur constantly in everyday life and are commonly called 'providential'. This is my own attempt to reconstruct what Dodd supposes may have happened, for his own indications are naturally meagre (he was considering the miracle at Cana).

Is there anything in what we have learnt in this present chapter which would interfere with the viability of this exceedingly interesting hypothesis? The answer must turn on the question whether the heart of the passage, namely the relationship between legal liability on the one hand and charitable duty on the other, which was not less interesting to early Christians than the vision of Jesus and his disciples as 'children' of the household of the divine

[1] Fr C. Spicq (*STh* 20 [1966], 50–1) rightly says that 1 P ii.13–16, specially the words '. . . as *free* men, and not using your freedom as a cover for wickedness, but like slaves to God: honour everyone . . . reverence the king', were inspired by the Capernaum episode.

[2] At p. 227.

Ruler (a point which needed no such elaborate exposition for its own sake), is suitable for exposition in a parable? I hardly feel that anyone would see it as such. Parables gain their force from their appeal to everyday, normal attitudes which can be subsumed in ordinary people. Freedom from taxation, immunity, was a highly abnormal and unusual privilege. No hero of a parable would be someone exempt from taxation, especially total exemption, such as we have found was contemplated here. In parables, Christian and rabbinical alike, a king of flesh and blood is frequently one of the dramatis personae: but it is normally the other characters, whose behaviour teaches us about people and their duties, upon whom the full light of attention is cast.

It is difficult to imagine the substance of our *pericope* placed in parabolic form without the question of immunity from taxation being raised. Consequently this *pericope* did not start its life as a parable, and we are not obliged to suppose this in order to remove the (to some people) objectionable element of the folk-tale and the miraculous. The same motive was at work when it was suggested that the blasting of the fig-tree (Mk xi.12–14, 20–5) was really not some strange thing that Jesus ever did, but a parable (like Luke's parable of the barren fig-tree, xiii.6–9?) which had somehow attached itself to traditions of Jesus's life. The *motive* for these hypotheses is not merely a desire to know more about the gospels, but rather to make the gospels, as not yet fully understood, less unpalatable to the untrained student. Students insensibly draw out from their teachers what they want to be told, and in protestant circles in particular it is no longer possible to say at the outset 'The gospel and all the gospel and nothing but the gospel . . . or out you go!' Once the end of the wedge had been inserted, and elaborate intellectual reasons had been found why certain portions could not be considered to be the authentic voice of Jesus, there was no end to ingenuity to remove from the gospel anything resembling a stumbling-block. Most unfortunately for these techniques they tend, again insensibly, to drift downwards until Jesus becomes a good man who came to a bad end due, *e.g.*, to academic jealousy(!) and who taught good behaviour, asking people to love one another. . . . When every challenging and paradoxical element is removed by critical techniques what is left is jejune and vapid. And this, we can be sure, is not the historical Jesus. Many unpleasing comments could fairly be made about the age and locality in which he lived and worked, but those Jews were certainly not a jejune and vapid people. Any critical techniques which serve to water down the oriental, archaic, and otherwise actual and factual reports of Jesus's life and times must be wrong, not only in motive, but also in results.

In the last decade another approach to the New Testament has made its appearance. To such scholars Jesus seems to have been a religious enthusiast who led some kind of revolutionary movement against Rome, but whose disappointed followers concocted some 'substitute'-myth, an imaginary biography, the gist of which is authentic only in those places where the evangelists' editing was incompetent—they were reliable (it seems) only by oversight. Such writers do not see in the gospels the Son of God acknowledged by the

Church. The Church itself is no doubt ultimately to blame for all this: it is contempt for the Church which has enabled this new kind of historical novel-writing to masquerade as history; but it would not have begun had not the guardians of the gospel themselves shown the way to build a house of cards by piling one learned (and often unnecessary) hypothesis upon another, and by failing to observe the elementary rule that before a decision is taken (and its effect put out as *teaching*) the burden of proof must first be enquired into—and then, and then alone, should the evidence be heard. 'Jesus the Zealot', or 'Jesus the Revolutionary' is not merely a figment of irreverent imagination, but also absurd. Whatever the difficulties with which the gospel text faces us we can be sure that the Jesus who superbly withstood the Temptations and who taught not to seek wealth, or power, or prestige, but to take the lowest seat, to swallow insults, to love enemies, *and to turn the other cheek*, was no Zealot, no politician! Difficult passages, like that of the Two Swords, should not be disposed of as signs, *e.g.*, that Jesus was a brigand chief (which is hopelessly incongruous), until more consistent and less anomalous explanations have been tried—in this case the possibility that Jesus was observing the working out in practice of a particular *midrash* about the Messiah's 'being handed over'. Such passages are indeed intellectually difficult, but those difficulties should not be utilised to whittle away the gospel story, or to turn it into something banal or grotesque. When we come to a difficult passage we should wait for an answer from the evidences provided (or still to to be provided) from Jewish history and culture of the first century. For the teacher who has a class of sceptical youngsters in front of him it is, no doubt, difficult to be patient: but elaborate intellectual hypotheses, however attractive and respectable, are not a substitute for academic patience.

Several readers may ask why I make these remarks in the course of a treatment of Professor Dodd's extraordinarily interesting conjecture about Peter's Penny. The fly buzzes round the elephant, and I can take a view of Dodd. The fly has little idea of the elephant's motives or potential, and to that extent my comments may well lack weight. One thing is certain, namely that the work of Dodd does not tend downwards so as to produce a jejune or absurd picture of Jesus: indeed he has done more than most to recover from St John's gospel abundant traces of historical tradition, and that tradition contains its challenging and paradoxical elements. But I am of course not aiming any particular shafts at Dodd himself. Rather I am compelled to comment on the techniques in which he has laboured for so long and to the viability of which he has contributed so much. Dodd, and a great many of his fellow theologians, were brought up in classical, that is to say Greek and Latin, studies. The addition of Hebrew to this produces an effect which is like what we should expect if an Indian, wanting to specialise in the study of Shakespeare, were trained from the age of seven to that of twenty in French, and then studied English from twenty to twenty-two. No doubt a thorough education through the medium of French would be an excellent thing, and would well prepare the mind for any minute and deep scholarly work. But what we should expect such an alien to read into Shakespeare, and what aspects of Shakespeare he would never appreciate would soon be revealed if his results were compared with those of his contemporary Anglo-Saxon colleagues. The position in New Testament studies is worse, in that we do not have abundant studies of the gospels and Acts and the epistles (for the most part) by unprejudiced *Jewish* scholars brought up in a Jewish (*i.e.* a non-occidental) environment. The possibility of comparing the results of our theologians with those of really well-equipped people is not yet open to us, and this allows the former a liberty which in other parts of the intellectual world would be regarded as extraordinary. Dr G. Vermès, however, has made it plain in a recent book that 'without the help of Jewish exegesis it is impossible to perceive any Christian teaching in its true perspective'. This, uncomfortably, is neither more nor less than the truth.

CHAPTER TWELVE

The Anointing at Bethany and the Story of Zacchaeus

IT HAS LONG BEEN EVIDENT that Mt xxvi.6–13; Mk xiv.3–9; Lk vii. 36–8; and Jn xii.1–8 are connected in some way.[1] Professor David Daube[2] offers an involved and ingenious reconstruction of a connection between them, indicating stages in a transmission of a 'funeral narrative'. Granted that Mark and Matthew stem from a source very close to that of the Lucan passage (an assumption that the present writer neither wishes to substantiate nor intends to doubt) a simple explanation of the behaviour of Jesus and his disciples in Mark and Matthew, which otherwise gives rise to comment (which may well have caused the fragmentation of the tradition), comes immediately to hand. It seems that no one has indicated it,[3] and it is worth while giving the outline of this explanation, even if the significance of it must be left to others to expound. If the reconstruction given here is sound the episode has nothing to do with a funeral narrative, though it does belong to the period shortly preceding the crucifixion. The attitude of the fellow-diners is shown as somewhat less crude than it appears at first sight, and Jesus's treatment of the woman, if less gracious than it is usually supposed to have been, is more rational, ingenious, and sympathetic.

[1] E. Klostermann, *Das Markusevangelium* (Tübingen 1950), 141 cites Origen, *in Mt. comm.*, Migne *PG* 17, who disagreed. So did Osiander, for example, but Beza took the now usual view. Tatian, *Diatess.* (*c.* A.D. 172), did not equate the events in Luke with the other passages: xiv.45–48; xxxvii.47; xxxix.7–17. The episode in John is believed by C. H. Dodd to relate to another theme: *Historical Tradition in the Fourth Gospel* (Cambridge 1965), 162–72 (John was not acquainted with the Marcan form, since the idea of an anointing which was also an embalming would have been congenial to his conception of the messianic king who reigns on the cross).

[2] *The New Testament and Rabbinic Judaism* (London 1956), 312ff.

[3] No trace of the explanation is seen in B. Weiss, Wellhausen, A. Schlatter (*Markus*, Stuttgart 1935), Klostermann, or Lohmeyer (*Das Evangelium des Markus*, Göttingen 1951, 292f.). E. Lipinski, 'De unctione peracta Bethaniae', *Ruch Biblijny* 12 (1959), 220–9, I was unable to use. St Bede, we note, commented, 'What she had used in the service of sin, she now uses in the service of Christ and in declaration of her penance' (in R. F. Stoll, *Gospel according to Luke* [Cincinnati, Pustet 1931], 137) which hits the nail on the head.

WHO WAS THE WOMAN AND WHAT DID SHE DO?

There is no doubt but that the actor in this little drama was a woman, that she opened or broke a container of 'ointment', *i.e.* highly perfumed or aromatic oil or compound of such substances,[1] and applied it to a part of Jesus's body without his permission. The symbolism of choosing the head, and (in view of her history) the appropriateness of choosing the feet (whichever be the truth) are evident. Whatever our doubts about the part of the body, it seems clear that the ointment was of very great value.[2] The action, apart from its evident attempt to honour Jesus, was one essentially of renunciation, abandonment of a valuable possession, dedication.

But was the woman not an ex-prostitute? 'A woman', as Mark and Matthew put it, seems very anonymous. John of course speaks of Mary, whose behaviour was extremely indecorous at the time but was otherwise, so far as we know, respectable. Luke's version preserves a tradition that the woman was exactly the sort of person whose conversion to the Kingdom and gratitude to Jesus gave rise to comment from all sides. He himself seems to have been proud of it. Unless this woman was an ex-prostitute the significance of the behaviour of the characters in the Marcan version is much diminished.[3] It may be remarked at this stage that whereas Mark or his source visualised the people present (Mark's τινὲς may be more true to fact than Matthew's more limited οἱ μαθηταὶ) as regretting the waste (ἀπώλεια), Luke's report that the host noticed rather the incongruity of the woman's past with her present would-be association with Jesus raises the question whether the original story did not leave the source of complaint vague. Both the Lucan and Marcan versions could have derived from a report like this: 'while Jesus was at dinner a woman of the town poured nard on him without his consent and the company were indignant—but Jesus said . . .'.

An expensive, a very expensive, container of 'ointment' in the hands of a woman recently living on the earnings of prostitution would be in

[1] S. A. Naber, ΝΑΡΔΟΣ ΠΙΣΤΙΚΗ, *Mnemosyne* 30, 1902, 1–15, and R. Köbert, 'Nardos Pistike', *Biblica* 29 (1948), 279–81, discuss the unsolved problem of πιστικῆς. A most interesting suggestion that πιστικῆς somehow reproduces **muta pistaqa* (pistachio nut oil) is made by M. Black, *Aramaic Approach* (*cit. sup.*) at p. 224–5. Billerbeck, *Kommentar zum Neuen Testament*, II (München 1924), 48–9. Dodd, *ubi cit.* 163 discusses the textual problem—it is probable that Mark and John originally had the rare πιστικῆς only. For costly 'ointment' on the head see Ps cxxxii (cxxxiii).2 and the allusion to Ex xxx.25, 30. K. Ziegler, *Kl. Pauly* III, 1969, 1572.

[2] John's estimate is apparently taken from Mark's source, where it is by no means certainly an 'embellishment'. Nard was fantastically expensive.

[3] Daube with good reason says, 'Luke on the whole stands nearest the original tradition'.

any case one of the most valuable and significant objects she would possess. Ointment to a prostitute must have been amongst the most useful 'tools' of her 'trade'. Had she been given it by an admirer? The great value of the container suggests rather that it had been bought by her (and by colleagues in partnership?) out of earnings. Even if it had been bought specially in order to honour Jesus, which is quite possible, she would have bought it with a professional taste and from a known dealer. The urge to make such a renunciation is quite understandable. No prostitute or ex-prostitute could pay tithes, or make gifts or offerings in the normal way. Her money was tainted, and that too in the highest degree. Dt xxiii.18 cuts off the prostitute (and by interpretation many others) from the self-taxing system of the Jewish people:[1] naturally the prostitutes formed a society to themselves and were despised as living on earnings which were so dirty that no respectable person would accept them as gifts, or participate in a tithe of them. We have already seen how Philo and the Dead Sea Scrolls community objected to participation in ill-gotten gains, and how the latter kept entirely apart from people whose wealth was tainted.[2] An opportunity to make a religious gift, so soon after release from the life of shame, would be eagerly awaited. But how could one be made under the orthodox system out of the paraphernalia or earnings of prostitution? If she had said to Jesus, or the disciples' treasurer, 'Please accept these alms', she would quite possibly have been spurned. Pouring the ointment on Jesus's head or feet would be a way of sacrificing something valuable, conferring a benefit of a more than negligible sort, without requiring the offering to be accepted deliberately. There was, it seems, some shrewdness in her choice of method. Let people think what they might after the *fait accompli*. Like the unconscious Jew who fell amongst thieves, Jesus would be expected not to object to a benefit, such as the Good Samaritan's objectionable wine and oil, offered with a good heart and actually doing no harm.

WHAT WAS THE NATURE OF THE DISCIPLES' OBJECTION?

In Lk vii.39–40 we are told that the woman's behaviour gave rise to doubt and discussion. There is no doubt but that, as T. W. Manson indicated,[3] the anointing was not without possible political reper-

[1] For the principle of Dt xxiii.18 (19) see below, p. 273 n. 4. The contemporary view of its meaning is reflected in Josephus, *Ant.* IV, 206 (IV, viii, 9), and indirectly in *ibid.* IV, 245 (IV, viii, 23), and better still in Philo, *De Spec. Leg.* I, 19, 104 and 51, 281–4. See above, p. 83 n. 1. b. Tem. 28*a* (*Mishnāh*), 29*a–b* (*Mishnāh*), 30*b*. Not so with a Gentile: Sifre Num. § 115.

[2] Above, p. 76.

[3] *The Servant-Messiah* (Cambridge 1961), 85.

cussions. But it is most unlikely that the disciples' objections related to such a consideration. The sinner's gift ought to be objectionable to a man who associated himself with the Holy One. One did not need to be a Pharisee to observe that. In Mark and Matthew 'some people', or 'disciples' objected, in John Judas objected, in an apparently ungracious manner, to the 'waste'. Of course they are not suggesting that the ointment is wasted on Jesus. The Marcan text is obviously allowed to be capable of bearing such an interpretation in order to bring out, ironically, the ignorance of people present in contrast with the unconscious 'prescience' of the woman and Jesus's approval of her act: it is a piece of artistry. Any merely ill-mannered remark would have failed to reach us. Of course we may understand that they will have suffered from the normal horror of Jews seeing a valuable object spent apparently to no purpose—*but why to no purpose?* This is the crux of the matter, which has not so far been noticed. Their suggestion was that since she could and should have acted otherwise her act was as good as useless. They mean what they say in so many words, namely that the ointment could have been sold at a great price, which should rather have been distributed amongst the poor, perhaps poor members of the community. Their point is sound. If she had wanted to make an offering (and others might be inclined, unless dissuaded, to follow her example) the proper course, they suggest, would have been to dispose of her assets on the open market, obtain money for them, and then donate it in charity. The objection which attached to the ointment as an offering to Jesus personally would not attach to its purchase price on the market (exactly the same point is latent at Mt xix.21 'sell that thou hast . . .'). Is not this an odd notion? Surely if the ointment were tainted, as all must have supposed (for they did not go into any enquiry as to its origin), any money received by the sale of it would equally have been tainted? This logical argument is not in accord with the ideas of the period.[1] Objects which are *extra commercium* for various reasons,

[1] First, the command in Dt xxiii.18 (19) was construed with extreme strictness (see b. cited in previous note); and only that object in consideration for which intercourse was obtained was within the verse. Secondly this was a rule, not of total prohibition (as in the case of flesh seethed in milk, from which no benefit of any sort might be obtained: Ex xxiii.19; xxxiv.26; Dt xiv.21; b. Ḥul. 115*b*), but of prohibition of a particular application. In the Talmud she is allowed to *dedicate* the object (and apparently its value may be given): b. 'Avod. Zar. 62*b*. A very useful comparison is provided by *Mishnāh*, B.Ḳ. X 1 (translators vary), b. B.Ḳ. 113*a*: one must not change money from the tax-gatherer's counter, nor from the tax-collector's purse, nor may charity be taken from them. If they offer charity from their own homes it may be accepted: but the actual coins tainted, or presumed tainted, by their unlawful dealings cannot be taken either in commerce (by the pious) or as charity. Our woman's ointment attracted a presumption of tainted origin or tainted purpose and association: but if anyone would buy it, the coins would not be within the same objection—no presump-

including objects as abominable as the hire of a harlot, *viz*. flesh cooked with milk or 'diverse kinds of a vineyard', may come to be sold, in which case the proceeds of the sale can validly be used for, for example, betrothing a woman.[1] Taint attaches to the earning itself, not to its substitutes or the products of its conversion *in specie*.[2] Any other rule would have rendered most objects of commerce untithable as time went on. In any case *pecunia non olet* is a convenient maxim in all civilisations. The disciples were quite prepared to accept assets of tainted origin in charity, provided (it seems) that the taint was at least one degree removed from the object actually offered. The Dead Sea Scroll sect seem to have been, or to have wished to be, more scrupulous: they were not supposed to take anything from those who do not obey the word of God *except for a price*; *i.e.* they would not even accept their charity.[3]

JESUS'S ANSWER TO THE OBJECTION

The benefit Jesus had received from the ointment struck him as timely and symbolic. Fortunately he had not been asked to accept it. The woman's intelligence deserved approval. But was it lawful for him to take such a benefit in such a way? Would not Jesus, like the Dead Sea enthusiasts, recoil in horror from 'a daughter of the Pit'? Was there anyone upon whom possibly tainted ointment could quite lawfully be poured? The unexpected and inauspicious case of a corpse comes to mind. When Jesus said 'she has done it to prepare me for burial' he referred to himself, and his cyming death, but also to the notorious position with regard to a corpse. Since a corpse is the most polluted and polluting thing imaginable,[4] there can be no ritualistic objection to

[1] *Mishnāh*, Ḳid. II. 9 (Danby, 324; Blackman, III, 463–4). See previous note.

[2] In the Talmud property attached to the soil (*e.g.* a house) may not be sold and its proceeds used for purposes of the sanctuary, but a thing not fixed to the ground (*e.g.* trinkets, etc.) may be used for secular purposes: 'Avod. Zar. 46*b*. A lax view that an animal given as hire to a harlot could be tithed direct, and another (a more strict view), that it could be tithed if it was bought back from her are reflected in the undeniably later doctrines of the Talmud: 'Avod. Zar. 56*a*–*b*, 57*a*. Contemporarily with Jesus there was doubt whether, when a harlot was hired with grapes, the wine made from them could be used as an offering in the temple. But Hillel took the less strict view (though a stricter interpretation of the verse of Deuteronomy) that as the wine was not the grapes it could be offered. This discussion is conclusive that the purchase-price of the grapes would have been lawful. See b. Tem. 30*b*, and B.Ḳ. 65*b*, Sonc. 380.

[3] 1 *QS* V, 15–17. Vermès, 79–80; Lohse, 18; Leaney, 174; Dupont-Sommer, 99. They cited Is ii.22, which the Targum connects with idolatry.

[4] On this it is sufficient to see Maimonides, *op. cit.*, *Book of Cleanness* (Yale Judaica Series, New Haven 1954); or App. IV to Danby's *Mishnah*.

tion could apply to them. See also 'Avod. Zar. 62*a* = Sonc. 303, and 54*b* = Sonc. 277: proceeds can effect a marriage. Here we are in the midst of true *halakic* disquisition.

using otherwise tainted materials on it.[1] A very objectionable object is a garment in which threads of mixed material have been woven. The regular rule, which we find preserved at b. Nid. 61*b*,[2] was that 'a garment in which *kil*^{e}*'ayim* was lost (so that the offending thread could not be pulled out) may not be sold to an idolater, nor may one make of it a pack-saddle for an ass, but it may be made into a shroud for a corpse'. It was objected that at the resurrection the former corpse would appear clad in unlawful attire! No, said R. Joḥanan (post-Tannaitic), for amongst the dead the commandments of the *Torāh* have no force (Ps lxxxviii.5 [6]): a dictum which he made his own, but which we are interested to see[3] was utilised by Paul in Rm vii.1, 4, *et alibi*. It is a work of charity to prepare a corpse for burial,[4] not an act of worship. Since a corpse cannot accept anything, the person to whom the body once belonged is not put to the embarrassment of refusing the doubtful gift proffered. The woman was inhibited from making gifts directly out of her tainted earnings, but the course open to her (ὃ ἔσχεν ἐποίησεν: Mk xiv.8*a*)[5] was the one she adopted—treating him (as Matthew emphasises) as the physical beneficiary from an act of self-sacrifice of which he could not be the acceptor. We note, as did Klostermann and Daube,[6] that the 'ointment' was applied from the container and not with the hand, an action which, however appropriate in any case to the head and to the head of a person whom one was not worthy to touch in so honourable part of the body, was undeniably fitted to the anointing of a corpse. The gesture had a certain ambivalence, of which a sharp mind could take advantage.

That Jesus recognised this is clear from the choice of words, as Daube noticed.[7] προέλαβεν implies an anticipation. What Jesus could not accept *in praesenti* he acknowledged as valid *in futuro*. The Jewish law knew the possibility of transactions the validity of which would mature in the future.[8] The two readings of the Johannine text present a problem, not because the more difficult reading[9] suggests that the

[1] The taint it would convey to anything that touched it would be far greater than anything that could be conveyed to it. The hire of a harlot was not a 'father of uncleanness' in any case.

[2] Sonc. 433–4; also b. Pes. 40*b* = Sonc. 189.

[3] See below, p. 466.

[4] Moore, *Judaism*, I (Cambridge, Mass. 1927), 71; Daube, *ubi cit.* 315. Burial takes precedence over feeding and clothing the living, whence Jesus's reference to the poor here (he cites Dt xv.11), and also the incident at Mt viii.21–2; Lk ix.59–60.

[5] Klostermann makes this point, *ubi cit.* 143.

[6] Klostermann cites *ZNW* iv (1903), 179f. Daube, *ubi cit.* refers to b. San. 101*a* (Sonc. 685) (?).

[7] *Ubi cit.* 313.

[8] Daube cites several instances at p. 313. A notable institution is the irrevocable gift to operate after death, which is dealt with at length by R. Yaron, *Gifts in Contemplation of Death* (Oxford 1960).

[9] On Jn xii.7 (where the *BFBS* text, Aland, and that followed by the translators of

woman should keep the residue of the perfume for Jesus's burial, which is banal, but because they *both* preserve the Jewish notion that she earmarked the valuable object for its purpose with a particular intention—an idea very difficult to put into Greek,[1] so that we cannot tell which reading is more likely to have been John's original text. Jesus wants his audience to *impute* to the woman a particular mental appropriation (a *keeping*, providently as opposed to a *wasting* or improvidently spending),[2] a particular intention (this last Bultmann observed): etiquette did not permit (even if Jesus had wished to do so) the woman's being interrogated as to her *actual* intention, which an interrogation or dispute might have obscured. Every offering must be made, in order to be valid, with an accompanying intention. This is well known. The Israelite who slaughters an animal must be mindful as he does so of exactly what he is doing and why.[3] The priest, as intermediary, must have the relevant intention while he takes the sacrificial offerings and does the ritual acts with them: it is the intention which counts.[4] Jesus did not therefore *accept* the gift, but admitted that her action was lawful in the context he mentioned, but of which she herself would not have been expected to have knowledge. 'Let us impute to her an intention that if anointing of my body shall be requisite hereafter (at my burial) her spending of this ointment shall be in performance of that charitable duty': a juridically as well as morally unanswerable comment, as kind to the woman as it was intellectually distinguished. This is not just a piece of sophistry. Upon the supposition that a corpse requires spices, a shroud, and soil upon which to lie, that corpse has a right like that of ownership in its requirements. It is a maxim of Jewish law that no one may derive any benefit from the requirements of a corpse.[5] Accordingly, once Jesus has shown that this ointment is destined for the preparation of his body for

[1] J. de Zwaan, *JBL* 57 (1938), 155ff.

[2] J. Jeremias, *ZNW* 35 (1936), 75–82. Examples of such mental appropriations were common in Jewish practice in Mishnaic times. 'The truly pious used to lay down money and say: "Whatsoever fruit is picked from here [a fourth-year vineyard] may it be redeemed by this money".' *Mishnāh*, M. Shen. V.1 (Danby, 80).

[3] 'An offering must be slaughtered while mindful of six things: of the offerings, of the offerer, of God, of the altar-fires, of the odour, and of the sweet savour; and, if it is a sin-offering or a guilt-offering, also of the sin': *Mishnāh*, Zᵉvāḥ. IV.6 (Danby, 473).

[4] *Mishnāh*, Zᵉvāḥ. II.2, III–IV (Danby, 469ff.).

[5] San. 47*b*; and the reference in 'Er. 31*a*, Sonc. p. 214, n. 8.

the *New English Bible* read the *lectio ardua* ἵνα εἰς τὴν ἡμέραν τοῦ ἐνταφιασμοῦ μου τηρήσῃ αὐτό) see Dodd, *ubi cit.* 167, 169; R. Bultmann, *Das Evangelium des Johannes*, 17th edn (Göttingen 1962), p. 318 n. 4 with additional references in his *Ergänzungsheft* (1957), 41. The *Jerusalem Bible* prefers the *lectio recepta*, with τετήρηκεν: 'she had to keep this scent for the day of my burial'. Arndt-Gingrich, s.v. ἀφίημι 4, say that ἄφες αὐτήν, ἵνα . . . τηρήσῃ αὐτό means 'let her keep it', which is (grammatically) attractive.

burial it follows as a matter of course that the living community, the Christian poor, whose rights must be postponed to the needs of the unburied dead, have no claim upon it. The analogy of the corpse with the unconscious person we have ourselves noticed in connection with the parable of the Samaritan. The unconscious, *i.e.* unaware, man's liabilities, and legal situation, often appear in the Talmud.[1] Jesus could lawfully benefit from this application of ointment without his consent just as an unconscious man can be a party to a legal transaction, and as a corpse can receive the charity of spices and a shroud. The woman could lawfully confer this benefit on the basis that she was anticipating a situation in respect of which her benefit would endure. Though John, or his source, had evidently forgotten that the woman was an ex-prostitute, so that the point of the story was hardly retrievable, he preserved in a garbled form the decision that the woman's act would be 'preserved', 'guarded'[2] until, and therefore be effective in respect of, the time of Jesus's death. So quite a difficult legal idea bridges the ages in not altogether inappropriate language.

It is very interesting that Mark, Matthew and John[3] (but not Luke), preserve the saying, 'You always have the poor with you, but me you do not have always'. It is generally realised that Jesus is citing Dt xv.11. One could go further and say that midrashically he distinguishes the 'poor' of that verse from the poor man of *vv.* 7ff. and so applies the latter to himself, thus justifying the woman's lavish and ungrudging expenditure which resembles what is recommended in such terms at xv.10, the immediately previous verse.

The woman would realise that the Master was giving one of his *halakic* opinions,[4] and the otherwise hurtful words, unthinkably inappropriate in the ears of one who loved him, would not be taken amiss. Luke's picture of the discussion as academic in tone is plausible. Jesus's admitting the lawfulness of her act was, as far as she was concerned,

[1] A striking example is the rule that an absent person can be benefited without his consent, but not inflicted with a liability: b. Giṭ. 11*b* (*Mishnāh*); 'Er. 81*b* (*Mishnāh*), 95*a*.

[2] Commentators discuss this ably. See Daube, *ubi cit.* 318–19.

[3] Bultmann, *ubi cit.* 318, thinks it probable that the phrase is a later addition at Jn xii.8.

[4] An actual (or apocryphal?) *halakic* responsum of Jesus of Nazareth on this very subject is reported somewhat comically at b. 'Avod. Zar. 17*a*, and less well at Midr. R., Eccl. I 8, 3 = Sonc. 27. He cites Mi i.7 (*cf.* Ho ii.5, 12; ix.1) to the effect that the hire of a harlot cannot be employed for any purpose, except perhaps the building of latrines! The notion that the hire of a harlot is utterly unfit for secular purposes is an extreme view which was evidently no part of practical law. The basic rule *quod fieri non debuit factum valet* is good Jewish law (*Mishnāh*, Ket. VIII.1, 2; b. Ḳid. 59*a*; B.B. 51*a–b*), and a transaction might certainly be valid though the court could never have ordered the act to be done through which the original title accrued.

the equivalent of a genuine acceptance. It is not a coincidence, one may suppose, that Luke follows this episode with an account of women who owed Jesus everything and served him (and his disciples?) with their goods; and equally appropriately Mark and Matthew continue from this story to the betrayal by Judas, an episode which undoubtedly includes the motif of unrighteous *mammon*. We are to understand the story as proof that Jesus interpreted the law strictly, and that his admission of publicans and sinners to his fellowship did not imply the casting aside of all regard for Jewish scruples.

Is there a reliable tradition in the prophecy (Mk xiv. 9) that she would be remembered personally for what she had done at that time? Why should her *personal* immortality be important enough for the Church to have included this? The theory that the act should be remembered as proof that his body did receive anointing notwithstanding its unexpected disappearance from the tomb ignores the phrase εἰς μνημόσυνον αὐτῆς ('for a memorial of her'). Evidently Luke and John had no use for this tradition, while Luke is concerned that the woman's act should have a benediction for its natural outcome. We have seen (if this reconstruction is correct) that what she did was intelligent. No doubt it was bold: the resentment of the disciples and other members of the company could have led to blows; the surreptitious applying of tainted offerings to one whom many regarded as a prophet (Lk vii.39*b*) could have had a painful sequel. She had faith that he himself would react favourably. What was so memorable was that she, a fallen woman, an outcaste from Jewish society, was the first to act upon the assumption which Jesus himself made, namely that he was very shortly to die and that this coming event deserved so vast an expenditure. She could not make offerings in the Temple; but to the temple of his body, as a *body*, she confidently made this offering. No doubt it should be remembered. What degree of prescience we are to attribute to her depends upon how far we believe that Mk xiv.9*c* is genuine and how far it represents Jesus as expecting that the woman herself would be remembered for what she *did*. She would not have done what she did had she not believed what turned out to be true: that much seems to be indisputable, and the rest would seem to follow as a matter of course. She was the first to act as if she saw the appropriateness of a solemn ceremonial anointing, as if she believed (for this was another case of the irony of actions during Jesus's last days) that he was to die and that his body deserved this worship in that light, and not in the light of other anointings with scented oils with which her previous life was familiar.[1] The paradox alone, seen in this way, is very striking.

[1] See Josephus, *Ant.* XIX, 239 (XIX, iv, 1) where anointing the head is treated as a

Jesus's reply turned away evil imputations and insinuations, and deflected attention on to the coming tragedy. This was not lofty condescension to the woman, still less pity, nor the crude disregard for her feelings which his words might otherwise imply. The mixture of the aloof and the welcoming is remarkable, and must have been an important factor in the life and happiness of that curiously assorted community.[1]

THE LUCAN VERSION OF THE STORY OF THE ANOINTING

Luke sets the scene[2] in the house of, not 'Simon the leper', but a Pharisee called Simon, who may or may not have been the same man. The Lucan story is a very extraordinary one, circumstantial and detailed. Its literary and linguistic content is greatly illuminated by the

[1] C. Montefiore (*Syn. Gosp.* I [1909], 315) lamentably comments 'the words are inconceivable in Jesus's mouth'. Before finding the evangelists' reports 'inconceivable' let us first see what they could mean!

[2] Lk vii.42*b*–43, 47*b*, gave me some doubt for a long time. I did not find it possible to accept that where a creditor forgave debts, 500 den. to one insolvent debtor and 50 den. to another, the first must be more grateful than the second. In the first place in my experience people take gifts very lightly (in contrast to bargains and to what they earn); and I could not see how gratitude could be measured proportionately in this way. Further I doubted how the debtors could feel such proportionate gratitude, or should do so, when in either case the creditor had simply forgiven what he could not collect! But the answers fall into two categories, both of which we must accept. Firstly the Jewish mentality which is depicted cannot be denied. Jesus's hearers might have a moment's doubt about it (ὑπολαμβάνω at *v.* 43), but they *did* feel more gratitude and affection for one who had forgiven them the larger amount. His personal loss was greater and thus the evidence he provided, whereby he might reasonably be supposed to feel an identity of interest with his donee, was more compelling. Secondly the law and practice of the country would put the debtor to personal inconvenience roughly in proportion to the amount he owed. His lands, if he had any, would be liable to be sold, and he himself would be liable to personal arrest. Naturally to recover his lands and goods, if any, and his personal freedom would be a much more difficult proceeding if his debt were large. We notice that the amounts have been chosen so as to suit the circumstances of people of no great resources. A man unable to pay 50 den. would indeed be a poor man, though not within the ranks of the chronic indigent. A man who accumulated a debt of 500 den. would be a man of some substance, but not necessarily of abundant credit. To get such a debt paid would mean social humiliation, and an ensuing obligation perhaps to a number of people instead of to the one. He would thus have frequent opportunity for remembering from what his kind creditor had saved him. Since he could not do much for him in point of cash he would be loud in his praises and effusive in his protestation of undying attachment (until the feeling wore off). J. Delobel, *Eph. Th. Lov.* 42 (1966), 415–75, is the main study here.

sign of having recently had intercourse with a woman (or attended a banquet, or party: ὡς ἀπὸ συνουσίας). Anointing the head was a characteristic of honouring a bridegroom, and he appeared at his wedding-feast anointed with oil. See also Jdt x.3; xxvi.8. Oil signifies rejoicing, its absence mourning (*e.g.*): 2 S xiv.2ff., Dn x.2–3; Pap. Eleph. 30 (Vincent, *La Religion des Judéo-Araméens d'Éléphantine*, Paris 1937, 503–4). Jesus at Mt vi.17 refuses to extend the rules about fasting so as to include the outward signs of mourning.

study of Professor M. Black.[1] It is not surprising that ingenuity has been used to reconstruct some kind of sequence of versions or reports of the original event. A suggestion was made above as to an original report which could have given rise to both sources of complaint against the woman's action; but that does not, and perhaps indeed cannot, account for the elaborate allegation by Jesus that his host had not greeted him in a particular way and that the woman had, as it were, made good the host's lapses, nor does it account for the presence of the little parable about the two debtors of one creditor. This is not the place to enter into the large number of hypotheses which could account for Luke's combination of elements. The one least likely to be given credence in the present state of New Testament studies is that Luke had a factual report of what occurred! That Jesus should accuse his host of not having shown him what would appear to have been elementary hospitality (at xvii.44–5) seems very odd, more odd if the words were false than if they were true, some would think. Moreover there is the extreme improbability of a Pharisee allowing a woman of bad fame to 'keep on', as Jesus puts it, kissing the guest's feet from the moment he arrived. Indeed these improbabilities alone might serve to explain why Mark does not retain anything of these details. But why does so well-informed an evangelist, with semitic scholars at his elbow, give so much space to this version of the events?

Perhaps the improbabilities, taken at their face value, should certify that the scene should be imagined as actually occurring in this way. The very extraordinary does happen. Life is certainly stranger than fiction. The woman's presence in the room would have been scandalous. Why was she not driven out? Because Jesus did not object to her presence. Why did he not object? This was a matter of speculation for the host and his other guests.

The host, being polite, did not presume to forbid what his eminent guest allowed; but he would naturally be in a quandary (as Luke indicates). Jesus was not puzzled either by the woman's flamboyant behaviour or by his host's alarm. Righteousness is taught by rabbis by their example, *i.e.* their lives, and by their teachings, *e.g.* in sermons and parables; and Jesus proceeds to justify his own conduct, to teach his host a lesson (quite in order in the circumstances, for he would not have been invited had not the host been ready for an edifying discourse under his roof), and to tell anyone willing to listen what was the sym-

[1] *Aramaic Approach* 181–3. The linguistic research is especially valuable as it confirms that the forgiveness of the woman was in the past—her demonstration of affection is a consequence of her having been forgiven. A. M. Hunter, *Interpreting the Parables* (1960), 55, noticed this: 'God must have remitted very great spiritual debts for her, since she shows so much gratitude.'

bolic, inside meaning of the curious little drama. Though the pericope could be, and has been, thought of as somewhat hard both on the woman and the Pharisee, we have seen that Jesus was kindness itself to the woman and Luke explains this very carefully ('Thy faith has saved thee. Go in peace!'). Similarly he was (though he might not appear to be at first sight) very kind to his uneasy host. The steps in his thought are typically spiritual–juridical. The very interesting and intimate question of a prostitute's repentance and forgiveness is beyond my competence and I must leave it at any rate for the present. But, as to the rest, the connection of ideas is clear. One cannot but point out how readily the Jewish mind turns to financial and material considerations as the readiest medium of communicating, by metaphor or simile, an abstract idea.[1]

(1) To understand the woman's behaviour and Jesus's in allowing her to behave as she did, one must grasp that emotional response towards a person is motivated, triggered off, as it were, by the previous history. A man given a large benefit is likely to be more grateful than a man given a small benefit, and is likely to feel and to show more emotion in consequence. The one who grants the benefit expects more emotion from the former than the latter, or at any rate is not surprised at it.

(2) The woman's emotional behaviour is conveniently contrasted with the host's sincere but conventional behaviour. The host *himself* did not do any of the acts mentioned, for a variety of reasons. Water for the feet was certainly provided, but the host had not poured it (a servant will have done that); the host had not kissed Jesus (it would have been frivolous and disrespectful to do so—one kisses relatives, equals, juniors, those returning from a long journey); he had not anointed him with oil[2] because the occasion was not so festive as to warrant it. But had he been intensely emotionally disposed he might have done all these. But he had no *reason* for such a disposition, and therefore he need not feel ashamed at not behaving in that way.

(3) He cannot, however, complain at the woman's behaviour because although she acted as she did for her own spiritual benefit in a wholly personal way, without the intention of conferring any benefit on Jesus's

[1] In what follows an entirely different approach is to be seen from that of G. Braumann, 'Die Schuldner und die Sünderin . . .', *NTS* 10 (1964), 487–93. The author there understands Lk vii.36–9, 44–6, 48f. and 41–3 as originally independent. *v.* 47 he would attribute to the connecting of the little 'parable' and the story. *v.* 50 he believes to be an addition which is to be explained from the early Church's call to baptism.

[2] Anointing with oil means a distinct anticipation of rejoicing (see above, p. 274 n. 1), but it is interesting to see how far back the connection between oil and banquets goes. A text from Mari (G. Boyer, *Archives Royales de Mari* VIII, 1958, cited by Z. W. Falk at *Ivra*, 17 [1966], 172) says 'They have eaten the bread, drunk the cup and rubbed the oil'—to celebrate a bargain and sale.

host (whom she may not have known), she performed on his behalf as it were acts which could be construed quietly as his duties—and he ought (if he had any 'reason' to do so) to ratify and adopt her acts. Jesus's extremely delicate way of suggesting that perhaps even his good host *might* have some weakness or lack of merit which could conceivably be remedied by an improvement in his attitude, whether to Jesus himself or to others, is marvellous. Although it seems that the host's objections to the woman included some doubt whether, after all, Jesus were the prophetic character he was supposed to be, Jesus does not include in his discourse one word of reproach. But if one reads it carefully one cannot escape the impression that the lesson would not be lost on the host or the assembled company.

Luke does not mention Jesus's burial. But the words relative to the woman's behaviour, the acts which are attributed to her, though they are made on the surface to refer to the reception of a guest at a solemn banquet, could as easily refer to the desperate grief of a mourner. The focal point of the story in Luke is the woman's love, and Jesus makes it quite plain that the woman's sins were forgiven *before* she manifested her emotion in all those ways. She did not spend her nard in order to be forgiven, but out of a state of mind which revealed that she had been forgiven.[1] Other people's attitudes towards Jesus lacked such exaggeration because in their cases either little had been forgiven or there was little to forgive—and a more tactful way of putting this complex idea it would be impossible to conceive.

It is often said that Jesus could be very rude. A retort commencing 'Thou hypocrite' would seem to substantiate the charge. His taking a whip to the moneychangers in the Temple is often alleged as an example of his capacity to be violent. However, there is evidence of great tact: the case of the so-called Young Enquirer would serve well as an example. And here we have had proof that in what pious Jews would regard as an extremely delicate situation (they were very sensitive to 'holy' men's dealings with women) Jesus could be the soul of tact without compromising his mission as a leader and a teacher.

THE STORY OF THE LODGING WITH ZACCHAEUS

It is unexpected that what seems to be the same lesson as we have learnt from Jesus's dealing with the ex-prostitute at Bethany is taught in the

[1] Since this is so she is no longer 'impure' and strictly there is no analogy with Jesus's kind treatment of the woman 'with an issue of blood' (A. Farrer, *Study in St. Mark* 1951, 168–9). Meanwhile, the correct translation of αἱ ἁμαρτίαι αὐτῆς αἱ πολλαί is not 'her sins, which are many' but 'her many sins' [*i.e.* there is no emphasis on the number] (Kilpatrick, *NT* 5 [1962], 112).

parable of the Pounds as Luke locates it at xix.11ff. Now we have already seen that the parable of the Talents or Pounds was not originally intended to teach anything about forgiveness as such, but rather to cope with the common excuses against getting on with the very serious business of doing God's bidding, and so showing him a profit—to re-employ the characteristic metaphor which Jesus's compatriots, and evidently Jesus himself, thought fit to employ in this context. In the parable the contrast is made between the capitalist's satisfaction with his partners' efforts wherever they brought a profit—even if that was relatively less dramatic—and the same capitalist's displeasure at the refusal of one partner to make any investment on behalf of them both. But it is possible to see the parable as an illustration of a hypothetical teaching to the effect that some Jews know what to do and do it, but woe betide those who, whilst knowing what to do, do not do it! And the story of Zacchaeus is a striking case where an improbable conversion takes place. Now if we assume that this is the main motive behind Luke's location of the parable in ch. xix, where we find it, the idea is quite reasonable. Great rewards are available to the servant who does his master's bidding when it was open to him to do nothing, to be idle and fearful and negligent. And the lesson of the Zacchaeus episode is that forgiveness and a change of heart (so as to be thenceforward 'profitable') can, in a very curious and unexpected way, seem to coincide—exactly as we found in the case of the woman with the ointment, whose behaviour could rationally be interpreted not (as she herself might have thought) as a search for forgiveness, but as proof that she had been forgiven. These subtle matters surely deserved authoritative and striking documentation, and in the episodes now being discussed we have it.

The story of Zacchaeus is particularly remarkable for its strict adherence to Jewish (indeed semitic and further eastern) ethics and, more especially, to the legalistic thinking of the people. It is not surprising that it has attracted the comparatively recent attention of Professor Dauvillier.[1] In his view Zacchaeus was a leading member of a partnership of publicans, and was responsible for the extortions of his subordinates. Professor Dauvillier continues with the suggestion that the extortion envisaged in our pericope was that of his subordinates (which, in fact, can hardly be proved), and that under the law as it is likely to have been laid down by the procurator, Pilate, he would have been liable to restore such amounts (if forcibly taken) with a threefold penalty superadded—always assuming that he could have been prose-

[1] J. Dauvillier, 'Le texte évangelique de Zachée et les obligations des Publicains'. *Recueil de L'Académie de Législation* (Toulouse), 5th ser., 1 (1951), 28–32.

cuted successfully. Later, certainly, there is evidence that such a penalty could lawfully be exacted from extortionate publicans under imperial legislation.[1] However, this may well be a coincidence for (as we shall see) Jews placed very differently from Zacchaeus used to think in terms of a fourfold restitution where they could be accused of causing loss, and there is no reason to suppose that first- or early second-century Jews imitated the Roman legislation in this respect. As we have remarked before, legalistic pedantry is strongly disliked today, particularly in the Anglo-Saxon world, and more especially in the English rather than the North American elements of that world. The (unhistorical) contrast between the 'spirit' and the 'letter' of the law has gripped our minds because our own tradition and our temperaments incline in that way. Yet Jesus himself fully appreciated the juridical fussiness of his nation, and in this episode we actually see him relying upon it, just as he did in the episode at Bethany.

The picture of the short-statured publican up a tree[2] to see Jesus passing is very attractive. The pun in his name (Zakkai means 'the Righteous') is amusing. We know about Zacchaeus's legal situation for we have already been studying aspects of a tax-gatherer's life. Since he was a *chief* tax-gatherer he will be presumed to have exercised force (an expression which includes menaces, etc.) in exacting money from the sub-collectors whom he had apparently under his control. We know that pious Jews objected to property obtained by *force* (*ḥāmaṣ*)[3] (violence being synonymous with injustice). Extortion (*'oshek̦*) is an expression as well known to the Bible as to daily life[4]—indeed in biblical terms *'oshek̦* and restitution are as closely connected ideally as they are remote from each other practically. We know that publicans were so suspect that no one should handle money found in their possession. The instances of the word 'publican' being linked with 'sinner', and of similar disagreeable associations, which have been ably gathered by Jeremias[5] are really impressive. It was not merely a matter of the publicans' being

[1] Dauvillier refers to Cicero, *In C. Verrem* II, 3, 10, 26. Paulus (*c.* A.D. 200) at Just. *Dig.* 39. 4 (de publicanis), 9.5 (per uim extortum . . . cum poena triplici). There is also an analogical rule at *Dig.* 39. 4, 1.3–4. It is relevant to note here that if a publican voluntarily restored what he had extorted he was *not* liable to the penalty. Under the edict of the urban Praetor (in Italy, not in the provinces) the penalty for forcible extortion was *double* si id restitutum non erit (Ulpianus, at *Dig.* 39. 4, 1). Whether Zacchaeus had Roman law in mind or the habits of his compatriots, it is clear his offer was histrionic: that does not, of course, necessarily mean grandiose and unrealistic—still less insincere.

[2] Kopp, *Holy Places* (1963), 260.

[3] On the distinction between a *ḥamṣan* and a *gazlan* (both of which could be comprehended in συκοφάντης) see b. B.Ḳ. 62*a* = Sonc. 361.

[4] E. Nestle, συκοφαντέω, at *ZNW* 4 (1903), 271ff.

[5] *Jerusalem zur Zeit Jesu* (Göttingen 1962), 346.

hated because they worked (as Zacchaeus seems to have done) for the Romans or even for the tetrarchal governments.[1] It was the overtone of force and fraud which constantly associated itself with the revenue system Palestine had known for centuries (*Mishnāh*, Ned. III.4) which rendered the gains, the riches, of the publicans suspect, and made association with them difficult for the pious.

Why should these people have been more or less outcastes? Jewish law (*i.e.* in courts under Pharisees' control) will not admit tax-farmers as witnesses in any lawsuit or case, and this is a ban at least as strong as any our New Testament language implies. The reason is simple enough. To the oriental mind it is wicked to eat the food of a person whose earnings are tainted. The concept *pecunia non olet* (which we have found useful in another connection) is not a distinctively oriental idea, unless confined strictly to coins, when in some cases it will be sufficiently at home in the East. We have already seen (Lk xvi.9) that tainted earnings (in the case of the usurious lender, etc.) can, in Jesus's view, validly be given to the poor—but there is no social relation between the donor and the object of charity, nor the reciprocity,[2] which would render participation in ill-gotten gains morally objectionable. But one who socially shares in the wealth of a man who earns unlawfully, or even unrighteously (if the distinction is ever significant), is a partner with him in unrighteousness, and shares his guilt. This is extremely obvious to one brought up in an oriental environment.[3] Associating with people means eating with them (*i.e.* as opposed to eating their leavings or accepting their charity). This indeed is exactly what the opponents of Jesus say in so many words: 'he accepts sinners and *eats with them*' (Lk xv.2). And eating with tainted people, simply swallowing their food, accepting non-charitable presents from them, seems to inflict *ipso facto* a taint

[1] The language of Lk xviii.11 (the Pharisee in the Temple) suggests that just to be a tax-collector was a sin over and above the immoral or illegal acts, including swindling, carefully listed in the previous clause. The great repertory of information on tax-collectors is O. Michel, τελώνης at *ThWzNT* VIII (2) (1965), 88–106 (Zacchaeus at pp. 97 n. 105, 105). Michel, however, supposes that Zacchaeus exceeds the required proportion; and remarks that Jesus promises 'salvation' before the penance is actually completed—this ignores the Jewish legal point made in our present chapter.

[2] Purchase from suspected persons was forbidden: *Mishnāh*, B.Ḳ. X, 9–10: all forms of exchange were avoided by the pious.

[3] For Islam see an instance cited by Holt (cited above, p. 76 n. 4). In India the concept is ubiquitous and helped to found the chief characteristic of caste: *Manusmṛti* VIII, 317 ('The abortionist wipes off his (or her) guilt on the one who takes his (or her) food . . ., etc.'); those who do not perform their penance must not be *eaten with*: *ibid.* IX, 236–8. A royal order of excommunication is phrased 'no one must eat in his house': Medhātithi on Manu IV, 226. Only excommunicated persons will eat in the house of the excommunicate, who may be quite cheerful otherwise, though he may find it difficult to get his daughters married, even with a large dowry: C. v. Fürer-Haimendorf, *Morals and Merit* (London 1967), 49–50.

indistinguishable from that borne by the unrighteous themselves. One must not eat with extortioners, says Paul (1 Co v.11). It is difficult to believe that Jesus did not share this point of view; it is difficult to see how he could have escaped this universal prejudice. It is a prejudice which is deeply rooted in the self-discipline of a community brought up to respect righteousness and not court-law. The judges may not be able to bring a robber to punishment, but social ostracism has, or at least had, some chance of being an effective deterrent. And just as the hole is necessary to the rat, and the receiver of stolen goods to the thief, so people who will take his food are a necessity for the extortioner or the corrupt politician. Unless these are deprived of their social potential there is, under normal eastern conditions, no hope of keeping them in check.[1]

The fact that Zacchaeus was interested in seeing Jesus tells (and of course told) its own story. A certain predisposition to be receptive was no doubt there. Jesus's reputation for not despising the people from whom the conventionally holy kept their distance was well known. Jesus accepted the 'sinners' not because he did not care for any taint they might communicate to him, but because, of course, he believed that his dealings with them converted and so purified them prior to any suspect contact that might arise. They were forgiven first and associated with afterwards. This could happen with lightning speed, as the Zacchaeus story shows. The humour of the situation is striking. Jesus tells the rich man that he intends to be his guest that very day. He reaches the house and is joyfully welcomed there (no doubt with multiple protestations of unworthiness to receive such a guest, etc.).[2] The bystanders, including those who would have been glad to have such entertainment themselves, are alarmed. Would Jesus actually accept the hospitality of a man whose goods were tainted with suspicion? At this point some of our predecessors have also stood at the door and hesitated. Sir Thomas More, for example, with lawyerlike caution, imputes to Zacchaeus an honesty and probity which remove the fears of the pious but destroy the value of Jesus's act. To More it seemed evident that Zacchaeus must have been an honest publican (his offer of restitution being so dramatic), who has not defrauded anyone, and who in giving to the poor removed at one blow the objection which had attached to his riches.

The truth of the matter, however, is otherwise. Zacchaeus could not know (nor could anyone else) how much of his private wealth was owed

[1] Pr xxix.24: 'He who divides with a thief. . . .'

[2] The centurion who dissuaded Jesus from actually visiting him (Mt viii.8, Lk vii.6–7) may not have been a theologian, but he certainly knew his Jews.

to extortion, menaces, and other examples of *violence, force* in the current language of the pious. He by no means *admitted* that he had 'blackmailed' or got property by any of those means (cf. *Mishnāh*, Ket. III. 9); he admitted that he was under suspicion of a presumptive character. It was proverbially difficult for anyone placed as he was to make a practical reality of repentance (which includes restitution).[1] But he did know that if his property (the unrighteous *mammon* we have discussed above) were purified as to its total corpus, there could be no possibility of communication of taint to his eminent visitor, and no scandal could arise from Jesus's dining with him. Zacchaeus knew perfectly well that Jesus was, in a respectable way, putting pressure upon *him* (Jesus was 'blackmailing' him!); and responded to that with the height of hospitality. If Jesus could find fault with his household on the ground of unrighteousness, then, as a good host, he would purify it for him. No one would think of admitting Jesus, who offered to be his guest, without making sure that that guest would suffer no real or supposed contamination thereby.

Zacchaeus says (xix.8): (1) 'I give half my property to the poor'; and (2) 'If I have extorted unlawfully anything from anybody, I restore it fourfold'. There can be no doubt that it was believed that failure to make appropriate gifts to the poor was sinful, and Jesus himself obviously disapproved of rich people, who would not have been rich had they made adequate provision for the poor around them. Zacchaeus will have known this. It would be an offence to his guest that the host was unpleasantly rich. It is moreover a fact that extortion, as a normal means of realisation of revenue, proceeded cumulatively as sub-contractors exacted their own commissions over and above their engagements to the head contractors,[2] so that the revenue system bore responsibility for the poverty of many of the poor. And a chief revenue collector would acquire money tainted by others' exactions besides his own. The gift, though it has not taken effect in fact is operative in law, for as soon as Zacchaeus formulated his intention the property became subject to it. Half the estate was no longer Zacchaeus's, and it would be left to future arrangements to determine which objects, what monies should

[1] Jeremias appositely cites (*op. cit.* 345–6) b. B.Ḳ. 94*b* = Sonc. 550. For shepherds, tax-collectors, and revenue farmers it is difficult to make repentance, *yet they must make restitution* to all those whom they know they have robbed (if the latter will accept from them). All the surplus (unclaimed) must be used to make public utilities, *e.g.* wells. Billerbeck, *op. cit.* II, 248 n. 2.

[2] *Cf.* John the Baptist's advice to publicans at Lk iii.13. The amount they are authorised to collect is a total reached in a bargain between them and their chief, but their authority can be used to extract much more, their emolument for their disagreeable (but profitable) task, irrespective of illegitimate gains made through manipulating exemptions from taxation.

be distributed and how. The meal already bought and possibly already cooking would naturally belong to the undedicated half and would cease instantly to be objectionable on the ground of the host's unbecoming prosperity. There could be no objection to ill-gotten gains being given to the poor: the rabbis encouraged[1] such behaviour just as Jesus did. And as for the idea that one could eat the 'purified' half there is a relevant precedent in the comical Jewish notion that one can eat from one end of a bundle, provided one has mentally intended to set aside tithe from the other end![2] But what of the presumption that he obtained his living by *violence*? In the same way he takes a step which no one could have forced him to take, and forms (and declares openly) his intention of restoring to any claimant, with a threefold amount as penalty superadded,[3] any sums which could be shown to have been extracted by him by means of false accusations, blackmail, menaces, and the sheer employment of imprisonment, or threats to sell up the defaulter and his family, and so forth—all normal weapons in the publican's armoury. 'I restore fourfold' seems to have been a standard undertaking, for it is found in contemporary 'bills' of divorce,[4] and may well be the origin of Josephus's statement that thieves must make *fourfold* restitution. This we should otherwise have attributed to Josephus's latent desire to report matters in a light which would obtain Roman approval, and the Romans (but not the Greeks) were indeed conversant with quadruple damages.[5]

[1] 'I, N., the son of N., scraped up such a sum by the fruits of the seventh year: and behold, I bestow it all upon the poor!' b. Sanh. 25*b* = Sonc. 147. J. Lightfoot *ad* Lk xix.8 (*Works*, 1823, XII, 183).

[2] b. Ḥul. 7*a* = Sonc. 28.

[3] The *biblical* command to restore fourfold can be found only where the thief of a sheep killed it or sold it (Ex xxi.37). By analogy from the reasoning (given in the Targum ps. Jonathan) one could extend this rule to cases where not only was capital robbed but the loss of its use was also inflicted. The *halakāh* is more mean than charitable: the biblical fourfold rule is restricted to the animals specified (b. B.M. III = Sonc. 208ff.; see also M. Jung, *Jewish Law of Theft* [Philadelphia 1929], 116–19, with references to b. B.Ḳ. 67*b*, 68*a*, 79*b*). Have we evidence of a pre-Mishnaic *halakāh* on the subject, which might well take the more logical and more equitable view? Perhaps the formula may have arisen as '*twice* the double'. The phrase *kif^{e}ley kif^{e}lāyiym* is evidenced from mediæval times, but may well have been a popular expression or had Aramaic counterparts. I owe this plausible explanation to Dr J. Rosenwasser. Such an approach is helped by the undoubted biblical metaphorical use of double compensation, *e.g.* at Zc.ix.12.

[4] And therefore not confined to restoration by a *thief*. See Pap. Murabba'ât 19, lines 10 and 23: *vmshlm lrb'yn* (presumably *l^{e}rab^{e}'iyn*). The husband is offering to restore to his divorced wife any property of hers destroyed or damaged (while under his care).

[5] Josephus says that 'the laws' bade the thief pay fourfold: *Ant.* XVI, 1, 3 (Loeb edn, Marcus and Wikgren, viii, 209). The passage is emphatic since he is condemning Herod for his selling thieves abroad. The point is discussed by Olitzki, 'Der juedische Sklave...', *Mag. für die Wissenschaft des Judentums* 6 (1889), 75 and B. Cohen

Once again, no actual amounts need be paid at once to anyone. The intention was enough to free his assets from the burden of the presumption, so that what was available for the guest was freed from the supposed taint. It could safely be left to claimants to come forward (if they were persuaded by Jesus's conduct or otherwise that Zacchaeus's expressions were made *bona fide*) and to establish on their own initiative how much the chief tax-gatherer had extorted from them in addition to what the law on the subject plainly allowed him to extract. And the implication is that Zacchaeus would faithfully (as a son of Abraham, and so presumably faithful) carry out his obligation to restore as under Lv v.21–4 (M.T.) = vi.2–5 and Ezk xxxiii.15: 'If the wicked restore the pledge, give again what he took by robbery, walk in the laws of life . . . he shall surely live—he shall not die'.

The story illustrates a number of points, factual and religious. It illustrates the great importance attached in Jewish ideas to expressions of intention. It is the intention which establishes the motive and the moral quality of the action; the practical consequences can be worked out afterwards. It was the woman's intention which determined the character of her act with the ointment. It was the publican's intention which purified his property and made him a fit host. It illustrates further Jesus's policy of relying upon the ability of the individual whose conscience has been touched to react appropriately, to know that he is forgiven, and to act in such a way as to demonstrate or to guarantee that fact. When Jesus says 'Today salvation (*i.e.* safety, wholeness, 'peace') has occurred in this house . . .' he acknowledges the purity of the household (including its property, of course), admits the validity of his host's two propositions and declarations, and certifies to the bystanders that reconciliation has been effected between the sinner and God. There can be no doubt that it was Jesus's initiative, and his general policy, which accomplished what many people must have viewed as a miracle no less astonishing than any other miracle which was popularly accredited to him.

Louis Ginzberg Jub. Vol., Eng. Sec. 117f. Greek law generally contemplated a penalty of double the amount of the damage and restoration. Plato only contemplated a fourfold penalty when incurable wounds were inflicted (*Leges* 878C). Philo therefore sticks to the double where Mosaic and Ptolemaic penalties appear to agree. E. R. Goodenough, *The Jurisprudence of the Jewish Courts in Egypt* (New Haven 1929), 146, 149. Philo, *De Spec. Leg.* IV, 2. In Roman law a praetorian action *in quadruplum* had taken the place of the scourging and bond-service with which the Twelve Tables had threatened the author of a manifest theft. Cicero, *pro Tull.* xxi, 50; iii, 7. A. H. J. Greenidge, *The Legal Procedure of Cicero's Time* (Oxford 1901), 208–10. Gaius III, 189, 190. On the word *quadruplator* ('informer', 'blackmailer', 'scoundrel') see the dictionaries and T. Mommsen, *Römisches Staatsrecht* II, 1, 3rd edn (Leipzig 1887), 599 n. 1.

CHAPTER THIRTEEN

The Parable of the Wicked Vinedressers

CONSIDERABLE STUDY has been devoted to this parable (Mt xxi.33–46; Mk xii.1–12; Lk xx.9–19) in recent years. Apart from the studies of Dodd and Jeremias we have a substantial monograph, several leading articles, and studies of topics in which the parable plays a part.[1] We have lacked, however, a reconstruction of the purely factual 'meaning' of the parable as it must have struck the original hearers. Until we have recovered this we can hardly dispose of the problems of the original form of the story, of the real point of the parable—was it, in particular, a 'story of our Salvation'?—and of the relationship, if any, of the quotation from Ps cxvii/cxviii to the parable. The great question, whether it is a *Heilsgeschichte*, has willynilly attracted to itself a greater question:

[1] S. M. Gozzo, *Disquisitio Critico-exegetica in parabolam N. Testamenti de Perfidis Vinitoribus* (*Studia Antoniana* II) (Rome 1949). This work deals with every aspect of the parable except the legal. C. H. Dodd, *The Parables of the Kingdom* (London, Fontana 1961), 93–8, 120; J. Jeremias, *Parables of Jesus*, Eng. trans. (1963), 70–7; E. Lohmeyer, 'Das Gleichnis von den bösen Weingärtnern', *Z. f. syst. Theol.* 18 (1941), 243–59; E. Bammel, 'Das Gleichnis von den bösen Winzern . . . und das jüdische Erbrecht', *RIDA* 3rd ser. 6 (1959), 11–17 (this interesting investigation of the question how the death of the son could permit title to vest in the tenants has recourse to the institution of 'gift in health', *mattᵉnat bāri*'; but unfortunately follows the wrong track in assuming that κληρονομία means strictly 'inheritance': the relevant parts of the Jewish law are not investigated); W. G. Kümmel, 'Das Gleichnis von den bösen Weingärtnern', *Aux Sources de la Tradition Chrétienne* (*Mélanges . . . Goguel*) (Neuchatel/Paris 1950), 120–31; B. M. F. van Iersel, *'Der Sohn' in den synoptischen Jesusworten. Supp. to Novum Testamentum* III (Leiden 1961), 124–45, ch. 3. M. Black, 'The Parables as allegory', *Bull. J. Ryl. Lib.* 42, 2 (1960), 273–87 is relevant to this parable, though nominally devoted to a new study of the Parable of the Sower. At p. 279–82 he criticises Dodd for running with the allegorical hare and hunting with the Jülicher hounds. In Black's view the tale was *originally* allegorical, and the servants must be the Prophets. W. O. E. Oesterley, *Gospel Parables in the Light of their Jewish Background* (London 1936), 117–22, is in some respects dépassé. F. Mussner, 'Die bösen Winzer nach Matthäus 21, 33–46', in P. Eckert, N. P. Levinson, M. Stöhr, *Antijudaismus im Neuen Testament* (Munich 1967), 129–34, finds anti-Pharisee tendencies in the parable.

is the parable genuine? If it is not a *Heilsgeschichte* one alleged ground for doubting its authenticity[1] would seem to disappear.

In what follows a reconstruction of the parable will be attempted, a reconstruction, that is to say, of the story contained in the parable. We shall speak of the parable as if it were a story of an actual event: this is in keeping with the atmosphere of most of the parables, and preserves the original illusion. If the reconstruction is authentic it will make a certain contribution to our knowledge of law in Palestine *temp. Christi*, which is in itself, apart from the theological aspect, not without interest.

There are admittedly certain doubts left. They are doubts which in many cases would have been present from the first, and only one of them is of any consequence. The exact contractual relationship between the owner and the tenants is in doubt. The original hearers of the parable will have had something of an advantage over us in that their imagination will have been slightly more specific. So also the precise time when the son arrived. But the most likely and the most probable is what Jesus will have expected his hearers to think of, and we shall do the same. We should have been warned by the text itself if anything unlikely ought to have been envisaged. Again, there is room for imagination at other stages. We are not obliged by the story as it stands to imagine one, and *only* one possible reason for the reaction of the tenants at a critical stage. But the most likely explanation, what would most normally account for it, is good enough, and we are no more in the dark than were the original hearers if we do not know whether the vines grew on trellises, and what was the price of dung or the cost of labour. It is the general principle that matters, and that is most informative.

It is quite another question with verse 5*b* of the Markan version. A good case has been made out for its having been inserted into the story at a stage midway between the original committal to writing and the publication of Mark,[2] and most theologians are content to dispense with

[1] The view that it is *not* a *Heilsgeschichte* is dominant, except amongst Catholic writers, *e.g.* Gozzo. R. Bultmann, *Geschichte der syn. Trad.* 191, 214, would have the passage (for the most part) a fiction. Kümmel (*ubi cit.* 131) says: 'Das Gleichnis kann daher nicht dazu verwandt werden, das Selbstbewußtsein Jesu oder seine eschatologische Erwartung zu erhellen. Wohl aber ist es ein wertvolles Zeugnis für die Geschichtsanschauung der Urkirche . . .'. Readers of this present book will obtain the impression that many of Jesus's parables carried, besides their purely objective lesson, indications, hints and implications which were of value independently. The early Church and the fathers seem to have been as keenly interested in the indirect teaching as in the direct and obvious; many of their ideas were conjectures, but while repelling these we must not deny Jesus's intention to combine many lessons in one parable. This approach is opposed to that of Jeremias, *op. cit.* esp. 76–7.

[2] F. Hauck, *Das Ev. des Markus* (*Synoptiker* I) (Leipzig 1931), 141. Dodd and Jeremias, both referred to by Kümmel, *ubi cit.* 124. Bammel, *ubi cit.* 12. Van Iersel, *ubi cit.* 132.

it. As we shall see, we are very much better off without 5*b*—indeed we shall positively require 5*b* to be omitted. Luke's version exactly fits law and common sense, and Matthew says nothing to the contrary. It has often been noticed that Luke had access to excellent material fitting relevantly and closely to the Jewish background against which alone the passages in question could be understood.

The method to be pursued here is to analyse the position of the characters in the story, stage by stage. We know much about them, partly from Jewish legal texts bearing upon the problems that must arise in the situation described, and partly from incidental observations in Talmudic material which, though they are often much later than our period in origin, show the traditional Jewish attitude to matters within the scope of the parable. Some may think that the most important element in the reconstruction is the recognition of the nature of a new vineyard: here we are in the world of incontrovertible fact—fact which can at one blow dispose of numerous common allegations made by readers of the parable ignorant of viticulture. Since the reconstruction is not simple, some patience is demanded of the present reader. The story cannot have been understood by the original audience 'in a flash'. It is an impressive parable, having many facets. It is not impossible that it has one 'point', but the 'point' is made to grip by several distinct edges. One cannot but be struck by the skill of the author. The parable is a mosaic, and must be viewed as a whole.

In contemporary scholarship the parable attracts attention by reason of its allegedly 'unreasonable' character. Critics note the 'utterly irrational' features.[1] The behaviour of the owner of the vineyard in sending again and again, and most notably in sending his son in such circumstances, seems crazy. The hope on the part of the vinedressers that by killing the son they would become owners of the vineyard is pointed to as not merely vain but even lunatic. If Jesus taught by irrational and inexplicable parables it would be a noteworthy feature of his mission. It will be seen from what follows that there is nothing unreasonable in the story: on the contrary the behaviour of all parties is reasonable and human. Ordinary Jewish people did manifest the sort of 'know-how' we find evidenced here: they were very conscious of rights and remedies, and they were quarrelsome and litigious. If a right were at stake they would litigate, even if the objects were trifling—or so many apocryphal

[1] Gozzo, *op. cit.* at p. 66f. depicts their difficulties in a masterly fashion with ample citation. Jülicher and Loisy in particular led the sceptics, if that is the appropriate label. Dodd, p. 93, seems more restrained. Jeremias, 58. I. K. Madsen, *Die Parabeln der Evangelien und die heutige Psychologie* (Kopenhagen/Leipzig 1936), 70ff. E. Hirsch, *Frühgeschichte des Evangeliums* I (1949), 129. Kümmel, *ubi cit.* 123, 124, 126. Van Iersel, *ubi cit.* 142.

tales in the Talmud would have us believe. The story of the rabbi who cheated his tenants of their *vine-prunings*(!) and whose wine went sour accordingly is eloquent witness: he was advised of his wrongdoing and admitted it, whereupon either (we are not told for certain) his wine turned back to its former quality, or the price of vinegar appreciated to equal that of wine![1] In any case Jesus would not be expecting too much expert knowledge from his audience.

Even less valuable objects than vine-prunings could be the object of a solicitude which was at one and the same time lawyerlike, pious, and mean. R. 'Abaye used to inspect his property daily. One day he met his tenant-farmer (*'āriyṣ*) carrying away a bundle of *twigs*. He asked, 'Where is this going?' The *'āriyṣ* replied, 'To my master's (*i.e.* your) house'. 'Abaye remarked, 'The rabbis have long since anticipated you!'[2] Everyone knew what a tenant might or might not 'get away with'.

THE OWNER AND THE TENANTS

One must realise that the choice of a *vineyard* is not dependent only upon a desirable allusion to Is v and other passages in the Old Testament.[3] There are special features about a vineyard which are not represented in, for example, an orchard, or a field. And this vineyard was no ordinary vineyard. The man, who we shall suppose was the owner of the land, planted the vines himself, made the boundary, provided the winepress, and built the 'tower' to serve as the vinedressers' home as well as a point from which to keep watch over the vines. He did everything he could to make the vineyard a profitable and self-sufficient affair: but it was a new vineyard, a speculation. Since he had to make the boundary and provide other structures it is clear that vines had not been planted there before, or at any rate within living memory. We have, therefore, not only new vines but also an untried soil. One must surely imagine that another vineyard might be on the same slope: but no one could be assured in those unscientific days that the wine would be drinkable, or at what price it would sell. One does not invest

[1] b. Ber. 5*b* = Sonc. 22. There is another translation at M. H. Harris, *Hebraic Literature* (New York 1946), 198.

[2] b Ḥul. 105*a* = Sonc. 583.

[3] The Old Testament references to vineyards are exhaustively considered by Gozzo. On Jesus's references to the 'true vine' and its biblical, particularly lectionary, implications, see A. Guilding, *The Fourth Gospel and Jewish Worship* (Oxford 1960), 50, 117, 120, 158. See also *Targum of Isaiah*, ed. J. F. Stenning (Oxford 1949), 16. A. Feldman, *Parables and Similes of the Rabbis, Agricultural and Pastoral*, 2nd edn (Cambridge 1927), 125–49, 132–4. G. Dalman, *Arbeit und Sitte in Palästina* IV (Gütersloh 1935), 323ff.

money in such a venture with hopes of an immediate return. If it were to be a success, which it might well not be, it would be an inheritance for succeeding generations.

Scholars have noticed already[1] that the vines would give no commercial profit for four whole harvests. A new vineyard is notoriously unprofitable. The investment, year by year, especially in the provision of supports, manure, and the like, many times exceeds the return—indeed there is no return worthy of mention until the fourth year is reached. In the fourth year it is unusual for the crop to equal the outlay for that year, but in the fifth year a profit can be expected.[2] These facts of nature, known to the Egyptians since long before the period of our parable and settled comfortably in our encyclopaedias for a generation or so, have a bearing on the Jewish law on the subject of the fruit of vines, and an obvious bearing upon our parable which, I am sorry to say, no theologian has noticed. In Jewish law the produce of the fourth year would be technically 'first-fruits' and would have to be redeemed, and could then be used subject to restrictions; that of the *fifth* year would be capable of being enjoyed as income by those entitled to the produce. The biblical law of *'orlāh,* which was strictly observed in the time of Jesus, provides that the fruit of trees and vines shall not be enjoyed until the fourth year, when in any case they must be redeemed if they are to be enjoyed.[3] Because travellers used to help themselves to grapes vineyards which were still *'orlāh* ought to be marked, and we are told they were marked with potsherds, but in the *fourth* year they were marked with clods of earth.[4]

Nothing is more natural than that the capitalist, the owner of the newly planted vineyard, should go away and leave it in the care of specialists in viticulture for at least four years. In the fifth year he would want to have some personal knowledge of how things were going. So the owner 'went away'. This is not, as has been imagined, for dramatic effect. It has been pointed out that ἀπεδήμησεν does not necessarily

[1] Hauck, *ubi cit.* 141. Lohmeyer, *op. cit.* 243f. W. Gundmann, *Das Ev. nach Markus,* 2nd edn (Berlin 1959), 239. Madsen, *op. cit.* 72.

[2] Expenditure in the first three years exceeds return fourfold. L. H. Bailey, *Standard Cyclopedia of Horticulture* III, 1380. This is cited by W. L. Westermann, 'Orchard and Vineyard Taxes in the Zenon Papyri', *J. Egypt. Arch.* 12 (1926), 38f. at 43.

[3] J. M. Powis Smith, *Origin and History of Hebrew Law* (Chicago 1931, repr. 1960), 79–80. Lv xix.23–5; *Mishnāh,* 'Orlah I, 8; III, 9. Danby, *Mishnah,* 795. Josephus, *Ant.* IV, vii, 19 (226–7) (Niese I, 208). Midr. R., Lev. XXV. 8 = Sonc. 323. b. B.Ḳ. 69*b* = Sonc. 401. In the fourth year the fruit is still holy, but it may be redeemed (the fifth of its value being added according to the School of Hillel: *Mishnāh,* Peah VII, 6, *cf.* B.M. IV, 8; Maas. Shen. V, 3). The fourth-year fruit (or the money with which it is redeemed) must be taken up to Jerusalem and there consumed under special restrictions which do not concern us here.

[4] *Mishnāh,* M. Shen. V, 1 (Danby, 80).

mean overseas,[1] but the word more naturally suggests a remote residence, or succession of residences, than sojourn in some other part of the land of Israel. Not much hangs upon the location of the owner: he was at all material times at an inconvenient distance for direct supervision over the vinedressers, and he needed to communicate with them through servants.

Of the three main classes of tenant our vinedressers were almost certainly *'āriyṣiym*, that is to say they were entitled to a fixed proportion of the produce, whatever that produce might amount to.[2] The status of the *'āriyṣ* is very little different from that of a servant. That they were *'āriyṣiym* is indicated by the circumstances, for their zeal would best be assured—at that critical stage in the vineyard's cultivation—by their financial interest in the entire net produce. Other classes of tenant would pay a fixed amount to the owner and keep the rest for themselves. The owner's share would be very small (see below) for the first four years, and he would be more concerned about the good management of his capital investment than about the income. Tenants who pay a fixed rent are notoriously careless about their landlord's property. It is fair to add, however, that nothing vital to the reconstruction of the parable hangs upon their identification in this case as *'āriyṣiym*.

The tenants took on a difficult and somewhat thankless task. We must know their situation in detail. They would, as we have seen, obtain no cash income from the vines themselves during the very period for which they would expect the owner to be absent. No doubt it would be cheap for them to live on the premises, but as we shall see, that was hardly a decisive advantage. They could have been a father and sons, or a group of brothers, in either case with their families. They were employed because they were knowledgeable about vines. Their duties were heavy. The phrase ἀμπελουργικὰ ἔργα we find in Egyptian papyri meant much in Egypt, but meant far more in the land of Israel. Everyone knew what these were and how vitally important they were. Jesus in celebrated passages draws upon his hearers' knowledge of the importance of pruning and the relationship between the stock, the living branch, and the fruit. Training vine-tendrils, pruning, setting up of poles or trellises, removing dead stems, and so on, would be time-

[1] Which Jeremias prefers (p. 75) with interesting citations of parallels (n. 97).

[2] Grotius understood them to be such: *Annot. in N. Test.*, ed. Windheim, I (Halle 1769), 414–15. Midr. R., Exod. XLIII. 9 = Sonc. 505 (vineyard), Eccl. V. 10 = Sonc. 148 (vineyard); B.M. 109*b* = Sonc. 625f. (vineyard); Sifre Deut. 312 (134*a*); Maimonides, *Mishneh Torāh* XIII (Civil Laws), I (Hiring), viii, 1–2 (trans. Rabinowitz, 27). G. Horowitz, *Spirit of the Jewish Law* (New York 1953), 325–6, 335. Feldman, *op. cit.* 39–44. J. H. Heinemann, 'Status of the labourer in Jewish Law . . .', *HUCA* 25 (1954), 263ff., 269–71.

consuming, and would have to be attended to meticulously. A Jewish vineyard was a special liability. The cultivation of the vines, of the young fruit trees (if any), and other crops in the spaces provided, was regulated by the very strict laws of 'mixed seeds'.[1] The public would interfere spontaneously if the rules were neglected. Prompt action was needed to destroy seeds blown by the wind under a vine-tendril. If the law were deliberately flouted the owner would stand to lose the vines themselves.[2] If a vine crept over the hedge or wall above growing crops belonging to a neighbour the latter would be forfeited, and the neighbour would have an action at law against the vinedressers for their negligence.[3] So a substantial boundary was needed, constantly kept in good repair, a barrier as much to roving vine-tendrils as to prying eyes.

No family of vinedressers would accept an employment unless they were covered against certain sources of loss: but since the owner himself stood to lose heavily if ritual laws were ignored he would not insure his tenants against their own negligence—on the contrary their efficient cultivation from the ritual as well as agricultural point of view would be a condition of their tenure, written firmly into their contract. During the period when the tenants' share of the produce would be nil the cost of cultivation would be at its highest, and would be most obvious. The owner naturally had to pay for this. Long before our period the Jewish people constantly reminded themselves that a vineyard, looked after by tenants *without* a share in the produce, *earns* for its keepers a proportion up to a fifth of its net annual value. We cannot take the figure too seriously, but the point was very plainly made in the ancient marriage-song captured for them, and for us, at Sg viii.11–12. If that was the principle for an old vineyard, how much more might the tenants of a *new* vineyard expect! We are not told how the owner proposed to pay them. He 'went abroad': we are not told of any plans to pay them, year by year, for their labour. On the contrary he sent, in due season, for the rent. The sending makes it clear that he did not leave a local agent to handle his accounts for him.

We should be much assisted if we could recover a specimen of a vinedressers' tenancy agreement. Documents from Israel have not yet included this particular type of covenant. Documents from Egypt are plentiful and illuminating, but they presuppose a different *lex loci*, and there are certain divergencies from Jewish drafting as evidenced from Israel and Persia in the rabbinical sources.[4] Amongst the documents

[1] Dt xxii.9. *Mishnāh*, Sheḳalim I, 1; Kil'aim IV, V, VI. Philo, *De Spec. Leg.* IV, 203–7. Josephus, *Ant.* IV, viii, 20 (229) (Niese I, 208). Dalman, *op. cit.* 326–9.

[2] *Mishnāh*, Kil. V, 8; VII; Sheḳ. I, 2.

[3] b. B.Ḳ. 100 = Sonc. 585.

[4] We have a mass of Egyptian leases and sub-leases of land of all kinds (see a list in J. Modrzejewski, 'Additional provisions in private legal acts', *J. Jur. Pap.* 7–8 [1953–4],

from Murabba'ât there is a Hebrew contract of farm dated in A.D. 133: but all it tells us is that the farmer undertook to cultivate for five years from the date of the document up to the end of the eve of the seventh year (was this a formality?) and to pay every year in good and pure grain a fixed quantity free from tithe.[1] This is not our sort of situation. Nevertheless common sense can be our guide. From the facts given in the parable itself, and from the usage evidenced in contemporary or near-contemporary documents we can draw up the heads of an agreement. They will have contained the following:

1. A statement that the owner admitted the tenants as tenants (the counterpart would state that the tenants were admitted by the owner);

2. an undertaking by the tenants to carry out the duties of vinedressers for a determined period or until such time as they are given notice to quit;[2]

3. an agreement that during the first four years the rent should be only one-tenth of the produce of the vineyard;

4. an undertaking by the tenants that thereafter they would pay in a particular month of every year one-half of the said produce;

5. an undertaking by the owner to reimburse the tenants for agreed

[1] Murab. 24B (Benoit, etc., *Discoveries* ii, p. 125) contains a term of the tenancy 'until the eve of the Seventh Year'. The rent is specified, the produce to be tithed after payment of tax. Murab. 24C (p. 129) is similar. 24E (p. 131) states the period of years as five.

[2] See last note.

211ff., at p. 214 n. 28) but in particular leases and proposals for leases of vineyards. In particular P. Oxyr. 729 (of A.D. 137) and P. B.M. 163 (A.D. 88) are to be recommended for study. In the latter the tenants pay to the lessor *two-thirds* of the produce. P. Ryl. 583 (vol. iv, 1952, 38ff.) is highly illuminating. P. Oxy. 1631 (A.D. 280), which deals with a palm-grove, is useful as it shows how tenants' obligations are stipulated; P. Ryl. 172 (A.D. 208) is also helpful: both are in A. S. Hunt and C. C. Edgar, *Select Papyri* in the Loeb Classical series (London/New York 1952)—see I, no. 18 and no. 43 (both of the third century). Many of the documents specify the rent in a fixed sum, whether in money, or partly in money and partly in kind. Reference may usefully be made to P. Giessen 56 (sixth century); P. Hamb. 23 (A.D. 569) and F. Preisigke, *Sammelbuch gr. Urk. aus Ägypten* I (1915), 4481–2, 4774. See in general S. Waszynski, *Die Bodenpacht* I (Leipzig/Berlin 1905) and J. Herrmann, *Studien zur Bodenpacht* . . . (Münch. Beitr. z. Pap. u. ant. Rechtsg. 41) (München 1958), 202–22. For a student of our parable the references to P. Soc. It. 393, 414 and P. Cair. Zen. 59300 given in the following article are invaluable: J. A. S. Evans and C. Bradford Welles, 'The Archives of Leon', *J. Jur. Pap.* 7–8 (1953–5), 29ff. at 53ff. ('Wine-production and trade in Ptolemaic Egypt'). Yet the material surviving in hypothetical rabbinical summaries of tenants' agreements seems to be more relevant. In particular one notes the schemes in b. B.M. 105*a* = Sonc. 600 ('I shall stand, plough, sow, cut, bind, trash, winnow, and set up a stack before you, and you will come and receive half; whilst I shall receive half in return for my labour and expenses.'), Maimonides *op. cit.* XIII, I, i, 3 (trans. Rabinowitz, p. 8); viii, 12 (trans. p. 30–1). See also Tos. B.M. IX, 13 (Zukermandel, 391–2). The document published at *J. Hell. St.* 35 (1915), 22–65 is not so useful as Deißmann and others have supposed.

capital expenditure, *e.g.* for propping the vines, during the first two years, after which owner and tenants would share the cost of capital expenditure equally between them;

6. an undertaking by the tenants to obey the *Torāh* in planting and maintaining the vineyard and its boundaries;

7. an agreement that in all matters not provided for the custom of the country should prevail;

8. an undertaking by the owner to defend and uphold the tenure of the tenants so long as they kept the covenant.

It is hardly conceivable that the covenant was not committed to writing. Such a step was not invariably taken, but one who was going abroad would certainly have a document drawn up, and both parties would have a copy.[1] How do we know that the owner's normal share was one-half? One-half was usual, but it might have been one-third. A simple arrangement, like that noticed at the end of this paragraph, is that owner and tenant should share costs and profits equally. In Malwā (India) the share-cropper (*bataī*) takes a half of the produce but supplies half the seeds; where he supplies only his labour he takes only one-third of the profits. In Babylonia the tenant normally took only one-fourth but by special agreement he could take more.[2] How do we know that during the first four years the proportion would be much lower? The vines then brought in no profit, the opportunities for producing commercial crops were limited (we return to this presently), and the normal proportion would leave the tenants with virtually nothing: it was not the function of the *'āriyṣ* to finance his landlord. Did the owner leave a cash payment for the four years with the tenants before he left? An *'āriyṣ* is never paid in cash, the essence of the relationship being that a share of the produce is his remuneration. While the owner is abroad his only security is his tenants' interest in working hard on the land in their own and their landlord's favour. If he had paid them in advance in cash they could easily have decamped and left him stranded. How do we know that the initial capital expenditure had to be met by the owner, though he was at a distance? It is a principle of Jewish custom that the landlord supplied what was needed for the fruitful cultivation of the land, the tenant supplying whatever was needed for the exploitation of the facilities provided.[3] Thus they would be expected to dig small irrigation channels, but not to finance the owner in respect of the young fruit trees and beams needed for the initial support of the vines. Fruit

[1] b. B.B. 167*b* = Sonc. 729ff.

[2] b. Giṭṭ. 74*b* = Sonc. 355.

[3] *Mishnāh*, B.M. IX, 1; b. B.M. 103*b* = Sonc. 591–2; A. Sammter, *Talm. Bab. Tractat Baba Mezia* (Berlin 1876) at 103*b*. j.B.M. IX, 1, 2 (Schwab X, 145). Maimonides, XIII, I, viii, 2 (trans. p. 27).

trees would not have had wide branches for at least two years. After that period he would have provided sufficiently for the vines' support. As for *recurrent* capital expenditure in respect of equipment, *e.g.* poles, it was a custom that the owner furnished them in proportion as he took the produce.[1]

We cannot approach the problem of how the owner was going to pay for the initial expenditure without thoroughly examining what is meant by the expression 'fruit of the vineyard'. We are told that the vineyard was properly laid out and bounded. The dimensions of vineyards had a certain inevitability about them. One knew how many rows one intended to plant, and the amount each row needed for weeding and manuring was fixed. Granted that the piece of land was of fixed dimensions the number of rows was therefore known from the outset. One naturally got as many rows in as possible. Assuming that the vines would eventually occupy much of the space, there were, nevertheless, spaces between the vine-stocks, and, if the vines grew to any height carried by trellis-work, cultivation in them was permitted by the ritual law. The distance allowed between crops and vine-material was established. The area open to cultivation with vegetables might diminish as time went on, but there would always be some cultivation of the vineyard with ground crops. 'Fruit of the vineyard' would not include fruit of the vines, *i.e.* wine, until the fourth year at the earliest, but it would have its maximum of vegetables in those early years.

Even in the first year it would have been possible for the owner to receive something by way of rent, but that something might be very small indeed. One-tenth (or, for argument's sake, even one-sixth) of receipts from sale of cucumbers would not amount to much. But in token of his rights as owner the latter would be prudent, or rather (as we shall see) virtually obliged, to send for it. We have already taken an interest in the priest in the Jewish parable who sent for two figs from his orchard (which, in the context, would be worth as much as 'two pins') and was furious with the tenants who refused them under the (false) impression that he would never come personally and chastise them.[2] One must keep an eye on one's tenants. The *'āriyṣiym* could pay in cash or kind, or both. In the early years the servants would expect to collect a token rent in cash. Later, when wine was sold to vintners they would expect to supervise the actual sales, and might even be expected to market the wine themselves, for vinedressers do not normally see to the marketing of their produce. But of course our parable never reaches that stage.

[1] *Mishnāh*, B.M. IX, 1; b. B.M. 103*a*–103*b* = Sonc. 590–2. Maimonides, *op. cit.* XIII, I, viii, 10 (trans. 30).

[2] See above, p. 216.

THE SERVANTS AND THE TENANTS

The first δοῦλος (servant) came to take the rent τῷ καιρῷ. With the definite article this could mean 'the time agreed upon', or 'the appropriate time'.[1] This would naturally be the time of the marketing of the principal crop. It is conceivable that for the first four years a different time was chosen, but this capitalist probably had other interests in the land of Israel and his servants may well have been expected to undertake numerous commissions connected with harvests. After reading that little was to be expected during the first four years the reader may wonder, was τῷ καιρῷ not the *fourth* harvest? This is not possible, since, as we shall see, the failure to apply for, and if possible collect, crops or a share of the produce of a piece of land was a definite step towards losing one's ownership in such property. An owner must meddle with every harvest, whether or not he takes a significant share of the crops. At any rate, at the expected time, the δοῦλος arrived. Note δοῦλος, not agent or steward. It is unfortunate that in New Testament parables this word is found both in its primary and, as we have seen twice in this book, in its secondary meaning of 'dependant'. In this case it must have its primary meaning, for otherwise the sending of the son loses some of its force. The owner preferred, having regard to the Jewish law of agency,[2] to employ persons bound to his service instead of a local agent, whom we ourselves would greatly prefer. Though δοῦλος is not unambiguous we are entitled to believe that he was a slave, and as such merely a messenger. The point of this will emerge presently.

What happened to him? Because of the climax that is evidently intended to be created in the story we must understand that he suffered in physical terms less than his successors. But he was at any rate 'beaten' and sent away 'empty'. *Beaten* because of his refusal to accept their account and go away quietly, and *empty* for two reasons: (i) whatever of value he had with him was taken from him, and (ii) he was furnished with nothing to take with him. This word 'empty' is most suggestive. The biblical parallels[3] leave us in no doubt but that the tenants stripped him of what he had, *i.e.* any valuable clothing or tokens of his position,

[1] Bauer–Arndt–Gingrich 3. Mt xiii.30, xxi.34, xi.12. Moulton–Milligan (p. 315) citing P. Lond. 974[5] (A.D. 305–6): τῶν κατὰ καιρὸν εἴδων ὀπωριμείων. Delling in *ThWzNT* III, 463 suggests *Termin—der Ablieferung des Ernteanteils*. Loisy's extraordinary obtuseness on this subject is handled by Gozzo, 75, 85–6, with restraint.

[2] M. Cohn, 'Die Stellvertretung im jüdischen Recht', *ZVR* 36 (1920), 124–213, 354–60, esp. p. 144. An advantage of sending a slave was that the master could repudiate the former's acts at will: Maimonides, *op. cit.* XII (Acquisition), I (Sales), xxx, 2 (trans. p. 107). The main difficulty with agents was that they were liable to compensate for only very limited categories of default. For the position in general see I. Herzog, *Main Institutions* ii, 142f.

[3] *reḳ*: Ne v.13; Dt xv.13; 1 S vi.3.

and the price of his lodging and travel. One speaks of sending away 'empty' a person who on leaving has no resources.[1] Why did the tenants do this? Obviously because so far from admitting that they owed the owner anything they actually claimed that he was indebted to them—which, as we have seen, was far from impossible, on the contrary most likely. The picture is best shown from an entirely imaginary balance sheet, such as the servant would have been expected to take back with him.

Income		*Expenditure*	
Sale of cucumbers:	12 den.	Purchase of props:	10 den.
Sale of pumpkins:	10 den.	Wages of gardeners:	15 den.
Miscellaneous:	2 den.	Manure:	6 den.
	24 den.		31 den.

If this is a reasonable illustration the tenants have certainly no rent to pay. The owner may well have been indebted *bona fide* to his tenants. The servant's clothing and ἐφόδια could quite properly be seized by the tenants in such circumstances.[2] The servant was beaten to prevent him seizing pledges from the tenants whom he suspected of cheating; and the tenants seized his clothing as the traditional pledge and evidence of indebtedness. The semitic races recognize at once an upper garment or a shoe as evidence of the owner's obligation to the possessor of them, and giving up a garment or casting off a shoe is the ancient ritual sign of releasing a right.[3] Why did the tenants allow the slave to go free? They wanted him to go back, eventually, to his master, to explain the situation, and show that the tenants were not to be trifled with.

In view of the creditor's lien on his debtor's *land* at Jewish law the tenants, so long as they claimed to be unpaid for their labour, had a right to exclude the owner and his servants from possession and from all the fruits until the debt was paid and the lien automatically released.

[1] Perhaps the best example is Lk i.53, where (in the image) the buckets that came up full are visualised descending empty.

[2] The law is beyond the scope of this article, but see L. Auerbach, *Das jüdische Obligationenrecht* (Berlin 1870) I, 168–9. 'A man's possessions are his surety' is a maxim. Boaz Cohen, 'Self-help . . .' (*cit. inf.* p. 299 n. 1), 126–7, citing *inter alia* B.Ḳ. 14*b* = Sonc. 62; 15*b* = Sonc. 67; 36*a* = Sonc. 200. E. Zingg, 'Das Schuld- und Vollstreckungsrecht . . . nach Moses', *Judaica* 16 (1960), 72–102, 156–71, 207–15. The rule is not later rabbinical law: Maimonides, *op. cit.* XI (Torts), III (Robbery), iii, 16 (trans. p. 101); nor Greco-Egyptian law: P. Oxy. III, 653 (b).

[3] The institution of *ḥalitsāh*, where the *yāvam's* shoe is loosened, will come at once to mind. See H. M. Weil, 'Gage et cautionnement dans la Bible', *Archives d'histoire du droit oriental* 2 (1938), 171ff., at p. 202, 223.

The protection of the lien is alone a sufficient explanation for the tenants' bellicosity.[1]

The owner might well doubt whether such an account would be honest, but it would certainly be plausible. If he wanted to submit the tenants to an oath[2] he would have to take the appropriate steps, and this, as we see, he hesitates to do. Next year the tenants might have done better with their crops; the capital expenditure might be less; his own liabilities smaller. Some rent there would surely be. He would have to claim it, for if he failed he would make an admission which would be damaging if eventually he had to take action against the tenants in court. So the second slave was sent.

We suppose that the second mission took place at the end of the second harvest, at the end, that is to say, of the second year from the commencement of the tenancy. Scholars have been satisfied that there were three separate sendings, each at the end of the agricultural year or similarly appropriate time. There would be no reason for sending a second messenger earlier. Moreover πάλιν ('again' at Mk xii.4) strongly suggests[3] a repetition in circumstances closely resembling the first, *i.e.* on the next appropriate occasion (καιρῷ), in other words, the next year.

Mark tells us that the second slave was 'beaten about the head' and 'insulted', 'shamefully ill-treated'.[4] Luke merely says that he was beaten, insulted and sent away 'empty'. What was the tenants' situation? Perhaps they could actually have afforded to hand over a small payment. Since it would in any case be small they doubtless felt that what had served to exonerate them the first time would serve the same turn again. The slave refused to accept their version of things. No doubt he had been ordered to make a show of getting some local help: but how could he enforce his master's claim? The accounts were in doubt, the *'āriyṣiym* probably had nothing of their own from which valuable pledges could be taken, and if he tried he would be treated as we are told he was. The beating must be put into perspective. The first slave would not necessarily have objected to it. Curious at first sight, the reaction makes good sense. The Jewish way of resisting unfair or

[1] The creditor's lien (*'aḥ^arāyūt, shī^{'e}būd*) was supposed to be of Pentateuchal origin, but its origin is obviously customary. The later rabbinical developments do not interest us. In fact a creditor could not have a lien over property which (like the fruit of a vineyard up to its fourth year) was in fact *extra commercium*: but this would not be relevant, since they held the land, with its capacity to grow vegetables—and its future value as a vineyard. Horowitz, *op. cit.*, ch. XXVI.

[2] *Mishnāh*, Shevū'ot VII. 8; b. Shev. 45*a* = Sonc. 276, 48*b* = Sonc. 300f.

[3] Bauer–Arndt–Gingrich 2.

[4] For difficulties with the word see Hauck, *ubi cit.* 141; Kümmel, *ubi cit.* p. 122 n. 11; Gozzo, *op. cit.* 41–2. M. Black at *Bull. J. Ryl. Lib.* 42, p. 281 suggests the word ἐκεφαλίωσαν means that they pulled out his hair and beard.

exaggerated claims was 'to break the teeth' of the other party.[1] Without showing some bruises the first slave could not convince his master that he had not drunk the rent at the nearest town. The fight was not necessarily a sign of ill-will, but of sincerity! Those who wanted to establish a claim, and those who felt that they were entitled to resist resorted, as a matter of course, to force. So there would be nothing remarkable in the first slave's returning without his equipment and with dramatic bruises. The second slave's position was somewhat different. His concussion and other injuries would be a very public demonstration of the tenants' repudiation of the owner's claims. This put an idea into the tenants' heads, as we shall see.

The owner's reaction can be imagined. It was still possible that the tenants did not really owe him anything. While that was doubtful there was no point in evicting them. They were probably men of straw. Even their tools may have been his. And if it turned out that they were right he would have difficulty in getting new vinedressers. As it was prudent to do, he left the matter until the third year and sent again.[2] Since he was expecting trouble he naturally sent several slaves. This is not inconsistent with Mark's ἄλλον, for the slave-collector would be accompanied by attendants, nor with Luke's ἕτερον for the same reason, nor with Matthew's ἄλλους. Naturally the tenants foresaw this; they would have their gardener or gardeners and some local ruffians ready before they admitted the third slave, if they admitted him at all. This time there was a riot. Wounds, not merely bruises, were received.

Now the tenants knew that they might plausibly claim that for three successive harvests they had refused to admit the owner's right to rent, his slaves having been sent away empty-handed. Could they not claim that, after all, they were owners, and not merely tenants? They might even tear up their document, and defy the owner to evict them. How

[1] Jb xxix.17; Ps iii.7. There is a valuable discussion at b. B.Ḳ. 27*b* = Sonc. 144ff. referred to by B. Cohen, 'Self-help in Jewish and Roman law', *RIDA*, 3rd ser., 2 (1955), 107ff., 120, and n. 64, 121 n. 67. (This article appears in *JRL* II, 624ff.) See also b. B.B. 99*b* = Sonc. 416; 126*a* = Sonc. 523–4.

[2] Whether there *were* three sendings has been raised by the *Gospel According to Thomas* (ed. and trans. Guillaumont and others, Leiden/London 1959), 93.1–16 (p. 59). See also R. M. Grant and D. N. Freedman, *Secret Sayings of Jesus* (London, Fontana 1960), 162. Two servants are sent and then the son. It is not the dominant opinion that 'Thomas' had access to pre-synoptic material. See W. H. C. Frend, *JThS* 18 (1967), 13ff. But even if he had would we be justified in assuming from his version that there was no allegorical element? See Jeremias, p. 77. Without the legal material arguments have gone in circles. As Kümmel, *ubi cit.* 122 seems to have realised, a *threefold repetition* is needed in Jewish law and custom to make a thing secure. This may actually explain the Matthew and Luke versions, or equally well account for the 'reduction' (?) to a total of three sendings in 'Thomas'. On the other hand the later 'gospel' may reflect an awareness of the legal point discussed in p. 302 n. 1 below.

this idea came into their heads needs investigation. Throughout we must bear in mind that they had in succession *two* ideas: an old one, which we shall notice immediately, and a new one, a brilliant one, which occurred to them only at the last minute. The modern eye sees little difference between a cheat and a thief, but, as we shall see, there is a substantial difference from the point of view of the Jewish law, upon which these rascals proposed to rely.

THE TENANTS AND THE FOURTH YEAR

They were in undisputed possession of the vineyard, and possession raises a presumption of ownership, a presumption to be rebutted only by proof that the possessors are in possession by permission, or by some title less than full ownership. *'Āriyṣiym* were known to try to convert their tenure into ownership dishonestly.[1] Owners were always afraid of this. The reason was the Jewish law of adverse possession, which seems very unfair until we realise the people's normal, and ready, recourse to violence when a right was hindered or denied. If a man goes overseas (*hālach li-m^ediynat ha-yām*) even the path leading to his field may be annexed by an adjoining owner and, not knowing which or how to recover it, he may (says the *Mishnāh*) have his choice between buying another right of way or 'flying through the air' to get to his field![2] The basic principle is that when a thing happens three times it is presumed to be normal;[3] the basic legal rule is that a claimant, who claims by a reasonable (even if false) title, is owner in law if he has enjoyed the produce for three successive harvests.[4] Thus one who had had three harvests could *prima facie* claim the full ownership of the usufruct, and

[1] b. B.B. 35*b* = Sonc. 159; 40*b* = Sonc. 174: the man in possession said, 'If you will sell it to me, well and good; but if not I shall suppress the mortgage-deed and say that I purchased it outright'. b. B.M. 110*a* = Sonc. 628–9. Note the cases reviewed in B.B. 33*b* = Sonc. 155–6, and the examples given by Maimonides, *op. cit.*, XIII (Civil Laws), IV (Pleading), xvi, 5 (trans. p. 256) and *ibid.* xiii, 3 (trans. p. 242), which applies to our own case.

[2] *Mishnāh*, Ket. XIII. 7 (Danby, 263; Blackman, III, 191).

[3] R. Simeon b. Gamaliel held that a presumption (*ḥazāḳāh*) is established only when a thing occurs three times. 'Rabbi' took a different view, that twice was enough. b. B.M. 106*b* = Sonc. 608. The rule is stated in San. 81*b* = Sonc. 540. *Cf. Mishnāh*, 'Oholot XVI, 3. Lk xiii.7 (if it could be presumed barren it would not be unlawful to cut it down: *cf.* b. B.Ḳ. 91*b*–92*b* = Sonc. 530–1; Billerbeck, *Kommentar*, II, 197–8). See also b. Yoma 86*b* (propensity to offend).

[4] *Mishnāh*, B.B. III. 1; b. B.B. 28*a* = Sonc. 138ff.; 35*b* = Sonc. 159. R. Zebid said, 'If he (the owner) plead, "I have installed him . . .", his plea is accepted *if made within three years*, but not later'. B.B. 38*a* = Sonc. 167. Maimonides, *op. cit.*, XIII, IV, ix, 6; x, 2, 4; xi, 1, 18 (trans. Rabinowitz, p. 228, 233, 234, 236, 240–1); XIV (Judges), II (Evidence), xxi, 7 (trans. Hershman, 1949, p. 132). Horowitz, *op. cit.* 346–8. I. Lewin, 'Die Chasaka des talmud. Rechts', *ZVR* 29 (1913), 151–298, esp. 162–8.

it is a small step from this to claiming that he was full owner. That the fruit of the new vines would be 'forbidden' would be nothing to the point.[1] One might say that an *'āriyṣ* has no chance of becoming owner by this method, since the very fact that he was an *'āriyṣ* stood in his way and precluded the claim:[2] no doubt, but that presupposes that he does in fact appear as an *'āriyṣ*. *'Āriyṣūt* may well develop into something else. One has to consider the hazards of litigation, when one party is abroad. From so ancient a period as Dt xx.6 it was normal to fear that if a planter of a vineyard did not 'eat of it' a stranger would oust him.[3] We have observed this in connection with disqualifications from front-line participation in the holy war.[4] Our tenants have paid nothing for three years. They have established that whatever rights were claimed by the owner were now extinguished. They might argue that originally the land had been sold to them with a reservation of a rent-charge. The owner, they might argue, claimed a proportion of the produce, but had in fact never possessed himself of any of it.

At this point a strange provision of law helped the owner. If he had been resident in the land of Israel, or within a reasonable distance from it, the expiry of three harvests without his participation, we may be sure, would have seen his right extinguished, once we assume that our tenants claimed that they were really purchasers. But since he resided abroad the law of adverse possession required that he should have had reasonable opportunity of protest, since the very theory of adverse possession is that the possessor possesses against the right of the opposite party to the latter's knowledge, and while he is competent to exercise his rights, or seek a remedy at law. The Roman law, as an imperial rescript of A.D. 199 shows, recognised that the period necessary for acquiring against the true owner (*longi temporis praescriptio*) should be longer if the latter resided 'abroad' than when he lived in the same region as the adverse possessor.[5] Conformably a Jewish owner abroad

[1] Lewin, *ubi cit.* 165–6, citing B.B. 36*a*. But Maimonides took a different view: XIII, IV, xii, 12 (trans. p. 239). Our tenants were not hoping merely to acquire the vinestocks or the fruit trees, but the land in which they were planted!

[2] *Mishnāh*, B.B. III. 3; b. B.B. 46*b* = Sonc. 195; 47*a* = Sonc. 198. Maimonides, *op. cit.* XIII, IV, xiii, 1. Bammel must take credit for first investigating *ḥazāḳāh* in connection with this parable (*ubi cit.* 15), though the point escaped him. Lewin, *ubi cit.* 164 (Es kann also keinem Zweifel unterliegen, dass auch eine durch Verpachtung getätigte und durch drei Jahre fortgesetzte Nutzung zur rechten *Chasaka* führt); also 223. He considers the *'āriyṣ* also at p. 203ff., 222ff., *q.v.*

[3] *Mishnāh*, Soṭāh VIII, 2, 4. Maimonides, *op. cit.* XIV, V (Kings and Wars), vii (trans. Hershman, p. 224ff.).

[4] Above, p. 130.

[5] πρὸς μὲν τοὺς ἐν ἀλλοτρίᾳ πόλει διατρείβοντας ἐτῶν εἴκοσι ἀριθμῷ βεβαιοῦται, τοὺς δὲ ἐπὶ τῆς αὐτῆς ἐτῶν δέκα. *Agyptische Urkunden aus den Museen zu Berlin: Grieschische Urkunden* (BGU) I, n. 267; P. Strassburg 22: both reproduced with commentary at S. Riccobono, ed., *Fontes iuris romani ante-Iustiniani*, I (*Leges*) (1941), 437–42; J. Partsch, *Die longi temporis praescriptio* (Leipzig 1906), 1, 109ff. These references are

could almost certainly claim a privilege of notice, and the three harvests were counted from the time when notice first reached him, or could have reached him, that the possessors denied his right, title and interest.[1] Thus time began to run against our owner from the moment the first slave was sent away, empty'. The fourth year was therefore the vital year.

If there was a likelihood that the *fourth* harvest would be denied him, at the moment when the vineyard was beginning to produce a crop having some value,[2] action must be taken during the third year from receipt of the 'notice'. Formal 'protest' (*m*ᵉ*ḥā'āh*) must be made before witnesses, warning the tenants that legal action would commence against them.[3] Slaves, however, could not make this protest, nor could slaves adjure witnesses[4]—a serious handicap in so involved a matter.

[1] The *Mishnāh*, B.B. III, 2, leaves us in some hesitation because, though the 'three countries' rule (b. B.B. 38*a* = Sonc. 167; Ket. 17*b* = Sonc. 96–7, 18*a* = Sonc. 99) is plainly intended to secure that the owner has notice of the adverse possession, R. Judah, a fourth-generation Tanna (*c.* A.D. 140–65) held that three years (*i.e.* three harvests) would operate even if the owner were in Spain and learnt of the possession a year late. R. Judah's rule presupposes good communications, peaceful conditions, and a sound system of agency. The rabbis in any case were anxious to support titles and tended to construe the three-year rule very strictly. However, the basic and essential principle that possession is adverse for the purpose of acquisition of title only when the owner is *aware* and *competent to sue at law*, is borne out conveniently by Maimonides, *op. cit.* XIII, IV, xi, 2 (trans. Rabinowitz, p. 231–2): 'If it was a time of war or of unsafe roads between the place where (the possessor) was and the place where (the alleged owner) was, the property is taken away from the possessor and restored to the owner, even if the possessor took its profits for ten years, because the owner may say, "I did not know that he was using my land".' *Ḥazāḳāh* is not *ḥazāḳāh* unless the owner could protest: R. Ḥisda at b. B.B. 47*a* = Sonc. 198. The point is so crucial that comparison with Hindu law is relevant. There a three-year period was anciently in use (Bṛhaspati cited in the *Vyavahāra-nirṇaya* and *Sarasvatī-vilāsa*: P. V. Kane, *History of Dharmaśāstra* III, Poona, 1946, 326 n. 467), and the owner's knowledge of the possession is required with every emphasis (Bhāruci on Manu VIII. 147, 148; Medhātithi on Manu VIII. 148 [trans. G. Jha, IV, 1, 176ff.]; Kane, *op. cit.* 320; L. Rocher at *Rec. de la Soc. Jean Bodin*, XVIII *La Preuve*, 1964, p. 355; A. Thakur, *Hindu Law of Evidence*, Calcutta 1933, 240–1).

The question may arise, why our owner did not protest while abroad. Rabbinical law by the time of the Talmud recognised a foreign protest as valid (Maimonides, XIII, IV, xi, 2, 5 [trans. p. 233–5]), but this seems to be in keeping with their attitude to *ḥazāḳāh*: that the protest must be brought to the notice of the possessor is not logically requisite, but it is practically essential. We note that a protest (n. 3 below) must announce the commencement of legal proceedings: a foreign protest then presumes excellent communications and a good state of public order. Though it is not essential to the argument of this paper I assume that *temp. Chr.* protests must be declared in the country of the possessor.

[2] See p. 290 above.

[3] Lewin, *ubi cit.* 168–72. b. B.B. 38*a* = Sonc. 169: 'X occupies my land wrongfully and *tomorrow* I am going to sue him'; 39*b* = Sonc. 172. Property of orphans was a partial exception: b. B.B. 32*a* = Sonc. 151–2. Maimonides XIII, IV, xi, 7 (trans. p. 235).

[4] *Mishnāh*, Shev. IV, 12.

owed to Professor Dieter Nörr. For the law under Justinian see his *Cod.* 7. 33, 12; and *Novella* 119. 8.

By that period it had not yet become possible to plead one's cause *through* an agent—one must actually transfer one's right to the 'representative'.[1] Therefore the son had to be sent. He is represented in the parable as if he really was the only son of the owner.[2]

The suggestion that the son came unattended is ridiculous. Naturally he came with a group of attendants, almost certainly including the very same slaves that had come before. They would not willingly have missed the opportunity. The son's errand, as the owner says, was to induce in the tenants some 'respect'. He would be able to recall them to their legal position in a way not open, for reasons we have shown, to the slaves. He could adjust the accounts, and knew, doubtless, what to do if the tenants were truculent.

The son was a menace to the tenants' schemes of claiming to have acquired the whole of the owner's interest by adverse possession. That scheme, for final success, required that all four harvests should have been taken in their entirety by the tenants, and that they should deny having commenced as *'āriyṣiym*. If they were relying upon their being unpaid workmen they must be able to show that their present possession was the result of a failure by the owner to redeem his land from them. All this required that proof of the original nature of the agreement should never be made successfully, and that their accounts should never be inspected. But here was a much better opportunity. The chance that the owner would come in person and produce his document was always hanging over their heads: but the presence of the son opened a better way. Something must be done about him or he would make the protest! Why not kill him? 'Come on, let us kill him, and then the inheritance will be ours!' This was a gamble, but the chances seemed to be in their favour. The killing of the son would be a splendid piece of evidence that the tenants utterly repudiated the owner's claims; but it would be more than that: it would enable them to acquire the vineyard, if the worst came to the worst, by a form of wrongdoing resembling robbery! Neither theft nor robbery of land is strictly speaking possible at Jewish law, but a kind of quasi-robbery is contemplated.

At this point it is necessary to notice the Hebrew root *yā'ash*, which

[1] b. B.Ḳ. 70*a* = Sonc. 402. Maimonides XII (Acquisition), IV (Agents and Partners), iii, 1–2 (trans., 215–16). It was also difficult to authorise an agent when the defendant had already denied liability. In our case the father need not have *given* the vineyard to his son (with the result that he would have inherited it from the son if the latter died childless); he probably transferred to him a small fraction (*e.g.* one-tenth), which would enable the son to commence proceedings for the whole, one-tenth in his own person, and nine-tenths as agent for his father. See p. 306.

[2] This is clear from the LXX citations adduced by Gozzo, *op. cit.* 111. For example Gn xxii.2, 12, 16; Jr vi.26; Am viii.10; Zc xii.10. And one must compare the important passage at Jg xi.34 (*cf.* Gn xxii.2, 12, 16).

means to give up hope of recovering something which one has lost or of which one has been deprived. This became in later centuries a fully-fledged legal concept, *ye'ush*. In the developed law one could not make *ye'ush* of, *i.e.* mentally abandon, *land*, but only moveables.[1] However, there is a strong suspicion, amounting to a probability, that this developed well after our period, in which physical enjoyment of land figured so prominently as evidence of title. We are left with the strong likelihood that an owner whose mind was elsewhere could be forced into a position in which he could be *claimed* to have abandoned his landed estate. This was highly undesirable, and it is easy to see why the rabbis later ruled against such an interpretation of mere inaction and so virtually excluded land from the operation of *ye'ush*.

One of the most curious features of the Jewish law was its tenderness to robbers. The position of a successful thief was enviable. We shall assume, as from the state of the Jewish law we have every right to do, that there was no way of bringing him before a judge and having him executed, flagellated or imprisoned. His advantage lay in the fact that if he *was* compelled to restore or make compensation the civil claim against him related to the value of the object when misappropriated.[2]

In a case of simple theft, if the owner gives up hope of recovery,[3] that is makes *ye'ush* (abandons it), the thief may wait until the value is enhanced, or do work on the thing, sell it at a profit, and still be liable eventually to pay (at most) compensation at the rate of the original value.

[1] Herzog, *Main Institutions* I (1965), 231. M. Jung, *Jewish Law of Theft*, p. 59 n. 134 cites Tos. B.B. 44*a* as indicating a contrary opinion.

[2] b. B.Ḳ. 65*b* = Sonc. 379. Maimonides, *op. cit.* XI (Torts), II (Theft), i, 12 (trans. Klein, p. 62): 'If the stolen object itself is in the possession of the thief and is unaltered, it must be returned to its owner whether he has abandoned hope or not, except that after hope has been abandoned, any improvement belongs to the thief. . . . But if the object stolen has been altered while in the hands of the thief, he acquires title to both the object and the improvement even before the owner abandons hope, and need only replace its value in money'. The first part would seem to throw doubt on the proposition that a thief acquires title as soon as the owner makes *ye'ush* (abandonment). But since the thief can give a good title to a third party (B.M. 22*a* = Sonc. 135) it seems idle to insist that he is bound to restore it. The confusion perhaps arises out of the theoretical proposition that a man who had made *ye'ush* can retract *ye'ush* (an impossibility) and sue for specific restitution of the object stolen. On the subject see M. Jung, *op. cit.* 59–60, where the third party's title to property disposed of by the thief after *ye'ush* is demonstrated. Horowitz, *op. cit.* 362, 612. The contrast of Tannaïtic law with that of the biblical periods is brought out if one compares Jung's work with F. Horst, 'Der Diebstahl im alten Testament', *Kahle-Festschrift* (*Studien z. Geschichte u. Kultur des nahen u. fernen Ostens*), ed. W. Heffening and W. Kirfel (Leiden 1935), 19–28.

[3] b. B.M. 21*a*–*b* = Sonc. 131–2; 22*a* = 135–6; B.K. 66*a*; 66*b*; 67*a*; 68*a*; 69*a*; 70*a*, 111*a*; 114*a*; 116*b*; Ḳid. 52*a*. Horowitz, 362–3, 612.

In the case of a new vineyard its value at the close of the fourth year would be many times greater than when the 'robbery' would have been presumed to have taken place, namely either in the first or the second year. Thus, even if the tenants were sued for appropriating the vineyard the owner would not recover the vineyard once he had given up hope of its recovery, and the vinedressers would have to fear at most a liability to make restitution at the value of the new, untried vineyard.[1] Thus the 'inheritance'[2] would be theirs, and the trick might seem well worth while. Actually they felt fairly confident that, time having operated against him so far, the owner would make *ye'ush*, and they would neither be called upon to restore the vineyard nor to pay compensation for loss of the crops meanwhile. The most the owner could obtain would be his land once again, and they thought this so remote a possibility that the risk was worth taking.

But what would make the owner give up hope of recovery? After three attempts and two fights, the last a riot, he had failed to obtain a small recognition of his rights. Thereafter he had sent his only son who was actually killed in the course of attempting to collect rent. It was, after all, for the sake of his son that the vineyard had been planted in the first place.[3] In a situation where accounts were in dispute, and he could have settled any of their legitimate grievances, he had preferred to handle the matter at arm's length. He is abroad, obviously has many interests, and can be expected to abandon the vineyard. If he feels so strongly about it, and takes action, the best he can then hope for is monetary compensation. The local judges in any case will see the tenants' point of view; perhaps, if necessary, their palms can be greased.

[1] Ex xxii.3, *Mishnāh*, B.Ḳ. VII, 1; *ibid.* IX, 1; b. B.Ḳ. 65*b* = Sonc. 379; B.M. 43*a* = Sonc. 256–8; Maimonides, XI, II, i, 14 (trans. p. 62). M. W. Rapaport, 'Der Talmud und sein Recht. 5. Teil. Obligationen aus einer unerlaubten Handlung', *ZVR* 16 (1902), 40ff., 83.

[2] Moulton–Milligan, *Vocabulary* (1957), *s.v.* κληρονομία P. Oxy. I, 76 (A.D. 179); P. Tebt. II, 319 (A.D. 248)—here Preisigke seems to give only the limited meaning (*Erbschaft*). *ThWzNT* III, 766ff., 767 (= *Besitz*); 776 (in LXX it constantly means 'property', 'possession'; *cf.* Sir ix.6, xxii.23, xxxiii.24); 781 (Ac vii.5 = 'possession'; cf. Ac xiii.33*d*; Heb xi.8). The word probably renders *naḥalāh* or *y^{e}ret.*). (Delitzsch has *y^{e}rūshāh.*) Grotius, *op. cit.* 65, 415. In papyri vineyards are often called simply κτῆμα. But it was the son's 'inheritance'. 'Inheritance', which is of course the symbol of entry into the world to come, has interesting overtones: *if* the Hebrew *y^{e}rūshāh* represents the original expression in our parable the suggestion is that it is a windfall, something one gets without working for it (the position of a son is a privilege): *Mishnāh*, 'Āvot II, 12 (Danby, 449; Blackman IV, 503): *she-'eynāh* (*torāh*) *y^{e}rūshāh lāch.* See p. 306 n. 1 below.

[3] b. San. 108*a* = Sonc. 742. A Tanna taught on the authority of R. Joshua b. Karḥa: '. . . a king prepared a banquet for his son . . . the son died . . . he arose and broke up the feast saying, "Have I prepared all this for any but my son? Now that he is dead what need have I of the banquet?" '

And there is another reason why he can be supposed already to have loosened his hold on the vineyard. The arrival of the son could be construed as evidence that he was making his last effort to retain his hold on his property: but it could equally be construed as a sign that he had transferred some, if not all, his interest to someone younger and fitter than himself. Wise and cautious tenants would not have contemplated this conclusion. But it was to this conclusion that they jumped, as we see from the phrase found in all three gospels, οὗτός ἐστιν ὁ κληρονόμος (Mk xii.7 par.) The word κληρονόμος is usually translated 'heir', and cognate expressions abound in the New Testament, usually translated 'inheritance'. Unfortunately it has escaped notice that although this is a possible translation, the normal implications of κληρονόμος are 'acquirer', 'gainer', whether of the estate of another person or indeed of property to which one had previously no shadow of a claim. The word is appropriate to one who takes under a testament or disposition.[1] And indeed this is what those foolish vinedressers had in mind. In order to prosecute difficult litigation it was usual for Jewish litigants to assign part of their rights to the agent who conducted the litigation for them; otherwise the agent would have no *locus standi*. In this case the tenants thought it quite possible that the son had come equipped not only with authority and instructions, but also with a title to the estate—they believed he might well be owner, and that the true owner had already assigned his rights. They did not stop to find out. Mark and Luke clearly show that the tenants did not bother to ascertain that the newcomer was merely the son—what struck them was that he might be the assignee of the estate. Matthew does indeed say that the tenants saw the son and then thought, etc., but he too does not say that they recognised the son for what he was, namely his father's representative. This was a very stupid mistake on their part. Out of greed one can jump to conclusions, or wishful thinking, and grievously misunderstand one's legal and moral position. They *wanted* the owner to abandon his vineyard and so grasped at an entirely illusory hint that he might have done so, or at least was on the point of doing so.

THE SON, THE TENANTS, AND THE OWNER

The discrepancy between the gospels on the exact situation of the son when he was killed is interesting. Quite apart from reasons for preferring one reading to another, the Mark version seems credible. The killing

[1] O. Eger at *ZSS* 55 (1935), 370. The Hebrew term, most probably underlying κληρονομία on this footing, would be *ḳinᵉyān* (*Mishnāh*, 'Āvot VI, 10.*q.v.*). P. 303.

would naturally be done in the 'tower' where they can corner him after ejecting his attendants. It would not be done near any part of the vines, because a death in their proximity would be a breach of a code of conduct which the vinedressers, particularly at that juncture, would certainly obey. They might well kill the son; but it would be unthinkable for them to endanger the sale of the wine when any of it could have been made from grapes grown on a vine which had overshadowed a corpse. The blood of a corpse entering the soil near the roots of a vine would in practice lower the value of the entire crop, and so of the vineyard itself. A scrupulous Pharisee would require the region over which the son's corpse had been carried to be excavated to some depth,[1] before he would purchase any of the wine. When the rules regulating the collecting of grapes from a vine growing in a 'grave area' were strict (a grave area is, popularly speaking, a stage less unclean than a grave or place of an actual interment),[2] the possibility of the tenants' burying a corpse in a vineyard is too absurd to contemplate. Where every foot of soil tells, no one in his senses would permanently incapacitate it. No, the death-blow would be delivered inside in the hope that the body could be carried alive as far as the wall. It is to be noted that the blood of a man at the point of death does not carry with it the problems adverted to above.

It is suggested that they did not bury him outside. This is likely. They would leave that duty to the first passer-by, or to the occupiers of the adjacent field.[3] There would be bound to be some complaint. Their reply would be simple: this man was the son of a person who claimed to be the owner of the land, against whom they had great claims outstanding, and who had been pestering them for several years—'he came with a group of servants and tried to oust us by force, and we naturally had to act in self-defence'. The more public the announcement of their act, the better. Local opinion would be enlisted in their support. A hole-and-corner burial would arouse suspicion that all was not above board!

Unfortunately for the tenants the absent landlord did not react as they had calculated. Filled with wrath he came, proved the nature of

[1] Earth receiving the blood of a corpse is as polluting as the corpse itself (see *e.g.*, Mishnāh, *'Oholot* XVI. 3). Mishnāh, *ibid.* XVIII, 15. b. San. 104*b* = Sonc. 709 n. 4: wine made from a vine whose branch trailed over a tomb smelt of death(!).

[2] Samaritans were as scrupulous as Jews about graves, but they disregarded Jewish rules concerning grave-areas. The three kinds of grave-areas and the disabilities each suffers and conveys are set out in Mishnāh, *'Ohol.* XVIII, 2–4. For gathering grapes there see *ibid.* XVIII, 1 (Danby, 674). The School of Hillel followed a rule entailing extra expense.

[3] For the corpse's right to burial where found see b. B.Ḳ. 81*a* = Sonc. 459; 81*b* = Sonc. 463–4.

the tenants' possession with the aid of his document and witnesses (if necessary), or merely utilised his right of self-help, ejected the tenants (he was in no position to put them to death—the word ἀπολέσει by no means suggests this), ruined them, and put others in their room. The killing of the son would have to be proved in a criminal court. While the tenants were in possession their gardeners would probably not give evidence against them; while the owner's slaves would hardly be accepted as witnesses in a capital case: the position would alter, however, as soon as the tenants were evicted, for their gardeners would be in need of fresh employment and would readily testify to what they had seen.

CONCLUSIONS

That the parable is 'pure allegory' seems now hardly to be accepted,[1] though, curiously, allegorical interpretation can be traced in the exegesis of even anti-allegorical exegetes of the parables. What, then, does it say? Let us apply the oriental principle of making the fewest assumptions, taking the 'shortest way'. This will not prevent us, at a later stage, from seeing implications and symbolism, provided neither hinders the understanding of the literal meaning.[2] Let us keep closely to the text. The factors which are *inevitably* within the parable are not few. They are these: (i) the ownership of the landlord and his concern for the vineyard, (ii) his patience with the tenants so long as there is doubt whether they are not acting *bona fide*; (iii) his willingness to risk something even more valuable to himself in the hope that the tenants would take the right path while there was still time; and (iv) his capacity to avenge the death of the son. Then we have (v) the weak position of the tenants and their exposure to temptation; (vi) their movement from a situation in which they might conceivably honestly deny a liability, or assert an adverse claim, into another, totally different situation, in which

[1] The matter was much disputed by Jülicher and Loisy, upon principles of their own construction, dealt with ably by Gozzo. But even Jülicher was prepared to admit the allegorical character of the setting. That it is mainly allegorical is accepted by Gozzo, whose exposition subsumes this. Hauck took a similar view. So W. Beilner, *Christus u. die Pharisäer* (Vienna 1959), 185. Dodd takes it as a parable (97–8). Jeremias (55, 60) as a 'parable bearing directly on a definite situation'. That situation is, he says, the offer of the gospel to the poor, not the situation of Jesus as one about to be murdered for doing his Father's errand. Black (as we have seen) is not afraid to take it as originally allegorical. The discovery of the Thomas version (*sup.*, p. 299 n. 2) does not automatically exclude the allegorical structure, nor does it tamper with the possibility that the Church saw the original form as a *Heilsgeschichte*. Hunter (no enemy of allegory in general) does not regard this parable as an allegory created by the early Church (*Interpreting the Parables* [1960] 116–18). The son's death did not *enable* the owner's re-entry!

[2] J. J. Vincent at *Studia Evang.*, 1959, p. 85. L. Sabourin, *Rédemption sacrificielle* (Brussels 1961), 195: our parable has a partially allegorical tendency.

they sought to deny the owner's rights entirely; (vii) their reliance on the local situation, underrating the intention and power of the absent owner, their willingness to speculate while greed deprived them of caution. Finally we have (viii) the obedience, but lack of authority, on the part of the messengers; contrasted with (ix) the obedience but full representative authority of the son. Do these points really need to be seen as a *Heilsgeschichte*?

The nine points, are they not both too many and too few for that purpose? They need not, it seems evident, be attached to the situation of Israel then and there. No doubt it was customary to apply scripture to the current situation, as Jesus seems to do in Mk xii.10. But the parable need not be an explanation of what had happened or was about to happen, whereas it could very well be an explanation of *authority* and *obedience*.

The owner of the vineyard no doubt represents God: but is the vineyard Israel? Some would have no hesitation in saying that it is the *Torāh*, in which 'tenants' have been working to little purpose but with ample cunning. Is it not easier to take it as the world?[1] Similarly the owner's patience may represent God's patience with not merely the Scribes but man, while he argues whether he owes God anything and, if anything, how he can avoid paying it, *e.g.* by asserting that God owes him a living, etc. Are the messengers the prophets—or rather the warnings which reveal God's continued interest in his 'garden'? The son need, therefore, not represent more than God's last opportunity, offered before a suggested possible fatal choice. The 'others' to whom the vineyard might be given need not be the Gentiles: they could equally well be another creation. One could indeed apply the story to Pharisees or Scribes. A final breach of the covenant (the *Torāh*—it is better so taken) by repudiating it was not to be thought of by a Jew; but the story suggests that interpreting it disingenuously might be only a step towards repudiating it. On the other hand one may take comfort from the observation that God's patience is only just, since he has 'gone abroad' and left the tenants to make the best of their situation.

Bearing in mind that the parable may not have been correctly understood by the evangelists, it is remarkable that its setting is accepted by all three. The citation of Ps cxvii/cxviii is generally regarded as an accretion,[2] due to an effort on the part of the early Church to see Jesus

[1] This is the view of pseudo-Athanasius (*Quaest. in N.T.*, Migne, *PG* 28, 714) and Irenaeus (*Adversus Haereses* IV c. 36, *PG* 7, 1091), disapproved by Gozzo (p. 117). W. Trilling, *Das Wahre Israel* (Munich 1964), 55–65, takes the parable in Matthew as an attack upon Israel for their guilt. For God's 'possession' see the Mishnāh referred to above at p. 306 n. 1.

[2] So Oesterley, *op. cit.* 120. Jeremias, 57 (a pre-Marcan addition). Not so Gozzo, who explains the parable and the quotation in conjunction.

proclaiming himself the Messiah and foretelling his rejection and triumphant resurrection. But it may be worth while to investigate once again the sequence of incidents: the episode of the fig-tree (in which Jesus behaves as Messiah); the question about authority; the parable we have just reconstructed; the citation of the challenging psalm. Jesus might have commented: God has the authority; he will exert it in his own time. Your duty is to see that you do not mistake the last warning for an opportunity to cheat God. The warning may not be rational; the credentials of the messenger may not be recognised for what they are; the clever ones may turn out to be wrong, for all their specialist knowledge.[1] Wonders are not for marvelling, but for use as a means of salvation.

Such an irritating answer to the question about authority (if it was made as suggested) would naturally produce the reaction which Mark says it produced. Even if events have been compressed and paraphrased by the evangelist, the same sequence of reactions and protests would produce the same effect. The result would be entirely consistent with the parable as reconstructed here with the aid of legal material.

In view of this reconstruction an Old Testament parallel comes to mind. That Jesus could not have had it in *his* mind is very unlikely. The question remains, what light does this parallel throw upon Jesus's intention in uttering the parable? If the legal explanation of the story of the Wicked Vinedressers is correct (as it is submitted it must be) we are at once taken back to the story of Adam and Eve, to the expulsion of the human race (not the Jews!) from the Garden of Eden.

Adam was put into the Garden to 'till it and keep it' (Gn ii.15); that is to say Adam was God's tenant, being both a guardian and a cultivator. Jewish commentators are clear that Adam was God's *'āriyṣ*. But the cultivation was minimal. This was the Golden Age, man was a fruit-gatherer, no digging or ploughing was required of him (*cf.* iii. 17–19). The tenant's pay was a share of the fruit of the trees, the share being the amount that he needed (ii.16). But there was a condition attached to the tenancy, explicit, and yet in a way not wholly arbitrary—the fruit of one particular tree was excluded, though, evidently, Adam was to 'look after' it. Adam is warned that his very existence depends upon his complying with that condition (ii.17). But temptation came. The circumstances created by God provided Adam's temptation, which came about by stages, and not directly. At some stage human guile,

[1] A somewhat similar understanding of the pericope (*mutatis mutandis*) was arrived at independently by N. Levison, *The Parables: their Background and Local Setting* (Edinburgh 1926), 226–9.

stimulated by external forces, corrupted what was initially an honest intention.

Then God, exactly like the owner of a garden which is tended by *'āriyṣiym*, 'walks in the garden in the cool of the day'. He calls Adam, apparently several times. The number of times is not given, and no special significance attaches to them—but we see that Adam hides because he cannot face the summons, giving a lame excuse (iii.10). Adam admits that he broke the commandment, blames Eve (who, we know from *v.* 6, experienced temptation from personal lust as well as the serpent's arguments), who blames the serpent. Breach of the condition of the tenancy leads to the pair's being expelled from the Garden, but, we note, it does not end Adam's status. Adam does not cease to be God's tenant. He loses the easy life and favourable terms of the Garden of Eden; yet he acquires a much larger field, with the harsh conditions which God sets for him in very explicit terms. One gathers from iii.17–19 that man has from God a permanent lease of the world (excepting Eden), with no conditions of obedience attached to it. Of course one learns later of the renewal of the relationship. Man, stage by stage, receives a re-grant of the tenancy, with explicit conditions: it is a commonplace that the conditions laid down for the sons of Noah (not the Jews!) were much less demanding than those later laid down at Sinai.

It might well be argued (the present writer has not seen evidence that it was argued) that the Fall of man had occurred long ago, and that a further worsening of man's relationship with God was not to be contemplated. God, so near the Beginning, had promised man his everlasting tenancy of the Earth (excepting Eden). A question remained, upon which a Prophet might well have much to say (and indeed we find the Prophets, through the marriage-image and otherwise, approaching the question),[1] whether God would regard himself as bound by his original declarations. How far was it true to say that the *Torāh* gave all that the 'tenants' needed to know, and that the construction and interpretation thereof was irrevocably in the hands of the Scribes or Pharisees, or, for that matter, messianic sects and other know-alls? Had God given over his territory, and gone away and left the responsibility with *them*?

When we compare the story of the Fall with our parable there is a striking difference. Adam in his simplicity hid. Had he been the crafty and wild creature that his descendants (*e.g.* Cain) became, he would not have been satisfied with hiding. God walked in the Garden like a human owner. Adam might have thought of strangling him and so becoming

[1] Above, p. 97.

owner of the Garden. Eve no doubt (*cf.* Ahab and Jezebel) would have lent a hand quite gladly, not to speak of the serpent, whose disloyalty to the Creator is depicted with picturesque detail. In dealing with the descendants of Adam God naturally has to assert his authority in a somewhat different manner. But the result is a foregone conclusion. Jesus (it would seem) has invented a series of episodes to take account of the lack of simplicity in man since the Fall, in contrast to the simplicity of Adam. The upshot, therefore, seems to be as suggested above: we are not to suppose that God will never exert his authority. But we can rely upon warnings until the (hypothetical) hour of repudiation.

Such is the conclusion we are entitled to form upon the basis of the parable itself. Are we inclined to waver when we consult the pseudepigraphical precedent which the evangelists, if not Jesus himself, almost certainly had before them? The *Psalms of Solomon* are dominated by the vivid recollection of Pompey's sacrileges in Jerusalem,[1] and Ps.Sal. viii depicts the Romans as God's instruments of righteous vengeance. The Greek version of *v.* 11 comes towards the culmination (not the actual pinnacle) of wickedness (on the Jews' part) with these words:

τὰ ἅγια τοῦ θεοῦ διηρπάζοσαν
ὡς μὴ ὄντος κληρονόμου λυτρουμένου.

"They plundered the holy things of God, just as if there were not an heir (able and willing) to redeem them." The enormities of the Jews are said to have been confirmed between them by covenants sealed with oaths (*v.*10b: συνέθεντο αὐτοῖς συνθήκας μετὰ ὅρκου περὶ τούτων). Impressive as this is, the fact remains that, under the guise of allusion to the just retribution which *may yet* fall upon the Jews at the hands of the Romans, the parable is conceived in much broader terms, and if it speaks to the Jews speaks in language applicable to all that defy God.

[1] G. B. Gray at Charles, *Apocrypha and Pseudepigrapha*, II, 629–30. Dupont-Sommer, 358–9.

CHAPTER FOURTEEN

'Render to Caesar . . .'

CHRIST'S TEACHING on the relations between the ruler and the subject on the one hand and between that subject and God on the other has been a matter of deep concern. The doctrine of the separation of Church and State which is in vigour in some predominantly Christian countries is founded upon a conception of that teaching which deserves to be re-examined, for it proceeds upon the hypothesis that Jesus distinguished between the claims of Caesar and God and placed these in some sort of balance or antithesis. Pope Leo XIII propounded anew a doctrine traceable through the fourth Lateran Council, Boniface VIII, and St Gregory II to St Gelasius—a doctrine to be found also in the works of St Thomas Aquinas.[1] In his encyclical *Arcanum* (10 February 1880) he says: 'No one doubts but that Jesus Christ, the Church's founder, intended the spiritual authority to be distinct from the civil, each free and untrammelled in the pursuit of its own concerns.' In his encyclical *Immortale Dei* (1 November 1885) he says: 'God divided the administration of the human race between two powers, namely the ecclesiastical and the civil, the former supreme in spiritual, the latter in secular affairs. . . . Therefore whatever in human affairs is in any manner sacred, whatever appertains to the salvation of souls or the worship of God . . . is entirely within the power and jurisdiction of the Church; but it is right that whatever falls within the category of the civil and political should be subject to the civil authority, since Jesus Christ ordained that the things of Caesar should be rendered to Caesar and those which belong to God should be rendered to God.' But did Jesus ordain this distinction precisely? Is it, for example, a distinction of which first-century Jews were capable? If not, it may be submitted that there must be the clearest evidence before we can attribute this idea to Jesus.

The pericope containing the famous *responsum* (Mk xii.13–17, Mt xxii.15–22, Lk xx.20–26) bristles with difficulties. This is unfortunate

[1] *De regim. principum* I, 14. A. Tanquerey, *Synopsis Theologiae Dogmaticae Fundamentalis* I, § 903.

as there is no passage in the New Testament which has so much to teach us about law. What, for example, is the meaning of the oily preamble with which, all three evangelists agree, Jesus's questioners attempt to trap him? Is it really evidence of what some of his contemporaries thought of him? If it is, it contains, perhaps by coincidence, some very odd words. For example, what are we to make of the extraordinary statement that οὐ μέλει σοι περὶ οὐδενὸς? The meaning often assigned by translators, namely 'you are not concerned about anybody' cannot fit in the context and is inappropriate to the person in general. Moreover the notion that οὐδενὸς is masculine, 'anybody', is a reflection derived from the following phrase which evidently refers to people, and the natural sense, as it would be heard by the first hearer, would be neuter, '. . . about anything', which is even stranger to us. Further, what is to be made of the extremely awkward, wooden, expression, 'for you do not look into the face of men'? Or is it not rather the case that πρόσωπον means not 'face' merely, but 'personality', 'person', in fact the Latin *persona* with its legal overtones? In short, there is ground for suspicion that the preamble, as we can call Mk xii. 14, is a construct, a fabricated entity, intended to prepare the reader for what follows, a clever and accurate fabrication—but of course no forgery in the sense that there was any intention to deceive, still less has it a deceptive effect.

Beyond the preamble, what of the act of Jesus and his *responsum* itself, which looks at first sight like an oracle, ambiguous, cryptic, a clever means of avoiding trouble? The attitude of the Church cannot be doubted. Jewish and Muslim communities have always held the acts and the *responsa* of the righteous to be precedents for others to follow, and the action of Jesus in asking for the coin, in asking about it also, and his immediate *responsum* will have been precedents for Christians. Every part of the story was thus intended to be instructive: not a tale about Jesus, but something which would guide Christians in their dealings with the world. A cryptic answer may thus be presumed to have had one or more clear meanings for those who treasured the pericope, far beyond their satisfaction at Jesus's keeping (for the while) out of the hands of his 'enemies'.[1]

But the oddity of the whole affair strikes one at once. Why should his questioners ask, as they do, 'Is it permitted to give *census* to Caesar or not?'? The Romans' demand for taxes of various kinds was a nuisance,

[1] In his *Trial of Jesus of Nazareth* (London 1968), S. G. F. Brandon, who believes Jesus was *rightly* executed for sedition, is surely correct in detecting (p. 67) that Jesus's answer must have been unambiguous when it was uttered. Brandon wrongly supposes Jesus meant that taxes should be withheld from Caesar.

for which some sort of compensation no doubt was evident in the internal security and the special status of Jews within the empire, neither of which would have been available without the same government which authorised the taxation. The Jews had a clear sense that before one can claim to be a king one must construct public works and fight wars on the people's behalf.[1] This the Romans were fully prepared to do, and they stood up for the Jews against their ancient enemies, the Greeks. True, nobody likes paying taxes, and some Jews had, or pretended they had, conscientious scruples against paying them. Some scholars have assumed that such objections were widespread and taken at their face value, that in fact such a problem was at the back of the questioners' minds. Or it might be contended that these questioners had only the intention of testing Jesus to see whether he were a Zealot, and if he gave a pro-Roman answer to discredit him with the populace who are supposed to have had more than a sneaking sympathy with the Zealots. But is there any ground for this? The question is framed as a question in Jewish law: 'Is it permitted, is it lawful. . . .' How odd this is! Was there any ground for supposing that the Jewish law would supply an answer? We might as well ask whether it is lawful for Britain to join the Common Market: what has the law of England to do with the Common Market? One would solve such a question by reference to expediency, provided that no authoritative prohibition were found. And here we come to a further objection. Why should the questioners who are variously called Pharisees' students (Matthew), Pharisees and Herodians (Mark), 'spies' (Luke—is he more cautious here than the others?) object to payment of tax to Caesar, or rather why should they presuppose that any intelligent person would object? Why should one object on the footing of the Jewish law? Perhaps even while the Temple still stood, Rabbi Ḥaniynā', deputy high priest, taught 'Pray for the peace of the kingdom . . .',[2] and this is the perennial attitude; while of course there can be no kingdom without taxes!

[1] *Mishnāh*, 'Āvot III, 2 (Danby, 450; Blackman, IV, 506). Loewe, 32. R. Samuel's saying, *diyna' d^{e}mal^{e}kūta diyna'* (the law of the state is [real] law, or paramount) found at b. B.B. 54*b*, 55*a*; B.Ḳ. 113*b*; Giṭṭ. 10*b* is mentioned by Loewe at p. 33, 53. The famous dictum of Mar Samuel (180–257) is something of a mystery in that its sources have not been discovered. But there can be little doubt but that it represents traditional learning, since it has never been contradicted. Its most interesting feature is that it has never been applied to any subject-matter beyond *diyney māmonot* ('matters of money or estate'). 'The law of the kingdom' is the law, but only in secular matters—as regards the spiritual and unseen aspect of Judaism and its law 'Caesar' has no rights. A profound and comprehensive study is provided by Herzog, *Main Institutions* I, 24–32. At p. 26 he refers to 1 S x.25, where there is a statement of the royal prerogative which, Herzog says, has been overlooked by those who discuss Mar Samuel's dictum.

[2] Mekilta, *Baḥod.* § 5, on Ex xx.2 (Lauterbach, ii, 230).

A review of Jewish history and legal thinking will solve these problems for us. First of all, there is ground for suspicion when the evangelist attributes evil motives to Jesus's questioners. This is, after all, some Christian's reflection or conjecture: we have no idea upon what material it was based. Evil imputations are normally *prima facie* plausible, especially with an under-educated audience who like to think of themselves as smart. But our text does not oblige us to start with the assumption that the questioners (whoever they were) intended to do no more than entrap Jesus. A *bona fide* doubt could well be used so as to have such an effect—but that is a rather different matter. Let us proceed without any presupposition as to the questioners' motives. They want to know whether it was lawful to give (note the colourless word, 'give', chosen with lawyerlike care) *census* (Luke says 'tribute') to Caesar or not. There had long been dissatisfaction with the Jewish State, in which for years various rulers had exercised functions *de facto*, and the expectations of the current 'tetrarchs', scions of a family of dubious origins and unholy habits, were very much in debate. Referring to anti-Hasmonean tendencies[1] Josephus indicates that it was claimed that the Jews had only one king, namely God. The Romans were still sympathetic to the Jews, as a very peculiar but industrious and worthwhile people. Embassies to Caesar might at any time obtain from him concessions of great utility. The choice of ruler was in fact his. He was the real ruler, and the puppets in office in the Land of Israel were his creatures, though they called themselves 'kings' and may well have fancied that their revenues were owed to them by virtue of rights more extensive than mere foreign appointment. Pharisees are known not to have concerned themselves much with the *de facto* sovereigns, Jewish or foreign. Individuals were not seldom on bad terms with the rulers, though what influence they might have in particular courts would depend on circumstances. It is generally believed that Pharisees, for the most part, did not take a violent objection to the Romans, as the Zealots did, and (as mentioned above) we know that Pharisees later accepted the jurisdiction of the State, even if non-Jewish, as valid for Jews in conscience—which has remained the Jewish law ever since.

It is notorious that the Romans were, at least until the time of Caligula, sympathetic to Jewish sensibilities about the Sabbath, for example, and concerning idolatrous objects (such as the standards of the legions) or objects that could be associated with idolatry (such as the shields that Pilate displayed and was forced to remove). This sympathy was reasonable and practical. What is not so well known is that the Romans took a positive attitude towards the conservation of indigenous

[1] *Ant.* XIV, 41 (Loeb edn, vii, 468).

religious feelings with which they sympathised. Not only is the celebrated inscription (now in Istanbul), which protected the heart of the Temple from pollution by the ingress of non-Jews, evidence of this attitude; but there is also the very interesting inscription which came from Nazareth (of all places) and which contains (in curiously Latinised Greek) an edict of Caesar, quite possibly Tiberius himself, if not Augustus, to the effect that disturbing graves shall thenceforward be a criminal offence punishable with death.[1]

It could, however, be argued that taxes were owed to the Jewish rulers, the immediate 'kings', and not the Roman emperor by way of direct taxation such as (we have every reason to suppose) the *census* was. It could be argued that Jews had been taxed by or in the name of kings, Hasmonean, Ptolemaic, Seleucid, as far back as anyone could remember. But it could be urged in reply that Jews would be justified in refusing, on conscientious grounds, to pay a direct tax to a remote ruler—while at the same time agreeing to pay taxes to any immediate rulers who actually gave (or purported to give) security in return. Such an outlook strengthened the claims of the 'tetrarchs', and accounts for the presence of the 'Herodians'[2] amongst the questioners, as Mark says, a presence which apparently was meaningless for the unquestionably later Matthew and Luke. We should not, however, forget that some pious extremists regarded the rule even of the Hasmonean priest-kings as having been unlawful (Gn xlix.10 as construed in the *Blessings of Jacob*).[3] It must be emphasised that the question was not 'Is it permitted to pay taxes . . .', but 'Is it permitted to give *census* to *Caesar*?' Quite so. If Caesar had appointed Archelaus or Antipas, for example, on terms that he should tax the Jews and pay a half to Rome, the Jewish lawyers would have no objection—that would be a question between the Roman and his puppets. And a Jewish legal opinion to the effect that Jews must not pay a tax direct to Rome, such as this *census* was, would not necessarily be, at the end of the day, hostile to Rome's interests, though that would naturally be open to argument.

Jesus is asked because he is thought to be a prophet, and must know all the answers to difficult questions. The Jewish Law was obscure

[1] L. Wenger, 'Eine Inschrift aus Nazareth', *ZSS* 51 (1931), 369ff. It is headed Διαταγμα καίσαρος and the death penalty is imposed for τυμβωρυχία. For tombs at Nazareth see Kopp, *Holy Places*, 50–1. But *cf.* Irmscher, *ZNW* 42 (1949), 172–84.

[2] H. H. Rowley, 'The Herodians in the gospels', *JThS* 41 (1940), 14–27. See also articles at *JBL* 39 (1920), 102–12; *R.Sc.Rel.* 28 (1938), 585–8; *R.B.* 47 (1938), 184–97. A strange suggestion has recently been made in the following article, on which it is not necessary to comment here: C. Daniel, 'Les "Hérodiens" du N. Testament sont-ils des Esséniens?', *Revue de Qumran* 6 (1967), 31–54.

[3] J. M. Allegro, *JBL* 1956, 174–6; Vermès, *Dead Sea Scrolls*, 224.

because it said, or appeared to say, nothing distinctly on the point. Such *lacunae* are to be filled from a prophet's wisdom. Jesus did not contend that his questioners were not entitled to ask him. We observe that he did not maintain silence. The evangelist or his source attributes to Jesus consciousness of the questioners' hypocrisy. But this did not influence, apparently, his conduct, which was to resolve the doubt. It was axiomatic with the 'righteous' then as it is with their counterparts still, that there is no question which the *Torāh* cannot answer, if properly interpreted. Payment of taxes too must come within the conduct of man a substantial part of which is regulated by positive and negative commandments. A thing is permitted or it is forbidden.

Now what rôle is played in all this by the coin? It is inconceivable that such high questions, tending to establish the general principle of civil subjection and obedience to the State, could depend even in a minor manner upon the coinage. Is it merely a matter, as has been thought, of Jesus seeking to convict or convince people out of their own mouths? Two adult males' admissions would be conclusive *pro tempore* in a contest or debate to which they were parties.[1] If this was his policy, which is by no means certain, he would hardly have answered in a manner which took advantage of the lack of intelligence or preparation on the part of his audience, for that would be no answer at all. This is apparently the reason why the original commentator on the episode, whose attitude is conveyed by the evangelist, inserts, as if to excuse Jesus, the notion that he was aware of their hypocrisy: yet that would not justify his adopting an indirect and perhaps casual method in solving their problem. The coin has deceived modern commentators one after another. But it is a fact of which Jesus was well aware, and we must not for a moment forget, that whatever may be said of the high constitutional questions in the abstract, payment of *census* was actually an activity performed by the human being with the aid of pieces of coined silver—the action of handing over, the motive for handing, and the object handed over must thus be thought of in turn if we are to know whether the payment was 'permitted', 'lawful', in the Jewish legal sense of these words.

The very varied interpretations given to the *responsum*[2] show that

[1] See above p. 160 n. 2.

[2] Cornelius à Lapide, *Commentarii in quatuor Evangelia* (Lyons 1681), I, 405–9. Origen (*in Luc. Hom.* 39, ed. Rauer, ix, 220–1): *imponite personam caelestis* (also *in Ep. ad Rom.*, ix. 26). Valentinian, Valens and Gratian on consubstantiality (A.D. 375: Theodoret, *HE*, iv, 8) repudiate the notion that the emperor's religion should be received as such. John of Damascus (A.D. 726–37: Migne, *PG* 94, 1297): the Church does not obey the king. S. Gardiner, *De vera obed.* (1535), ff. 12*b*–13*a*, 24*a* (ed. Janelle, 98, 133), opined the contrary, that obedience to kings must be unlimited. Beza (*ad*

for the most part it is understood not, as it should be, by reference to the pericope itself, so much as by referring to what Jesus *could* have

Mt xxii.21): the hearers must bear patiently the burden owed to their sins. H. Grotius, *De Iure Belli ac Pacis*, I, iv, 4.1: obedience is due to Gentile kings no less than to Jewish (correct). S. Pufendorf, *De Iure Nat. et Gent.*, VII, viii.9: Christ required obedience to the *de facto* ruler. Wetstenius *ad* Matt. xxii.21: *pecuniam Caesari reddendam* (*esse*) *quoquo modo se res haberet, sive dominus Judaeorum esset, sive non esset.* O. Gierke, trans. F. Maitland, *Pol. Theor. of the Middle Age* (Cambridge 1900/1958), p. 109 n. 15: divine institution of worldly magistrature. See also J. E. E. D. Acton, *History of Freedom and other Essays* (London 1907), 29: inauguration of freedom [absurd]; G. E. Fasnacht, *Acton's Pol. Phil.* (London 1952), 30–1; A. N. Whitehead, *Adventures of Ideas* (Cambridge 1933), 68–9 (God now a principle of organization); E. Barker, *Princ. of Soc. and Pol. Theory* (Oxford 1951), 7; *From Alexander to Constantine* (Oxford 1959), 395–6, 400–4, 456–7; G. H. Sabine, *Hist. of Pol. Th.*, 3rd edn (London 1951), 162; F. Gavin, *Seven Cent. of the Prob. of Church and State* (Princeton 1938), 8–9 (no abiding principle). F. Dvornik, *Early Christian and Byzantine Political Philosophy* (*Dumbarton Oaks St.* 9) (Washington 1966) I. 432: the keystone of all political development down to the present day; the basis for every theory concerning the relation between the Church and the State. While it could be urged that Church and State were coterminous those who objected to items of legislation in England were loud in their appeals to Christ's saying (*e.g.* P. S. Belasco, *Authority in Church and State*, London 1928, 112–14): but was it the *basis* of Quaker theories, or rather a convenient argument—for they denied the moral validity of human legislation as such? For H. Loewe see below p. 332 n. 2.

W. L. Knox, 'Church and State in the N.T.', *J. Rom. St.* 39 (1949), 23–30 (not the origin); O. Cullmann, *The State in the N.T.* (London 1957), 3, 9, 18, 20 (also *Der Staat im N.T.*, 2nd edn, Tübingen 1961) (zealot movement), *ibid.* 35 (like Tertullian, Erasmus: give the State money, God your self); *Early Church* (London 1956), 127 (Caesar within the *regnum Christi*); *Vorträge u. Aufsätze* (Tübingen 1966), 296. M. Rist, 'Caesar or God? A Study in *Formgeschichte*', *J. Rel.* 16 (1936), 317–31 (a Gentile-Christian redaction). L. Goppelt in *Studia Evangelica II* (*TuU* 87, Berlin 1964), 183–94 (call to eschatological existence). K. Barth, *Against the Stream* (London 1954), 24–5. P. S. Watson, *The State as a Servant of God* (London 1946), 34, 84ff.; M. Dibelius, *Jesus* (London 1963), 115; *Rom u. d. Christen*, S. B. Heid. A.W., Phil.-Hist. Kl. 1941–2, N. 2 (1942), 3–4 (the pericope plays no rôle). J. S. Kennard, *Render to God . . .* (New York 1950) (Jesus ironically *refuses* to pay the tax (!)). L. Wenger, 'Über erste Berührungen der Christentum mit dem Römischen Rechte', *Misc. G. Mercati* 5 (*Studi e Testi* 125) (Vatican 1946), 569–607 (the hearers knew no god but Caesar). T. M. Parker, *Christianity and the State in the Light of History* (London 1955), 17–19. Dvornik (*cit. sup.*) sees Jesus as condemning the Zealots' theocratic régime, allotting to the political organisation and to the members of the 'kingdom of God' spheres which each must respect. C. D. Morrison, *The Powers that be . . .* (*Stud. Bibl. Theol.* 29) (London 1960). H. Conzelmann, *Rel. Ges. u. Geg.*, 3rd edn, III (1959) *s.v.* 'Jesus': Jesus did not compare the two duties—that to God is absolute. R. Schnackenburg, *The Moral Teaching of the N. Test.*, 2nd edn, trans. (Freiburg/London 1965), p. 117–19 (the State has rights in its sphere; there is no reservation in regard to God). G. Bornkamm, *Jesus of Nazareth*, 2nd edn, trans. (London 1966), p. 120–4 (there are no two realms, no ideal State: God's reign alone comes, to survive). The best all-round treatment remains that of E. Stauffer, *Christ and the Caesars* (London 1955), 112–37. Pastor Richard Wurmbrand, who knows heathen 'Caesars', warmly contended (in a television interview given to the B.B.C., 7 May, 1968) that Tiberius had done nothing for Palestine; he was a usurper to whom no one owed anything; and Jesus's words mean virtually that 'Caesar should be "given" a kick in the pants'!

meant, to his life and death, and to the prescriptions of St Peter and St Paul.[1] The opposite fault can be incurred. Some scholars reconstruct Jesus's meaning by inference *ab extra*, some say Jesus's words are inconclusive, impenetrable;[2] and then again another has said that by 'Caesar' he meant the kings known to him, and that he could not have said the same of Nero or other persecuting emperors: he had not had acquaintance with the totalitarian State!

The pericope is set in the middle of a discussion of Jesus's personal authority.[3] He is the stone that was rejected by the builders/scholars. Thomas (Aland, App. I, § 100) and the Egerton papyrus (*c.* A.D. 140)[4] cannot help us much here, but the synoptics are more or less agreed as to the position of the episode. Matthew (xxii.15–22) places it after the parable of the Great Supper which he sees as a development of the theme in that of the Wicked Vinedressers; Mark (xii.13–17) places it after the Wicked Vinedressers; Luke (xx.20–6) likewise. All the synoptics place the Sadducees' question about the resurrection after this passage. The scene is thus set for Jesus to give a clever, conclusive, and unchallengeable answer. Previously we have parables and the saying about the 'stone' in which Jesus teaches somewhat darkly; subsequently an argument in which biblical material and *haggadāh* are employed to remove the nominal objections to the resurrection. In our pericope he uses his authority to settle the conflicting claims of Caesar and the kingdom of God, the first earthly and practical, with aspirations in religious spheres, the second not the less earthly for its being heavenly and moral. Is it conceivable that he could have satisfied his enquirers without biblical authority? None is cited, but is there not one lying under the surface?

Our instincts confirm that such an argument there must have been, and hence the intense interest in Jesus's question and in his apparent reaction to the answer. In fact Matthew's ἀπόδοτε οὖν and Luke's τοίνυν ἀπόδοτε (whereas Mark has only ἀπόδοτε) prove that even very early readers felt that the *responsum* must have derived directly from the reply, 'Καίσαρος'. This instinct directs attention to the question of Jesus, τίνος ἡ εἰκών . . ., and this has precipitated a rash of expositions on the Jewish attitude to 'idolatrous' coins.[5] At least two notions have

[1] Rm xiii.1–7; 1 P ii.13–17.

[2] Klostermann's comment on the saying.

[3] G. Kittel, *Christus und Imperator* (Stuttgart 1939), 16. The argument of D. Daube (*New Testament and Rabbinic Judaism*, London 1956, 158ff.) that this is one of the four types of question analogous (in Mark's eyes?) to four questions for four types of son in the Passover Haggadāh may not throw light on our immediate problem: but his identification of the question of one of *ḥochma*, and *halachic* (159) is obviously right.

[4] Stauffer, 112. Rist, 338–9 (pre-Marcan form?); Dibelius, 5.

[5] Stauffer, Rist, Loewe, Kennard.

arisen out of this, namely that the coins are Caesar's, and should go back to him(!),[1] and that in return for the use of Caesar's money the Jews should recognise his authority and therefore pay his taxes.[2] These have a superficial plausibility, but they melt before a closer examination.[3]

The enormous importance attached to 'Render unto Caesar the things that are Caesar's and to God the things that are God's' only confirms what a careful inspection reveals, namely that the *responsum* has nothing to do with coins as such. Would it *really* have been different if Caesar had agreed to make yet another concession to Judaea and had allowed scrupulous Jews to pay the *census* in *e.g.* unobjectionable (*e.g.* Tyrian) tetradrachms? Caesar could easily have done so: would that have affected the relations between our duty to 'Caesar' and our obligations towards God? Previous studies have not attended to this question because the clue was missing—namely the biblical authority. Once this is identified, and its midrashic potentialities are investigated, difficulties are removed. The exceptional appropriateness of the Marcan version becomes apparent. The author of the pericope wrote so that readers should be alert to the biblical authority and should admire how scrupulously Jesus was able to use it so as to provide reliable guidance whilst avoiding personal exposure to calumny, so far as he might.

The story is in fact simplicity itself, and it takes very little space; we shall need space to work out the facts, however. To start at the beginning, the questioners, having warned Jesus that they expect him to answer without fear or favour,[4] ask him 'Is it lawful to give *census* to

[1] This appears in various forms in Cullmann, Stauffer, also M.-J. Legrange, *Évangile selon Saint Marc* (Paris 1947), 315. Cranfield, *cit. inf.*, p. 333 n. 2 at p. 372.

[2] Billerbeck, *Kommentar* I (p. 884) (taking up a hint at Wetstenius on ἀπόδοτε): Als allgemein anerkannter Grundsatz galt: das Herrschaftsgebiet eines Königs deckt sich mit dem Gültigkeitsgebiet seiner Münzen. But this has deceived many. Indians used Roman coins and the English have used, *e.g.* Portuguese coins (and *cf.* the currency of Maria Theresa dollars in Ethiopia). Did the Temple at Jerusalem, which used Tyrian silver, recognise the sovereignty of Tyre? The idea goes back to J. Lightfoot or earlier. Stauffer, 130. V. Taylor, *The Gospel according to St. Mark*, 2nd edn (London 1966), 480. B. Orchard, etc., edd., *A Catholic Commentary*... (1953), 736*g*. P. Gaechter, *Das Matthäus Evangelium* (Innsbruck, etc., 1963), 703. J. Bowman is more subtle (*Gospel of Mark*, Leiden 1965, 227) but the error is the same, b. B.Ḳ. 113*a*: one who issued coins had authority to levy tax (?): 'He was convicting them... of enjoying both the gifts of Roman civilisation and the benefits of religion; both in their different ways were in debt to each.' *Cf.* Adeney at Hastings, *DB*, I, 336. The contemporaries of Christ were cunning or intelligent, but whether they were so sophisticated is doubtful.

[3] A coin belongs to its possessor or it is no coin. There is no evidence that coins belonged to the ruler. A *figurative* right on his part would not serve us, as the rights of God are surely not viewed as figurative. Use of a king's coinage does not amount to acknowledgement of his rule, as the mixed hoards in the Holy Land testify clearly: many issues of a wide provenance were in circulation and saved.

[4] *I.e.* to answer 'no': so, rightly, St Chrysostomos on the passage.

Caesar or not? Shall we give or not give?' Rabbis expect questions to be phrased in such a way, 'Is it lawful?' The stock answers are 'It is permitted' or 'It is forbidden'. The questioners want a further answer in confirmation, 'You should give' or 'You should not give'. They do *not* expect reasons, because it is not etiquette for a rabbi to give reasons except in scholarly debate with his colleagues.[1] The answer would be enough for their purposes, and some might think that they have him in a fork.

In order to answer such a question it is necessary to have an authority. *Halakāh* cannot be stated unless the rabbi has a precedent, or a direct authority, or at worst a *haggadāh* from which a reasonable and relevant inference can be drawn. Even the *Mishnāh* does not have an halakic statement to the effect that taxes must be paid to *Caesar*. Whether R. Ḥaniynā' 's dictum could be construed to this effect is another matter: it is in any case not contemporary with Jesus. The Bible certainly has no direct authority. Jeremiah's 'Seek the peace of the city . . .' (xxix.7) is, though relevant, too general. In the absence of direct authority, in the written or even the oral law, where shall one turn to? Obviously to Jesus, as a supposed prophet, and supposedly the man to whom Isaiah referred in ch. xi, who will judge impartially in all such fundamental and abstruse matters.[2] The question was in order as a question, whatever the motives of the enquirers themselves. The evidence that there was opposition to the Roman tax-system is well established.

Jesus, when approached with the question, must himself refer to the law. Moses tells us nothing to the point: to make matters worse the coinage contemplated by the Old Testament had become associated with a coinage other than the imperial coinage, and the Romans had provided that the census amount should be paid in imperial coinage,[3] in fact the imperial *denarii* which, we know, circulated in the Holy Land as elsewhere in the East alongside Greek and Tyrian coinage of various ages and provenances.[4] The imperial coins were objectionable to some Jews

[1] See above, p. 176 n. 2.

[2] '. . . and his delight shall be in the fear of the Lord. He shall not judge by what his eyes see or decide by what his ears hear; but with righteousness he shall judge the poor. . . .'

[3] Rescript of Germanicus Caesar, A.D. 17–19, quoted in the Palmyra tariff, col. IV, 41ff. (*Hermes*, 19 [1884], 520; *ZDMG*, 42, 370): δεῖ πρός ἀσσάριον Ἰταλικόν [or εἰς δηνάριον] τὰ τέλη λογεύεσθαι. A. N. Sherwin-White, *Roman Society and Roman Law in the N.T.* (Oxford 1963), 126–7 is very brief on our topic.

[4] C. H. V. Sutherland, 'The pattern of monetary development in Phoenicia and Palestine during the early Empire' (to be published in) *Proceedings of the International Numismatic Convention*, Jerusalem 1963–4, is excellent on the money circulating at our period. D. Sperber, 'Palestinian currency systems during the second commonwealth', *JQR* 56, no. 4 (1966), 273–301, corrects in important respects F. Heichelheim in T. Frank, *Economic Survey of the Roman Empire* IV (1959), *Roman Syria*, 211–23.

on the ground that they came within the prohibition against making images,[1] because they bore an excellent portrait of the emperor (Augustus or Tiberius himself). The point, which later became significant, that a profile (showing only one eye) is not strikingly a representation of a human face, like the similar point that images in relief but not in the round are not forbidden objects, was surely a quibble and should not detain us. Therefore *halakāh* seems unable to instruct that we should pay such money to Caesar. It does tell us not to *make* such money, and many pious people would not handle or even look at such money. The objection will be mentioned again below, but for the present it is enough to realise that so long as the tax was associated with the coins no command to pay them could be derived directly from the *Torāh*. In the circumstances some teachers would be prepared to answer that they had not received any traditions on the subject from their elders, and leave it at that. I and perhaps all my readers would take, in such a context, such a path. But Jesus knew that although the question might not have been sincerely posed, it was a genuine question; and he knew that there was a biblical passage (Qo viii.2) which, when exhaustively studied, gave all the necessary guidance.[2] This text he must have used, as we shall see, and gave his *responsum*, which is unquestionably in strict accordance with it.

THE PROLOGUE

Before we pass to it we should compare the verse which precedes it with the prologue which the questioners apply. Qo vii.29 is in many versions included with Qo viii, and one should read on before proceeding to Qo viii.2, the source of Christ's *responsum*. 'Behold, this alone I found, that God made the Man upright, *yāshār*. But they have sought out many devices. Who is like the wise man? And who knows the interpretation of a thing? A man's wisdom makes his face shine, and the hardness of his face (or 'his impudence')[3] is changed (or 'hated').'[4] The 'wise man' is variously interpreted by the rabbis. The Targum says it means Adam as created. Others say it means a rabbinical scholar whose face shines when he can answer a difficult question,[5] others again

[1] Ex xx.4.

[2] Non-Jewish scholars have ignored this text, to which Abrahams (*Stud. Phar. Gosp.* I, 1917, 62–5) and C. G. Montefiore (*Rabb. Lit. Gosp. Teachings*, 1930, 311) drew attention so long ago, not to mention Loewe himself.

[3] *'Azzūt pāniym, cf.* Dt xxviii.50. *Mishnāh*, 'Āvot, V, 20 (Danby's *Mishnah*, 458: R. Judah b. Tema, end of second century). Vulg.: et potentissimus faciem illius commutavit.

[4] Ta'an. 7*b* = Sonc. 29, read *yesuneh*. So LXX: μισηθήσεται.

[5] Midr. R., Eccl. VIII.1 = Sonc. 215f.; Midr. R., Lev. XXXVI.2 = Sonc. 458.

that it means Moses.[1] Others again make out that the whole passage refers to God,[2] and still others to the story of the Creation and fall of Adam.[3]

The questioners in their prologue are made out to tell Jesus, as *teacher*, (1) he is true; (2) he is not concerned for (*'ēyn ḥēphets b^e*) anything,[4] because (3) he does not look into the face (πρόσωπον) of human beings, but (4) teaches in truth the way of God. The last may be a reference to Is ii.3 (it is in any case a commonplace), but the antithesis of 'human beings' (especially their 'faces') to the way of God prepares us for the dilemma with which they are to confront the man they are questioning. Certainly they are asking him for an 'interpretation of a thing', the great art of the rabbinical scholar, *pēsher dāvār*. The wisdom of the successful scholar 'makes his face shine' and has as one of its results that the insolence of the others (whoever they are) is abashed. The author of our pericope almost certainly had these ideas in mind when he constructed the obviously plausible prologue to the affair.

The questioners' insistence on Jesus's *lack of concern* deserves a closer examination, as was hinted at the beginning of this chapter. A search through instances given in Liddell–Scott–Jones's *Greek–English Lexicon* reveals an interesting series of facts about μέλει. It is used of deities interfering or taking responsibility. What we are to understand is that the questioners suggest that Jesus does not meddle in matters which are no real concern of his, because he does not recognise or take account of the legal status or rank or political character (all these ideas lie within the word πρόσωπον) of individuals and can therefore be the ideal referee on matters of religious and moral obligation. The two-edged character of this preamble and the hidden comedy of the word πρόσωπον (face) seem to prove that the wording has been artfully contrived. Christians will have been gratified to see that Jesus's future enemies admitted (if only with the irony of history) that he was totally impartial, a man whose devotion to God had (in the metaphor of Jewish piety) relieved him of the 'yoke of worldly care' (*'ol derech 'ārets*) if not the 'yoke of the kingdom' (*'ol mal^{e}chūt*) also.[5]

THE MEANING OF ECCLESIASTES viii.2

The modern translator of the Old Testament text[6] is not much con-

[1] Midr. R., Eccl. VIII.1 = Sonc. 216f.; Midr. R., Num. XIX.4 = Sonc. 754; b. Sot. 13*b* = Sonc. 71. The *hāchām* at Qo viii.17 can be the Messiah: *Midr. on Ps.*, Ps cvi, §2 (Braude II, 188).

[2] Midr. R., Eccl. VIII.1 = Sonc. 213; Midr. R., Num. XIX.4 = Sonc. ii, 754, also b. Ber. 10*a* = Sonc. 54.

[3] Midr. R., Eccl. VII.29, § 1 = Sonc. 212, cf. *ibid.* VIII.1 = Sonc. 213f. The Targum tells of Adam and Eve's reasonings, found out to destroy humanity.

[4] οὐ μέλει: *cf. ḥēphets* Qo viii.6; Ws xii.13.

[5] See below, p. 338 n. 1.

[6] See references at the next two notes. For *'aniy* Kittel suggests *'attā*, but perhaps *'anna'* fits.

cerned with the meanings which it had in the time of Christ, but rather with the original meaning so far as this can rationally be recovered. He is also in the difficulty of all modern translators of any document, namely to put down on paper the best or most appropriate meaning. The contemporaries of Christ, like most orientals at all ages, did not select one meaning to the exclusion of others, and, when faced with alternative readings and corrupt passages tended to be eclectic, to use any reading that suited the immediate purpose, and to use the imagination to turn the corrupt text to edifying spiritual purposes: it was the antithesis of modern scholarship. This is the perpetual essence of Jewish sermon-making, *haggadāh*. Best of all was the interpretation (*pēsher*) which drew out the literal, obvious, symbolic, metaphorical, and imaginative meanings at one and the same time. This was work of genius, and one not seldom achieved in the Jewish world: one thinks at once of R. ‘Aḳiba.

The Masoretic text of our passage was already ungrammatical by Jesus's time. It started with a suspended 'I'—the *'aniy* which at once announces a divine pronouncement. Our modern translation, 'I [counsel thee] to observe the king's command', is feeble, and would not have been accepted as final in the time of Christ. Knowledge of the Septuagint must be attributed to the author of the prologue (whose structure can be understood more immediately from the LXX version of Qo vii–viii than otherwise) but the LXX after all was a version of Jewish traditions of the meaning of the M.T., and these will have survived in Palestine independently of the LXX. The Targum, even if post-Christian in date, is extremely relevant to the Aramaic-speaking synagogue which Jesus knew, for its tradition will be of very great age. The version of Symmachos indicates how the text could have been understood by first-century scholars, and this is not based upon conjecture alone. Moreover the rabbinical tradition of the meaning of the passage is a living witness of extreme importance: the Jews were in conflict with non-Jewish regal power for centuries, the conflict between God and 'Caesar' was endemic, and it continued, with Caligula, Trajan, Hadrian and the Antonines taking the place of our Tiberius. So we may use the rabbinical *midrashim* with sympathy. And what do we obtain? A very different impression of Qo viii. than what is presented in our current translations and commentaries. Let us first set out the effect of the different versions:

(1) *'^{a}niy piy-mélech sh^{e}mor v^e-'al div^{e}rat sh^{e}vū'at '^{e}lo-hiym. 'al-tibbāhel* . . . Literally: 'I . . . Mark (watch, observe) the mouth of the king, and on account of the oath of the Lord.[1] Be not hasty. . . .' 'Mouth' of

[1] *'^{e}lohiym* may mean conceivably either the human or divine master, according to one's understanding of the phrase (see P. Humbert, *Recherches sur les Sources Égyptiennes*

course suggests 'face', and there are two mentions of face, that of the wise and that of the shameless in the immediately preceding verse. 'Mark' means 'look intently at'. The same words are used of watching the mouth of a person at 1 S i.12. The literal meaning is that one must watch, *i.e.* obey, serve, the king for various reasons (prudential and otherwise) not least of these being one's recollection of the oath of God. The oath of God[1] supports, justifies, explains, the need to obey the king, for *piy-*, 'mouth', also means 'command'.[2] In the M.T. 'be not hasty' belongs to the next sentence, but rabbis would not hesitate to interpret it also with the previous . . . 'be not hasty in dealing with the king's commands, out of respect for the oath which God took. . . .' Now all this has to be put into elegant words in any translation, with any additional reflection that experience of the life of the Jews may suggest.

A seventeenth-century translation and explanation of Qo viii.1 may be mentioned here, not only because it anticipates the teaching which will be attributed to Jesus below, but because it demonstrates that Old Testament studies of an older generation could have led scholars to the correct answer long before this:[3]

Praestitutum meum, praestitutum regis observa. sed pro ratione juramenti Dei. The world is vain, its administration uncertain. Human wisdom cannot define the relationship between human administration and divine law. This verse is the chief proposition of human duty towards superior authorities. The second sentence moderates men's duties towards the latter: one must obey, he says, but only according to good faith and conscience—for there is no authority except from God . . . and therefore no *potestas* has the right to diminish men's obedience to God.[4]

(2) στόμα βασιλέως φύλαξον, καὶ περὶ λόγου ὅρκου θεοῦ μὴ σπουδάσῃς (LXX). Literally: (Omitting the 'I') 'Guard the mouth (words) of the king, and be not eager about discussion (question) of the oath of God.' In other words obey the king, and do not exert yourselves to dispute his

[1] For various interpretations see H. W. Hertzberg, *Der Prediger* (Gütersloh 1963), 161–4; R. Pautrel, *L'Écclesiaste* (Paris 1958), 31; E. H. Plumptre, *Ecclesiastes* (Cambridge 1890), 174–5 (citing 1 Ch xxix.24); H. Ranston, *Ecclesiastes* (London 1925), 37–8; G. A. Barton, *Ecclesiastes* (Edinburgh 1908), 149–52. I would rather prefer to refer to Jr xi.1–8; Lk i.73; Ac ii.30; Heb vi.16–17.

[2] Ex vii.1. Rupertus (Migne, *PL* 108, col. 1271): videtur quidem praecipere regibus et potestatibus juxta Apostolum obsequendum (Rm xiii). Sed ego puto de illo rege nunc dici, de quo David ait—Ps lxxi—et in alio loco—Ps xx.

[3] I. Tremellius and F. Junius, *Testamenti Veteris Biblia Sacra* (Hannover 1624) *ad loc.*

[4] quia non est potestas nisi à Deo; ac proinde ius non habet homines ab obsequio avocandi, quod Deus à suis jurejurando exigit, et illi fide data se exhibituros receperunt.

---

de la Litt. Sap. d'Israël, Neuchatel, 1929, 119). The Vulg. reads: ego os regis observo et *praecepta* iuramenti Dei, on which see Cornelius à Lapide.

authority by appealing to the sacred bond between God and yourselves.

(3) ἐγὼ παραινῶ ῥήσεις (or ῥῆσιν) βασιλέως φύλασσε καὶ παραβῆναι ὅρκον θεοῦ μὴ σπεύσῃς. Symmachos here keeps the 'I', careless of grammar, explains *piy* as 'words' (or 'word') and takes the second half to mean 'be not zealous to transgress the oath of God', *i.e.* in your obedience to the king follow exactly what God requires of you (for the oath was not unconditional), neither opposing the king without righteous grounds nor obeying him in defiance of God's requirements from you.[1] In other words, remember to balance the two demands (which of course gives no guidance in a dilemma).

(4) *hwy zhyr yt pwmch 'l gzyrt mlk' lmyṭr mh dy pḳdynch w'l 'yṣḳ mwmt' dyhwh 'zdhr wl' tymy bshwm mymryh 'al mgn.* The interest of the *Targum* lies in the fact that it interprets viii.2*a* with the help of 2*b*, and then 2*b* independently, which is entirely normal from a rabbinic point of view. We may paraphrase as follows: 'Keep a guard over your mouth in respect of a decree of the king, to observe all that he enjoins upon you and also in respect of business sealed with an oath by God; have a care not to take the name of the Memra in vain.'[2] The double use of the word 'mouth' is important, showing that the literal meaning was taken as well as the common metaphorical meaning, 'command'. The *Targum* is in part followed by the midrashic interpretation employed by the rabbis whose renderings have been preserved:—

(5) The chief haggadic allusion is to the three saints whose faith in God kept them unharmed in the fiery furnace, Shadrach, Meshach, and Abednego, who abused Nebuchadnezzar to his face when he required them to bow to idols.[3] This is our first overt contact with kings and idolatrous practices. Jews of the time of Christ must often have thought of the book of Daniel in their conflicts with Pilate and others over idolatrous Roman usages. In one *midrash* the three saints cite Pr xxiv.21 ('My son, fear the Lord and the king, and do not disobey either of them') which is quite relevant,[4] but is hardly of use to us in

[1] It is possible Symm. may have understood 'do not hastily break an oath taken in the name of God', not unlike the Targum. For the first part of his version see Field's *Origen's Hexapla* II, *Auctarium*, 26.

[2] A similar rendering of the LXX is found in Gregorios Thaumatourgos (d. *c.* 270) (Migne, *PG* 10, col. 1008).

[3] Midr. R., Lev. XXXIII.6 = Sonc. 425; Midr. R., Num. XV.14 = Sonc. ii, 656. *Tanḥuma* cited p. 337 n. 3 *inf. Cf.* 1 Baruch (i.10ff.; ii. 22ff.). Knox, 24. The saints obey the King literally, except when he commands anything contrary to the *Torāh:* Qo viii.2 is explained carefully in this sense at *Tanḥuma* (ed. Buber), Noaḥ, 19*b*–20*a*, trans. Montefiore and Loewe, *Rabb. Anthology* (1963), §.660. Jos., *Macc.* §§.200, 220 (Nab.).

[4] Cornelius à Lapide, *Comm. in Ecclesiasten* (Antwerp 1725), 239ff. (good on interpretations of Ecclesiastes) cites Pr xxiv.21 quia Dominus (he says) iussit ut regi obedias.

a suggested conflict between the two. The saints, however, assert that where obedience to Nebuchadnezzar means disobedience to God they are under no obligation to the king.

R. Levi, whose *midrash* is cited not less than three times in two slightly differing versions,[1] said as follows: '"I: keep the king's command" means I will keep the command of the Supreme King of kings, the Holy One, blessed be he, the *mouth* which uttered "*I* am the Lord thy God" (Ex xx.2: the first *commandment*). "And that in regard of" means (as an independent phrase) "Thou shalt have no other gods before me" (Ex xx.3); and "the oath of God" means "Thou shalt not take the name of the Lord thy God in vain" (Ex xx.7).' The result is that Qo viii.2 is a restatement in antithetical form, relative to a human king, of the propositions delivered by Moses at Sinai so far as these are relevant to the question. Here the rule of foreign, and specifically idolatrous kings is looked to, and particularly in view of any temptation to commit idolatry.

But this is not the end of midrashic ingenuity with the passage. R. Levi is reported as having reinterpreted the second half of the verse. '"In regard of the oath of God", in regard, that is, of the verse "And God spake all these words saying" (Ex xx.1).'[2] Once again we find a deliberate linking of Qo viii.2 to the ten commandments, this time to their prologue which itself emphasises the spoken word. Again elsewhere the rabbis hold that the apparently superfluous 'I' has the function of asserting the sovereignty of God, which we must dread.[3] Let the king do what he will, the 'I' remains. But the 'I' may require obedience, as he did in the case of Joseph, paragon of virtue. The righteous Joseph feared Pharaoh, whom God appointed, and who addressed him with the words '*I* am Pharaoh' (Gn xli.44).[4] We should also read our verse 'Supreme is the commandment of the oath of God' in which case the reference is to Joseph who did not shake off the yoke of heaven but feared God (Gn xlii.18) notwithstanding the great power which his earthly sovereign had given him—and we remember that he kept chaste (in token of his obedience to the divine commandment).[5]

Before we come to Jesus's behaviour, which is explicable on the basis of this text and its current interpretations, we must diverge for a moment to consider the coinage and the *census*.

[1] Midr. R., Ḳoh. VIII.2, 1 = Sonc. 217; Midr. R., Lev. XXXIII.6 = Sonc. 425. Midr. R., S. S., II.14, 1 = Sonc. 129.

[2] See Midr. R., Lev., *cit. sup.*

[3] Midr. R., Num. XIV.6 = Sonc. ii, 588. It is of interest that the rabbinical glosses are continued with augmentation by Olympiodoros Alexandrinos (sixth century, A.D.: Migne, *PG* 93, coll. 573–6).

[4] Midr. R., Num. XIV.6 = Sonc. ii, 594–5.

[5] *Ibid.*

THE CENSUS COIN

As the coin obviously plays a special rôle in the little drama it is important to know which one it was. The amount of the λαογραφία (= census) in Egypt was 16 denarii the year or 8 denarii the half-year.[1] It is uncertain what the amount of the *census* was in Palestine, and how frequently it might be levied. In spite of frequent statements by commentators to the contrary it is unknown even whether *census* was a poll-tax at all.[2] It will certainly have resembled one. At any rate the discussion about *census* is in essence about the payment of tribute and so Luke is justified in writing φόρον instead of κῆνσον.

The suggestion that *census* might not be obligatory rested in reality upon an attitude similar to that of Judas of Galilee,[3] namely that the Romans were usurpers and had no jurisdiction to tax Jews in Judaea and other parts under Roman rule in Palestine. Such a case could not have been substantiated if the *Torāh* had plainly required that Roman taxation should be paid. The argument that the coins were objectionable objects has to be taken seriously, though it might be held by only a small minority, and in reality as an excuse for fanning anti-Roman feeling. The point was not that the Romans were idolaters, nor that they were compelling the Jews to become idolaters, for they were not: the argument was that the coins were made in defiance of the command against making images, and were therefore objects of no commercial value for the pious Jew. The notion of coins which were demonetised either totally, or for certain purposes was well known at the time.[4] The

[1] *Corp. Pap. Jud.* II, 111 (CPJ 230, 231, 233, 239).

[2] F. X. Steinmetzer, *Census*, *RAC* II (1954), coll. 969–72. Same title in Pauly–Wissowa, *Real-Encycl.*, and the recent *Der kleine Pauly*, I. A thorough study of the beginning of the story appeared in 1961: E. Stauffer, 'Die Dauer des Census Augusti. Neue Beiträge zum lukanischen Schatzungsbericht', in *Studien zum Neuen Testament und zur Patristik . . . Klostermann* (Berlin 1961), 9–34.

[3] Jos., *Bell. Jud.* II, viii, 1. (118) Wetstenius, *ad* Mt. xxii.17. The wording is important: κακίζων εἰ φόρον τε Ῥωμαίοις τελεῖν ὑπομενοῦσιν καὶ μετὰ τὸν θεὸν οἴσουσι θνητοὺς δεσπότας. *Cf. Bell.* II, xvii, 8 (433), *Ant.* xviii, i, 1 (23). Origen, *In Matth.*, XVII.25 (M. *PG* 13, col. 1552). Goppelt, 185. E. Klostermann, *Das Markusevangelium* 4th edn. (Tübingen 1950), 124–5.

[4] Coins in the possession of tax-collectors are forbidden: b. B.Ḳ. 113*a*, *Mishnāh* X, 1 (Danby, 346), but this is a temporary and conditional bar. M. R. Lehmann, *Revue de Qumran*, no. 17, vol. 5, pt. 1 (1964), 102–4. The Copper Scroll refers to numerous places where *ḥerem* money was hidden. *Figured* ('TSLM) coins are referred to (though Lehmann argues otherwise and adduces b. 'A.Z. 13*a*, Bek. 53*a*, Yoma 66*a*, Sheḳ. 22*a*, and also Pes. 28*a*): col. xi 1, 4, 15: J. M. Allegro, *Treasure of the Copper Scroll* (London 1960), 53, 148, n. 109. In his view the rebuilding of the Temple was expected, whereupon the hidden coins would be paid to the Temple, being redemption money. Coins with which things were redeemed could be thrown in the Dead Sea or otherwise hidden in water. The matter requires further investigation. Note that if 'TSLM < *tsélem* (idol) the circumstances there and at col. v. 7 (Allegro, 41) seem to be met.

likening of any image of a living creature to an idol was a notorious part of contemporary thinking on the more enthusiastic fringe of orthodox Jews.[1] The passage in Deuteronomy[2] which requires that idols should be destroyed notwithstanding their being overlaid with silver and gold could be cited here tellingly: 'the images of their gods ye shall burn with fire, etc.' Moreover Ex xx.23, '. . . gods of silver and gods of gold ye shall not make unto you', is understood in Jewish law to forbid the making of *ornamental* figures of human beings irrespective of idolatrous worship.[3] It was notorious that Augustus and Rome, the genius of Augustus, or even Augustus himself, were objects of worship, and temples had been erected for such cults even in Palestine by Herod.[4] It seems practically certain that Pontius Pilate had just erected or dedicated a temple to the emperor Tiberius in his headquarters at Caesarea, a fact which would have been notorious.[5] Thus the beautiful little portraits of Tiberius or Augustus, completed by the inscriptions which announced what they were, were unquestionably images of gods. One must not admire them because of the text 'Turn ye not unto idols' (Lv xix.4). That Essenes, or the more scrupulous of them would not handle them or even look at them, is quite understandable.[6] To them

[1] The incident of the two rabbis and Herod's eagle on the Temple: H. Mantel, *Studies in the History of the Sanhedrin* (Cambridge, Mass. 1961), 278–9. Jos., *Ant.* XV, ix, 1–2; viii, 7, 5; *Bell. Jud.*, I, xxxiii, 2; II, x, 4.

[2] vii.25.

[3] See Maimonides's 4th negative commandment at Chavel, II, 3–4 (p. xxxvii above). It is believed that *paintings* (images on coins are in relief) were *not* within this prohibition (*ibid.*).

[4] L. R. Taylor, *The Divinity of the Roman Emperor* (Middleton, Conn. 1931), 151f., 160f., 168f., 171f., 205ff. Jos., *Bell.* I, xxi, 2–7; *Ant.* XV, ix, 5 (Loeb edn, viii, 157). On this subject the eloquence of Kennard is justified, in the context. C. Lattey, *Texts Illustrating Ancient Ruler-Worship* (London 1924). C. Habicht, *Gottmenschentum und griechische Städte* (Zetemata 14) (Munich 1956) puts the notions in historical and geographical perspective.

[5] The inscription of Pilate. A. Frova, *L'Iscrizione di Ponzio Pilato a Cesarea* (Rend. Ist. Lomb., acc. di scienze e lett., cl. di lett. 95) (Milan 1961). E. Stauffer, *Die Pilatusinschrift von Caesarea* (Erlanger Universitätsreden, N.F. 12) (Erlangen 1966). Imbert (1968) refers to studies by Nicolet and Pflaum. Pilate was both *procurator* and *praefectus*, with a plenitude of power. There is no basis, of course, for the view that Roman authorities accepted complacently the divine honours accorded to them in the eastern Mediterranean area: there are instances of their refusal (refusal was good taste in the period: references are given by R. Merkelbach, *Die Quellen des griechischen Alexanderromans* [*Zetemata* 9: München 1954], 97). We cannot attribute to Jesus or his contemporaries ignorance of the tension between the respective psychologies or political consciousnesses of the Levantine subjects on the one hand and of their Roman masters on the other.

[6] Hippolytos, ed. Wendland, iii (1916), 26 (p. 260) = A. Adam, *Antike Berichte über*

Another word for figured (coins) (*tsūrāh*) is quite possibly the original of εἰκών in our text, but though it implies any figure or representation it does *not* imply an idol, and coins which bore a *tsūrāh* were not necessarily objectionable (b. 'Erub. 31*b* = Sonc. 218).

they were forbidden objects. The *Mishnāh* and the Talmud do not list such coins amongst forbidden objects; it would have been odd if they had. Commerce would have been crippled. There is evidence, however, of scrupulous Jews through the ages refusing to look at,[1] and sometimes even to receive,[2] portrait coins. In the eyes of these enthusiasts the coin, as an 'idolatrous' object, had no commercial value whatever.[3] There could be no objection to giving away one to a Gentile (who could not thereby be encouraged in idolatry); but the point was that good money or labour had to be given away, *i.e.* wasted, in order that such coins should be available for paying the tax. From this it might appear that some benefit had been[4] had by the coins, whereas one was not permitted to have any benefit whatever from an idol, which, if obtained by accident, should be thrown in the Dead Sea. Now for this compulsory loss of money or labour no direct biblical authority was forthcoming.

It might be objected that surely *force majeure* could be pleaded, and the conscientious mind could be set at rest? What the emperor commanded would exempt the subject from scruple? But this is to ignore the Jewish mentality. If a powerful Gentile forces a Jew to keep something which his religion forbids to him, and can insist on his treating it

[1] Nahum or Menahem b. Simai: j. 'A.Z. 3, 1 (f. 42*c* top), b. 'A.Z. 50*a* = Sonc. 251. Loewe, 88, 95. Tos. Pes. 104*a*. Rashi on M.Ḳ. 25*b*. Cited by Kennard, 96, Stauffer, 126. Friedlander, *Laws and Customs of Israel*, 187, § 2 states that for the face to be forbidden it must have both eyes as well as the nose (*cf.* the action of Samuel who required a colleague to put out the eye of a head on his signet: b. R.H. 24*b* = Sonc. 106f.) and this, Dr H. J. Zimmels, Principal of Jews' College, London, writes (19 May 1967), can be traced back by stages to R. Asher b. Jehiel (thirteenth–fourteenth century), commenting on 'A.Z. III, no. 5. The statement that 'one is forbidden to gaze at the graven image of a person, as by doing so he transgresses the precept "Turn ye not unto idols" (Lv xix.4)' is traced back, Dr Zimmels explains, to b. Shab. 149*a* = Sonc. 759, which forbids looking at images. R. Menahem's piety in not looking at a coin proves that in practice the images on coins were allowed to be looked at. But the attitude persisted. A scholar of the sixteenth century in Safed would not touch or keep Venetian coins called crusads (Zimmels, in *Festschrift Krauss*, Jerusalem 1937, 182).

[2] R. Judah and the Caesarean denar (*c.* A.D. 250): 'A.Z. 6*b* = Sonc. 27 (cited by Kennard at p. 94–5). Wetstenius, *ad* Mt xxii.21.

[3] Of thirteen classes of forbidden things only things of idolatry, seventh-year produce and leaven at Passover may not be used or enjoyed or profited from in any way whatever (Lv xxv.12): b. 'A.Z. 54*b* = Sonc. 277; the difference of opinion relating to meat seethed in milk does not concern us here. *Mishnāh*, Ḳid. II, 9; b. Ḳid. 56*b* = Sonc. 281ff.; Ḥul. 114*b*–116*a* = Sonc. 630–5.

[4] No benefit may be had from idols even though they are no longer in worship, and *e.g.* have been used to pave streets: that was the pious view. If by paying a coin in tax one had acquired rights or immunities one was clearly obtaining benefit from the payment.

---

die Essener (Berlin 1961), 47–8: ἕτεροι γὰρ αὐτῶν τὰ ὑπὲρ τὸ δέον ἀσκοῦσιν, ὡς μηδὲ νόμισμα βαστάζειν, λέγοντες μὴ δεῖν εἰκόνα ἢ φέρειν ἢ ὁρᾶν ἢ ποιεῖν (cited by Rist, 324). Dupont-Sommer, 43 n. 4.

as valuable (*i.e.* hold him responsible for it) the Jew's acceptance of the fact that he will be held liable is tantamount to his accepting ownership of it. But if the object belongs exclusively to the Gentile, and the Jew does not accept any responsibility for its loss, the position is otherwise.[1] Those, therefore, who actually objected to the imperial coinage but were confronted with an enforcible demand to pay taxes in it were in a genuine dilemma so far as the *Torāh* was concerned.

No one will suggest that the questioners did not know their Bible. Qo viii.2 has escaped all except Abrahams, Montefiore and the pious and learned Herbert Loewe, whose praiseworthy book on this topic[2] was given a cool reception.[3] But it will hardly have escaped those who had the courage to beard Jesus on the subject. We have already seen how the text appears to direct attention to the ten commandments—at any rate that is how rabbis took it, if not actually at that time, at least not long afterwards. *Ecclesiastes* is a respectable biblical source, relied upon in several places in the *Mishnāh*. Amongst the Dead Sea Scrolls a longish passage was found closely agreeing with the M.T., but unfortunately breaking off before it reached the end of chapter vii. There was a question about the book's canonicity, which the School of Shammai doubted, but the other view has prevailed.[4] Amongst the commandments believed to be referred to by the verse were the first, the second, and the third: for God 'spoke all these words...'. It was possible to argue that the word 'king' must be read twice in two senses: read as 'God' it informs us that the supreme king must be obeyed and should have no rival. What the questioners objected to is not the idolatry of the Romans, nor the Roman cults, but the tendency to transfer to Caesar, a more than life-size figure apt for hero-worship

[1] The reason is that by accepting responsibility (even unwillingly) the Jew has a financial interest in its safety (or possession) and therefore to that extent it is 'his'. See b. Pes. 5*b*–6*a* = Sonc. 20–1. Maimonides, *Mishneh Torāh*, III (Seasons), V (Leavened Bread), iv.2–4 (trans. Gandz and Klein, p. 337–8).

[2] H. Loewe, '*Render unto Caesar*'. *Religion and Political Loyalty in Palestine* (Cambridge 1940): 141 pp. Loewe was Reader in Rabbinics at Cambridge at the time of his death in 1940. The book repays careful study, going, as it does, further than Abrahams; but the following tentative conclusions are unsound, *viz.* that Christ's attitude was unclear; that the text is wrong ('gaze upon the face *of a coin*'); that Christ turned the coin over. He also misunderstands (as does Kennard) the meaning of the temple-tax pericope, on which see above.

[3] Grant, *Ang. Th. R.*, 22 (1940), 226; Enslin, *J. Bib. Lit.*, 54 (1940), 430–1; Rist, *J. Rel.*, 21 (1941), 200–2; Mattingly, *J. Rom. St.*, 32 (1942), 142f. *Cf.* T. M. Parker, *Christianity and the State* (*cit. sup.*), p. 18 n. 5 (reserve). Loewe is ignored by standard commentaries.

[4] *Mishnāh*, 'Eduy. 5.3. The story of the objections to Ecclesiastes and its attaining 'canonicity' is told from mishnaic and talmudic sources by H. E. Ryle, *The Canon of the Old Testament* 2nd edn. (London 1899), 206–9; S. Zeitlin at *Proc. Am. Ac. Jew. Res.* 3 (1932), 121–58.

(itself a well-known instance of 'idolatry' in rabbinical thought), part of the obedience that the Jews, by reason of the covenant, owed to God, or if not to God at any rate to the kings who actually ruled in the Land of Israel. God's commands were *prima facie* comprehensive. Qo viii.2 could be construed to mean that there is no king other than God,[1] with the result that Caesar's commands to pay taxes are a nullity. But which interpretation of Qo viii.2 was right: or could both constructions be used? One could not know until a specific case arose—and it had arisen.

Jesus recognises and resents the examination to which he is submitted, and it is conceivable that he said τί με πειράζετε; in order to suggest that an adequate knowledge of scripture would have obviated the difficulty. In polite language he says φέρετέ μοι δηνάριον. φέρετε implies that respectable Jews will not have a *denarius* on their persons, and one will have to be fetched (from the less pious, presumably!). It also shows that he did not believe that it was wicked to handle or display the coin. ἵνα ἴδω, which Matthew and Luke neglect, has a substantial meaning. Jesus wants to 'mark the mouth of the king'. *Piy-*, 'mouth', indicates the source of command; it also can mean a side or edge, especially the 'face' of a precious stone (*'Āvot d^e R. Nathan*, ch. 28): *piy-mélech* is metaphorically the king's proclamation, and literally both the king's mouth and the profile on the actual coin ('heads', in fact!). This appears comically as if it were an answer to the questioners' οὐ βλέπεις εἰς πρόσωπον which is (oddly) not perfectly idiomatic for 'you are no respecter of persons'.[2] Of course, there can be little doubt that it was *not* in order to answer the questioners' compliment, but rather to enact, to mime, the biblical instruction. And quite naturally his next task is positively to identify the mouth as that of the earthly sovereign.

JESUS'S RESPONSUM

Having acted to show his literal reliance on Qo viii.2 he speaks in conformity to it: 'Whose image and superscription is it?' Not only does the coin reveal the 'mouth' but its owner has something to relate about his identity, inscribed around it. For example, T. CAESAR DIVI AVG. F. AVGVSTVS. The coin which, as Matthew correctly, as if a commentator, reminds us, was alone fit to pay the *census*, was not merely 'of Caesar' in the sense that it was issued by a Caesar, a Roman imperial coin, but

[1] The opposite is claimed: Jn xix.12–15. Ecclesiastes was himself a king: 1.12.

[2] C. E. B. Cranfield, *The Gospel according to Saint Mark* (Cambridge 1959), 370. For 'respect of persons' (*massū' pāniym*, 'lifting up of the face') = partiality see, *e.g. Mishnāh*, 'Āvot iv, 22.

was a thing unknown to Jewish Law, a thing of the Gentiles, a thing appertaining to the king in the sense that it was ordered by the king (like the *census* itself). The coin bore the *piy-mélech*, but it also existed by reason of the *piy-mélech*. Jesus looks upon the face of the king, whose identity with the foreign source of law he establishes to his satisfaction (coin 'of Caesar' does not mean coin of Tiberius, but coin of the Roman administrative and political dominion), and proceeds to observe the king's commands. Public baths, bridges, aqueducts, and gymnasia were things of the Gentiles in much the same sense, *i.e.* that the *Torāh* did not provide for them, ignored them: but of course they were not backed with jurisdiction, compulsion, they were merely a matter of taste and style. The coin serves as a perfect illustration of the class of business which falls right outside the *Torāh* but which is the proper province of all kings from Ezra onwards, Jewish and non-Jewish alike. The Law of God does not prescribe how city corporations are to collect their dues, but no one would suggest that because such rules are not in scripture all such arrangements are *ultra vires* and void. For this very reason the Pharisees went a very long way in their attempts to attach practical and prudential rules by slender threads to Old Testament texts of various kinds, often with dubious relevance and appropriateness. Their starting point was the belief that the actual practices of which they approved must have been valid, and that therefore the divine Law must somehow have authorised them. Had the coin shown to Jesus been other than that of a Roman emperor he could as well have said ἀπόδοτε τὰ τοῦ βασιλέως τῷ βασιλεῖ, the τά referring not to the coins, or even taxes, but to the 'rights'[1] of the king in general. Just as τὰ τοῦ θεοῦ cannot mean only tithes and oblations, so τὰ Καίσαρος does not refer to taxes as such. This fits well with the Jewish legal point we have already observed about where Gentiles insist upon custody of forbidden things. If we accept that these coins are, or represent, Jews' debts or duties to Caesar, to that extent the scrupulous can safely acquire figured coins on the footing that though they are in Jews' possession they at all times belong (potentially) to Caesar. Thus one is not really deriving profit from them at all. This reasoning would be very neat and would coincide with the basic requirement to obey the sovereign's behests. Now as it happens there is a perfect biblical precedent[2] for distinguishing the rights of the king and the rights of God.

[1] ἀποδοῦναι does not mean 'give back' (as Cullmann) but 'render' in the sense of 'make over' as is proper, due (Stauffer, 129; also Bornkamm, Schnackenburg). See with ναῦλον Aristophanes, *Ran.* 270; φερνήν fourth-century B.C. papyrus from Elephantine. *Cf.* the Lat. *reddere* in the same sense, *et horrenti tunicam non reddere servo* (Juv. I, 93).

[2] In purely historical terms the episode can be approached sceptically—but that is a

Both can be the object of dispute, and Jehoshaphat (at 2 Ch xix.11) when setting up a court of justice carefully distinguishes the individuals who are to be chairmen, so to speak, respectively in 'matters of the Lord' (*d*^{e}*var-yhvh* = τὰ τοῦ θεοῦ) and in 'matters of the king' (*d*^{e}*var-ha-mélech* = τὰ τοῦ βασιλέως, here *placita coronae*). The distinction reminds one of the judicial functions in early Tudor England of the Archbishop of Canterbury (often also Chancellor) and the Chief Justice of the King's Bench. But the point is that under Jehoshaphat these two recognised classes of rights could not conflict, and no clash of jurisdictions was contemplated.

Such royal commands as are not repugnant to the *Torāh* are binding upon the subject under Qo viii.2 (*cf.* 5).[1]

There is some virtue in a doubt which someone has expressed, whether Jesus *did* utter the name of Caesar, or the name (or a periphrasis for the name) of God. We have concentrated here, as did the evangelists, upon what Jesus *meant*. But, if any importance were to hang upon the actual words, one might think it well worthy of conjecture that Jesus formulated his *responsum* in mishnaic Hebrew in the same manner as R. 'Eliezer of Bertota,[2] namely *t*^{e}*nū lo mishelo v*^{e} *t*^{e}*nū lo mishelo*,[3] which neatly avoids mentioning either name, and could be translated into Greek only as we have it before us.

The original meaning is therefore not an evasion, nor an equivocation, but simply 'Obey the commands of the king and obey (thereby) the commandments of God'. There is no dichotomy between God and Caesar, nor between the 'world' and the kingdom of God,[4] but a straightforward application of the pregnant biblical verse. Obedience even to non-Jewish rulers is within one's comprehensive obedience to

[1] Cornelius, *ubi cit.*: observa os, id est praecepta regis, sed magis observa juramenta, quibus obstrictus es Deo, ut si rex aliquid Deo contrarium praecipiat, dicas: obedire magis oportet Deo, quam hominibus.

[2] See below, n. 4.

[3] Literally, 'Give to him from the things that are his and give to Him the things that are His.' At the first 'him' it is conceivable that Jesus pointed to the coin.

[4] As St Ambrose and Severus of Antioch, for example, seem to have thought. Compare the opinion of a contemporary of R. 'Aḳiba at *Mishnāh*, 'Āvot, III, 7 (Danby, 451; Blackman, IV, 509; noticed by C. Schöttgen at *Hor. Hebr.*, *ad Mt* xxii.21: 'Render unto Him what is His (*ten lo mishelo*) for thou and what thou hast are His, as [king] David has said . . . (1 Ch xxix.14).' The maxim is well treated by Cornelius, *ubi cit.* He quotes Ambrose, *epist.* 3 (Migne, *PL* 16, 999.19): respondeo: Noli te gravare, Imperator, ut putes te in ea, quae divina sunt, imperiale aliquod jus habere. Noli te extollere, sed si vis diutius imperare, esto Deo subditus. Scriptum est: *Quae Dei Deo, quae Caesari Caesari.* Ad imperatorem palatia pertinent, ad sacerdotem ecclesiae. Publicorum tibi moenium ius commissum est, non sacrorum.

different matter. W. F. Albright, 'The judicial reform of Jehoshaphat', *Alexander Marx Jub. Vol., Eng. Sec.* (New York 1950), 61–82.

God. The Pauline and Petrine passages can easily be reconciled with this and could with real plausibility be traced back to this attitude. If indeed Caesar's orders implied disobedience to any one of the divine commandments, Caesar's order was not binding upon the conscience and consequences follow which are outside the scope of this present study, but the promises of God will not be jeopardised thereby,[1] because (of course) the promises do not relate to terrestrial existence and as Caesar cannot give paradise so he cannot take it away.

In short Jesus taught what oriental teachers (especially Hindu and Muslim scholars)[2] have taught for millennia and still teach, namely that the ruler may pass decrees and orders to which we owe implicit obedience, provided that in obeying them we do not disobey God. As S. Rosenne has recently written in an excellent survey,[3] 'Jewish law, by its very nature and in the light of its very purpose, has the concept of the limitation of sovereignty built into it'. In other words laws passed and enforced by human beings are valid in conscience and in law provided they are not repugnant to the divine and revealed Law.

There is a *responsum* of the Prophet Muḥammad which is worth comparing with this. A woman whose mother had died without performing her vow to go on pilgrimage asked the Prophet whether she

[1] It is important to realise that the temple-tax episode teaches, not so much that Jesus was not liable to the tax but that action should be taken so as to prevent opponents from being provoked into sin. See the discussion of Mt xvii.27 in the light of 1 P ii.13 by C. Spicq, 'La Iª Petri et le témoignage évangélique de saint Pierre', *St. Th.* 20 (1966) 37ff., at p. 50–1. Above, p. 262.

[2] So far as Muslims are concerned the matter is beyond doubt. Legislation contrary to the express provisions of the Koran is nearly impossible in Muslim countries and legislation contrary to the opinions of specialists in *fiqh* is rare and cautious. The Koranic passages relevant to this theme are iv.59, 80; v.92; xlii.10, 13; lix.7. See Badr al-Dīn al 'Ayni, '*Umdat al-Qāri* XVII, 314; XIV, 221, cited in S. Mahmassani, *The Philosophy of Jurisprudence in Islam* (Leiden 1961), 106, 109, 126–9. In fact in Iran, where it is not constitutional to promulgate any law contrary to the sacred precepts of Islam and laws laid down by the Prophet, an attempt was made recently to reform the law of divorce by an interesting expedient. The earlier law had been based on the Ithnā 'Asharī school. The means adopted were a statutory alteration of the marriage document in the form of a condition of the contract and an irrevocable power of attorney for the wife to execute a divorce. Thus lip service is paid to the *sharī'a*, and the husband's prerogative is retained in form if not in substance. (Iran) Family Protection Act, 1967: see D. Hinchcliffe at 17 *ICLQ* (1968), 519. On the normal identity of political and religious society before our era see the remarks of E. Pritsch, 'Vom Wesen des islamischen Rechts', in K. Bünger and H. Trimborn, *Religiöse Bindungen in frühen und in orientalischen Rechten* (Wiesbaden 1952), 37: not to speak of orientals, Greeks and Romans too regarded the State as the focus of the national religious cult. For traditional Hindu ideas see Derrett, *Religion, Law and the State in India* (London 1968), 167, 191.

[3] 'Jewish law' in A. Larson, C. W. Jenks, edd., *Sovereignty within the Law* (New York and London 1965), 141ff. at p. 163. See also *ibid.* 164 and S. Baron, *Social and Religious History of the Jews*, 2nd edn, I (1952), 74.

needed to perform this vow on her mother's behalf. Answering affirmatively the Prophet pointed out that if the woman would have paid her mother's *pecuniary* debts so, *a fortiori*, 'Repay God's debts, for God is more entitled to redemption'.[1] The obligation to God must in any case be fulfilled.

LUKE xxiii.2

There has been some discussion whether the contentions made against Jesus before Pilate were basically genuine or not: 'We found this man . . . hindering us from giving tribute to Caesar. . . .' No one can read the text in Luke without grasping that Luke intended this particular allegation to be understood as false witness. But could any colour of justification be offered?[2]

As our passage appears in the synoptic gospels it is unquestionably evidence that Christ advised everyone to pay tribute to Caesar as Caesar. The Church must have valued it for this reason, if not for others. But could any competent bystander argue that Jesus's reply tended to support those who argued against Caesar's taxing power? The cryptic nature of the reply, especially when heard by one whose mind was already prejudiced, might lead to many conflicting interpretations as it has obviously done down to our own day. But if we return to Qo viii.2, of which Christ's *dictum* is an application, a theory or principle presents itself which could, paradoxically, be understood in the way stated.

The command of the king is to be observed, and that out of regard for the oath of God. Caesar does not rule the Jew because of his *imperium*, his *potestas* as the Romans see it; he has no *jurisdictio* except so far as God gives it to him. He is God's agent *de facto*, and his demands have no more validity than God's law allows. God's relationship to Caesar can be posited in several ways, provided it is realised that God is at all times superior to Caesar.[3]

[1] al-'Ayni, *'Umdat al-Qāri* X, 212, 214, quoted by S. Mahmassani (*op. cit.*), 81.

[2] As Kennard thought, 139. That the charge that Jesus prevented payment of tribute to Caesar (Lk xxiii.2) might have been proffered *bona fide* is the opinion of W. De Vries, *De Dood van Jezus* (Kampen 1967), 30–4 (in his opinion the answer ἀπόδοτε τὰ Καίσαρος . . . was intentionally ambiguous, and meant 'Return imperial things to the emperor and your *thanks* to God'). S. G. F. Brandon, *The Trial of Jesus of Nazareth* (London 1968) at p. 67, 144–6, insists that Jesus taught decisively that tribute should not be paid to Rome, whereas Mark deliberately distorted the account in order to hide the fact that Jesus was a revolutionary rabble-leader. The superficiality of this view of the factual situation, let alone of the pericope itself, need not be emphasised here.

[3] Abrahams cites *Tanḥuma* on Gn viii.16, *Noah* 10, ed. Buber, 33. Note Pr viii.10–21, esp. 15: 'by Me kings reign'. So Rm xiii.1–7, 1 P ii. 13–17 (Selwyn, *First Ep. of St. Peter*, 1946, 172–3) and 1 Clem iv.5 may be taken. There is a negative as well as a

R. Nᵉhūnᵉyāh, who is believed to have flourished between about A.D. 70 and 130, said:[1] 'He that takes upon himself the yoke of the *Torāh*, from him shall be taken away the yoke of the kingdom (*'ol malᵉchūt*) and the yoke of worldly care; but he that casts off the yoke of the *Torāh*, upon him shall be laid the yoke of the kingdom and the yoke of worldly care.' Ignoring the *double entendre*, we gather that those who are obedient to God's laws need fear no molestation from the kings of this world, whom God appoints.

Where a conflict might arise between *census*, or any other tribute, and God's right to, for example, tithes and the Temple half-shekel, Caesar's right must take second place. Occasions might well arise when the tax-collectors had no right, even in Jesus's own view of their situation, to enforce payment. In that sense Jesus's teachings were contrary (as of course they were bound to be) to the constitutional law of the Roman empire. Many a case which is good in principle is spoiled by perjury and bad pleading: and the allegation at Lk xxiii.2 is an example of this. In reality Christ allows a limited place to Caesar, a proposition which Caesar, on principle, cannot possibly accept until he himself, of course, accepts Christ.[2]

[1] *Mishnāh*, 'Āvot III. 5 (Danby, 450; Blackman, IV, 508).

[2] When I thought (as many had before me) that the answer to the problems lay in the coin I communed much with numismatists. Mr Carson of the British Museum and Drs Sutherland and Kraay of the Ashmolean Museum gave me their time and advice and showed me coins and reference works. I am much obliged to them. Dr Zimmels (mentioned above) was exceedingly prompt and complete in his reports on the relevant questions of Jewish piety, and greatly increased my confidence. Dr A. D. H. Bivar helped me by many an apposite reflection on the pericope.

---

positive way of putting the same matter. G. Dalman was right in his analysis (*Words of Jesus*, Edinburgh 1902, 138): 'His verdict . . . shows that he did not consider the political dominance of the Romans to be any infringement of the sovereignty of God. It is not the rule of foreigners over the nation, but the rule of all ungodly powers in the inner life of men, that the sovereignty of God aims at removing. . . .' And, we may add, if Caesar supports the ungodly powers Caesar is acting *ultra vires*. Abrahams would agree. See also Philo, *Leg. ad Caium*, xxxii, 236 (Colson, X, 123). To the same effect Maimonides, *Book of Divine Commandments*, Chavel, I, 297–8—but note that the privileges of the kings (commandment 173) are due to their having been chosen in strict accord with the *Torāh* (Dt xvii.15, etc.). The last word may remain with St. Chrysostomos: σὺ δὲ ὅταν ἀκούσῃς ἀπόδος τὰ Καίσαρος Καίσαρι, ἐκεῖνα γίνωσκε λέγειν αὐτὰ μόνον, τὰ μηδὲν τὴν εὐσέβειαν παραβλάπτοντα. ὡς ἐάν τι τοιοῦτον ᾖ, οὐκέτι Καίσαρος, ἀλλὰ τοῦ διαβόλου φόρος ἐστὶ καὶ τέλος τὸ τοιοῦτον.

CHAPTER FIFTEEN

Herod's Oath and the Baptist's Head

KLOSTERMANN'S 'MARKUSEVANGELIUM'[1] reveals how the depressing scepticism about Mk vi.17–29 persists. He cites Windisch who concluded his enlightening essay (1917)[2] with the words 'Nur Phantasie würde zum Ziel führen, besser ein Ziel vorspiegeln'. Many would be inclined to suppose that the gospel retains an imaginative elaboration of an incorrect version of an event of which Josephus gives an unverifiable account (*Ant.* XIV, v, 2). That the formerly supposed improbable elements in the gospel version, namely the princess's dance and the lordly promise, could be paralleled from Athenaeus and Herodotus did not do more than verify the plausibility of the folk-tale aspect of the version. It is difficult to doubt, however, but that when the pericope was inserted into Mark, and accepted in substance by Matthew, the Church believed that the story, down to its details, was true and edifying; if the version contained an obviously improbable feature it would have been recognised and either explained or ejected. Let the style of the pericope be what it may, persons able to influence the use (and thus the content) of the text, some of whom had Josephus available to them, were satisfied that it contained no obvious absurdity. Klausner's reconciliation of Josephus with the gospel[3]—a reconciliation along lines acceptable to many—leaves one element (which he regards as legendary) undiscussed, but its discussion is overdue, for the pericope contains a glaring curiosity. It is Herod's oath.

It is desirable, in the interests of clarity, to state shortly at the outset what the position was regarding that oath. The position is so curious that it cannot but throw light on the original intention of the author who adopted the incident into the gospel. Many may feel that the very existence of this curiosity throws light on the genuineness of the facts

[1] 4th edn, Tübingen 1950, 58–60.
[2] 'Kleine Beiträge zur evangelischen Überlieferung. 1. Zum Gastmahl des Antipas': *ZNW* 18 (1917) 73–81.
[3] J. Klausner, *Jesus of Nazareth, his Life, Times, and Teaching*, transl. H. Danby (New York, Macmillan 1959), 248ff. J. Blinzler in *Herodes Antipas und Jesus Christus. Die Stellung des Heilands zu seinem Landesherrn* (Stuttgart 1947) is cited below.

alleged: authors of legends do not normally introduce into their fabrication embarrassing and discordant elements without explanation.

Let us first accept certain facts, assuming that the story is substantially true:

1. Pharisaism was the leading school of interpretation of Holy Scripture,[1] and Pharisees claimed numerous *ḥaveriym* amongst the influential citizens both of Judaea and Galilee; but Pharisees were not the majority of the groups exercising authority, and will not have been dominant in Antipas's court (Mk iii.6). Antipas's advisers on Jewish Law will have been inclined to a more literally strict (and thus often more morally lax) view of the *Torāh*, and will have included some Sadducees. That his guests at the banquet included Pharisees can hardly be doubted; that the majority of the orthodox Jewish guests were Sadducees or inclined away from Pharisaism is virtually certain.

2. Pharisees were on the whole not well disposed towards John the Baptist, nor could he count upon Sadducees as admirers.[2] John's following lay chiefly with the public at large, though he had made something of a conquest with Antipas himself.

3. John's success with the multitude and his propaganda against Antipas's marriage would tend to arouse fears of a political and international character.

4. At constitutional law, whether of a Jewish[3] or a non-Jewish nature, acceptable *prima facie* in all quarters, John had risked a death sentence by his contempt of convention in dealing with the lawfully constituted authority,[4] and in stirring up popular discontent against Antipas.

We may now proceed to the oath. The notion (in a late work noticed by A. Mingana),[5] that Antipas swore by the emperor's life is to be rejected as improbable, since the oath was not taken in such solemn circumstances as to require a deviation from the customary profanity known to the inhabitants, who were for ever taking oaths for all sorts of purposes. The oath must have been taken by the name of God,

[1] For the standing and claims of the Pharisees and literature on them see now M. Gertner, 'The terms pharisaioi, gazarenoi, hupokritai: their semantic complexity and conceptual correlation', *BSOAS* 26 (1963), 245–68. For Jesus's relationship to them see above, pp. 75–6, 84, 275ff.; below, pp. 370, 379.

[2] Mk xi.27–33.

[3] Jos i.18b; 2 S xvi.5, 7, 9. b. San. 49*a* = Sonc. 326; *Mishnāh*, San. IX, 3. Maimonides, *Mishneh Torāh*, XIV (Judges), V (Kings and Wars), iii, 8 (trans. Hershman, 213–14). The sentence must be carried out, according to rabbinical law, by *decapitation*. Brandon's comment (*Trial*, 1968, 48) on the death of James (Ac xii.2) that the implication is that he was put to death as a political offender is correct (one could add that this is the point of Hb xi.37): but that does not prove, of course, that any real offence against the law of the State was actually committed by the condemned men.

[4] On the Jewish law on this subject in general see above p. 335.

[5] 'A new life of John the Baptist' in *Woodbrooke Studies* 1 (Cambridge 1927).

most probably under the cover of some customary euphemism.[1] Our text says that Antipas refused to ignore the request 'because of his oath and the guests'. The reason is altogether extraordinary and suggestive. The usual explanation of our own day, that Antipas was afraid to look small in front of such and so many important witnesses,[2] cannot be accepted. He is depicted, from this episode, as a weak-willed character: but for this there is no corroborating evidence.

Let us examine the position from two angles, *A* from the point of view of a scholar of *c.* A.D. 30, and *B* from the point of view of a scholar of *c.* A.D. 130.

A

1. The oath cannot have obliged Antipas, situated as he was, to take away the life of the Baptist. A man who swears to do something which turns out to be to his disadvantage can for practical purposes absolve himself from his oath. If a penance was necessary for breach of the oath Antipas was rich enough to pay for it.

2. Strict Pharisees would regard the breach of any oath as sinful; Sadducees would regard it as worthy of the death penalty. But, as we have said, Antipas could perform a penance (if he was so scrupulous), and even the Pharisees admitted that kings were not amenable to human courts.[3]

3. Contrary to the Sadducees' opinion, Pharisees were developing the doctrine that oath-takers could be released from their oaths (as they could be released from vows) for defect in the intention. Assuming that this new doctrine was admitted to be valid, debate would continue upon the question who might release the oaths of kings. Their relations with their superiors (if any) and with one another frequently depended upon no stronger foundation than their oaths.

4. In view of the uncertainties and conflicts mentioned above there was no question but that his oath did not oblige Antipas to put the Baptist to death. The handing over of the Baptist alive would not have complied with the request of the girl, and there were difficulties about enslaving Jews.[4] That the Baptist's head might be valued at more than the half of the 'kingdom' was impossible in view of the fact that Antipas

[1] *Mishnāh*, Shev. IV, 13 (Danby, *Mishnāh*, 415), b. Shev. 35*a*–36*a*, Sonc. 202ff. S. Belkin, *Philo and the Oral Law* (Cambridge, Mass. 1940), 141–3; F. X. Kortleitner, *Archaeologiae Biblicae Summarium* (Oeniponte 1906), 151–4.

[2] The present writer feels it unnecessary to refer in detail to the views of previous commentators, most of whom lean to this view of Herod's conduct.

[3] After Herod the Great's time: Josephus, *Ant.* XIV, ix, 4; after Alexander Jannaeus's time: b. San. 19*a*, *b* = Sonc. 98–9. Maimonides, *op. cit.* XIV, I, ii, 5 (trans. p. 8).

[4] Herod the Great criticised: Josephus, *Ant.* XVI, i, 1 (Niese iv, 4–5).

did not own the Baptist. The oath was an oath to give, but was converted by the request into an oath to perform, to act and give.

5. Since no scholar could understand how Antipas would be moved by the oath alone to give the Baptist's head (the very idea is ridiculous), the phrase 'because of his oath and the guests' acquires a new significance. It was because of the way in which the guests reacted to his situation that he acted as he did. This is what is indicated.

B

1. A Jewish scholar of *c.* A.D. 130 will have accepted the Pharisaical doctrines now enshrined in the *Mishnāh* and developed therefrom in the Talmud. To him the oath is typically an oath of exaggeration and was not binding at all, *ipso facto*.[1] It was not a serious promise, and could readily have been ignored.

2. If it were to be taken as a serious promise, the intention was defective because Antipas when he made the oath could not be understood to have willed to do anything in itself contrary to God's will. An oath plainly contrary to any commandment is no oath, and is null and void.[2] It is against God's will (as interpreted by the *Pharisees*) that a man not under any criminal charge shall be put to death to satisfy a girl's request, without any trial and without any formalities. According to the *Torāh* two or three witnesses are necessary, and a decision by a properly constituted court. No one can take an oath to put an 'innocent' person to death: it is no oath.

3. If one who had taken, in ignorance, an oath which turned out to appear to oblige him to transgress any fundamental provision of the *Torāh*, such as Lv xix.18 ('thou shalt love thy neighbour as thyself'), was troubled in conscience, a *bet-din* must release him from his oath. Developed Talmudic law understood that any rabbi might release.[3]

4. At Talmudic law (see b. Giṭṭin 74*b*) a man may release himself, *without consulting a rabbi*, from a vow (and therefore from an oath) if failure to perform it would deprive him of a benefit anticipated. An example would be self-release from a vow such as this: 'Korban be anything which you might have had from me unless you give me this house': by mentally releasing the stipulation one becomes free to benefit (*e.g.*

[1] R. Mari said: We have also learnt thus (in a *Mishnāh*): Four vows did the Sages permit (to be deemed null and void without absolution: b. Ned. 20*b*): vows of urging (by merchants), vows of hyperbole, vows made unwittingly, and vows accidentally unfulfilled. So b. Shev. 28*b* = Sonc. 155f.

[2] *Mishnāh*, Shev. III, 6 (*cf.* 4) (Danby, 412); b. Shev. 27*a* = Sonc. 145ff.

[3] *Mishnāh*, Ned. IX, 1–5 (Danby, 264–5), especially 4 (R. Meir: *flor. c.* A.D. 140–65). Oaths (like vows) annulled: b. Ket. 77*b* = Sonc. 488. Moses absolved God from his vow(!): Midr. R., Exod. XLIII. 4 = Sonc. 498–9 (on Ex xxxii.11). Maimonides, *op. cit.* VI (Asseverations), I, xii, 12 (trans. Klein, p. 53).

maintain) the person so spoken to. In our case Antipas was advantaged socially and morally by recompensing the dancer: forgoing his right to reward her (thus remaining in her debt) he could have annulled his oath.

From these two expositions it appears that *at all times material to a study of this pericope and its history* the oath taken by Antipas would be well known to scholars to be of no sufficient effect to lead to the Baptist's death. Would non-scholars have thought differently? Perhaps amongst Greeks, but not amongst Jews, for the custom of the *'amme hā-'ārets* was to take oaths upon all sorts of occasions and to absolve themselves automatically; and a rascal like Antipas could not be expected to be more scrupulous than the general public. But the presence of the guests and the nature of the occasion made all the difference, and this we must investigate. Origen, whose general contact with living Jewish tradition is evident, notes that the reference to the guests warns us that not the oath alone but also the presence of the guests was responsible for John's death.[1]

From this summary it appears that if the episode of Salome is legendary the legend has been implausibly and embarrassingly constructed. Let us now see whether this doubt throws light on Mk ix. 13*b*, *c*. 'And they did to him whatever they wished, according as it is written concerning him' obviously looks back to our pericope. The apparent reference was (as Klausner emphatically accepts) to 1 K xix.2, 10, 14. Let us inspect these verses and compare them with our story—divergencies will be to the advantage of our story's authenticity, but they need not invalidate the justice of Jesus's comment.

We note with satisfaction that Jezebel swears by false gods (*cf.* Judith's oaths at Jdt xi.7; xii.4). We notice that her oath that Elijah should be slain with the *sword* was not fulfilled because God enabled him to escape; could it be argued that whenever Elijah reappeared such a fate would befall him? It is impossible at present to deny this possibility. That the messianic age would repeat in detail the experiences of the biblical pattern undoubtedly existed as a theory, which Paul, for example, shared.[2] Klausner[3] insists that John modelled his life upon Elijah down to the closest details. The wicked queen's enmity and the oath are common to both stories. Another coincidence is the ambivalent

[1] At Migne, *PG* 13, 472 (col. 896). A similar point is made by Photius of Constantinople (*c.* 820–91), see J. Reuss, *Matthäus-Kommentare aus der Griechischen Kirche* (*TuU* 61) (Berlin 1957), 311.

[2] Illustrations: 2 Co iii.7–11; Ga iv.21–31; similar (?): Heb. ix.18–28; xi.32 to xii.6; xiii.11–12. The attitude of mind is illustrated in Jn i.46; vii.41, 52 on Nazareth or Galilee as a whole being a possible home of the Messiah.

[3] *Op. cit.* 248. See also G. Richter, 'Bist du Elias?' (Jn i.21)', *BZ* 6 (1962), 79–92, 238–56. C. Kopp (*Holy Places*, 140–1) plausibly suggests that John may have confronted Antipas like Elijah (1 K. xviii.1, 18).

attitude of Ahab towards Elijah and that of Antipas towards John; we note too that the idolatress Jezebel is ambiguously but distinctly accused of 'whoredoms' (2 K ix.22). Victims of Antipas might well accept the theory that he was a reincarnation of Ahab, and Herodias of Jezebel; but it is enough if they noted the resemblances.

The divergencies between our pericope and Mk ix.13 are, however, plain. Not only did Jezebel not succeed, but there was no question of her utilising Ahab himself for her purpose. The main features of the story, the lordly promise, and the prize for dancing, even the banquet, all are missing in the supposed prototype. The true correspondence appears to lie in the fact that but for the will of God, exerted where necessary for the divine purpose, prophets are at the disposal of the earthly powers, and are liable to suffer at their will and pleasure. On the whole there seems no likelihood that a tradition of Jesus's comments on John's death produced or foreshadowed a circumstantial account of how it all happened. A forger, intent on reproducing a pattern conformable to the Elijah story, would have made the oath the oath of Herodias and not of Herod.

Jesus's written authority can hardly have been other than biblical. For this reason the source behind Ps. Philo, *Bibl. Ant.* 48 (trans. M. R. James, 1917, 59, 210–11) cannot be relied upon implicitly. The text asserts that Phinehas, returning as Elijah (see above, p. 188), shall taste of death. Popular belief in the atoning power of the death of saints (Ps cxvi.15) may account for this notion.

THE OCCASION

The mistake about the identity of Herodias's first husband seems unimportant. The age of the girl perhaps less so. If she were about 14 the needs both of the occasion and of propriety would have been met.[1] Antipas is unlikely to have been so far intoxicated as not to be able to comprehend what he was about. The information, which John's disciples appear to have had from the men under the command of the officer who carried out the sentence,[2] sounded bizarre to them, as it must have done ever since: but that does not argue that the participants in the drama were too intoxicated to cope adequately with the situation. The likening of the tetrarchal court to that of the Persian emperor (by

[1] So rightly C. Kopp, *Holy Places* (1963), 138–9.

[2] Windisch *art. cit.* 80. W. L. Knox, *Sources of the Synoptic Gospels*, Cambridge 1953, I, 50f. suggests a 'History of the Herods' as the source. Our *v.* 29 is evidently intended to provide the authentication of the story. The fact that the disciples buried a πτῶμα, that the Baptist was decapitated, no doubt had a symbolic significance (see D. Daube, *New Testament and Rabbinic Judaism*, London 1956, 309f.), but that is beyond our present concern.

deliberate allusion to Est v.3, 6; vii.2), a feature which the author of the pericope accepted with dramatic effect,[1] was hardly out of keeping with the frustrated ambitions of that court. Antipas cannot have doubted that he could fulfil his oath. He, as the host, offered remuneration to the young dancer both for himself and his guests (who in view of his and her rank could not remunerate her themselves); and his act was a compliment to Herodias: that the girl should have asked her mother what to ask for was entirely fitting and is a plausible element favourable to the authenticity of the story. What he expected to be asked for was jewellery, or better still the release of prisoners, relief of the people from taxation, or something auspicious. Herodias's odious request was absolutely enabled to be made by the oath. Without the oath and the embarrassment it would be likely to cause at that time and place she would not have dared to make the suggestion, and Antipas would merely have rejected it.

We are told the occasion was that of the king's birthday: the suggestion which is at first sight very plausible, namely that the feast was that of Purim,[2] does not, on further reflection, turn out to fit our story adequately. The connection with Esther has no doubt occurred at some point in the transmission, but that is too slender a basis upon which to embellish still further a highly dramatised tale.

Birthdays were days of rejoicing.[3] The day a man was released from the womb, the day he obtained life, he should release others, for example prisoners (as Pilate is said to have released a prisoner in celebration of the Jews' release from Egypt), and should grant life (as Esther's boon gave life), for example by reprieving condemned persons from their death sentences.[4] Not invariable was this respect for a birthday or similar auspicious day, but the exceptions were often emphatic, and we

[1] Compare Mk vi.21 with Est i.3. For the type of reward see 1 K xiii.8.

[2] On Purim itself see above, p. 145. The suggestion was made by A. Guilding, ***Fourth Gospel***, 168, as she feels the whole passage in Mark belongs to the Passover and the Spring, but her main argument rests on the similarities of this pericope with Esther.

[3] γενέσια means only 'birthday' in Jewish sources, but can mean 'anniversary of death' in classical sources: S. Krauss, 'Zur griechischen und lateinischen Lexicographie aus jüdischen Quellen', *Byz. Zeits.* II, 3–4 (reprinted Leipzig 1893), 538–9. Censorinus, *De Die Natali* (ed. Hultsch, Leipzig 1867, § 2, p. 5) is usually cited: 'cum die natali munus annale genio solverent, manum a caede ac sanguine abstinerent, ne die qua ipsi lucem accepissent alii demerent'. It has been suggested that the day was the anniversary of Antipas's accession: this is not impossible, but the word suggests his true birthday, and the result would not differ greatly. See H. Lindenbrogius's notes to Censorinus (Leyden 1743), 11–12; W. Schmidt, Γενέθλιος ἡμέρα: Pauly-Wissowa, *Real-Encycl.* 13th Halbb. (1910), 1138f. (Fürstengeburtstage).

[4] Josephus, *Ant.* XIX, vii, 1; Chrysostom (344/54–407), *In Matth. hom.* 48/49 (Migne, *PG* 58, col. 490): ὅτε γὰρ αὐτὸν εὐχαριστεῖν ἐχρῆν τῷ θεῷ, ὅτι κατὰ τὴν ἡμέραν ἐκείνην εἰς φῶς αὐτὸν ἤγαγε, τότε τὰ παράνομα ἐκεῖνα τολμᾷ· ὅτε λῦσαι ἐχρῆν δεδεμένον, τότε σφαγὴν τοῖς δεσμοῖς προστίθησιν. *Cf.* T. Innitzer, *Johannes der Täufer* (Wien 1908), 354.

note that they were made by the persons whose day it was.[1] Herodias would have been punished for this insult to her husband's birthday, if not to himself; but his grief (at the insult) would be worth while if she could obtain her wishes. The impropriety of killings on auspicious days was obvious to Jews and one emphatic *midrash* illustrates it.[2] It has been urged[3] that Herodias cannot have asked for the head in such terms. But this is to misjudge the Jewish sense of humour.

The idiom is found in a later Jewish *midrash*. It is forbidden to cut down trees unless they are barren. An owner wanted some trees destroyed as they were weakening vines. He would not say, 'Cut them down', which seemed to break the commandment. He therefore said to his tenant, 'Bring me their roots tomorrow'.[4]

One may even go so far as to say that no self-respecting Jewish ruler would put to death even a self-confessed *rebel* on an auspicious day, a day celebrating some inauguration. Saul was a mature person when he began to reign, and he was the first of the Israelite kings, and his inauguration was an inauguration *par excellence*. We know how Saul's temper developed. At 1 S xi.12–13 we read the following: 'And the people said to Samuel, "Who is he that said, Shall Saul reign over us? Bring the men that we may put them to death". And Saul said, "There shall not a man be put to death this day: for today the Lord has wrought deliverance in Israel".' The word translated 'deliverance' (*t^eshū'āh*) implies 'salvation' (as indeed the LXX translates it). The day was so auspicious that even the 'sons of Belial' (x.27), who did not believe that Saul could 'save' Israel, could escape the otherwise appropriate punishment. And lest the reader of the historical books should miss the point, it is affirmed dramatically by David himself at 2 S xix.22–3. The men who counselled David to put Shimei to death are reprehended, because the day was David's inauguration (or was regarded as being David's inauguration). Obviously the guests of Herod Antipas forgot this warning, which it would not have been so difficult to draw to their attention. To counsel such an act was to deny the king's sovereignty (or so David seems to have implied).

THE OATH

Our summary has introduced us to the complexities of the law, and its

[1] See Lindenbrogius cited at p. 345 n. 3 above.
[2] A king, wanting to kill his daughter's *shosh^eviyn* (see above, p. 230) said he could not do it on her joyous occasion, but he would do it at one of his own (a birthday?): Midr. R., Lev. 20, § 10 (transl. J. Israelstam and J. J. Slotki, London, 1939, 262). See also Origen, *In Levit hom.* 8 (Migne, *PG* 12, 229, col. 495B).
[3] By Klostermann *loc. cit.* The request '. . . on a dish' must be original.
[4] b. B.Ḳ. 92*a* = Sonc. 531.

uncertainties, especially in view of the development of the Pharisaical doctrines which achieved maturity and the right to pose as the typically Jewish doctrines only after the destruction of Jerusalem. Now a fuller exposition is required.

Iurare est aliquid Deo teste affirmare.[1] One who fails to fulfil an oath or vow is guilty of taking the name of God in vain. Perjury is a sin. But worse than perjury is the fulfilment of an impious oath; and the common semitic view seems to have been that an oath which would involve the breach of the will of God is (in an apparently older view) to be broken on payment of a penance, or (in a more developed view now accepted by Christians as well as Jews) is *ipso facto* of no binding force.[2] The older view survives in Islam, where an oath to do evil must not be kept, but expiation for the breach of the oath is obligatory![3] Muslim and Jewish jurisprudence on this subject are very much alike.[4] The Talmud calls such an oath a 'vain oath'.[5] Philo, whose discussions of the subject are fundamental to any study,[6] was aware that non-Jews (and Jews that imitated them?) used oaths as a cover for otherwise unjustifiable acts.[7] Ac xxiii.12–15 provides an example.

Failure to fulfil an oath to perform something was equivalent to a denial of the existence of God. Punishment would be at the hands of God or at those of men.[8] According to Philo the 'more pious', *i.e.*

[1] Philo says (*De Spec. Leg.* II, 9–10, Colson, VII, 311–13): ὅρκος γὰρ οὐδὲν ἄλλο ἢ μαρτυρία θεοῦ περὶ πράγματος ἀμφισβητουμένου. θεὸν δὲ μὴ ἐπ' ἀληθεῖ καλεῖν πάντων ἀνοσιώτατον.

[2] See p. 342 n. 2 *sup*. The doctrine at the time of Christ is not perfectly clear. The Zadokite Document only says that a vow to depart from the *Torāh* must not be kept even at the price of one's life (see below, p. 350 n. 3). Philo's opinion is not free from ambiguity, which it would have been had the doctrine been undisputedly as indicated in our *Mishnāh*. He says 'to swear concerning anything not forbidden by the law', at *De Spec. Leg.* II, 9, which has not been translated absolutely correctly by Belkin at *op. cit.*, 157. See also b. B.Ḳ. 91*b* = Sonc. 528. It is unnecessary to give Christian references which echo the developed rabbinical opinion.

[3] I am obliged to Professor A. S. Tritton for citing to me Tabari's commentary on Qur'ān 2, 224–5. He who swears to disobey God has not taken an oath (no oath is on him): 442. But he who swears to commit sin and does not do it must make an atonement: 439. A saying of the Prophet is 'I never take a vow without being prepared to expiate it if I see that another is better and adopting the better'. Expiation is called *kaffāra*, *e.g.* by feeding ten poor men or three days' fasting. It is important to carry out oaths, but these must give way to higher considerations. The two views are that a sinful oath is invalid, according to others it is valid but must be broken and expiated. See J. Pedersen, art. '*Ḳasam*' in *Encyclopedia of Islam* (1925), also 'Nadhr', *ibid.* (1936), also the same, *Der Eid bei den Semiten* (Strassburg 1914). In Islamic law an inconsidered expression (*laghw*, a rash oath) can always be broken, but must be expiated.

[4] S. Rosenblatt, 'The relations between Jewish and Muslim laws concerning oaths and vows', *Proc. Am. Ac. Jew. Res.* 7 (1936), 229–43, at p. 236.

[5] *Mishnāh*, Shev. III, 8–9 (Danby, 413).

[6] See Belkin, *op. cit.*, ch. 6.

[7] *De Spec. Leg.* II, 12–13 (Colson, VII, 313).

[8] *Ibid.* 28, quoted by Belkin, 144.

apparently the Sadducees, inflicted the death penalty; the milder, less good view, which generally agrees with the tendencies of the Pharisees, led to a public flogging.[1] Punishment at the hands of God would await those whose fault could not be proved adequately, or was not amenable to human justice. The latter (including, we have seen, kings and the like) might fear a natural calamity in divine vengeance[2] for their unexpiated misdeeds. Antipas might or might not await divine vengeance for his marriage, which, in the eyes of some, if not all, non-Pharisees could possibly be extenuated;[3] but breach of an oath might come, or might be thought to come, in a different category.

Thus, if we view the matter from a non-Pharisaical standpoint, Antipas's oath placed him in some danger even if, as events turned out, the fulfilment of his oath would have been contrary to the divine law (itself a debatable question). The danger of course was hypothetical, and of a spiritual character, such as would be unlikely to have affected

[1] *De Spec. Leg.* II, 28; the better or more pious are identified as Sadducees by Belkin, 149. Maimonides, *op. cit.*, VI, I, xii, 12.

[2] The destruction of towns of Jannaeus was caused by vain oaths: Midr. R., Num. XXII, § 1 = Sonc. 853f.

[3] Because the marriage (which was not unexampled in that family) is criticised by Josephus, *Ant.* xviii, 5, 4, it is assumed that the Baptist's rebuke represented the Jewish Law. If it were so there would be evidence that Antipas cared nothing at all for divine vengeance, and this would have a bearing on his behaviour generally. However we must note that Herodias's first husband was only a paternal half-brother of Antipas. The scriptural law is not to be interpreted by analogy, though Pharisees certainly did so interpret it in a few contexts. Curiously the divorced wife or widow of a *half*-brother is not in terms forbidden in scripture. The sister-in-law does not appear at all in Lv xx.11–21. Where she does appear, namely Lv xviii.16, the text calls for interpretation in the light of xviii.9. Marriage with the two types of half-sister is distinctly forbidden, but the sister-in-law is not so qualified. David in fact married his paternal half-sister (2 S xiii.13) and Sarah was Abraham's half-sister. That paternal half-sisters were sometimes married *de facto* is evidenced (it seems) in Ezk xxii.11. The evidence of Dt xxviii. 20, 22, 23 could also be read negatively. A Pharisaical text, *Mishnāh*, Yevāmot I, 3, makes such distinctions. Though the School of Hillel and that of Shammai differed (interpreting Lv xviii. 18 differently), they were agreed that marriages were void that took place with the consanguine (paternal) half-sister and the 'wife' (*i.e.* widow) of a consanguine half-brother. That is, while the Pharisees would not regard marriage with the uterine half-brother's widow as null and void, they fulminated against the particular type of marriage which Antipas had made. Yet if 'brother's wife' in Lv xviii.16 meant wife of a full *or* half brother this point of view would be untenable. If the Pharisees were prepared to make a distinction of this character we can be sure that Sadducees would be willing to allow the Herodian family to take advantage of any loophole left by the words of the *Torāh* read strictly. Pharisees will have been against the marriage with Herodias, but it does not follow that others were. Meanwhile the Zadokite Document shows that the Dead Sea sect at any rate were prepared to interpret Lv xviii strictly. 'Although the laws against incest are written for men, they also apply to women'—from which it would seem to follow in our case that if marriage with the two kinds of half-sister is literally forbidden marriage with the two kinds of half-brother is analogically forbidden. *CD* V, 8–10 (Vermès, 101–2; Lohse, 74; Dupont-Sommer, 144–5).

Antipas himself if he were not prompted by other considerations. The possibility cannot be denied, indeed it amounts almost to a certainty, that Pharisees present will have drawn attention to the doubt whether a boastful oath, intended for dramatic effect and not literally, a 'rash oath', oath in name only, could be binding at all.[1] But Philo seems to be of the view that such oaths were effective to create an obligation in the taker; only the grounds for his release from it would be substantial, or, to put the procedure in other words, its annulment. The Old Testament, which supplies the ultimate authority on such vexed subjects, is singularly confused on the subject of oaths and vows. Pharisees' doctrines which later developed along the lines indicated above cannot have weighed at our period decisively in the Baptist's favour either at that place, or, except amongst Pharisees, anywhere. For, after all, reliance would be placed in the cases of Jephthah and of Samuel and Jonathan.

RELEASE FROM AN OATH

Let us turn to the question of release from oaths. David was persuaded not to fulfil his oath, fulfilment of which would not have subserved his motive.[2] Now David was so placed that he might have found it difficult, if at all possible, to have his oath annulled. Perhaps Antipas's situation was comparable? Could Pharisees present not have urged him to release himself from his oath? The actual wording of Mk vi.26 strongly suggests (Mt xiv.9 does not) that attempts to persuade him were actually made.[3] But the difficulty was this: for an important man in an important matter, a matter which had to be handled with delicacy, to release himself like a common shepherd was unseemly; and to receive annulment of his oath would be requisite in contrast to the situation of David, since Antipas's predicament differed from that of David in that his terms of appointment differed, and a constitutionally agreed method of absolution from oaths nominally existed at Antipas's time. If Antipas could be released as easily as a shepherd or fisherman his oaths would thenceforward be worthless, and the publicity of the affair underlined this embarrassing point. The common people did not give their oaths and asseverations much thought (hence the Pharisees' concern with such matters in the vast tractate called Sh^{e}vu'ot). We even see St Peter

[1] See p. 342 n. 1 above.

[2] 1 S xxv.22 (for form of oath *cf.* Jezebel's oath to kill Elijah), *ibid.* 24–35. David swore to kill Nabal but was restrained by Abigail's prayers. Augustine says, *juravit temere, sed non implevit jurationem majore pietate . . . David . . . de duobus peccatis elegit minus.* David's oath regarding Shimei (2 S xix.23) seems to have been no great hindrance to him (1 K ii.9).

[3] οὐκ ἠθέλησεν ἀθετῆσαι.

swearing (with the mild euphemism εἰς τὸν αἰῶνα used by Jesus mainly in promises, blessings and the like, in general imitation of the divine 'oaths' of the Old Testament)[1] that Jesus shall not wash his feet (Jn xiii.8), yet afterwards he broke his oath, for an adequate reason.[2] But the people of consequence had a recognised method of dealing with inconvenient oaths, namely an approach to the priest. The priest as God's agent might reject offerings and might annul oaths and vows. A daughter or wife was not *sui juris* in this respect and the father or husband could release her from them.[3] Upon this ratio the Pharisees built the doctrine that a rabbinical court or even a rabbi might release an individual from his oath, for in such matters the non-rabbis were not *sui juris*. It followed that the High Priest in Jerusalem could have absolved Antipas from his oath if his self-respect would not have permitted him to release himself.

There is a discussion of Jephthah's vow in an old (but of course Pharisaical) *midrash*. 'But surely he could have had his vow disallowed by going to Phinehas? He thought: I am a king! Shall I go to Phinehas? And Phinehas argued: I am a High Priest and the son of a High Priest! Shall I go to that ignoramus? Between the two of them the poor maiden perished, and both of them incurred responsibility for her blood.'[4] Josephus would have concurred[5] that Jephthah sinned against God in keeping his oath, for human sacrifice was not consistent with the *Torāh*. The notion that an oath-taker's oath could be released is here taken as a matter of course.

[1] The phrase is used as an oath by Paul, 1 Co viii.13; by Jesus at Jn viii.51, 52; x.28; xi.26; as a curse at Mt xxi.19 = Mk xi.14; Mk iii.29. G. Stählin, 'Zum Gebrauch von Beteuerungsformeln im Neuen Testament', *NT* 5 (1962), 114–43.

[2] Ps. Athanasius, *Quaestiones ad Antiochum Ducem*, q. 130, Migne, *PG* 28, 246 (col. 679). St Peter was not so delicate *out* of Jesus's presence, and reverted to plebeian habits in an emergency: Mk xiv.71 = Mt xxvi.74.

[3] Nb xxx.3–16. *Mishnāh*, Ned. X (Danby, 277ff.); b. Giṭṭ. 83*b*. J. Jeremias, *Jerusalem z. Zeit Jesu*, 3rd edn, Göttingen 1962, 400, 405. See b. Shab. 46*b* = Sonc. 212. The rabbinical rules 'hover in the air' because of their tenuous support from this text: *Mishnāh*, Hag. I, 8 (Danby, 212). For an example see b. Shab. 127*b* = Sonc. 634. Z. Tauber, 'Die Auflösung des Gelübdes', *LGWJ* 73, 1929, 33–46 is not wholly correct. See *ibid.* 326–9. The Zadokite Document says '*Concerning the oath of a woman*: Inasmuch as He said, "Her husband may invalidate her oath" (Nb xxx.9), no husband shall invalidate an oath unless he knows whether it is to be confirmed or invalidated. If it tends to a transgression of the Covenant [of the Community], he shall invalidate it and not confirm it. And such is the law for her father.' The Dead Sea Scroll Community, to judge from this document, did not allow Priests to annul vows or oaths in general: Vermès, 109; Lohse, 98–101; Dupont-Sommer, 178.

[4] Midr. R., Levit. xxxvii, § 4 (trans. p. 470), a part of the commentary on Lv xxvii.2.

[5] Jos. objects to Jephthah's act (Jg xi) at *Ant.* V, vii, 17 and *cf. Contra Apionem* vii, 37. Ps. Philo, *Bibl. Ant.* 40, 3 (trans. James, 192): Seila says, 'Now therefore annul not anything of that thou hast vowed', implying that personal release from such a vow was possible.

Jesus seems to have agreed with the Pharisees, rather than the Dead Sea Community, in the view that a sage might release the Israelite from his oath: Mt xvi.19*b*.[1] It may be argued that the Zadokite Document says that a man must keep his oath even at the price of death,[2] but this was not somebody else's death, and the Community were professedly strict. There is a passage of Josephus dealing with the oath not to give daughters to Benjamin (Jg xxi.1, 16–25); it strongly suggests[3] that in Josephus's time there was doubt whether such an oath could be held binding or not—which altogether accords with our reading of Philo who clearly antedates the Talmudic view that such rash vows and oaths are void.[4] But the discussion is not inconsistent with our contention, for it is only a binding oath which can be annulled or released. But that great rabbis *did* release the people from oaths at the time of Christ cannot really be doubted, for the notorious case of Simeon ben Sheṭaḥ seems to prove it. That case also illustrates the prestige difficulties which could arise in such a situation as Antipas's:

The historicity of this story found in the Jerusalem Talmud has never been doubted,[5] and any experience of Alexander Jannaeus will have served as a useful precedent for the Herodians. Belkin says, 'the law of dissolving vows was not a Pharisaic innovation. It had already existed before the time of this sect [*sic*] and was vested . . . in the High Priest. As Alexander Jannaeus was both King and High Priest, the right to dissolve vows belonged to him'.[6] After inducing Jannaeus to pay for the fulfilment of the vows of half the number of Nazirites in need of this charity, Simeon (who disapproved of Naziritism) dissolved the vows of the remainder, thus escaping his obligation to pay for their offerings. He was thus casting aspersions upon Jannaeus's fitness to be a High Priest, and simultaneously asserting the rabbi's power (which the

[1] 'Binding' and 'loosing' are especially appropriate for decisions relating to oaths and vows. Vows (and therefore oaths) may well be annulled by an agent: b. B.M. 96*a*.

[2] *CD* XVI, 6–9 (Vermès, 109; Lohse, 98): 'And as He has said (Dt xxiii.23 [24]) "That which is gone out of thy lips thou shalt observe" to confirm it; every binding oath that a man has taken to do something from the *Torāh* he shall not redeem even at the price of death. When a man has taken upon himself to depart from the *Torāh* he shall not, even at the price of death, fulfil it.' Belkin, *op. cit.*, 147–8. A reforming tendency is at work at Ps xv.4*c* (MT): where the oath would operate to the swearer's hurt the just man keeps his oath. The original reading is surely represented in the text translated at ψ xiv.4 (where οὐκ ἀθετῶν correctly means 'does not annul his oath'). See *Midrash on Psalms*, on Ps xv.5 (Braude, I, 191, 193–4).

[3] Jos., *Ant.* V, ii, 12, quoted by Belkin at p. 164–5.

[4] The final view was that an oath to do something one has no legal right to do was void *ab initio*: b. Ket. 59*a* = Sonc. 349; 66*a* = Sonc. 399.

[5] Belkin, 167. The story is repeated in J. Mann, 'Oaths and vows in the synoptic gospels', *Am. J. Theol.* 21 (1917), 260, 272.

[6] *Op. cit.* 167.

Pharisees ultimately sanctioned exclusively when the high priesthood vanished with the temple).

Philo says,[1] 'Release from a promise can only be in the most perfect way when the High Priest discharges him from it; for he is the person to receive it (in the case of a vow) in due subordination to God'.

Thus the notion that his oath bound Antipas to cut off the Baptist's head could not possibly have been accepted by any contemporary, however learned or unlearned; still less could there have been any hope of its being accepted by generations after the fall of the Temple, unless the reader was to suppose this was further, and very subtle, evidence of the wickedness of Antipas and all his court, and kingdom, whence (?) the calamities that fell upon him and it. But the reference to the guests puts the affair in a different light.

THE GUESTS

To investigate what the guests must have said is not to wander into fantasy. They had a distinct interest in what happened. Herod had placed his guests in a predicament which must gravely have embarrassed those who were capable of being embarrassed at all. Even the least pious could not be assumed to take no notice of a perjury (however technical) committed brazenly in front of them. Philo gives utterance to a rule which has no identified Old Testament textual basis, but which we can accept as good law then, as it is good sense to this day.

He emphasises (and it will serve for all streams of opinion) that 'a person who sees one violating an oath and does not inform against him or convict him, because he is influenced by friendship or respect or fear rather than by piety, is liable to the same punishment as the perjured man himself, for to range oneself on the side of the wrongdoer is just the same as committing the wrong'.[2]

The guests had sufficient interest in the affair for a debate (the conventional ornament of a banquet) to have been inevitable. The presence of Pharisees and Sadducees and others will have made it a lively debate. Let us adopt the old-fashioned, but handy practice of putting a hypothetical advice to Herod into the form of a speech. In this now somewhat unusual manner we can overcome the otherwise formidable obstacles to the imagination which a historical reconstruction imperatively demands.

St Augustine did this in a minor way:[3] Dicit mihi aliquis: quid ergo

[1] *Hypoth.* cited by Eusebius, *Praep. Evang.* VIII, 7, cited by Belkin at p. 166.
[2] *De Spec. Leg.* II, 26, quoted by Belkin, 151–2.
[3] Sermo CCCVIII, Migne, *PL* 38, 1408.

debuit facere Herodes? Demus illi consilium. Si dixerimus, Parce Joanni, ne facias scelus; perjurium suademus. Si dixerimus, Noli perjurare; ad scelus implendum provocamus. Mala conditio. Yet the position was more complicated than that.

After all possible discussion, this is the sort of advice which Antipas's advisers would have given him:

'Your step-daughter has asked for the head, and it is evident that it would be inexpedient for you to annoy your wife by refusing. Was your oath a "rash oath" and so void? Most of us cannot accept this: your intention was to give anything asked for, and we cannot accept, placed as this gathering is, that you should contemplate breaking it; we would dissuade you from committing perjury, since perjury might undermine, or, what is much more important, might be thought by your rivals to be an excuse for undermining, your kingdom, which we are bound to uphold. Much as the populace of Galilee loves John they are addicted to religious extremes, and, inconsistent as faithfulness to your oath might seem to be with John's welfare, it is possible to argue that Galileans would resent open and flagrant perjury.[1] The matter is complicated by the fact that the head asked for is John's. Whatever may be thought about John by the majority of us here, the public are inclined to regard him as a prophet: upon that footing the most scrupulous adherence to the divine law would be entirely in order; John himself could not object if you treat him in a manner which the *Torāh* sanctions or requires.

'Pharisees urge that John (towards whom they cannot be accused of partiality) cannot be killed because, even if the oath is not void as a "rash oath" it is a "vain oath". But we cannot accept this. Whether it is a "vain oath" is doubtful (we return to the point presently); but even if it were, perjury would be involved in breaking it unless one of two courses were followed. The first suggested is that you should absolve yourself from the oath on the ground that the consequences are undesirable, just as the common people do. Whether a king should treat his oath so lightly is most doubtful. If one cites the case of David, we oppose the case of the marriages with the tribe of Benjamin. Moreover Samuel would have kept his oath, but the people prevented him.[2] Jephthah must have regretted his oath, but the abhorrence with which his act is regarded is due to his making a human sacrifice rather than to his obstinate piety. If a king were entitled to release himself from

[1] Rains are withheld in punishment for four kinds of sin, including the sin of pledging *gifts* (*e.g.* charity) in public and not honouring the pledge(!): *Midr. on Psalms*, Ps xvii, trans. I, 223–4 (Pr xxv.14); *cf. ibid.*, Ps lii, trans. I, 474.

[2] 1 S xiv.39, 43, 45.

oaths to the nobility all the bonds of society would be loosened. The second course suggested is that you should approach the High Priest for a release from your oath.

'Jannaeus insisted that the High Priest alone was entitled to do this, and, against our Pharisee friends' opinion, we think it unsafe to assume otherwise. But should you submit your problems to his jurisdiction? If he absolved you, well and good; but this would place all the prestige of your government within the power of a man who is not appointed by you, nor subordinate to you, but actually open to influence by your brother's Roman successors, a step which would provoke the gravest repercussions. Unfortunately your powers are circumscribed by Rome. Rome controls your arms. Is Jerusalem to guard your conscience? Even if the High Priest were to consent the precedent would be disagreeable and possibly fatal to your rule. But what if he refused? Herodias would approach him. The breach between you two would have become apparent. The relatives of your former wife would be encouraged. And would the High Priest care to do a service for John the Baptist? If your application for release is refused your situation is worse than before. You would be obliged to put John to death, and you would have admitted the High Priest's authority over your court and your prestige would have been undermined.

'Since self-absolution would be plebeian or tyrannical or both, and since an approach to the High Priest is not to be contemplated, it remains to investigate the notion that the oath is a "vain oath". The view that such an oath can be ignored with impunity is not widely held. Even those who hold it would require you to pay a penalty of some kind. You would (in their view) have to offer a handsome sacrifice in Jerusalem in exchange for the life of John the Baptist, which, quite apart from Herodias's objections, would place an unexpected value upon John's safety. But the biblical text "to do evil or to do good"[1] is capable of another interpretation, which we prefer. No oath, in our view, is *ipso facto* invalid: God's name is not to be taken without effect. You would not wish your own act to be a bad example to your subordinates. It was, after all, with the object of preventing hasty swearing that the divine legislation assumed that remarkable form. But even assuming that the Pharisees' position on this subject has some reason behind it—unlike their doctrine of release from vows it does not hang by a thread—it by no means follows that the oath is void as unpleasing

[1] Lv v.4 (see *Mishnāh*, Shev. III, 5; Danby, 412). The Christian interpretation of the verse, which may follow the rabbinical, is not that there can be an oath to do evil to another, but that one can swear to inconvenience oneself, mortifying the evil inclination, abstaining from unlawful pleasures, etc.

to God. Obedience to kings is required of every subject. John has stirred up sedition and has more than justified the supreme penalty. His plain speech is not excused by his reputation as a prophet: rather he should know better. Our own opinion is that he is a lunatic,[1] and to rid the tetrarchy of a fomentor of rebellion would be a national service.

'Since it is doubtful whether the oath is a vain oath you would be well advised to be on the right side and act in accordance with it. People will be satisfied that you were tricked into doing the act, and the stricter their piety the more they will sympathise with you. John might well have restricted himself to general moral questions and left alone the matrimonial affairs of princes: the outcome might have been anticipated by a true prophet. Those whom they are pleased to call "the men of the Pit"[2] are not even rebuked publicly by so scrupulous a sect as that of the Dead Sea.

'Quite apart from all these considerations, political, ethical and religious, there remains the obvious objection to the revoking of a royal oath. It is unkingly for a king to revoke his oath, even if he has the best of reasons for doing so, and could ethically be excused for doing it. Even an obscure princeling would seek a device to avoid breaking his oath, however absurd.[3] We note with satisfaction that no device could be adopted to evade the literal fulfilment of the oath which you have taken.

'The dilemma however is at an end once you treat John as a political offender, due to die for his crimes. Order his execution in exercise of your constitutional power; Herodias will be satisfied, the girl will be honoured, your oath will not be broken, your guests' qualms will be set at rest, and the tetrarchy will be rid of a troublemaker. A simple solution.

'Admittedly it could be urged that this tetrarchy is not a safe place for "prophets" of the calibre of John the Baptist. We do not feel that Pharisees' qualms about your following our advice will cost your country anything of value. When the Pharisees are in the majority (if ever) will be time enough to give these religious maniacs licence to turn the world upside down.'

CONCLUSION

The importance of the passage in Mark can be found out, no doubt,

[1] Lk vii.33, *cf.* 29–30. [2] I *QS* IX, 16 (Vermès, 88; Lohse, 34).

[3] *Midr. on Psalms*, on Ps vi.2 (Braude I, 97). Alexander the Great promised to kill that one of the Indian holy men he had captured who answered his conundrums worst. Clever answers achieved that if he adhered to his promise none would die. Alexander proposed to kill all. No, said the gymnosophist, οὐ βασιλικόν ἐστι ψεύδεσθαι . . . (P. Berol. 13044 = Jacoby, *F. Gr. Hist.* II B 153. F. 9. p. 828). See above, p. 34 n. 6.

from a full reconstruction of the two as yet unsolved problems, the importance to the gospel of parallelism between Old Testament precedents and the development of the redemption story; and the importance of the Trial itself, and the place of Antipas in those proceedings. It would be improper to enter such fields here, and it would be superfluous to speculate on the meaning of this pericope for disciples of John and their own disciples, who were to be absorbed into the cult of Jesus. That the death of John was in some way explanatory of not only the movements of Jesus prior to his last journey to Jerusalem but also the behaviour of the principal parties at the last, critical moments of his life, seems highly likely, if not certain: but how precisely it served to explain the latter has yet to be shown.

Meanwhile we may rest assured that the novelettish tone of the pericope could not have acquired its oath element by a simple process of legend-making. There is nothing legendary about that very difficult and embarrassing episode. Understood as we have understood it above Josephus and the gospel are virtually in agreement. The suggestion that Josephus would have liked a means of abusing or ridiculing Salome who was still alive falls flat when it is realised that Salome was a mere intermediary, and that the real culprit was Herodias, who had, with her wretched husband, suffered abundantly before Josephus began to write. Moreover a third source has been recovered,[1] which shows that behind both the gospel and Josephus there may lie a third account, which definitely attributes the Baptist's death to his denouncing Antipas's marriage with Herodias.

What is the meaning, meanwhile, of Jesus's remarks at Lk xiii.31–3? Apprently Pharisees, fearing that the same fate would overtake Jesus as had overtaken John (ix.9), warned him that he was in danger. Jesus's answer has many features, only some of which deserve discussion here. He refers to Herod as 'that fox', a most opprobrious designation. 'Fox' does not mean a cunning, wily person (such as would perhaps send agents in the guise of friends), but a miserable, low-spirited, worthless

[1] A. A. Neumann, 'A note on John the Baptist, and Jesus in Josippon', *HUCA* 23, 2, (1950/1), 137–49. The text reads, 'He took unto himself the wife of Philip his brother while the latter was still living, and though she had children from his brother he wedded her. He killed many of the Sages of Israel. He also put to death John because he upbraided him, saying, 'it is forbidden unto thee to take in wedlock thy brother Philip's wife'. And so he put him to death. This was John who practised baptism (*hu' yoḥanan 'asher 'asāh ṭeviylāh*). For an earlier study see S. Zeitlin, *Josephus on Jesus* (Philadelphia 1931). On the baptist and his baptism we may see I. Abrahams, *Studies in Pharisaism and the Gospels*, I (Cambridge 1917), 30–5; also A. H. W. Brandt, *Die jüdischen Baptismen* (*Beih. z. ZATW* 18) (Gießen 1910), 69–85. C. H. H. Scobie, *John the Baptist* (London 1964), at 183–4 accepts the usual resolution of the discrepancies, with which this writer on the whole agrees.

creature. The word emphasises low birth,[1] as it subsequently indicated ignorance and low cultural status.[2] While the lion which had overcome Israel was Rome, Antipas was the fox, or jackal,[3] which possessed the remnants of what it could not catch for itself, a status it did not deserve. Indeed, the fox would not do to Jesus what Rome was eventually to do. Jesus's message to 'that fox' also calls to mind the popular saying, 'A fox in its hour—bow down to it!' Just as 'every dog has his day', so one may, rarely, be justified in showing respect to the worthless.[4] Secondly Jesus pointed to the contrast between John's activity and his. John cast out no devils, nor performed cures; neither did he 'walk'. Still more important is the fact that John was not 'perfected'—when Jesus says, 'the third day I am perfected' he alludes[5] to a programme for which John's could show no parallel. A problem is posed by the attribution to Jesus of the remark that a prophet cannot perish out of Jerusalem, which amounts to a denial that John was a prophet. Perhaps the solution is, as many translators have observed,[6] to be found in the words οὐκ ἐνδέχεται which, though common enough in Greek, are found only here in the New Testament. Jesus can hardly have denied that John was a prophet (Lk vii.26) and Luke cannot have been ignorant that John did not die in Jerusalem. From this it follows that the entire expression is intended to look at Jesus in contrast to John, and the words do *not* mean (as would otherwise be attractive) 'it is not possible', 'it cannot be', but rather 'it is not fitting', or 'it is not admissible'. In *his* case what is fitting must happen, whereas in John's there was room for an alternative. No doubt Jesus's words, spoken after all to Pharisees, must contain a biblical allusion, most likely a *midrash*. It has yet to be identified.

In anticipation of the required identification we may however suggest the following interpretation of xiii.31–3:[7] the Pharisees, who had sufficient contact with Antipas's court to know whether there might be

[1] b. B.M. 84*b* (bottom) = Sonc. 485: 'he is a lion, and the son of a lion, whereas you are a lion, the son of a fox'.

[2] b. B.Ḳ. 117*a* = Sonc. 699–70; *Mishnāh*, 'Āvot IV, 15.

[3] It is not clear whether *shū'āl* means fox or jackal, but in any case it means a contemptible animal. There is, curiously, a possibility of a covert reference to the Egyptians who were drowned in the hollow (*sho'al*) of the sea: Midr. R., S. S., on II, 15. For an explanation of the paronomastic character of the original Aramaic (facilitating memorisation) see M. Black, *Aramaic Approach*, 233.

[4] b. Meg. 16*b* = Sonc. 98; G. Dalman, *Jesus-Jēschūa'* (Leipzig 1922), 208.

[5] M. Black, *cit. sup.* considers that τῇ τρίτῃ (third) means 'one day soon', and the perfection alluded to is Jesus's death, since πορεύεσθαι in his view means to die.

[6] *New English Bible* (unthinkable); Schonfield (it will never do); Rieu (it is not right); Phillips, following Moffatt (it would never do); Knox (there is no room for . . .); *Jerusalem Bible* (it would not be right).

[7] J. Blinzler, *Herodes Antipas und Jesus Christus* (Stuttgart 1947), 16–20.

any danger, out of fear for Jesus's safety, or desire to see him out of Galilee, or both, tell him of his danger. Jesus, repudiating the suggestion that he is in danger, replies (1) Antipas is not destined to be the end of me, for he is only a fox—and you may tell him so if you should learn that he has such plans; (2) there is no need for these fears since my behaviour is not analogous to that of John; (3) my movements are set for me, and may not be interfered with upon any consideration—in particular Antipas will not catch me and hold me for it 'is necessary' that I 'walk', *i.e.* there is a predestination with which he cannot meddle; and (4) I shall journey towards Jerusalem since (whatever may have happened in John's case) 'a prophet must perish in Jerusalem'. This does not tell us anything about Jesus's actual movements, whether he remained in Galilee or left it. At any rate the passage throws no light on the place of John's death, or its circumstances. It can however legitimately be used as evidence that Pharisees did not desire that Antipas's actual rule, with its political, constitutional, religious, and sectarian aspects, should claim another victim, should add a further and more notorious (if possible) precedent to the list of bad precedents with which the court of that ruler embarrassed them. Though we know that persons close to Antipas's court had Jesus's interests and his mission at heart (Lk viii.3) this passage cannot be relied upon as proving that Pharisees would act purely, or even chiefly, out of regard for Jesus's personal safety; but that they were concerned about the administration of law by princes can in any case be accepted as indisputable.[1]

APPENDIX

'Elijah comes first to restore . . .'

It is necessary to revert to Mk ix.13 (which, as often, has a commentary embodied in it in the version of Mt xvii.12, *q.v.*) in order to do justice

[1] The prevailing opinion, that the passage is gossip in which no deep implications ought to be sought, does not account for the problems raised by the oath. Previous studies of the pericope have tended to be obscured by preconceptions about the Jews' notions about the character of an oath, by incomplete investigations of Philo before 1940 (Grotius's study in his *Annotationes* might have been followed up more intently), by suppositions that Christian learning was, or ought to have been, applicable, and by confusion of Jewish with pagan practices, many of which undoubtedly fostered folk-tale and legend. A concise, interesting, and valuable study of oaths, which serves to explain why our pericope has not been better investigated in recent centuries is the widely translated and publicised S. von Pufendorf's *De Jure Naturae et Gentium* (*Law of Nature and Nations*) IV, 2, 13–14 (orig. edn 1672). R. Hirzel, *Der Eid: ein Beitrag zu einer Geschichte* (Leipzig 1902), gives the Greek vocabulary and ideas: it does not assist with our pericope. Joh. Schneider's valuable articles ὀμνύω and ὅρκος, etc., in Kittel-Friedrich, *ThWzNT* do not deal with Herod's predicament except in passing (V, p. 185 n. 6). A comprehensive study of oaths in the pagan Levantine world is W. Kunkel's article at *ZSS* 51 (1931), 222 ff.

to an important *Mishnāh* which, although well known, has not hitherto been employed to throw light either on the fate of John the Baptist or on the vexed question of the sufferings of the Messiah.

Mishnāh, 'Eduyot VIII, 7 embodies[1] an extremely ancient tradition, amounting to an *halakāh* (law) that Elijah will come to 'expel and draw near', which cryptic formula (as so often, obviously antedating its explanation or explanations) means, we are told, not (one explanation) nor (another explanation) but the expulsion of those that entered by violence and the reinstating of those who were expelled by violence. Writers who accept the Talmudic tradition assume that the tradition relates to questions of illegitimacy, a very limited object not in itself inconsistent with the function attributed to a prophet, but far short of it in scope.[2] All are agreed that Elijah's activity consists in a turning topsy-turvy. Force occurred, and force will be countered (by force?). The mature rabbinic view, contained in the same *Mishnāh*, is that Elijah's function is 'to do peace in the world'.[3] The expulsion and reinstating means putting an end to injustice and wrong.

The scriptural basis for this view, as given *ibid.*, is Ml iii.23/iv.5, which may well have been the basis for the more restricted rabbinical expectations of Elijah. It is clear that Elijah was seen as he who comes before (see also Ml iii.1*c*), and his coming is to turn the hearts of the fathers... (as at Lk i.17). Jesus's own interest in Malachi has been indicated above, pp. 15–16.

Malachi sees the activity of Elijah as prior to a visitation by God. In iii.22/iv.4 we are given to understand that remembering the Law is helpful prior to Elijah's coming (this agrees with Lk xvi.16), but in preparation for the visitation Elijah will bring about a reformation which exceeds the requirements of the law as such.

Nothing is said about Elijah's personal future. His coming is associated with the restoration. There is no assurance that there will be no violence in his time, nor that he shall not suffer. On the contrary, since his coming imports a reform, wrong and violence are very much in the picture. Two types of wrong are specifically mentioned in Ml iii.24

[1] Also Midr. R., S.S., IV, 12, 5 = Sonc. 224.

[2] The text is cited by W. D. Davies, *The Setting of the Sermon on the Mount* (Cambridge 1964), 159. G. F. Moore, *Judaism*, II, 358–9. D. Daube, *op. cit.* 297–8. This interpretation is very old, because it seems to lie behind the paraphrase of Malachi's text given in Sir xlviii.10, which may support the M.T. reading, though this is far from certain. C. G. Montefiore described the gospel passage as a 'confusing and useless quotation from Malachi'. Before making such comments it is necessary to know what part biblical studies played in the intellectual justification of Christ to his contemporaries, and on that subject we have much research to do.

[3] *la'asot shālom bā'olām*, which we note is exactly equivalent to βαλεῖν εἰρήνην ἐπὶ τὴν γῆν (Mt x.34) or εἰρήνην ... δοῦναι ἐν τῇ γῇ (Lk xii.51), on which see below.

itself: the M.T. shows unnatural feelings between father and son, and *vice versa*, which is not very attractive; and this is the reading which the *Mishnāh* adopts. But all the Greek translations (so far as we know) did not read 'the heart of the fathers towards their children and the heart of the children towards their fathers' (which would support the narrow interpretation of the ancient saying about Elijah's 'expelling and drawing near'), but read, for the second turning, '. . . the heart of man towards his neighbour'. The Hebrew original must have been *'al-'aḥeyhem* instead of *'al-'avotām*, and the previous *bāniym* must have been read as if it were *b^e^ney-'ādām*, which is unobjectionable. Thus at the time of Jesus there was excellent authority for understanding that the coming of Elijah would right (perhaps in the midst of force?) two different sorts of wrong, namely unpaternal feeling towards sons (*i.e.* any dependent people), and unfraternal/unfilial feeling between equals. At Elijah's coming the superiors wrong the inferiors, and man oppresses his neighbour, but his coming will attend to this. The expression Jesus uses, 'restore', in Mark in the present (uncompleted) tense (reconverted perhaps to the future by Matthew who has consulted the LXX), represents the Hebrew *v^e^-heshīv*, which can certainly have this sense. 'All things' summarises the wrongs that are comprehended in the two sorts of evil alluded to by Malachi as read in the Greek versions. The effect of Elijah's coming is to make this restoration: but meanwhile the two wrongs exist. In a sense the coming of the forerunner and these two types of wrong are connected, and not incompatible. To say that John the Baptist did *not* restore all things would seem to miss this point.

If this is correct, it is small wonder that the Messiah himself must suffer from unpaternal and unneighbourly treatment (which would otherwise be surprising). Matthew actually understands this, and is satisfied that Mark's text implies it: '. . . so also the Son of man will suffer at their hands'. That Elijah should suffer would by no means be excluded. To revert to Lk xvi.16, that God himself ('the kingdom of heaven') should suffer force, and his Son suffer its effects, would not be improper. In Elijah's time force exists (as the rabbis indicate) and it is he who effects the setting right of all wrongs. The process which Elijah/John the Baptist starts ends in the reconciliation of mankind within itself, and with its heavenly Father, and protects it from the curse referred to by Malachi at the end of his book (in the Hebrew version).

I should like to insert a tentative conjecture for what it is worth. The structure of Mk ix.12*b* has caused difficulty, the word πῶς particularly. We have seen that the Greek versions of Ml iii.23 (24 in the M.T.)

take *bāniym* to mean 'sons of men', 'man'. It is possible to argue that Jesus connected midrashically 'man' in Ml iii.24 with Dn vii.13. One does not have to search for a justification. The first part of Malachi's text dealt with sonship, paternal responsibility; the second must deal with sons exclusively in their quality as the collective human race (and note that the LXX gives καρδίαν ἀνθρώπου without the article). If the heart of man must be restored towards his neighbour (lit. 'brother'), if this was the work of Elijah, and if Elijah had to restore what was done by force, man must suffer force from his neighbour, and if the man mentioned here is a personification of humanity with which the prophet Daniel associates the Messiah the argument is complete.

Has this text, and its interpretation, anything to do with Mi vii.6, as quoted in Mt x.34–6, Lk xii.51–3? At first sight these passages are contrary to the one with which we have been dealing. If it is the character of Elijah to 'restore all things', and if this means, as the rabbis say, making peace, what is Jesus doing in predicting internecine strife of much the same kind as that which Malachi specifically says Elijah will quell? In the Lucan version Jesus says 'For there shall be from now onwards five divided against one another in one house, three shall be divided against two and two against three.'

The context relates the saying to Jesus's identity and to the disciples' duty to acknowledge it. The language, especially the word 'come', directly relates this passage to our passage about Elijah who must 'come', moreover 'peace on the earth' links Elijah and this passage. Jesus was in danger of being confused with Elijah himself. Elijah was supposed to bring 'peace', as we have seen. Jesus denies this of himself. He cannot but bring division, *dissension* (Matthew's picking up the word 'sword' (perhaps from Mi vii.2?) is yet another example of his commenting on his text). What sort of division? Luke's very curious *v.* 52 was too much for Matthew (and he understandably omitted it?). It is a curious example of midrashic work, the chief key to which is so far missing. But upon the surface the source of the idea is plain. Micah instances three types of rebellion and follows it by a generalisation in the plural (*q.v.*). The three rebellions are all examples of the younger generation rebuking or 'dishonouring', the elder generation, implying opposition and disobedience by way of dissent. But the three rebellions are against two people. Hence three against two, and two against three! Hence also the notion that the household consists of five persons, as it might well do, for the son, presumably, is the husband of the daughter-in-law. The 'man' mentioned in *v. 6d* is obviously the head of the household, which (apart from his wife) is rebelling against him.

This rebellion, exactly like the wrong we noted in Malachi, precedes the visitation of God. It is symptomatic of the period before the end: so, at great length the *Mishnāh* itself, Soṭ. IX, 15 (b. Soṭ. 49*b*), concerning the coming of the Messiah. Are these two symptoms not irreconcilable, for Elijah is supposed to make peace and to restore, to correct these wrongs? Not necessarily. But surely there is an inconsistency here? No. The restoring which Elijah was to do concerned (i) the paternal attitude towards the younger generation, and (ii), in the Greek versions we have been following, the brotherly attitude between equals. Now Micah, as understood by Jesus, does not envisage any lack of parental fondness for the younger generation; still less fraternal strife between members of that generation. He most specifically excludes these! If at a later age one were to assume that Micah was predicting the chaos of the Jewish War which might be attributed to the Jews' hostility to John and to Jesus, one might well think that Jesus alluded to the various types of disorder and civil strife which his coming would foreshadow. But Luke seems to have an earlier version of the saying which by no means suggests this. Thus, even when Elijah's work is done, there is still room for the younger generation, touched by Jesus's teaching, to dissent from, be divided from, their elders, whom they would have been obliged by the decalogue to honour (and obey) but for the new dispensation which Elijah's and Jesus's coming brings with it. If the parents' hearts are turned towards their children the bitterness of their grief at their children's conversion is understandable. If men are turned towards their brothers the comradeship of the faith, which facilitates such a rebellion, is facilitated. The reference to the sword of Matthew is not present in Luke. To him the reference is to division and dissent, not hatred as such. Jesus intends, it would seem, to give a spiritual and would-be-historical interpretation to Micah, aware that it does not conflict with Malachi's reference to Elijah: the two in fact fit together very neatly. Jesus is not the one who should bring 'peace' to the earth in the sense understood by the rabbis of Elijah. Whatever the function of Elijah as the righter of wrongs, discipleship in the company of Jesus means a readiness to sever, if need be, the bond of peace with an elder generation which does not accept the gospel.

CHAPTER SIXTEEN

The Teaching of Jesus on Marriage and Divorce

ONE HEARS IT SAID that conceptions of Jesus vary with the person. A peaceable man emphasises Jesus's mildness. A vigorous man emphasises Jesus's determination. An authoritarian points to Jesus's certainty and forthrightness. A man whose life has lacked strictness welcomes signs that Jesus was tender with offenders. How far can this many-sidedness be stretched? How far may wishful thinking determine the picture of the historical Jesus? Again, there is the problem how far his teaching, directed to the people of his day, with their taboos and their own prejudices and peculiar oriental social system, can be applied literally to us in our own day. The first stage is to find out what his teaching was, but our difficulties start when we realise that the evangelists themselves must be reflecting, to however small a degree, the same tendency to propound Jesus's words in a form suited to contemporary inclinations.

No topic is so 'near the bone' as sex. Had it been certain that Jesus concentrated on the moral, rather than the purely physical aspects of sexuality, the antagonism to Christ and the Church through the ages would have been immensely reduced. 'Sin' is popularly equated with 'sex'; and Jesus's kindness to the repentant prostitute and his fairness to the woman taken in adultery are not enough to prove that he took a lenient view of sexual aberration. Indeed his distinct pronouncements about the eye which offends leave us in no reasonable doubt on the subject. To make matters worse, there is a strong suspicion in many quarters that Jesus's teaching on divorce was of the strictest character, stricter than even Pharisees would accept. If this suspicion is well-founded the implication is that Jesus was actually cruel to people, for to keep together those whose marriage has 'broken down' is a form of cruelty. Some might argue that Jesus did not care if people chose death rather than sin, for to him death in itself was not the greatest evil. This argument merits careful examination. Suffering, provided sin were avoided, was not necessarily an evil. However, it can hardly be doubted that Jesus referred all such difficult questions to a particular test, of some considerable complexity and subtlety (not yet fully understood) and if by that test the conduct argued for was bad—*i.e.* against the will of God—that conduct must be disallowed.

Disallowing conduct is not the same thing as penalising it. The conduct disallowed is disapproved, it is not void in law. The society, in its own way, may deal with offenders: there is no assumption that the courts of law will take action; but this assumption may well be true in the rare cases where the society and the political unit are the same (as, for example, in a sectarian colony).

The great importance of knowing what Jesus's teaching was on the subject of Marriage and Divorce is universally accepted. It is felt in many quarters that there is no necessity for Christians to compel obedience to that teaching in our society, which is not consistently Christian in complexion, and indeed contains within its geographical limits numerous adherents of other faiths, such as Hinduism and Islam, let alone Judaism. But Christians can as a Church, as a matter of conscience, be guided by Jesus. And thus it becomes a matter of urgency to know what he really thought on this delicate subject of which, interestingly enough, he had no personal experience.

Further, some scholars are of the view that Jesus taught a double standard, one rule for the *élite* and one for weaker vessels. It is alleged that this would be a distinction known to Jewish law.[1] For my part I do not find a trace of such a distinction in Jesus's teaching, which is a teaching of righteousness, unitary and (ultimately) quite simple. It put divorce in its place and makes one piece (as juridical interpretation should) of all sources of obligation.

MARRIAGE AND LAW

At the outset we must arrive at a correct appreciation of what is being discussed.[2] A failure in this obvious preliminary is responsible for innumerable mistakes in studying the gospel texts. Unions between

[1] D. Daube, 'Concessions to sinfulness in Jewish law', *J. Jew. S.* 10 (1959), 1ff., at p. 11–12, itself cited by the same author at his *Collaboration with Tyranny in Rabbinic Law* (London 1965), 12–13. In the present writer's view all civil laws must be viewed against the background of a law of creation; but there is bound to be a difference of opinion as to whether any *law* can properly enforce a kind of sexual life which, if conscientiously carried out, effectuates transcendental and not merely mundane requirements.

[2] E. O. James, *Marriage and Society* (London 1952), 54, 93.

men and women happen, due to forces which they themselves imperfectly understand. The mating urge is difficult to control precisely because it is not the fruit of reason or prudence, but of forces operating upon the parties, forces for the effects of which, wretchedly, they are often called upon to account, though they are manifestly not of their own making nor under their own control; and so it has been from the beginning of the world. Unions happen, but they are not marriages! What then is 'marriage'?

'Marriage' is a human institution. The ancient Chinese long debated whether marriage was a human or a natural institution and the settled Confucianist position is (rightly) that it is the former. Marriage is principally concerned with property, and with the securing of a maintenance to a woman while she is bearing and rearing children. Take away the economic dependence of women and you weaken the institution of marriage. Of this there are already abundant examples in the West Indies, the United States (especially amongst Negroes), and in the emerging independent territories of Africa, not to speak of the contemporary population of Great Britain, and we need say no more about it. Where women are, for reasons best known to themselves or perforce economically dependent on men, and where there is abundant paternal property to be inherited, the concept of 'legitimacy' is extremely relevant, and of course for the most part legitimacy has meaning in the context of an actual or a presumptive legal marriage. Marriage is thus an institution of law, its general character being unitary throughout most of the world's societies living and dead, but its details varying very much from society to society and from region to region and from period to period. People can be united physically and psychologically without being married; and people can be married in the eye of the law without either a physical or a psychological union.

'Divorce' is likewise a human institution. Men tiring of their women, and women wishing to transfer themselves to other men, have been exemplified as long as man has been human. The mating urge has a limited object, but the intimacy which is a direct result of sexual contact (as distinct from issue, who are of course a by-product of it) has psychological ramifications which outlast the mating urge, and, though they might be said to have natural sources beyond the control of the individuals, are much more open to rational consideration than the urge itself. One is in a position to consider whether one loves a particular individual enough to tolerate his or her defects; and what the emotional cost would be if one discarded the unsatisfactory partner. But in societies which have a use for marriage there must be some regulation, in terms of law, of the termination or dissolution of that relationship.

Thus some societies allow divorce on easier terms than others; but most recognise divorce as something which cannot be allowed to take place without grounds or formalities. Divorce does too much damage to established rights and expectations for it to be granted as readily as the marital status is granted.

Thus the question whether, in religious law, in, that is to say, a society which has its religious code as the formal source of its legal institutions, divorce should or should not take place in any particular circumstances, presupposes that marriage exists, marriage (that is to say) as opposed to mere unions. But since there cannot be a marriage which is not also potentially or actually a union, and since marriage is a social, legal recognition or validation or certification of a particular class or classes of unions, the first step to understanding the nature of marriage (and thus of its hypothetical dissolution) must be to understand unions, and what they are all about. How far has a sexual union a purely casual and how far an *exclusive* character? Do men and women in sexual intercourse impliedly (at any rate at the time) exclude others from their mutual enjoyment? Is the concept of 'adultery' present in human terms even before it becomes a legal concept? Psychologists and sociologists may have various notions about this. However, we are now in a position to see how Jesus set about the question. It could be argued historically that the concept of adultery arose out of a right to avenge injury to the husband's property in his wife. But this is to tack one legal conception onto another, and the question in terms of the aetiology of human beings is completely open.

The reader will have grasped that the Jews have two sources of information. The first, and most immediate, is the Law of Moses, written and oral, which tells us about the Jewish legal institution of marriage and divorce. The second, less immediate, but fundamental, is the law of human nature, the character and meaning of sexual union, about which the Book of Genesis has a very great deal to say. A truly legal mind, in construing the meaning of the Law of Moses, will go first to the law apparent in Genesis, and then see what, against that background, Moses had to tell the Jews. Every structure has its foundation. The foundation of all human laws about marriage and divorce must, in the Jewish scholarly view, be found in Genesis. Upon that foundation municipal and social laws of great variety may be built; and upon it, and nothing else, is the Jewish municipal law built, namely the law attributed to Moses. Therefore no interpretation of Moses which conflicts with the fundamentals can possibly be right. This is juridical interpretation, and the subject of marriage and divorce is without question its most searching test.

THE QUESTION PUT TO JESUS

In Mark (x.2) Pharisees come to Jesus and ask him 'whether it is permitted for a man to release (divorce) his wife'. This is supposed by the evangelist or his source to be asked as a test for Jesus (as it may well have been). The Matthaean version (xix.3) is slightly different, and the difference has caused much excitement. There the Pharisees ask Jesus 'whether it is permitted to release (divorce) one's wife *on any ground*'. As we know Matthew's method of reproducing Mark, *i.e.* inserting a commentary as he goes along, we have no hesitation in assuming that this is what Matthew understood the Pharisees to have *meant*, supposing them actually to have *said* what Mark shows them saying. However, it has been open to modern scholars to assume the reverse, namely that Matthew and his readers would have no doubts about a Jew's right to divorce his wife; they could only be in doubt whether that right could be exercised capriciously. In any event the question is merely a prelude to Jesus's answer, which virtually denies both the more restricted and the more ample assumption: he corrects *either*, namely that the right itself might be exercised, and likewise assuming it to be open to the husband, that it might be exercised on any and every ground.

It is assumed that the reader has available the principal pericope on divorce (Mt xix.3–11, Mk x.2–12) with the parallel texts together (as in Aland's *Synopsis*, § 252). Moreover the four logia on divorce have to be seen synoptically, as below:

Mt v.32	Lk xvi.18
Πᾶς ὁ ἀπολύων τὴν γυναῖκα αὐτοῦ παρεκτὸς λόγου πορνείας ποιεῖ αὐτὴν μοιχευθῆναι, καὶ ὃς ἐὰν ἀπολελυμένην γαμήσῃ, μοιχᾶται.	Πᾶς ὁ ἀπολύων τὴν γυναῖκα αὐτοῦ καὶ γαμῶν ἑτέραν μοιχεύει, καὶ ὁ ἀπολελυμένην ἀπὸ ἀνδρὸς γαμῶν μοιχεύει.
Mt xix.9	**Mk x.11–12**
Ὃς ἂν ἀπολύσῃ τὴν γυναῖκα αὐτοῦ μὴ ἐπὶ πορνείᾳ καὶ γαμήσῃ ἄλλην, μοιχᾶται.	Ὃς ἂν ἀπολύσῃ τὴν γυναῖκα αὐτοῦ καὶ γαμήσῃ ἄλλην, μοιχᾶται ἐπ' αὐτήν· καὶ ἐὰν αὐτὴ ἀπολύσασα τὸν ἄνδρα αὐτῆς γαμήσῃ ἄλλον, μοιχᾶται.

The texts were thoroughly examined recently by Dr Abel Isaksson.[1]

[1] *Marriage and Ministry in the New Temple* (Lund 1965).

Not all his results are satisfactory,[1] and indeed the entire literature is confused and hampered by misunderstandings and pre-judged conclusions. But we are indebted to him particularly for his demonstration that Ml ii.14–16 does *not* throw light on divorce as a topic of family law.[2] Very thorough attention was devoted to the topic and its vast literature by Dom Jacques Dupont, whose results are none the less to be respected for their appearing *cum approbatione ecclesiastica.*[3] We shall proceed from the argument of Jesus, demonstrated in this present work for the first time in its true shape, to the individual logia. The demonstration reveals that the question with which the pericope starts, differing significantly, as Dupont shows, in Matthew and Mark, is not to be reconstructed with certainty from the argument, because either method of commencing would serve equally well.

The subject has greatly perplexed the churches: evidently Matthew's 'except on the ground of unchastity' was always ambiguous. Scholars of all complexions contend that passages are corrupt, that phrases are spurious, or that the text has been incorrectly transmitted or misunderstood by the evangelist or evangelists. The reconstruction offered for the first time here has been described by a friend as an example of *pilpūl* (recherché dialectic). Whether or not it is so, it seems to be correct: and this is the point. That intimate moral questions could be sought to be solved with reference to biblical texts which do not in fact apply themselves directly to the solution, and that the author of the argument should reach down to fundamental considerations for the purpose is in itself very interesting.

Jesus himself in his valedictory remarks on the subject is found (Mt xix.12) seriously offering the standard which he requires for the hearer's free acceptance: 'Let those accept it who can!' This seems at first sight very diffident teaching, and has given scope for Christians throughout the ages to take the whole passage as a piece of perfectionism which communities may try to enforce so far as is practicable in the circumstances. The very odd ending will make better sense when we realise

[1] In particular his narrow interpretation of πορνεία (135). It is very difficult to argue that πορνεία excludes μοιχεία—on the contrary the latter seems wider than the former. The mention of both together does not imply that the one must exclude the other. There are certain objections to be taken to the narrow concept of πορνεία found in J. Bonsirven's otherwise useful *Le Divorce dans le Nouveau Testament* (Tournai 1948).

[2] Isaksson, *op. cit.* 27–34. At p. 31, however, he implies that Malachi is referring, if he refers to marriage at all, to a marriage by commercial negotiation (a point strongly emphasised in the book)—whereas, *pace* the learned author, what seems to be in question on his own showing is a (metaphorical) union of a highly primitive type in which what counted was the physical union.

[3] *Mariage et Divorce dans l'Évangile* (Bruges 1959).

that the disciples' rational suggestion that 'it is better to refrain from marriage' is *not* based on the discreditable reflection[1] that if one cannot divorce, in ninety-nine cases out of a hundred, without incurring sin, and if one cannot guarantee that one's wife will use this security entirely to one's satisfaction, it is better to remain unmarried—but rather upon the reflection that sexual relations carry with them the multiple inconveniences which we shall describe below, so that abstention from intercourse is indirectly recommended by the teacher. This Jesus denies, consistently with the doctrine he has been explaining: those[2] whose natures exempt them from the state of affairs set out in Genesis, the natural eunuchs or genetic hermaphrodites and the individuals whose temperaments disincline them to sexual activity, will alone be able to abstain from intercourse. The result is not a stiff teaching followed by a flaccid reservation, but a bald statement of fact, which anyone can recognise as no less than the truth. The 'old crux' has, therefore, a simple solution, requiring no recondite interpretation.

The teaching as set out below has not been accepted by any church. The reasons do not concern us here, but if the text has been regarded as perfectionist, and if the matter concerns (as it does) the individual conscience, divergencies in canon law are understandable. Moreover it is worth pointing out at this stage that Jesus envisaged an oriental society in which first marriages were almost invariably with virgin brides and these were married not long after puberty. If no one could, with safety to conscience, marry anyone but a virgin or a widow, the effects on western society would have been catastrophic, a point which can be left for others to pursue if they wish.

The method of proceeding here is unusual. First the superficial interpretation of Jesus's teaching will be outlined, more or less as a casual reading of Matthew will permit. Then the chief weakness in this will be pointed out and discussed. Then, since the subject is of great general importance, irrespective of our present juridical concern, the whole argument will be gone over and in the footnotes occasional reference will be made to the flaws in previous research and to misunderstandings which have bedevilled the innumerable otherwise admirable treatments of this perplexing passage. At the outset let us accept that Matthew was probably intentionally ambiguous, was anxious to leave room for the incorrect (soft) interpretation with which we shall start, and had more theological (allegorical) objects in mind than appear on the surface.

[1] W. D. Davies, *Setting of the Sermon on the Mount* (Cambridge 1964), 393. C. G. Montefiore, *Synoptic Gospels*, ii (London 1909), 690, calls it 'exceedingly naïve and candid'. He adds (691) that Jesus's reply is in bad accord with the purpose of the section. But is it?

[2] Blinzler, *ZNW* 48 (1957), 254–70.

Any spiritual teaching on divorce brings up the allegory of God and his people,[1] just as Paul uses the identical topic to emphasise the relation between Christ and the Church.[2] But we are not to depart from the words of our text: the evangelist may have been devious, but we have no reason to do what so many have done before us, namely to excise or abandon portions the use of which we cannot understand. Our argumentation needs no distortions of the text, and is as happy with Matthew, for all its faults, as it is with Mark.

Asked about divorce, Jesus points to the constitution of Creation. Man and his wife become one flesh. Thus no human being can purport to divorce them. What then of Moses's provisions (Dt xxiv.1)? These were a concession. When can this concession be utilised? We are not told, but one infers that since adultery is, according to Jesus, committed by remarriage after divorce, the ground for the use of Moses's concession which Jesus permits must be unchastity in the wife. The biblical text literally supports this, though according to the Bet Hillel it would support an even wider scope for the husband's use of his customarily established right.[3] Therefore our guess that this was the scope Jesus intended is reasonable. To continue with the superficial view, if the concession is availed of otherwise than in such a case (Matthew specifically says 'except on the ground of unchastity')[4] adultery is committed

[1] See below, p. 465.

[2] 1 Co vi, citing Genesis. Ep v.31. *Cf.* Rm i.

[3] The right is alluded to correctly at Mt i.19. I cannot accept the statement in I. Abrahams' illuminating essay (*Studies in Pharisaism and the Gospels*, 1st ser., Cambridge 1917, 72) that Joseph had no option as to discarding Mary. He could still have kept her—as he actually did. The implications of his situation deserve separate treatment. Works dealing with marriage and divorce include E. Neufeld, *Ancient Hebrew Marriage Laws* (London 1944); D. W. Amram, *Jewish Law of Divorce according to Bible and Talmud* (Philadelphia 1896); M. Mielziner, *Jewish Law of Marriage and Divorce* (Cincinnati 1884); L. M. Epstein, *Marriage Laws in the Bible and the Talmud* (Cambridge, Mass. 1942) (our texts are considered at p. 14–15); M. Duschak, *Das Mosaisch-Talmudische Eherecht* (Vienna 1864); M. Cahn, *Le Divorce dans la Législation Talmudique* (Paris 1901); L. Blau, *Die jüdische Ehescheidung und der jüdische Scheidebrief* (Strasburg 1911–12) (esp. Pt. 1, 45–72). Several of these works, especially where they deal with divorce initiated by the wife would have gone far to obviate theologians' difficulties with Mk x.12 (see below). Among more recent studies are R. Yaron, 'On divorce in Old Testament times', *RIDA* 3rd ser. 4 (1957), 117–28; Z. W. Falk, *Hebrew Law in Biblical Times* (Jerusalem 1964), 154–7. Z. W. Falk, *Jewish Matrimonial Law in the Middle Ages* (Oxford 1966) is rich on earlier law. In his view the practice of Jewish women taking the initiative to divorce their husbands (120) was a result of exposure to Greek law. This is almost certainly true in part, but Jewish and Islamic law reacted in the wife's favour irrespective of heathen models. K. Kahana, *The Theory of Marriage in Jewish Law* (Leiden 1966) is strong on principle, less so in detailed information. B. Cohen, 'Concerning divorce in Jewish and Roman law', *Proc. Am. Acad. for Jew. Res., N.Y.*, 21 (1952), 3–34 is reprinted at his *JRL* I, 377–408.

[4] For the endless controversies over these words see U. Holzmeister, S.J., 'Die Streitfrage über die Ehescheidungstexte bei Matthäus . . .', *Biblica*, 26 (1945), 133–46.

by the husband in remarrying, by the wife in remarrying, and by a third party marrying either of them (Mark is silent about the third party, but this may not be as significant as it seems).[1] Or so one supposes. These adulteries seem to afford the reason why divorce is not permissible except within the scope deduced above. Jesus thus agrees with Bet Shammai. A woman properly divorced was available for remarriage without fear of adultery on anyone's part: this was (and remains) the common Jewish view. So much for a superficial reading, which would alarm very few readers.

But Mark alone would not allow this reading to be taken, and indeed the Catholic Church has preferred to take Mark literally and Matthew's exception-clause as referring to separation other than divorce, an awkward subtlety. Other faults appear. Is *no* 'adultery' committed when one divorces on the ground of unchastity? We are in some difficulty over basic terms. The fundamental commandment, Ex xx.13(14), is in that half of the Decalogue which deals with offences against God.[2] It says simply *lo' tin*^{e}*'āf* ('Thou shalt not commit N'F'). This is normally translated 'adultery', but since intercourse between unmarried people who are not able or willing to marry each other by that means (as was theoretically always possible at Jewish law) must be forbidden, though it does not come within the English concept of 'adultery' (which is confined to intercourse between parties not married to each other, one or both of whom is already married to another) it is to this commandment that we allot it. The explicit prohibition of a man's adultery appears at Lv xviii.20, and it is to be observed that coveting the neighbour's wife is separately dealt with at Ex xx.17, while incest and whoredom are distinctly forbidden by various other commandments. Hence 'sexual irregularity', or 'fornication' will approach nearer to the meaning of N'F than 'adultery', and this is confirmed by the constant biblical use of this root for the metaphor of religious unfaithfulness, unconfined to gender or marital status. Did Jesus mean, by μοιχεία, what we mean by 'adultery', or did he not rather mean the concept N'F, which by his

[1] It is relevant to interpose here and to explain that Jewish juridical technique places a very special importance upon commandments' bearing individually upon *both* parties to a prohibited activity: see the discussion at b. San. 54*b* = Sonc. 368 and Maimonides's 350th negative commandment (at Chavel, II, 315), and his 347th negative commandment (at Chavel, II, 312–13).

[2] J. J. Stamm and M. E. Andrew, *The Ten Commandments in Recent Research* (London, 1967), 100: legitimate marriage is presupposed (quoting Procksch); but Reventlow goes more deeply into the commandment—the committing of adultery brought into view the whole field of sexuality (with the dangers lying therein for a way of life comformable to faith in God). *N'F* is pronounced, by the way, *na-ấf*.

Dupont, 81–114. H. Baltensweiler at *Th.Z.* 15 (1959), 340–56 suggests πορνεία (which really refers to unlawful sex relations) meant forbidden unions amongst the heathen.

day (outside criminal contexts)[1] meant the whole range of sexual experience, including notions far beyond intercourse with a neighbour's wife (a point to which we return in detail)? It is inconceivable that he should have warned his hearers against N'F in the criminal sense but forborne, in a highly moral context, to warn them against secondary and applied N'F, which were equally sinful with the first, and indistinguishable from the moral aspect. An objection more immediately striking is the question whether Moses, by permitting divorce and apparently contemplating remarriage thereafter by a stranger, thereby purported to put an end to the 'one flesh'. *This is the crux.* If he did, valid divorce ends the objections to intercourse with strangers. If he did not, the possibility is excluded of forming a valid one-flesh relationship with another party: whereupon the sexual intercourse with that third party is outside marriage as conforming to the statements of Genesis on the subject, and so within the concept of N'F, forbidden in the Decalogue, as understood by moral teachers of Jesus's period.

The difficulty seems to have been observed in apostolic times. It is otherwise difficult to account for the curious translations of *sépher k^e^riytūt* at Dt xxiv.1. The N.T. follows the LXX, βιβλίον ἀποστασίου which implies a cessation of cohabitation. The competing translations (see Field's *Origen's Hexapla*, *ad loc.*) prefer words implying the 'cutting' in the sense of 'destruction', a human destruction of the conjugal relationship, such as would purport to put an end to the one flesh. We cannot press these metaphorical niceties too far, but the point was obviously a sensitive one: as well it may have been, because the Jewish teaching was that divorce, though legally possible, was morally deplorable.

MOSES AS LEGISLATOR

If we are to proceed logically it is plain that no act of Moses could have abrogated the constitution of humanity, which was not committed to him to revise. No part of the covenant at Sinai could have enabled man to break a bond which nature itself created, it could only afford him machinery for his convenience, or for the better performance of his moral duties. Just as the one flesh is not created by the passing of money

[1] It is most important to bear in mind (as R. H. Charles in his *Teaching of the New Testament on Divorce* (1921) and *Divorce and Nullity* (1927) and others did not) that the criminal definition (Lv xx.10, Dt xxii.22) for the purposes of inflicting a penalty is quite another matter, and has nothing to do with the concept N'F as such. The highly unqualified terms in which the seventh commandment is framed ought to have warned against this confusion.

or a promise of money (as in Adam's case where there was no betrothal) so it is not broken by the delivery of a piece of written paper: thus it follows that N'F (μοιχεία) may be committed by means of ending conjugal relations. Whether the husband or the wife initiated this, under any law, customary or otherwise, or *de facto* with no law at all, the moral position was unchanged: the one flesh remained and the pair were still obliged to remain faithful to each other. The one-flesh doctrine is obviously and literally the basis of Jesus's reasoning, and divorce cannot end it, even in cases where Moses's concession may be availed of. Thus adultery is committed even in cases where on any current doctrine amongst the Jews the husband would be entitled to divorce his wife, does so, and marries again. What of cases where, without the excuse of her unchastity, he divorces, say, out of pique? The answer proceeds *a fortiori*: the one flesh is not broken. The text of Mark is thus literally correct. Luke agrees with him. One who divorces and marries again is an adulterer *vis-à-vis* his first wife, for he breaks the commandment against N'F. The Matthaean version, which has given constant trouble, is equally correct, though embarrassing as it can give rise to the incorrect inference we indicated above. One who divorces *for unchastity* is avoiding 'adultery' at home. There is something distinctly to be said on the moral side for his preferring to clean his home, to avoid temptation, rather than to keep the wife with him out of fear of responsibility for her misadventures abroad. He cannot be accused of sexual immorality in sending her away if at that moment he is in moral danger at home.[1] Admittedly it is up to him, though no more to him than to the lover, to see to the woman's welfare after he has divorced her: they are still one flesh and the welfare of the divorced wife should be a righteous Jewish husband's concern (see Midr. R., Gen. XVII.3 = Sonc. 134). At any rate he can divorce her to *avoid* adultery, and if she is unchaste already the recurrence of unchastity can be presumed to lie at *her* door. The position is exactly the reverse with one who divorces *without* that justification. By definition his home is clean. Thus by turning her out of doors he faces one or more of the three types of N'F. Thus the Matthaean statement makes excellent sense, but not of course in the way in which it is usually taken. The fault of our exegetes is that they have not envisaged the true course of the argument and thus do not see the silent contrast between the husband who is authorised and him who is not authorised to divorce, and the relative moral dangers to be incurred in each case.

This systematic but novel interpretation is backed by the teaching of Paul (1 Co vii), who forbids divorce and deprecates separation, though

[1] There is a saying. 'Can fire be near tow without singeing it?' b. San. 37*a* = Sonc. 232.

he likewise deprecates intercourse as such. He makes small concessions to those married people who are not both Christians, and who, if they are not willing to remain united, may be separated. To him, at any rate, the moral objection in such cases was not important: but this was a marginal case. It is also backed by the principle in the *Shepherd* of Hermas, whose teaching[1] is unquestionably based on the doctrine of one flesh, which subsists after adultery, even after divorce, and on the taboo against two men having or appearing to have intercourse with one woman. Paul's reference to the doctrine (1 Co vi.16) that a man becomes one flesh even with a prostitute fits this way of thinking.[2] There is no ground for supposing that this is a late development, since Paul is not asserting something new, but relying on what will not be denied. Intercourse itself, between marriageable people, may make a marriage at Jewish law[3] but Jesus is not speaking only of *marriage*. In the one-flesh relationship which has not been defiled sexuality finds its natural end. The discovery of a sexual plurality, a moral monstrosity, either by reason of pre-marital unchastity or post-marital adultery, interrupts, though it does not end, innocent sexuality. There one flesh is superseded by something else; in consequence the sexual community must cease; the husband must abstain; he should not divorce her against her will; if she is unrepentant and wants to go to her lover he cannot keep her and enjoy her, he may divorce her, to ease his own moral burden; but she may not marry the lover while the husband lives (Jewish law later says never); nor may the husband marry again while she lives. In effect all Israel must practise the scrupulousness of the priests (Lv xxi.7, 13–15) who may not marry divorced women or keep with them even their wives married as virgins if these have fallen under any suspicion. And bishops must be *almost* equally scrupulous: the 'husband of one wife' phrase referring to these requirements (and not

[1] Mandate 4, xxix (Goodspeed, *Ap. Fathers*, 1950, 125–6; Joly, *Le Pasteur* [1958], 153–5). The text belongs according to Goodspeed to *c.* A.D. 100, according to others to about 150. On its authorship note the theory of S. Giet at *Studia Patr.* 8 (*TuU* 93) (1966), 10–24. The passage (known to theologians: see, *e.g.* Kirsopp Lake, *Expos.* 7th ser. 10 [1910], 423–4) is important and should be given in full: εἰ γυναῖκα ἔχῃ τις πιστὴν ἐν κυρίῳ καὶ ταύτην εὕρῃ ἐν μοιχείᾳ τινί, ἆρα ἁμαρτάνει ὁ ἀνὴρ συνζῶν μετ' αὐτῆς; Ἄχρι τῆς ἀγνοίας, φησίν, οὐχ ἁμαρτάνει· ἐὰν δὲ γνοῖ ὁ ἀνὴρ τὴν ἁμαρτίαν αὐτῆς καὶ μὴ μετανοήσῃ ἡ γυνή, ἀλλ' ἐπιμένῃ τῇ πορνείᾳ αὐτῆς καὶ συνζῇ ὁ ἀνὴρ μετ' αὐτῆς, ἔνοχος γίνεται τῆς ἁμαρτίας αὐτῆς καὶ κοινωνὸς τῆς μοιχείας αὐτῆς· τί οὖν, φημί, κύριε, ποιήσῃ ὁ ἀνήρ, ἐὰν ἐπιμείνῃ τῷ πάθει τούτῳ ἡ γυνή; Ἀπολυσάτω, φησίν, αὐτὴν καὶ ὁ ἀνὴρ ἐφ' ἑαυτῷ μενέτω· ἐὰν δὲ ἀπολύσας τὴν γυναῖκα ἑτέραν γαμήσῃ, καὶ αὐτὸς μοιχᾶται.

Delling, at *NT* 1 (1956) 263, describes this doctrine as a misunderstanding of Jesus's teaching, whereas in fact it is very much closer to the core of it than other expositions.

[2] R. Kempthorne, *NTS* 14 (1968), 568–74 explores this with reference to 'incest', *sed quaere*?

[3] *Mishnāh*, Ḳid. I. i. Dt xxii.28–9.

alluding to polygamy as a custom).[1] That the infant Church had similar standards even for the laity is clear from the same source: no widow could be enrolled as such unless she possessed a good record, positive virtues *and* the qualification (one would suppose the somewhat accidental qualification) of having been the wife of one husband.[2] Such is the effect of going to fundamental considerations, going to Genesis to construe the various provisions of Deuteronomy.

The whole of this turns on the concept of 'one flesh'. This one flesh is made by nothing but sexual intercourse, and there is no sexual intercourse which does not make one flesh. An interesting idea has found some adherents; it seeks to explain Gn i.27 as indicating that Adam was originally androgynous. In spite of the age and reasonableness of this interpretation it is at Gn. ii.24 that the 'one-flesh' doctrine is propounded and that doctrine derives from the mating of *two* beings. The one-fleshedness of a couple does not prevent either or both becoming one flesh with others. No ceremony is needed to make two people one flesh. The idea is not based so much on an observed psychological fact, as upon the texts of Genesis themselves. No doubt that fact corroborates the text. The couple become one flesh physically, not mentally, not conditionally upon their awareness of the bond; nor does that one flesh disappear if the bond is denied. The institution of marriage presupposes this law, and no part of the law of marriage and divorce can proceed without accepting this as its basis. One flesh does not make a marriage in all cases; just as not all marriages make one flesh. But it is the one flesh that determines whether it is sinful to engage in any of the activities which are comprehended in the concept N'F as understood in the relevant period. All this might be challenged. It might be urged that 'his wife' at Gn ii.24 implies that only with a wife can a man make one flesh (in which case Paul's allegation is false). But in the beginning (to which Jesus emphatically refers) a man made a woman 'his' who was not previously 'his' or 'another's', and the woman whom a man carnally knew was 'his wife' for only the word 'his' was necessary to turn 'woman' into 'wife'. The institution of marriage must not be allowed to cloud the constitution of humanity, which it subserves. The various elements of biblical law, looked at from this point of view, bear Jesus out. A bridegroom who finds his wife not

[1] The 'polygamous' interpretation of 1 Tm iii.2 and Tt i.6 never seemed very plausible. What is required is that he shall not utilise the civil law to live in a union which righteousness would abhor. He will not marry a divorcee whose previous husband is alive. I do not think it conceivable that the early Church would reject a widowed prestige-bearing candidate who had married, for his second union, a *widow*. Hence 'husband of one wife' must have the technical meaning explained above.

[2] 1 Tm v.9.

to be a virgin may not, in all parts of the Jewish world, have had her stoned: but he was entitled to divorce her, quite apart from the action he might take because his 'goods' are 'spoiled'. Jewish morality and law do not contemplate a man sharing a woman (Jr iii.1). In essentials the doctrine of no divorce except for unchastity appealed to the fundamentals of Jewish morality. The remarriage of a divorced woman is a sinful and socially disreputable affair which Moses can be taken in Dt xxiv to have noticed without approval.[1] Of course marriage comprehends other aspects besides sexuality: the husband is not necessarily suspected of having intercourse with a wife who has been adulterous; if he can abstain from intercourse and can persuade his neighbours that he is not setting a bad example he can maintain her at home and enjoy the other benefits of conjugal life. If, however, he cannot abstain, and suffers from hardness of heart,[2] unwilling to conform to his contractual obligations towards her and his moral obligations towards righteousness, then he can utilise the concession which, in Jesus's view, Moses designed for him. Sexuality outside the uncorrupted unity of the sexuality of Adam and Eve is in breach of the will of God, who constituted man and woman in such a way that sexuality itself subserved the one-fleshedness of the couple. Whether or not the customary law of marriage condones other instances of intercourse will not influence a teacher of righteousness; and Jewish usage (rightly) did not condone intercourse with one

[1] T. Walker, *cit. inf.* p. 380 n. 1, in a treatment of the subject, discusses (275) an inference to be drawn from Jn iv.18. The passage is curious. The woman says she has no husband. Jesus replies that she does well (inadvertently) to admit this, for she has had five men/husbands and the one she now has is not her husband. The Samaritans were scrupulous people in their way, and her reaction shows that she admits his law. The most natural way to take Jesus's comment is in the sense which the present writer takes his teaching on divorce, namely that though a woman may have intercourse with various men in succession (obviously here by divorce amongst other possible methods of release from the marriage bond) she cannot be the wife of any other man while any previous man/husband is still alive. But we cannot rely on this. It seems inconceivable that the woman was a whore in the normal sense, for she would not be at the well and would not object to giving Jesus water merely on the technical grounds which she alleges if that were the case: thus she purported to be a divorced woman or a widow whilst actually consorting with a man secretly. Jesus can hardly be praising her for admitting something that was obvious, therefore he wants her to know that he knows that her union is not a lawful one (whether or not some ceremony or documentary act had been performed may be beside the point). Yet it is not impossible that all her previous husbands had died in succession and that Jesus did rely on the lack of intention of the current lover actually to marry her, whence intercourse (though it would make one flesh) would not effectuate a marriage.

[2] The meaning of this phrase, about which there has been speculation, is settled by Dupont, *op. cit.* 18–19, but he is wrong in suggesting that Moses was unable to effect God's will entirely—a comical notion. The point is that through inability to conform to the requirements of righteousness the husband might sin: to avoid this, a concession to his weakness, divorce was permitted. Customary divorces are only permitted if they conform to this pattern (very few will).

woman by two men: obviously because it accepted that she was one flesh with both. This did not authorise intercourse with both (the Jews were not polyandrous barbarians) but prohibited intercourse with either during the life of the other. Where the Jewish law went wrong was in the failure to perceive that the one flesh persisted after divorce, or where it was perceived (as illustrated at Midr. R., Gen. *cit. sup.*) the implications were not carried over into a thoroughgoing condemnation of the customary law. Gn ii.24 shows that one is not entitled sexually to enjoy a woman who is not 'his', and 'his' means exclusively his. So the argument is complete. Let us now recapitulate the argument with our eye on Matthew's text, since it is the harder.

JESUS'S TEACHING

What we must note for our present purpose is that Jesus did not abrogate, nor did he disapprove of, the legislation of Moses.[1] On the contrary, he saw Moses as conceding what was required by the Jews of the time of Sinai, and afterwards, for their moral comfort. The churches have regarded Jesus as attempting to set aside Moses's rule, in keeping with Matthew's picture of Jesus as a second Moses: but this is otiose and contrary to the reasoning here.[2] We need not see Jesus's teaching

[1] Dupont, *op. cit.* 21–2. Dupont and Bundy are incorrect (p. 23 n. 2) in supposing that Jesus is opposing Scripture with Scripture: he is harmoniously construing them. The notion that God was opposed to Moses as legislator (*ibid.* 32), and that Jesus doubted the validity of the Mosaic Law (*ibid.* 34) is otiose. D. W. Riddle, *Jesus and the Pharisees* (Chicago 1928) thought Jesus 'undercut the Mosaic Law'. B. H. Branscomb, *Jesus and the Law of Moses* (London 1930), 153–4: Moses's 'concession' must be disregarded as imperfect and incomplete. This is followed by H. J. Schoeps at *Rev. d'Hist. et de Phil. Relig.* 33 (1953) at p. 13ff. This is all mistaken. See also Gutbrod at *ThWzNT* IV, 1056 (sin not to be presumed). In an important lecture entitled 'Marriage in the Bible and in the Early Church' delivered by Professor W. Rordorf of Neuchâtel in the University of London on 21 November, 1968 the point of view expressed was that Jesus said that God wanted the couple to remain one flesh so long as they lived; the ethical imperative to love the neighbour took priority over Moses's rule about divorce, because that imperative was not consistent with divorce and remarriage—but on the other hand Jesus did not teach that marriage was indissoluble. This point of view is interesting as it seeks to construe Jesus by reference to fundamental propositions (turning the tables on him, as it were), as it goes a long way to conform to current sentiment, and as it goes some way towards recognising that Jesus addressed himself not to the human institutions of marriage and divorce in the first instance, but to the divine provision for the unification of male and female. However, the learned professor failed to observe that the doctrine of the 'one flesh' is objective and absolute, and though Jesus may obtain forgiveness for a sinner who repents, he does *not* offer to the unhappy spouse an opportunity to put an end to his or her 'one-fleshed' status (with its positive and negative obligations) whenever it becomes evident that love of the 'neighbour' has ceased to be possible.

[2] J. Dauvillier, *Le Mariage dans le Droit Classique de l'Église* (Paris 1933) gives the pre-1918 western canon law. Apart from Dupont the present situation may be found

as a recommendation, either, to the *élite* to do something extra, nor should we understand Jesus to have described Moses's work as a concession to sinfulness (it was a concession provided to avoid sin). These were possible interpretations but it is ultimately easier to see Jesus as interpreting Moses's work so as to consist with righteousness.

'Have you not read that the Creator, from the beginning, made them male and female? And He said "for this reason man shall leave the father and the mother and shall be attached to his wife, and the two shall become one flesh". So that they are no longer two but a single flesh. Accordingly that which God joined together man must not separate.' There is a *midrash* here. Gn i.27 is interpreted with the aid of Gn ii.24: people were made in two genders and it is on this account (ἕνεκα τούτου) that the adherence to parents, which is equally natural and is commanded by the fourth commandment, is abrogated so far as necessary to achieve adherence to the wife, so that man and wife become one flesh. Professor David Daube has another interpretation, but he prefers to suppose that Jesus originally cited only Gn i.27 and the reference to Gn ii.24 was added later—in his view it is the androgynous nature of Adam which can, unaided, explain the objection to divorce. But we should take another path, which does not need that supposition, but rather pursues the simple fact that divorce as a human institution is only tolerable if it is used in accordance with God's will. Nothing is said about love. Correctly. After intercourse the husband loves his wife, and the emotional adherence follows the fact of physical adherence. The latter was taken extremely literally: one nakedness, one flesh.[1] Sexuality, sexual behaviour belongs to the one-flesh concept, and is meaningless, apart from being prohibited, outside it. Here Jesus claims that man, the husband, or men, *i.e.* a court, cannot purport to end, in the eye of morality, a union which God himself directed and provided. The inconvenience of the result does not diminish the logic of the teaching.

'They say to him, "Why then did Moses command to give a docu-

[1] Lv xviii.8, 10, 16, xx.21, etc.

in Cardinal J. MacRory, *New Testament and Divorce* (Dublin 1934); G. H. Joyce, S.J., *Christian Marriage: an Historical and Doctrinal Study*, 2nd edn (London 1948) (see 302); P. J. O'Mahony, ed., *Catholics and Divorce* (London 1959); and, for an Anglican point of view, in T. A. Lacey and R. C. Mortimer, *Marriage in Church and State* (London 1947); K. E. Kirk, *Marriage and Divorce*, 2nd edn (London 1948); also in F. C. Grant's article at *Ang. Theol. Rev.* 22 (1940), 169–87. Useful notes appear also in J. Simon, 'The biblical background to marriage and divorce', *Law Soc. Gaz.* 62 (1965), 80–4. For specialists A. H. van Vliet and C. G. Breed, *Marriage and Canon Law* (London 1964) is a concise and complete account of its subject, as applied by Roman Catholic courts.

ment of divorce and divorce (her)?" He says to them, "Moses permitted you to divorce your wives in view of your hardness of heart, but this was not how it was made in the beginning".' The very text of Moses is intended to subserve the taboo. It is concerned with preventing the first husband from resuming intercourse after his wife has been discarded even though she was one flesh with himself (and remains so). The intention of the passage is to prevent loaning of wives and other immorality,[1] and the spirit of this must be read into the beginning of it. That is why it requires that he should have seen some 'unseemly thing' or lewdness, for that is obviously what it originally meant. This view contradicts the tendency and teaching of the Bet Hillel.[2] Hardness of heart, we have seen, has nothing to do with human compassion but implies human weakness in front of moral temptation. If *H* has had intercourse with his virgin wife *W* they make a unity, *HW*. If *W* has intercourse subsequently with an adulterer, *A*, the result is not two units, *HW* and *WA* only, though it is certainly that, but also a monstrosity *HWA*, in which all sexual activity is forbidden. Therefore *H* is entitled to use Moses's concession, whereupon he is commanded to give *W* a *get*, wherefrom it may be ascertained that *H* has no claims on her. One might argue that in Jewish usage *H* would signify in the document that as far as he was concerned *W* could marry any Jew:[3] but even if he did, the responsibility lay with *W* and any man who offered to marry her to observe the prohibition of sexual intercourse so long as *H* lived. If *H* had any responsibility for sin resulting therefrom, as for example by encouraging her to marry a man who would have intercourse with her, he broke the commandment against N'F, for although *W* ceased to be 'his' so far as conjugal rights in general went (for he had abandoned those in the interests of his moral comfort) she did not cease to be 'his' in the sense of one-fleshedness.

Jesus was anticipated in his reliance upon Genesis for this purpose by the Dead Sea Scroll Community, who quite possibly took the same view of divorce as he took, and they certainly agreed with what he obviously inferred, namely that polygamy was prohibited.[4]

[1] J. Breslawi in an article in the *P. Korngruen Volume*, 44–56 (as reported in Z. W. Falk, *Current Bibliography*, 2) explains that the practice prohibited by Dt xxiv.1–4 was current and persisted until the law of the Qur'ān was enforced. Biblical reform does not necessarily prove social reform, though it of course affected the ideal considerably.

[2] The Talmudic position is concisely given at *Mishnāh*, Giṭṭin IX.10, b. Giṭ. 90*a*–*b* = Sonc. 436–9.

[3] *Mishnāh*, Giṭ. IX, 3 and surviving bills of divorce. Benoit, etc., *Discoveries* II, no. 19, 104ff. Daube, *N.T. and Rab. Jud.* p. 76 n. 1.

[4] Zadokite Fragment (Damascus Document), *CD* IV, 20–V, 2 (E. Lohse, *Die Texte aus Qumran*, Munich 1964, 74–5) thoroughly studied by P. Winter, 'Sadoquite Fragments IV, 20, 21 and the exegesis of Genesis i.27 in late Judaism', *ZAW* 68

As Professor Daube rightly points out, in a potentially polygamous society it is inconceivable that the husband should be guilty of adultery if he marries again while his first wife lives: so that it is evident that Jesus took it as certain that polygamy was an evil and abhorrent custom.

Further light on the non-availability of intercourse between *W* and *H* after *W's* intercourse with *A*, so long as *A* lives, is available from a literal reading of Gn ii.25, which is automatically called up by Jesus's mere citation of verse 24. 'And the two (may be) both naked, *the man and his wife* and (may be) not ashamed.' The explicit words indicate that where there *would* be shame, as in sexual relations common to *H*, *W* and *A*, there can be no intercourse. The residual one-fleshedness of the spouses cannot authorise intercourse in such a situation. Hermas takes a view approaching this, though not as strict as Jesus's.

Since the concession is to be used when an 'unseemly thing' is seen, and the husband cannot abstain, the relation between these ideas and the seventh commandment, which is the key to the whole, must be explored. N'F, by the time of the Second Commonwealth, though not in biblical times,[1] comprehended several different classes of sexual activity, and the prohibition could be broken by acts which were not adultery in any modern sense. The commandment could be broken by (i) orgasm outside the one flesh, or, to take the narrower Jewish view, outside marriage;[2] (ii) by placing oneself within temptation to commit (i)—for the fence must be maintained around the law[3] and (iii) by causing others knowingly or unwittingly to commit (i).[4] Jesus explicitly teaches (ii) at Mt v.28. It is impossible to argue that he was exaggerating, for the same doctrine is unquestionably traditionally Jewish,[5] and fits the further-eastern asceticism of the period. These extensions are in

[1] Note the attitude reflected in Judah's dealing with Tamar (Gn xxxviii). And see Jg xix. But *cf.* Test. Iss. VII. 2 (cited effectively by T. Walker, *Jesus and Jewish Teaching* [London 1923], 234).

[2] b. Niddāh 13*b*. Note the phrase *ha-m^{e}nā'afiym b^{e}yad*. Note also the development of the seventh commandment in the *Didache* (ii.2) and the *Ep. of Barnabas* (xix.4) which enumerate adultery, pederasty, and fornication. L. M. Epstein, *Sex Laws and Customs in Judaism* (New York 1948), 11, 114, 117, 146, 167–8, 203. Dupont, *op. cit.* 107–10.

[3] *Mishnāh*, 'Āvot, I, i.

[4] The pander is prohibited by the seventh commandment: b. Shev. 47*b* = Sonc. 291 (Simeon b. Tarfon, who lived *c.* A.D. 100, read *lotin^{e}'āf* as *lo-tan^{e}'iyf*). Interference between husband and wife is a breach of that commandment: Midr. R., Num. X.2 = Sonc. 345.

[5] See Midr. R., Lev. XXIII.12 = Sonc. 302, a teaching of Resh Laḳish. Jb xxxi.3. Sir ix.5–8, xli.20–1. Epstein, *Sex Laws*, p. 114, 115, n. 53.

(1956), 71–84 (an important study which greatly strengthens the suspicion that the community abhorred divorce—the myth of bisexual creation does *not* appear to have influenced Jesus's teaching). Isaksson, *op. cit.* 57–63. Daube, *op. cit.* 81, gives an account of a variant reading at Gn ii.24 which suggests that certain interests wished (by omitting the word 'two') to leave the door open for polygamy.

any case legitimate interpretations of the unpointed word N'F. Moreover the *yetser ha-ra'* must be overcome: temptation or incitement to commit any of these classes of N'F is also to be avoided as a religious obligation in itself.

No problem now remains with the four logia. Matthew's insertion of the exception-clause was explained above. One is entitled to divorce for the wife's unchastity, if one cannot keep her as a housekeeper. This is plain on the reasoning in Mark alone, where that clause does not appear. The clause emphasises that where the excuse for taking advantage of Moses's concession is not present the divorcing husband plainly incurs sins in one or more kinds of breaches of the commandment against N'F. The differing formulation of the risks incurred, at which the disciples reasonably quail, need not be too closely observed for hidden motives. There remains the famous 'anomaly' of the Marcan formulation. How could Mark speak seriously of a wife 'releasing' or divorcing her husband and marrying another man?

The debate has been keen.[1] This writer thinks help could have been had from Jewish usage relative to matrimonial disputes and from notorious Islamic usage and even from a recherché and unique passage in an Indian document. In all three civilisations the initiative to effect (but not necessarily to negotiate) a divorce lies with the husband. There is no debate about this. In India, where the one-flesh doctrine (older than normative Judaism) has taken command of marriage law and sentiment amongst the culturally educated classes, divorce was impossible but the wife could be separated from conjugal intercourse on the husband's initiative, and not *vice versa*. In Islam the husband's power has been the subject of continual complaint in recent times. But although the law itself leaves the power in the husband's hands, means of securing the wife's safety have always been open to parents or guardians or, in the case of a widow marrying, the bride herself (in India widow-remarriage was theoretically impossible as the one flesh lasted even after the death of one spouse). The husband can agree in his marriage contract to divorce the wife if he marries again, to pay her a huge sum if he takes the initiative in divorcing her otherwise, and to give her the freedom to take the initiative in cases stipulated or unstipulated, *e.g.* to consider herself divorced if he fails to return from a voyage within a specified period. Social customs would determine how much freedom the wife ought to have, which at law would be derived from the husband himself. Thus divorces actually initiated by the wife are far from unheard of. Certain cases of divorce in Islam are well

[1] Delling, *NT* 1 (1956), 266; Yaron's 'refutation' of Modrzejewski at *Ivra* 13 (1962), 170ff.

known to be in the wife's hands and the husband's formal co-operation is taken for granted.[1] In Judaism, apparently by Jesus's time, if not much earlier, a court could compel a husband to divorce his wife on grounds accepted in the community,[2] and it is impossible to rule out collusion or complacent action by such a court, which might act quite informally. The behaviour of Jews in Palestine would be influenced by non-Jewish practices and documents, for matrimonial affairs might at any time come before non-Jewish courts; in the diaspora this would be even more markedly true. Greek influence (*e.g.* in the Decapolis region) will have been great, not to speak of Egypt? Therefore marriage contracts giving the wife the right to effectuate her own divorce would by no means necessarily infringe the Jewish Law, which in theory left the initiative with the husband, as it still does, to the great embarrassment of many in modern Israel. Thus when we find in Elephantine long before our period,[3] and apparently, but not quite certainly, in C. P. Jud. 144 during our period,[4] and in a second-century document found at Murabba'ât[5] that a Jewish wife may take the initiative in divorcing her husband, or apparently do so, this can be read consistently with the basic Jewish law. There is thus no anomaly in Mark's speaking of a woman divorcing her husband, whether or not Paul prefers to

[1] Sufficient details are given at Abdur Rahim, *Principles of Muhammadan Jurisprudence* (London 1911), 338–9; F. H. Ruxton, *Maliki Law* (London 1916), 121–33. The logical last step was reached in Pakistan in 1966 in the (highly controversial) case of *Khurshid Bibi* v. *Muhammad Amin* [1967] *Pak. Leg. Dec.* 97 (S.C.): a wife can insist on a divorce by paying compensation to her husband and the court will divorce her. A. A. A. Fyzee at (1936) 38 Bom.L.R., *J.* 113–123, is instructive.

[2] The concept of standard of treatment for a wife is voiced at Ex xxi.7–11. *Mishnāh*, Ket. VII, 9, 10; Giṭṭ. IX, 8; Yev. XIV, 1; 'Arāk. V, 6.

[3] E. Volterra, 'Osservazioni sul divorzio nei documenti aramaici', *Studi Orient. . . . Levi Della Vida* II (Rome 1956), 586–600. R. Yaron, *The Law of the Aramaic Papyri* (Oxford 1961), 53–64. Vincent, *La Religion des Judéo-Araméens*, 505 (ref. to Pap. Eleph. 15 line 23). I have not had access to A. Verger, *Ricerche giuridiche sui papiri aramaici di Elefantina* (*Studi Sem.* 16) (Rome 1965).

[4] J. Modrzejewski, 'Les Juifs et le droit hellénistique: divorce et égalité des epoux . . .', *Ivra*, 12 (1961), 162–93. Yaron is evidently right when he contends (p. 381 n. 1 above) that none of the documents prove that the spouses were juridically equal; and of course the Marcan passage does not contend that this was so. V. Taylor, *Gospel acc. to St. Mark* (London 1963), 421 alleges that Jesus placed husband and wife in a position of equality, which goes too far. The attitude adopted by the present writer avoids the problem which, in this connection, was faced by D. Daube, *New Testament and Rabbinic Judaism* (London 1956), 365–6, provided ἀπολύειν is taken simply to mean 'divorce'. Daube's study of the vocabulary involved is basic. See *ibid.* 362–72. His treatment of our subject *ibid.* 71ff. and later, leads to the suggestion that Matthew altered the Marcan account. This seems not to be necessary, if one takes the point of view adopted here.

[5] P. Benoit, J. T. Milik, R. De Vaux, *Discoveries in the Judaean Desert II, Les Grottes de Murabba'ât* (Oxford 1961), document 20 (Aramaic marriage contract), lines 5–6, is not so conclusive as one could wish. The learned editors are satisfied that the wife is envisaged as having the right to terminate the marriage and to recover her dowry.

speak of her 'deserting' or 'separating from' him, for that is exactly what happened, whether one looks at those documents, or consults the rabbinical law on divorce on grounds proffered by the wife. This non-existent conflict[1] between Jewish law and Jewish usage is a parallel with the law on διαθήκη. In theory a man could not alter the law that would operate at his death, so as to vary the succession, and give, for example, an equal share to all sons. But everyone knows that documents were executed which were not testaments in reality but which had an effect as like that of a testament as made no difference. The practice and the law stood together and it was not necessary for the Jew taking advantage of a hybrid institution to draw attention to the anomalies or apparent anomalies in the document itself.

But whether the wife, hiding behind her husband's permission, or a court's resolution, was less sinful than a husband divorcing her out of hand remained a proper question for a Jewish casuist. Of course the prohibition of N'F had applied to both parties: a woman can be as guilty of N'F as a man. If she takes the initiative she is guilty, even though the law would purport to place the responsibility somewhere else, because it is she who in that case severs what God has joined. It is the *de facto* severance that counts.

Jesus's *responsum* is a veritable judgement of Portia. 'By all means use your facility if you must, but take care that no N'F is committed. So much for your freedom of divorce and remarriage, so much indeed for your concept of marriage; and so much for your marriage contracts and the schemes sometimes envisaged in them!' Those who seek after righteousness have another standard to live by: and only those to whom the Almighty has given deficient sexuality or who have implanted in them a zeal to control sexuality in the interests of righteousness can ignore the commandment at Gn i.28, are exempted from the consequences as stated at ii.24, and may expect to avoid the risks which mankind as a whole has to face. Jesus leaves the topic, not with flaccid permission to the disciples to sin if they desperately want to, but with a warning that only a very few are exempt from the spiritual peril against which they must be ever on their guard. This would *not* be to reduce what is radical to the possible.[2]

[1] In the delightful idiom of our day this is a 'non-problem'. There is no reason for supposing that Jesus or his disciples contemplated an *irregular* or quixotic self-divorce by the wife. See App. II to this chapter. The point is that even if she properly used her civil rights she would be in danger of sin—a perfectly valid point for a religious teacher to make.

[2] On the chapter of Matthew see W. D. Davies, *Setting of the Sermon on the Mount*, 212–13. At p. 394 the learned author most interestingly compares a rabbinic principle of not demanding the impossible: but was this Jesus's point? I very much doubt it.

CONCLUSION

Moses, as legislator, had no greater power than Moses as mediator. He did not grant rights which the nature of things precludes by its true implication.

Jesus proved that the *Torāh* taught a stricter way of righteousness than anyone could have desired. Gentiles became one flesh, so that his doctrine had its scope even for those to whom the covenant at Sinai was not relevant.

But what of this method of argumentation? It should be judged by results. Jesus's doctrine, which involves the belief that even casual intercourse creates a relationship rendering sinful any further intercourse with others during the partner's lifetime, is not at present accepted by any church. The strictest church[1] actually contemplates a husband having intercourse with a wife who has a lover, though it faithfully adheres to the view that a divorced person cannot remarry in the lifetime of the former spouse.[2]

APPENDIX I. AN OBJECTION NOTICED

To the argument that in Jesus's view man and woman become 'one flesh' by intercourse alone without any ceremony (which I have shown to be the basis of his thought), it is possible to object as follows: even if such a position could be posited on the basis of the text of Genesis, it was not the rabbinical view at the time of Jesus. Now to this there are two answers, a short one and a long one. The short one is that we are not very sure of the rabbinical *views*, for the surviving Pharisaical view is not evidence for the whole of Jewish thought at the period; and even if we were sure what would that have to do with the subject? Jesus was at liberty to take a stricter view of such taboo questions than the Pharisees did, just as the sect known from the Dead Sea Scrolls differed from the 'seekers-after-smooth-things at Jerusalem' and the 'men of the Pit'. The sectarians of the Dead Sea had no more respect for the Pharisees than for the Sadducees; and it remains an open question how far Jesus sided with Pharisees in religio-legal questions and how far he found fault with them: there are passages to be cited on either side.

The long answer is equally valid. The rabbis visualised the union between Adam and Eve as a marriage. Why? The very fact that they did so concedes,

[1] See p. 377 n. 2 above, also S. B. Kitchin, *A History of Divorce* (London 1912). It is fair to comment that judicial separation (*divorcium a mensa et thoro*) was and is available to a spouse complaining of the other's adultery—but what if no such complaint is made (the *ex officio mero* procedure is obsolete)?

[2] On one of the aspects of Jesus's teaching which is explained in this chapter Prof. Joyce (*op. cit.* 289) says: 'Had Christ really so taught, it is inconceivable that the Church should have been completely ignorant of it.' But see Hermas. Where ignorance is bliss . . .!

in a way, our argument. They thought that the Genesis story was part and parcel of the institution of marriage, and that in a way confirms Jesus's approach as one which many of his contemporaries would have regarded as admissible. But why exactly did the rabbis so regard that union? Simply because prestige, good manners, the larger health of society, all urge the formation of marriage by a betrothal, followed by a 'hallowing', in other words a ceremony. From the beginning of the world unions have turned into marriages by the operation of legal presumptions, without any ceremony. Yet society, thinking such private arrangements barely civilised and derogatory to the prestige of the girl's family, has insisted on a ceremony wherever possible. The history of Indian law, with which we are not much concerned here, except that it provides a distant parallel, gives a striking illustration; and the law of Scotland went the same way in living memory. It is of course clear that since the capacity to enter into a legal marriage is not present in every case of intercourse we cannot make unions into marriages in every case—but only where the intention and capacity is there, and ancient societies as well as our own greatly preferred a ceremony to obviate doubts in so important a matter. Thus the rabbis read back into the union of Adam and Eve the legal institution of marriage which of course, upon any showing, cannot have existed in a society of two; and which has no purpose whatever when (1) woman was not economically dependent upon man, and (2) there was no question of issue prior to Adam's fall, and therefore no inheritance to be thought of!

Rabbis thought Adam and Eve had a canopy, and a blessing.[1] A pretty thought, but an illogical one. The idea of faithfulness, however, *was* present in the Adam and Eve relationship, and perhaps that was a sufficient nucleus for their pleasant *haggadāh* on the subject.

For both these reasons, the short one and the long one, rabbinical ideas about Adam and Eve cannot exclude the validity of Jesus's approach to the subject. And to crown all our arguments on this topic, it is notorious that Jewish law accepts without question that a man and a woman *can* be married by mere intercourse, without any ceremony.[2] Under conditions admitting of the capacity to marry in both parties mere union makes a valid marriage, Unfashionable, primitive, derogatory to the prestige of the families: perhaps, but still good Jewish law. Even the rabbis admit that becoming one flesh in fact can amount to a marriage without any ceremony. It is thus useless to argue that Jews regarded a ceremony as indispensable before a couple might become one flesh. Desirable in social terms, perhaps, but not indispensable.

[1] This is an implication of the remarks at *Targ. ps. Jon.*, Dt xxxiv.6 (Etheridge, II, 683); Midr. R., Gen. XVIII.3 (Sonc. 142). The story is summarised and references indicated in L. Ginzberg, *Legends of the Jews* I (1909), 68–9. *Targ. Jer.* on Gn xxxv.8 (Etheridge, I, 280).

[2] See p. 374 n. 3. Epstein, *op. cit.* p. 18 n. 7. This is the basis of the saying that if two (non-Jewish) men have intercourse with a woman the first is not culpable but the second is: Midr. R., Gen. XVIII.5 (Sonc. 144) (citing Gn xx.3). b. Kiḍ. 9*b*–11*a* = Sonc. 35–42. One who betrothed by intercourse was punished by 'Rab' (*ibid.* 12*b*).

APPENDIX II. THE WIFE'S ACT OF DIVORCE

Since theologians of the standing of Professor Delling have formed the opinion that Mk x.12 is an insertion, and that Jesus cannot have referred to a woman's divorcing her husband, and since Professor Daube has given great attention to the terminology and concepts relating to divorce and separation as known in the New Testament, it is high time that the mystery should be cleared up once and for all. What is the objection to Jesus's speaking of a woman divorcing her husband? In Islamic law a divorce initiated by the wife is possible (1) when the husband grants her a conditional divorce which operates when the condition is fulfilled and when she herself desires this, (2) when the wife purchases her release from her husband, and (3) according to the Maliki school of law if the wife proves certain charges against her husband, in fact a judicial divorce. We have seen that in the ancient documents found at Elephantine and in the less ancient documents of Murabba'ât unmistakable traces have been found of women initiating divorces from their husbands. What peculiarity would prevent a Jewish woman from putting an end to her marriage *de facto*? Hebrew is even equipped with a vocabulary for such action on a woman's part. What is *not* available to a woman is a unilateral repudiation of her marriage such as would free both herself and her husband for a future legal marriage: a woman could not independently and *sua sponte* put an end to her marriage. But in actual fact she could bring her marriage to an end *in Jewish law* in one or other of the following ways:

(1) She could provide at the time of her marriage for her husband to undertake to divorce her should he marry again. Indeed she could provide for her own security in more ways than this.[1] Under the terms of her marriage-settlement he would then be obliged to grant her a bill of divorce if he broke his undertakings. The favourite method of securing the wife was to force the husband-to-be to stipulate a large sum in her *ketubāh*, which would become payable at once on divorce.

(2) She could make a vow not to have any further intercourse with her husband, whereupon he would be forced to divorce her.[2] Whether or not he wanted to do this he would in some circles at least be compelled to do this.

(3) She could approach a court for matrimonial relief, and if her com-

[1] A wife could virtually buy her divorce by forgoing her *ketūbāh* (as in the Islamic *Khul* divorce). The document at b. *Giṭṭ.* 35*a* (Cohen, 'Concerning divorce...', 33) shows a wife instigating her divorce on such terms. There is an example at b. B.M. 66*a* = Sonc. 387. She can write out her own divorce deed and get him to sign and deliver it to her: *Mishnāh* at b. *Giṭṭ.* 22*b* = Sonc. 87–8 (Epstein, 203). For a Jewish comment on a wife buying her freedom see Midr. R., Gen. XVIII.5 = Sonc. 145. For restrictions written into the *ketūbāh* contract see Epstein, 53–4, 196ff. Some *ketūbot* might give the wife a right to divorce herself: j. Ket. 60*b*, j. B.B. 16*c* (Epstein, 198, 204).

[2] *Mishnāh* at b. Ned. 90*b* = Sonc. 279. Consider how easy it was for the wife to take such a step in a moment of anger, and for her husband to refuse to annul it afterwards!

plaints against her husband were sufficiently grave the court would compel him to give her her bill of divorce.[1]

It is most important to realise that the court in question was not some formal tribunal of seventy judges, not even the rabbinical court known in Israel or other similar courts in other countries today. Three reputable persons could be convened for this purpose, though it depended naturally upon the state of public order and the sophistication of the judicial administration how regular and formal the procedure was. It is precisely for this reason that since a Jewish woman could obtain relief in the nature of a bill of divorce either upon the operation of a condition in her marriage settlement, or, if that was not in question, by approaching a court or by forcing her husband to seek the aid of the judiciary, such as it was, there was no practical reason why a Jewish woman of standing should not arrogate to herself the right to divorce her husband by mere notice or intimation, which is exactly what Salome did (Josephus, *Ant.* XV, vii.10). What is shocking about such conduct is, as usual, the brazen assumption that what is illegal or against the theory of the law but tolerated indirectly could be practised openly as if it were legal. Small wonder that Professor Nörr says after a careful review[2] of the old Babylonian law, 'the surface hides contradictory forces at work'. Law has not outgrown the ancient prerogative of the husband, yet some security for women must be devised or at least tolerated. And of course the Jewish law left the initiative to grant a divorce squarely with the husband.

In modern times both Jews and Muslims have felt the inconvenience of the ancient taboo (for it is little better). Writing recently in the *Muslim Bulletin* (Jerusalem),[3] Mahmūd al-Māḍī, Director of Shari'a Courts in Israel, notes that the Shari'a permits the wife to set conditions to the husband at the time of their marriage contract, such as not to take an additional wife or not to transfer their residence to another city; and if the husband infringes such a condition, the wife may dissolve the marriage. The position of an unsatisfactory wife is different in that the husband has the right to divorce her. In al-Māḍī's opinion the exercise of the husband's right belongs exclusively to the husband and should not be exercised on his behalf by the Shari'a court—in contrast with the Christian religious law, which vests jurisdiction to grant divorces exclusively with the court. It follows from this that the husband can refuse to grant the divorce (this does not, of course, follow the Maliki view on the subject).[4] In Morocco, under the French,

[1] Amram, ch. 5, 6. See above, p. 382. The twelve grounds cannot, in sum, be regarded as narrow. Falk, *Jewish Matrimonial Law*, cited above, at p. 120 and references there given. After the advent of Islam Jewish courts allowed divorces to wives without formality, lest they should turn Muslim to annul their marriages: Falk, 'Jewish Law' in Derrett, *Introduction to Legal Systems* (London 1968), 34–5. Even annulments were possible where the marriage was conditional: E. Berkovitz, *Tenai Nisu'in we Gerushin* (Jerusalem 1966).

[2] 'Die Auflösung der Ehe durch die Frau nach altbabylonischem Recht', *Studi . . . Emilio Betti* III (Milan 1961), 507–26.

[3] *Mus. Bull.* 10, 1–2 (1966), 5–6.

[4] For the recent attempt in Iran to overcome this intractable legal difficulty see above, p. 336 n. 2.

Jewish wives who obtained decrees in their favour in rabbinical courts found themselves damaged by their husbands' refusal to grant the bill of divorce as authorised and required by the court. Unable to force the husband's hand otherwise the wives sought the aid of the French judiciary. The latter developed an interesting and valuable rule, under which the husband would be liable financially for the injury he had inflicted on his wife by withholding the *get*.[1] Thus the man's hand was forced. Curiously this effectuates Mishnaic Law: 'A bill of divorce given under compulsion is valid if it is ordered by an Israelitish court, but if by a Gentile court [in the Land of Israel or elsewhere] it is invalid; *but if* the Gentiles beat a man and say to him, 'Do what the Israelites bid thee', it is valid.'[2] Money would speak, and influence would tell in first-century Palestine as it does in areas governed by similar laws today. The wife could, in fact, initiate proceedings for a divorce: and often, we can be sure, she would be successful. And it is to this that Jesus alludes.

[1] A. Zagouri, *Le divorce d'après la loi talmudique chez les Marocains de confession israelite et les réformes actuelles en la matière* (Paris 1958), 111.
[2] *Mishnāh*, Giṭṭ. IX. 8 (Danby, 320). Amram, 59.

CHAPTER SEVENTEEN

The Trial of Jesus and the Doctrine of the Redemption

IN THE WORLD OF SCHOLARSHIP there is no more difficult question than that of the history of the trial and death of Jesus. Just as the question has agitated scholars, in recent years particularly,[1] whether Jesus did call himself the 'Son of Man' and, if so, what he meant thereby, so in the same period there has appeared a flood of books and articles on the trial of Jesus. Some very extraordinary things have been written on that subject by scholars who have, in their zeal, brought in a considerable amount of learning and the fruits of learning. There is no doubt but that when the result is achieved in course of time, after the publications have been sifted and shaken down by that final and only true tester of such hypotheses, far more solid residue will be found than is suspected by any reader who finds these bizarre studies unpalatable at present. But meanwhile the lay reader is puzzled by the confident assertions of a Zeitlin,[2] a Winter,[3] a Carmichael,[4] or a

[1] The topics are connected because Mk xiv.62 is the most crucial of the sayings. The books of Higgins (1964), Tödt (1965), Borsch (1967), and Miss M. D. Hooker, *The Son of Man in Mark* (London 1967) show no sign of stemming interest in the topic. G. Vermès in M. Black, *Aramaic Approach*, 3rd edn (1967), 310–28 goes into the Aramaic background deeply, but doubts the Messianic possibilities of the phrase—a doubt which Black himself contradicts at *ibid.* 328ff. J. Jeremias at *ZNW* 58 (1967), 159–72 introduces comparisons between sayings having the phrase 'Son of Man' and those which, apparently dealing with the same subject-matter, do not.

[2] S. Zeitlin, *Who Crucified Jesus?* (1947/1964); *JQR* 55 (1964), 1–22; *Rise and Fall of the Judaean State* II (1967), 163–75.

[3] P. Winter, *On the Trial of Jesus* (1961) (well reviewed at *Biblica* 43 [1962], 87–93). Winter reiterates his position at, *e.g.*, *Das Altertum* 9 (1963), 159–64. A similarly sceptical treatment is E. Lohse's *Die Geschichte des Leidens und Sterbens Jesu Christi* (Gütersloh 1964), 71–88. Winter is in the line of J. Juster, *Les Juifs dans l'empire Romain* (Paris 1914) and H. Lietzmann, *Der Prozeß Jesu* (Berlin 1931), as J. Blinzler points out in detail and Sherwin-White also. In view of the Zeitlin–Winter–Brandon approach some attempt has been made to ban books containing hymns or folksongs making reference to Jewish complicity in the death of Jesus!

[4] J. Carmichael, *The Death of Jesus* (London 1963). Reviewed with justified hostility by W. G. Kümmel at *Frankfurter Allg. Zeit.*, 1 March, 1966 (p. 20) and Judge W. De Vries, *De Dood van Jezus* (Kampen 1967), 73–4. Pilate himself determined against

Brandon[1] to the general effect that Jesus was, or was mistaken for[2] a revolutionary or a Zealot,[3] and was put to death *therefore* as a political offender against the Roman State; and by the equally confident counter-assertions of those whom we may call the 'orthodox' (for what that term is worth in a discipline where such variety of opinion exists), and who cannot see in the Jesus who was crucified any other Jesus than the teaching and healing Son of God, whose worship by the Church the previously mentioned scholars tend to see as a curious phenomenon of misplaced zeal. In addition to those named a no less zealous scholar, Hugh Schonfield, has made an elaborate case for Jesus's having engineered his own crucifixion in what is called, appropriately, the 'Passover Plot'.[4] It would not be so surprising if we found that those who take this 'secular' and 'sceptical' point of view are in fact Jewish: that would be in keeping with the history of the whole affair. But there are numerous Christian scholars too who find it to their taste to adopt what may be called broadly the 'sceptical' course. This has been opened for them in recent decades by the well-intentioned activities of the 'critical scholars' who have taught them[5] to discard as unauthentic any text against which any sort of hostile case can be made, and to treat with the greatest freedom the undoubted (though as yet unmeasured) hiatus that exists between the gospels and the recollections of the apostles.

The 'orthodox' detect immediately that the 'sceptics' are not adherents of the creeds, except (if their faith is nominally Christian) under some intellectual subterfuges. They resent the attempt on the part of

[1] S. G. F. Brandon, *Jesus and the Zealots* (Manchester 1967). This, and his earlier book, *The Fall of Jerusalem and the Christian Church*, have some relation to R. Eisler's *The Messiah Jesus and John the Baptist*, and are strange productions. The latest of the series, *The Trial of Jesus of Nazareth* (London 1968), though it appears in a respectable historical series, is not based on the application of canons of history as used by historians—far too many assertions depend on circular arguments.

[2] This is the view of Cullmann, who would not be persuaded by the above-mentioned works, and by a historian such as Dvornik, who might be.

[3] On whom see W. R. Farmer, *Maccabees, Zealots and Josephus* (New York 1956); M. Hengel, *Die Zeloten* (Leiden/Cologne 1961); A. Stumpff, *ThWzNT* II, 886ff.; K. H. Rengstorff, *ibid.* IV, 262–7. The nature of the Zealots claimed additional interest when the fortress of Masada was excavated recently.

[4] H. Schonfield, *The Passover Plot* (London 1967).

[5] In a fine review of Marcello Craveri's negative *Life of Jesus* (London 1967) in *The Times Literary Supplement* for 18 April, 1968 (p. 396) the point is made that to attribute the important features of the evangelists' accounts of Jesus's life to myth is to strain credulity more than even the most fanciful story in the gospels. Yet the last step along the road paved by the 'critical scholars' has still to be taken. I. Baer, in *Zion* 31 (1966), 117–52 argues that the gospel accounts of the trial of Jesus reflect the time of Roman persecutions of Christians, while the *Mishnāh* reflects the law obtaining before A.D. 70.

this viewpoint (Lk xxiii.13–16, *cf.* Jn xviii.38, xix.12) and if we reject that evidence which shall we retain?

the 'sceptics' to make money by sensational appeals to a public incapable of determining for itself which approach is right. But at the same time they are powerless to resolve the contradictions in the gospels' narratives, and are at the mercy of any scholar who asks them to prove positively that Mark was not a fraudulent propagandist and John a dreamer. Their situation is like that of the historian when confronted with the claim that Hitler is alive in South America or that Alexander the Great still lies in his tomb under a mosque in Egypt. The 'sceptics' accuse of being led by blind faith anyone who shows astonishment at their own reconstructions. They regard any failure to agree with themselves as tantamount to being an obscurantist. The theologians (whom I myself have no special desire to protect) are accused of turning their backs on history in order to maintain their social and intellectual situations, which (it is supposed) would be undermined by disclosures of the allegedly bogus foundations upon which the Christian faith rests.

In this disturbing morass, made extraordinarily difficult because upon any showing the gospel-writers *did* have motives and did have cases to make (they were not pure narrators), it would be advantageous to take a firm grip upon basic principles of research. If these are not accepted, it is submitted, all enquiries are vain, from whichever standpoint one starts and even if (better still) one has no standpoint at all.

(1) First, we should keep close to the earliest authorities, namely the references in the epistles of Paul, the gospels, and other very early Christian literature.

(2) Where the meaning of these is plain we should take them as evidence of what responsible people believed (on a matter of great importance to them) during a period when there were plenty of individuals still living who both *could*, and, given a chance, *would* have mocked the Christians for their version of events had it been substantially wrong, not to speak of the possibility of correction by sympathetic contemporaries and eye-witnesses (some of whom were not permanent residents in the Land of Israel and will have survived the first Roman war and lived perhaps as late as A.D. 85!).[1]

(3) Since the authors of these passages had an interest in the implications which they place upon them, the colour they give them or the

[1] It is one of Brandon's notions that the Mother Church (*sic*) at Jerusalem was destroyed with its archives in A.D. 70; nevertheless St Mark, while fabricating his gospel, felt bound to incorporate (or failed to excise) numerous elements he obtained from an 'apologia' put out by that Church, which was committed to the notion that Jesus was a holy martyr falsely accused of threats against the Temple and of blasphemy (whereas, says Brandon, he attacked the Temple in collusion with the insurrectionary leader Barabbas[!]). In fact Christians with personal knowledge were domiciled before A.D. 70 throughout the Levant and even further west, not to speak of Galilee itself!

use they make of them, we are entitled to ask ourselves whether the factual kernel of each passage could have other meanings and implications when extracted from its immediate environment. If this is so we must keep an open mind as to the implications which we may ourselves entertain when we read the passages *in situ*.

(4) Where the meaning of the text is not plain we may take help from other quarters. Which shall these be? Primarily similar material, written in similar language and style, provided that this too is subjected to the test mentioned at (3) above. But if the doubts we have of the meaning are of a more substantial character, regarding for example the history, law, or habits of mind of the people concerned, we are entitled to take advantage of any learning which may be relevant.

(5) In determining the relevance of any such aids we must have regard to the setting of the events, and see them, as far as possible, through the eyes of contemporaries. We should not, for example, suppose that the Jewish leaders were governed by mishnaic law, when there is good evidence they were not, and no evidence, apart from an ambiguous remark attributed to Jesus himself, that they ought to have been. Nor should we suppose that Pilate did out of weakness what he could as easily have done out of malice or meanness: the evidence about him would be consistent with the latter, not the former. We should not suppose that the crowd which called for Jesus's death did so because they were disappointed at his having fallen tamely into the hands of his captors, when we know that one of the popular heroes of the Jews, Samson, was at his best when blinded and in captivity.

(6) Lastly, when approaching the task of reconstructing what happened we must treat all available pieces of evidence with respect, not excluding the bits which do not seem to fit the puzzle, nor grasping at variant readings or other slight coincidences. The thing should work on broad lines or it will not work at all. And in fitting the pieces together we must not erect artificial criteria for evaluating them when they appear to conflict, on the footing that one evangelist is trustworthy and not another, for that is highly implausible. In short, only a hypothesis which takes account of *all* the material will serve: and the result must be plausible in terms of the civilization, its qualities and its weaknesses.

The trial of Jesus when read in even one gospel is highly fascinating. When read synoptically it is intriguing beyond measure. Small wonder that scholars, even those who have no particular interest in Jesus, including even those who do not believe that the historical Jesus can be recovered for us, have not stinted pains to produce well-documented accounts of their own explanations of the events. In a single chapter, though a long one, it is not possible to give the wealth of detail or references which are to be found in the works readily available on this subject: but this chapter does contain what no previous treatment has had, namely an objective (though sympathetic) reconstruction which does not require that any piece of the text should be eliminated, and which sees the story through the eyes of contemporaries (beyond whom it is impossible to go). Many of these saw those sombre and sordid happenings as proof that God's plans were working out, that the long-awaited divine drama had at last been staged. Now with our knowledge of the midrashic technique as commonly used by the Jews of various schools of thought we realise that it is quite possible for a tendentious account,[1] even several concurrent tendentious accounts, to be written, using factual or near factual reports or what were thought by competent judges to be reliable reports. A motive and a bias may be detected, but this does not mean that the material, the very stuff of the account, is fabricated or forged.

I have not mentioned in the previous paragraphs the work which has been done up to now by lawyers and judges.[2] Their works come in a

[1] At App. III below I give a trivial example of such composition in order to explain to those unfamiliar with this problem that dramatic reconstruction in the course of narration is fully consistent with factual veracity.

[2] The work of the Canadian judge, McRuer, is unscholarly. It is mentioned below, p. 433 n. 1. The finickings of scholars are nearly always objectionable and sometimes boring: but unscholarly works, written out of good intentions but without adequate acquaintance with the sources or the means of evaluating them or their implications, come within range of being described as frauds upon the public. The magistrate F. J. Powell wrote an elaborate *Trial of Jesus Christ* (London 1949) in which he found, in a characteristically English manner, that 'justice was not done and was manifestly and undoubtedly seen not to be done' (p. 135). He relied extensively on mishnaic law, and believed that Jesus underwent two formal (but ill-conducted) trials. The banal outcome of such an investigation never struck the author as incongruous. The redemption of the Jews could, in purely Jewish terms, conceivably be envisaged in an innocent man's being 'done down': but this is altogether too naïve a view of what happened and what was recognised as having happened by contemporaries. Judge Mr W. De Vries's *De Dood van Jezus van Nazareth in het Licht van Geschiedenis en Rechtspraak* (The Death of Jesus of Nazareth in the Light of History and Jurisprudence) is a work of a different order, the result of deep research, and contains an elaborate and restrained imaginative reconstruction. In particular his handling of the question of the competence of the so-called Sanhedrin reveals the quality of the investigation: the theoretical position is unimportant given the facts of the situation; and there was no trial there. He also notices that Pilate ordered Jesus to be crucified *not* as judge, but as governor (a distinction most scholars have failed to make). M. J. Imbert, Professor in the Faculty of Law and Economics at Paris, gave a lecture in Paris on 23 February, 1968 entitled 'Le procès de Jésus. Essai de mise au point'. I was favoured by the author with a copy of his text. He points out that strictly speaking the *ius gladii* may not have belonged to Pilate himself—but his *coercitio* would amply suffice for death sentences in political contexts. He clarifies the constitutional position then obtaining. He also moderates the claims of critics that the accounts of the gospels are improbable. In his view Pilate yielded to fear of the mob. And the 'Sanhedrin' acted chiefly to discredit Jesus in the eyes of the public.

class by themselves. In some cases these have used original sources, though usually in translation. They often lean somewhat heavily on the theologians, and as a class (and this includes Jewish writers)[1] they are unaware of the tendentious character of the sources, or of the theological biases and tendencies under the influence of which the sources were written. They tend to take the accounts of Jewish law too seriously where in fact little reliance is to be placed upon it; and where Jewish or at any rate oriental approaches are needful they forget at times that they are not dealing with a western society. That is why they seem to concur that Jesus had two trials, which he did not; and that both (or the sole trial) were mockeries of justice, or judicial murders—which they (or it) certainly were not.

There is, no doubt, one further question to be asked, which I do not intend to answer here: and that is what was it all *for*? The strange events were followed by still stranger, the Resurrection and the post-resurrection life of the apostles, the Ascension and Pentecost. It is by no means impossible to tackle these in the same objective and matter-of-fact way as the trial and death of Jesus must be tackled: but the present is not the book in which to do it. I should however like to add at this point that just as Jesus's teaching was matter-of-fact and practical, so his last days were faced, and undergone, in a practical, matter-of-fact manner. Jesus was prepared for his ordeal not, as Schonfield would have it, because he engineered a superb hoax,[2] but by his conviction that in him culminated all the hopes and potentialities of the religious sense of the Jews who, in addition to being very religious, were (as they still are) some of the hardest-headed people on earth.

THE REAL PROBLEM

I commence with two quotations. They typify the incomprehensibility of holy scripture when one approaches it without prior orientation. The First Epistle to the Corinthians was written about a quarter of a century after the crucifixion. This was long after the first Christian communities

[1] Justice Haim H. Cohn, writing in the *Israel Law Review* for July 1967, refutes the accounts of the gospels, and exculpates all the Jewish actors in the drama. The 'Sanhedrin's' part was to persuade Jesus not to plead guilty before Pilate! The High Priest rent his robe at Jesus's obstinacy (or stupidity?)!

[2] Can one engineer anything so complicated in an Asian environment? Administrators and businessmen universally report that Asian society, with its impediments to individual responsibility and personal achievement, and its partial elimination of predictability of behaviour, and other factors separating promise from performance, makes nationals of these developing countries much less 'reliable' and less amenable to 'organisation' than their counterparts in advanced countries. The Americans have found this out in Vietnam in what must surely be the most dramatic example of all time. That Jesus could have organised his 'hoax' Schonfield-style is incredible.

had made up their minds what happened, objectively speaking and symbolically, that Passover-time in the year 30.[1] There St Paul says[2] ὅτι Χριστὸς ἀπέθανεν ὑπὲρ τῶν ἁμαρτιῶν ἡμῶν κατὰ τὰς γραφάς ... 'The Messiah died for our sins according to the scriptures.' Jesus had made a not altogether dissimilar remark about the death of St John the Baptist (Mk ix.13), but of course he did not suggest that John died for anybody's sins. How and why should the death of a man be for, or indeed in any relation to, anybody's sins; and to what extent and how was this, or indeed could it be, authorised or required by the Hebrew bible? Such questions have occupied theologians to distraction. Recent studies, especially the exhaustive book of Fr Sabourin,[3] attempt to clarify the picture for one who reads a Bible, and does not lack faith in it.

Then the prophet Isaiah, to whose text Sabourin gives close attention, sang the following cryptic words[4] early in the Song of the so-called 'Suffering Servant' of Yahwe: *ḥinnām nimᵉkarᵉtem vᵉlo' bᵉchéṣef tiggā'ēlū.* 'You were disposed of[5] for nothing, and you shall be redeemed without money.' This text does not seem at first sight to have much to do with the first I have quoted. Yet anything to do with disposition or sale and redeeming recalled the Exodus of the Jews from Egypt, which took place 'without money', and with the Exodus, the pattern which that event laid down for all Jewish religious thought, a pattern upon which Professor David Daube has written. The Exodus and its yearly re-enaction in the *Peṣaḥ*, or Passover, had overtones not merely of redemption of the new members of the people but of redemption in a religious and eschatological sense, a redemption in which the Messiah was vaguely involved, a picture expounded for us in Fr Notker Füglister's valuable book, *Die Heilsbedeutung des Pascha.*[6] The scriptures, taken as a whole, had much to say about the Exodus-pattern, about the Passover, and, in less precise terms, about that other redemption which should make permanent what had, at the historical Exodus, been only provisional.[7] The redeemer then too would redeem 'without money'.

[1] The extreme likelihood that the crucifixion took place in A.D. 30 is demonstrated with all the necessary detail by J. Jeremias, *Eucharistic Words*, 41 (4th edn, p. 35). Friday, 7 April, 30 or 3 April, 33 would be the 14th Nisan in which we are interested. S. Zeitlin prefers the less probable year, 34.

[2] 1 Co xv.3. Wolff (1950), 151. Sabourin (1961), 227–8.

[3] Especially his excellent ch. 7.

[4] Is lii.3. Daube (1947), 41. Bonsirven (1963), 97. But *cf.* Is xliii.3. Füglister (1963), 177 n. 149. [For the full references to these secondary works please see Bibliography to Chapter 17 below.]

[5] Z. W. Falk, 'Hebrew legal terms: II', *JSS* 12 (1967), 242–3. Ps xliv.12, 26.

[6] Especially at p. 174–9.

[7] So Tanḥ. B. § 18 (36*a*) quoted Billerbeck IV, 2. Wiencke (1939), 25. *Midrash on Psalms*, on Ps xxxi, § 2 (Braude, I 393).

But the statement of St Paul I quoted suggests something further. The scriptures *in toto* were fulfilled in the death, that is to say the manner of death, just as they indicated the purpose of that death. Soteriologically, for Christians, the death and the resurrection form a unity, but it is plain that the death alone is the chief point of inquiry, since Christ *died*, and did not *rise from the dead*, for our sins. Perhaps Paul's words can be understood if we first recall the nature of the subject-matter and the intellectual climate and discipline in question.

PAUL AS AN 'ORIENTAL LAWYER'

Paul belonged to a class of scholar which we should now call 'oriental lawyers', to distinguish them from the lawyer, or indeed the jurist, known to the West. An oriental lawyer is (as we have seen) primarily occupied with scripture, *i.e.* texts and their interpretation, and hardly ever with expediency or considerations other than those arising out of his materials and the needs of applying them to contemporary life. If life does not harmonise with the texts as technically understood, then it is life that is wrong. Custom went on under the shadow of religious disapproval, and religious teachers could take advantage of their audiences' knowing this. But faith in scripture never wavered, and it was scripture that was the teacher's primary tool and support. The scriptures had always their literal meaning, but gradually gained additional meanings from fanciful as well as rationalistic interpretation and expansion. The whole was then handed down as venerable treasure, the gloss being as important as the text. If a scholar could derive three or more meanings from his text by rearranging the words or pronouncing them in different ways, each meaning consistent with the spirit of the law, he was performing the function which the science and its divine Author demanded of him. Thus when scholars laugh at the fanciful, unhistorical, and unphilological notions which the rabbis derived from scripture, they are turning their backs on the schools in which Paul learnt and subsequently taught and, as it seems to me, on the schools in which Jesus himself learnt and subsequently taught.

We are now in a position to approach Paul's statement about Christ's death in the proper spirit. Paul's pupils must obtain an emotional, intellectual, and finally moral stimulus from this formula. The statement must be true objectively, spiritually, and on the planes of the metaphors themselves. We approach the subject with every confidence because, though Paul is often obscure to us, his stature as a thinker and as a man is beyond question.

If we can understand what Paul is saying we possess an independent means by which we can understand the teaching of his own master, Jesus himself. One might suppose that the gospels, which purport to give histories of Jesus, would be more direct evidence. But these are for the most part later than Paul's writings, and those portions that are not are, as we shall see, far from direct evidence on the very subject which now concerns us. Such an independent approach is desirable, especially since the reality and vitality of Paul have never been questioned.

Paul is very direct. He preaches Christ crucified and glories in the cross.[1] At first sight this is fantastic. That the king Messiah, the worker of the eschatological redemption, should have been crucified by Romans at an historical moment was bad enough: that one should speak of it not in terms of pity (as Jews might well do),[2] nor as a deplorable incident (as Josephus apparently does),[3] but with positive joy, is alarming. Paul blandly works out the meaning of that event in a strictly legal framework. His use of legal metaphors is not surprising since he was in any case brought up as a jurist, and legal metaphor was good style in an age when law was the prestige-bearing discipline. But he uses them readily, as if the minds of his readers were entirely prepared for such language, and the metaphors cascade smoothly, interlocking and mutually supporting, as if the intellectual structure were already well established. The appeal is not directly to the emotions, but to existing belief in relationships known indeed to the law, though by no means all of them (as we shall see) wholly contemplated by the rules of the *Torāh* itself, read literally. Christ died, he seems to say, in order to achieve realities which can only be expressed in terms of law, and which are fully and adequately so expressed. We, with our lack of interest in law and a long-inherited dislike of lawyers, find it hard not to regret this choice of language.

Gustav Wiencke in 1939 thoroughly investigated Paul's metaphorical

[1] 1 Co i.23; ii.2.

[2] The Jewish War had not begun. Even at its end compassion was still capable of being utilised: see the proposed crucifixion of young 'Eleazar at Jos., *B.J.* VII. vi. 4 (200, 202: Loeb edn, iii, 563): τοῖς δ'ἀπὸ τοῦ φρουρίου τοῦτο θεασαμένοις ὀδύνη τε πλείων προσέπεσε, καὶ διωλύγιον ἀνῴμωζον οὐκ ἀνασχετὸν εἶναι τὸ πάθος βοῶντες. . . .

[3] Jos., *Ant.* XVIII, iii, 3, § 64; XX, ix, 1, § 200. It is well known that the *testimonium Flavianum* (see S. Zeitlin, *Josephus on Jesus*, Philadelphia 1931, 66ff.) is of doubtful authenticity, but the present writer finds it less plainly unacceptable than do most scholars since, from the Dead Sea Scrolls, it is apparent that a far wider range of notions about the Messiah persisted in the first century than had previously been suspected. Nevertheless we shall not go far astray if we say with L. H. Feldman (at his edition of *Josephus*, Loeb Classical Library, ix, 1965, p. 49—he provides a useful bibliography on the subject at p. 573–5) that 'our text represents substantially what Josephus wrote, but that some alterations have been made by a Christian interpolator'.

thinking on this subject,[1] but he did not trace the metaphors to their source. He did, however, find something which we shall welcome. Paul and the convictions of the early Church seemed to him to be consistently in harmony,[2] and this was plausible, since we know that Paul, though never himself a student of any of the apostles, was accepted by them (with one painful exception) as a teacher as well qualified as themselves. Yet it appears that he had never seen their common master in the flesh. We shall have to go beyond Wiencke and find out not only what Paul's ideas were, but what their authority was.

THE DOCTRINE OF THE REDEMPTION

The oriental lawyer, faced with the rich vocabulary of Paul and of his contemporaries and juniors whose work is available for us in the non-Pauline epistles, soon detects eight metaphors, two of which coalesce, leaving seven in all. It is quite extraordinary how these metaphors, so far from jostling or hindering each other, actually combine to point in one direction. This would seem to be the work of a towering genius, were it not the case, as we shall see, that scriptural origins must be posited for them. All scriptures were pondered over until every aspect of significance had been derived from them, and it is quite unimportant how much of any result can really be attributed to an original author or authors. The doctrine of the redemption, which is the central doctrine of Christianity, in the mouth of Paul, the Church's first and ever-greatest theologian, was a seven-fold but compact notion.[3]

The seven metaphors were these:

1. *Redemption*[4] from the debt arising out of sin. By reason of the breaches of the covenant entered into between God and the children of Israel at Mt Sinai the latter were desperately in debt.[5] God's anger at their disobedience in the past had led to their slavery under other nations. Bondage for debt was a familiar notion. Now some kind of exchange was thought to have taken place whereby God released his rights under the pre-existing contract. The notion that God himself,

[1] At 65–8 he relates one metaphor to Is liii.

[2] 194–5.

[3] *Cf.* Jeremias, *Eucharistic Words of Jesus* (1966), 231.

[4] Rm iii.24 (?); 1 Co i.30; Ga iii.13; iv.4–5; *cf.* Ep i.7 (?). Wirtz (1906), 5. Richard (1959), 59. Füglister (1963), 270, 274ff.

[5] ἀπολύτρωσις: Erlösung nicht Loskaufung. Büchsel (1943), 354–7, emphasises absence of price. Daube (1947), 41. Proksch (1943), 334, finds λυτροῦσθαι from sins only at ψ 129.8. ἐξαγοράζειν (Ga iii.13; iv.5); ἀγοράζειν (1 Co vi.20; vii.23) emphasise the redeemer's rights, referring back to Dt xxxii.6, Ps lxxiv.2 (MT)? Käsemann (1964), 49. The sin–debt image is apparent from *Mishnāh*, 'Āvot, and from Jesus's parables *passim*. Dalman (1930), 334–7. Deißmann (1926), 168ff.

as a super-relative of all his people, should and would redeem them from this condition of indebtedness, certainly existed.[1] Even a friend, as a quasi-relative, should redeem a friend:[2] how much more such a relation! Paul contended that this had been done, and it followed logically that the redeemer obtained rights over the redeemed similar to those which a redeemer for cash would obtain over any insolvent debtor whom he had in actual fact released from his creditor's possession.[3]

2. This redemption was an act similar to a *rescue from a hostile power*, such as a non-Jewish power, which kept slaves, whether won by force or self-sold.[4] Whether by persuasion or by force these captives are set free: not necessarily by any exchange in point of value. Paul viewed Jesus as triumphing over the forces that held the people bound. But of course the freed slave acquired at the point of his release not freedom as such, but a new master, unless that master otherwise provided.[5]

3. Neither redemption nor rescue would be of any value if the debt or slavery could once again be incurred (as was highly possible). Therefore we must suppose the creation of a new relationship in place of the old. The old was impracticable or harsh. The debts under it have been wiped out in order that the two parties may again enter into contractual relationships upon better terms. These terms are negotiated by a middleman who not only represents the formerly defaulting party, but is able to *guarantee* the performance in some such terms as these, 'If he does not fulfil the terms, I shall'.[6]

4. The release from the sin-debt involves appearance before the creditor–judge–king (for in oriental laws, as so many of Jesus's parables show, the plaintiff or prosecutor may also be the judge),[7] and advocacy

[1] Proksch (1943), 331. Job xix.25. [2] Stamm (1940), 10.

[3] Daube (1963), 42. Yaron (1959), 155, 164, 167. 1 Co vii.22.

[4] Rm vi.18, 22; 1 Co xv.57 (?); Ga iv.8; v.1; Co ii.15. Ep iv.8. 1 P i.18–19. Proksch (1943), 334. *C.I.J.* 709–11. Lewis, *JSS* 2 (1957), 264ff. *C.P.J.* III, 473, p. 33 (community redeem: A.D. 291). Sacral manumission *via* a temple is not the source of the image (as Deißmann [1923], 270–87, etc.). The implications are objectionable (temple-slaves, prostitutes, etc., see Latte [1920]). Elert (1947). Christ's 'price' is not fictional; Paul's slaves were insolvent; when redeemed they were not destined for freedom. P. Oxyrh. 1205/7 is far from conclusive. Deißmann influenced the *NEB*: Dodd (1961). Improperly? Wiencke (1939), 45–6.

[5] Deißmann (1926), 173–4. Elert (1947). Daube (1947), 51. 2 P ii.1; Rm vi.22; *cf.* Ep vi.5f.; 1 P ii.16. See αἰχμαλωσία image: Lk iv.18–21 (*cf.* Rm vii.23; 2 Co x.5; 2 Tm iii.6). Ga v.1 as explained by Rengstorf (1951) with ref. to *Mishnāh*, Giṭṭ. IV, 4. Yaron (cited above).

[6] Weil (1938), 229ff. 1 Tm ii.5–6; Heb ix.15 (*cf.* viii.6), leading to Rm v.9–10? For *fidejussio* in other systems, the *fidejussor* freeing the debtor, see J. H. Wigmore, *Harv.L.R.* 10 (1897), 321ff., 328.

[7] Boecker (1964). A common lawyer may be permitted to comment how appalling,

before him. Christ is seen by Paul as both *vindex* and *patronus*.[1]

5. The *patronus* would be unable to obtain the release of the debtors or to conclude the new agreement unless the anger of the creditor against the debtors were first abated. He must say 'Leave them alone, I will repay'.[2] By promising satisfaction the transactions were enabled to be done, which was possible only if *vicarious punishment* was offered. The idea of vicarious punishment, offensive to many western theologians, makes perfect sense in the setting of semitic society: the blood-community still in theory (as not so long ago in fact) pay compensation for their member's wrongs and take compensation for his injury or death. The tribe is not exclusively the receptacle of such rights and duties, for the effective social organisation may assume this rôle.[3] The act of offering to be punished in the place of others is the act of a blood-brother, who, even though he may have no solidarity in point of the debt, has solidarity in point of integrity of blood—the great fundamental conception of semitic society.[4] Naturally, the extent of the punishment would depend on the case this *patronus*, this *advocatus*, can make on behalf of his clients and himself. Vicarious punishment is not accepted in biblical law, but the notion was only another side of the concept of the 'avenger of blood', who certainly survived all biblical legislation on that subject.

6. In so far as sins had made the children of Israel unfit to present themselves for a new covenant, especially before God, not merely must vicarious punishment be envisaged but even an *expiation*. Christ's death was therefore also an expiation.[5]

[1] Rm v.18; viii.27 (?), 31–4 (citing Is l.8–9). *Cf.* 1 Jn ii.1; Heb vii.25. Elert (1947). Daube (1947), 59.

[2] Explicit is *Mishnāh*, B.B. X. 8. Weil (1938) *ubi cit.*; Weil (1947), 195. The vicarious punishment theme: 1 Co i.30; 2 Co v.14–15. Rm iv.25 is ambiguous, while v.11 is doubtful. For Jesus 'made sin' see below in the text.

[3] The Caliph 'Umar ibn al-Khaṭṭāb, the founder of the Islamic State, ordered that blood money should be the liability of the military regiment. Iraqi jurists accepted this. The Imām al-Shāfi'i rejected it, and confined the responsibility to the tribe.

[4] Proksch (1943), 331, citing E. Merz, *Die Blutrache bei den Israeliten* (BzWAT. 20: Leipzig 1916); O. Proksch, *Über die Blutrache bei den vorislamischen Arabern* (Leipzig 1899). For an example of the blood-feud in Palestine see Josephus, *Ant.* XVI, ix.1, 277 (Loeb edn, viii, 321). Daube (1947), 47, 59: 'The result that I wish to stress is that the idea of God or Jesus redeeming mankind from sin and damnation, apparently a purely religious idea, derives from those ancient rules on insolvent debtors and victims of murder, on the preservation of the existing clans and the patrimony of clans.' *Midr. on Ps.*, I.224. *Cf.* 2 S xxi.4ff. The richest and most comprehensive study of solidarity of blood in semitic societies is J. Scharbert (1958), 25ff., 88ff.

[5] Rm iii.24–5; 1 Co i.30; 2 Co v.18; Col i.20; 1 Tm ii.6; *cf.* Ep ii.13–16. Käsemann (1950/1). Dodd (1954), 94.

---

yet how typical, this is. *Mishnāh*, 'Āvot IV.22: '... he is God ... he is the Judge, he is the Witness, he is the Complainant, and it is he that shall judge ... for all is his' (a saying of R. 'Eleazar ha-Kappar [c. 165–200]).

7. All these metaphors lead up to another. The first covenant at Mt Sinai was negotiated through a marriage-broker,[1] Moses. The second may be seen in the same light. The blood-brother who can act as 'avenger of blood' is entitled to marry the masterless woman whose marriage has ended by the termination of her marriage-contract. Perhaps it would be better to say that he is under an *obligation* to do this. The redeemer, who would in any case have rights against the redeemed and would be interested in any assets of the latter, may very well be thought of as a 'marrier' (God remains the husband so that that word is not strictly applicable),[2] and this role also Paul unhesitatingly attributes to Christ.[3] In some ancient societies the delinquencies of women were liable to be punished by action against their husbands, and so the metaphors (3) and (7) are consistent. This is not in fact the Jewish law, but it reflects actual behaviour.

Difficulties have abounded in understanding the implications of these metaphors. If redemption was some kind of repurchase (as Paul graphically insists),[4] what was the price?[5] Some say it is better not to ask these embarrassing questions. They rightly point out that even in Old Testament times the notions *g'l* and *pdh* do not imply consideration or equivalent necessarily, but contemplate unilateral manumission. Thus *price* is not to be taken too seriously. How can the death of a man act as redemption, release, guarantee, vindication, vicarious punishment, expiation, or marriage? If a *death* could do it, why would poisoning or mere battery not have served? The likening of the crucifixion to an expiatory sacrifice is particularly objectionable to traditional sentiment and to the intelligence. Yet Paul and his colleagues have no doubts about it. If the arrangement of metaphors given here is correct, an atonement was effected for the children of Israel at the moment of Christ's death, and there is no reason to suppose, as many do,[6] that the effect is postponed until the end of days.

LAWYERS' ATTEMPTS AT INTERPRETATION

Attempts to interpret the legal metaphors of the redemption in legal

[1] See below, p. 465 n. 1. Jr xxxi.31–4. *'Al-tiḳᵉrey* at b. Ber. 57*a*: at Dt xxxiii.4 read not *morāshāh* (inheritance) but *mᵉ'orāsāh* (betrothed). *Midr. on Ps.*, on Ps xiv, § 6 (Braude, I, 187) (ref.: Is lxiii.4). Midr. R., Exod. XXI, 5 (Sonc. 266).

[2] Below, p. 468. The apparent inconsistencies are there explained.

[3] Rm vii.4; 1 Co vi.17; 2 Co xi.2; *cf.* Ep iv.25–33. The *Song of Songs* was a synagogue lection during Passover: Füglister (1963), 24 n. 40, 185.

[4] 1 Co vi.20; vii.23.

[5] Rivière (1931), 16.

[6] Jeremias (1947), 263–4; Käsemann (1964); Wiencke (1939), 25.

terms have been very few.[1] St Anselm of Canterbury wrote his *Cur Deus Homo* in the last years of the eleventh century.[2] This original genius explained the redemption in strict legal terms which have commanded admiration notwithstanding doubts. In his view sin is failure to render to God what is due;[3] restitution is called for and a penalty also. As every sinner owes satisfaction and God is just, either punishment or satisfaction is essential.[4] Man's total inability to pay is his own fault, and God cannot be compelled to give salvation. This stark picture of an angry God's severity accords with the picture which Jesus gives of the state of affairs prior to his own coming death,[5] though this fact has not been seen to defend St Anselm against his critics. Man, according to him, is alone bound to make satisfaction, though unable to do it, and only God has the resources to make satisfaction. Therefore a God–man should make it, for he alone will be sinless.[6] The sin done by taking Jesus's life outweighs other sins, therefore the life, if given for them, was worth more than all sins. To this theory there are several objections. Apart from Jesus no room for divine mercy appears; a certain circularity is apparent in the argument, and the multiplicity of the metaphors in Paul's exposition is not observed. However, due justice is done to the chief metaphor, that of *redemption* properly so called.

Another scholar with a legal turn of mind, the famous and controversial Johannes Coch, alias Coccejus (1603–69), professor of theology at Leiden, explores a wider range of metaphor. His leading theory[7] was upon the pact between God and Christ (not between God and man), which is mediated and guaranteed[8] by Christ in a dialogue taken from scriptural passages. Coccejus's speciality was his extensive literal knowledge of scripture, which enabled him in a quasi-rabbinical fashion

[1] Three of the metaphors are handled, differently, by Bultmann (1956), 295–8.
[2] Rivière (1931), 313ff. Anselm, *Cur Deus Homo*, text and trans., ed. Schmitt (Darmstadt, 1956); trans. E. Prout (London n.d.). Mazzarella (1962), 448–72. Criticised by E. Brunner, *Dogmatik* ii, 2nd edn (Zürich/Stuttgart 1960), 309.
[3] Mazzarella (1962), 455. Sabourin (1961), 68–9.
[4] Mazzarella (1962), 457.
[5] Rich Man and Lazarus (Lk xvi.19–31); Wicked Husbandmen (Lk xx.9–18); Unmerciful Servant (Mt xviii.23–35); Virgins (Mt xxv.1–12); Composition with the Adversary (Lk xii.27–9); Fig-tree in the Vineyard (Lk xiii.6–9); Talents/Pounds (Mt xxv.14–30; Lk xix.12–27); Two Servants (Mt xxiv.45–51; Lk xii.41–6). Even the Prodigal Son (Lk xv.11–32)?
[6] Mazzarella (1962), 460.
[7] 'Federal' theory. *Summa Theologiae ex Scripturis Repetita* (last edn 1662), cap. 34. *Summa Doctrinae de Foedere et Testamento Dei* (last edn 1660), cap. 5, § 88. Metaphors neatly aligned: *Catechesis Religionis Christianae*, § 54 (qu. xviii). G. Schreck, *Gottesreich und Bund* . . . (Gütersloh 1923).
[8] Heb vii.22; Ps cxix.122: *S. Doct. Foed. Test.*, edn of 1701, vol. vii, p. 61, col. i, bottom.

to see Christ and his work in every corner of the text. He notices that Christ, by being a blood-brother of man, is able to redeem, expiate, and guarantee; but he insists that the virgin-birth was necessary to preserve Christ from the sin which would have tainted him had he been a normal descendant of Adam. There are some inadequacies. In his view the sins under the new covenant would be exigible only from the sponsor, which does not seem to be correct. He was also of the opinion that the *price* with which the redemption was effected was the blood of Christ, which some phrases in Paul might lead us to suppose, but which is in fact incompatible with the metaphors when seen as a whole.[1]

Others who have contemplated the divine mystery leave us in the dark as to how God was brought to accept this unconventional offering, to accept this unique 'case', to decree this strange novation of his old contract. The usual explanation is that God did all this of his grace. That grace enters into the picture is certain. It is yet another metaphor, indicating goodwill or a present of some kind, to which we must return.

ISAIAH AND THE REDEMPTION

The oriental lawyer wishes to know whence Paul's ideas came. From dreams, hallucinations, 'visions'? His consistent work, the general agreement of his colleagues, and finally the acceptance of the Church would indicate nothing so personal. Paul's direct allusions to the prophet Isaiah put us on inquiry whether that is not the quarter in which first to look.[2] That by itself will not serve, for the oracles of the prophets were plastic and could be made to fit many occasions, the psalms likewise. Further corroboration must be searched for. The claims of Isaiah are very strong. The Song of the Suffering Servant served as the beginning of Philip the Evangelist's preaching to the Ethiopian eunuch (Ac viii.27–35).[3]

Before we examine it and its implications we must pause to notice the vehement argument of Harry M. Orlinsky[4] to the effect that the subject of Is liii is no one but the prophet himself; that vicarious suffering is a theological and scholarly fiction, the result of an eisegesis

[1] *Cat. Rel. Chr.*, qu. xxxiv. Blood was not in reality the price, but the instrument whereby God was 'obliged' to accede to the offers of satisfaction, etc. But the metaphor emphasises the redeemer's rights over the redeemed: so Ac xx.28.

[2] Is lii.7 and liii.1 are quoted at Rm x.15f. Is lii.15 is quoted at Rm xv.21. Ph ii.7 recalls Is lii.3. On 1 P ii.21–5 see below.

[3] Euler (1934) would identify Isaiah's figure and the Messiah, Philip's teaching with the Church's.

[4] 'The so-called "Servant of the Lord" . . .' in *Studies on the Second Part of the Book of Isaiah* (*Supp. to N.T.* 14) (Leiden 1967), 17, 23, 51, 54–5, 73. His approach was anticipated by B. W. Bacon, *JBL* 48 (1929), 40–81; L. Waterman, *JBL* 56 (1937), 27–34; C. T. Craig, *J. Rel.* 24 (1944), 240–5.

(as he calls it) by interested theologians ignorant of the spirit of biblical law and the teaching of the prophets; and that the so-called Song of the Servant is in reality nothing of the kind, merely a hyperbolical statement that a prophet who points out Israel's transgressions is bound to be abused and thumped. Orlinsky says that neither the Old Testament nor the Judaism of the intertestamental period knew anything of the concept of the Servant of the Lord, Suffering Servant, and Vicarious Suffering and Atonement as they came to be developed by the followers of Jesus some time after his death. Orlinsky does not study the psalms in this connection, especially Ps cxvi. It is true that that psalm can be taken in a non-sacrificial sense (as by S. Daiches in a study of some thirty years ago);[1] but when it is supported by Tannaïtic *midrashim* and Dead Sea Scroll material the position seems very different. The plain fact is that a rational–historical–philological study of the Old Testament does not take us into the minds of first-century Jews in Palestine.

The kernel of the material is Is liii and immediately adjacent verses but we must remember that, unlike modern Old Testament scholarship, the contemporary scholar would call up as sources of elucidation any part of Isaiah, indeed he should do so, and other sources, especially the psalms dealing or apparently dealing with related topics.[2] It turns out that if we use the available versions of Is liii and related material, applying to the extremely cryptic text the midrashic techniques which were available in Paul's day, every one of our seven metaphors turns up. No one doubts but that all the Greek versions have to be looked to, including those written with an anti-Christian tendency,[3] and the Aramaic Targumim. Fortunately, a synoptic study of the versions is already available to us. Yet all the possibilities have not been exhausted. Even far-fetched possibilities must be entertained, since in rabbinical circles to be far-fetched is by no means to be suspect, indeed a *midrash* which is far-fetched may often be the more admirable for that. The claim of Is liii to exhaustive treatment is an obvious one.[4] These verses for the first time bring out in combination ideas otherwise separate in Judaism, namely redemption in a practical sense and forgiveness in a religious sense.[5] And it is in a combination of metaphors that we are especially interested. When we review them it is, of course, desirable

[1] *Gaster Anniv. Volume* (London 1936), 64ff.

[2] Rabbinical technique eluded Miss Hooker (1959), 90. The word *nivᵉzeh* at Is liii.3 would call up *vᵉzūy* at Ps xxii.6 (the root *ma'aṣ* at Ps cxviii.22 is different).

[3] Jeremias (1954); Jeremias (1950), 117. Aquila belongs to A.D. 110 at latest. Euler (1934), 35, notes Symmachus. Hoad (1956/7) would go ever further than Jeremias in coupling Is liii with 2 Co v.21, Rm viii.3–4.

[4] Romaniuk (1962) has a parallel study.

[5] Stamm (1940), 147.

to bear in mind that a legal term will not necessarily convey to later ages the exact juridical force which it originally had (and only that force). But even poetry uses juridical ideas only if it may conjure up a practical notion which people are used to.

1. *Redemption* appears at xliii.1, liii.9 (LXX) and 11 (cf. l.1*b*); it also appears at lxi.2 (taking *rātson* as 'satisfaction'). lxi.2, which according to Mt xi.5, Lk iv.18–19, vii.22 is cited by Jesus himself, was obviously an important text for the early Church.

2. A triumphal *freeing from slavery* appears at liii.12, at liii.8 as understood in the Targum, at lxi.1 (the importance of which, being next to lxi.2, we have incidentally observed), and at xlii.6.

3. *Suretyship*, which we came across in both the Pauline metaphors numbered (3) and (5) above, can be seen in the idea of intercession at liii.12. The new covenant itself appears at Is xlii.6 (to be read with lxi.1 and xlix.8). The actual concept of surety appears at Ps cxix.122.

4. The concept of *vindex* lies also within 'intercession' at liii.12, but it is more plainly present at l.8–9, li.22. In the Targum liii.4 is relevant.[1] Is xlix.4 shows that the Servant expects *judgement* and *reward*.[2] Ps lxxii.14 shows the Messiah[3] saving the endangered 'poor'.

5. The *vicarious punishment* undergone by the blood-brother (*i.e.* 'avenger' in reverse) occurs by a combination of liii.5, 6, 8 with lxi.2 (which we have noted twice above).

6. *Expiation* is clearly referred to at liii.10 (*'āshām*).[4]

7. The 'husband' (or rather 'quasi-husband') metaphor appears in the plainest terms at liv.4–8 and lxi.10.

A further conception confirms the reliance of Paul upon Isaiah. Professor Daube has drawn attention to the fact that at the Exodus the children of Israel were given a present. A redemption should be accompanied by a present, 'grace', from the former master or creditor-enslaver. True enough, Is xlii.6 says, most relevantly, 'I have *given* you (the Servant) as a covenant to the people'. Paul at Rm iii.24, v.15, and viii.32 (*cf.* vi.23) emphasises that Christ was a free gift, who, in fact, brought 'justification' and 'eternal life'. The *shālāl* which we shall presently discuss is 'prey' or 'spoil' in at least two other senses, but it can legitimately recall Ex xii.36 ('they spoiled Egypt'), where Israel received presents.

All these metaphors occur in respect of the Suffering Servant. Modern scholarship is not unanimous that these prophecies were intended to

[1] Hegermann (1954), 94: Rm viii.34, Heb vii.25 in this sense.
[2] Porúbčan (1958).
[3] *Mid. on Ps.*, Ps. 72, § 3 (Braude, I, 560); *cf. ibid.* §§ 4, 5.
[4] Euler (1934), 119–21.

refer to the Messiah. Perhaps they refer to Israel collectively. But this will not serve our turn. We want to know what is the significance for Paul of what we can suggest for purposes of argument is a coincidence between his group of metaphors and those we have found in his 'scriptures'. Even if it can be shown (as it can) that Palestinian Judaism was prepared to see the prophecies as referring to the Messiah, that does not take us home: we must see whether Paul could have thought that they did actually refer to the man Jesus whom he calls Christos, Messiah.

THE CHARACTER OF THE NEW TESTAMENT ACCOUNTS

The real test is whether the Church between A.D. 30 and about A.D. 45 (by which time Paul's ideas were mature) believed that the death of Jesus fulfilled (not necessarily finally and exhaustively, but at all events perfectly) what was prophesied of himself or of Israel by Isaiah in the Song of the Servant, or was voiced in the psalms and other obviously oracular places of scripture. The contention that this was so appears in the plainest terms at 1 P ii.21–5, a document containing many Pauline ideas. The First Epistle of Peter has never conclusively been proved to be pseudonymous and may well be as old as A.D. 63.[1] At any rate it is an ancient authoritative work. Meanwhile Paul himself saw the 'betrayal' or handing-over of Jesus (to his 'enemies') as nothing but the fulfilment of what was said of the Servant (Rm iv.25 = Is liii.12*e* (LXX)).[2]

There were two levels upon which the matter could be tested. Were the facts of the trial and death of Jesus similar to what Isaiah and the psalmist contemplated? The oriental thinker does not dismiss coincidence as coincidence: on the contrary it would be a want of coincidence which would alarm him, for it is coincidence which reveals the pattern and makes the temporary and fugitive one with the eternal—and therefore meaningful. Further, did the events of the trial and death when seen as a pattern produce an impression that the purpose and drift of the scriptures was actually being effected? We must revert for a moment again to Isaiah. Paul constantly speaks of the justice of God and of the justification which the death of Jesus has somehow produced. No doubt he refers to an imaginary scene in which Jesus as *vindex* and *patronus* obtains in the court in which his father, God, is judge, a decree favourable to his clients, who are thereby justified.[3] This notion appears in

[1] W. G. Kümmel, *Introduction to the New Testament*, 14th edn, trans. Mattill (London 1966), § 28, finds its date of composition between 90 and 95 (p. 299), giving multiple arguments for pseudonymity.

[2] Sabourin (1961), 229.

[3] C. H. Dodd, *Epistle of Paul to the Romans* (London 1959), 75, *ad* Rm iii.23–6.

Isaiah. After the recital of the woes which the Servant is to endure, we hear that justification must follow (liii.11), and the reason follows at once in the chief verse of the whole passage, liii.12. Thus we must see whether the trial and death of Jesus could have followed the literal pattern of Isaiah to any substantial extent, and also whether the events could have enabled this set of metaphors to have found a factual pattern to which they could prospectively have belonged.

One might suppose that the gospel narratives would settle this question at once. The major difficulty is that they were, from their earliest detectable strata, coloured by an historical, that is to say a tendentious, sense. Two examples will suffice. At the nocturnal meeting, sometimes (wrongly) called the Trial before the Sanhedrin,[1] at which the decision was taken to send Jesus to Pontius Pilate, the utterance by Jesus which was the mainspring of the action leading to his death produced what has since been called an undignified or even incredible outburst from the influential persons present. They cover his head and hit him asking him to tell who had done so.[2] We must realise that physical reaction to

[1] It seems to have been an *ad hoc* meeting, hardly a council or a committee, still less a formal Sanhedrin. The presence of witnesses, their being discarded (correctly according to mishnaic law) for non-congruence, and the decision that Jesus was *ḥayyāyv* do not certify that it was a trial. Failure to observe mishnaic forms is inconclusive. There has been a good deal of perplexity about the committee or group which interviewed Jesus, and which found itself fixed with the responsibility to have him put to death. Some scholars have seen it as a regular Sanhedrin, a court with jurisdiction to hear accusations and to condemn (and the rejection of the witnesses who did not agree in their testimonies made it seem as if it was such a court); others have seen it as not only an informal but also an irregular body, proceeding in a manner which no self-respecting Jewish jurist could accept for a moment. The view put forward here is that it was a group convened *ad hoc* to enquire into the question of Jesus and to determine whether any official action should be taken and if so what it should be. It is necessary to draw the reader's attention to an aspect of the constitution of the Jewish State prior to A.D. 70 which has been overlooked. There was, no doubt, a court of seventy (the Sanhedrin proper); there were, in Jerusalem and throughout the Land of Israel, courts of three handling religious and religio-social and religio-political questions. Divorces, and the determination of the first day of the lunar month, for example, were handled by such courts. But a residual authority remained with a permanent priestly aristocracy, which might take the initiative and exercise judicial and/or executive functions independently of the court of seventy. The latter was obviously primarily a judicial assembly convened only for cases of gravity and in an atmosphere of deliberation, free from precipitation or haste. Such a court could not be swayed easily (in the nature of things), nor readily managed. Jesus was not brought before such a body, but before the priestly committee, which exercised the political leadership of the nation. Evidence for the existence of this priestly body is to be found at *Mishnāh*, R.H. I.7 and Ket. I.5, and 'Ohol. XVII.5. Mark's use of ὅλον τὸ συνέδριον at xiv.55, xv.1 (not followed literally by Matthew or Luke, but *cf.* Lk xxii.66) does not in fact prove that all the Sanhedrin proper were summoned at any stage, for συνέδριον (= "court") is used much more loosely (*cf.* Mt v.22, Mk xiii.9!).

[2] Mk xiv.65. It is of great interest that only Mark preserves the haggadic idea undamaged. On the passage see P. Benoit, 'Les outrages à Jésus prophète', *Neotestamentica et Patristica* (Fest. O. Cullmann) (Leiden 1962), 92–110.

events was normal and indeed conventional: had the elders not struck Jesus or at least spat on him (we are told they did both), they could not have cleared themselves from the implications of condoning his (apparently) outrageous behaviour, which every pious Jew must abhor. Next, *haggadāh* told them that the true Messiah had the power of prophecy, and could 'prophesy' by smell without the need of sight—a curious piece of folk-belief the origin of which is a *midrash* on Is xi.3.[1] There is nothing, therefore, improbable in their conduct as reported.[2] But the real significance of the story, which seems to have been missed, is the weaving into the tale of the betrayal by Peter. We are not told of Peter's threefold denial except as contemporaneous with Jesus's rejection as Messiah, and the scene is unbearably loaded with irony. At the very moment when the Jews are casting scorn upon his claim to be Messiah Jesus's incredible prophecy that Peter, of all people, would solemnly and deliberately deny him was coming true. No one will doubt but that Peter himself authorised, if he did not actually construct, this version of the events.[3]

One may take another episode which has escaped attention for what it is. This is the so-called purchase of Jesus by the Temple. Every reader of the gospel stories knows that Judas Iscariot was given money as an inducement to indicate where Jesus could be taken with the minimum of fuss. This was not a purchase of Jesus, though in a double sense Jesus was handed over (traditionally 'betrayed') to those who turned out to be his enemies. The monetary transaction subserved plausibility in the actual situation, and placed some obligation on Judas to play his part. The 30 shekels were not a *valuation* of Jesus,[4] nor were they really blood-money in the sense of compensation for his loss: though it would be falsifying the impression given by the passage if we were to neglect to notice that for the 'twelve' to receive blood-money (by way of their representative) in compensation for the loss of their leader, who was no less their member for being their leader, made

[1] 'His smell/delight is in the fear of the Lord.' When Bar Koziba could not 'smell and judge' they slew him: b. San. 93*b* = Sonc. 627. J. Lightfoot *ad* Mt xii.25 (*Works*, 1823, XI, 197). The Targum *ad loc.* goes far to clarify this. *Midr. on Ps.*, Ps. 72 § 3 (Braude, I, 560) links Ps lxxii.4 and the Messiah with Is xi.1, 3, 4. The Dead Sea Scrolls people said that Is xi.3 meant that the Messiah would judge according to the teachings of the priests (not the 'scribes'): Vermès, p. 227 (a fragment of a commentary on Isaiah not dealt with by Lohse). Dupont-Sommer, 287.

[2] *Pace* Burkill (1963) and previous writers cited by C. G. Montefiore, *Syn. Gospels*, i, (1909) 356–7. Klausner (1959), 344.

[3] In Brandon's view the account of Peter's denial is an interpolation by Mark intended to denigrate Peter, in the course of his scheme to minimise the relevance of the 'Mother Church' and original Christians, who were nationalistic (75, 79, 81). In this view Peter's denial was 'an incident quite irrelevant to the trial' (85). The superficiality of this explanation is striking.

[4] Yet the gospel refers to Zc xi.12–13.

sense. No doubt the Jewish authorities will have wanted to act righteously, and, by paying a sum to the community through their treasurer, they will have settled all claims upon themselves from that quarter—and this may well be the genesis of the idea we are about to consider.

St Matthew relates a story of flawless ambiguity. Judas abandoned the coins and the Temple officials refused to credit them to the treasury because it was 'the price of blood'.[1] The legal minuteness is entirely plausible, as also their making no difficulty about appropriating the abandoned property and putting it to the use specified. On the footing stated plainly by Judas and apparently not denied by the officials (Mt xxvii.4) the money was a bribe to betray the innocent and therefore tainted (Ps xv.5). Such money could not be accepted by the divine treasury, but could quite lawfully be expended on the needs of the dead.[2] However, the actual phrase 'price of blood' does not itself indicate bribe or corrupt inducement: on the contrary it points to quite another idea, itself entirely consistent with the decision taken regarding the coins. What lies behind this anomalous choice of phrase is the notion, allegedly on the part of the officials (who were evidently experts in such matters), that Jesus had virtually been bought by the treasury (whence the coins had obviously come)[3] as a sacrifice. Whether or not the officials could have admitted this at that stage, Matthew would see in the pronouncement a recognition, perhaps partly conscious, that Jesus died as an atonement for the whole nation, a sacrifice even in the eyes of his enemies. Rightly on that footing the coins could not be paid into the treasury, for the sacrifice would thereby be nullified! Whether the officials were admitting by their conduct that the 'betrayal' of Jesus was a sin; or whether they admitted that he was a sacrifice on behalf of Israel, the fact remains that irony is heavily written into the story as Matthew presents it, so that a straightforward and literal reading is hardly rewarding to the historian.

The gospel accounts having been arranged in this spirit, it is naturally difficult to disentangle what happened. The vast literature on the trial

[1] Mt xxvii.6: τιμὴ αἵματος.

[2] This point of Jewish law is explained above, pp. 270–1.

[3] Mt xxvi.15. Action taken in reliance upon the High Priest's *responsum* at Jn xi.50 (discussed below)? The applicability of Lv xxvii.29 ('None devoted . . . shall be ransomed; he shall surely be put to death') to these discussions has not been examined. It could be argued that the death of Jesus was required, if his 'enemies' had him 'delivered into their hands' (like the Canaanites to the Israelites at Nb xxi.2–3, *cf.* Jephthah's situation at Jg xi.30, 34–6, 39). Now it happens that a possible translation (see below, p. 423 n. 1) of *CD* IX, 1 (T. H. Gaster, *Scriptures*, 83, following C. Rabin, *Zadokite Documents* p. 54 n. 8) would insist that according to the Dead Sea Scroll community and their co-sectarians one who is condemned on a capital charge (as in Jesus's case) is not to be ransomed (under Lv xxvii.29) but must be handed over to the Gentiles for execution!

has been sifted and examined by Professor Blinzler. Scholars are preoccupied with fruitless searches after the responsibility for Jesus's death. The early Church was concerned about this in a constructive way. The downright accusations[1] recorded as made by Peter and others ignore the excuses the actors could have urged in their own defence—but of course the Resurrection had intervened, and the apostles' own miracles threw a special light on their considered view of what had happened. To the apostles the Roman soldiers were mere agents for the Jewish people who, so their minds seem to have run, could slaughter through the executioners' weapons as directly as they could through a priest's knife. The Jews, the Church seems to have said, were all ultimately determined to send Jesus to his death: they thus fulfilled the prophecies of Isaiah and the psalmist, and now they must follow out the consequences and be baptised! No doubt the Jewish wars later added a certain colour to this point of view. But we cannot follow that line of thinking here. We must see whether the outlines of the affair support Paul in his metaphors, all of which were complete while the Temple still stood.

Meanwhile the reader must be told that, quite apart from the tendency (which we shall see is Pauline) that underlies the narrative of the trial and death of Jesus, the synoptic gospels show clear traces of a bizarre interest in quite a different theme. To the Jewish mind there is nothing incongruous in a story's having two tendencies or implications, for both may be true and inconsistencies are of little moment. Many of the quite unnecessary details of the story are there (irrespective of whether they were *true*) since they linked Jesus's sufferings with the usual dramatic preparation of the High Priest, on the Eve of the Day of Atonement. The latter was taken to an *upper chamber*, where he communed with the 'elders of the priesthood', having left the custody of the 'elders of the Court'. He was *adjured*, and was kept awake all night. The tending of the Altar *fire*,[2] which normally took place about *cock-crow*, was advanced, and before cock-crow the Altar was made ready for the High Priest's personal sacrifice.[3] During the ceremonies the

[1] Ac ii.36; iv.10 (Ac ii.23 is more circumspect); x.39. But throughout note that Zc xii.10 'showed' that the Jews crucified Jesus!

[2] No one has explained the gospels' interest in the fire in the High Priest's hall (Mk xiv.54, 67; Lk xxii.55, 56; Jn xviii.18). It seems utterly irrelevant. But the fire and cock-crow are linked and it is by cock-crow that Peter's sin occurs. The High Priest's atonement for himself and his house begins at cock-crow. Peter himself (I suggest) is responsible for this highly subjective interpretation of Jesus's prophetic reference to the cock-crow. Peter was Jesus's 'star pupil', as we should say. That the notion did not remain infertile is seemingly revealed by Jn xviii. 19–23: Jesus talked to the High Priest as if he denied his authenticity or the validity of his function.

[3] *Mishnāh*, Yoma, I, 1–8. The fire was raked and stirred up. Are we to understand that Peter poked the fire in the hall?

High Priest was robed and disrobed several times and his final vestments were glorious. The gospel texts have retained the coincidences, some of them trifling in themselves, because the rôle of the High Priest and the outlines of his ritual were perfectly well known, and because a succession of mere hints was enough to make the point that Jesus was the *real* High Priest and was just about to effect the *real* (and everlasting) Atonement. That he was interrogated by the High Priest and elders in the High Priest's dwelling (and we note in passing the gospel's stumbling over the place of the meeting and the exact identity of the chief interrogator) is a perfect piece of New Testament irony. And that the Day of Atonement and Passover have little in common seemed irrelevant, on the theory that Jesus's life summed up and gave meaning to all the *Torāh*.

Should any reader doubt whether the evangelists were capable of incorporating material selected and arranged in this fashion, blending two inconsistent themes, he has only to turn to the story of the Crucifixion itself. That the death of Jesus was in some way like the deaths of the paschal lambs is a notion well embedded in the framework of the story of the Redemption (as we shall see). Yet the events were also thought to fit the theme of the slaughter of the Red Heifer (Nb xix), which is a sin offering. That is why we are told of Simon of Cyrene's carrying the cross (Mk xv.21), there is some dealing with pieces of cloth (*v.* 24), and chief priests are present (*v.*31)—and this is the reason why only one authority reads ὑσσῷ at Jn xix.29 for the otherwise unanimously testified ὑσσώπῳ. Probable as Camerarius's conjecture was, that the sponge offered to Jesus should have been placed, if not on a *reed* as the gospel of Mark says, then on a *javelin*, the fact remains that hyssop (a bush), which is to be used at Passover,[1] is also to be used at the burning of the Heifer (Aland recognises this at § 347, p. 488 f.n.). The Heifer must not have borne any yoke, and must be killed in the presence of the priest, and wood, hyssop, and red cloth are associated with the ceremonial burning. The bizarre recognition of the Crucifixion as analogous to the slaughter of the Heifer is confirmed by what is said plainly at Hb xiii.11–13, and less plainly at Hb xii.24: we see, in fact, that it was present before Mark was compiled; and John insists that the correspondences were, unexpectedly, even more complete.[2] Thus the incongruous collocation of inconsistent themes is perfectly in accord with the evangelists' technique, and, of course, does nothing to weaken the probability (rather the reverse, it strengthens the probability) that Simon

[1] Midr. R., Exod. XVIII.2 = Sonc. 213

[2] That the vinegar (Mk xv.36, Lk xxiii.36, Jn xix.29) was linked with Ps lxix.22(21) is explained by Dodd, *Historical Tradition* 33, 41–2.

did perform the function, that a chief-priestly party *were* present, and that hyssop (instead of a javelin) *was* (for whatever motive) actually used.

THE DATE OF THE LAST SUPPER

As for the chronology, it is obvious that the story of the trial of Jesus starts not with the arrest in the garden but with the Last Supper. Was this a Passover meal, a ceremony after a Passover meal, a ceremony in lieu of a Passover meal, or a ceremony on the evening before the Passover and thus chronologically independent of the Passover ritual? The early Church did nothing to dispel the confusion caused by a passage in St Mark which suggests that Jesus ate the Passover with his disciples and then instituted the Eucharist. But for this passage[1] we should all be content to believe with St John's gospel that Jesus and his disciples never ate that Passover, for Jesus was crucified when the Passover lambs were being sacrificed in the Temple on the Friday afternoon, so that he might be likened to a sacrificial lamb. His disciples might have been able to eat the Passover at the second Passover which was available for people disqualified from eating the Passover at the correct date, but the gospels give us no indication that they did. While in mourning for their lost teacher, they would not have pursued the ritual on the day for which all their preparations had been made. This complicated problem cannot be pursued here unless I suggest, what should surely have been suggested before, namely that the troublesome passage from Mark, which has valuable information and should not be discarded lightly, does not, in fact, *say* (though no doubt it can be held to imply) that Jesus ate the Passover at all. He was concerned that preparations such as would have been required for the Passover and which took not less than one complete day, should be regularly made. During the period of preparation the 'company', *i.e.* Jesus and his 'family' selected for the purpose, would have to eat, and unleavened bread would begin to be available. Jesus will have had, as we shall see,

[1] Mk xiv.12–16. Burkill (1963), 261. In my view (as distinct from Jeremias's—he sees the Last Supper as a Passover meal)—Mark's 'first day of Unleavened Bread' is the festal day when all leaven must be removed, *i.e.* 14th Nisan. The Last Supper took place after dark on the 13/14th Nisan. In this connection it is important to recollect that the day of preparation for the Passover was itself semi-holy, that is to say it was on the way to becoming a sacred occasion as the developed law of the mishnaic period shows. The *Mishnāh* (Pes. I, 1ff.) shows that leaven was removed on the night of the 13/14th Nisan: and at any period when or in any circles where mishnaic law was observed leavened bread would have ceased to be available by the evening on which I understand the Last Supper to have taken place. It perhaps will not strike everyone immediately, but 'leaven' does not mean only yeast in its natural form but any object containing leaven, hence leavened bread was taboo.

an interest in the availability of unleavened bread which was presumably difficult to obtain in the ordinary way except during and after the period of preparation for the Passover. Jesus's own very peculiar words about his anticipation of that particular Passover[1] are capable of two meanings: either that he did expect to eat the Passover regularly that year, or that the Passover to which he had been looking forward was his personal and peculiar Passover 'before I suffer', namely the special ritual which he instituted. This is my view: Jesus's Passover was in two parts—the ritual meal on the night of the Preparation for the Passover and his personal sacrifice during the ensuing afternoon; thus he was present for his disciples (as representatives of Israel) in the meal which itself anticipated (and as we shall see authorised) his death. The paschal lamb was normally killed first and eaten afterwards: Jesus was first eaten and then killed—that was the difference; hence the different chronology! The early Church, under doctrinal influences, seems to have wished not to see Jesus's ritual in any other light except as a substitute for (in fact a mirror-image of) the Passover for Christians who had a redemption to celebrate additional to that celebrated by all Jews.[2] Hence the ambiguous passage in Mark was allowed to produce the impression that the Last Supper took place on the evening of the Passover. A scholar has recently shown that Paul seems to have believed with St John that the crucifixion took place on the eve of the Passover.[3]

Jesus himself seems to have expected his crucifixion at the precise time the lambs would be slaughtered.[4] The extremely cryptic passage known as the Lament over Jerusalem,[5] differently placed by Matthew and Luke, can be taken, as often hitherto, as a promise of an eschatological acceptance[6] of the Messiah by those who reject his offer of salvation at the moment of speaking or earlier. But this is forced and does not take account of the close association of the passage with references to the blood-guilt of the people (Mt xxiii.36) and to the Temple (Mt xxiv.1). In Luke's view the passage relates to the welcome

[1] Lk xxii.15–16 ('With desire I have desired to eat this Passover with you before I suffer: for I say unto you, I will not eat it, until it be fulfilled in the Kingdom of God'). Was this anticipation of Jesus's own ritual because a cosmic Passover would prevent his participation in the normal ritual? A cryptic comment.

[2] The *Quartadecimans* observed the 14th Nisan as the Passover, but as a fast for non-believing Jewry. B. Lohse, *Das Passafest der Quartadecimaner* (Gütersloh 1953). Jeremias (1966), 19, 83.

[3] H. Montefiore, *Expos. Times* 72 (1960), 53–4. 1 Co xv.20 fits with 1 Co v.7. Jeremias (1966), 74.

[4] 3 p.m. to 5 p.m., 14th Nisan. Josephus, *Bell. Jud.* VI, 423; *Mishnāh*, Pes. V, 1. Jeremias (1966), 74.

[5] Aland, *Synopsis*, §§ 213, 285. H. van der Kwaak, *NT* 8 (1966), 156–70.

[6] Jeremias (1966) understands the passage as referring to the Second Coming (p. 259).

given to Jesus at his triumphal entry into Jerusalem, which he would place later chronologically; but this is excluded by Matthew's arrangement: in the latter Jesus, himself abandoning the Temple, refers to an event in the uncertain future.[1] I should suggest the following interpretation, in which a *midrash* on Jr xii.7 occurs: 'Jerusalem kills the Prophets. Jesus wanted to take her inhabitants under his wing like a bird[2] (a gesture which should be visualised), but they would not consent to this. Yet now "there is being abandoned to you your house". This is the leaving or forsaking of his house by God that is foretold by Jeremiah, "I have deserted my house, I have abandoned my inheritance". Now the Temple is being deserted by the Presence. But the abandoning is to you and for you, for God's temple is really *your* temple, and this is being given up for you, namely the body of Jesus. For, says Jesus, you shall not see, *i.e.* know, me until you (all) say, "Blessed is he that cometh in the name of the Lord", as they will next do in the Temple courtyard at the slaughtering by the sacrificers (all Jewish males can then be priests) of the paschal lambs.' The key to the *midrash* would be the fact that the Hallel (the words cited are near the end of it) is recited and repeated at that very time, the first after the winter solstice and the next before the recitations, company by company, on the Passover evening itself.[3] The synoptic gospels, taking Jesus's death to be the second Exodus, wished the crucifixion to be seen (actually or notionally, it is not clear for want of explicit statement) as happening on the Passover day—so that, of course, the Last Supper would already have taken place on the Passover night and would have more or less coincided with the Passover meal. This will have had its own effect in shrinking or obscuring the cryptic passage I have been discussing. Yet the actual words as reproduced both in Matthew and Luke preserve a midrashic handling of the idea in Jr xii.7, and once this is taken up and the double meaning is explored, the sequence of ideas becoming plain, a prophecy of the actual time of the crucifixion is revealed. For at the very moment when the lambs were being slaughtered Jesus was put to death, his death providing atonement for the blood-guilt belonging to the Jews, a perpetual means of atonement which entirely superseded the Temple. The temple of his body, as is well known, could be represented later as affording a salvation which the Temple built with hands could not do. But the supersession could not be effected unless

[1] Aland, § 269. The comparable 2 Esd i.25–36 (of Essene provenance?) possesses Christian *midrashim*. W. J. P. Boyd, 'Mt xxiii.38f. = Lk xiii.35 "You shall not see me . . . Blessed is he . . ." ', forthcoming in *Studia Evangelica* IV, shows that the logion was originally a theophany which the gospel authors partly obscure.

[2] Alluding to Dt xxxii.11–12 and Rt ii.12. *Cf.* Ml iii.20 (iv.2). See previous note.

[3] Lightfoot, *Works* (London 1823), ix, 140–3. Segal (1963), 259.

the Jews came under the wings of the cross, seeing Jesus for what he was. Thus the notion that the crucifixion itself was a perpetual redemption could, if this explanation is correct, be attributed to Jesus himself in a passage so cryptic that the evangelists were unable totally to obscure its purport. There is evidence, which we have seen in connection with the rod or staff of Moses,[1] that Jesus found out midrashically how the objectionable, alien means of execution could be a means of salvation. The paradox can thus be traced (it would appear) to Jesus himself. The boldness of such an interpretation of scripture is obvious.

Many a critically-minded reader of this page may ask himself whether Jesus *really* believed that the ugly gibbet-like method of execution, unknown to Jewish law and an intrusion (if ever there was one) into the native culture, could have been foreshadowed in biblical literature. The instance of the 'wings' could conceivably be argued away as a metaphor which need not be visualised in a concrete form. The rod or staff of Moses on the hill above the field of battle with Amalek could be explained away as a pious association of ideas—for many believe that the Church introduced the logia about 'taking up the cross', fathering upon Jesus an idea which originated in its own desire to obtain comfort in persecution. But there is yet another instance of Jesus's endeavouring to 'naturalise' the cross, trying, as it were, to acclimatise his disciples to the idea that it could be, must be, the proper method of salvation. This is equally bizarre, and I do not see how it can be argued away by any of the methods dear to the 'sceptics'. St John, at i.51, places in the mouth of Jesus the words 'You shall see the heaven opened and the angels of God ascending and descending upon the Son of Man'. It is well known that this alludes to Jacob's dream of the ladder. Professor C. H. Dodd describes the passage as having nothing to do with apocalyptic visions of the future, but having reference to the ministry of the incarnate Logos.[2] He refers to a *midrash*, the antiquity of which is unknown, but which is in fact found in several places,[3] to the effect that when Jacob (*i.e.* Israel) dreamt of the angels going up and down he saw them not merely on the 'ladder set up on earth', its top reaching to heaven, but actually ascending and descending *on him*, for the word *bo* can mean 'on it' or 'on him'. He also shows how in this *midrash* the idea of ascending and descending is not confined by the rabbis to movement, but is taken to imply the angels' reflections about Jacob. In fact in one

[1] Above, p. 148.

[2] *Interpretation of the Fourth Gospel*, 245–6; *Historical Tradition in the Fourth Gospel*, 407n.

[3] Midr. R., Gen. LXVIII.12–14 = Sonc. 625–9; Midr. R., Exod. XLII.2 = Sonc. 483. *Targ. ps. Jon.*, Gn. xxviii.12 (Etheridge, I, 253) shows that aspects of this *midrash* go back to a very early period.

place we are told that God said to Jacob 'If thy offspring will be righteous they will be exalted in the world, and they and their messengers will rise higher and higher; but when they suffer a decline, then will their messengers share in their downfall.' And again, when they were ascending and descending some were exalting Jacob and some maligning him. In other words the dream of Jacob could be taken rabbinically in many different ways. In one way Jacob himself was seen as a method by which angels, messengers, passed between God and man, and was himself the cause of their exaltation or depression. In fact this comment refers to the crucifixion. This has not occurred to anyone because it would be difficult for the occidental to visualise the cross as a ladder. But it fits very well, since in the Middle East, Iran, the Himalayan regions, and into further Asia wherever wood is scarce and the labourer is disinclined to exert himself unduly, a ladder which is basically a single trunk with rough battens affixed, notches cut out, or rungs tied on crosswise is the most common (and in some regions the only) kind of ladder. The cross, with its victim affixed, at one and the same time degraded and exalted, is thus seen as that special means of communication between God and man which Jacob, the progenitor of the Jews called by the collective name Israel, saw in his dream.[1] Scholars who have been attending to the question whether 'Son of Man' means the ideal Israel, and remarking on Jesus's solidarity with his followers, have, apparently, missed the point Jesus himself wanted to make, namely that those who are prepared, like Nathanael, to see Jesus as 'Son of God', 'King of Israel', must be prepared to see him in the paradoxical rôle of executed criminal and saviour at one and the same time. That John himself knew that this passage likened the cross to the ladder seems clear enough, for he sees the 'lifting up' of Jesus (viii.28, xii.32, 34) as a metaphorical exalting as well as a physical erecting like that of the serpent which Moses erected in the wilderness (iii.14). John says Jesus accepted the prospect of being gibbeted on the cross: the synoptic gospels preserve a tradition that he knew when it would take place.

Our explanation of the apparent discrepancy between the synoptic gospels and St John as to the date of the Last Supper (it took place on the Thursday night, 13/14th Nisan) totally avoids the unfortunate plethora of hypotheses recently put forward to the effect that Jesus used a special calendar,[2] that there were alternative calendars in vigour in

[1] Justin Martyr, *Dialogue* § 86

[2] J. L. Lauterbach, *Proc. Am. Ac. Jew. Res.* 12 (1942), 48–9. A. Jaubert, *La date de la Cène* (Paris 1957). An early Jaubertine bibliography: M. H. Shepherd, *JBL* 80 (1961), 123–32. Jaubert, *NTS* 7 (1960/1), 1–30; 14 (1968), 145–64.

Jerusalem,[1] or overseas[2]—hypotheses rejected (rightly) by Jeremias,[3] fraught with error for the unwary,[4] and otiose.

Critics are well aware of the handicaps under which we labour in using the gospel materials. Sometimes they fear an obscure or apparently nonsensical passage is corrupt or even spurious. A sceptical approach is no doubt a healthy one, but one would always need better reasons for discarding a passage than a suspicion that the evangelist's opinion of it disagreed with one's own. It is worth adding at this point that the Johannine story of Jesus's trial and experiences at the hands of his 'enemies' is silently influenced by the vocabulary of Esther, as Professor A. Guilding explains.[5] The striking correspondences between St John's account of the Passion and both Esther and lections for the season of Purim could be urged as evidence that his account was corrupted in an effort to depict Jesus as a redeemer of the Jews from the Gentiles. But it could equally be claimed that, as Jesus was emphatically and obviously nothing of the kind, the textual correspondences, though not coincidences in themselves, confirm the Church's zeal to gather every scrap of coincidence between the events and biblical counterparts, without too sharp an eye to relevance. And this was not an irrational perversity on their part, since the technique was part of the culture and had been used with the utmost boldness by Jesus himself.

THE TRIAL (IN OUTLINE)

We may now consider the outlines of the trial and its implications as a practical affair. Let us leave the symbolic implications aside for the present. There is no dispute but that Pilate put Jesus to death on the footing that Jesus was, politically speaking, a person deserving of death. No one doubts, and our gospels go to great lengths to emphasise, that Pilate came to this conclusion tardily and unwillingly. As 'King of the Jews' Jesus was crucified.[6] There is doubt, however, as to how Jesus

[1] G. R. Driver, *Judaean Scrolls* (Oxford 1965), 331–2, criticised by S. Zeitlin, *JQR* 57 (1966), 28ff., 40–5. Zeitlin attacked Torrey's idea (*JQR* 42 [1951/2], 237–50) at *JQR* 42 (1951/2), 250–60.

[2] M. H. Shepherd, *JBL* 80 (1961), 123–32.

[3] *Eucharistic Words* (1966), 24–5.

[4] M. Black, 'The arrest and trial of Jesus and the date of the last supper' in *New Testament Essays . . . T. W. Manson* (Manchester 1959), 19–33. Professor J. Imbert's lecture (referred to above, p. 393 n. 2) evidences influence from Mlle. Jaubert.

[5] *Fourth Gospel* (1960), 168–9.

[6] Jn xix.14–15. So the *titulus*, discussed by P.-F. Regard, *Rev. Arch.*, 5th ser., 28 (1928), 95–105. The Messiah was a 'King' according to the *haggadāh* common to Pharisees and the Dead Sea Scroll community (*Blessing of Jacob*, Vermès, 224). He was not a political King but a spiritual, ideal King—though such subtleties would be beyond a Gentile responsible for government in Palestine.

came into Pilate's hands and what induced Pilate to take the course he did.

A source of error is the notion that Jesus was aimed at by 'the Jews', as if his antagonists were a homogeneous group, incapable of division or difference of viewpoint. It is too often supposed that this imaginary body was predisposed to get rid of Jesus by almost any possible method. On the contrary there are traces of very different attitudes, and the actual behaviour of the meeting when it took its fatal decision raises numerous inferences which deserve exploration in the light of this. We have evidence that in influential circles there were some who believed that Jesus was some kind of prophet.[1] There were those who believed in Jesus perhaps as the Church itself later believed in him, or at least tended to accept him as a saviour figure.[2] These may not have been more than a substantial minority. There were Pharisees and Scribes who were intellectually convinced that Jesus was a dangerous, false teacher.[3] There were those who, after forming this view, believed it their pious duty to remove him from the scene.[4] There were those who were curious about him.[5] There were those who had no opinion one way or the other and would need to be convinced by evidence whether there was need for action and then would consider what action needed to be taken.[6] There were those to whom fear could be attributed that if such a teacher, with radical views, were allowed to inflame the mob, the Romans would be forced to take action such as would subvert what little of Jewish freedom remained.[7] But some seemingly wished that Jesus, as a sinless man, could be *allowed* to be put to death (by anyone?) in order to do the nation good.[8] Whether St John is right or not in his report of the High Priest's ideas about Jesus (to which we come presently) the passage he hands on to us unquestionably evidences this superstition. This last notion must be carefully explored. It is uncongenial to the western mind and must therefore be enlarged upon here.

Perhaps from before Judaism itself God's justice was reconciled with experience by supposing that the sufferings of the good, and particularly their death, could atone for the sins of others, which sins would otherwise lead to the destruction of the people.[9] This does not

[1] Mk vi.15–16; Lk ix.9; xxiii.8. [2] Lk xxiii.50–1; Jn xii.11, 42.
[3] *e.g.* Jn ix.16. [4] Lk xix.47–8; xxii.1–2. [5] Jn xviii.13, 19–23.
[6] The episode of the witnesses. *Cf.* Nicodemus's attitude at Jn vii.51.
[7] A possible interpretation of Jn xi.48 and therefore an indication of what could rationally be believed.
[8] Jn xi.49–50. συμφέρει ὑμῖν ἵνα εἷς ἄνθρωπος ἀποθάνῃ ὑπὲρ τοῦ λαοῦ καὶ μὴ ὅλον τὸ ἔθνος ἀπόληται (on which *vid. inf.*) followed by St John's own commentary. It must be emphasised that 'one man' could die 'on behalf of the people' more naturally in a spiritual (*i.e.* superstitious) sense than in any other: but see D. Daube, *Collaboration* (cited below, p. 420 n. 3).
[9] See b. Ber. 62*b* = Sonc. 393. Dalman (1914), 28–9; Büchsel (1943), 343; Stamm (1946): but Is lii.13–53. 12 does *not* stand alone. Jeremias (1947), 255; (1966), 215–16,

mean that one could *kill* a man to make atonement (for that is human sacrifice), but one could accept his death at the hands of others as if it were an atonement for sin. Judaism, popular and scholarly, accepted this theory.[1] Martyrdom had supernatural power. The reason seems to have been that the shedding of innocent blood put God, the Almighty, in the wrong; for God is amenable to complaint arising from man.[2] R. Meir said, 'If Scripture speaks thus (at Dt xxi.23 about the man hanged on the tree) "I am troubled at the blood of the wicked", how much more at the blood of the *righteous* which is shed'.[3] The belief is an oriental one not confined to the Jews. The political sufferings of the Jews were attributed by many people to the nation's sins. Redemption from them would remove the foreign power and the frustrations it caused. Against this background we must read the Christian gloss (Jn xi.51–2) put on a *dictum* attributed to the High Priest (*ibid.* 50) which on the surface is a straightforward *responsum* of Jewish law founded on 2 S xx.18–22 generalised with the aid of Ps lxxii.14 ('He shall redeem their soul from oppression and violence; and precious shall their blood be in his sight'). I do not think we can doubt but that St John wished to imply that the Jewish leaders' hands were forced by political necessity: but the passage itself can be read easily without this implication and is better so read, for the oft-repeated charge that the Jews were afraid of Jesus as a rebel-leader seems to be largely imaginary.[4] What the High Priest most probably meant, at that early stage in the discussions, was this: 'Jesus's miracles may well produce a dilemma (*ibid.*

[1] Ps lxxii.14; cxvi.15; 1 S xxv.24; 2 M vii.37f.; 4 M vi.28–9, and especially xvii.21–2 (the work belongs to *c.* A.D. 35 or at any rate, according to E. J. Bickerman, to A.D. 18–55). *Midr. on Ps.*, on Ps cxvi (Braude, ii. 225–7). b. M.Ḳ. 27*b* = Sonc. 181; Midr. R., Deut. VI. 5 = Sonc. 124 (vicarious atonement). *Cf.* Rm v.7 (but Paul's acceptance of the belief is doubted: Bonsirven [1963], 98). G. Vermès, *Scripture and Tradition in Judaism* (Leiden 1961) at p. 198 insists upon the relevance of this theory.

[2] By his own wish (see p. 437 below). The credit for connecting the blood-feud, martyrdom, and Is liii belongs to Dr J. Scharbert (1964), 294ff.

[3] *Mishnāh*, San. VI, 5 (Danby, 391; Blackman, IV, 264–5). The passage is much the more interesting because the context does *not* concern the righteous.

[4] It is said clearly that they feared a riot only if they took him publicly! Μὴ ἐν τῇ ἑορτῇ, μήποτε ἔσται θόρυβος τοῦ λαοῦ (Mk xiv.2). As Jesus himself is made to point out, he could have been arrested in the Temple in broad daylight. The irony of the story is that, hoping to avoid a riot and determined to bring the business to an end *before* the Passover if possible, the authorities unwittingly provided that Jesus should be 'betrayed', *i.e. handed over*, which had biblical–messianic implications. History would unfold itself irrespective of the intentions of many of the participants: that is the idea. On ἑορτῇ see Jeremias (1966), 71.

226–31. Midr. R., S.S., 1, 14, § 60: the righteous are ransom, mediators, and sureties (Jerem. 254). Miss Hooker (1959), 55ff., cannot link this notion of atonement with the Messiah before the Hellenistic period of the Church. But see Richard (1959). Moreover the Dead Sea Scroll community shared in the notion that the sufferings of the righteous are an atonement: *CR* VIII, 3–4 (Vermès, 85; Lohse, 28–9; Leaney, 214).

47), but *if* it is true that his religious teachings tend towards rebellion, and *if* that would itself tend to the destruction of the Temple (τόπος) and the City, and *if* the ensuing Roman supremacy would testify to God's wrath against the nation (ἔθνος), you may rely, on the footing of expediency and in the interests of peace (that fundamental maxim of the Law), on the precedent set by the wise woman of Abel in recommending the threatened citizens to throw the rebel Sheba's head to Joab.[1] If those contingencies emerge, the pious, including Jesus's followers, cannot object to our putting Jesus to death, charge or no charge, upon *bona fide Torāh* considerations.' Of course things took a different course, but the stage was set with a pronouncement (possibly as much sarcastic as sententious) which could immediately be misinterpreted in popular terms as (unconscious)[2] recognition that a single man may die for the people.[3] That the early Church found the story of Joab and Sheba reconcilable (somewhat unexpectedly) with the doctrine of the atoning power of the death of the innocent (Sheba was *not* innocent, of course, but he was under protection by the city which ultimately betrayed him) is indicated by St John's immediate, and altogether unnecessary, dispatch of Jesus to a place called Ephraim (*cf.* 2 S xx.21), for Sheba was an Ephraimite, and whether history or geography enters into this 'coincidence' it is quite superfluous to ask.[4] Jesus

[1] Discussed at Midr. R., Gen. XCIV.9 = Sonc. 878. See n. 3 below.

[2] Aquinas II^a II^{ae} q. 173, a. 4 *sed c.*

[3] In the sense of the last *śloka* of the *Bṛhaspati-smṛti*: one man may lawfully be put to death to effect the safety of many (J. Jolly, *SBE* xxxiii [1889], 390)? The proposition that a city may be saved at the expense of a guilty life is still *halakāh*: J. L. Kadushin (comp. and trans.), *Ḥoshen ha-Mishpaṭ. Jewish Code of Jurisprudence*, pt. 1 (New York 1915), p. 189 = §§ 41–2, 4th edn (New York 1923), 434*a*. Maimonides, *op. cit.* I (Book of Knowledge), I, v, 5 (ed. and trans. Hyamson [Jerus. 1965]), 40*b*. On Jn xi see Bultmann (1959), 314, also W. Bauer, *Das Johannes-Evangelium*, 3rd edn (Tübingen 1933), 156–7. Commentators, including R. H. Lightfoot, fail to perceive the significance of the precedent at 2 S xx (though it is known as such). Josephus's idea of what the woman's wisdom was is shown at *Ant.* VII, xi, 8 (289–93). The principle alluded to appears at his *Bell. Jud.* II. xii, 5 (237). D. Daube, *Collaboration with Tyranny in Rabbinic Law* (Oxford 1965), fully discusses the episode of Sheba, its later history and implications (p. 18ff.). The relevant teaching (see j. Ter. 46*b*, Midr. R., Gen. XCIV = Sonc. 878) is found at least as early as A.D. 100 that 'if the demand is for a named individual like Sheba son of Bichri, then, in order to avoid wholesale slaughter, he should be surrendered'. The topic is raised again by Dr G. Vermès in a letter to the *Observer*, 21 April, 1968. Reliance on the biblical authority would be justified if the Romans had *demanded* Jesus to be surrendered to them—but the behaviour of Pilate as represented in all the gospels firmly negatives any such suggestion. Brandon's hypothesis that Pilate engineered Jesus's arrest is without foundation. The High Priest's *responsum* was therefore hypothetical (if we are to take it literally, as perhaps we should).

[4] Guilding, *Fourth Gospel*, 150 connects Ephraim not with 2 S xx.21 but with Jo xxiv.30, 33 (the implication is that Jesus's death is like that of Joshua as Lazarus's was like that of 'Eleazar [for 'Eliezer as one who returned from the dead see above, p. 99 and for Phinehas as an immortal see above, p. 188]).

was thus, whether as the great scapegoat (as some at least of his pious followers were prepared to believe) or as politically dangerous or a 'security risk' (as his enemies believed), fit to be 'put to death'. Throughout all these discussions the Jewish maxim *māh naf^eshăch?* is to be inferred: from whichever point of view you commence, the ultimate decision must be the same.

High Priests, of course, as the great officiants at *Yom ha-kippūriym*, were experts in atonement. When they died their deaths released persons under restraint due to guilty shedding of blood.[1] And they were, in ideal cases at least, *ex officio* prophets.[2] We do not know whether the alleged *responsum* quoted above was reported to the people prior to the trial before Pilate, but if it had been its effect would have been electrifying. More probably this information, like that of the treasurer's comment, obtained currency and significance after the Resurrection. But, apart from the legalistic aspect of the pronouncement, the strange passage in Jn xi shows us that, whatever the implications, people in high places might plausibly be supposed to believe that at a time when there was no imminent *political* danger worthy of mention Jesus was still a person whose death would be expedient for them and would save the whole Jewish people. In other words, in the time of St John's immediate source Jesus's death could still seriously be suggested as having been beneficial for all Jews, and this could only be in a spiritual sense. He died to save his nation—from what?—from their sins. Suggestions that he died in order to save them from anything else cannot be taken seriously. There is absolutely no evidence that the Romans had on foot any anti-Jewish political programme of note, still less had they any interest in Jesus at that point. Pilate's few well known attempts to accustom Jews to the artistic representations symbolic of Roman authority cannot be enlarged so as to appear to have been a scheme intended to subvert the Jewish religion.

But what of the plausibility of any scheme against Jesus's life? Jesus was alleged in some quarters to be a false teacher, a fomenter of sedition, one who foretold the collapse of the Temple or at any rate of its profitable cult. If one felt that his original notions on Jewish Law could call down the wrath of God and thus indirectly an increase in the Roman tyranny, irrespective of other possible upheavals reminiscent of Herod Archelaus's reign, how could one be *sure* that engineering Jesus's death might not be a worse sin, with worse consequences? The group or body

[1] Rowley (1952), 170–1, citing Nb xxxv.25, 28, 32. Wiencke (1939), 56.

[2] Josephus, *Ant.* XIII, x, (of John Hyrcanus). Dodd (1962), 139. Tos. Soṭa XIII.5–6 is a good example. John's idea may have been, in company with the synoptics, that the High Priest, without realising it, acted prophetically.

before whom Jesus was brought, which is usually (no doubt wrongly) called the Sanhedrin must have known their law, or at any rate the High Priest would authoritatively pronounce on it for them in case of doubt. In the case of a prominent man they would know and observe their constitutional powers and the 'margin of the law' (*shūrat ha-diyn*) which Jewish jurists, provided their mental balance was not disturbed, ever sought to keep within. No doubt if the Jewish elders, whatever the ground or inducement, stoned or otherwise made away with the true Messiah, they would be in grave danger; but the situation would be otherwise if they induced someone else to do it. The general law of responsibility is clear: only he who, not being disqualified from legal responsibility, actually does and performs the act is liable for it or its consequences. Pharisee rabbis would, no doubt, order a man to be flogged who instigated a crime. But the scriptural law did not penalise one who merely counselled a wicked act. If an independent mind (such as was Pilate's) intervened, the act could not be laid at the counsellor's door.[1] In the especial context of judicial mistakes of law, we know that it was believed that a judge was liable only if he himself executed (as in a 'lynching') judgement on the innocent victim.[2] Thus, if Jesus were the Messiah and his death were not transcendentally ordained as pro-Jesus enthusiasts may have urged, and if Pilate killed him, Pilate would take the consequences (hence Pilate's insistence that the Jews accept moral responsibility?).[3] If Jesus were a false teacher, Pilate would have rid the country of a dangerous rascal, and the Jews would have done what they afterwards constantly did, namely used the Gentile ruler to carry out Jewish sentences. The Jewish willingness to hand

[1] *Mishnāh*, Sanh. IX.1; Hor. I.1. The school of Shammai took a view more congenial to our notions, but it did not prevail. The principle is expounded *a fortiori* by Maimonides, *Mishneh Torāh* XI, V, ii, 2 (trans. Klein, p. 199). The law of agency operated similarly: responsibility could not be passed on: see above, p. 52 n. 3. If in the interests of public order one who urged the commission of murder was to be flogged, this lay within the discretion of the Jewish judicial authority.

[2] b. Bek. 28*b* = Sonc. 182; B.Ḳ. 100*a* = Sonc. 584–5.

[3] This seems to be the true explanation for the hand-washing which has caused such scholarly alarm. The scene at Mt xxvii.24–5 (confined to St Matthew) was understood by the evangelist himself to show that the Jews *alone* were responsible for Jesus's death and that the Roman thought that execution a *crime* (ἀθῷος ἀπὸ τοῦ αἵματος: a thoroughly Jewish expression, *cf. Mishnāh*, San. IV.5 [Danby, 288] *ad fin.*). But when the tradition reached Matthew, perhaps in almost identical words, it could have meant something significantly different: 'As an official I can arrange his execution, but I choose to do so provided you fully understand that I am not your cat's paw and provided you reconsider your acts and appreciate that any moral responsibility for this irregularity is entirely yours.'—'By all means: we are prefectly willing to accept this.' Mr De Vries interestingly suggests (68–9) that the hand-washing enraged the crowd. His suggestion that Pilate followed Dt. xxi.6–9 in order to impress upon the people that Jesus was innocent ('this innocent blood': Kilpatrick, *NT* 5 [1962], 114) is impressive. But this innocence related only to the Jews' charge . . .

over offenders to a heathen ruler has not perhaps aroused as much interest as it deserves, but it goes back well beyond the time of Christ to the pre-Hasmonean period.[1] On the other hand those who believed that the death of a sinless man was an atonement would welcome, rather than shun, Pilate's killing the Messiah in ignorance of what he was. And so, strange as it seems, opposite notions could lead to one and the same result.

Thus, long before Jesus was brought before the 'council', the groundwork was there. A decision to hand Jesus over to Pilate would satisfy different shades of opinion: yet hardly the opinion of those who sat on the fence and professed indifference to the whole discussion. They may have been sceptics. The popular belief in atonement by suffering may have seemed to them folly, as it must have seemed to many philhellenes. They did not believe that Jesus was sinless, for they had no knowledge on the subject. Neither did they see why a Jew should be handed over to the Gentiles, itself a notoriously wicked act unless fully justified by circumstances.[2] It was, no doubt, for the purpose of coping with such reservations that witnesses were produced whose evidence would convince the sceptics, one way or the other. If he were convicted he could be sent to the gallows with a quiet conscience: a majority for handing him over to the Romans could then be obtained. Unfortunately the witnesses, who are called 'false' but may in fact have been telling the truth,[3] did not agree, and according to regular Jewish practice had to be disregarded entirely. Jesus's failure to provide material helpful to the meeting left them frustrated. But in all cases of witchcraft and other secret offences, or matters in which evidence is difficult to obtain, the method of eliciting admissions known as 'adjuration' existed. We are told by St Matthew that the High Priest adjured him to tell whether he was the Messiah.

[1] Zad. Doc. (*CD*) X, 1 (Vermès, 110; Lohse, 82–3; Gaster, see above, p. 409 n. 3; Driver, *Jud. Scrolls*, 70, 367, 585) is variously translated, but it is clear that the sect (and others besides) regarded execution at the hands of the Gentiles as not only lawful but in certain circumstances obligatory. However the difficult sentence is construed, complete authority is given *bᵉḥūḳey ha-goyim lᵉhāmiyt hū'* (which is all we need for our present purpose). The *halakāh* as explained by Maimonides, *op. cit.* I, III, vi.14(9) (trans. Hyamson, 64*a*) is that it is sinful for one Israelite to testify against another before a Gentile judge unless the sentence would agree in effect with what the *Torāh* would have prescribed. *Aliter* I. Rabinowitz at *Rev. de Qum*, 6 (1968) 433ff. Falk. *ibid.*, 569.

[2] The excitement over Herod the Great's selling thieves (contrary to Dt xxiv.7) is sufficient illustration of this belief: Jos., *Ant.* XVI, i, 1 (Loeb edn, viii, 209), *cf.* Falk, *JSS* 12, 243. See Daube cited on p. 420 n. 3 above. Meyer, *NTS* 14 (1968), 545–51.

[3] Mk xiv.57–9. 'False' may mean 'incompetent', *i.e.* inadmissible, or those found not to have been eye-witnesses: above, p. 173 n. 6. This answers the doubt raised by Miss Hooker, *The Son of Man in Mark* (London 1967), 165. Threatening to destroy a place was an offence even in angels: Midr. R., Gen. on Gn xix.13.

The actual formulation of the question is in doubt, also its precise import. One cannot help suspecting that the High Priest adopted a formula which he had been told Jesus would accept, and which upon his own construction was criminal. But suspicion is not proof, and the man may have been innocent of corrupt intention. That the formula does not obviously agree with known Jewish notions about the Messiah is not in any case a fatal objection to the truth of either gospel version. Whether Jesus was adjured, as Matthew says, is not certain either, if Matthew also supposed that Jesus would not have consigned himself to death without powerful cause. We may doubt his inference. Many will think that Jesus, at this crisis, would speak the truth whether adjured or not.

But besides Jesus's polite admission,[1] which in itself hardly serves the purpose of the drama, Jesus volunteers explanation which, according to the dominant school of Jewish law, was evident blasphemy: καὶ ὄψεσθε τὸν υἱὸν τοῦ ἀνθρώπου ἐκ δεξιῶν καθήμενον τῆς δυνάμεως καὶ ἐρχόμενον μετὰ τῶν νεφελῶν τοῦ οὐρανοῦ ('... and you shall see the Son of Man sitting on the right hand of Power and coming with the clouds of Heaven').[2] Pharisaical hesitations assure us that much more definite words are needed to support a prosecution for blasphemy: the name of God must be pronounced—such is the mishnaic law. But since 'blasphemy' (*ḳᵉlālāh*) meant diminishing the honour of the person blasphemed,[3] these statements are unequivocally blasphemous. The Son of Man, whatever else he was, was obviously a *man*. The suggestions

[1] 'Thou sayest' (Mk xv.2), sometimes understood as indeterminate, is rightly taken as an admission at Lk xxii.70–1, as the exactly similar phrase at Mt xxvi.25 obviously is. F. C. Grant, *Translating the Bible*, 155–6, shows how understanding has wavered. The form is a euphemistic avoidance of the tabooed (see b. Ket. 104*a* = Sonc. 664, but death is not the only tabooed subject).

[2] *Cf.* Mt xxiv.30. Mk xiv.62 is a midrashic combination of Dn vii.13 with Ps cx.1. So exactly (?) at *Midr. on Ps.*, on Ps ii.7 (I, 40, § 9). The last was known to Edersheim (*Life* [1901], 716), but since it became generally available in translation (1959) scholars have ignored it. Not only Ps cx and Dn vii are put together but Is lii.13 and Is xlii.1 as well! So much for Orlinsky's negative arguments. Moreover here (*ibid.* I, 41) R. Yudan is reported as saying, 'All these goodly promises ... the King of Kings will fulfil them for the lord Messiah. Why? Because the Messiah occupies himself with the *Torāh*!' See also the 'Four Nights' (of 14/15th Nisan) dealt with by M. Black at *Aramaic Approach*, 237. Also *ibid.*, on Ps xviii, § 29 (I, 261). b. San. 98*a* = Sonc. 663f. R. Joshua opposed two verses: it is written, 'And behold, one like the son of man came with the clouds of heaven'; whilst it is written, '[behold, thy king cometh unto thee ...] lowly, and riding upon an ass'. If they are meritorious [the generation of those to whom the Messiah will come] 'with the clouds of heaven', if not, 'lowly and riding upon an ass'. See App. II below. For Mk xiv.62 as an alleged Christian fabrication see N. Perrin at *NTS* 12 (1965/6), 150ff, and F. H. Borsch at *NTS* 14 (1968), 565–7.

[3] b. Nid. 52*a* = Sonc. 362. Note the use of the word by Josephus, *e.g. B.J.* II, viii, 145, 154. P. Lamarche, 'Le "blasphème" de Jésus devant le Sanhedrin', *Rech. Sc. Rel.* 50 (1962), 74–85. Jaubert (1965), p. 12 n. 2. See App. II below.

were shocking that (1) he should be at the right hand of God, *i.e.* honoured by God (*cf.* 1 Esd iv.29–30), whereas any human must be flat on the face before God if at all in his presence, and (2) that human beings should see, face to face, what Moses had not been permitted to see properly even from behind.[1] The High Priest's reaction was correct.[2] The meeting knew that the law required them to put the guilty person to death. But if they took him out and stoned him, which they should have done immediately, though it was night time, they might be endangering their own safety should Pilate get to hear of it. In the subsequent case of Stephen, whose conduct requires much fuller examination than it has had,[3] the bystanders could not find patience enough to think of their own possible danger. Next the meeting conscientiously applied the 'smell and judge' test[4] with a negative, or perhaps inconclusive, result: their *abundans cautela* failed to provide a way out for any of them. They must decide what to do, for the decision that Jesus deserved death did not settle the question. Some may have argued that Jesus was mad, or even that the Messiah *would* behave as he had behaved. There is no trace of such arguments: everyone was in a hurry. That he should be disposed of promptly would satisfy several shades of opinion. A scholar has recently pointed to the haste shown in the Marcan and Matthaean versions and has plausibly argued against its credibility: but this was no ordinary trial.[5] At the most sceptical level it would be observed that the corpse must not be displayed during the Passover night itself (a Sabbath night), however advantageous it might be for pilgrims to see for themselves that messianic enthusiasts got prompt treatment at the hands of an alert government. A few hours' display would serve for this. Another reason which urged the immediate handing over of the condemned man to Pilate was the fact that a stoning could not practicably be carried out. The mob, which plays an important part in such ceremonies, might refuse to co-operate, and the

[1] Ex xxxiii.18–23. Note how Is lii.8, 'They shall see, eye to eye, the Lord returning to Zion', is treated at *Midr. on Ps.*, on Ps xvii, § 13 (I, 219). It can scarcely be doubted that Jesus's blasphemy was prompted by Is lii.8. But still the *Torāh* did not contemplate the survival of a man who spoke so. The passage attributed to 'Eliezer, who is depicted (b. San. 108*b* = Sonc. 747) as saying he saw Abraham at the right hand of God in battle (citing Ps cx.1), is interesting: 'Eliezer was surely authorised to take such liberties!

[2] Mk xiv.63. 2 K xviii.37. *Mishnāh*, San. VII, 5. j. M.Ḳ. iii, 7, p. 341. Luke (xxii. 69–71) understood that Jesus distinctly admitted that *he* was to be seated at the right hand of God.

[3] His words go beyond Is lii.8 and he did not have the Messiah's justification (there was no 'excuse' in either case). He could have urged that the *Torāh* was (?) suspended, nullified *ad hoc*. The matter is nowhere discussed. Ac vii.55–8: 'Behold, I see the heavens opened, and the Son of Man standing at the right hand of God.'

[4] See above, p. 408 n. 1.

[5] Jaubert (1965).

promoters of the execution might be endangered themselves.[1] Thus Jesus was sent to Pilate, before whom the most intriguing parts of the drama unfolded. Before we take up the story there we must recollect that Jesus had not yet, strictly speaking, been on trial. In front of a body of persons convened to discuss a serious religious, social, and political emergency, with powers to investigate matters not yet clear, Jesus had volunteered statements which placed upon the hearers the obligation of effecting his death; and he had declined to pass a traditional test of Messiahhood, which might otherwise have saved him.

Pilate could not be expected to grasp all this: on the contrary, his law did not contemplate such a situation at all. Therefore he would not co-operate unless his co-operation were obtained by indirect means. The plausible charge was ingeniously put up that Jesus called himself King of the Jews. Whether Jesus actually used that very phrase is immaterial: his behaviour and tendency to identify himself with the Messiah, eagerly accepted by his followers, served the same turn. People called him 'son of David', which had royal implications, and they had not been effectively silenced by Jesus or his disciples. We are told that Jesus admitted the Jews' charge;[2] Pilate could, had he wished to do so, have condemned him there and then. It was later felt that an explanation was called for. Pilate's reluctance was then attributed to an explanation by Jesus that his kingdom was not of this world;[3] it is certainly possible that Pilate grasped that Jesus would not have admitted the charge except on the footing that no offence had been committed at Roman law. But a further consideration, emphasised by the evangelists, carried weight. Pilate, about whom a great deal is known, would not believe in doing something for nothing. That he took bribes from Caiaphas seems certain. The way to handle the Jews was to keep on top of them. To feel the pulse of public life he will have required a complicated system of precautions about which we know very little but which cannot for a moment be doubted. Pilate must have had informers, spies, and advisers, and can have had more than an inkling of what was going on. He was not disposed to allow the Jewish leaders to use him as a cat's paw; and the more they pressed him the more he sought to evade their scheme. Ingenious methods were used in turn to achieve this end. The gospels give the impression that so inevitable was the *dénouement* that nothing anyone could do would prevent it. If a popular hero were saved against the Jewish leaders' wishes, this would be conducive to Pilate's security on the principle *divide et impera*, and the last

[1] Lk xxii.2*b* (Mk xiv.2*b*). On mobs and stonings see above, pp. 165–6.
[2] See p. 424 n. 1 above.
[3] Jn xviii.36.

thing the Roman wanted was to pleasure the High Priest and the rest. So he sent Jesus to Herod Antipas,[1] who used Jesus as a means of reconciliation and did not seriously utilise the jurisdiction so implausibly and dangerously offered to him by his former enemy. The return of Jesus was then treated as proof that the charge was false (disingenuously, of course, for the return meant nothing of the kind). The leaders felt that they must not turn back, and further charges were pressed. Pilate knew that Jesus was envied by the leaders and was popular amongst the people: and the extremely clever idea occurred to him of presenting Jesus to the people as a gift. The method derived from a ceremony which either Pilate or his predecessors invented or followed, of releasing a prisoner to the people on the eve of the Passover[2] as a sign that the governing power recognised the Jews' national birthday and did not accept analogy with the Egyptians: a courteous and harmless gesture. If Pilate had released Jesus the leaders would not have dared to pursue their schemes, but would have had to start again from the beginning, and Judas would have had to be bribed twice, had not remorse already claimed him as a victim.[3]

We are entitled to utilise St John's account of the trial and death of Jesus alongside the synoptic accounts provided we do not assume that the Johannine material is direct evidence of the events, but rather evidence of how, at John's period, surviving traditions were thought worthy of being saved from oblivion. It is now a commonplace that a considerable amount of early tradition is buried in Johannine structures, and that a recognisable proportion of that tradition has synoptic parallels. St John's evidence therefore, though necessarily studied with

[1] Lk xxiii.6–12; Ac iv.27–8. Imbert (1968) cites J. Colin to show that such arrangements were known to Roman practice (*Dig.* 1.18.3, 48.3.11, 48.2.22). Imbert's own conjecture is (contrary to the gospel story's tendency) that Pilate wanted Herod to help him out by finding some material against Jesus.

[2] Mk xv.6 revised (?) at Jn xviii.39. M. Black, *op. cit.* 228 on Lk xxiii.17 which is almost certainly genuine. It appears that this *was* a Jewish custom, irrespective of Roman precedents (Blinzler, 220–35) and is not in the least incredible (Imbert [1968] citing Aulus Gellius and A. Steinwenter, *JJP* 15 [1965], 1–19), as Brandon, ignoring evidence, would have us believe.

[3] Judas, the greatest mystery in a story fraught with mysteries, is often sought to be explained as a Judaean disappointed to find that Jesus was not the political liberator he had supposed, or as a man who feared that if he did not precipitate matters Jesus would never play his destined rôle properly. I see him as a victim of teleological thinking. One of the 'twelve' had to 'hand over' Jesus so that he might be crucified. This act was, by its inherent nature, an affront to fundamental semitic social ideas in general and to Jewish beliefs in particular. He was thus obliged to sin (a situation which can only arise in oriental juridical thought) and a penance was necessary. In his case penance was a dreadful death, the exact particulars of which may never be known. Jesus, foreknowing this, felt acute sorrow for him (Mk xiv.21) and attributed his destruction to the divine prescience (Jn xvii.12).

caution, must be treated as seriously as any synoptic passage. A typical passage is xviii.31*b*, upon which much unjustified reliance has been placed by others, and upon which, as has been seen above, we have placed a more cautious but nevertheless distinct reliance. The immediately preceding half-verse comes in the same category, and must be compared with xix.6 ('Take him yourselves and crucify him: for I find no crime in him'). Winter would have us believe that Pilate invited the Jews to save him the trouble of putting Jesus to death. On the surface this seems a possible interpretation. But there are other possibilities. First of all, it is transparent that St John's main object is to place beyond all possibility of doubt Pilate's reluctance to condemn Jesus: the superficial reason being that he could not find Jesus guilty by the law by which he supposed himself governed. This of course does not exclude other reasons which may be read (as we read them) quietly between the lines. St John however intends us to understand that Pilate did not wish to handle the matter at all, so that if there were any bias on his part it was against condemning Jesus, come what might. This evangelist goes further than the others in elaborating the theme that Pilate wriggled desperately to avoid inflicting the death penalty, and he was more or less blackmailed into doing it because of a threat to denounce him to Caesar (xix.12–13). There are other elements in the story which work out literally the symbolic overtones which can in any case be drawn independently from the synoptic accounts, so that the sacred drama unfolds with all its technically 'tragic' qualities. But there is something more, which not all non-lawyer observers have grasped.

Ulpianus, who came from Tyre and died in 228, was one of the most important of the Roman jurists of the classical period. There is no reason whatever for supposing that opinions of his cited by the compilers of the *Digest* of Justinian centuries later do not, in their original form, represent Roman law of the imperial period long before Ulpianus's own day. In any event the principle which he states (*Dig.* 50, 17, 70: from the first book of his work *On the Office of the Proconsul*) is of such a nature that we can be sure it was standard Roman practice.[1] *Nemo potest gladii potestatem sibi datam uel cuius alterius coercitionis ad alium transferre*, 'No one is able to commit to another the power to inflict capital punishment, or indeed the power to inflict any other form of punishment'. The upshot of this is that no intelligent member of the Church for which St John was writing could for one moment have supposed that Pilate was offering the Jews an opportunity which they

[1] Compare what Sherwin-White says, *Roman Society and Roman Law* (1963), p. 4, referring to the related passage, *Dig.* 1. 16.6 pref. Blinzler, *Prozeß*, 3rd edn. (1960), p. 243 n. 31.

did not legally possess. In other words, xviii.31*a* and xix.6 must imply something quite different. Pilate could never be believed to have offered to delegate his powers to the Jews: he must have had something else in mind. Or at any rate St John's first hearers must be understood so to have received the passages in question. Hence St John must have understood his own tradition in this sense. Removing the element of drama and the liturgical tone, we arrive at a perfectly practical hypothesis, at once plausible and probable. Pilate says to the Jewish leaders, 'I am not unwilling to attend to business which properly falls within my jurisdiction. But you must satisfy me that you have exhausted your own jurisdiction and your own powers first. The matter is *prima facie* one which falls specially within your domestic competence, and only when you have satisfied yourselves in due course that your powers are insufficient are you entitled to call upon me to exercise mine. I understand that you have hurriedly investigated the question: what hinders you from proceeding to a regular trial?' The strange exclamation, 'Take him yourselves and crucify him . . .' is an elaboration of the idea that if, when at length Pilate *has* accepted jurisdiction, he acquits Jesus, and if the Jews are still not satisfied, there remain no legal means whereby a Roman can condemn Jesus, and illegality must follow—in which the Jews would, of course, be acting at their own peril. 'If he is to be crucified *you* will have to do it, for I shall not . . .' Pilate is still speaking as judge: he has not yet grasped that it will be necessary for him to act as governor. The political factor had not yet appeared in a clear light; and we see St John (xix.12–16) introducing the political factor in between the two episodes. None of this, of course, for one moment supports the notion that Jesus really was, or indeed was seriously supposed by any responsible body of people to have been, a revolutionary, a nationalist, a brigand, or any other seeker after the things of this world—and historians who would explain the story in that fashion are gravely misled.

Why did the people present before the tribunal, a substantial crowd, refuse to have Jesus? The gospel, in order to make the point plain, shows that the people were given a choice, they might have Jesus or Barabbas. Pilate's advisers will have told him, 'Jesus is so popular that they will surely choose him'. To Pilate's dismay the crowd insisted on having Barabbas,[1] a common murderer, and went further, requiring that Jesus

[1] A. Bajsić, 'Pilatus, Jesus und Barabbas', *Biblica* 48 (1967), 7–29. He rightly comments, 'Wir haben also nicht die Bosheit einer Partei, die sich trotz allem Widerstand durchsetzt, sondern ein Mitspielen von verschiedenen Motiven'. Brandon, characteristically, assumes that Barabbas was an insurrectionary *leader* and had murdered *Romans*.

should be crucified. This uncharitable addition has never been satisfactorily explained. It is perfectly true to say that crowds are unpredictable and react to a mass psychology, but they could (theoretically) have moved the other way. It was suggested to some puzzled inquirers—and the suggestion survives in Matthew—that the chief priests stirred up the crowd poisoning their minds against their hero, though Mark (xv. 11) says only that they recommended the choice of Barabbas, while Luke leaves out all hint of the accusation. But those who were partial to Jesus had already been warned against the 'leaven of the Pharisees' (Mk viii.15, Lk xii.1), and will have treated reports of Jesus's blasphemy with suspicion or indifference. The gospels are not unanimous about the terms in which people advised Pilate to crucify Jesus. One evangelist adds the double-edged, and gratuitous, comment, 'His blood be on us and on our children', which gives a clue.[1]

Following St Matthew's line of thought, the people of Israel deliberately accepted responsibility for Jesus's death, but presumably for their benefit and as a sign that they welcomed the new covenant, consecrated with blood like the old, that new covenant which Christian theology understood his death to effect for them. Perhaps, in retrospect, they could also appear like the sons of Levi reconsecrated with a brother's blood deliberately shed with that object.[2] Historical irony was apparently at work again. Yet we may be more historical in finding another significance. The people believe that Jesus is the Messiah, they know that the suffering of the innocent is an atonement, they believe that the Passover is the time of redemption, and they are impatient for Roman power to be removed. This is not a crowd of Greeks or Romans, but of orientals, many of them strictly Asians—they are living during *Peṣaḥ* in a timeless period which links them with Moses and the people's escape from Egypt. Blood must be shed, so that these supernatural workings can start, and so they look forward eagerly to Jesus's 'sacrifice' at the hands of Gentile executioners. However improbable the method, the early Church believed that Jesus had frequently foretold exactly this happening, and no one doubted but that, in view of his miracles, his faithful contemporaries would have supported the project with all their power when the opportunity duly arose. While the early Church wished to see the crowd as paschal slaughterers *par excellence*, the crowd

[1] St Matthew only: xxvii.25. 'Children' = 'households', secondarily 'posterity'. Scharbert (1958), 100ff. W. Trilling, *Das Wahre Israel* (Munich 1964), 70–1 (citing Jos ii.19, 1 S ii.32–3: the reference to *Mishnāh*, San. IV, 5 does not seem entirely relevant).

[2] Ex xxxii.27–29, M.T. and LXX. I reserve an opinion on the question whether here we have not the 'sons of Abraham' *not withholding* Jesus, in conformity with Gn xxii.17.

themselves believed Jesus to be their redeemer in the political sense, because in a spiritual sense he, as the supremely innocent one, could alone atone for them by being slaughtered by the Gentiles. In my view this notion is borne out by the accounts of the trial and death. If the crowd yelled for the crucifixion not out of black-hearted wickedness but out of a desire that Jesus should perform for them a function they passionately (if irrationally) believed in,[1] the whole story fits. As we shall see it makes good, if unexpected, sense of the Last Supper.

The idea that the sacrifice of a just man at the Passover would operate as a redemption was by no means a strange idea to the Jews and would have existed even if Jesus had not approved of it and put it into effect. The tradition went that Isaac's willingness to offer himself as a sacrifice, in obedience to God, was a redemption. It was believed that he shed some blood and thereby earned the right to immortality. The Temple sacrifices were supposed to remind God of the binding of Isaac (supposedly in the month of Nisan) and were connected thus with the redemption theme. In prayer to God the Jews reminded him of the merit earnt by Isaac. Isaac, as well as the much vaguer character, the Suffering Servant, was a pattern for a redemption sacrifice.[2]

But this does not tell us why Pilate acquiesced. Did he give in through weakness?[3] The picture of his washing his hands[4] can be read in more than one way. The presumption is that here, as elsewhere, Pilate was a hard, harsh man. The gospels sought to explain[5] what on the face of it seems clear enough. Other governors in Palestine might have done the same. Here is a popular hero, and the crowd is yelling excitedly for his death by crucifixion. A lesser penalty, which should have satisfied them,[6] and which actually terminated the judge's powers judicially speaking, has not had the desired effect. Nothing but cruci-

[1] K. H. Schelkle in P. Eckert, etc., *Antijudaismus im N. Testament* (Munich 1967), 148–56 says, 'Das Blut Christi ist nicht Unheil, sondern Gnade und Segen'.

[2] Though to some extent he was anticipated by I. Lévi (1912), H. J. Schoeps (1946) and S. Spiegel (1950) the credit for linking Isaac with the gospel story (even including Mk i.11 and Jesus's Eucharistic Words) belongs to Dr G. Vermès, *Scripture and Tradition in Judaism* (Leiden 1961), 197ff. J. E. Wood, 'Isaac typology in the New Testament', *NTS* 14 (1968), 583–9 (drawing attention to the 'third day' motif).

[3] As Imbert (1968) believes quite possible. He refers to J. Colin, who refers to *Dig.* 48.8.16, etc.

[4] See p. 422 n. 3 above.

[5] Pilate's exchanges with the crowd were not part of a judicial proceeding.

[6] If St John's sequence is correct: Jn xix.1; *cf.* Lk xxiii.22. See Sherwin-White (1963), 27–8. I believe it is important to grasp that Romans at this period were brutal and sadistic. This aspect of their natures (brought out firmly and convincingly by Michael Grant, *Gladiators* [London 1967]) not only explains the scourging of Jesus and his humiliation as facts, but greatly strengthens our admiration for the Romans' undoubted zeal to achieve a perfect Rule of Law. I do not believe that the evangelists were *ashamed* of Pilate: quite the contrary.

fixion will serve. Why? Because, the astounding answer is offered, they think there will be a miracle and the nation will be freed from its sins and you and your court and your army and the tax-gathering system will disappear! *Functus officio* as judge,[1] Pilate must now act as governor. A dangerous situation, where superstitious belief and rebellious tendencies join hands . . . subject peoples and the Jews in particular are prone to such movements. . . . How shall it be put down? Surely by doing what they ask! Crucify the man and show them that the King of the Jews does not have the power to remove the Roman government. And in order that there shall be no doubt about it, the identity of the crucified must be written up for all to see, his charge and his title: 'Jesus of Nazareth, King of the Jews'. Naturally, the Jewish leaders were scandalised. 'King of the Jews', whatever else it is, is a religious conception. There was no need to show the wretched victim in such guise. They repudiated the popular fallacy. This man is not King of the Jews, they say, but Pilate refuses to alter the inscription—as if, the evangelist implausibly and somewhat unnecessarily hints, to show that he too, even if uninstructedly, was somehow aware of what had been done.

It is quite unnecessary to suppose he ordered Jesus to be crucified because he was afraid of the Jews falsely reporting him to Tiberius, with whom he may not have stood on a good footing then: but it can be regarded as certain that had he *not* taken effective measures to quash this Messianic movement he would have been truthfully delated to the emperor and would have been in serious difficulties, as actually happened later on. The necessity of government required Jesus's death—not as a rebel, or Zealot, or would-be political alternative to the Romans, or as a rabble-rouser—but as the human focus of Jewish popular belief in redemption.

THE TRIAL AND DEATH OF CHRIST, AND THE SUFFERING SERVANT

This novel view of the affair should at once be tested, to see whether it could be said to offer an analogy with the Suffering Servant and the metaphors which his Song includes. But we are detained by a consideration which has hitherto received abundant attention and cannot be ignored here. Many have contended that the Jewish leaders never did either condemn Jesus for a religious offence or take such a part in his condemnation by Pilate as would implicate them substantially in guilt,

[1] Judge W. De Vries has an excellent impression of Pilate's competence and integrity as judge (*De Dood van Jezus*, 72–3).

assuming that his execution was unlawful. As we have seen, this way of looking at the affair is uncalled for. There is no proof that either the Jewish leaders, whatever the motives of some of them, or Pilate, acted without due care and attention or improperly. The hangers-on certainly acted brutally and vulgarly, but the age was both brutal and vulgar. Certainly it cannot be proved that Jesus's death was a judicial murder.[1] Had it been such it would have been a straightforward contest between goodness and evil in which evil wins on the earthly plane but loses on the transcendent. But it was something far more interesting. Such an interpretation of the death of Christ could hardly have supported Paul's metaphors or the Church's theology.

It is alleged that that part of St John's gospel is false which depicts the Jews as saying to Pilate that they had no jurisdiction to handle a capital trial of a Jew,[2] and that, by implication, *he* must handle the case. We have already seen that persons holding quite distinct points of view will have been prepared to accept Jesus's death at the hands of the Romans, whereas there were difficulties about Jesus's being done to death by means other than the one actually adopted. The story makes it abundantly clear that the delegates of the meeting we have alluded to were insistent that Pilate should carry the responsibility, and we have surmised their reasons. Scholars have argued heatedly that the allegation that they had no jurisdiction was false. Why? We need not be concerned whether it was true or false. The text says that they denied jurisdiction. It does not say that in other capital cases they would have hesitated to assume it if they could do so with safety. In fact it seems nearly certain that they had no jurisdiction,[3] even in the unique case of Gentiles penetrating into the Temple, for the famous and oddly phrased Greek inscriptions which warned Gentiles of the death-danger that awaited them if they trespassed[4] do not tell us that the Sanhedrin itself would inflict the death penalty, and there is every reason for doubting whether so important a breach of the normal constitution of a Roman province would have been allowed. Moreover, it has not always been observed that the gospel accounts do not in so many words pretend that that meeting was a constitutionally competent court convened for a criminal case: the determination against Jesus could as well have been made

[1] As is urged in a series of semi-popular works the latest example of which is J. C. McRuer, *The Trial of Jesus* (London 1965).

[2] Jn xviii.31*c*. ἡμῖν οὐκ ἔξεστιν ἀποκτεῖναι οὐδένα, with the evangelist's explanation subjoined.

[3] Sherwin-White, 35–47. Jaubert (1965), 7, takes the opposite view.

[4] See now S. Zeitlin at *JQR* 56 (1965), 88–9. Kopp (*Holy Places*, 290 n. 29) rightly says, 'They [the notices] only imply that the Romans refrained from taking action against lynch-law in such a case'. *Supra*, p. 317.

(indeed, from a *non*-Pharisaical point of view, must have been made)[1] had he spoken the same words in the presence of two or three Jewish adults on the top of a hill or in the middle of a desert, and no one pretends that Roman law conceded jurisdiction to take a subject's life to any such *ad hoc* tribunal. But this is beside the point. The delegates denied jurisdiction because they knew that in the face of that plea Pilate could not pass the case back to them, but was forced to retain it or at most to seek expert help in using his powers. He might invite Antipas to act as *ad hoc* assessor or even to accept jurisdiction, but he would not, in the face of this plea, give a Jewish body a prerogative that ought not to belong to it.

At this point a further argument ought to be raised, the inferences from which are subtle, but none the less important. The point helps us to understand the *weight* behind the actual decision not to deal with the case of Jesus themselves, but to hand it over to Pilate. Jewish law is fully aware that any tribunal or committee may sin. When a body makes a decision which turns out to be wrong, all the members are tainted with sin. But they can clear themselves by a collective expiation, by sacrifice.[2] Thus even if the Jewish elders who heard the blasphemy were wrong in determining that Jesus should die, they could cure the defect by steps which would not see them greatly out of pocket. This useful safety-valve for the joint conscience could work both ways. If they had wanted to kill Jesus by other means than the immediate public stoning which the *Torāh* required, they could have gone ahead, and either satisfied themselves that the exigencies of the moment justified such a step, or, if this view did not prevail, buy the sacrificial animal which the law required in such a case. The fact, which we know, that they insisted heavily on the case going to Pilate, shows that they were at least as much concerned with Pilate's disposing of Jesus on any count (it did not much matter as long as the object was achieved), as they were with the putting to death, as such, of Jesus himself. And the safety-valve entirely protected them in so doing. It is part of the irony of the position that if the notions, independent in origin but agreeing at the final point, that Jesus should be handed over to the Romans, turned out to be misdirected, and the meeting were left with the sin of handing a Jew over to the Gentiles, the collective expiation would take care of that difficulty as well. We are thus strengthened in the view already voiced that several points of approach coincided *if in nothing else* at least in an agreed policy of inviting Pilate to do his worst. Hence Pilate's extreme

[1] *Cf.* Lk iv.28–9 (no question of trial).

[2] Lv iv. *Mishnāh*, Hor. I.5; II.6, 7. For complications regarding Temple questions see *ibid.* II.4 (uncertain whether relevant).

and entirely justifiable reluctance, which an otherwise unscrupulous and hard-hearted member of that grim race could hardly have been expected to show.

Could this trial and subsequent crucifixion, then, bear out the Servant's story; and could the events support a metaphorical interpretation such as Isaiah provides for us? The answer is unhesitatingly yes. The petty details were thought suitable for such a comparison by Jesus himself. The episode of the two swords shows Jesus applying to his and his students' situation a prophecy in Is liii.[1] True, this application does not agree[2] with that which the early Church evidently looked for when they sifted Is liii for correspondences. But we have already noticed that the technique of midrashic teaching is to derive all possible meanings from a text, and a text is not exhausted if it is applied in one situation. An example of this would be a hypothetical *midrash* which I am about to give concerning the Last Supper. Leaving the petty details aside, the sufferings entailed in the crucifixion, which are expressed in apparent detail in Ps xxii, are referred to aptly at Is liii.12. The Servant achieves his object by 'pouring out' his soul to death. But this dying is by way of crucifixion, for the word *h^{e}'erāh*, which means 'poured out' (a word appropriate to emptying a cup),[3] has both in biblical and in Talmudic Hebrew the sense of shameful exposure,[4] which meets the case. The befouling of the body with blood is much more important than the surface correspondences with Is liii suggest. The key word *go'el*, which means *vindex*, blood-kin, and so avenger, redeemer of persons or property, marrier of widows of kindred, and so forth, comes from the root *ga'al* which also provides the meanings 'foul' or 'polluted', *e.g.* with blood (Is lix.3, lxiii.3).[5] This very ancient semantic meeting of blood and marriage can safely be left to the anthropologists to explain. Jesus was depicted by Paul and Paul's colleagues as

[1] Lk xxii.35–8 (ἀνόμων = οἷς παραδίδοται). Jesus rejected force (Mt xxvi.52). Why were the swords needed? Were they (as Winter and others think) Zealots, bandits, after all? μετὰ should be taken in the sense of juxtaposition, not identification (Bauer–Arndt–Gingrich A II 3–4; Blass–Debrunner–Funk § 227 citing Lk xxiv.5 and Mk i.13). Jesus will forcibly be made to consort with wicked people, and foreseeing this he knows that his disciples must be prepared to face the 'wicked'. The incongruous appearance of the two swords confirmed the prophecy. The righteous did carry swords in those days, διὰ τοὺς λῃστὰς ἔνοπλοι, as the Essenes: Josephus, *Bell. Jud.* II, viii, 4. Brandon's failure to notice this (though he figures as an expert on Josephus) vitiates an important element in his work.

[2] As the use of Is liii.4 at Mt viii.17 does not preclude its use in the 'vicarious punishment' metaphor. Nor that of liii.12 at Mk iii.27 (Is xlix.24) in the version of Lk xi.21–2. See App. I below.

[3] *Cf.* ἐκχύνω at Mk xiv.24. See Gn xxiv.20; Lm iv.21 (LXX).

[4] *'er^{e}vāh.* Is xx.4; xlvii.3; Ezk xvi.37; xxiii.10, 29. Jastrow, *Dict.*, *ad verb.*, 1114.

[5] Johnson (1953), 72. The argument is that the two roots are really one.

pre-eminently the *go'el* of whom Isaiah and others had spoken, and the ghastly spectacle at Golgotha (of which our crucifixes give no adequate impression) was far from inconsistent with the prophetic notion.

How, then, could it be believed, to return to our original question, that by dying on the cross Jesus, if he was the Messiah faithfully portrayed by Isaiah, redeemed Israel by the method referred to? How could he free Israel from her bondage to the old covenant and to the sins it produced, enable her to enter into a new one, enable her to become dependent upon him, her intermediary who made these transactions possible, and take them purified by his blood into a fruitful union? It is impossible to answer this question so long as we view the trial and death of Jesus in the light that has hitherto been usual. Jesus the victim of wicked men, whom God allowed to maltreat him for some otherwise unnecessary play-acting, is a feeble figure. But what Paul saw, and his contemporaries evidently accepted, was that God had no alternative, once he had admitted the children of Israel into the first covenant, from which they emerged hopelessly sinful, but to give them the means of redemption and a new standard of life with new means of achieving obedience. This he promised (Isaiah *passim*), and this was bound to happen. In order to obtain release from former sins and to obtain a new covenant they must have a mediator who could approach God with a powerful argument. The blood of Christ, our brother according to the flesh, but sinless and pure in a spiritual sense, cannot be shed without consequences of powerful importance.[1] His blood 'cries out better than Abel'.[2] All mankind is interested in the blood of Christ just as he is interested in them. An injury done to him will give mankind a complaint against God. If God injures his servants they are free from his charges against them, just as a master who injures his slave forfeits his rights over the latter.[3] By injuring Christ God falls into wrong.

But, it will be argued, the drift of the discussion has been to show that Jesus's death was nobody's fault! His blasphemy settled the official Jewish decision, and the shouts of the crowd derived from, amongst other sources, misguided loyalty. However, this is to ignore the fact that Jesus's blasphemy was only blasphemy because as a man he contravened the *Torāh*. Likewise the crowd's attitude was derived from a doctrine which the scriptures sanctioned. The holy *Torāh*, which is perfect,[4] made no allowances for the Messiah. The Messiah is a man, and he is bound to tell the truth: yet if he is asked his nature and his

[1] Wiencke (1939), 60, thinks the idea was not used by Paul.

[2] Heb xii.24. Koch (1962), 407, 409, 414.

[3] L. Gulkowitsch, 'Der Kleine Talmudtraktat über die Sklaven', ΑΓΓΕΛΟΣ 1 (1925), 87–95.

[4] Ps xix.7. Rm vii.12.

relationship to God he is bound to commit blasphemy.[1] So the holy *Torāh* does wrong in this one case.

Not that this could be claimed in so many words. The *Torāh's* failure to permit a Messiah to survive can be accepted upon the footing that the Messiah's suffering is preordained and that the *Torāh*, in thus requiring the slaughter of an innocent person by what purports to be judicial means, is evidence of God's thought for man's predicament. And this is the interpretation which a student of Isaiah and the Psalms (messianically understood) will place on this paradox. Unless I am mistaken, Paul grasps the nettle. For our redemption it was necessary that the Messiah should not merely *appear* to be, but actually *be*, guilty. The transcendental innocence of Jesus is, for a messianic purpose, hidden behind *Torāh*-given guilt. 'For our sake (God) made him to be sin who knew no sin, so that in him we might become the righteousness of God' (2 Co v.21). God (by the *Torāh*) condemned sin in Jesus in the flesh—therefore Paul admits that Jesus was sinful, though by God's will: Rm viii.3–4. Indeed, he goes further and asserts that in Jesus's hanging on the cross he enacted the part delineated at Dt xxi.23, becoming therein a 'curse', a 'curse' within the meaning of the *Torāh*: Ga iii.13.[2] To use a modern metaphorical expression: at the moment of his blasphemy Jesus is not so much an innocent man condemned, as a guilty man whose guilt condemned the law by which he must be guilty. The law is condemned because (naturally) it does not provide for the Messiah's self-revelation to be an exception to the general prohibition of diminution of God's honour.

Turn now to Pilate. Gentile governments hold sway by God,[3] if only for the punishment of wickedness,[4] and both Pilate's reaction to the crowd's behaviour and the Roman constitution which he embodied existed only by divine sufferance. The two cultures in union must destroy the Messiah. That is why Jesus asks God to forgive the executioners since they act under a false impression of justification, an impression which God himself has permitted.[5] The death of the Messiah is therefore the preordained method by which God, for the first time a debtor to his beloved Israel (debtor, because he has wronged an innocent

[1] Jn x.36.
[2] Sabourin (1961), 24, 142ff.
[3] Pr viii.15; Rm xiii.1–4, etc.; Jn xix.11.
[4] 1 P ii.13–14. Above, pp. 319–20, 336.
[5] Lk xxiii.34 (an understandably difficult passage: see crit. app. to text). No injury requiring forgiveness was done to Jesus himself (and therefore he did not forgive them himself *quoad se ipsum*), for they were protected by *bona fide* pursuance of superior orders. The sin against God was inadvertent (not presumptuous, *cf.* Jn ix.41), since the *Torāh* was wrong upon which the whole story had hung: but inadvertent sins must be expiated, or forgiven. The former (in the case of those pagans) was improbable; it was charitable, therefore, to beg for the latter. Ignorance can be pleaded as an excuse: 1 Tm i.13.

creature of his), is, if he is just, bound to cancel the *Torāh* in their favour, to rescind his decrees against them,[1] to allow them to be purified from their taints, to take them into a new relationship, and all by means of this man, their blood-brother, who can guarantee their obedience and can take the blame if they are disloyal to him and betray him. Thus the holy *Torāh*, fault and all, is the means whereby redemption comes, and is at the same time the source of its own relegation to the background for those who, by faith in Jesus, accept him as their surety and enter into a new covenant with God, with new standards and new hopes of success.

On this footing, the role of Jesus can bear comparison with that of Moses. Moses argued with God[2] (Ex xxxii.7–14) and secured thereby the preservation from destruction of the children of Israel who had made and worshipped the golden calf, by pleading (i) the fact of the redemption, (ii) the probable reactions of the Egyptians, and (iii) the promises to Abraham, etc.: and finally propitiated God (*v.* 14 LXX). The text taken as a whole shows that God accepted his plea after Moses had himself destroyed the tables of the Law (*v.* 19, *cf.* Dt ix.17) and asked to be classed, though otherwise innocent, with the idolatrous people (Ex xxxii.32); and the rabbis understood Moses to have offered his life in this manner in order to preserve the people as a whole.[3] The Dead Sea Scrolls contain the idea that Moses atoned for the sins of Israel in a document supposedly pre-Essene.[4] Meanwhile, the text itself shows the avenger-of-blood concept used as it were inside out, as the sons of Levi (to whom we have referred in passing above) purchase their continuing 'service' of God by themselves slaughtering, evidently as substitutes, their own sons, brothers, and closest relations (Ex xxxii.25–9).[5] Propitiation, vicarious suffering, advocacy, expiation, and perhaps vindication also, appear in this chapter in close and evidently deliberate proximity. It is impossible to say whether or not they served as a model for Isaiah, but the similarities between the rôle of Moses and the Suffering Servant have been noted fully.[6]

[1] Visualised as a bond at Co ii.14 (Jesus, agent of *creditor*, acts on behalf of the *debtor*).

[2] Who actually says 'Permit me . . .' (*hannīḥāh lī*) at *v.* 10. Scharbert (1964), 86.

[3] Daube, *N. Testament and Rabbinic Judaism*, 11–12. Füglister (1963), 194. Rm ix.3 = Ex xxxii.32. Moses pleaded for Israel for forty days and nights: Midr. R. Exod. XLIV, 1–2 = Sonc. 507–8.

[4] *Words of Heavenly Lights* (Vermès, 202).

[5] It must be remarked that the episode can be read differently. The slain can be seen as enemies of God eliminated by the elect; the suffering can be seen merely as merited punishment and as in no way vicarious. But there is no end to the way in which such texts can be construed, and rabbinical *midrashim* show Moses (like Isaac) as suffering vicariously.

[6] Sabourin (1961), p. 207 n. 3. W. D. Davies, *The Setting of the Sermon on the Mount* (Cambridge 1964), 117. b. Soṭ. 14*a* = Sonc. 73.

THE LAST SUPPER

Jesus's own acts, perhaps more convincingly than the words (though naturally both must be taken seriously), plainly link himself and his sacrifice with the Suffering Servant. The Last Supper, as the gospels emphasise, is the commencement of the trial-and-death story. The differences between the Marcan account and the Lucan–Pauline account amount to this, that the vow at Mk xiv.25 is isolated and developed for what it is,[1] and the legal importance of the explanation of the (second) cup (placed by Mark *after* the drinking, a fact Matthew hastens to gloss over by reading πίετε instead of ἔπιον: Mk xiv.23, Mt xxvi.27) is brought out by a more deliberate sequence (Lk xxii.20; 1 Co xi.25). The legal and midrashic mind is more obviously to the fore in Paul and Luke (as one would expect). Taking the Lucan–Pauline account (wrongly shortened in some western texts) as the basis, the mime which Jesus conducts links Ps cxvi.12–19 ('What shall I render unto the Lord? . . . I will take the cup of salvations . . .') firmly with Is liii.12 ('Therefore I will divide him a portion . . .'). The Jesus-Passover, for which preparation had to be made just like any other Passover,[2] was the performance of the acts in those two places followed by the factual 'handing over' or 'betrayal' which is foretold at the very end of Is liii.12 (LXX), and completed with Jesus's death on the cross.

Let us start with Lk xxii.15–18. This corresponds to Ps cxvi.13, 14, 17, 18. It will be recollected that it is Ps cxvi.15 ('Precious in the sight of the Lord is the death of his saints') which is the biblical recognition of the popular doctrine of atonement by the death of the innocent. Ps cxvi.16 emphatically explains that he who does the acts mentioned in the earlier verses is the Lord's Servant: the link with Is liii and connected passages is definite from a rabbinical standpoint. The Servant thus first 'raises the cup of salvation(s), and calls upon the name of the Lord'.[3] Next, he promises to 'pay his vows'. Not only are two or more

[1] The objections to Luke's longer reading as a 'Western non-interpolation', and Pauline (F. C. Grant, *Translating the Bible*, 119–20) are ill-founded. Jesus's self-offering was not 'sacrificial worship', the longer text is not non-Lucan, and Pauline ideas pervaded the narrative from the start.

[2] One might ask if the Jesus-Passover imitates a real Passover *seder* where are the 'bitter herbs'? They are present in the sadness with which the whole ritual is infused—the episode is near the bottom of the disciples' experience (they reached bottom in their subsequent exhaustion and flight). *Mishnāh*, Pes. X, 5 (Danby, 150), b. Pes. 116*b* = Sonc. 595. Midr. R., Exod. XV, 12 = Sonc. 175. Philo, *Supp. II. Questions on Exodus* (ed. Marcus, Loeb, 1953), 24–5.

[3] Ps cxvi.13 (LXX: 115). Why, literally, 'of *salvations*' has never been explained. *Two* redemptions therefore: Peṣaḥ and Last Supper? Ps cxvi is a central scriptural authority. *v.* 15 is the 'vicarious atonement' verse, while *v.* 16 links with the Servant what goes before, and the suggestive words that follow. *Midr. on Ps.* (Braude I, 333) links this cup with the full cup of Ps xxiii.5*b* (both messianic).

vows in question, but, as if to remove doubt, the point of payment of vows is emphasised by repetition. The first vow Jesus makes is the unexpected one of not eating Passover again until the kingdom of God is fulfilled.[1] To 'eat Passover' is of course to celebrate the Exodus. Jesus naturally will not celebrate the Exodus again in the ordinary way, but since he himself makes perpetual redemption the vow, which is otherwise odd, makes very good sense. The celebration of the last of all Passovers must be at the messianic banquet. The cup of salvation he probably did not partake of himself for two reasons, first because as they drank it they accepted his salvation of them—to drink a cup is to accept and undergo an experience[2]—and secondly because of his immediate vow as a Nazirite, which is what the reference to 'produce of the vine' (*cf. Mishnāh*, Nazir; based on Nb vi.3–4) clearly means. This vow, which created great sanctity,[3] ought not to be taken lightly so as to deprive oneself of lawful enjoyment, and Jesus properly leaves it to the end of his life. It is interesting that in his rôle as a sin-offering and a guilt-offering his own death in a sense fulfils that vow. He observes the vow later: Mk xv.23 (refusing the wine mingled with myrrh); and note Jn xix.32–3, *cf.* Nb vi.9. After the Resurrection his live body must not be defiled by the touch of one who has recently handled his corpse (cf. Nb vi.6–7), as we see from his words, 'Touch me not . . .' (Jn xx.17), which indicate that the vow was in another sense incomplete until he had reached the 'courts of the Lord's house' (Ps cxvi.19).[4] Curiously, the unleavened cakes (or wafers?) actually used at the Last Supper fit with the Nazirite's vow. Actual Nazirites, when the period of their vow was over, rendered a special offering in the Temple and ate part of this themselves. The animals they offered (one for a burnt offering, one for a sin offering, and one for a peace offering—the blood of all of these would be offered as part of the sacrifice) were accompanied by ten unleavened cakes and ten unleavened wafers. One of each of these last was 'waved' by the priest together with the boiled shoulder of the peace offering.[5] The point which comes to mind is that Jesus's sacrifice should be accompanied by unleavened bread which is part of a sacrificial offering. It is very curious that Nazirites at the termination

[1] M. Black, *Aramaic Approach*, 229–36.

[2] Mt xx.22–3; xxvi.39, 42; Jn xviii.11; 1 Co x.21; *cf.* Ps xi.6; xvi.5; lxxv. 8; Is li.17, 22; esp. Jr xxv.15–29. *Midr. on Ps.*, on Ps lxxv. § 4.

[3] H. Salmanowitsch, *Das Naziräat nach Bibel und Talmud.* (Diss.) (Giessen 1931). In Jeremias's view Jesus renounced festive celebration as a fast for those who persecute him (*Eucharistic Words*, 218).

[4] Various renderings of Jn xx.17 discussed by F. C. Grant, *Translating the Bible*, at p. 154 are alike in missing the point. The suggestion that she should not restrain Jesus, so as to prevent his return to the Father (like tying down a rocket) is ridiculous.

[5] Nb vi.15, 19; *Mishnāh*, Naz. VI, 9 (Danby, 289).

of their vow could be imagined as using their wafers to fulfil their duty to eat unleavened bread at Passover,[1] from which we may conclude that Nazirites sometimes had such bread baked prior to Passover with the object (not simply of saving money, doubtless!) of celebrating their release from their vow (and so being entitled once again to drink wine) at the period when Jews celebrated their national release.

The vows taken, the Servant passes to the handing over of himself to the representatives of Israel. Let us deal with the cup first. We know what drinking a cup means, and we need not waste thought on *drinking blood* or any similar distasteful notion.[2] As the explanation of the cup shows, they accepted and admitted by partaking of it that his death (blood means death)[3] effected a new covenant for them.[4] Their consent is necessary: just as bondmen for debt must be asked whether they consent to a lamb's being slaughtered for them.[5] They appoint him, therefore, their mediator when he arrives in the heavenly court. The 'dividing' (Lk xxii.18) which is mentioned in connection with what I have identified as the cup of salvation(s) of Ps cxvi, links the ritual with Is liii.12, where two dividings are mentioned (as we shall see). The 'pouring out' of 'spirit' or 'life' in the same verse obviously fits the second cup.

The bread likewise should have a scriptural authority. Bread is not mentioned plainly in Is liii or Ps cxvi. If the bread represents Jesus's body, to be eaten as a memorial of *his* Passover, it obviously contains, and yet does not contain, his blood, so that we are in a difficulty. σῶμα does not mean flesh to the exclusion of blood, but the paschal lambs (like other meat) were not eaten with the blood. And this distinction exists independently of the well-known Jewish phrase 'flesh and blood'.[6] St John is careful to keep flesh and blood apart, for the sacrificial analogy is uppermost in his exposition. Nevertheless, since we know that blood in the (second) cup meant 'death', to be accepted in quasi-legal terms, the body meant nothing other than 'body', *i.e.* Jesus committed himself *in toto* to and for Israel, as his words plainly convey

[1] *Mishnāh*, Pes. II, 5 (Danby, 138).

[2] Which, in fact, a civilised oriental would *not* accept. Such ideas belong to a very primitive mind, more fit for the anthropologist than the sociologist. Sabourin (1961), 249. *Targ. Jer.* on Gn xl.32 (M. Black, *op. cit.* 298: Etheridge, I, 300 has a different trans. but 'cup of death' is plain). For this very reason the words implying drinking blood like wine at Zc ix.15 (dāmām, well attested) must be taken esoterically.

[3] *Cf.* κοινωνοὶ ἐν τῷ αἵματι at Mt xxiii.30.

[4] The phrase τὸ αἷμά μου τῆς διαθήκης is odd Greek but can be rendered in Hebrew as *damiy shel b^{e}riyt* or in Aramaic as *'idmī diḳeyāmā'*. J. A. Emerton, *JThS* 6 (1955), 238–40. H. Gottlieb, *STh* 14 (1960), 115–18.

[5] Tos. Pes. VII, 4, cited by B. Cohen, *L. Ginzberg Jub. Vol., Eng. Sec.*, 128 (reprinted in *JRL* I—see p. 174 n. 84).

[6] Jeremias (1966), 200.

(Lk xxii.19; 1 Co xi.24; Jo vi.51*c*).[1] It will be appreciated that it was the committing of the body that counted, not the verbal accompaniments as such. Since the committing of the body led up to the 'betrayal', it is quite intelligible that in the ritual the body was given first, and the acceptance of his death insisted upon afterwards. However, since at a true Passover meal unleavened bread must be the last thing eaten,[2] it is natural to doubt whether the bread was not eaten last—nevertheless Luke and Paul agree that a cup was given last, as is logical.

But where is the authority for this ritual? We need a recondite suggestion (for no source has hitherto been found, for all the centuries' desperate searching) which yet accords with an oriental technique of interpretation. This conjecture has no warrant from any direct indication. Yet we shall find that it is consistent especially with the formula given by Paul,[3] and indeed makes sense of a juxtaposition of ideas which has so far been a puzzle.

Let us turn to Is liii.12, the chief verse of the Song we have been studying. The beautiful and cryptic beginning runs as follows: *lākēn ᵃḥalleq-lo bārabbiym vᵉ'et 'ᵃtsūmiym yᵉḥalleḳ shālāl*, which the Revised Standard Version translates, 'Therefore I will divide him a portion with the great, and he shall divide the spoil with the strong.' The notion of triumph and victory is clear, but the actual sense eludes us. In such a case one must look minutely at the words and see whether another or other meanings are also permissible. For the first half one could equally well translate 'therefore I shall divide him among the many', taking, as in several places,[4] the preposition *lᵉ* as a sign of the object. Next, the word *'et*, which can be taken to mean 'with', is more commonly the sign of the object of a verb, and is in fact in this very place so taken in both the LXX and the Targum. This enables us to translate, 'And he will divide (or apportion) the *'atsūmiym* as spoil (or prey).' At first sight this is of little help, but the validity of this method is apparent when one realises that *'atsūmiym* could equally well have been written without the *vāv*, and a different pointing produces the word *'atsāmiym*, which means 'bones' in the collective sense, the body.[5] Nor is this enough. It is to be observed that *Midrash on Psalms*, which is of unknown age but contains apparently unexpurgated Christian *midrashim*,

[1] Jeremias (1966), 107.

[2] If we are to trust b. Pes. 119*b*–120*a* = Sonc. 617. Maimonides, *Mishneh Torāh* III (Seasons), V (Leavened Bread), vi, 11 (trans. Gandz and Klein, 1961, 349).

[3] 1 Co xi.23: ὅτι ὁ Κύριος Ἰησοῦς ἐν τῇ νυκτὶ ᾗ παρεδίδετο ἔλαβεν ἄρτον. . . . The act of communicating *publishes* (or is there only a ritual rehearsal, proclamation: Schniewind, *ThWzNT* I, 70?) the death (not resurrection). Füglister, 137. On the significance of 'night' see Le Déaut (1963).

[4] Jr xl.2, v.2.

[5] Gesenius, *ad v.*, *'etsem.*

when commenting on Ps xxvii, takes the words as 'I shall divide the spoil' but proceeds to interpret them as 'I shall *be* divided *as* spoil'. Such liberties with the text were quite in order. Again we find that at the period with which we are concerned the words *y^e^ḥalleḳ shālāl* were actually interpreted in an esoteric sense. These very words occur in one other place only in the Bible, namely in the blessing pronounced upon Benjamin at Gn xlix.27. We are entitled to obtain light on the one cryptic passage from the traditional interpretation of the other. The Genesis passage was understood to mean that *in the evening* the priests divided, that is to say distributed, the portions of sacrificial meat. This accounts for the fact that the LXX translation of *shālāl* is τροφήν, 'food', which would otherwise be inexplicable. The key to that traditional gloss is to be obtained from Aramaic versions now available to us. For this reason it remains highly likely that at Is liii.12 students could be taught that the Servant would divide his body as not merely 'prey' but actually like portions of meat deriving from sacrifices! Even without the possible reading *'atsāmiym*, he would be dividing portions of food.

If one is disposed to read Is liii as referring to an event to take place at Passover time, it is impossible to neglect a further, very fanciful, but none the less striking, interpretation for *'atsūmiym*. The Greek word ἄζυμα 'unleavened bread' provided the name of the festival itself. The use of Greek words to explain the Hebrew text is far from unknown,[1] though it is hardly common and would astonish many readers. Rabbis were occasionally content to employ this method, on the footing that the Almighty knew that Palestine and the Dispersion had two main languages, as it had two main cultures. Thus it could be argued that the Servant understood himself to be under obligation to be 'divided' or apportioned. Jesus himself divided his 'body' in the form of unleavened bread. This division had to take place at that very time, one

[1] Gertner (1963), a learned pun circulating in the time of Christ: *paṣḥā'* = πάσχειν Füglister, 165. *Midr. on Ps.*, i, 52, 441; ii, 20. Citations by Jastrow, *op. cit.* 748–9: *morā'* 2; *moreh* 2, 3; *moroṣ* (?). j. Talm., Sukk. iii. 5, Schwab VI, 25 (also Levit. Rab. 30): Aquila rendered *hadar* (beautiful) at Lv xxiii.40 by ὕδωρ (water) in order to obtain the sense 'tree growing by water'. j. Talm., Hag. ii, 1, Schwab VI, 276: R. Samuel b. Naḥman said *b^e^yāh* at Ps lxviii.5 meant βίος (life), for Providence is life. On βία, βίος in midrashic literature see I. Wartski at *Tarbiẓ*, 36 (1967), 239–56. At 2 Enoch xxx.13 (Charles, *Apocrypha and Pseudepigrapha* ii, 426, 449 n.) Adam's obviously semitic name is explained by initials of Greek words. 2 Enoch belongs to *c.* A.D. 1–50. Even more striking are the following examples: Gn xxxv.8, *'allon bāchūt* is explained as 'another (ἄλλον) weeping'—this is old, as it is found in *Targ. ps. Jon.* (Etheridge, I, 279) and appears in Midr. R., Gen. LXXXI, 5 = Sonc. 750. R. Ishmael (*c.* A.D. 120–40) said that in Lv xx.14 *'et^e^hen* (they) means 'one of them (shall be burnt)' because ἕνα (*hena*) means 'one' (b. San. 76*b* = Sonc. 518)! Ps xlviii.3 is explained with the use of Greek at Midr. R., Exod. XXXVI, LII.

may suggest, because the 'betrayal' was to happen then. The gospel stories insist on the chronological implication of the giving of the body, or at any rate of some food (as in St John), and the effective steps to 'betray' or hand Jesus over to a band of 'wrongdoers'. The word *shālāl* would then explain this. Jesus had to give a portion of his body as future 'booty' to each of the twelve in order that one of them could, and must, at once hand him over. Of course Jesus must be handed over, as 'prey' (therefore Mk xiv.48*b*: 'with swords and staves to seize me?'), on that very night and no other, because he is to be crucified on the eve of the Passover. This would explain why the famous question, 'Is it I?', which has an otherwise incredible ring (for students could not suppose that one of them *must* betray their teacher), comes immediately after the division of the 'body' in the form of pieces of unleavened bread. Only after the symbolic acts are they ready to face the possibility, and this because Jesus must have explained to them some scriptural authority underlying the action. Indeed, the gospels show Jesus associating betrayal and eating, for which St John produces a scriptural authority from another quarter.[1] Paul himself, at 1 Co xi.27, appears to say that anyone who at any time eats the body and drinks the blood of the Lord without mental attention and spiritual preparation is left, (as it were, residually) *guilty* of his death (rather than merely desecrating the elements)—for the immediate impression of acceptance of body and blood remains, namely complicity in killing: the twelve would have consented to a killing had they not *discriminated* (1 Co xi.29) what they were about.

At this point it may be argued[2] that Jesus was authorised to make ritual play with the unleavened bread because already by his time some sectarians, if not the general body of Israel, treated the bread eaten at the end of the Passover meal as symbolic of the Messiah. The name *afikoman* is given to this, and in the Passover *haggadāh* the 'wise' son asks about it and is given a cryptic answer. If this were certainly traceable to popular symbolism of Jesus's time it would be a very significant argument. But two points must be made here. Firstly, the *haggadāh* itself does not go back to the time of Jesus, nor do the questions of the four sons as there set out necessarily belong even in embryo to that period—the *haggadāh* bears too many traces of a cultural acclimatisation to leave us with any confidence about its antiquity[3]—with the result that we cannot be sure that Jesus could rely upon the

[1] Jn xiii.18 citing Ps xli.9 = ψ xl.10.
[2] D. Daube, 'The significance of the Afikoman', *Pointer* 3 (1968), 4–5.
[3] D. Daube (1956), 158ff. would assign the scheme of the Seder service to New Testament times (or earlier). This is not supported by the study of S. Stein, *JJS* 8 (1957), 13–44. See J. B. Segal (1963), p. 241 n. 2–3.

inner meaning of his act being apparent without specific teaching and preparation on his part. Secondly, the *haggadāh* and the *afikoman* itself are, as portions of Jewish tradition, valuable evidence of a continuity of symbolism of a much wider character, of which we can take advantage.

What I mean is this: the *Peṣaḥ*, the Passover proper, reminded all Israel of the redemption from Egypt; that the unleavened bread was highly symbolic in that connection is also certain, both positively because eating unleavened bread was desired and negatively in that removal of leaven was obligatory; we are also certain that the ceremony was intended to heighten anticipation of the coming of the Messiah, since the redemption from Egypt was only the first stage of a process of redemption in a multitude of senses. Now if my reconstruction of what happened is correct Jesus imitated down to small details the elements of the *Peṣaḥ* meal, except for the paschal lamb. In his view *his* Passover would resemble a normal Passover except that his death would take the place of the paschal lamb's. The body of the lamb would be eaten at a genuine Passover, and so his body must be eaten at *his* Passover. The lamb was a symbol of something greater than a lamb; and his body was to be symbolised. The eating of unleavened bread was also symbolic, and he fused the two symbols, making his companions eat the bread as if they were eating his body. Thus, knowing that they would not be able (because of mourning) to eat the Passover meal that year, he caused them to eat a special meal which he himself understood to be the true Passover, to which the biblical texts had pointed. The fact that the unleavened bread had never before represented the body of the Messiah was no obstacle, because the Messiah had never come before. Now that he had come and was performing the function of redemption the Jewish insistence that the bread must be eaten last at a true Passover meal could be observed,[1] and the bread could be given a symbolism which, Jesus seems to have been teaching, was latent until that point. Had it been the case that the bread eaten at the end of the meal was already supposed to represent the Messiah, the action and words of Jesus would have been of no more significance than an additional (or, according to the viewpoint, a specially explicit) assertion that Jesus was the Messiah. Now it is noticeable that Jesus asks for the ritual to be repeated in remembrance of him. The *Peṣaḥ* was in remembrance of the redemption from Egypt, and was yearly. But the Jesus-Passover was to be remembered, re-enacted, on a different footing. Now that the final redemption had come, and expectation of that redemption had ceased, yearly celebration was irrelevant. There

[1] b. Pes. 119b.

was no longer any point in the Passover proper. But as God had bidden the Israelites to celebrate the Passover yearly, so Jesus bade his followers to remember his act of redemption in a homely ritual which, detached from the paschal lamb, was detached from the characteristics of the Passover.[1] But much more important than the eating was Jesus's own act of handing himself over symbolically to his companions, committing himself to them. This he was authorised to do by the symbolism of the Passover ritual and by the esoteric interpretation he was prepared to place upon the words of Isaiah.

It is of interest that although St John would see the body and blood of Jesus as strictly 'flesh and blood', the flesh being a manna of perpetual efficacy (Jn vi.51–8) just as, in the common view, Christ's death was an Exodus of perpetual efficacy, the same evangelist insists with the synoptics that the 'handing over' of Jesus was bound up with the actual giving of bread (Jn xiii.26–7). Indeed, a more emphatic association of the apparently incongruous elements of feeding and betrayal (in John Judas was fed like a child) would be impossible.

A shrewd suggestion which has been published very recently demands that we look at this feeding more closely.[2] Jn xiii.26 is, in view of St John's special view of the sacred meal, very strong evidence that the early Church had a tradition that Jesus said that he would be 'handed over' by someone who *dipped* with, along with, in very close association with, himself. The word for dipping (Matthew ἐμβάψας, Mark ἐμβαπτομένος: Luke has only ἡ χείρ, etc.) alerts us at once. There is unquestionably a cryptic reference here to some purification, symbolic no doubt, sacramental perhaps, of transcendental significance, the scriptural basis of which still has to be traced. The notion that Jesus is actually *in* the dish (grotesque as it may seem) can by no means be excluded in the present state of our knowledge: all puns, however grotesque, must be investigated sooner or later. But we should now explain the notion of 'along with', *simultaneity*, which no one had thought odd (because St Mark, perhaps improperly, or perhaps rightly in order to bring out the otherwise hidden allusion to ψ xl.10, obscured the point with the ὁ ἐσθίων μετ' ἐμοῦ, 'the one who eats with me' at xiv.18).[3] It is not necessary to suppose that the bread, which, when given, authorised the 'twelve', or any one of them, to 'hand' Jesus 'over', was in fact *dipped*. The exact chronology of the actual and the sacra-

[1] The congruence with, and divergence from the *Peṣaḥ* and the evangelists' failure to make this plain in so many words is noted by Segal at p. 246. He does not trace the confusion to Jesus himself, as he might have done.

[2] F. C. Fensham at *Rev. de Qumran* 5 (1965), 259–61.

[3] On the manner of citing Ps xli.10 (9) at Mk xiv.18 and Jn xiii.18 see J. de Waard, *Comparative Study* (1965), 67, where *1 QH 5*, 23–4 is cited.

mental meal was in dispute throughout the period while the gospels were being compiled. Mark understood that that bread was given while the actual meal was in progress, so that *dipping* would not be excluded. But, however that may be, Jesus's words, as represented, along with commentary (as is usual), in the synoptics and, as we have noticed, well evidenced in John, emphasise that the one who hands Jesus over will have *dipped* along with him in a (common) dish. Yet Luke felt that the emphasis must be on the hand and not on the dipping, possibly fearing the purification overtones of 'dipping', and disbelieved or disregarded the point which I am now about to make, thinking that what was significant was only that the 'betrayer' was actually a fellow diner, a notion extremely repellent to the oriental mind, and seemingly in no need of embellishment. However, it is a fact that to dip simultaneously implies equality, friendship. Students would not dip simultaneously with their teacher. Whether any of the twelve actually did so may well be doubted. Mark by adding 'one of the twelve' admitted that it was supposed that all of them could not have been believed at the time to have abstained from this breach of etiquette. Jesus's point will then have been, not (as the recent writer suggests in accord with the Psalm cited above) that the designated individual was rebellious, contemptuous of the teacher he was about to betray (which would be in direct opposition to the scene depicted by St John), but that Jesus will have accomplished between himself and his disciples, especially the twelve to whom he committed his body, a perfect equality. And, as if to bring this or a similar point out in the fullest detail, all the gospels are agreed that at this very time Jesus insisted that his former subordinates, previously inferiors and now friends, should love one another in perfect equality, as he had loved them. This almost mathematical proposition is by no means self-evident, and the symbolic activities which were expected to hammer the point home may well have required support from teaching directed to the same end.

In this view of the Last Supper Jesus does what Isaiah said the Servant would do, and does it as an immediate preliminary to his sacrifice and atonement for the 'many'. The ceremony worked out in detail the pattern which the principal verse in the Song lays down.

A 'RANSOM FOR MANY'

To all this it may be objected that Jesus did not actually see himself as the Suffering Servant, either exhaustively or identically. Instances of Jesus's behaving as if he were a servant are not conclusive: the Servant after all is God's servant. Yet we have the leading text, Mk x.45, the famous λύτρον logion.[1] Jesus is depicted as saying: καὶ γὰρ ὁ υἱὸς τοῦ ἀνθρώπου οὐκ ἦλθεν διακονηθῆναι ἀλλὰ διακονῆσαι καὶ δοῦναι τὴν ψυχὴν αὐτοῦ λύτρον ἀντὶ πολλῶν. A careful translation would read as follows: 'For the Son of Man did not come' (note the past tense) 'to the end that he should be served[2] (or 'waited upon'), but to the end that he should serve (or 'wait upon people'), and to the end that he should give his life as a ransom in the stead of many.' This pronouncement wraps up no less than four distinct ideas.[3] It is unfortunate that the learned discussions of the relevance of this verse and its genuineness have not taken midrashic techniques into account. First the Son of Man, the figure of Daniel, ch. vii, has *come*. The relationship to Jesus is left vague, but it is evident that in so far as Jesus is or represents the Son of Man the characteristics of the latter belong to the former. We have seen that the High Priest knew that by 'Son of Man' Jesus meant himself, at any rate for that limited purpose.[4] Next, the logion says that the goal or object of the coming (which has happened) is not to have ministers or servants but to serve. To whom the service is to be given is not indicated and is probably left vague, so that one could move imperceptibly from the impression which such vagueness naturally gives, *i.e.* that he is to serve God,[5] into the next notion, where the service operates for the benefit of men. That such a movement would be a genuine notion of Jesus's everyone will accept who has grasped a constant feature of Jesus's teaching, namely that love of God's creatures is an essential part of genuine service or worship of God. The third section of the logion tells us that the life is to be given (whether pledged or given up, or handed over as in the Last Supper ritual is not made

[1] Daube (1947), 60. Jeremias (1947). Mk x.45 when compared with 1 Tm ii.6 has a semitic ring. Jeremias sees complete correspondence between our logion and Is liii.10–12. Jeremias (1929), 118. Wolff (1950), 54. Barrett (1959): the theme of ransom is common, the logion does not refer to Is liii? Attempts to tie down λύτρον to *'āšām* rather than ***kopher***, or indeed to be too definite linguistically, interfere with midrashic thought. For λύτρον as strictly 'ransom' see, *e.g.*, Jos., *Ant.* XIV, 107. Jeremias in 'Die älteste Schicht der Menschensohn-Logien', *ZNW* 58 (1967), 159–72 shows that a dual tradition existed, in which logia of Jesus were reported with 'Son of Man' and with 'I' respectively. Mk x.45 is amongst them (p. 161). The form without 'Son of Man' may be earlier, but this does not exclude Jesus's having authorised the identification of himself with the 'Son of Man', and is inconsistent with his having distinguished himself from the Son of Man.

[2] *Infinitiv des Zwecks.*

[3] Büchsel (1943), 344: there is some discrepancy. Euler (1934), 121, 141: martyrdom underlying Is liii operates as an atonement and is a historical redemption. *Cf.* Jn i.29; 1 Jn iii.5; 1 P i.19. Sabourin (1961), 247, would see two principal ideas. Wolff (1950), 146, would see Is lii.13–liii.12 'transformed' in this formula.

[4] Mk xiv.62–4; Mt xxvi.64–5; Lk xxii.69–71, esp. 70.

[5] The double paradoxes are lost on those unacquainted with midrashic techniques.

clear and is no doubt left vague intentionally)[1] as a ransom.[2] This choice of the word links the Suffering Servant of Is liii.12 with the popular superstition to which we have referred.[3] The word λύτρον would mean also an atoning sacrifice, a notion obviously present in Is liii.[4] 'For many' is an obvious semitism for 'for all'.[5] One who atones for many atones for all, unless they dissociate themselves from his act. Furthermore, a legal metaphor is present in our logion. λύτρον meaning 'rescue' could embrace also our notion of suretyship. The idea is explained in Ecclesiasticus, so that we are in no doubt.[6] The logion thus wraps up numerous ideas which might previously have been entertained in isolation. It appears to be Jesus's original scholarship *in parvo*. Palestinian Judaism had already connected the Son of Man with the Servant in Isaiah.[7] Likewise a connection had been made between that Servant and the Messiah (a fact fully presented in the Targum, which, as a post-Christian document in its present form, could have been expected to expel Christian *midrashim* if at all possible).[8] But the implication that in a rôle of Son of Man, Servant, and Messiah Jesus himself would not enjoy government in the normal sense, and would need no human ministers or servants, but would perform his function by humble service of God and humanity, must have been original.

[1] Jn x.11; xv.13. τιθέναι = pledge, place at risk (*cf.* Sir xxix.15).

[2] Büchsel (1943), 343. Jonah and David 'gave' their lives for Israel: the idea behind Jn x.11 (the good shepherd lays down (?) his life for his sheep) exhaustively discussed in the light of Mekilta on Ex xv.1 (Lauterbach, ii, 4) by P. Fiebig, ΑΓΓΕΛΟΣ 1 (1925), 58–9.

[3] Barrett (1959), 43–4. I accept Sabourin's comment (226 n. 1, citing J. Dupont) on the point of view represented by Miss Hooker (1959), *viz.* that Jesus did not refer to Is liii. Meanwhile Wolff (1950), 149–50, seems perfectly correct.

[4] Ex xxx.12; Nb viii.19; Lv xvi.30; Nb viii.21. See especially Is xliii.3 and xliii.1. Whether *kopher* was a *propitiatory* offering is still controversial (Dodd, 1954).

[5] Büchsel (1943), 344. *Cf.* Mk xiv.24; Mt xxvi.28. Jeremias (1947), 260, 263; (1966), 179–82. Sabourin (1961), 242–6.

[6] Weil (1938), 226; Weil (1947), 195. Falk (1964). Sir xxix.14–20, esp. 15: χάριτας ἐγγύου μὴ ἐπιλάθῃ· ἔδωκεν γὰρ τὴν ψυχὴν αὐτοῦ ὑπέρ σου. 16 . . . ῥυσάμενον.

[7] The Ethiopian Enoch-book (*c.* 37–71 B.C.) and R. 'Aḳiba's teaching (*c.* A.D. 50–135) as explained in Jeremias (1950) and (1954), the last being the major reference. Sabourin (1961), 220, 254. On the exact information to be obtained from the various versions of Enoch there still seems to be some obscurity. At *NTS* 14 (1968), 551–65, J. C. Hindley argues powerfully for a date about A.D. 115 for this work, but his conclusion, that it should be 'ignored altogether' in assessing the background of 'Son of Man', is not proved: ideas survive, and later references need not be original, need they?

[8] Dalman (1914). *Midr. on Ps.*, on Ps xliii.3 (I, 445): 'Send two redeemers like them (Moses and Aaron) to this generation. "O send out Thy light and Thy truth; let them lead me" (Ps xliii.3), *Thy light* being the prophet Elijah of the house of Aaron . . . (Nb viii.2); and *Thy truth* being the Messiah, son of David . . . (Ps cxxxii.2). Likewise scripture says "Behold, I will send you Elijah the prophet" (Ml iii.23) who is one redeemer, and speaks of the second redeemer in the verse "Behold My servant whom I uphold" (Is xlii.1).' Sabourin, 216ff. 4 Ezr [2 Esd] vii.28–9 and the fragment 4 *QFl.* b. 1–3 quoted by Driver, *Judaean Scrolls*, 468.

One might ask whether all this justifies Paul's metaphors. Is redemption, after all, a servant's function? Obviously, yes. The humblest function a slave can perform for his master is to be pledged or sold to release his master from debt. The famous saying, 'Greater love hath no man . . .', makes this oriental notion clear. Friendship, which orientals do not differentiate from love, is an extension of the idea of family relationship. A member of a family would proudly risk himself for another member's sake; the institution of the blood-feud bears this out. Students and teachers formed a family for the purposes of their science. Jesus defied convention in insisting that his students formed so close a family with him that their conventional respect for their teacher (which he himself acknowledged)[1] must give way to the requirements of 'friendship'. To enable their teacher to give himself for them and for their nation they must fully obey him, even when it came to his requiring them to accept his death and to admit responsibility for his 'betrayal'. Scripture, in which everyone believed, required this. Scripture fulfilled itself in minute details, sometimes several ways over, which the early Church lovingly gathered.[2] Paul saw the effects of Jesus's walking to his death only in terms of Isaiah's metaphors, which the actual facts of the case, seen through an oriental lawyer's eyes, justified. Accept Jesus as your surety, by faith in him, and he has done for you retrospectively the service he did for Israel on that day in the year 30; so the teaching seems to run.

Is there any more nearly contemporary evidence that Jesus himself believed he would act on sinners' behalf in such a way? Indeed there is, though it is to be found in a somewhat neglected place, and might be thought the more reliable on that account. The people in every sense nearest to Jesus at the climacteric were the two thieves. The second thief confessed, when his pains permitted continuous thought, three things: (i) his own punishment as due reward for his sins (Lk xxiii. 40*b*–41*a*); (ii) Jesus's sufferings as (*a*) unmerited and (*b*) consistent with his alleged status as Messiah (Lk xxiii.41*b*); and (iii) Jesus's power to do something valuable for him at some point in the future when Jesus's kingdom' would arrive—obviously after the thief's own death. This faith is the more interesting as we can be sure that what he looked forward to was nothing like the messianic banquet of which the rabbis so often talked, at which the guests would entertain one another with endless jurisprudential discussions. The response of Jesus to this threefold confession may have been the last words the thief heard, probably the last to which he paid any attention: '*Today* you shall be with me in

[1] Mt. x.24.
[2] See App. I below.

Paradise!' The Garden of Eden ('The Lord . . . hath made her wilderness like Eden, and her desert like the garden of the Lord . . .': Is liii.3 M.T., LXX) was a notion the thief could understand;[1] and we can visualise what rôle the rescued client would play there, a prospect he might entertain with confidence even without his agent's oath (ἀμήν σοι λέγω: Lk xxiii.43).

What sort of 'with-ness' was that? How would the thief and the rescuer be together? The day of the Passover is, as far as that thief was concerned, unexpectedly the day of his personal redemption. Why? Because of his faith, set out so carefully for us in the form of his broken utterances from his own cross. So far as *he* is concerned a new chapter is beginning. The disciples' new chapter was inaugurated somewhat earlier, when Jesus committed his body to them. What sort of 'with-ness' did they have thereafter? This too can call for a juridical explanation, and with it (in the ensuing chapter) this book will end.

APPENDIX I. THE NARRATIVE OF THE TRIAL AND ISAIAH

The search for similarities is not new.[2] The extent and number of them has not been appreciated. The correspondences are often forced and trifling. There is no question that the narrative has been falsified to fabricate a similarity with Isaiah. Yet the arrangement may have been affected. St Luke, for example, combines Peter's grief (xxii.62) and the Jews' mocking of Jesus (*ibid.* 63–5) immediately before the transaction which is usually called a trial (*ibid.* 66–71), so as to reproduce the priority of Is liii.3 ('He was despised and rejected by men . . .') to *ibid.* 4–8, which appear to correspond to the trial of Jesus. It is to be noted that Isaiah's language distinctly suggests two *trials*.

The following instances of similarity have struck me. We can be sure that even more far-fetched similarities were observed. To avoid prolixity reference is made to K. Aland's *Synopsis Quatuor Evangeliorum*. Is l.6 (smiting,[3]

[1] On *Pardeṣ* see A. Feldman, *Parables and Similes of the Rabbis*, 86–99. Also P. Grelot at *RB* 1967, 194–214.

[2] Previous sceptical work: Montefiore, *ubi cit.* Feigel (1910). Wolff (1950), 75–8, mentions four. Miss Hooker (1959), 62, isolates seven and dissociates them from Is liii (unnecessarily?) by various expedients at p. 88ff. No doubt Professor C. F. D. Moule is right in saying (*Birth of the New Testament* [London 1962], 81–3) that Is liii is less often used in the synoptics than one would expect, provided one takes 'used' as verbally used or cited—hidden allusion, as we have seen, must also be counted as 'use'.

[3] R. H. Grundry, *Rev. de Qumran* 2 (1960), 559–67. For 'reviling' see *Midr. on Ps.* (Braude II, 233), citing Ps lxxxix.52. 'Likewise, when the Messiah comes . . . the Children of Israel will not sing this song until the Messiah will have been reviled, of whom it is said "Thine enemies . . . O Lord . . . have reviled the footsteps of Thine anointed".'

shame, spitting: § 332); lii.13 (lifted up = crucifixion, *cf.* Jn iii.14; xii.32–3: § 344); lii.14 (disfigured: § 340); lii.15 (kings shut their mouths, *i.e.* are amazed: Mk xiv.60; xv.4–5; § 337: therefore Lk xxii.68?); liii.6, 12 (LXX) (given up for, or because of, sins: § 331); liii.3 (dishonoured, forsaken:[1] Mk xiv.50; § 332); liii.7 (silence: see at lii.15 above);[2] liii.7 (shearing: § 340); liii.8 (two 'trials' and a taking away: §§ 332, 336, 341); liii.8 (judicial killing: § 344); liii.9 (burial with wicked/rich: § 350, esp. Mt xxvii.57); liii.9 (no violence: § 331, esp. Mk xiv.48); liii.9 (no deceit: § 332, esp. Mk xiv.62); liii.10 (seeing a generation: Jn xix.26); liii.12 (nakedness: § 344, esp. Mk 15.24*b*); liii.12 (numbered with transgressors: § 345);[3] liii.12 (entreating for the wicked: Lk xxiii.34).[4]

By another approach one would leave the actual sense of the passage and merely catch up the words. Thus 'carrying' at Is liii.4 recalls the incident of carrying (a part of) the cross (§ 343) and 'esteemed him stricken, smitten by God' recalls the episode of the women of Jerusalem (*ibid.*), who are addressed in words in any case reminiscent of liv.1. Needless to say, upon the view of the matter taken in this chapter, Jesus was indeed smitten by God (as Ps xxii.1 recalls). The different words 'wounded', 'bruised', 'chastised' in liii.5 recall the frequent instances of Jesus's suffering, which have been suspected to be duplications: it could as well be argued that a natural tendency to abridge and generalise was halted by a desire to give Is liii.5 full scope. The most curious analogy is at liii.9 (LXX), where the rendering, 'I will give the wicked for his burial', performs two functions. First, and more obviously, it supports the theory of vicarious suffering and atonement for the wicked (which in any case appears in the key verse, 12), but secondly it suggests an exchange, which actually occurred. The extraordinary episode of Barabbas, which is necessary to show Pilate's motive and the crowd's enthusiasm (Aland, § 339), does indeed show that a wicked man's life was saved through Jesus's sentence of death. Jesus throughout his ministry steered clear of being confused with a Zealot or revolutionary, whilst taking advantage of 'revivalist' enthusiasm to obtain soil for the seed of his message: it was the height of irony that he should face this objectionable confusion to the last.

Perhaps the most important part of this survey is the relationship of Is liii.12 to what goes before. The translations and versions understandably vary and wander in attempts to obtain intelligible and edifying messages from it. But in all versions now available the relationship of the end to the remainder is the same. The great metaphors of triumph, self-sacrifice, vicarious suffering, and atonement derive from the suffering described in

[1] Philologically (but not necessarily midrashically?) the word should have meant 'avoiding men' or 'not recognisable as a man': D. Winton Thomas, *Understanding the Old Testament* (London 1967), 20.

[2] Brandon is of the view that Jesus is represented as silent because the 'record' said that he refused to divulge his accomplices or give other information about his 'movement'!

[3] Jesus's own different application has been noted above.

[4] Noted above, p. 437 n. 5. For the word 'wicked' *cf.* Ac ii.23.

the earlier verses. The achievement expressed metaphorically in that way is the result of the detailed suffering which, at any rate in the Hebrew and Greek versions, stems from the official condemnation and punishment of one who was in a transcendental sense innocent. And this agrees with the outline of Jesus's experience so far as we have been able to disentangle it.

APPENDIX II. JESUS'S BLASPHEMY BEFORE THE MEETING

The words Jesus is represented as having uttered (Aland, § 332, p. 465) are unquestionably blasphemous, for reasons briefly set out above. Since this was the crux of the whole affair, and without it Jesus would not have been sent at once to Pilate (if we follow the gospel picture of what happened), and since Jesus's predicament is, as I suppose, the pivot upon which the trial and so our 'redemption' turned, it is imperative to deal, if only shortly, with the principal reasons which have hitherto led the vast majority of scholars and others to believe that Jesus was unjustly declared guilty of blasphemy, 'worthy of death', and that the proceedings were a mockery of justice—which (in my view) is far from being the truth.[1] The main source of error is *Mishnāh*, San. VII, 5, and the *gemara* thereon. The Pharisees supposed that the strictest possible interpretation of Lv xxiv.10–17 was the only proper one in view of the possible loss of an Israelite's life by stoning. The method adopted was to read the several verses as if they controlled each other and mutually narrowed each other's application. The Name must be distinctly uttered and must be cursed with a formula such as 'May G. curse G.', or some other folly. Undoubtedly, this is a possible method of interpretation, and it has alone survived as evidence of Jewish scholarship on the subject: except for Mk ii.7 *par.* and Mk xiv.63–4 *par.* St Luke's decision not to use the Greek word βλασφημία[2] in this context is suggestive, and likewise not to explain by 'blasphemy' the hostile verdict (xxii.71) of the council, but such negative evidence cannot be pressed far.

Now when we come to the *scriptural* texts,[3] and, for the while, forget the Pharisaical method of interpretation, two separate notions appear. First, the penalty of stoning must be inflicted on one who 'pierces' the name of God (*noḳev shem*); and death is, further, the penalty for everyone who defames God (*yeḳallel 'elohāyv*). Instead of taking these as a compound crime, let us

[1] See O. Linton, *NTS* 7 (1961), 258–62.

[2] See H. Beyer, *ThWzNT* I, 620ff. βλασφημεῖν also *could* translate, *gādaf*, which means 'revile', 'abuse', also as to tendency, *cf.* Nb xv.30. Is xxxvii.6, 23 (all about God). Schippers uses this as a possible translation of βλασφ. at Mk iii.28–9, Lk xii.10*b*: see Schippers at *Ex Auditu Verbi* (*Fest. Berkouwer* 1965), 247ff. However, according to S. Krauss (*Gr. und Lat. Lehnwörter im Talmud, etc.*, 1898, I, 212) this word is used in a religious sense and never in the sense of 'calumny'. He refers to 1 M ii.6, *cf.* 2 M viii.4, x.35, xv.24; and Ezk xxxv.12 where the Hebrew is *ne'ātsāh*.

[3] D. W. Amram, *Leading Cases in the Bible* (Philadelphia 1905), 91ff.

take each independently. The result is that the Torāh requires the death of one who *yᵉḳallel 'elohāyv* without 'piercing' the name. What does *yᵉḳallel* mean? There has hardly ever been any doubt. The root *ḳālāl* means to undervalue and say so, to defame, to *diminish the honour of* someone. It is the opposite of to honour, or to bless. It certainly does not have any technical signification of *blasphemy* to start with. It is only when one defames God that one comes within the crime defined in Lv xxiv.15, and must 'bear one's sin', *i.e.* be put to death. The Latin equivalents for *ḳālāl* include *alleviare vel pondere vel honore vel existimatione, detrahere, maledicere, vilipendere*, and, best of all, *elevare*. Quite ordinary defamation or 'depriving of honour' are within the meaning of this word. The best illustration is exactly the same phrase as in our Lv xxiv.15 which occurs at Lv xx.9, where the dishonouring (too strongly translated 'cursing') of parents is rendered capital: Ex xxi.17 uses the same word in the same context. The general idea is contained in Gn xii.3, where God himself promises to slander those who slander Abraham. A very mundane example occurs at Qo vii.22. Thus to diminish God's honour by attributing to him qualities not belonging to him, or by depriving him of rights to which he is entitled (as at Mk ii.5–9), does certainly come within Lv xxiv.15 as construed by any person not already determined to make stonings for blasphemy almost impossible.

This investigation of the root *ḳālāl* has a further use of importance. We have seen how Paul refers to Christ as having become a curse, in a striking phrase which must always have been offensive to an unprepared hearer. Turn κατάρα back into Hebrew and one obtains *ḳᵉlālāh*. This means *levificatio sive honoris sive bonorum*. Usually translated 'curse', its meaning is surely much wider, namely any attempt to diminish in point of honour or fortune. True enough, the hanged man is called *ḳilᵉlat 'elohiym* at Dt xxi.23. The hint is evidently this: Christ at that crucial moment became a 'cursing of God', not in the sense that he cursed God, for he did not, but that he diminished God's honour within the meaning of Lv xxiv.15. Meanwhile the phrase 'cursing of God' at Dt xxi.23 is ambiguous, meaning either a derogation from God's honour (so Targ. ps. Jonathan), or a curse inflicted by God (so LXX).[1] In either sense it was appropriate that the crucified who was 'hanged' within the meaning of that verse should himself have been guilty of derogating from God's honour. In fact Targ. Onḳelos (the so-called official Aramaic Targum) renders Dt xxi.23 *'al dᵉḥāv ḳādām yᵉyā 'itsᵉṭᵉlav*, 'because he was convicted (or guilty) before the Lord he was impaled'. The root *tsālav* was used for crucifixion and *ḥāv* ('guilty') is of course ἔνοχος (Mt xxvi.66). Though Paul

[1] See H. Danby, *Tractate Sanhedrin: Mishnah and Tosefta* (London 1919), p. 91 n. 3. At b. San. 46*a* = Sonc. 304 (*Mishnāh*): 'for he is hanged (because of) a curse against God, as if to say why was he hanged? Because he cursed the name; and so the name of Heaven is profaned'. Passers would enquire why he was hanged: the answer would be that he cursed God, and so the name of God would be profaned. C. Schöttgen I, *ad loc.* p. 734 cites Bechai fol. 211.4 (1546), the same, adding 'He would not have been hanged unless he had been a blasphemer or idolater', also 'the word *ḳᵉlālāh* means both 'curse' and 'vilitas' (*i.e.* a cheapening of God)'.

does not, in fact, translate Dt xxi.23 after the fashion of either Targum, we can assume that his readers were at least as familiar with Aramaic versions as they were with the LXX, which in any case he chooses not to follow exactly (the ὑπὸ θεοῦ is missing).

This rabbinical playing with the text of scripture is to be tested by the question whether the result fits both the facts (if discoverable) and reasoning. In this case, Paul's notion that Christ voluntarily underwent the sin (see above, p. 400) and its Law-sent punishment and death receives confirmation from the gospel account of what happened. Thus one should understand that the non-Pharisaical and literal interpretation of Lv xxiv.15 was in use—exactly as the gospel would seem to depict; and that Jesus did 'blaspheme'.

The early Church evidently took very seriously the contemporary tradition that Jesus blasphemed before the meeting in Caiaphas's house: Jn x.33–6. They grasped the bull by the horns, for if *legally* guilty Jesus was transcendentally innocent (*ibid.*). Boldly the debate is arranged in St John to be read immediately in connection with Lv xxiv.10ff., the *locus classicus* on blasphemy (Aileen Guilding, *The Fourth Gospel and Jewish Worship*, 1960, p. 131), and it must be observed that Dt xxi.23 (above) is the passage to be read with it in the next year of the lectionary cycle! To the author of St John's gospel and his Church the relevance of the charge against Jesus both to the pentateuchal law on blasphemy (not the Pharisaic) and to the text on him who is hanged on a tree was therefore well known.

APPENDIX III

Since it is necessary to understand the mental process whereby a factual tale may be told accurately and also in such a guise as to induce a spiritual apprehension, there may be some advantage in giving a humble and trivial example, which will serve equally for the purpose of elucidating parable-construction and for the purpose of explaining how the Church could, and would, hear of events in the life of Jesus as combined symbol and event.

To compose a parable is not within everyone's powers, and I often tried without success, until recently I wrote the following simple specimen:

A packman with a heavy pack sought shelter with charitable folk in a part of their sumptuous hospice. They were politeness itself. One asked after his health. Another said, 'Have you not been this way before?' Yet another said, 'You must have some interesting things in your pack.' Later another poor wayfarer came. He said, 'Open your pack and show me what you have'. The packman undid his pack. 'You have many beautiful things', said the stranger, 'but I cannot buy them.' 'Never mind', said the packman, 'Accept this one as a gift.' And he picked up his pack and went on his way.

This relates a perfectly factual tale. The 'charitable folk' live thirty miles from the spot where I am at the time of writing. It would be no great difficulty for me to list their initials, or for that matter their names. The 'hospice' is certainly real enough. The date of the occasion was July, 1967. The 'stranger's' initials are 'V.T.' I will give three guesses who the 'packman' was, and one will not have to look far for the 'pack'. For the covert scriptural allusions look, not under 'pack' in the concordances, but under 'merchandise'. Many a biblical allusion has been missed from real parables by such an accident as that.

The emotionally fervent and the imaginative, the poetic and the dramatic, recall the fairy tale and the oriental: but the groundwork is as practical and real as the typewriter on which I am now typing. But if the tale reproduced above in dramatic form had been told in bald English it would have raised at best a laugh, and would have left no impression, certainly not the impression which the above will have created and which will not soon be lost.

There is one element which is missing from any such fictitious simulations of biblical style, and that is the liturgical. As the Last Supper lived on (as Jeremias has shown in his *Eucharistic Words*) in the worship of the early Church the story of that event has been handed down to us under the subtle and silent influence of liturgical usage—they read back their own practice into the finer details of the ritual and that has affected some of the texts. It would be impossible to reproduce a colouration of that kind deliberately.

BACKGROUND BIBLIOGRAPHY TO CHAPTER 17

St. Thomas Aquinas, *Summa Theologiae*, III[a], qq. xlvi–xlix.

Bandas, R. G., *The Master-Idea of Saint Paul's Epistles, or the Redemption* (Bruges 1925).

Barrett, C. K., 'The background of Mark. 10. 45', in *New Testament Essays: Studies in Memory of T. W. Manson* 1893–1958 (Manchester 1959), 1–18.

Benoit, P., *Exégèse et théologie*, 2 vols. (Paris 1961).

Billerbeck, P.: Strack, H., and Billerbeck, P., *Kommentar zum Neuen Testament aus Talmud und Midrasch*, 4 vols. (Munich 1926–1961).

Bligh, J., 'Typology in the Passion narratives: Daniel, Elijah, Melchizedek', *Hey. J.* 6 (1965), 302ff.

Blinzler, J., *Der Prozeß Jesu*, 3rd edn (Regensburg 1960). Trans. McHugh, *The Trial of Jesus*, 2nd edn (Westminster, Ma. 1959).

Boecker, H. J., *Redeformen des Rechtslebens im Alten Testament* (Wiss. Mon. z. A. N. T., 14: Neukirchen 1964).

Bonsirven, J., *Theology of the New Testament*, trans. S. F. L. Tye (London 1963).

Büchsel, F., λύω, etc., in G. Kittel, *ThWzNT* IV (1943), 337–59.

Bultmann, R., *Theology of the New Testament* i, trans. K. Grobel (London 1956).

—— *Das Evangelium des Johannes*, 17th edn (Göttingen 1962).

Burkill, T. A., *Mysterious Revelation* (New York 1963).

Coccejus (Coch), J., *Opera Omnia*, 3rd edn, 10 vols. (Amsterdam 1701).

DALMAN, G. H., *Jesaja 53: das Prophetenwort vom Sühnleiden des Gottesknechts mit besonderer Berücksichtigung der jüdischen Literatur*, 2nd edn (Leipzig 1914).
—— *Die Worte Jesu, I*, 2nd edn (Leipzig 1930).
DAUBE, D., *Studies in Biblical Law* (Cambridge 1947).
—— 'For they know not what they do', *Studia Patristica* (Texte u. Unters. 79: Berlin 1961), 58–70.
—— *The Exodus Pattern in the Bible* (London 1963).
DE BOER, P. A. H., *Second Isaiah's Message* (Oudtestamentische Studiën 11: Leiden 1956).
DE VRIES, W., *De Dood van Jezus van Nazareth* (Kampen 1967).
DEISSMANN, A., *Licht vom Osten*, 4th edn (Tübingen 1923).
—— *Paul, a Study in Social and Religious History*, trans. W. E. Wilson, 2nd edn (London 1926).
DODD, C. H., *The Bible and the Greeks* (London 1954), 82–95.
—— 'Some problems of New Testament translation', *Expos. Times* 72 (1961), 268ff.
—— 'The prophecy of Caiaphas. John 12, 47–53', *Neotestamentica et Patristica* (Festschrift Cullmann: Leiden 1962), 134–9.
DOEVE, J. W., *Jewish Hermeneutics in the Synoptic Gospels and Acts* (The Hague 1953).
ELERT, W., 'Redemptio ab hostibus', *Theol. LiteraturZ.* 72 (1947), 266–70.
EULER, K. F., *Die Verkündigung vom leidenden Gottesknecht aus Jes. 53 in der griechischen Bibel* (Stuttgart 1934).
FALK, Z. W., 'On surety in Hebrew Law', (1964) *Recueils de la Société Jean Bodin*, 28, *Sûretés personnelles* (to appear).
FEIGEL, F. K., *Der Einfluß des Weissagungsbeweises und anderer Motiven auf die Leidengeschichte* (Tübingen 1910).
FÜGLISTER, N., *Die Heilsbedeutung des Pascha* (Munich 1963).
GERTNER, M., 'Terms of scriptural interpretation: a study in Hebrew semantics', *BSOAS* 25 (1962), 1–27.
—— 'Midrashim in the New Testament', *J. Sem. St.* 7 (1962), 267–92.
—— 'The terms *Pharisaioi, Gazarenoi, Hupokritai . . .*', *BSOAS* 26 (1963), 245–68.
GOLDIN, H. E., *Hebrew Criminal Law and Procedure* (New York 1952).
HANSON, A. T., *Jesus Christ in the Old Testament* (London 1965).
HEGERMANN, H., *Jesaja 53 in Hexapla, Targum und Peschitta* (Gütersloh 1954).
HERZ, M., *Sacrum Commercium* (Munich 1958).
HOAD, J., 'Some New Testament references to Is. 53', *Expos. Times* 68 (1956–7), 254–5.
HOLLMANN, G., *Die Bedeutung des Todes Jesu nach seinen eigenen Aussagen auf Grund der synoptischen Evangelien* (Tübingen/Leipzig 1901).
HOOKER, Miss M. D., *Jesus and the Servant* (London 1959). See also p. 389 n. 1 above.
IMBERT, J., 'Le procès de Jésus. Essai de mise au point' (1968) (to appear).

—— *Est-ce Pilate, qui a condamné Notre Seigneur . . .?* (Paris 1947).
JAEGER, H., 'La preuve judiciaire d'après la tradition rabbinique et patristique', *Recueils de la Soc. Jean Bodin*, 16, *La Preuve* (1965), 415–594.
—— 'Les sûretés personnelles dans la pensée patristique dans leurs rapports avec les droits rabbinique et romain', *Rec. Soc. Jean Bodin* (to appear).
JAUBERT, A., 'Les séances du Sanhédrin et les récits de la Passion', *Rev. Hist. Rel.* 166 (1964), 143–69; 167 (1965), 1–33. (For earlier works see p. 416 n. 1 above.) ,
JEREMIAS, J., 'Erlöser und Erlösung im Spätjudentum und Urchristentum', in *Deutsche Theologie, II. Der Erlosungsgedanke*, ed. E. Pfennigsdorf (Göttingen 1929), 106–19.
—— 'Das Lösegeld für Viele', *Judaica* 3 (1947), 249–64.
—— 'Zum Problem der Deutung von Jes. 53 in palastinischen Spätjudentum', *Aux sources de la tradition chrétienne. Mélanges offerts à Maurice Goguel* (Neuchâtel–Paris 1950), 113–19.
—— παῖς θεοῦ, in *ThWzNT* V (1954), 653–713, also published in W. Zimmerli and J. Jeremias, *The Servant of God* (London 1958).
—— *Die Abendmahlsworte Jesu*, 4th edn (Göttingen 1967).
—— *The Central Message of the New Testament* (London 1965).
—— *The Eucharistic Words of Jesus*, 3rd edn, trans. Perrin (London 1966).
JOHNSON, A. R., 'The primary meaning of G'L,' *Suppl. to Vetus Test.* i, *Congress Vol.*, Copenhagen 1953 (Leiden 1953), 67–77.
KÄSEMANN, E., 'Zum Verständnis von Römer 3, 24–26', *ZNW* 43 (1950–1), 150–4.
—— 'Erwägungen zum Stichwort "Versöhnungslehre im Neuen Testament" ', in *Zeit und Geschichte: Dankesgabe an Rudolf Bultmann* (Tübingen 1964), 47–59.
KILPATRICK, G. D., *The Trial of Jesus* (Friends of Dr Williams's Lib. Lect., 6: Oxford University Press, 1953).
KLAUSNER, J., *Jesus of Nazareth*, trans. H. Danby (New York 1959).
KOCH, K., 'Der Spruch, "sein Blut bleibe auf seinem Haupt", und die israelitische Auffassung vom vergossenen Blut', *Vetus Test.* 12 (1962), 396–416.
KRAUS, H.-J., 'Erlösung im Alten Testament', *Relig. Gesch. Geg.*, 3rd edn, ii (1958), coll. 586–8.
KUHL, E., *Die Heilsbedeutung des Todes Christi, eine biblisch-theologische Untersuchung* (Berlin 1890).
LATTE, K., *Heiliges Recht. Untersuchungen zur Geschichte der sakralen Rechtsformen in Griechenland* (Tübingen 1920).
LE DÉAUT, R., *La Nuit pascale* (Rome 1963).
LINDBLOM, J., *The Servant Songs in Deutero-Isaiah* (Lund 1951).
LYONNET, S., *De Peccato et Redemptione, II, De Vocabulario Redemptionis* (Rome 1960).
MANSON, T. W., 'The Son of Man in Daniel, Enoch and the Gospels', *B. J. Ryl. Lib.* 32 (1949), 171–93.
MANTEL, H., *Studies in the History of the Sanhedrin* (Cambridge, Mass. 1961).

MAZZARELLA, P., *Il pensiero speculativo di S. Anselmo d'Aosta* (Padova 1962).
MICHEL, O., *Der Brief an die Römer* (Göttingen 1963).
MORGENSTERN, J., 'The Suffering Servant—a new solution', *Vetus Test.* 11 (1961), 292–320, 406ff.
NORTH, C. R., *The Suffering Servant in Deutero-Isaiah* (Oxford 1950).
PORÚBČAN, S., *Il Patto Nuovo in Is. 40–66* (Rome 1958).
PROKSCH, O., λύω in G. Kittel, *ThWzNT* IV (1943), 329–37.
RENGSTORF, K. H., 'Zu Gal. 5, 1', *Theol. LiteraturZ.* 76 (1951), 659–62.
RICHARD, L., *Le Mystère de la Rédemption* (Tournai 1959).
RIVIÈRE, J., *Le Dogme de la Rédemption* (Louvain 1931).
ROMANIUK, K., 'L'origine des formules pauliniennes, "Le Christ s'est livré pour nous", "Le Christ nous a aimés et s'est livré pour nous" ', *Novum Test.* 5 (1962), 55–76.
ROWLEY, H. H., *The Servant of the Lord and other Essays on the Old Testament* (London 1952).
SABOURIN, L., *Rédemption sacrificielle, Une Enquête exégétique* (Brussels 1961).
SCHARBERT, J., *Solidarität in Segen und Fluch im Alten Testament und in seiner Umwelt* (Bonner Bibl. Beitr. 14) (Bonn 1958).
—— *Heilsmittler im Alten Testament und im Alten Orient* (Quaestiones Disputatae 23–4: Freiburg i. Br. 1964).
SCHUMANN, H., 'Bemerkungen zum Prozeß Jesu vor dem Synhedrium', *Z. der Sav. Stiftung, rom. Abt.* 82 (1965), 315–20.
SEEBERG, A., *Der Tod Christi in seiner Bedeutung für die Erlosung: eine biblisch-theologische Untersuchung* (Leipzig 1895).
SEGAL, J. B., *The Hebrew Passover* (London 1963).
SELWYN, E. G., *The First Epistle of St. Peter* (London 1946).
SHERWIN-WHITE, A. N., *Roman Society and Roman Law in the New Testament* (Oxford 1963).
SPICQ, C., *L'Épitre aux Hébreux*, 2 vols. (Paris 1952–3).
STAAB, K., *Die Lehre von der stellvertretenden Genugtuung Christi* (Paderborn 1908).
STAMM, J. J., *Erlösen und Vergeben im Alten Testament: eine begriffsgeschichtliche Untersuchung* (Bern 1940).
—— *Das Leiden des Unschuldigen in Babylon und Israel* (Ab. z. Th. A. N. T., 10: Zürich 1946).
STAUFFER, E., *Jerusalem und Rom im Zeitalter Jesu Christi* (Bern–Munich 1957).
STENNING, J. F., *Targum of Isaiah* (Oxford 1949).
TAYLOR, V., *The Gospel according to St. Mark* (London 1963).
WEIL, H. M., 'Gage et cautionnement dans la Bible', *Archives d'Histoire du droit oriental* 2 (1938), 171–241.
—— 'Le cautionnement talmudique comparé aux institutions correspondants de l'ancient Orient', *Arch. d'Hist. dr. oriental* 3 (1947), 167–208.
WHALE, J. S., *Victor and Victim* (Cambridge 1960).
WIENCKE, G., *Paulus über Jesu Tod. Die Deutung des Todes Jesu bei Paulus und ihre Herkunft* (Beitr. z. F. Chr. Theol., Ser. 2, 42: Gütersloh 1939).

WINTER, P., *On the Trial of Jesus* (Stud. Jud. 1: Berlin 1961).
WIRTZ, J., *Die Lehre von der Apolytrosis* (Trier 1906).
WOLFF, H. W., *Jesaia 53 im Urchristentum*, 2nd edn (Berlin 1950).
YARON, R., 'Redemption of persons in the ancient Near East', *Rev. In. Dr. Ant.*, 3rd ser., 6 (1959), 155–76.
ZEITLIN, S., *Who Crucified Jesus?* (New York, Bloch 1947, reprinted 1964).
—— '... II. The Crucifixion, a libellous accusation against the Jews', *Jewish Quarterly Review* 55 (1964), 1–22.

[BETZ, O., *Was wissen wir von Jesus?* (Stuttgart, Kreuz, 1965), known to me from a review, appears to have an approach similar to that of WINTER (above).]

CHAPTER EIGHTEEN

Romans vii. 1–4. The Relationship with the Resurrected Christ

THE NOTORIOUS CRUX provided by these verses of Paul has called forth a variety of attempted solutions. Commentators vary in the degree of politeness they are willing to show the author.[1] Ever since Origen, the lack of clarity and logic in the argument has proved troublesome. There is no room for fanciful interpretation, and the suggestion is freely made that Paul was not at home with his analogies, or dictated too rapidly and did not check the transcript. In view of the fact that Paul was a lawyer writing for lawyers, as he says himself explicitly,[2] and in view of the fact that lawyers are (or should be) masters of concise, accurate language the first suggestion is challenging. The second will not bear examination in view of the nature and purpose of 'Romans'.

[1] C. Gore (1915) claims that the thought is clear. O. Michel, *Der Brief an die Römer* (Meyer's Comm. on the N.T.), 12th edn (Göttingen 1963), 165–7, ignores the difficulty by treating *vv.* 2–3 as a mere example from actual juridical life. F. J. Leenhardt, *The Epistle to the Romans* (London 1964), 176–9, passes over the passage as if there were no problem. Lightfoot, *Epistles* (1895, 301), clearly exposes the difficulties. R. A. Knox (1954) speaks of juggling with metaphors. C. K. Barrett, *Romans* (1957) speaks of 'careless use of metaphor'. C. H. Dodd (*Epistle of Paul to the Romans*, 1959, 120–1): '... confusion worse confounded ... the illustration has gone hopelessly astray ... Paul lacks the gift for sustained illustration of ideas through concrete images ... probably a defect of imagination ... laboured and blundering allegories ... flounders among the images he had tried to evoke ... unmanageable puppets ...'. The effort to make Paul intelligible to the layman produces an understandable sense of frustration, particularly where Paul relies upon knowledge and attitudes which we do not share with his correspondents. For example, the doctrine that the *Torāh's* function is, *inter alia*, to demonstrate (or, more accurately, to effectuate) the righteousness or justice of God (for he would not have this attribute without it) sounds nonsense to the non-Jew. We cannot enlarge here. Dodd's apologies for Paul are very intelligible (*op. cit.* 70–1, 75, 116–17).

[2] I take the words γινώσκουσιν γὰρ νόμον λαλῶ at *v.* 1 to mean that Paul claims not merely that his correspondents knew law in general (as Michel supposes) but that they knew the *Torāh*, they were '*Torāh*-understanders' (at least so far as *halakāh* went). He would not presuppose a full knowledge of the spiritual implications of the *Torāh*.

I believe the passage to be an extremely clever one. In my view, the method of exposition wraps up together with marvellous ingenuity numerous ideas stated or hinted elsewhere. But the task of demonstrating what Paul meant was, and remains, that of the theologian; and the function of this chapter is merely to show what seems to have been in Paul's mind as he progressed from vi to vii.5 and following.

To remind the reader of the difficulty: we are told (i) that the law binds an individual so long as he lives; (ii) that a married woman is freed from the law of husband and wife when her husband dies, in fact that the death of the husband frees her from the possibility of being an adulteress if she consorts with another; and finally (iii), that one is to conclude that the Christian at Rome was put to death as to the law through the body of the Christ with the result that he gained a new consort, namely the resurrected one, with the object of the Christians' (including Paul's) producing fruit to God. Some sort of hiatus between point (i) and point (iii) seems to have occurred, and it has been noticed that there would seem to be a parenthesis by way of (ii). This parenthesis (if it really is one) is embarrassing, for it can have no purpose whatever, if it is not relevant to either (i) or (iii). To suggest, as some have done, that all we are to understand is that 'a death has intervened', and that 'death changes status', is rather desperate.[1] And no one is quite satisfied. I give my own attempt at a retranslation at the end of this chapter, but I must first show how I arrive at it.

The clues to Paul's meaning must lie in *legal* thinking. He is professedly writing for a group in which persons trained in the Jewish Law were represented, and almost certainly influential. He is utilising their legal skill to make a point: therefore the reference to adultery must be of substantial value, and not redundant. That he is certainly concerned with union between genders in a metaphorical sense appears from γενέσθαι . . . ἑτέρῳ in *v*.4 which picks up the γενομένην . . . ἑτέρῳ[2] in 3. This link proves that 3 is distinctly and essentially relevant to the understanding of 4. To throw 3 away because it does not harmonise with 1 and 4 (which seem in harmony) is to concede the battle almost before it has begun.

It is a great help to us if we realise that Paul is writing to his intellectual equals, whose opinions of his gospel were not gratifying to him. Romans is apologetic in character. He cannot be sure that he will visit Rome, though he has many reasons for wishing to do so: yet while he

[1] A. Schlatter, *Gottes Gerechtigkeit* (1935, 224–8); A. Nygren, *Commentary on Romans* (Eng. trans., 1952, p. 269–72). The *Jerusalem Bible*, which is liberally furnished with a helpful apparatus of notes and references, neatly avoids the problem without mistranslation ('you . . . are now dead to the Law').

[2] See p. 468 below.

is away there is a chance that he may be misrepresented and misunderstood. No one can concoct a lengthy, detailed, argumentative, imaginative and bold *apologetic* letter without anticipating his correspondents' objections. The rhetoric of the times expected the orator to anticipate objections and forestall them. Paul had, we know, learnt of the views concerning his gospel which had recently been current in Rome. He knew what sort of objections they would raise to his methods of preaching. It would be foolish to imagine that he was not well supplied with news of the discrepancies that had emerged there as they had emerged elsewhere: and this no doubt was the source and inspiration of Romans itself. Once this has dawned upon us we are a long way towards explaining vii.1–4.

The translators and paraphrasers have distorted and spoiled the text by their attempts to make it read logically.[1] They have not hesitated to mistranslate words, and the most frequent victims are the particles. Notions of what the passage ought to mean seem to have played havoc with it. A dead, straight, literal translation has much to offer in all such difficulties. We ought (as the translators of the King James version generally did) to confess our ignorance and wait until the clue arrives.

Willing, now, to depart from the style of the current translations and paraphrases we approach the text. We must begin with chapter vi. By baptism the Christian was baptised into Christ's death,[2] and spiritual death is followed by a spiritual burial. When he rose again we did not spiritually rise again with him. This coming to life by him and by us is reserved for the future (Col iii.3–4); but meanwhile he died to sin (and to the law) and lives to God, and we have lost our sinful selves so that we are no longer slaves to sin. Dead to sin, and alive (pending the second coming) to God, we are in union with Christ. As if we were resurrected, our living bodies must be yielded to God. Obedience to sin has given place to obedience to God. The reward is eternal life, in union with Christ, who lives for ever.

Before we continue we must notice that Paul here, as elsewhere, shows the baptised individual as a person united with Christ, and distinguishes that situation from that of the slave bound to a master, sin. He undoubtedly envisages the soul as a female, bound to Christ as a male, as if to a husband. This, indeed, he is going to say in vii.4, but the notion is already adumbrated, and is stated clearly elsewhere.[3]

[1] Barrett (cited above); G. O. Griffith, *St. Paul's Gospel to the Romans* (1949), 44.

[2] On this whole question: R. T. Tannehill, *Dying and Rising with Christ. A Study in Pauline Theology* (Berlin 1967). Passing through the water (like a proselyte) with the intention of discarding the previous life, the convert simulates a re-birth and is born again (the waters of the womb being visualised as symbolic).

[3] 1 Co vi.15–20; 2 Co xi.2–3. One may compare Ep v.22–9. Unless I am mistaken,

The emotional and ethical importance of this notion cannot be overestimated, and there seems little doubt that Paul personally felt the force of it. Obedience to God is possible, he has said, because of the attachment to Christ and service to him. The emphasis on service to Christ is very slight, and indeed it would be fair to describe it as more of a hint than a downright declaration. But union, and love, are distinctly postulated. The status of widows in the Church was regarded by some as a union with Christ on their part very closely resembling a marriage.[1] No one can doubt but that this must have been objectionable to orthodox Jews and to Jews recently converted to Christianity.

What after all is the relationship between God and Christ? The straightforward identification of Christ with God is not present in our text. Christ is the Son of God, and still a distinct person, though he represents God's power.[2] If this is the case, say Paul's opponents at Rome (and perhaps elsewhere), what becomes of the first commandment? You are indeed not recommending us to worship the Christ as God, and on that account we shall absolve you from the charge of preaching polytheism. But what about Dt vi.4–5 ('The Lord our God is one Lord...'), to which Jesus, according to the synoptics, gave prime importance? He regarded it as the 'first' commandment (Mt xxii. 37; Mk xii.30; Lk x.27).

This raises a serious problem on Paul's own showing. Nothing is worse for a lawyer than to be tripped up by his own admissions. It is Paul's theory (no doubt held very widely at the time) that idolatry is the *cause* of sexual depravity and perversion, the latter evidently a burning topic of the time. Further (see Rm ii.18–22) sexual depravity brings with it, as a consequence, numerous other sins, so that, in effect, idolatry and breach of the remaining commandments go together. If the Jew sticks firm to the first commandment there is a chance he can recover himself from the tendencies towards breach of the remainder, from which the Gentiles cannot hope to extricate themselves without conversion. In the new religion the Jewish members were distinctly

[1] The author of 1 Tm v.11–12 goes to the length of using the words καταστρηνιάσωσιν τοῦ Χριστοῦ of them when they want to remarry (as in law and morals one would have supposed—see above—they might have done). καταστρηνιάω, the more emphatic for being rare, means (apparently) 'to behave brazenly with indecent suggestions', so, of course, as to humiliate the person to whom one should be faithful (ἔχουσαι κρίμα ὅτι τὴν πρώτην πίστιν ἠθέτησαν: the Christian widow in the infant Church owed her first allegiance to Christ—the previous husband is forgotten).

[2] 1 Co i.24.

---

the allusions at 2 Co v.16 (see 15–17); and at Col i.22 are blurred by the *NEB* version. If this is correct the translators have either failed to grasp, or have deliberately ignored Paul's imagery. See also 1 Th v.10.

senior, leaders and teachers. They had reason, as Paul says, to be proud of their law.

Unions with Christ might not be idolatrous in the first instance, but if it meant loving one other than God it was idolatrous at one remove, which was every bit as bad. Everyone knows that at Mount Sinai Moses hallowed, *i.e.* betrothed, the Jewish people to God.[1] God became the 'husband' of the people, and the *Torāh* was the marriage-instrument. The people were ὕπανδρος and were bound to the law by the law (*cf.* δέδεται νόμῳ). Thus idolatry and disobedience to, or unfaithfulness towards God was referred to by the prophets as adultery, 'whoredom'.[2] The nexus between breach of the first commandment and adultery was complete and notorious.[3] The *Midrash Rabbāh* on Exodus shows how God's rejection of the people, his 'divorce' of them was feared: but it was thought that he would never 'divorce' them but only chastise them.[4] He would not bring the marriage to an end, and as he could not die the status of wife would last for ever. There would be no question of καταργεῖσθαι ἀπὸ τοῦ νομοῦ. Paul himself has made it plain that in his view this marriage has been barren. Any issue have been abortive.[5] One could say that the former relationship with the *Torāh* was itself within the borders of sin. In an isolated passage R. Judah b. 'Ila'i equates with 'harlotry' intercourse with a woman known to be incapable of conception.[6]

[1] *ḳiddashātem.* So also Ex xxxi.13: *m^eḳaddish^echem.* So Paul himself at 2 Co xi.2*b*. Midr. R., Num. XII.4 = Sonc. 466; XII.6 = Sonc. 475. There is the best of authority for the image: Is xlix.18; l.1; liv.5, 6 (*kiy vo'^alayich . . . v^e-go'^alĕch ḳ"l . . .*). We notice that marrying and redeeming appear in the same verse, completely justifying Paul's images in this section of Romans. Also Is lxii.5; Jr iii.14; Song of Songs. Ezk xvi.8f. completes the link between the covenant and adultery/idolatry. The point has been taken up already by Mirjam Prager, 'Israel in the Parables', *The Bridge*, iv (1962), p. 44ff., 65 n. 35, where she refers to R. Josē's interpretation of Dt xxxiii.2, *the Lord came from Sinai*—as a bridegroom; and she cites Mekilta (Lauterbach ii, 218–19 (see also 262)). See also *Pir^eḳē d^e R. Eliezer*, 41, cited by Billerbeck, *Kommentar*, I, 970 (on Mt xxv.6), where God comes to the Israelites as a bridegroom.

[2] Ex xxiv.15, 16; Lv xvii.7, xx.5, 6; Nb xxv.1–2; Dt xxxi.16; Jg ii.17, viii.27, 33; 1 Ch v.25; Ezk vi.9, xvi, xxiii.20; Ho ii.19–20 *et passim*; Ws xiv.12, 22–7. Dr M. Gertner tells me that Jm iv.4–6 is a reference to Gn vi.3 (LXX). He approves Delitzsch's translation of the James passage. God is jealous of idolatry and fornication. Noah was humble, and grace was shown to him. See also 2 Esd ix.30–7.

[3] For Paul himself see Col iii.5–6; 2 Co vi.14–16 (read with 1 Co vi.19), and *cf.* Ep v.3, 5.

[4] XXXI.10, discussed above at p. 97.

[5] *Cf.* 2 Esd ii.20. The product of sin being death. But *cf.* Paul's alternative image in Ga iv.24–7 where the barren wife produced the legitimate heir that typifies the Church which, in Christ, is the 'heir' to whom the promises were made: a magnificent citation of the paradox in Is liv.1. See above, pp. 124–5.

[6] *Mishnāh*, Yev. VI.5. The reference is to Ho iv.10. In secular contexts too much weight should not be attached to the dictum, which could be countered *aliunde*. But we are entitled to compare Philo, *De Spec. Leg.* III, 36 (Colson, VII, 497; trans. Yonge, iii, 312) who condemns as impious men who deliberately marry women 'tested by

Thus Jewish thinkers had used the metaphor of the husband–wife relationship, and the law relating to divorce and the dissolution of marriage by death, as a means of understanding God's patience with the Jews. Paul now asserts that God has made provision for the marriage to become something nearer what he had intended, and Paul is about to explain in what way the *Torāh* was inadequate, by itself, to serve its purpose: the promises were, it seemed, self-frustrating under the conditions laid down; but, without abrogating them, a new state of affairs had come about by which the individual Jew could escape the former barrenness and become full of life. This was by means of the physical presence, suffering and death of the Christ, and the possibility of participating in that death. While the body lived on as the former slave of sin the soul was freed by a spiritual death, with a glorious future and an immediate hope of fruitfulness as the servant of a new master. It followed as a matter of course that Jews unused to Paul's teaching would stumble at this. We know, they would say, what God demands of us; and we know that, as 'wives', we have been 'unfaithful'. We accept our deliverance from sin by our baptism; but how can our union with Christ be other than adulterous? Spiritually dead we may be with Christ: so we are spiritually adulterous, which is exactly what is in point in the idolatry/adultery concept. Here Paul commences chapter vii.

His correspondents are perfectly aware, he says, that the *Torāh* binds an individual so long as he lives. That is to say the *Torāh* is a code for the living and not the dead. It is notorious that the commands do not apply to the dead. For example,[1] if a corpse is dressed in a garment made of mixed threads the person, at the general resurrection, will not be unlawfully dressed because the Psalm tells us, '*Free among the dead*'.[2] One cannot commit sins after one is dead. If, therefore, one is spiritually dead, having undergone a spiritual killing, one does not in that state retain allegiance to commands of the *Torāh* relating to actual living people. This applies as much to metaphorical relationships as to real ones.

[1] b. Nid. 61*b* = Sonc. 433–4.

[2] Ps lxxxviii.5 (6). LXX (Ps lxxxvii.6) agrees with the Masoretic: ἐν νεκροῖς ἐλεύθερος. *Mishnāh*, Kil. IX, 4 = Sonc. 136. The principle appears to have been a favourite one of the (third century) R. Johanan. b. Shab. 30*a* = Sonc. 132; 151*b* = Sonc. 772. W. Gutbrod at *ThWzNT* IV (1942), p. 1047 n. 135, would deny the parallel between Shab. 30*a* and Rm vii.1ff. on the ground that the rabbinical principle applies only to study and by death one is freed not from the commandments but from the opportunity to perform them. Dodd, *op. cit.* 111

other men and ascertained to be barren'. They are enemies of God and nature. And to a similar effect is Maimonides's 360th negative commandment (see Chavel, II, 326–7).

God is of course bound by the *Torāh* (as the husband is by the *k^e^tūbāh*), which discloses (somewhat imperfectly) his nature. He has chosen the marriage metaphor, and from the provisions of the *Torāh* relating to adultery we are entitled to know how far God regards union with 'another' as adulterous. The *Torāh* defines adultery with scrupulous care. One cannot, for example, commit adultery by consorting with an angel.[1] It is not by union with any person whatsoever that adultery is committed. What is the rule then? *It is true* (the particle γὰρ is not used here in the sense '*because*', '*for example*':[2] Paul is not illustrating the first point: he is indicating that he proceeds to set out the material which was in his mind when he called up the proposition in *v.* 1 in the first place) that a married woman is bound by law to a *living* (*i.e.* living human—notice the repeated ἀνδρί) husband; whereas if he were to die she would be rendered unanswerable[3] to the law of husband and wife (*i.e.* it would become a nullity so far as she is concerned). This indeed involves the proposition that she becomes an adulteress if she unites with another man during the husband's lifetime, but if the husband dies she is free from the legal provision in question, so that if she consorts with another man she is not an adulteress. Thus the *Torāh*

[1] Lv xx.10 emphatically says *'et-'ēshet rē'ēhū*. See the Hebrew *Encyclopedia Talmudit*. ii, 6 *s.v.* *'lyhw*.

[2] This particle, as shown by Arndt and Gingrich at no. 4, has the effect of expressing a continuation or connection, and this is exemplified at Rm i.18; ii.25, for example, in the sense of '*indeed*', '*to be sure*'. Blass–Debrunner, § 452, refers to classical usage. Our instance, since it occurs in an imaginary dialogue, would seem to come within the scope of Denniston's VIII (1st edn, 1934, 86f.) which he derives from his V (3), (4), etc. (*ibid.* 75f.). γὰρ here would seem to have the effect of introducing material in a tone of assent by way of taking up the point which is alleged to be in the mind of the opponent, to whose point of view he makes a direct appeal in the immediately previous sentence. This interpretation of γὰρ naturally affects our anticipation of the succeeding particles. ἄρα οὖν (Blass–Debrunner, 451 (2*b*)) is well attested (Arndt and Gingrich at no. 4) as '*so then*', '*consequently*'. Thus the whole of our *v.* 3 is adduced as the consequence of *v.* 2; Paul eagerly draws from his opponents' main proposition the conclusion which is very much in their minds—and then crushes them with his own ὥστε: '*that is precisely why . . .*', '*for this very reason . . .*'. Here ὥστε is not Arndt and Gingrich's no. 2*a*, α ('*so that*', '*with the consequence that*'), but their no. 1*a*. Indeed they (following Bauer) take our instance in this sense and compare numerous Pauline examples. Of these 1 Co xi.27 seems a parallel: the consequence is unexpectedly derived from the previous assertion, with which the correspondents will have been ready to agree. If this is correct, we must attempt to prise the καὶ away from ὑμεῖς, to which it adheres idiomatically; the καὶ does not mean '*you, too*', but 'for this *very* reason', or '*it was actually for this reason that . . .*' See Denniston, καί, II B (3), (4), 298–9 (1st edn). *Cf.* διὰ τοῦτο καὶ Blass–Debrunner, § 442, p. 229 (12). The intervening ἀδελφοί μου may not be fatal to this suggestion.

[3] The technical term καταργεῖν should be visualised as in general opposed to ἐνεργεῖν. See Arndt and Gingrich and Sophocles' Dict. It should be contrasted with διασκεδεῖν, καταλύειν, which are the proper terms for repealing or abrogating a law. In Paul the word means '*to render null from the point of view of*', '*to render inoperative in respect of*'. See 1 Co xv.24, 26; Rm vi.6.

actually provides that adultery is possible only when a married woman consorts with a third party when her husband is alive. Apply this to the heavenly marriage. The Jews would be bound to God for ever, and any association with anyone *other than* an earthly living spouse would be adulterous in a spiritual sense. As union with the dead and resurrected Christ is not adulterous for the Jewish wife of the living husband; so union with a living wife is not adulterous for the male Jew married spiritually to God. What is objectionable is the consorting of a Jew with a spiritual being other than God. No doubt this is so: Paul concedes that his opponent correctly states the law and the analogies that are to be drawn in our situation, so far as they go. But we must take this in the light of the first proposition.

Because the baptised Christian is dead to the *Torāh* in his spiritual death, spiritual adultery is theoretically possible only if he were to worship idols. The earthly living body can still commit adultery within the meaning of the *Torāh*; but the spiritual soul which has undergone the spiritual death is beyond the *Torāh's* reach. Therefore the commands relative to adultery cannot be applied by analogy to the soul's new situation. Moreover, since we are united with Christ until the second coming it is highly doubtful whether spiritual adultery is possible. We are with Christ in heaven, where presumably temptation to worship idols is unlikely to arise. Since we are not spiritually resurrected the question of adultery to God cannot reappear. Union with Christ in his death has taken us beyond not only the metaphor of idolatry/adultery, but also beyond the scope of actual idolatry.[1]

The outcome of this is simple. The Jews' fear that union with Christ implies a breach of Dt vi.4–5, whereupon all the commandments would eventually be broken and the Jewish converts would be as far from God as the Gentiles, is dispelled by appeal to the *Torāh's* own provisions on the subject. The marriage with God subsists, and cannot be broken, but this union with Christ, which was itself contemplated by the *Torāh* (Ga ii.19*a*: ἐγὼ γὰρ διὰ νόμου νόμῳ ἀπέθανον ἵνα Θεῷ ȝήσω) and which is emphatically *not* a marriage (whence the vague word γενέσθαι which does not[2] imply the married state), provides us with an opportunity to be fruitful. The fruit will not, of course, belong to Christ, for he is not the husband, but to God, who is.

This rather scandalous, and unexpectedly bold concept ought perhaps

[1] We are concerned with a spiritual metaphor, and customs relating to 'idolatrous' behaviour are neglected for the moment.

[2] Arndt and Gingrich's great caution (following Bauer) at γίνομαι II, no. 3 is abundantly justified. The Hebrew parallels adduced by no means prove that γίνεσθαι ἀνδρί could mean specifically 'to marry a man', and the very context of our *v*. 3 shows that that is exactly what is *not* meant.

to be approached with some caution. Modern Christian societies are familiar with the rule that a child born of a valid marriage is presumed to be the legitimate child of the husband. But that was not in fact the position at Jewish law. That system, generous on the whole to children whom we should call illegitimate, eventually defined the *mamzer* as the child of an adulterous or incestuous union,[1] and excluded him from succession to his mother's husband, if any, whatever his rights might be in succession to his natural father. But two points must be borne in mind. Firstly, if this picture were an earthly situation the husband would be entitled to recognise, and must in fact often have recognised in practice, the child as his own child.[2] If he did not repudiate him the presumption would be that, if the husband brought him up, he had recognised him. Since the redemption of mankind was according to God's will, and for God's own purposes, it is ridiculous to suppose that he might repudiate the fruit of the union he had procured. But, in reality, all this is otiose. The status of the *mamzer* depending strictly upon adultery or incest, which are concepts of the *Torāh* applicable only to earthly life, the fruit of the union with Christ cannot be bastards.

What would be an adulterous relationship were it an earthly, physical situation is free from sin since death carries us beyond the scope of the *Torāh*; and as we are not, for this purpose, alive to any law (even to that of the descendants of Noah) there is no residual law according to which we can be adulterous. Having established this, Paul proceeds to expatiate on the fertility which this new union can work in us, and the fact that the death in question came about ultimately through the *Torāh* itself is hinted at, and wrapped up in passing in the phrase 'put to death to (or by) the *Torāh*', for Paul, like any Jewish exegete, revels in significant ambiguities, and will take advantage of double meanings, puns, which are hardly to our modern taste.

To summarise this attempted exposition: Paul, aware that his correspondents are sceptical of his doctrine of spiritual union with Christ, warns them that the death of baptism has invalidated their fundamental assumption. He shows that that is the effect of his warning in the parenthetic references to the doctrine upon which they rely for the analogy that traditionally shows God as the husband of the Jewish people. Having shown that he understands their ground, he proceeds to show how his warning removes their difficulty. The particle γὰρ introduces the doctrine of the opponents in a guise which both accept, though no doubt phrased so as to put it in a light favourable to

[1] Dt xxiii.2. *Mishnāh*, Yev. IV. 13.

[2] Though citation is hardly required, Midr. R., Num. IX.12 = Sonc. 260 may exemplify this position.

himself; the particle ἄρα οὖν completes the exposition of their case by setting out specifically and clearly what they are aiming at. *Only if the husband dies is the wife freed from the possibility of being an adulteress.* He does not bother to add, 'whence, my brothers, you would conclude that the eternal husband, God, cannot tolerate our union with another', for this would be unnecessary when writing to correspondents whose attitude and doctrines are common ground. If he had put it in, our non-Jewish commentators would have been spared much uneasiness and fruitless speculation.

He concludes by asserting that it is just because of these apparently rational objections that baptism effected a spiritual death, and so, all at once, destroyed the applicability of the analogy. The rare expression, *You have been put to death* . . ., strongly suggests that Paul wishes to imply that the process is God's work, achieved in order to overcome what would otherwise have been a fatal objection. God foresaw not merely our moral, but also our intellectual limitations. To enable the promises to be fulfilled he provided means consistently with his nature, and so *ipso facto* with the *Torāh* itself.

A draft translation incorporating this suggested solution follows.

(vi.22) '. . . but now, being set free from Sin and enslaved to God you retain your profits with a view to holiness, and the outcome is eternal life. The wage Sin paid was death, but God's bounty is eternal life in union with Christ Jesus, our lord. You are, my brothers, well aware—for I am speaking to men who know law—that the *Torāh* rules an individual no longer than he lives. It is true that a married woman is bound by law to her living husband, and that if he comes to die she is placed beyond the power of the law of the husband's rights. This certainly leads to the proposition that while the husband lives she is technically to be declared an "adulteress" if she consorts with another man, whereas, should the husband die, she is then free from the provision,[1] so that she is no "adulteress" when she consorts with another man. It is precisely, my brothers, for this reason that you were put to death in the eye of the *Torāh* through the means of the body of the Christ, in order that you *should* consort with another—I mean him who rose from the dead—in order that we may be profitable for God. For while we were alive merely in the flesh our limbs were activated by sinful passions created through the means of the *Torāh*, so that we could be profitable only for Death. Now, on the contrary, we have been placed beyond the scope of the *Torāh*. We have died in the eye of that which held us under restraint. The result is that we are slaves under a new master, the Spirit, instead of under the archaic one, the Document.'

[1] As we say collectively 'the Halakāh', and individually 'a halakāh', for a specific rule.

As if to confirm that this passage was not addressed to Latins or Greeks, innocent of Jewish concepts, Paul artfully inserts into his exposition a further characteristic Jewish metaphor which, so far as I know, no commentator has noticed. With a deft touch, a glancing insinuation, he brings before us the powerful institution of *yibbum*. We are accustomed to think of *yibbum*, the so-called 'levirate marriage', as meaning nothing more than *ḥalitsāh*. The *y*ᵉ*vāmāh*, the childless widow whose deceased husband's brother (the *yāvam*) is competent to marry her, is visualised as having no choice but to 'loosen the shoe' (*i.e.* induce him to release his right over her publicly), whereupon she is free to marry a stranger. But it seems by no means to have become usual by Paul's time, for the *yāvam* either to refuse to take his *y*ᵉ*vāmāh*, or for the community to persuade the couple to perform *ḥalitsāh*. Shortly, what Paul insinuates is that the death to the *Torāh* is practically a death of the *Torāh* to the individual[1] (for his ability to use such *vice versa* concepts *cf.* Ga vi.14), whereupon the *Torāh's* surviving 'brother', Jesus, is ready and willing to cohabit with the widow, who, of course, is 'fruitless' and therefore under an obligation to accept the *yāvam* if he is willing. The metaphor is not completely consonant with the remainder of the passage, but the degree of appropriateness is quite striking. Jesus is everywhere taken as the substitute for, and superseder of, the *Torāh*: both of them seen as emanations from God. It is appropriate that he should be obliged to make the unfruitful bride at Sinai fruitful; and it is appropriate that she should be obliged to marry him, and indeed be incapable of marrying elsewhere so long as he stands ready and willing. The fruit of a levirate marriage is of course, as we know, the child not of the *yāvam* at all, but of the first husband. Thus the fruit of union with Christ is the progeny of the Law.[2]

[1] R. F. Weymouth (ed. E. Hampden-Cook) (1917) says (365): 'So, my brethren, to you also the Law died . . .' (!). One may refer to Col iii.5 where the expression is 'Put to death what is earthly in you . . .', and earlier, at ii.20–22, Paul implied that the Christian died to 'human' precepts, *i.e.* the taboos and observances of pre-Christian religions. The former would complete the process initiated by the later 'death'.

[2] *Mishnāh*, Yev. II.8; IV.5. The tractate *Yevāmot* in the Babylonian Talmud. Midr. R., Gen. LXXXV. 5. L. M. Epstein, *Marriage Laws in the Bible and Talmud* (Cambridge, Mass. 1942), ch. III. Marcus Cohn, art. *Leviratsehe*, *Jüdisches Lexicon*, III, 1076–8. P. Cruveihlier, 'Le Lévirat', *Rev. Bibl.* 1925, 524–47. S. Belkin, *Philo and the Oral Law*, p. 251.

Index of Biblical References

1. OLD TESTAMENT

2. NEW TESTAMENT

Index of Greek, Hebrew, and Latin Terms

GREEK

HEBREW AND ARAMAIC

(The Roman alphabetical order has been observed so far as may be.)

LATIN

Index of Names and Topics

Printed in the USA
CPSIA information can be obtained
at www.ICGtesting.com
LVHW010254261123
764936LV00008B/461

9 781597 522311